The Solitary Singer

WALT WHITMAN DURING THE CIVIL WAR
Photograph by Brady. Courtesy of National Archives, Records of the
Office of the Chief Signal Officer, Washington, D.C.

The Solitary Singer

A CRITICAL BIOGRAPHY OF

WALT WHITMAN

by

GAY WILSON ALLEN

NEW YORK UNIVERSITY PRESS
1967

COPYRIGHT © 1955, 1967 BY GAY WILSON ALLEN

This edition is published by arrangement with
The Macmillan Company

First Edition 1955
Reissue with revisions 1967

Published by New York University Press
Washington Square, New York
Library of Congress Catalog Card Number 67–23414

MANUFACTURED IN THE UNITED STATES OF AMERICA

Solitary, singing in the West,
      I strike up for a New World.

TO

E V E

as much her book
as the author's

PREFACE

No AUTHOR in American literature has been a greater puzzle to his biographers and critics than Walt Whitman. There have been well over fifty attempts (counting books only) to interpret his life, and yet most students of Whitman agree that still another biography is needed. This is no reflection on the competency or integrity of all previous biographers. There have been several good ones—Bliss Perry, Henry Bryan Binns, Emory Holloway, Jean Catel, Frederik Schyberg, Henry Seidel Canby, and Roger Asselineau, to mention the best—but each year since Whitman's death in 1892 new letters, manuscripts, information, and—most important of all—new insights, have become available for a more complete, more exhaustive, and therefore a *truer* life of Whitman than anyone has yet achieved. This is the justification for the publication of the present detailed biography to mark the first centennial of *Leaves of Grass*.

I began studying and writing about Whitman nearly twenty-five years ago without any intention of becoming a "specialist" in the field, but Whitman's literary achievement was so great that he has drawn me on from one investigation to another. In order to understand his ideas and art I have been led into the study of philosophy, comparative religion, mysticism, prosody, esthetics, mythology, history, comparative literature, and other related fields. This is but one evidence of the breadth and depth of the man and his works. One can quite literally spend a lifetime studying Walt Whitman without exhausting the subject, and this can be said only of such supreme artists and great minds as Shakespeare, Goethe, Dante, or Homer.

Although Walt Whitman possessed one of the most remarkable personalities of the nineteenth century, his life is primarily of interest and importance to later generations because he wrote *Leaves of Grass*, one of the truly great books in world literature. Therefore, I have attempted to trace consecutively the physical life of the man, the growth of his mind, and the development of his art out of his physical and mental experience. Other biographers have attempted this integration, but never on quite so ambitious a scale. I have also tried to show the relations of these concomitant developments to the national life, which it was Whitman's special ambition to express through his poems.

But as great as Whitman was, both as man and poet, his life was crowded with failures and disappointments, many but not all of which he overcame. In order to write truthfully of him, therefore, I have had to write critically. The first books about him were more hagiography than biography, and later biographers have often been blindly partisan, either for or against Whitman. I have perhaps striven for the impossible, but my sincerest purpose has been to be strictly impartial, believing that truth, whatever it may be, leads to understanding, and ultimately to appreciation.

I am, of course, deeply indebted to all Whitman scholars and biographers, past and present, including many in foreign countries, but most of all to two Americans, Emory Holloway and Clifton Joseph Furness. Holloway has laid the foundation for all modern Whitman scholarship, and will be gratefully remembered as long as the poet is studied. Professor Holloway has generously advised and aided me since I was a graduate student.

To the late Clifton J. Furness I am more personally indebted. Until I learned after his untimely death that he had not been able to complete his biography in publishable form, I had not thought of undertaking the staggering task of writing one myself. For twenty years he had assiduously collected material for a life of Whitman, and I had no doubt that it would be "definitive." He did live to complete a manuscript, but his heavy academic duties and many distractions prevented his assimilating the huge stack of documents and data which he had assembled. His was one of the most tragic failures I have known among scholars. Yet it has been my fate to profit from it, for Furness's literary executor, Moreton Abbott, decided that I was worthy of receiving the notebooks, transcriptions of manuscripts, and bibliography collected by his friend. Mr. Abbott kept the unpublished biography (it was useless to me anyway), but Furness's raw materials have been of inestimable value. I hope later to revise and publish his bibliography.

Space does not permit the adequate acknowledgment of my many other indebtednesses, but I should like to mention the late Danish critic Frederik Schyberg, whose method taught me to read Whitman more closely and perceptively. I do not always agree with him, but many times I have found his shrewd guesses confirmed by my own discovery of documentary evidence. And since my biography is based so far as possible on objective fact, I have methodically footnoted each chapter so that anyone may readily examine the evidence, though these notes have been placed at the back of the book, where they will least annoy the incurious reader. I have not refrained from speculation where it seemed to be called for, but I have tried to indicate clearly where fact ends and my interpretation begins.

I am grateful to many private collectors and to curators of Walt Whitman letters and manuscripts, all of whom have most generously shared their treasures and information, such as Charles E. Feinberg, T. E. Hanley, Oscar Lion, Mrs. Harriet Sprague, Milton I. D. Einstein, Edward Naumburg, Jr., William D. Bayley, and Clifton Waller Barrett; and the curators of: The Walt Whitman Foundation, Camden, N. J.; the Trent Collection of Duke University Library; the Van Sinderen Collection, Yale University Library; the Berg Collection and the Rare Book Room of the New York Public Library; the Rare Book Department of the University of Pennsylvania; the Harned Collection of the Library of Congress; the John Pierpont Morgan Library, New York City; the Long Island Historical Society, Brooklyn; the Huntington Historical Society, Huntington, Long Island. Librarians in the New York University libraries, the New-York Historical Society, the Pennsylvania Historical Society, the American Antiquarian Society of Worcester, Mass., the Boston Public Library, and the Houghton Library at Harvard University have also generously assisted. Mrs. Martha K. Hall, of Huntington, supplied genealogical information; Mrs. Katharine Molinoff donated legal data she had collected; Joseph J. Rubin and Charles H. Brown permitted quotation from *Walt Whitman of the New York Aurora*; the Brooklyn *Daily Eagle* made available the files of the Brooklyn *Times* and Edwin D. Wilson and William Boyle helped locate the files in a warehouse. I have made use of a thesis on Whitman's Camden years by Henry Chupak, and of information supplied by the State Museum of Louisiana.

The Rockefeller Foundation made possible a year of research during a crucial year of my Whitman studies, and a Guggenheim Foundation fellowship enabled me to complete the writing of the book. My academic superiors and colleagues, Dean William B. Baer and Professors E. L. McAdam, Jr., Oscar Cargill, William M. Gibson, and Charles Davis, have aided in various ways. Arthur Zeiger, Stephen Stepanchev, Joseph J. Rubin, Norman Holmes Pearson, Cleveland Rodgers, Roger M. Asselineau, and Anne King gave helpful criticism of the manuscript, in part and in whole.

Ralph Westcott, Sculley Bradley, and Harold Blodgett gave encouragement and assistance. I am also indebted to Professor Blodgett and the Librarian of Union College for locating copies of the New York *Tattler* which Whitman edited. Mr. Nathan Reingold located valuable material in the National Archives in Washington, D. C., and the General Services Administration kindly supplied photographic copies. Professor Fredson Bowers, who is editing the "Valentine" manuscripts (now in C. W. Barrett's collection), generously permitted me to use his transcriptions and gave me the benefit of his expert judgment. Mr. Jesse Merritt, Nassau County historian, donated maps, clippings, and historical data.

But the contribution of my wife, Evie Allison Allen, exceeded all others; she did research, typed, translated from several languages, read proof, and helped to shape the biography from beginning to end.

ORADELL, N.J.   G. W. A.

CONTENTS

CONTENTS

ILLUSTRATIONS

The Solitary Singer

❧ I ❧

THIS THEN IS LIFE

This then is life,
Here is what has come to the surface
    after so many throes and convulsions.[1]

I

One of the earliest dates that Walt Whitman remembered was May 27, 1823, the day his family moved to Brooklyn from West Hills, a little farming community on Long Island. Although this event took place four days before his fourth birthday, the day became indelibly stamped on his infant consciousness, not only because of the novelty of the thirty-mile trip from the country to town but also because this was a day long remembered by Brooklyn residents, for it was the occasion of one of the most exciting horse races held in America up to that time. Many years later Whitman merely recorded in an autobiographical note that it was the date of a "Race between Eclipse and Henry," [2] but the details can be found in the contemporary newspapers.

Eclipse was the most famous race horse in the North, owned by Van Ranst.[3] Colonel W. R. Johnson, of Virginia, had selected the fastest horse he could find in the South to match against him. Thus sectional pride had been aroused, and the stakes were high. The result of the prolonged publicity given to this "match race" can be judged by the descriptions printed in the newspapers next day,[4] as in the following paragraphs from a long account in the New York *Advertizer*:

Yesterday the great race between Van Ranst's horse ECLIPSE and Long's HENRY was run at Jamaica on Long Island. An immense number of people from different parts of the United States were collected on the occasion. The bet was twenty thousand dollars aside. The interest felt in the race caused more betting than ever took place on any similar occasion in our country. It

1

is calculated that not less than some hundred thousands of dollars were staked on the result.

The day was remarkably fine, and from sunrise till 12, immense crowds were passing to the ferries to cross over to the island. The city was in a great measure deserted. Vehicles of every description had taken their stations at the ferries [in Brooklyn] to convey the multitude to the race ground, but many could not obtain seats, and were obliged to walk a distance of eight miles.

Little Walt's maternal grandfather, Major Cornelius Van Velsor, a breeder of horses, and gregarious by nature, may have attended the race, but we may be sure that his stern father, Walter Whitman, Sr., did not, though he would have done well not to have planned to move on the same day. The highway between West Hills and Brooklyn ran right by the Union (that is, Jamaica) race track, and on the morning of May 27 the Turnpike was jammed with such a stream of traffic coming from Brooklyn as the countryside had seldom if ever seen before.[5]

Walter Whitman's stubbornness and unreliable judgment had caused him to fail so many times in the past that he felt himself to be an unlucky man. A good carpenter, a hard worker, and only thirty-four years old, he had already become soured and irritable by his losing struggle to support his rapidly growing family on a small farm at West Hills, and it was just like him to choose such a day as this to move to Brooklyn. Whether he himself drove the wagon loaded with his family and scanty household possessions or hired a teamster for the trip, we do not know. But his tall figure and bony face must have twitched with vexation as the oncoming tide of vehicles slowed his progress to a snail's pace, or forced him off the road altogether. Ordinarily he was taciturn and undemonstrative,[6] but his wife feared his terrible temper when aroused, or—almost as much—his silent spells.[7] He was of English stock, descended from Puritans who had moved to Huntington in the seventeenth century. She, Louisa Van Velsor, was Dutch and Welsh, with the Dutch strain predominating in her build and temperament. She had blue eyes, a round pleasant face, and a sunny disposition.

Probably Mrs. Whitman needed all her Dutch patience and good humor to calm her husband on that memorable day, or to control her three excited children. The oldest, Jesse, was only five; little black-haired, blue-eyed, pink-cheeked, roly-poly Walter was fifteen months younger (born May 31, 1819); Mary was two and a half; and Mrs. Whitman was expecting her fourth child in November.[8] Life in the country had been hard, and she was not unwilling to leave the house at West Hills, near

Huntington, which her husband had built and to which she had gone as a bride in 1816. He had tried hard to earn a living as a carpenter, but for the past few years there had been little building on Long Island except in Brooklyn, and he had been reduced to farming in summer and cutting and selling firewood in the winter.[9] Maybe living in town would be easier. People said Brooklyn was beginning to grow, and a good carpenter should have no trouble in making a living there. Walter knew more about life in town than his wife for he had spent three years of his apprenticeship in New York City.[10] However, Brooklyn was not a strange place to her, for every week her father, Major Cornelius Van Velsor, drove his combination stage and vegetable wagon to the market near the ferry, where he either sold his produce or drove his horses onto the ferry boat and thus crossed the East River to the New York markets.[11]

The race at Jamaica finally got under way at one o'clock, and in the early afternoon Front Street, where Walter Whitman had rented a house,[12] was relatively quiet, though it was near New Ferry, at the end of Main Street. During this lull the newcomers could have unloaded their furniture and eaten their lunch. But at three o'clock the noisy, jubilant throng —for Eclipse had won—began flocking back from Jamaica, arriving by stagecoaches, carriages, horseback, and on foot. By nine o'clock that evening twenty thousand people had passed through Brooklyn, five thousand of them crossing at New Ferry.[13] While waiting for passage on the crowded ferries, many, of course, celebrated in Brooklyn. Front Street was surrounded by taverns and grog shops, some on the short street itself near the water front, and others at both ends of the street to which the Whitman family had just moved. The largest taverns were to the south, near the end of Old Ferry Road (Fulton Street), but several grocery stores on the lower end of New Ferry Road (Main Street) also sold grog, and in all these places many a toast was drunk to the winner of the race. Next day the New York *Evening Post* reported, "During the afternoon and evening utmost harmony prevailed, a number of appropriate toasts were drunk and several excellent songs were given with good taste." But the *Post* did not say where this decorous celebrating took place—not likely on Front Street in Brooklyn.

Walter Whitman had not brought his family to a quiet country village. Although Brooklyn had only six or seven thousand inhabitants, because of its position and harbor facilities it had the activity and noise of a small city. On Clover Hill (soon to be known as Brooklyn Heights) there were fine estates with well-kept gardens, and half a mile east were real farms;

but near the ferries the taverns, livery stables, tar sheds, tanneries, slaughterhouses, tenements, and a few once-decent houses huddled together indiscriminately. Here lived bargemen, oyster dealers, small shopkeepers, Irish day laborers, and manumitted Negroes. James Street, which angled up the hill from Front, was heavily populated by Negroes, whose children mingled with the white ragamuffins on Front and adjacent streets. Theoretically, this should have fostered a democratic feeling of common interests, but anyone who has observed the life of children in the slums knows that frustrations and tensions were created instead of tolerance.

The house into which the Whitmans moved was almost beneath what is now the eastern end of Manhattan Bridge. Only a short distance north was the busy United States Navy Yard, where the marvelous new steam frigate *Fulton* was moored when in port. Thus even though the bridge was not to be built for many years, in 1823 the Whitman family lived right beside one of the main traffic lanes between Brooklyn village and big New York City, which already had a population of a hundred and twenty thousand.

Rivalry between the village and the city had just reached a new intensity of bitterness because New York owned the ferries and land adjacent to the landings, and Brooklyn citizens resented this outside control of the ferry rates and regulations.[14] However, this friction was not without its benefits, for hitherto Brooklyn had been almost destitute of civic consciousness and now its leading citizens were stimulated to plan for the future. The village had no street lights, no night watch, almost no sidewalks, no systematic police force, a makeshift volunteer fire department, and of course no municipal water supply or sewage disposal. A few pumps in the middle or along the edge of the unpaved streets supplied water for drinking and cooking. Garbage was thrown into the highways to rot or to be eaten by the hogs that ran wild—though in this practice Brooklyn was no worse than New York City. Even the better homes a few blocks from the ferries had barns and cowsheds near the main dwellings.[15] Every man of means kept a horse or two, and many residents owned pigs, goats, geese, and chickens. Naturally, epidemics were common. During the Whitmans' first summer in the village ten people near them died of yellow fever, and in succeeding years there were outbreaks of cholera.[16]

The Whitman family arrived in Brooklyn just at the time when it was beginning to expand rapidly on both sides of Fulton Street. The village was a good location for manufacturing as well as shipping, and each year new factories were being built and put into operation, thus providing additional employment and swelling the population. One of the largest distilleries in the nation was situated near the harbor. The business district was gradually shifting from the water front up Fulton Street, and the value of real estate on both sides of Fulton was increasing so fast that speculative buying and selling was becoming a major enterprise. To the north of Fulton, gradually extending eastward toward the limits of the incorporated village, cheap frame houses were being built for the families of the day laborers. There Walter Whitman found employment as a carpenter, first as a wage earner, and later as a contractor or speculative builder.

South of Fulton Street, a few blocks from the river, were the large estates of the Hicks, Middagh, and Pierrepont families. This region, still called Clover Hill but already re-named Brooklyn Heights, was the aristocratic section of Brooklyn. In addition to being free of the squalor of the crowded ferry district, the elevation gave a splendid view of lower Manhattan and the forests of masts at the piers; on a fair day one could see clear across to the wooded shores of New Jersey and Staten Island. Hezekiah Pierrepont had already begun an advertising campaign to induce New York business and professional men to buy lots on the Heights, where they could establish a home in a "select neighborhood," healthful, spacious, and inexpensive.[17]

The lots readily sold, and fine houses began to go up in this increasingly exclusive neighborhood. Of course, as the former New York City residents increased in numbers, the cleavage between Heights and native villagers became more pronounced. And Walter Whitman's work and interests were almost always on the other side of the village. For a while in 1824 the Whitman family did reside on Cranberry Street,[18] the only time they ever lived on the south side of Fulton, but this was on the outskirts of the Heights, and if the rent had not been low they could not have afforded to live there. They never felt any identity with the elite section, from which they were excluded both by economic and by social barriers. The older Dutch families scattered throughout the village enjoyed a certain amount of prestige both as established citizens and as well-to-do landowners; but the residents of the Heights soon became the social aristocracy. It was not a rigid caste, and anyone who could accumulate enough money to build a good house there and buy a pew in one of the fashionable churches, such as St. Ann's (Episcopal), could change his social status. Here were no "Brahmins" as in Boston. Yet as far as the Whitmans were concerned, the barrier might as well have been hereditary.

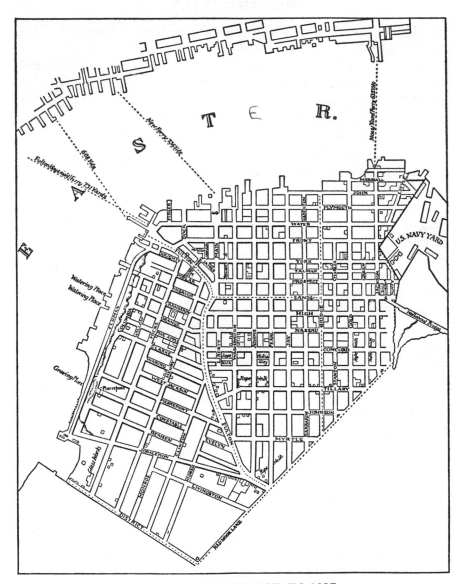

BROOKLYN VILLAGE IN 1827

Reprinted from Ralph Foster Weld's *Brooklyn Village: 1816–1834*, courtesy of Columbia University Press and the Long Island Historical Society.

Probably during most of his first year in Brooklyn, Walter Whitman continued to work for carpenter's wages, which were something like a dollar a day. But on September 1, 1824, he and Mrs. Whitman bought a lot on the corner of Washington and Johnson streets, near the outskirts of the village, for $250, and for several years following he continued to buy a lot, build a house on it, move into the house for a few months or a year, then buy, build, sell, and move all over again.[19] Thus the family lived on Johnson Street in 1825, on Van Dykes in 1826, Adams in 1827, and then Tillary from November, 1827, until November, 1831.[20] Seldom were they again to live in one house for four years, but this unusual stability was evidently not the result of prosperity. It is likely that Walter Whitman was again working for wages, because he did not buy any property between February 13, 1826, and March 3, 1831. Others were making fortunes in real-estate transactions, but he was never successful in his speculations. Walt later recalled that the houses on Johnson and Tillary "were mortgaged, and we lost them."[21]

By this time Mrs. Whitman had borne four more children: Hannah Louisa in 1823, an infant in 1825 that died before receiving a name, Andrew Jackson in 1827, and George Washington in 1829. Perhaps during these years Walter, Sr., was becoming more patriotic, if the names of his sons are any indication, but he was as unlucky—or at least as unsuccessful—as ever. Many years later Walt thought that at one time his father drank heavily,[22] and this may have been the period, though whether drinking was cause or effect of the financial difficulties we do not know. Possibly the latter, for Walt also said that his "straightforward father was nearly swindled out of his boots" by a Methodist "elder," [23] and both the lot on Johnson Street and the one on Tillary were bought from men listed in the deed as "minister." [24] Probably this experience intensified the dour carpenter's free-thinking tendencies, as it certainly did his son's.

Walt also said that his father had been a friend of Tom Paine.[25] That would have been around 1807–1809, the last years of the old patriot's life, when he was living in the neighborhood of Bleecker Street in New York and Walter Whitman was a carpenter's apprentice in the city. Elias Hicks, the radical Quaker preacher from Jericho, Long Island, and a lifelong friend of the Whitmans, had been kind to Paine during those years, and his defense of the author of *The Age of Reason*, at a time when the clergy of all churches were vilifying him, was at least partly responsible for the schism in the Quaker Church in 1826.[26] Elias Hicks became the leader of the more liberal branch, which was for many years known as the Hicksite

Quakers. Walter Whitman did not take an active part in any church, but his sympathies were always to remain with the Hicksites, and he heard Elias preach whenever he was in the vicinity.[27] In addition to reading Paine and admiring Elias, Walt's father also owned and read Count Volney's *Ruins*,[28] an epitome of the political and Deistic philosophy of the French Revolution, and subscribed to the *Free Inquirer*, published by the notorious socialists Frances Wright and Robert Dale Owen.[29] Thus through his father Walt early came under the influence of rationalism and liberal political thought, and combined with these intellectual influences was the personal animosity against the Methodist "elder" who had trimmed his father in business.

Mrs. Whitman had probably received as much formal education as her husband, which was very little, but she was too busy bearing children and trying to provide a home for them to have time for reading. She was a good cook, an industrious housekeeper, and the peacemaker of the family[30]—and the family needed a peacemaker, for all indications are that it was always uncongenial. Walter Whitman was not a kind or loving father, and his eldest son, Jesse, was excitable, jealous, and often hysterical, even from infancy.[31] Walt was a direct contrast, phlegmatic and even-tempered, perhaps at times a little moody, but never disagreeable or aggressive in his wants or aversions.

It was already a family of great diversity in temperament, intellect, ability, and interests, and destined to become more diverse with the passage of time. Of games or amusements together we hear nothing. Each child apparently went his own way, and his parents made little effort to control his going or coming. Perhaps it was good training in self-reliance, but it was a gamble with character. The results, however, were not completely dependent on mere chance, for innate disposition is also a kind of fate. Good-natured little Walt was relatively safe anywhere. Petted and "deadheaded" by the gatekeepers and deckhands of the ferries,[32] he amused himself by riding back and forth across the river. He loved crowds and spectacles of all kinds. The East River became his backyard and he never tired of watching the ships and barges on the water, or the stevedores, teamsters, hucksters, and loafers ashore. During all his youth he was never seriously injured or ill. Considering his environment and the freedom he enjoyed even as a small child, this fact is only a little short of miraculous.

II

Two years after the Whitmans moved to Brooklyn, Walt had a fortunate experience that made a profound impression on his six-year-old mind. A local committee had raised funds to build an Apprentices Library,[33] which was also to be used as a public hall for lectures and cultural activities, and a corner-stone-laying ceremony was planned for July 4, 1825. General Lafayette had been touring the States and was coming to New York. To the great delight of Brooklyn residents, he agreed to lay the corner-stone, and the whole town was nearly as excited as it had been over the horse race two years earlier.

On the eagerly awaited day the weather was splendid—clear, bright, and not too warm. Old soldiers and prominent citizens met the hero of the Revolution at the ferry and escorted him up Fulton Street. He rode in an old-fashioned yellow coach and waved his hat to acknowledge the applause. At Market Street a formal procession, including school children, fell in line behind the carriage and marched to the corner of Henry and Cranberry streets, where the ceremony was to take place.

It is not certain whether little Walt had yet begun to attend public school, but he was a Sunday-school pupil, and he marched with the children. At the location of the projected library the stone and dirt excavated for the foundation walls and basement had been piled high on all sides, and many of the men in the crowd volunteered to lift the smaller children down the banks of the cellar in order to place them in positions where they could hear and see in safety. Lafayette joined in this assistance of the children, and Walt had the good luck to be picked up and carried by "the old companion of Washington." The experience lingered in the boy's memory, and as he grew older it took on symbolical significance. After he became a poet he wrote three separate versions of it, in the later versions adding a kiss from the general as a prophetic blessing.[34]

In his accounts of this occasion Whitman mentions both school and Sunday-school children. The Sunday-school movement had been started in Brooklyn around 1815 as part of an anti-vice campaign—during the first half of the century Brooklyn was always having moral crusades of some kind—but the plan called for instruction in reading and spelling as well as for the Bible and religion. Nearly half of all Brooklyn children of school age did not attend any school, and many of the civic leaders believed there was a direct correlation between illiteracy and crime. By 1825 nearly all churches in Brooklyn had Sunday schools, and at various times

Walt attended several, but the one that made the deepest impression on him was at St. Ann's, although neither of his parents ever showed any interest in the Episcopal Church, and they would certainly have felt out of place at aristocratic St. Ann's, where the pew rent was beyond their means.

Perhaps soon after the church was built in 1824 the members of St. Ann's Church made special efforts to enroll needy children in its Sunday school. When the blue stucco building at the corner of Sands and Washington was torn down in 1880 to make way for a more imposing structure, Whitman wrote that old St. Ann's was "twined with memories" of his youth.[35] He recalled nostalgically the stately building he had known as a child, with its spacious grounds, well-kept lawn, fashionable congregation, kindly clergyman, "and the long edifice for Sunday-school (I had a pupil's desk there), and the fine gardens and many big willow and elm trees in the neighborhood." What he learned there he did not say, but the place was always to be associated in his memory with grass, shady trees, and kindness. Public school never had such pleasant associations for him.

At least by the autumn of 1825—and possibly earlier—Walt was attending a public school, which in a reminiscence he located at Adams and Concord streets.[36] Public schools were still a novelty in Brooklyn, and were regarded by many citizens as a form of charity and a nuisance. There were a number of private schools, and nearly all parents who could afford the tuition sent their children to them.[37] In theory a small fee was charged in the public schools for parents able to pay, but in practice most parents paid nothing. Whether Walter Whitman, Sr., paid anything for his children we do not know, but Walt attended public school for six years and probably most of his brothers and sisters were enrolled for similar periods.

The Brooklyn public schools were operated on the Lancastrian plan, which enabled one teacher with the assistance of student monitors to instruct from one to three hundred pupils. The children sat on backless benches at curved desks, ten children to each desk, and a monitor—one of the older children—sat at a little desk nearby. He policed the group and drilled it on the "lesson" which he had previously had drilled into him by the teacher in charge of the room. The youngest children met in the basement, the older girls on the next floor, and the older boys on the top floor. In some schools the Negro children were segregated from the whites.

The instruction, confined mainly to arithmetic, geography, reading, and writing, was routine and tiresome almost beyond endurance; rote was the principal learning technique. Discipline was strict, and corporal chastise-

ment was the usual penalty for talking in the classroom, swearing anywhere on the premises, fighting, or playing truant. Whether Walt was
often whipped is not known, but he grew up with the conviction that
corporal punishment was the worst crime in education. His schoolmaster
remembered him as a boy large for his age, a "good-natured lad, clumsy
and slovenly in appearance, but not otherwise remarkable." [38] And Walt
remembered his boyhood as restless and unhappy.[39] It is not likely that his
monitors and teachers did anything to lessen his uncertainty and unhappiness.

III

None of the events of his school years that Whitman later recalled in
print had anything to do with his studies. One of these occurred in 1829,
in his tenth year. An "exasperated sailor," as an act of vengeance, fired
the magazine of the steam-frigate *Fulton* on June 4, 1829, and the resulting explosion killed, in Whitman's words, "between forty and fifty persons [the Long Island *Star* reported forty-three]. The writer of these paragraphs, then a boy of just ten years old, was at the public school, corner of
Adams and Concord Street. We remember the dull shock that was felt in
the building as of something like an earthquake—for the vessel was
moored at the Navy Yard." [40]

He also distinctly recalled the funeral held two or three days later at
St. Ann's:

It was a full military and naval funeral—the sailors marching two by two,
hand in hand, banners tied up and bound in black crape, the muffled drums
beating, the bugles wailing forth the mournful peals of a dead march. We remember it all—remember following the procession, boy-like, from beginning to
end. We remember the soldiers firing the salute over the grave. And then how
everything changed with the dashing and merry jig played by the same bugles
and drums, as they made their exit from the grave-yard. . . .[41]

Wherever there was a crowd and excitement young Walt was likely to
be found. But in all his numerous reminiscences he never mentioned going anywhere or doing anything with his brothers and sisters during
this period. He did, however, accompany his parents to hear Elias Hicks
preach. In the autumn following the *Fulton* explosion this famous old
Quaker, at the end of a two-year tour that had taken him as far west as

Indiana, preached in the ballroom of Morrison's Hotel on Brooklyn Heights.

Though it is sixty years ago—and I was a little boy at the time in Brooklyn, New York—I can remember my father coming home toward sunset from his day's work as carpenter, and saying briefly, as he throws down his armful of kindling-blocks with a bounce on the kitchen floor, "Come, mother, Elias preaches tonight." Then my mother, hastening the supper and the table-cleaning afterward, gets a neighboring young woman, a friend of the family, to step in and keep house for an hour or so—puts the two little ones to bed—and as I had been behaving well that day, as a special reward I was allow'd to go also.[42]

Earlier in this account Whitman says that the event took place in November or December, 1829, and in his *Journal* Elias Hicks recorded that late in November, 1829: "On second day [Monday] I had an appointed meeting at Brooklyn," which he described in his Quaker language as "a large and very favored season." [43] This meeting must have been held either on November 16 or 23, both Mondays in 1829 (it could not have been earlier because Hicks did not arrive back in New York from his trip until November 14). It is rather surprising, however, that Mrs. Whitman felt like attending the meeting on either date, because on November 28, 1829, she gave birth to another son—George Washington.[44] But Walt's date checks so closely with Elias Hicks's *Journal* entry that we must assume his accuracy in this detail. The "little ones," then, were Andrew, two and a half, and Hannah, six years old. Where was Jesse? Had he not behaved well that day? Or was he out with his companions? Mary, three months short of nine, would perhaps have been restless during the sermon, but she is not mentioned or alluded to either.

Anyway, with the care of the children arranged, Walt and his parents start for the meeting. They arrive at "a large, cheerful, gay-color'd room, with glass chandeliers bearing myriads of sparkling pendants, plenty of settees and chairs, and a sort of velvet divan running all around the side-walls." The room fills rapidly, including "many fashionables [who have come] out of curiosity," and "the principal dignitaries of the town. . . . Many young folks too; some richly dress'd women," one group accompanied by officers in uniform, possibly from the Navy Yard. "On a slightly elevated platform . . . sit a dozen or more Friends, most of them elderly, grim, and with their broad-brimmed hats on their heads. Three or four women, too, in their characteristic Quaker costumes and bonnets. All still as the grave." The boy from Tillary Street is obviously dazzled by the splendor, novelty, and solemnity. Hicks himself is an impressive figure. Though over eighty, he is tall, straight, dressed in plain clothes, face clean-shaven, with broad forehead, black eyes, long white hair covered by a Quaker hat. Then, slowly and dramatically, he begins "in a resonant, grave, melodious voice, *What is the chief end of man?* I was told in my early youth, *it was to glorify God, and seek and enjoy him forever.*" The boy "cannot follow the discourse." But presently it becomes more fervid and the preacher takes off his broad-brimmed hat and dashes it to the floor.

Years later, though remembering vividly the whole scene, Whitman could not "repeat, hardly suggest the sermon." But we know that Elias Hicks did not believe the purpose of life to be to glorify God endlessly; rather it was to make the life here on earth as full and joyous as possible, while heeding the "Deity-planted" intuitions of one's own soul. The attentive boy must have at least been aware of the general drift of the sermon, however little it meant to his immature mind. After he became a poet Whitman always felt a strong bond of spiritual kinship with this Quaker minister.

But Elias Hicks was not entirely responsible for Walt's boyhood sympathy with the Friends. His grandmother "Amy" (Naomi Williams Van Velsor) had observed many of the old Quaker customs. She had died in 1829, and Walt still felt her loss very deeply. Like her daughter, Walt's adored mother, she had been mild, gentle, sweet-tempered, and fond of children.[45] Her Welsh father, Captain John Williams, had been master and part owner of a ship engaged in the West Indies trade and Walt never tired of hearing about his adventures. He was serving under John Paul Jones when the *Bon Homme Richard* met the *Serapis* on September 23, 1779, and Whitman later wove this incident into a passage in "Song of Myself":

> Would you hear of an old-time sea-fight?
> Would you learn who won by the light of the moon and stars?
> List to the yarn, as my grandmother's father the sailor told it to me.

Of course, the poet was giving an imaginary source, for he actually got the story from grandmother "Amy," not her father. And she was not the only grandparent who had such stories to tell. The "Major" (how he got the title is not known) was also descended, on his mother's side, from a picturesque sailor, "Old Salt Kossabone," whose death Whitman also described in a poem. In his retirement "Old Salt" lived on a hill overlooking

a harbor, and he died one evening after watching an out-bound brig
struggle with the crosstides for several hours:

At last at nightfall strikes the breeze aright, her whole luck veering,
And swiftly bending round the cape, the darkness proudly entering, cleaving, as
     he watches,
"She's free—she's on her destination"—these the last words—when Jenny came,
     he sat there dead,
Dutch Kossabone, Old Salt, related on my mother's side, far back.[46]

Such were the stories and traditions that little Walt eagerly absorbed in
Grandfather Van Velsor's jolly home. The Major himself was "a hearty,
solid, fat old gentleman, on good terms with the world."

For over forty years, he drove a stage and market wagon from his farm to
Brooklyn ferry, where he used to put up at Smith & Wood's old tavern on
the west side of the street, near Fulton ferry.—He was wonderfully regular in
these weekly trips; and in those old fashioned times, people could almost tell
the time of day, by his stage passing along the road—so punctual was he.—I
have been up and down with him many times: I well remember how sick the
smell of the lampblack and oil with which the canvas covering of the stage
was painted, would make me.[47]

Apparently these trips were not an unmixed joy to the boy. And he did
not find the same pleasure in visiting the Van Velsor farm after the death
of his grandmother. In the same journal quoted above, Whitman stated
that his grandfather promptly re-married, adding, "but did not make a
very good investment." This Whitman deleted, without giving any clue
for the basis of the suppressed opinion. But it hardly seems likely that he
became very fond of his step-grandmother.

Walt never knew his Grandfather Jesse Whitman,[48] but he respected and
admired Grandmother Hannah Brush Whitman. She had once been a
schoolteacher and Walt was particularly impressed by her manners. Probably she was also a good storyteller, for from her he learned a great deal
about life on Long Island during the time of the Revolution, and especially about the part his Whitman ancestors and his Grandmother Hannah's family had played in it. His boyish heart swelled with pride as he
listened to the accounts of their bravery and patriotism. All the Whitmans,
like most Long Islanders, had supported the war for independence, and
one of Walt's great uncles was killed in the battle at Brooklyn.[49]

From his Whitman grandmother Walt also liked to hear stories about his great-grandfather, Nehemiah Whitman, who was said to have owned five hundred acres and slaves enough to farm them. Under Nehemiah and his vigorous, strong-willed wife, Sarah White, the Whitman line reached the peak of its prosperity. "She smoked tobacco, rode on horseback like a man, managed the most vicious horse, and, becoming a widow in later life, went forth every day over her farm-lands, frequently in the saddle, directing the labor of her slaves, in language in which, on exciting occasions, oaths were not spared." [50] Perhaps later unconventional, unorthodox Whitmans owed something to this colorful ancestor, though none of them inherited her financial competence. By the time the ancestral estate reached Walt's father, it had been divided and subdivided so many times that Walter Whitman could not make a living on his share.

So far as known none of the Whitmans ever held town or county office, or became distinguished as leaders. Walt's Grandfather Whitman was a close friend of Elias Hicks, and this suggests that his views and his general temperament were something like those of Walt's father. For at least two or three generations the Whitmans had been uncompromising individualists—probably too uncompromising for their own worldly success.

Though none of the Whitmans had been seamen, like Captain Williams or romantic "Old Salt" Kossabone, they also loved the ocean in their own way. The highest elevation on Long Island is at West Hills, from which the sea is visible in several directions, Long Island Sound lying only a few miles to the north, the Great South Bay ten or twelve miles to the south, and the Atlantic Ocean about fifteen. On still nights it can be heard from the heights of West Hills, especially after a storm. Walt Whitman said of his forebears that "all hands, male and female, went down frequently on beach and bathing parties, and the men on practical expeditions for cutting salt hay, and for clamming and fishing." [51] Walt inherited the Whitman farmers' love for the ocean rather than the nautical spirit of Captain Williams and "Old Salt" Kossabone.

Walt visited his grandparents at every opportunity, in all seasons, not only for their companionship but also because he loved Long Island and the surrounding ocean. In cold winters the shallow waters inside the outer bars on the Great South Bay froze into thick ice, and Walt "often went forth with a chum or two, on those frozen fields, with hand-sled, axe and eel-spear, after messes of eels." The boys would cut holes in the ice, "sometimes striking quite an eel-bonanza, and filling our baskets with great, fat, sweet, white-meated fellows." [52]

Another youthful sport of which Walt was fond was going on "a bay-party in summer to gather sea-gull's eggs." It was probably in his later boy-hood that he used to go down to the eastern end of Long Island, in the Peconic Bay region, where he fraternized with the "blue-fishers." Some-times, too, along Montauk peninsula he met the unkempt, half-barbarous herdsmen who had charge of large droves of horses, cows, and sheep owned by farmers of the eastern end of the island. All along the Island and its shores Whitman "spent intervals many years, all seasons, sometimes rid-ing, sometimes boating, but generally afoot, (I was always then a good walker,) absorbing fields, shores, marine incidents, characters, the bay-men, farmers, pilots— . . . went every summer on sailing trips—always liked the bare sea-beach, south side, and have [had] some of my happiest hours on it to this day." [53]

Here we have clues to the developing mind and character—and later genius—of the poet of *Leaves of Grass*. Even as a boy, his companions were outdoor men, especially uneducated herdsmen, farmers, pilots, fish-ermen. He always felt at home with them and they took readily to him, willingly feeding and sheltering him, the fishermen and pilots taking him on sailing trips around the Island. But we hear of no special friends or boon companions. The genial youngster could strike up an impromptu comradeship almost anywhere among these crude but good-hearted peo-ple, but it was all casual and temporary. He had genuine affection for all of them, yet his most precious experiences were the sense impressions of "the soothing rustle of the waves, and the saline smells—boyhood's times, the clam-digging, bare-foot, and with trowsers roll'd up—hauling down the creek—the perfume of the sedge-meadows—the hay-boat, and the chowder and fishing excursions. . . ."

Whitman's youth was a prolonged boyhood. Even though at sixteen he was as large as a grown man, emotionally and intellectually he remained adolescent for years afterward. In fact, he never lost his childlike wonder or his boyish relish of sensory stimulation. And of all his senses, his sense of touch—such as he experienced when he bathed naked in the warm ocean—was so acute that it would bring him repeated ecstasy and torment until the end of his life. Though indiscriminately gregarious, he was nat-urally hedonistic and narcissistic.

IV

Young Whitman's carefree life in the fields and streams and bays of Long Island was balanced by other experiences in the town and the practical workaday world. At the age of eleven he went to work as an office boy, first for two prominent lawyers, James B. Clark and his son Edward,[54] members of St. Ann's church. If Walt was not already attending Sunday school at St. Ann's, they would certainly have encouraged him to do so, but it is possible that they first noticed the large, serious boy at their church and offered him employment because he aroused their sympathy and interest.

Leaving school did not mean the end of Walt's education; that, in fact, had scarcely begun, and would continue more rapidly in office, print shop, newspaper office, and before many years in his own schoolroom. He was especially lucky in his first position, for the Clarks took a personal interest in him. They gave him a desk and window nook to himself, and Edward Clark helped him with his handwriting and composition. Even more important, the younger lawyer gave him a subscription to a circulating library, and now much of the time he lived in the world of romance. He read Walter Scott's novels one after another in rapid succession, and then his poetry, the first poetry that had interested him. In old age Whitman also remembered with pleasure the trips his lawyer employers had sent him on with messages for Aaron Burr, who lived across the Hudson in New Jersey. "Burr was very gentle—persuasive. He had a way of giving me a bit of fruit on these visits—an apple or a pear. I can see him clearly, still—his stateliness, gray hair, courtesy, consideration." [55]

After leaving the Clarks, Walt was employed in a doctor's office, but exactly when or how long cannot be determined. The fact that in old age he remembered so vividly his experiences in the law office but failed to mention the name of the doctor for whom he worked is an indication that his second employment either was of short duration or was uncongenial or both. But he was fortunate again in his third employment, during the summer of 1831, which was in the printing office of Samuel E. Clements, editor of the Long Island *Patriot*. There he became interested in journalism, which in turn aroused literary ambitions. Walt's father subscribed to the *Patriot* and shared the editor's political views, a fact which may have influenced him in apprenticing his son to Clements.[56]

The *Patriot*, like its older rival, the Long Island *Star*, edited by Alden Spooner, was a small four-page weekly. Each newspaper was written and edited almost entirely by one man, and both were violently partisan. The *Star* was Whig, and supported the business and manufacturing interests of Brooklyn and the nation, though Alden Spooner was often independent on local issues. The *Patriot* was only ten years old, having been founded in 1821 by Tammany politicians, to whom it was completely subservient. It attempted to appeal to the growing population of mechanics and artisans in Brooklyn, the majority of whom adhered to the "Bucktail" [57] faction of the Democratic party. One of its slogans was "the right of the people to rule in every case."

The first editor of the *Patriot*, George L. Birch, had been given a juicier political plum in 1829, the inspectorship of customs, and in the summer of 1830 he had resigned the post office and the newspaper to Clements, whom Walt regarded as a "good fellow" personally, but eccentric, "A great, lank, lean . . . hawk-nosed Quaker and Southerner (he often boasted of his Southern blood)." [58] But Clements did not last long as editor because his indiscretions created so much rancor and opposition that the politicians who had secured his appointment saw fit to get rid of him in November, 1831, less than six months after Walt had become his apprentice. In one of his more fantastic escapades Clements and the sculptor Henry Kirke Brown disinterred the body of Elias Hicks, soon after his burial in Jericho, in order to make a plaster cast of his face and head.[59] After making the moulds the two men quarreled, and either by accident or by intention the casts were destroyed. The friends and relatives of Hicks instituted legal proceedings, and Clements fled to New Jersey, where he was soon editing a Whig paper.

One might well doubt the beneficial influence of such a man on a twelve-year-old apprentice. But Clements appears to have been indiscreet rather than unscrupulous. And one indication that he was particularly sympathetic and kind at least to one of his apprentices was that Walt was permitted to contribute "sentimental bits" to the *Patriot*.[60] The items were certainly unimportant, and cannot now be identified, but this was the first appearance of Walt Whitman's writings in print, his first faint beginning of authorship—at the remarkably early age of twelve.

Moreover, it was not the editor but the foreman printer who made the most lasting impression on Walt.[61] This man was William Hartshorne, who had come to Brooklyn from Philadelphia toward the close of the eighteenth century. Unlike Clements, he was small, almost fragile in appearance —though he lived eighty-four years—and in temperament quiet, unassuming. He was not a politician and had been employed only for his skill. Until his death in 1859 Whitman often saw him strolling on Fulton Street, wearing a broad-brimmed hat, carrying a cane, and chewing his quid of tobacco. Whitman's own character was almost certainly influenced by his admiration, as boy and man, for the cheerful, sagacious old printer in the broad-brimmed hat, with the eighteenth century manners.

It was Hartshorne who gave Walt his first instruction in typesetting, and the poet never forgot his novice sensations of holding the composing stick, locating the letters in the case of type, and "the first experience in 'pi.'" This printing office was a lively and exhilarating place for the apprentice. Years afterward Whitman recalled that there he first met the young writer and later political "boss" Henry Murphy, and he wondered if Murphy, now ambassador to The Hague, remembered the "carrying on" in the printing office, the cigar smoking, the animated political discussions, and the arguments over some article contributed to the "Pat." Despite the boyish capers that Whitman doubtless participated in, it would seem that at twelve he had some interests beyond his years.

Walt and several other apprentices boarded with Hartshorne's granddaughter, though the Whitmans lived only ten or twelve blocks from the printing office of the "Pat" on Fulton Street, near Nassau. Hartshorne himself had lived in Philadelphia during the Revolution, and Walt "listened with a boy's ardent soul and eager ears" to his reminiscences of Washington, Jefferson, and other heroes of the early years of the Republic. On Sunday the apprentices accompanied Hartshorne to "a great old rough, fortress-looking stone church, on Joralemon Street," [62] at that time still surrounded by broad fields and country roads. This was the Dutch Reformed Church, the oldest in Brooklyn, with a tradition extending back two centuries, before the British occupied New York. Though the building seemed so old and "fortress-looking" to Walt, it was actually less than twenty-five years old, having been erected in 1807.[63] Perhaps its gloomy, ugly, and formidable exterior made it seem older—and the appearance was not out of keeping with the Calvinistic theology still preached there, which Walt never mentioned, perhaps because he was impervious to it, as his later poem "A Child's Amaze" suggests:

Silent and amazed even when a little boy,
I remember I heard the preacher every Sunday put God in his statements,
As contending against some being or influence.

The Dutch Reformed Church drew a large part of its membership from the surrounding farms, as it had done for six generations, and thus linked town and country.[64] The Dutch farmers, butchers, and small merchants were notoriously stubborn in holding on to old customs and ideas. St. Ann's was more progressive, more responsive to social change and new needs. Before the Revolution it had, of course, been Anglican, but now, as an Episcopal church, it attracted the best educated and most progressive men and women in Brooklyn. Whitman's preference for exclusive St. Ann's was not typical of him, for most of his life he was opposed to all social and intellectual elites, but in his childhood this was his favorite church. Though he later took much pride in his Dutch inheritance, he could never stomach Calvinism.

The members of the Presbyterian Church on Cranberry Street were beginning to exercise great influence on the civic and cultural development of Brooklyn, and Walt's next employer, Alden J. Spooner, was one of its most prominent members.[65] But, like the Methodist Chapel on Sands Street, it was strongly evangelical, and piety and evangelism never appealed to Whitman. He did attend some of the Methodist "revivals," and apparently enjoyed the emotional singing and looking at the "pretty girls," but we may be sure that he was not one of those who went to scoff and was irresistibly drawn to the altar, there to spend "the night in tears and mental wrestling." [66] Mrs. Whitman was the only member of the family who felt a special need and desire to attend church, though she attended irregularly and was not a member of any church. Childbearing and the frequent moving from house to house might explain her irregular attendance, for she was genuinely religious. Her son George later said, "She pretended to be a Baptist," [67] and when her husband died she got a Baptist minister to conduct the funeral service. The Baptist church, like the Methodist, included a large number of people in her own social and economic class; and another special reason for her loyalty to the Baptists may have been that they, unlike most of the other churches, did not sell or rent pews.[68]

After he became a poet, Walt Whitman liked to think that his mother was a Quaker, but despite his father's sympathy for the Hicksites (they had no church in Brooklyn), he and his wife never formally joined any Quaker group. In the Whitman home there were no religious exercises or observances of any kind. But when Walt came to write *Leaves of Grass* he felt the religious motive to be one of the strongest features of the poems. It is significant, therefore, that he grew up in a town which prided itself on its churches and whose prominent citizens—several of whom employed Walt during his most impressionable years—actively supported the temperance movement and the numerous moral crusades of the time.

V

After Clements fled Brooklyn, the *Patriot* was edited by John T. Bergen and Joseph Moser, the latter also becoming postmaster. So far as known, Walt Whitman continued his training under Hartshorne, who was retained as foreman printer for the *Patriot*. But the printing office did not absorb Walt's whole interest. In the evenings and on Sunday he often took the ferry to New York, which was far more exciting—and dangerous too—than prosaic Brooklyn. He was always to remember "a sharp, bright January day" about 1832 when he saw John Jacob Astor, "a bent, feeble but stout-built very old man, bearded, swathed in rich furs, with a great ermine cap on his head, led and assisted, almost carried, down the steps of his high front stoop" and seated in his gorgeous sleigh "drawn by as fine a team of horses as I ever saw." [69]

By the summer of 1832 Walt had begun working for another Brooklyn printer, Erastus Worthington, a close friend of Alden Spooner, from whom he had taken over a bookstore and circulating library. Of course, Walt made good use of the library. But he stayed with Worthington only through the summer. In the autumn he was employed by Spooner himself, the most successful printer, editor, and publisher in Brooklyn, and one of the town's most active civic leaders. He had helped found the first bank in the village, had used the *Star* to encourage the establishment of a competent night watch, and had agitated for improvements of the streets, to mention only a few of the reforms he supported. By 1832 the town had graded, graveled, and paved a considerable number of streets, and sixteen were now illuminated by oil lamps. Since the Whitmans' arrival the population had more than doubled, now numbering 15,000.

In 1832 George Hall won the village presidency on two main issues: clear the hogs from the streets and reduce the licensing of grog shops. [70] A cholera epidemic in the summer aroused the town to the danger of its polluted streets and its contaminated water supplied by communal pumps, and some of the churches seized upon the cholera scare to advance the doctrine that drinking spirituous liquors increased susceptibility to the disease. The Presbyterian editor of the *Star* eagerly supported these health and temperance movements, and the *Patriot* was equally vigorous in advocating reforms. Usually the editors of both papers agreed that New York was more wicked, but Spooner once declared of Brooklyn that "there never was a place more incorrigibly *crooked*. . . . Nothing flourishes there but meeting-houses and porter-houses; and the women fill the former and the men the latter." [71]

Brooklyn citizens had long resented the control of the ferry rates by New York companies, but animosity between the village and the city reached an unprecedented intensity during 1832–1833 as a result of Brooklyn's deciding to incorporate its various communities under a single administration and to apply to the State Legislature for a city charter. New York real-estate dealers became alarmed over the rapid growth of Brooklyn, and with the aid of their Board of Aldermen they managed to block legislative approval of the charter until 1834. But the delay did not curb the boom in Brooklyn real estate, and prices continued to rise fantastically.

In fact, when Andrew Jackson was inaugurated in March, 1833, the whole nation was enjoying an exhilarating prosperity after several years of wide unemployment and slack business. It was not, therefore, because of "hard times" that Walter Whitman, Sr., decided in May to move his family back to the region of West Hills.[72] The exact location of the first stop is not known, but in 1834 the family was living at Norwich (now East Norwich), near Oyster Bay, probably only five or six miles from the home of Major Van Velsor. Mrs. Whitman's eighth child was due in July, and she was in poor health. From Walt we learn that she was "very ill for a long time," [73] but he did not indicate the nature of her illness or whether it began before or after the birth of her son, Thomas Jefferson, on July 18. Many people in Brooklyn were apprehensive over another outbreak of cholera in the hot weather, and this may have influenced the move.

But returning to the country was also another proof that Walter Whitman, Sr., was not a businessman. He lacked both the judgment and the businessman's point of view. His sympathy was with the workingmen who attended Frances Wright's lectures in New York and subscribed to her militant *Free Inquirer*, which she had started in 1829, after two winters of great hardship for day laborers in all the large Eastern cities. Walt was perhaps too young to take much interest in the lectures (though he may have attended a few with his father), but he read his father's copy of the *Inquirer*, and at some time in his youth he evidently studied attentively Frances Wright's little book on Epicurean philosophy, *A Few Days in Athens*, which his father also owned.[74]

When the Whitman family moved back to the country, Walt remained in Brooklyn. Jesse had possibly already gone to sea,[75] though details of his early life have not survived. Major Van Velsor was still making his weekly trips to Brooklyn, and of course Walt could always ride back to West Hills with him, and probably did so at every opportunity. But he was in Brooklyn in June, when President Jackson, accompanied by the Vice President and the former Governor of New York, visited the town. On the first anniversary of the ex-President's death, Whitman said in an editorial in the Brooklyn *Eagle* (June 8, 1846): "We never saw him but once. That was when we were but a little boy, in this very city of Brooklyn." [76] The President came over to Brooklyn on a bright summer morning, rode up from the ferry in an open barouche, and was greeted much as General Lafayette had been on that other memorable occasion. He saluted the crowd with his broad-brimmed white beaver hat, the women waved their handkerchiefs, and the men shouted.

Walt may have been in the country during the great meteor shower in August, 1833, when the whole sky seemed to be filled with falling stars.[77] Of course superstitious people regarded this phenomenon as an omen of disaster, and in the autumn something did occur that brought distress to the whole nation. After several years of political wrangling over the issue of the United States Bank, which President Jackson wished to abolish in order to establish an independent Federal treasury, the President suddenly withdrew government funds from the United States Bank in Philadelphia, thereby touching off a series of bank failures and precipitating an economic crisis. Eventually this would affect Walt, perhaps change his life plans, but so far as known he continued throughout the fall and winter to work for Spooner.

At fifteen Walt Whitman was as large as a grown man, and he was beginning to acquire some of the tastes and habits that were to influence and characterize his adult life. After contributing to the *Patriot* he had "a piece or two" published in George P. Morris's "then celebrated and fashionable *Mirror* of New York City. I remember with what half-suppressed excitement I used to watch for the big, fat, red-faced, slow-moving very old English carrier who distributed the *Mirror* in Brooklyn; and when I got one, opening and cutting the leaves with trembling fingers. How it made my heart double-beat to see *my piece* on the pretty white paper, in nice type." [78] These contributions were anonymous and cannot now be identified, but they were important to young Whitman as his first ventures in authorship.

While still employed in a Brooklyn printing office, Walt began attending performances at the Bowery Theater in New York, probably on passes distributed to local newspapers. One of the earliest plays he saw was a thrilling melodrama, *Jonathan Bradford, or The Murder at the Road-side Inn,* but this was soon followed by Shakespearean productions. He was so favorably impressed by seeing the elder Booth (Junius Brutus) play Richard that he ever afterward believed *Richard III* to be one of Shakespeare's greatest dramas. At first Walt went to the theater with other boys of his age, but they were not as attentive as he was, and he soon began attending by himself in order to avoid their distractions. He would go early in order to get a good seat in the pit, and while he waited for the dark green curtain to go up "with quick and graceful leaps, like the hopping of a rabbit," he observed the "animal specimens" around him. But as soon as the curtain was up, he lived in "a mimic world of heroes and heroines, and loves, and murders, and plots, and hopes." [79]

Toward the end of his employment in the *Star* printing office Walt also joined a debating society in Brooklyn,[80] a new form of education and recreation combined. And by this time in his reading he had become "an insatiable romance devourer." At Worthington's circulating library he could obtain the latest works both of English and of American authors, but he read novels primarily. This does not sound like the life of a boy who was taking advantage of the separation from his parents but rather of a serious and bookish youngster whose chief delight was to escape from the drab world of work and responsibility into the realm of literature and fantasy. "Illusions of youth," he later called his amusements of this period.[81]

VI

Some time around his sixteenth year, having completed his training and become a full-fledged "journeyman printer," Walt Whitman went to New York to work as a compositor. This was probably in the spring of 1835, though the exact date cannot be determined, or the location of his boardinghouse.[82] At that time New York was a restless, dangerous, but no doubt exciting place for a boy like Walt. Famine in Ireland had caused thousands of Irish immigrants to inundate the cities of the Eastern coast; many of them could not find employment of any kind and the charitable organizations were overwhelmed by their numbers. The Whigs accused Tammany politicians of buying their votes with grog or with dishonest promises, and certain rabble-rousers kept them in a constant frenzy. In the April election of 1834 groups of the Irish and fanatically nationalistic Americans clashed in bloody riots. Gangs of thugs and criminals, recruited mainly from destitute immigrants, lived downtown at Five Points in an abandoned brewery and other ramshackle buildings. Decent citizens avoided like a plague certain corners and alleys of the region, and most New York streets were unsafe at night.

On July 10 there was a brutal riot at Walt's favorite Bowery Theater when an English actor was billed to appear on the stage. The building was nearly destroyed, and a great deal of property around Astor Place was damaged. During the summer there were also anti-abolition riots in the city, abolitionists being very unpopular both in New York and in Brooklyn. Conservative citizens thought the nation was on the brink of disaster, and blamed the Jacksonites for arousing the ignorant masses, while the laboring class in general regarded the President as its savior and bitterly hated his enemies.

Probably at the time Walt Whitman did not realize that the social unrest and economic uncertainty would directly affect him; and indeed, he might have continued indefinitely working in New York if two of the greatest disasters in the history of the city had not taken place in 1835 within a few months of each other. On August 12 the worst fire in thirty or forty years broke out in Paternoster Row.[83] Although this was the center of the printing, binding, and publishing district, it probably did not affect Walt immediately, for he continued working in the city until the following spring. But on December 16 and 17 a still more disastrous fire ravaged the whole area from Wall Street to Coenties Slip. So many business firms were totally burned out that all the fire insurance companies were bankrupted, thereby affecting the whole region and even the national economy, not yet recovered from the bank failures. Thus these fires aggravated the financial depression that had begun two years earlier, and even the weather increased the misery of the poor. The winter of 1835–1836 was so severe that ice on the Connecticut River was forty inches thick, and Philip Hone recorded in his diary that in New York "the high banks of ice in the streets have the appearance of solid walls of black marble."[84] Unemployment increased alarmingly; goods were scarce and prices high. Spring brought relief from the cold, but no abatement of the economic distress.

VII

In May, 1836, Walt joined his family in Hempstead, where they were now living. Probably his father was farming, because farm produce was bringing good prices in the city, and it is not likely that much building was being done anywhere near Hempstead. Walt did not record that he had lost his position in the New York printing offices, but the less experienced printers were undoubtedly first to be dismissed, and employment of any kind was becoming increasingly hard to find. A strong indication that Whitman had lost his position is that in June he began teaching a country school at Norwich[85] (today called East Norwich), a few miles from Major Van Velsor's farm near Cold Springs. The Whitmans had recently lived at Norwich before moving to Hempstead on the southern side of the Island. Walt did not, therefore, begin teaching in a strange community.

Most critics agree that the stories and sketches that Whitman published in the 1840's contain a considerable amount of autobiography, and one of these, "The Shadow and Light of a Young Man's Soul," [86] is particularly revealing. The hero of the story, Archibald Dean, is mentally depressed because as a result of the great fire of 1835 in New York he has had to leave the city and go "down into the country to take charge of a little district school." That Whitman's morale was as low as Archie Dean's we can only guess, but under the circumstances he might be expected to be discouraged, for country schoolteaching was not well paid or very much respected. The hero of this story "had too much of that inferior sort of pride which fears to go forth in public with anything short of fashionable garments, and hat and boots fit for fashionable criticism." In the earliest photographs we have of Whitman, made only a few years later, he is modishly dressed, wears a well-trimmed beard, and carries a cane. Very likely at this time Walt, like Archie, "looked on the dark side of his life entirely too often; he pined over his deficiencies, as he called them, by which he meant mental as well as pecuniary wants."

Here is Walt Whitman, barely seventeen, recently journeyman printer in New York City, teaching a district school not far from his grandfather's farm, where he had spent some of his happiest days and nights before his grandmother's death. He could have been describing himself when he wrote of Archie Dean: "the discontented young teacher's spirits were eventually raised and sweetened by his country life, by his long walks over the hills, by his rides on horseback every Saturday." Walt probably rode one of his grandfather's horses on Saturdays, and he too found something "to admire in the character and customs of the unpolished country folk." Later he would call these associations "one of my best experiences and deepest lessons in human nature." [87]

By modern standards Whitman's qualifications for schoolteaching were

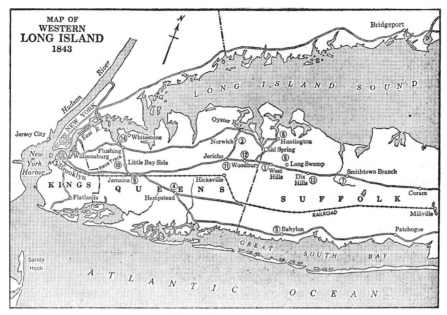

LONG ISLAND, 1843

(1) West Hills, birthplace of Walt Whitman; (2) Brooklyn—youth and early manhood; (3) Norwich (East Norwich)—taught school, summer of 1836; (4) Hempstead—lived with family, spring, 1836; (5) Babylon—taught school near Babylon, winter of 1836–37; (6) Long Swamp—taught school, spring of 1837; (7) Smithtown (Smithtown Branch)—taught school, autumn and winter, 1837–38; (8) Huntington—edited newspaper, 1838–39; (9) Jamaica—worked on newspaper, late summer and fall of 1839; electioneered for Van Buren, fall of 1840; (10) Little Bay Side (near Jamaica, on highway to Flushing)—taught school, winter of 1839–40; (11) Triming Square (not on map, near West Hills)—taught school spring of 1840; (12) Woodbury—taught school, summer of 1840; (13) Dix Hills—Whitman family lived here in 1840; (14) Whitestone—taught school, winter and spring, 1840–41.

certainly meager; nevertheless, in printing and newspaper offices he had acquired far more competence in the basic subjects than most country schoolteachers of the time possessed. Schoolteaching in general was held in low esteem in America, and the rewards were small indeed. The law required each district to operate a school for three months of the year, and many districts did not exceed this minimum. The average compensation for a three-months' term was $35 to $40 and board. The latter was particularly unsatisfactory, because the custom was for the teacher to "board round," [88] that is, a day or two at each home in rotation, the parents thus saving the authorities the expense of paying for the teacher's room and meals at an inn or boardinghouse. The subjects taught were those of the primary grades, spelling, reading, writing, and sometimes a little geography and public speaking.[89] A few texts, such as Webster's "blue-backed speller," were more or less standard, but the individual student usually recited out of any textbook his parents happened to own or could easily procure. Thus each child pursued his studies in haphazard independence. With this system, twenty was said to be as many pupils as a teacher could efficiently manage, for in addition to hearing each child recite he was also supposed to make or re-sharpen every quill that the children used in writing, set down models of handwriting for the pupils to imitate, keep the fire going in cold weather, and of course maintain order and discipline, which usually required a considerable amount of birching. Yet in some schools Whitman taught forty or fifty students, and in at least two over eighty, ranging in ages from five to fifteen, some of the students almost as old as the teacher.[90]

The buildings were one-room box-like structures, with an open fireplace. If the fire went out, the teacher might send one of the boys to a nearby house to borrow live coals. Those who sat closest to the fire roasted while those in other parts of the room shivered. There was no janitor, and at the end of the day the teacher or some of his pupils swept out the room. The school day was long, from eight o'clock in the morning until four or five in the afternoon. The children sat on backless benches and naturally became restless long before the daily session ended. If the teacher taught four quarters (as Whitman did part of the time, though in different schools), he had no vacation except a day or two spent in transferring from one school to another. Traditionally, the district schoolteacher was also expected to sit up with all corpses! A teacher who had preceded Whitman by a few years in one school declared, "Many think a schoolmaster's employment an easy one—the teacher that makes it so is not fit for one, and whoever undertakes to perform half a schoolteacher ought to do will find a laborious and wearisome task." [91]

At the end of each term a committee appointed by the school board visited the school to ask questions and inspect the progress of the pupils. This day was dreaded by the whole school, and the report of the committee was a spur to the teacher as well as the students, since it might determine whether he was re-employed. However, the visits of the inspection committee may not have been responsible for Whitman's frequent changing of positions. In view of the instability of the teaching profession—if it could be called a profession—there might have been other reasons, and it is significant that Whitman apparently had little difficulty in finding new appointments.

According to his own record, Walt was not employed in the fall of 1836, but this may have been because he wished to rejoin his family. The Whitmans moved from Hempstead to the vicinity of Babylon in August, 1836,[92] near the end of Walt's term at Norwich. This was probably the time when, according to George's recollection,[93] Walt's father tried to make him work on the farm, and Walt rebelled. It was a tempestuous summer anyway, for a very bitter presidential campaign was getting under way, and the Whigs were using every means possible to defeat Martin Van Buren, President Jackson's choice for his successor.

During this campaign there was one subject on which Walt and his father agreed, and that was Frances Wright, who was vigorously supporting Van Buren. She had returned to America late in the preceding year and throughout the summer of 1836 lectured in Philadelphia, Boston, and New York.[94] Although Walt may have heard her in 1828 and 1829, when she was preaching rational education, equal rights for all men, and urging the workers to organize, he was probably too young to understand her radical ideas. In 1836, however, he could not have read the newspapers without being aware of her, and it is likely that he heard her speak in New York. Paid thugs tried to break up some of her meetings, and the Whig press attacked her in violent language, calling her atheist, Negro lover, she-Locofoco, and an immoral woman. But the more she was attacked, the more loyally her supporters rallied around her, and she deserved part of the credit for the election of Van Buren—though she warned that the split which had developed in the Democratic party in New York City and State would enable the Whigs to return to power in 1840.

The role that Frances Wright played in American politics and cultural life from the summer of 1836 until her final return to Europe on June 16,

1839, endeared her to Walt Whitman and thousands of other young men with similar political views. Years later Walt glowed with enthusiasm every time he mentioned her name. He called her "a woman of the noblest make-up . . . a most maligned, lied-about character—one of the best in history though also one of the least understood." [95] She was not beautiful, but she had good features, a majestic poise, a strong clear voice, and she knew how to control an audience. In his reminiscences Whitman showed how deeply she had stirred his emotions: "She has always been to me one of the sweetest of sweet memories: we [who heard her speak] all loved her: fell down before her: her very appearance seemed to enthrall us." [96] And again: "I never felt so glowingly toward any other woman." [97]

Soon after the election of Van Buren, Walt began teaching a three-months' term in a school near Babylon, and George, who was now seven, was one of his pupils. Probably Walt continued to live with his family during the winter of 1836–1837, but there are strong indications that he was not at this time a harmonizing influence. He was absorbed in his teaching and experiments in writing, kept to himself, confided in no one, and his father, still irritated by his refusal to do farm work, was critical and sarcastic. Walt resented his father's attitude, and at times there were emotional outbursts.[98] Mrs. Whitman, the "peacemaker," intervened and calmed the men down, but she could not remove the friction. Though Walt loved her more than anyone else in the world, he did not confide in her, but they trusted each other, and Walt felt sustained and comforted by her love and faith.

With the exception of his older brother Jesse, who was probably not at home, Walt felt a deep affection for his brothers and sisters, though he may have been a bit dictatorial toward them at times. He often helped his mother take care of the younger children, and, according to George, it "seemed as if he had us in charge"—adding, "now and then his guardianship seemed excessive." In a thinly disguised allegory, called "My Boys and Girls," [99] which Whitman wrote in 1835 or 1836 to satisfy the sentimental magazine taste of the day, he described three of his brothers and his two sisters, even giving their correct names. Louisa (Hannah) he called "the fairest and most delicate of human blossoms"; she was always his favorite, as George asserted. Walt did not identify a "fat, hearty, rosy-cheeked youngster . . . an imp of mischief," though it was undoubtedly Jeff. The young author played facetiously upon the patriotic names of his brothers: George Washington, whom he had carried on his shoulders; Thomas Jefferson, whom he had held in his arms while teaching him to spell; and Andrew Jackson, who had often wrestled with the author.

That "My Boys and Girls" was a picture of family relations at this period is indicated in the age given Mary: "She is a very beautiful girl in her fourteenth year." That would have been 1835, the year Edward (the mental defective) was born; he is not alluded to in the sketch. But Walt seemed to have strange intimations of unhappiness in store for Mary. "Flattery comes too often to her ears. From the depths of her soul I now and then see misty revealings of thought and wish, that are not well. I see them through her eyes and in the expression of her face." He feared "the dim phantoms of Evil standing about with nets and temptations" to ensnare her. Whether there was any basis for these premonitions, or whether they were merely sentimental moralizings, we have no way of knowing. At the age of nineteen Mary married a Long Island mechanic, Ansel Van Nostrand,[100] two years before the publication of this sketch. Before her marriage she may have gone with boys against her parents' wishes, and this might have caused her older brother to think her headstrong and reckless —though in his own way he was certainly as stubborn as she could have been.

VIII

Walt had scarcely finished his one term near Babylon before he began teaching a new school in the spring of 1837 at Long Swamp,[101] a few miles east of his birthplace at West Hills. He was thus still in familiar territory, but no further information about this school has survived. And what he did during the following summer is completely unknown. It is likely that he tried to secure other employment, but by this time the nation was in the grip of the worst economic depression in its history. Land speculation and Jackson's financial policies had contributed to the collapse, but there were other causes, such as crop failures in this country and bankruptcies of firms in England that had invested in American land and industry. In New York and Brooklyn unemployment reached staggering proportions. In May all banks suspended specie payments, and money practically stopped circulating. Walt may have returned to his parents' home, though of course Walter Whitman, Sr., was hard pressed to feed his large family. In old age Walt told a friend that at one time he had been a gardener on Long Island,[102] and possibly this was the way he spent the summer.

In the autumn, however, Walt returned to schoolteaching, this time at Smithtown (that is, Smithtown Branch), about ten miles east of West Hills. Here he taught two terms instead of the usual one. Soon after his arrival he joined a debating society—perhaps, more accurately, it was revived for his pleasure—and in this organization, which elected him secretary, he associated with some of the most prominent men of the town, including two judges, a congressman, a member of the New York legislature, two physicians, two justices of the peace, a dentist, several businessmen, and some prosperous farmers.[103] These mature men accepted the eighteen-year-old schoolteacher as an intellectual equal, and of the sixteen debates held during the autumn and winter of 1837–1838 Whitman took part in eleven, his side winning six times and receiving two tie decisions. The subjects debated were serious and important, such as the advantages of military training, vocational versus liberal education, soldiers' bonuses, imperialism, the practicality of settling national disputes without war, and "Has Nature more influence than education in the formation of character?" On the last question the schoolteacher appropriately defended the negative—though this was one of his three defeats. His debating record as a whole was creditable, especially considering the fact that the speakers who opposed him were older and more experienced. In later life he was always a slow thinker, seldom at his best on the spur of the moment, and it is surprising that he made so good a record in the Smithtown Debating Society.

In the spring of 1838 Whitman decided to start a newspaper in nearby Huntington. Some of his friends in Smithtown may have loaned him the money for this venture, for he certainly could not have saved enough during his few terms of teaching, and he evidently found no difficulty in launching his weekly paper, the *Long Islander*. Many years later Whitman wrote this account:

I went to New York, bought a press and types, hired some little help, but did most of the work myself, including the press-work. Everything seem'd turning out well (only my own restlessness prevented me gradually establishing a permanent property there). I bought a good horse, and every week went all round the country serving my papers, devoting one day and night to it. I never had happier jaunts—going over to south side, to Babylon, down the south road, across to Smithtown and Comac, and back home. The experiences of those jaunts, the dear old-fashion'd farmers and their wives, the stops by the hayfields, the hospitality, nice dinners, occasional evenings, the girls, the rides through the brush, come up in my memory to this day.[104]

Here we have one of Whitman's few references to "girls." While he was an apprentice he had noticed the pretty girls who attended the Methodist revivals, and here he mentions them along with the "nice dinners" and the pleasant rides. That there were any love affairs at this time, however, seems doubtful, because Walt's younger brother, George, who was assisting him on the *Long Islander,* states emphatically, "I am confident I never knew Walt to fall in love with young girls or even to show them marked attention." [105] And this opinion is corroborated by the memory of two of Whitman's friends in Huntington who were interviewed many years later by Daniel Brinton and Horace Traubel. To the inquiry "whether Walt was a gay lad among the lassies of the village—a beau in the rustic society of his day," the reply was, "He seemed to hate women." The interviewers thought this a "hard and . . . quite too strong expression, but one which forcibly shows how alien even to his hot blood of twenty summers were all effeminate longings." [106]

But Walt did like amusements. He lived with George in a room over his printing shop, and at night groups of his friends would gather there for talk, storytelling, games, and frolic. Yet there was no dissipation, if we can believe the statements of these old cronies, who declared that he did not "use tobacco in any form. He drank no liquor. He was in no way profane." George adds that Walt liked to play cards, but he never attended dances. One gathers that he spent most of his evenings in his office, or in the room upstairs. George remembered that, "He once had a ring suspended from the ceiling. The point was to throw this ring on a hook driven in the wall. On one occasion the prize was a mince pie or twenty-five cents, and I recall that I had to go for the pie." But Walt "cared little for sport." He had no use whatever for hunting. "He would fish now and then, but he was not carried away with it. He was an old-fashioned ball-player and entered into the game heartily enough." Once while fishing Walt was provoked into thrashing a boy with his rod for scaring the fish away. First the boy threw stones into the water near Walt's line, and then got into a boat and rowed around the line. Walt managed to catch and thrash him, and for this assault he was haled into court, but the verdict was, in the cockney English of the foreman, a fisherman himself, "We find that 'e did not 'it 'im 'ard enough." [107]

It is difficult to understand why Whitman became so restless that he gave up his pleasant life in Huntington at the end of a year, but of course country newspapers were not very profitable. He may have believed, too, that his experience in editing and printing his own paper would make it easier for him to secure a position in New York City. At any rate, in May, 1839, he sold his newspaper and equipment, disposed of Nina, his horse —that was hardest of all because he had become attached to her—and left Huntington. After visiting his family and loafing for a while on the beaches, he went to New York to look for work; but printing offices and newspapers had not yet recovered from the depression—as a journalist should have known—and Walt was unable to find employment in the city.

IX

James J. Brenton, editor of the *Long Island Democrat*, published at Jamaica, had reprinted several of Whitman's essays and poems from the *Long Islander;*[108] and probably on the strength of this approval, and correspondence which it had involved, Walt applied to him for employment. Actually, it is impossible to determine which took the initiative, but in August, 1839, Whitman went to Jamaica and began working for Brenton and living at his home. It is not unlikely that the room and board constituted a large portion of the compensation for setting type and writing for the paper. Apparently Whitman gave his full time to Brenton from late August until about the first of December, when he took charge of a nearby school at Little Bay Side, a short distance down the highway toward Flushing.

The months spent at Jamaica were crucial ones for Whitman. He was near a crossroads in his life, and he did not know which road to take. We might guess this from his literary juvenilia, but the testimony of Brenton's daughter-in-law, Mrs. Orvetta Hall Brenton,[109] confirms this hypothesis. Some exaggerations and inaccuracies may have crept into this woman's account, for she got the details years later from Mrs. James Brenton, but in the essentials it is probably reliable. According to Mrs. Orvetta Brenton, her mother-in-law was "a practical, busy, New England woman," who disliked Walt Whitman intensely and regarded him as a "dreamy, impractical youth, who did very little work and who was always 'under foot' and in the way." Part of the dislike may be attributed to a difference in social background. Walt's parents had no regard for formality in dress and manners, and he probably resented Mrs. Brenton's making him wear a coat at the dinner table. She thought him sloven, crude, and "inordinately . . . lazy." Perhaps he was reacting to this opinion when he wrote an essay on the joys of loafing, in which he declared, "How I do love a loafer!," though Brenton did not publish this until Walt had left Jamaica.

Brenton himself liked Walt and made allowances for his faults, but even he is reported to have said that he wondered how he could make the young man realize that he must work for a living. We are told that Walt would often lie under an apple tree for two or three hours after he was supposed to be at the printing office and that Brenton would have to send his "printer's devil" after him. "When spoken to, he would get up reluctantly and go slowly back to the shop."

Another cause of Mrs. Brenton's dislike was Walt's "disregard of the two children of the household—two small boys—who seemed to annoy him when they were with him in the house." The daughter-in-law did not believe that anyone who disliked children as Walt did could have been a good teacher. But of course we cannot accept this opinion at face value without knowing something about the two boys. However, it is significant that Mrs. James Brenton regarded Whitman as "dreamy, quiet, morose" and never "bright or cheerful," though the younger Mrs. Brenton admitted that she "never heard a word against his habits." And Brenton "was sorry to have him go, for, even in those early days, he showed marked ability as a writer and was of great value to the 'literary' end of the newspaper work."

There is some evidence that Walt was a more successful teacher than Mrs. Brenton could imagine, for one of his students at Little Bay Side, a boy of ten named Charles A. Roe, later testified to his effectiveness in the classroom.[110] According to Roe, Whitman discarded the usual methods of rote and depended to a considerable extent on conversation and oral instruction. He gave his students much practice in "mental arithmetic," played "twenty questions" with them, and participated in their games at recess and lunchtime, paying special attention to the younger children. He had novel methods of discipline, too, and never used corporal punishment. If he detected a student in a falsehood, he exposed him in a story told in such a way "that the guilty fellow knew who was meant" without having his name mentioned. The teacher never betrayed "by anything in his manner that he felt above us, or condescended, or wished in any way to put on a tone or an air of superiority." It is not surprising that his students "were all deeply attached to him, and were sorry when he went away."

This same witness also gave other pertinent information about Whitman in his twentieth year. "The girls did not seem to attract him. He did not specially go anywhere with them or show any extra fondness for their society . . . He did not care for women's society—seemed, indeed, to

shun it. Young as I was, I was aware of that fact." But "I do not think he
became very closely acquainted with our young men of his own age. He
seemed retiring, diffident, yet he was friendly to everybody—was not
offish—made no enemies." Perhaps Whitman preferred the companionship
of older people, because Roe remembered that his teacher enjoyed discussing books with his father. On Sunday he stayed away from church,
and the woman with whom he boarded, who had four daughters, regretted
that he was not more religious. "I had heard her speak of his views on religion as being rather atheistic. Very friendly to him otherwise—just a trifle
suspicious, or sorry, that was all." Of course he was no more "atheistic"
than Frances Wright, who by this time was giving lectures on "the religion
of humanity" and advocating religion as the foundation of all culture, [111]
but heterodoxy is not usually tolerated in rural communities. One is astonished that there was not more opposition to Whitman, but "He was not
aggressive—did not talk of his religion."

Whitman's personal appearance at this time was conventional; he "always dressed in black—dressed neatly—very plain in everything—no attempt at what would be called fashion. He wore an old style frock coat,
vest and pants black . . . He dressed mainly as other people dressed . . .
His hat not out of the usual at that time." And his personal habits were
equally conventional. "He was never sick; did not smoke; never, that I saw
or heard of, drank any liquors. As to his eating, I never knew him to have
had any peculiar habits."

Roe's recollection of some verses that Whitman assigned his students to
memorize gives unexpected proof of the accuracy of this witness' memory.
In old age he could still recite the poem, one stanza of which went:

> Oh he was pure! the fleecy snow
> Sinking through air to earth below
> Was not more undefiled!
> Sinless he was, as fleeting smile
> On lip of sleeping child.

The family with whom Whitman boarded told the little boy that his
teacher wrote poetry and that this was his own composition. "That was
the rumor. The poem was quite long, having a number of stanzas. My
version is very faulty, no doubt, but the lines I have given you are substan-
tially correct." They were indeed, for they were very close to a version of
the poem that Whitman published two years later, [112] and the minor variations between the memorized and the printed poem might easily be ac-

counted for by Whitman's revisions. The whole poem, called "The Punishment of Pride," was excessively moral and sentimental, in accordance with contemporary taste, and it proves that the young schoolteacher's mind was still as conventional and undistinguished as his dress and conduct.

From Little Bay Side Whitman returned to the West Hills region, where he taught during the spring of 1840 at Triming Square (no longer found on Long Island maps) and the following summer at Woodbury, three or four miles from West Hills. Whitman entered these places and dates in his notebook but gave no details. In 1890 two English friends of the poet made a trip to America just to see their idol and visit his birthplace. Near West Hills they met an old man named Sandford Brown, who said that Walt Whitman was his first teacher. He did not give the name of the school, but it was probably either Triming Square or Woodbury. According to Brown, Whitman was not a successful teacher. "He warn't in his element. He was always musin' an' writin', 'stead of 'tending to his proper dooties . . ." [112a] But it is difficult to know how much credence to give to this witness. Whitman's novel disciplinary and pedagogical methods might have influenced rural folk to think he was lazy and incompetent. And there may have been other reasons for suspicion and misunderstanding. During the Civil War Whitman once confessed to a friend that "the grown up son of the farmer with whom he was boarding while he was teaching school became very fond of him, and Walt of the boy, and he said the father quite reproved him for making such a pet of the boy." [113] This was evidently an early example of the affection for men that Whitman was later to express in his "Calamus" poems.

X

There was, perhaps, some truth in Sandford Brown's belief that his teacher was more interested in his "musin' an' writin'" than in his schoolroom, for in the spring of 1840 Whitman began a series of essays called "Sun-Down Papers from the Desk of a School-Master," that Brenton published in the *Long Island Democrat*, along with six more poems. [114] These essays continued to appear occasionally throughout the winter of 1840–1841 and into the following summer. Though Whitman called them ". . . Papers from the Desk of a School-Master," they did not deal with school matters, and were highly didactic, sentimental, and oppressively moral. One of the earliest was a little sermon on the evils of smoking and drinking coffee. In another the author wondered "How many persons go down to the grave, praised by the world and pointed to as examples, who were still far, very far, from good men!"

Some of the "Sun-Down Papers" reveal the vague ambitions beginning to form in the twenty-one-year-old young man's mind. In No. 7 he thinks of composing "a wonderful and ponderous book . . . And who knows but that I might do something very respectable?" [115] The nature of this book is extremely ambiguous, and the author is well aware that he has yet to produce visible evidence that it is not an absurd dream; hence he is half facetious about it himself, as when he remarks, though possibly with more truth than he realizes, that he "would carefully avoid saying anything of woman; because it behoves a modest personage like myself not to speak upon a class of beings of whose nature, habits, notions, and ways he has not been able to gather any knowledge by experience or observation."

Another essay, No. 8, is revealing in a different way. The subject is an allegorical dream in which the author wanders over the earth in search of "Truth." In general style and diction it is trite and amateurish, but the writer is stumbling in the direction of the "catalog" technique of *Leaves of Grass*, with which he would survey all creation and annihilate time and space.

The poems that Whitman wrote and published during this time and the next few years showed little promise. The themes, images, and conceits were borrowed from the eighteenth century "graveyard" poets; the mawkish sentiment was that of the poetry columns of the various weekly newspapers on which Whitman had worked; and the didacticism was labored. He wanted to write poetry, but he had as yet no subject matter of his own, no depth of emotion, no experience that must be expressed. Occasionally, however, we glimpse a spark of genuine feeling through the derivative verbiage, as in this use of the friendship theme:

> O, mighty powers of Destiny!
> When from this coil of flesh I'm free—
> When through my second life I rove,
> Let me but find *one* heart to love
>   As I would wish to love.
>
> Let me but meet a single breast,
> Where this tired soul its hope may rest,
> In never-dying faith; ah, then,
> That would be bliss all free from pain,
>   And sickness of the heart.

For vainly through this world below
We seek affection. Nought but wo
Is with our earthly journey wove;
And so the heart must look above,
 Or die in dull despair.[116]

Already this young man felt a premonition of his destiny to be the "solitary singer." Despite the friendly faces around him, he was beginning to wonder if he would ever find the one person capable of responding as he himself "would wish to love."

The crucial presidential campaign of 1840 gave Whitman a temporary escape from the classroom. Probably through his friend Brenton he received an appointment as Democratic electioneer for Queens County. There have been many bitter presidential contests in American history, but few more reckless than the battle between the supporters of Martin Van Buren and William Henry Harrison in the fall of 1840. And though Walt Whitman's contribution was a very minor one, he shared fully in the intensity and scurrility of that political battle.

Jamaica had two newspapers, the Whig one being the *Long Island Farmer*. On September 24 Daniel Webster spoke at Jamaica, to an estimated audience of two thousand, in support of the Whig ticket, and he was followed on the platform by Charles King, son of Rufus King, editor of the New York *American*. The *Long Island Democrat* reported [117] Webster's speech as "a complete failure. . . . The man was sick, his cause was bad, and moreover his stomach was out of order," an obvious jibe at the great man's fondness for alcohol. As for Charles King, he was Satan in the shape of a pursy gentleman with a husky voice. "He *lied* up hill and down. He asserted that Mr. Van Buren was 'in favor of having all things in common—property, wife and children.'"

A few days later the local officials of the two parties staged a debate between John Gunn and Walter Whitman. On October 6 the *Long Island Farmer* reported this affair as "A Loco Foco Defeat," the "champion of Democracy" having been "completely stumped."

He called Mr. C. King a "liar and a blackguard." We warn this man how he again indulges in public attacks of this kind; personal slanders are not to be allowed in this manner. We say to *him* beware. The friends of the gentleman alluded to, will not allow such things. The writer of this is authorized in saying, and *he says it with emphasis*, that *another* such provocation, *another* such encroachment on the decencies of life, and this loco foco, or any other may meet with severe and deserved chastisement.   BUCKEYE[118]

Whitman replied to these threats in a signed letter to the *Long Island Democrat*.[119] "From my very soul," he wrote, "I look with sorrow on the pitiable and blacksouled malice which actuates such men as this young Gunn, who has lately been uttering the most reckless falsehoods, and endeavoring to stain, by mean and ungentlemanly misstatements, the standing of our most reputable citizens." Whitman denounced the editor of the *Long Island Farmer* for "sending forth, week after week, the basest lies, upon the character of our country and countrymen." Then in no unmistakable words he repeated the charge that had provoked the threat on his person and safety: "I publickly reaffirm the truth of all that I said at the discussion alluded to. I openly and without qualification assert that Charles King, at the late Webster meeting, in saying that Mr. Van Buren and the democratick party uphold the doctrine of a 'community of goods, wives, and children,' uttered a *lie*, and acted as no *gentleman* would act."

Evidently Whitman successfully called "Buckeye's" bluff, for no one replied to his repeated accusation, and so far as known no attempt was made to execute the threat of violence. In the November election the Whigs carried New York State and the nation, as Frances Wright had warned, but Jamaica went Democratic. How much credit Whitman deserved for the local victory it is impossible to estimate, but he was hardly a failure as a political campaigner. However, he had won a pyrrhic victory, because his party was unable to reward his efforts. He must now return either to the printing office or the schoolroom. For the moment he chose the latter, and he secured an appointment at Whitestone, a few miles north of Brooklyn, for the winter of 1840–1841.[120] But again we have no details for this school term. No matter how successful he may have been in teaching, however, he was still in a very poorly paid profession. This was sufficient cause for his deciding at the end of the term to return to the printing trade in New York City, and this time he would be fortunate enough to secure a position.

◦§ II §◦

ROOTS AND LEAVES

Roots and leaves themselves alone are these,
. . . they will become flowers, fruits, tall
branches and trees.[1]

I

NEAR his twenty-second birthday Walt Whitman took one of the ferries from Brooklyn to bustling, raucous New York City, which despite fire, pestilence, and economic depressions now had nearly half a million inhabitants. In his notebook he simply recorded that he "went to New York in May 1841 and wrote for *Democratic Review*, worked at printing business in *New World* office [,] boarded at Mrs. Chipmans." [2] This notation does not list the events in chronological order, and its barrenness of detail conceals the excitement and importance of four of the most influential years in Whitman's personal and literary development.

The young man arrived almost exactly a year after the beginning of one of the hottest newspaper battles in the history of American journalism, the effects of which would be felt for many years. Vituperative editorials were nothing new, but this was organized warfare, the result of rapid changes taking place in city journalism. The establishment of the "penny press" in the previous decade had greatly enlarged the newspaper-reading public, and thereby encouraged the starting of new papers. Until recently all newspapers had been partisan, and their very existence had depended upon the patronage of a political party or of an influential officeholder.

The old order of journalism was challenged, therefore, when James Gordon Bennett founded the New York *Herald* in 1835 as an independent daily.[3] And he was such an able and enterprising editor that his competitors became alarmed. One of these, Park Benjamin, editor of the aggressive *Evening Signal,* opened battle in the spring of 1840 with a violent attack on Bennett's character, calling him "an habitual liar," an "active utterer of obscenities," a "notorious scoffer" at religion, and other papers quickly enlisted in the "moral war." Then the editors tried to form an alliance with merchants, ministers, and politicians to deprive the *Herald* of advertising, but Bennett prospered beyond all precedent despite the combined efforts of his enemies.

The most important result of these journalistic developments was the growth of the independent press and the rapid multiplication of daily papers in New York City. Whitman arrived in an off year, for only two new papers were started in 1841, the *True Sun* and the *Tribune*, as compared with nine in 1839, the same number in 1842, and twenty in 1845. However, the founding of new papers did not greatly increase the demand for journalists, because one editor with the assistance of one or two less experienced men usually comprised the whole editorial staff. But the type had to be set tediously by hand; consequently there was a growing need for printers. This was especially true of Park Benjamin, who edited not only the daily *Signal* but also the large literary weekly the *New World*, which made a specialty of pirating famous British authors,[4] and it was in Benjamin's large printing office that Walt Whitman found employment.

Although Benjamin was one of the most successful, though erratic, editors of the period, he was irascible and treacherous, and Whitman never indicated a liking for him. As a result of illness in his youth (possibly poliomyelitis, though the disease was not yet named) one leg was shorter than the other, and this handicap may have caused his nervousness and irritability. He had inherited a fortune (which he later lost in a publishing failure), had attended several colleges, and had studied law both at Harvard and at Yale. In Boston he was a highly successful editor before coming to New York. Enterprising, adventurous, and extremely aggressive, he had advertised *Brother Jonathan*, which he had recently edited, as "the largest and cheapest newspaper in the world," and he now claimed the *New World* to be "not only 'the largest and cheapest,' but the handsomest newspaper in the world." The size was twenty-four by thirty-three inches —sometimes in a special issue thirty by fifty inches—well printed on good paper and liberally illustrated. In 1840 Benjamin also began printing an additional library or quarto edition, and some of the books he published in magazine form were still smaller. For several years these variable-size editions of the *New World* outdistanced all competition and nearly drove the book publishers into bankruptcy, but a change in the postal rates in 1843 finally caused the death of the *New World* in 1845.

Several other papers also reprinted whole books in "extras," thus competing with the American book publishers. A work that Harper sold for one dollar or a dollar and a half a copy, these papers would sell for six and a half, twelve and a half, or sixteen and three-quarter cents; and the *Herald* might even include the work in its regular news edition for two cents. Dickens's *American Notes* was thus pirated and sold for ten cents. Benjamin specialized in obtaining advance copies of a British book by a London or Liverpool steamer, setting up and printing a special edition overnight, and selling it on the streets next morning. Such speed necessitated his employing many typesetters; thus Walt Whitman found a position in the busiest printing office in the city.

But the former schoolteacher, country journalist, and political campaigner did not intend to hide his talents behind a typecase. He lost no time in getting acquainted with Democratic political leaders as well as with a number of editors and journalists, and scarcely two months after his arrival in the city he made a speech, on the evening of July 30, at a Democratic rally in the Park near City Hall. Next day the *New Era*, the official Tammany newspaper, and the *Post*, edited by William Cullen Bryant, quoted Whitman's speech at length.[5] It was a heady beginning for the young man whom Mrs. Brenton only two years previously had thought lazy and unambitious.

As a speaker, however, Whitman was no spellbinder, and would never become one. The words quoted in the newspapers do not contain anything likely to provoke prolonged cheering. Yet they were commendable, revealing the speaker as a person of high integrity, and containing some wise political advice and prophecy. He urged the Democrats not to try to raise "this or that man to power," but to battle for "great principles," to stand for the right "measures, policy and doctrine, and leave to future consideration the selection of the agent to carry our plans into effect. My firm conviction is that the next democratic candidate [for the Presidency], whoever he may be, will be carried into power on the wings of a mighty reaction." The advice was sound because it was still too long before the next presidential election to foresee the possible strength of any one candidate, and the reaction envisioned by Whitman actually did, three years later, sweep James K. Polk into the Presidency over Henry Clay. But Tammany politicians were doubtless not interested in idealistic principles, and Whitman did not make any more speeches for them. He was not destined for a political career in New York City—or anywhere else.

Moreover, Whitman's main ambition was not in the field of politics. For several years he had been writing and revising stories, essays, and poems, which of course he had brought with him to New York, and he had not been in the city many weeks before he sold his first story to the *Democratic Review*. Although his employer published some work by American authors, for which he paid what was at the time considered to be a fair price, he naturally found it more profitable to pirate the more famous British writers. Whitman may have submitted some of his manuscripts to Park Benjamin, but perhaps he wanted the approval of the best literary magazine then being published in America, and that was unquestionably the *Democratic Review*, in which the contributions of Poe, Bryant, Hawthorne, Lowell, Whittier, and other eminent Americans, frequently appeared. Founded in Washington, D.C., by John L. O'Sullivan as the *United States Magazine and Democratic Review*, it had only that year moved to New York. O'Sullivan, an ardent Democrat and patriotic to the extreme of jingoism, hoped through his magazine to stimulate the growth of a native, democratic culture. A few years later he became one of the leaders of a movement called "Young America," [6] the purpose of which was to spread democratic ideas throughout the world, and especially to undermine European monarchies. He was the editor who was to invent the phrase "Manifest Destiny" in 1845 during the dispute between the United States and England over the Oregon territory.

Whitman was naturally elated over placing his story in the *Democratic Review*,[7] and it was published without delay in the August number. Evidently O'Sullivan thought his readers liked it, because he accepted two more of Whitman's stories for the November and December numbers. The first, "Death in the Schoolroom," [8] told a lurid tale of a sadistic schoolmaster who unwittingly thrashed the corpse of a frail schoolboy. In the second, "Wild Frank's Return," [9] the hero left home because of a stern, unfeeling father, and on his return was accidentally killed by his favorite horse. The moral was: "Oh, it had been a mistake of the farmer that he did not teach his children to love one another." In the third story, "Bervance," [10] presented as "more truth than fiction," the father hated his son and almost drove him insane by having him committed to an asylum, but the son escaped and left home forever. The young author seemed to have almost a compulsion to write about cruel fathers.

Perhaps Park Benjamin was impressed by the appearance of Whitman's writing in the *Democratic Review*. At any rate, in the fall he published two of his employee's poems in the *New World*, "Each Has His Grief," [11] on November 20, and "The Punishment of Pride," [12] on December 18.

Both were tiresomely didactic and showed no literary advance over the poems that Brenton had printed in the *Long Island Democrat*. In fact, Whitman was now revising some of those earlier poems for republication, and the revisions throw some light on his psychology if not his literary growth. The January 29, 1842, issue of *Brother Jonathan* contained a revision of "Fame's Vanity," [13] now called "Ambition," [14] with added lines at the beginning and end in blank verse. The new introduction might well have been an autobiographical confession:

> One day an obscure youth, a wanderer,
> Known but to few, lay musing with himself
> About the chances of his future life.
> In that youth's heart, there dwelt the coal Ambition,
> Burning and glowing; and he asked himself,
> "Shall I, in time to come, be great and famed?"

A specter then preaches to the youth the old sermon on the vanity of fame (using the lines of the earlier poem), but this time the youth is not reconciled to the doctrine of resignation:

> And as these accents dropped in the youth's ears,
> He felt him sick at heart; for many a month
> His fancy had amused and charmed itself
> With lofty aspirations, visions fair
> Of what he *might be*. And it pierced him sore
> To have his airy castles thus dashed down.

The live coal "ambition" was burning with increased heat, and could no longer be quenched by the tag-end doctrines of an outmoded romantic idealism. But scarcely had this revealing poem appeared in print before a new longed-for opportunity opened up for the "heartsick" youth.

II

Some time in February, 1842, Whitman began writing for a twopenny daily paper, the *Aurora*,[15] started the previous November by Nelson Herrick and John F. Ropes, who also published a successful Sunday paper called the *Atlas* and two other weekly papers. They owned a well-equipped printing office at 162 Nassau Street, near Tammany Hall, in a region known as "Printing-House Square," where most of the Democratic papers were published. The first editor of the *Aurora* was a New Englander,

Thomas Low Nichols, who had worked for the *Herald* and had acquired Bennett's impudent, egotistical, slam-bang style. The publishers explained in their first issue: "The leading editor is a Yankee from the Granite State [New Hampshire], and, without the slightest feeling of proscription, American writers, of equal talent, will always be preferred to foreigners, simply because they understand better the genius of the people for whom they write." [16]

In his first editorial Nichols announced that the *Aurora* would be politically independent but "democratic, in the strongest sense of the word." The paper, therefore, gave small space to political subjects, and made little attempt to cull European news from the papers received from abroad. But it specialized in social activities, prize fights, lectures, art, and sensational murder trials. The editor's greatest ambition was to be sophisticated, and he fancied that the *Aurora* was "the acknowledged journal of the *beau monde*, the Court Journal of our democratic aristocracy."

In *Specimen Days* Whitman said that he went to the *Aurora* as "a sort of free lance," [17] which must have meant that he was writing at space rates, one of its "penny-a-liners." On March 18 the *Aurora* published a parody (in imitation of the Reverend Charles Wolfe's "The Burial of Sir John Moore") entitled "The Death and Burial of McDonald Clarke" and signed with Whitman's initials—later acknowledged by him.[18] Clarke was a contemporary eccentric, known as "the mad poet," who lost his mind and died in prison at the Tombs. Apparently it was also Whitman who wrote a violent attack on Park Benjamin, his recent employer, that appeared in the *Aurora* on March 24 under the title "Bamboozle and Benjamin." Before this the *Aurora* had ridiculed Benjamin, who had abused enough of his rivals to deserve some of his own medicine, but this latest outburst of invective sounded like the result of a personal grudge. Benjamin, like many another editor of his day, was notorious for quarreling with his employees and associates,[19] and he had probably had a tiff with Walt—possibly discharged him, though he later commissioned him to write a "temperance novel." [20] In the *Aurora* Benjamin was called a literary quack, "possessing some little tact at stringing together sentences, and very great tact of impudence, conceit, and brazen assumption . . . one of the most vain pragmatical nincompoops in creation—[he] sets himself up for a poet!" [21] He was also accused of being a pious fraud and hypocrite. And in typical *Aurora* fashion, "He is not a native of the United States, but came here a foreigner." He has no "caste among the refined and accomplished circles of our city."

Although Whitman would hardly have attacked his former employer in this fierce way without some personal motive, it is a curious coincidence that only two days later an equally blistering attack on Benjamin's dishonest advertising methods, captioned "Newspaper Quackery," appeared in *Brother Jonathan*,[22] which Benjamin had recently edited with Rufus Griswold but which was now hostile to both men. Aside from the rivalry between this weekly and the *New World*, the immediate cause of this outburst was frustration over the pirating of Bulwer-Lytton's *Zanoni*. *Brother Jonathan* had widely advertised its intended publication of this work, but Benjamin had managed to get an advance copy from Harper and had printed it complete in one large extra before *Brother Jonathan* could run the first installment. Since a weekly paper like *Brother Jonathan* was edited and printed less rapidly than the daily *Aurora*, Whitman probably knew about the impending attack on Saturday when he published his on Thursday. This implies friendly or professional relations—or collusion if one wishes—between him and the editorial staff of *Brother Jonathan*. This "coincidence" is trivial in itself, but it implies a good deal about Whitman's acquaintance with the game he was now playing and his willingness to play it.

Though Benjamin was certainly in many respects a "literary quack" and actually had "degraded the very name of literature by a series of clap traps and low vulgar tricks to advance the interests of his paper," the publishers and staff of the *Aurora* had little right to point an accusing finger. But Walt was now struggling for recognition in this quagmire of scurrilous journalism, and he was learning rapidly. Nichols got himself into trouble by printing libelous charges of graft against the city in connection with a pipe-laying project. He was promptly discharged and Whitman made editor. On March 28 the publishers announced the employment of "Mr. Walter Whitman, favorably known as a bold, energetic and original writer, as their leading editor," who, they were confident, would "sustain the dignity and interests of our country." [23]

Thus two months before his twenty-third birthday Walt Whitman found himself in charge of one of the metropolitan dailies, and he set to work with youthful vigor. The Brooklyn *Eagle* commented on March 30 that, "A marked change for the better has come over this spirited little daily since the accession of Mr. Whitman to the 'vacant chair.' There is, nevertheless, a dash of egotism occasionally." [24] On the very day that the *Eagle* made this comment Whitman provided an example of the "dash of egotism," though he doubtless intended it as humor. He had not been recognized by the doorman at a market festival and had had to argue for ten minutes before gaining admission as a member of the press. Next morning he declared in his paper, "When any one connected with the *Aurora* takes the trouble to visit public places—he considers that if there is any favor in the matter, it certainly does not come from them to him." [25]

The young editor also attempted to live up to the dignity and importance of his new position by dressing like a man of fashion. William Cauldwell, a seventeen-year-old apprentice in the *Aurora* printing office, recalled many years later that at that time Whitman "usually wore a frock coat and high hat, carried a small cane, and the lapel of his coat was almost invariably ornamented with a boutonniere." [26] In an April 6th editorial Whitman described with intended facetiousness how he strolled down Broadway to the Battery in his fine toggery after dining sumptuously at Mrs. C.'s at two o'clock. But "nobody said 'there goes *the* Whitman of the *Aurora!* . . . the man that uses up the Great Bamboozle!'" (that is, Park Benjamin).[27] Down the street the self-conscious young editor came to a group of children playing a game in which they formed a ring by holding hands. "Ah! said one, with a peevish air, to a companion, 'We shall have to break the line. There comes a gentleman.'" But of course "the gentleman" walked around them without disturbing the game. He felt so pleased with himself and enjoyed the fine spring day so much that at half past eight he had still not written his editorial for next morning, but in a few minutes he dashed off this account of his walk, and his stint was finished—or at least so he pretended.

Walt Whitman was certainly taking his editorial duties in stride, but the nonchalance was deceptive. While the paper was ridiculously small, six columns wide, with a printed page about 24 by 16 inches, Whitman had the help of only one reporter, who covered the courts and police stations. The long social accounts, on which the *Aurora* prided itself, were written by penny-a-liners. But, the editor informed his readers: "Most of the principal articles are concocted by one Whitman, whilom little known in these diggings . . . It requires no great stretch of ingenuity to suppose that in order to keep some eight or ten compositors employed, a man's pen might fly glibly, and still be by no means too much in a hurry. Something or other *must* be 'set up.'" [28] Thus if he loafed after his two-o'clock dinner, he put in extra time later. As a matter of fact, morning papers are almost always edited in the later afternoon and evening hours. Cauldwell, the young printer, remembered that the editor usually reached his office around eleven or twelve in the morning, spent a short time looking over the exchanges, and then "it was Mr. Whitman's habit to stroll down Broadway to the Battery, spending an hour or two amid the trees and enjoying the water view, returning to the office location about 2 or 3 o'clock in the afternoon." This report does not take into account the dining at Mrs. Chipman's at two, but it establishes the fact that Whitman began his editorial duties in midafternoon. Yet he never became so busy that he did not have a cheery word for the printing staff. He became "quite chummy" with young Cauldwell. "Frequently, while I was engaged in sticking type, he would ask me to let him take my case for a little while, and he seemed to enjoy the recreation . . ." [29]

Whitman felt that his efforts with the paper were being rewarded with success. He had edited the *Aurora* scarcely two weeks before he boasted that the "regular edition has been completely exhausted by eight or nine o'clock every morning; and we have made arrangements to increase it next week to a thousand beyond what it has hitherto been," [30] which was probably five thousand, a circulation surpassed by the *Herald, Tribune, Sun,* among the twopenny papers, and by several of the older sixpenny papers. To his readers Whitman confided: "Editing a daily paper, to be sure, is an arduous employment. The consciousness that several thousand people will look for their *Aurora* as regularly as for their breakfasts, and that they expect to find it an intellectual repast—something *piquant,* and something solid, and something sentimental, and something humorous—and all dished up in 'our own peculiar way'—this consciousness, we say, implies no small responsibility upon a man. Yet it is delightful. Heavy as it weighs, we have no indisposition to 'take the responsibility.' " In fact, "we have full confidence in our capacities to make *Aurora* the most readable journal in the republic. We are hourly accosted in the streets, in hotels, in places of mercantile resort, everywhere, with compliments, and praises of the boldness, beauty, and merit of our paper." [31] After one makes due allowance for the commercial brag, it is still obvious that the young editor was almost intoxicated with his apparent success. The future, he innocently believed, held unlimited opportunities for him, and he meant to take full advantage of them. In this buoyant mood he re-asserted the *Aurora's* policy of "Americanism" and his own emerging patriotic ambitions:

We glory in being *true Americans.* And we profess to impress Aurora with the same spirit. We have taken high American ground—not the ground of exclusiveness, of partiality, of bigoted bias against those whose birth place is three thousand miles from our own—but based upon a desire to possess the republic

of a proper respect for itself and its citizens, and of what is due to its own capacities, and its own dignity. There are a thousand dangerous influences operating among us—influences whose tendency is to assimilate this land in
thought, in social customs, and, to a degree, in government, with the moth
eaten systems of the old world. Aurora is imbued with a deadly hatred to all
these influences; she wages open, heavy, and incessant war against them.[32]

During Whitman's editorship of the *Aurora* he wrote several feature articles (illustrated) for the front page on typical New York characters, such
as butchers and their boy assistants, firemen, and horsecar drivers. In
other articles he described scenes in the market and life in the boarding-
houses. He estimated that half the inhabitants of the city lived in boarding-
houses, from the three-dollar-a-week houses for mechanics to the six-dollar
or more places like Mrs. C.'s, where he himself was living in comfort or
even luxury, compared to his previous experience in the cheaper places.
"In our rough and tumble through the world," asserted the young editor,
"we have taken up quarters in all the various kinds, and therefore 'speak
from experience.' " [33]

At no time in his life did Whitman take greater delight in the varied
sights and activities of the roaring city. In the course of a single day he
might visit a gymnasium—but more to observe than to exercise—stop at
a pistol gallery, take his usual stroll down to the Battery, drop in at the
American Museum and have his palm read by a gypsy girl, attend a temperance or literary lecture in the evening, and then work late at the office
that night. During this period he occasionally mentioned the theaters,
but probably his editorial duties prevented his attending as often as he
had while a typesetter or as he would later. He saw J. R. Scott in *Macbeth*
and *Coriolanus* at the Chatham and he heard the opera *Norma*;[34] he was
already a great devotee of the opera and folk music. He praised Charlotte
Cushman's efforts to create a national theater, and declared, "Let us have
an international copyright law, and we shall have a national drama and
literature also." He was now fully aware of the harm being done by publishers like Park Benjamin. This situation also made him hypercritical of
British authors and patriotically loyal to American writers. He called
Longfellow "one of the best of American bards" and Bryant the greatest,[35] an opinion he never changed throughout his life. He planned to
start a department of weekly literary criticism in the *Aurora*, but left the
paper before he could carry out the plan.

In the short time that he was the editor of the *Aurora*, Whitman also
participated in a political controversy that tested his basic philosophy of

government and soon brought him into collision with Tammany and the Democratic party in New York City. The Irish population had grown so fast in recent years that an energetic young bishop, John Hughes, decided to organize it into a political group to force the state to appropriate part of the school funds for the support of parochial schools, and in the spring of 1842 he succeeded in injecting this issue both into city and into state politics. Whitman was fundamentally opposed to supporting sectarian education at public expense, regarding it as a violation of the ancient democratic doctrine of separation of church and state, but what especially aroused his anger was the conduct of the Irish at a rally held in the Park on March 16. The presiding officer was struck on the head and other officials were injured by the unruly mob. Whitman saw—or thought he did—Irish priests "looking on and evidently encouraging the gang who created the tumult," and he angrily asked: "Has it come to be, that the American people cannot gather together for the purpose of an orderly expression of sentiments, without being broken in upon by a gang of foreign outcasts and bullies . . . ?" [36]

Tension throughout the city increased with Whitman's own wrath. Tammany hesitated but finally capitulated to the Irish pressure, whereupon Whitman denounced the Democrats as cowards and hypocrites. Nevertheless, the bishop got his school bill approved by a narrow margin in the State Senate and the incumbent candidate for mayor was re-elected though Whig aldermen carried ten out of seventeen wards. But even after the election, riots continued. The Irish believed that the Protestants were going to assault their cathedral, and for several days there was an uproar in Mulberry Street in the region of St. Patrick's. These disorders increased the strength of the "Native American" party, which opposed all foreign influence and even the enfranchisement of immigrants. On April 18 Whitman reasserted the position he had recently taken, but repudiated Native Americanism. [37]

Whitman also took a keen interest in all evidences of oppression of the poor, the innocent, or the helpless. On one occasion he was greatly stirred by the mass arrest of about fifty prostitutes on Broadway, on orders of a police court magistrate. He apparently went too far, however, in his editorial denunciations, for next day he "apologized" in this manner:

The language we used in our article of yesterday, denouncing the kidnapping of women in Broadway, by the police authorities, was not intended and does not apply to them as citizens. We meant only to say that the kidnapping and imprisoning of these women, on Wednesday night, was a ruffianly, scoundrelly, villainous, outrageous and high handed proceeding, unsanctioned by law, justice, humanity, virtue, or religion; and yet the justices and officers may be decent, upright, well meaning, and faithful in their duties as public servants and as citizens. The whole proceeding was villainous—wrong—but perhaps we may have used rather hard words in denouncing it.[38]

It is not clear whether the editor was protesting against the arrests or the manner in which the officers carried out their orders, perhaps without proper warrants. But young Whitman's sympathies were obviously with the women, much as Stephen Crane's were many years later. Such compassion and sympathy he was later to express in his poem "To a Common Prostitute," and in the notorious lines in "Song of Myself":

The prostitute draggles her shawl, her bonnet bobs on her tipsy and pimpled neck,
The crowd laugh at her blackguard oaths, the men jeer and wink to each other,
(Miserable! I do not laugh at your oaths nor jeer you;) . . .

Anyone who takes the time to study Whitman's later editorials, or his mature poetry and prose, will be astonished at the number of his seasoned convictions that first appeared in the *Aurora*. On April 20, for example, he expressed the belief that morality cannot be legislated. The New York legislature had been considering but finally tabled a bill, as Whitman described it, to make "all practices of licentiousness penal," punishable by "the severest terrors of the law." Whitman reminded his readers: "Were communities so constituted that to prune their errors, the only thing necessary should be the passage of *laws*, the task of reform would be no task at all . . . You cannot legislate men into morality." [39] He believed implicitly in the Jeffersonian motto of the *Democratic Review*: "The best government is that which governs least." He would extend this to the theory "that every being with a rational soul is an *independent man*, and that one is as much a man as another, and that all sovereign rights reside within himself, and that it is a dangerous thing to delegate them to legislatures." [40]

This extremely self-reliant individualism resembled the doctrines of the New England Transcendentalists, though it more likely derived from the Jeffersonian tradition. However, in March Emerson gave a series of six lectures in New York on "The Times," and someone on the *Aurora* commented March 7 regarding the lecture on "The Poetry of the Times," saying that it was "one of the richest and most beautiful compositions, both for its matter and style, we have heard anywhere, at any time." [41]

This was probably Whitman, for he later mentioned[42] having heard Emerson lecture in the halls of the Athenaeum and Historical societies on Broadway, which could have been in 1842.

While editing the *Aurora* Whitman was probably too busy to do much reading, but he occasionally quoted Shakespeare, Homer, and Coleridge. Dickens had also become a favorite, and he replied to an attack in the April number of the *Democratic Review* on "the atrocious exaggeration of his bad characters." Whitman's argument was that there were wicked men in the world, and they should be exhibited in their "unclothed deformity." [43] This was a plea for realism long before the movement by that name. Whitman's own literary theory was, of course, still embryonic, but he had already acquired some of the stylistic mannerisms of his later years, such as using French words and phrases, giving *mélange* descriptions (that is, unorganized enumeration), and using the ambivalent "his or her" construction.

Exactly when or why the owners of the *Aurora* discharged Whitman is not certain. William Cauldwell reported that he refused to let Herrick "tone" his leaders and that a violent quarrel resulted. Whitman is said to have told his publishers, "If you want such stuff in the *Aurora*, write it yourself," and Herrick called him the "laziest fellow who ever undertook to edit a city paper." [44] It is likely that Whitman's nonchalant manners and habits irritated his employers, and they used this excuse to get rid of him. On May 3 they stated in print: "There is a man about our office so lazy that it takes two men to open his jaws when he speaks . . . *What* can be done with him?" Yet the disagreement seems to have taken place in April, for on May 16, 1842, the paper carried this announcement: "Mr. Walter Whitman desires us to state that he has been for three or four weeks past, and now is, entirely disconnected with the editorial department of the *Aurora*." [45]

James Robinson Newhall, who worked beside Whitman on some of the papers published by Herrick and Ropes (they published three besides the *Aurora*) gave in his reminiscences[46] two possible causes for Whitman's discharge. "Though affable and unassuming in personal intercourse, he was occasionally so trenchant with his pen that the proprietors had, now and then, to broadly hint that some restraint would be desirable." On another occasion Whitman arranged with Newhall to take his place on the morning paper (that is, the *Aurora*) while he enjoyed "a stroll on Long Island." One of the owners, when he learned of this arrangement, called Whitman a "lazy devil!" though he said he had no objection to the substitution. Newhall, in recalling the incident, insisted that Whitman was not lazy; he merely felt the need "to indulge uninterruptedly in some train of thought, the fruit of which might soon appear in print."

Though Whitman may have been provocative or even disrespectful to his employers, his short tenure of office was not an unusual occurrence for editors of the period. His predecessor on the *Aurora* had lasted only three months,[47] and in the precarious state of the newspaper profession at the time, that was about average. Even a prominent editor and publisher like Park Benjamin might start or work on a dozen papers in as many years. Only the most successful, like Bryant and Bennett, continued editing the same paper year after year, and they were proprietors, not mere employees holding office at the whim of capricious owners.

III

Whitman did not remain long unemployed. Within a few weeks he was editing another paper, the *Evening Tattler*, a small daily published at 27 Ann Street (right across the street from the *New World* office) by the same firm that issued *Brother Jonathan*—a fact that increases our suspicions regarding the almost simultaneous attack in March on Benjamin in the *Aurora* and *Brother Jonathan*. In fact, Whitman's co-operation in lambasting the editor of the *New World* may have helped him to secure the editorship of the *Tattler*. This newspaper had been founded and first edited by Park Benjamin and his crony and associate editor Rufus W. Griswold, the same Griswold who a few years later was to betray Poe as his literary executor and first biographer. In 1839 Griswold and Benjamin had started the *Tattler* as a noon paper, aimed to catch the street sales in the lull between the editions of the morning and evening papers. They announced it as politically independent, but within three months they quarreled with their publisher and withdrew to launch the *Evening Signal* and the *New World*.[48]

This new position enabled Whitman to prolong his feud with Herrick and Ropes. When the editor of the Hartford *Review* accused them of failing to pay a bill for woodcuts and called them hard names, Whitman delightedly reprinted the charges and insults. Finally, on August 29, Herrick and Ropes were stung to reply that an abusive editorial in a Hartford paper had been quoted by "a small, 'obscure daily' now under control of a 'pretty pup' once in our employment; but whose indolence, incompetence,

loaferism and blackguard habits forced us to kick him out of the office."
The "pretty pup" then retorted:

There is in this city a trashy, scurrilous, and obscene daily paper, under charge
of two as dirty fellows, as ever were able by the force of brass, ignorance of
their own ignorance, and a coarse manner of familiarity, to push themselves
among gentlemen. Not capable . . . of constructing two lines of grammar or
meaning, they are in the habit, every month or so, (for no man can remain
longer than that time in their concern,) of engaging some literary person to
"do" their paper. We—ill-starred by Fate—were, some six months since, unfortunate enough to allow ourself to be induced by the scamps in question, to
take the editorial charge of their sheet. During the few weeks we continued
there, we saw, in the instance of these two ill bred vagabonds, more mean selfishness . . . more low deceits—more attempts at levying "black mail"—heard
more gross blasphemy and prurient conversation, than ever before in our
life.[49]

Herrick and Ropes merely commented on this: "This fellow tells his
own story. We were fine fellows as long as we consented to pay him for
loafing about our office; but we didn't happen to want him, and 'of course'
we are 'dirty fellows.' " Here the dispute stopped. Maybe there was nothing else for Whitman to say, or maybe he was already having trouble
with the owners of the *Tattler*, Dillon and Company.

In one of the extant copies of the *Tattler*[50] at the time of Whitman's
editorship, the editorials sound very much like those of the *Aurora*. On
August 11 Whitman devoted one to "An Hour at the Bath," in which he
described a ship sailing up the harbor and a French steamer anchored two
furlongs off, whose sailors and officers had come to shore in a boat the
observer much admired. When the editor's cobbler gave out and the sun
sank behind the Jersey shore, the essay ended. What pleasanter way to
earn a living? In the same issue we find Whitman, as in the *Aurora*, once
more defending Dickens. Americans, he says, are too ready "to pet and
caress a foreign lion" and deserve such a lesson as Dickens is giving
them; he came over to effect an international copyright law, which he did
not get and is understandably disgruntled; and he correctly exposes "the
flimsiness of our American aristocracy."

IV

During his editorship of the *Aurora* and the *Tattler* Whitman had continued to publish in the *Democratic Review*, which printed five of his

stories between January and September, 1842.[51] These were still in the vein of his earlier experiments, and were probably from the batch of manuscripts he had brought with him from the Island. The earliest of these stories, "Tomb Blossoms," dwelt on the romantic pleasures of the country life and told of an old woman who decorated two graves because she did not know which contained her husband's remains, he having died and been interred while she was seriously ill. What especially marks this as an earlier composition of the young writer's "grave-yard" period is not so much the story itself as the didactic conclusion in which the author asserts: "I do not dread the grave. There is many a time when I could lay [*sic*] down and pass my immortal part through the valley of the shadow as composedly as I quaff water after a tiresome walk." This sentiment he had expressed in several early compositions.

The next two stories dealt with legends of the Revolution on Long Island. They have no obvious biographical significance. But in the fourth story, "A Legend of Life and Love," the cruel-father motif reappeared. A grandfather on his deathbed advised his two grandsons never to love or trust anyone. The boys separated, and when they met many years later one had blasted his life by following the advice while the other had enjoyed some happiness by disobeying it. But the moral is so trite that perhaps one should attach little importance to the story.

Two biographers [52] have thought they detected the influence of Poe in "The Angel of Tears," but the didacticism is certainly not Poesque, though the names and symbolism might be so interpreted. The Angel Alza was sent down to earth to visit the People of the Black Souls. A companion spirit grew faint merely by looking "abroad through these guilty places" of the world. "He pointed, and Alza, turning, saw rooms of people, some with their minds maddened by intoxication, some uttering horrid blasphemies—sensual creatures, and wicked, and mockers of all holiness." [53] Alza visited a murderer in prison, and when he, "the Angel of Tears," glided away, "a thousand airy-forms, far and near, responded in the same tongue wherewith Alza had spoken: 'Beautiful to the Eye of the Centre, is the sight which ushers repentance!'" Nothing could be less characteristic of the later Whitman than this sentimental allegory of holiness and repentance, though it may have given some intimations of a latent vicarious sympathy and Messianic love.

By the time "The Angel of Tears" appeared in the September number of the *Democratic Review* Whitman had either lost or was about to lose his second editorial position in New York. He might continue to sell a story or a poem occasionally to one of the popular magazines, but that would be a precarious way to live. However, his luck had not entirely run out. The thought occurred to Park Benjamin that Whitman would be just the person to write a temperance novel. In England such novels had been very profitable, and in America the Washington Temperance Society had been flourishing for two years. A second organization, the Sons of Temperance, formed only two months previously in New York, already claimed a national membership of 300,000. Here was a market ready for exploitation. One might suppose that Benjamin would still hold a grudge against his former printer for those attacks last spring, but he could forget personal feelings when money was to be made. He would print the novel as a supplement to the *New World* and sell it for a few cents.

How much Whitman was paid, or how long it took him to write the story, is not on record, but *Franklin Evans, or the Inebriate*, "A Tale of the Times.—By A popular American Author," was announced in the *New World* on November 5, 1842, to be "issued in an Extra *New World*, (octavo,) on Wednesday, Nov. 23, at 12½ cents single; ten copies for $1, or $8 per hundred." [54] Whitman's name did not appear in this first advertisement, but when the novel was printed the title page read "By Walter Whitman." Benjamin evidently expected to dispose of the edition wholesale, and Whitman later said that 20,000 copies were sold[55]—not improbable, considering the fact that the work was still being advertised the following August. However, Whitman's old-age statements about the book must be regarded with some skepticism, for he was then so ashamed of it that he wanted to minimize the whole incident. Once he garrulously asserted that the offer of "cash payment" to write it "was so tempting—I was so hard up at the time—that I set to work at once ardently on it (with the help of a bottle of port or what not). In three days of constant work I finished the book. Finished the book? Finished myself. It was damned rot—rot of the worst sort—not insincere, perhaps, but rot, nevertheless . . ." [56]

Doubtless *Franklin Evans* was rapidly and certainly carelessly written, but hardly at the rate of 20,000 words a day. One evidence of the haste is that Whitman padded his manuscript by inserting several stories that he had on hand—for example, the Indian tale in Chapter I, the story of Little Jane in XIV, and probably the allegorical dream in XXI. On another occasion Whitman claimed he wrote the novel in the reading room of Tammany Hall, fortifying himself with gin cocktails in order to keep going.[57] Again some possible truth: he was well acquainted with Tammany Hall, and may have completed the manuscript there, but whether he patronized the Tammany bar at that time is by no means certain. In Brooklyn as an apprentice he had signed the pledge of total abstinence; while a schoolmaster on Long Island he had been an ardent prohibitionist; and there is no reason to suspect that he did not honestly believe in temperance at the time he wrote *Franklin Evans*.

Franklin Evans is just the kind of work that we might expect this young man to write in the fall of 1842. His self-confidence and self-importance had expanded while he was "Mr. Whitman" of the *Aurora* and the *Tattler*, but unemployed and discouraged he would be likely to revert to his former introspective, sentimental personality. Of course, Whitman knew that Benjamin's motives were mercenary, and he had agreed to a contract because he was "hard up," but the moral earnestness of the introduction still sounds sincere today, and when Whitman reprinted the novel in the Brooklyn *Eagle* four years later under the title "The Fortunes of a Country Boy, by J. R. S." he editorialized: "We consider temperance one of the grand regenerators of the age; and that all who, in truth of heart, labor in its promulgation, deserve well of heaven and men." [58]

As with most of his short stories, Whitman claimed: "I narrate occurrences that have had a far more substantial existence, than in my fancy." This claim may have been intended to make the story seem more convincing—and he was well aware of a moral prejudice against fiction among the kind of people who would read his book. But it is difficult not to give some credence to the author's further assertion that "There will be those who, as their eyes turn past line after line, will have their memories carried to matters which they have heard of before, or taken a part in themselves, and which, they know, are *real*." [59] And *real* it certainly was in some senses, though obviously not a "true story" throughout.

The story was of a country boy from Long Island who went to New York to make his fortune, was introduced to saloon life by a sophisticated acquaintance, became a drunkard, broke the heart and caused the death of the "good woman" he married, wandered to the South with the intention of reforming but returned to drinking under the influence of a plantation owner—and on and on through an interminable "soap opera" plot. Evans fell in love with an attractive Creole on the plantation and married her—after the plantation owner had obligingly freed her—only to fall in love with a seductive blond widow, thereby setting the avenging furies to work and eventually causing the death of both the widow and the Creole wife. Evans then drifted North, got into more trouble, but rescued a child from drowning, was finally redeemed from drink, and was rewarded with a fortune—the earthly equivalent of repenting and going to heaven.

It is no wonder that Whitman later was ashamed of this melodramatic, maudlin story. In their combined sequence the events were utterly improbable, but individually they had and have happened many times. Some of them may have been, as the author claimed, recognizable to living inhabitants of Long Island and New York City. But of more importance are possible biographical revelations in *Franklin Evans*. The hero started out from his Long Island home in a "country-market wagon which also performed the office of stage-coach," such as Walt Whitman's grandfather had driven[60]—an indication that to some extent at least the author was drawing upon memory. In the beginning the descriptions are clear and vivid, but after the young hero arrives in the city his will is like a feather in the wind and his life has the quality of a dream. In fact, the author makes frequent use of dreams, as in some of his short stories. This device may be attributed in part to Whitman's amateurish art—or lack of it—but the itinerant schoolmaster had felt that life was a dream, and at the time of writing *Franklin Evans* he had still better reasons for the sensation of unreality. He could be stubborn in holding on to an idea or a moral principle, but his specific ambitions were still amorphous. His dreams were therefore both a compensation and, as with Evans, an indication of a relaxed will. Whether Walt Whitman himself had succumbed to temptations in the city we do not know, but if he had he would have felt that this was something unreal that had happened to his body; in his "soul" and his conceit of himself he was "pure." He had not yet reached a degree of sophistication that enabled him to avoid these moral clichés in his thinking.

One critic has interpreted Whitman's "tendency to spin the story from a dream" as an indication of the "sentimental, introverted, egocentric mind of the narrator." [61] He thinks it significant that "only two years before writing 'Franklin Evans' Whitman had declared in print that neither by experience nor by observation had he learned anything about women; yet in this dream-like story the future author of 'Children of Adam' passes through a varied experience with the sex: a back-stage disillusionment, an unreal marriage, an illicit flirtation, an idealization of the wife and mother, and even a drink-inspired entanglement with an octoroon, whose chief recommendation is her voluptuous appeal to his senses." This critic sees in these details a forecast of what might or could happen to Whitman himself. It would seem, however, that the very haziness and unreality of their presentation is an indication that Whitman had still learned little about women either by "experience or observation" and was not even able to imagine sexual temptations with any convincingness. Here the autobiography is entirely negative. The extreme artificiality of this prominent part of the novel may have been another reason for Whitman's violent revulsion against it later.

The introduction to *Franklin Evans* contained a forecast of a very different kind that should be mentioned. In bragging that his publisher had the "power of diffusing it more widely than any other establishment in the United States," he was merely helping to advertise the book, but in his insistence that it was "being written for the mass" we have a prophecy of the poetic role that he would later try so desperately and vainly to fill in *Leaves of Grass*. He was not entirely trying to disarm the critics by declaring that the book was not written for them "but for THE PEOPLE," because he was already groping for an art that would somehow circumvent art and establish a direct communication with the "divine average," as he would later think of his audience. For this reason he hoped that his novel would sell and make further communication possible. Ironically, he was here on the right road to the kind of expression by which he could establish contact with the masses. But after his intellect and judgment had grown sufficiently for him to realize what literary "rot" *Franklin Evans* really was, it would be impossible for him to reach this mass audience.

V

Whitman's notebooks contain no clues to his activities during the winter of 1842–1843—except for his boarding with "Mrs. R. in Spring Street," [62] which does tell us that he was still in New York. He probably worked on some of the numerous papers in the city—at one time during these years he wrote for the *Sun*[63]—or he did anonymous hack work. For recreation he may have frequented Tammany Hall, because it was about this time that he met Colonel Fellows there.[64] Fellows, a tall, white-haired, refined man in his late seventies, had known Tom Paine during his last years, and Whitman liked to draw him out on this subject "over a social glass of toddy, after his day's work" as constable in one of the upper courts. While listening to this stately old gentleman reminisce about the man whom Walt's father and Elias Hicks had known, he experienced the same sensations he had felt as a boy while Hartshorne talked of Washington and Jefferson. This was the way he liked to learn history.

At Tammany Hall Whitman of course also met Democratic editors, journalists, and politicians, and as a consequence he was offered the editorship of another Democratic paper, the *Statesman*, in the spring of 1843. But apparently he was in charge of this paper for only two or three months. Maybe it was a short-term appointment—but it is useless to speculate when the facts are completely missing. There are one or two indications, however, that he was busy during 1843: one is that he published almost nothing in the magazines—only one poem, "Death of the Nature Lover" [65] (a revision of the earlier poem "My Departure"), in the March 11 issue of *Brother Jonathan*—and the other is that he was boarding near the printing and publishing center of the city, though he moved often, as if restless or frequently changing positions. Thus, "Spring of 1843 boarded at Mrs. Bonnard's in John st.—Also at Mrs. Edgarton's in Vesey. Summer of '43 at Mary's and at Brown's in Duane st. October 1843 commenced with Winants'." [66]

Early in 1844 Whitman had sufficient leisure to write more stories. Possibly he was unemployed and had begun free lancing again to earn a subsistence, but he had also found new markets for his writings in magazines recently started, and this fact alone could have reawakened his literary ambitions. The March number of the *Columbian Magazine* contained a story of his called "Eris; a Spirit Record," [67] a somewhat Poesque account of an angel, Dai, who was assigned by God to guard the soul of a young girl on earth named Eris, but Dai fell in love with her, neglected his duty, and caused her death, for which God made him blind. Her soul went to Heaven, where she waited patiently for the soul of the mortal whom she loved to join her. The angel Dai continued to love her, but she always turned quickly and sadly away from him. Thus throughout eternity, "Wandering in the confines of earth, or restlessly amid the streets of the beautiful land, goes Dai, earnestly calling on one he loves. Wherefore is there no response?" Then the pious ending: "And haply Dai is the spirit of destiny of those whose selfishness would seek to mar the peace of gentle hearts, by their own unreturned and unhallowed passion."

It is a little difficult to believe that Walt Whitman, not yet twenty-five, in excellent health, and surrounded with hundreds of friends and acquaintances in journalism and politics, was, like the Angel Dai, searching for love and finding no response. And yet this was to be one of the paradoxes of Whitman's gregarious and lonely life. In writing this "Spirit

Record" he was imitating the popular authors of the day, who were also writing about angelic creatures in Heaven and angelic children on earth, but it also symbolized a dimly felt condition of his own spiritual life. And his idealization of children was both a response to contemporary taste and an expression of his affection for children, especially those most closely related to him. His thinly disguised sketch of his own brothers and sisters, called "My Boys and Girls"—which was mentioned in Chapter I—appeared in the April 20th issue of the *Rover*, a small magazine edited by Seba Smith. The May number of the *Columbian Magazine* contained "Dumb Kate," the story of a beautiful deaf girl who was betrayed by a selfish boy and died of grief and shame.[68] In September the same magazine published "The Little Sleighers," [69] a sentimental description of children sleighing on the frozen Battery during especially cold, blustery weather, with a moralizing end on the beauty and uncertainty of life.

There was also a great paradox in the fact that the decade in which such stories as these were popular was one of the maddest, roughest, and crudest in American history. Every spring in New York there were noisy conventions of abolitionists, prohibitionists, believers in women's rights, free-love advocates, vegetarians, and universal reformers. Whitman attended many of these meetings in the Tabernacle, "a great turtle-shaped hall" with an immense gallery, on the east side of Broadway near Pearl Street. There he heard Wendell Phillips, Emerson, Cassius Clay, John P. Hale, Henry Ward Beecher, Fred Douglas, William Lloyd Garrison, and many others.[70] But also he saw "a fierce politician . . . with a band of robust supporters" try to break up some of these meetings, and admired the speakers for being "tough, tough," who "always maintained their ground, and carried out their programs fully."

The "fierce politician" was actually Isaiah Rynders (Whitman spelled it "Rhynders"), Tammany boss of the Sixth Ward, which included the notorious tenements at Five Points, near what is now the northwest corner of City Hall Park, where lived gangs of murderers, prostitutes, petty thieves, and degenerates of all kinds.[71] Rynders had come to New York in the 1830's after a career as a gambler and fighter with pistol and knife on the Mississippi River. In 1843 he became proprietor of the Empire Club at 25 Park Row, a gathering place for the Five Points gangsters, whom he organized politically and thus made himself a powerful figure in Tammany Hall. On election day his gangs not only controlled voting in the Sixth Ward, but terrorized other wards and voted repeatedly at the polls, a practice used by both parties but most successfully by these thugs.

Thus when Whitman described the reform speakers and leaders as "tough, tough," able to maintain their ground, he was referring to conduct that was nothing short of heroic. Except for his indignant denunciation in the *Aurora* of mob violence in the elections of 1842,[72] Whitman left no detailed comments on the gangs, though they were one of the ugliest phenomena of the period. Those controlled politically by Rynders were not the only ones. The Bowery Boys[73] were almost equally tough, and they frequently fought in the streets with the Five Points gangs, using bricks, clubs, paving stones, or any other lethal weapons readily available. They wore heavy hobnailed boots and often stamped or kicked their rivals to death. The volunteer firemen were also a brawling, riotous bunch of men, who often took part in these gang wars, or fought crews of rival fire stations. When a fire alarm sounded several crews might race to the scene of the fire and then fight over the hydrants while the building went up in flames.

It is difficult to imagine kindly, peaceful Walt Whitman living amid the almost incredible brutality of New York life at that time. That he himself was not a frequenter of low dives or a brawler in saloons is indicated by his dress, such glimpses as we get of his habits, and his moralistic editorials. Yet the swagger of the butchers[74]—who were at that time the aristocrats of the "sports"—the bravado of the volunteer firemen, and the belligerency of the Bowery Boys were not entirely without influence on the future author of the first two editions of *Leaves of Grass*. In fact the Americans as a whole were a swaggering, brawling nation of exhibitionists, as the folklore of the period plainly reveals. On the frontier the "gamecocks of the wilderness" fought loudly with epic boast and utter disregard of life and limb.

The Bowery, too, had its legendary hero. He was Mose, an actual leader of the Bowery Boys in the 1840's, who was to appear a few years later in B. A. Baker's play *A Glance at New York in 1848*, in which Frank S. Chanfrau would act the role of "Mose, a true specimen of one of the B'hoys." [75] In legend Mose was a giant, eight feet tall, with hands the size of hams which in repose hung below his knees. On his ginger-colored head he wore a huge beaver hat over two feet high, and his feet were so large that a ready-to-wear shoe would not hold his big toe. The hobnails in his specially made brogues were an inch long and were the terror of the Five Points gangs. He had the strength of ten men and fought with a wagon tongue, an iron lamp post, a butcher's cleaver, or, when pressed, the trunk of a tree, which he would uproot with a mighty yank and wield like a flail. Such was the folklore of the expanding nation, whether the story was of Mose the Bowery B'hoy, John Henry of the Lower Mississippi, Davy Crockett of the frontier, or Paul Bunyan of the Northern and Western lumber camps.

In the 1840's Americans gulped their food, as Dickens and other visitors from Europe complained, picked their teeth in public, and the men spat tobacco juice everywhere. On the frontier and in the city slums bullies fought like wild animals, gouging out eyes, biting off ears or noses, and engaging in mayhem generally. President Jackson overthrew the ruling class of bankers and financiers, but he inaugurated the spoils system, and in New York men like Rynders organized the underworld into a political machine that finally reduced the finances and administration of the city to utter chaos. Whitman was not alone, however, in ignoring these ugly facts in his stories and poems. Despite the screaming demands for a native literature, the actual output of the period was characteristically sentimental and romantic.

VI

Both as a journalist and an associate of politicians Whitman knew the life of the city, but he had not given up hope of doing some good himself, as well as earning a livelihood, in party journalism. In the summer of 1844 he accepted the editorship of the New York *Democrat*.[76] This must have been an exciting and arduous summer, for Whitman used the paper to advocate the nomination of Silas Wright for governor, in defiance of the political "bosses" of the city.[77] Wright was one of the most remarkable men in American politics at that time, able, honest, almost worshiped by liberal Democrats of his state, but hated by the Conservatives, or "Old Hunkers," as their enemies called them.[78] Wright was then in the United States Senate, and William C. Bouck, a "Hunker," was governor of New York. The Democratic party in the state had been torn by internal strife for many years, but was now more split than ever both over local and over national issues. Rivalry between New York City and upstate politicians for control of the party had existed for a long time, but now new schisms developed as the nation drew nearer to a showdown on the problem of slavery in the new territories. Conservative Democrats were either sympathetic with the extension of slavery or justified the *status quo* on arguments of "states rights" and constitutionality.

The "Old Hunkers" were in a dilemma because Governor Bouck was so unpopular in the summer of 1844 that even many of his friends despaired of winning the next election with him. On the other hand, though all the liberal and "free soil" Democrats wanted Wright, he did not wish to leave the Senate, and until the Democratic Convention in September he tried in every way to discourage his nomination.[79] He was finally persuaded to accept, however, in order to strengthen the national ticket, for James K. Polk faced a hard struggle to beat Henry Clay, and New York's electoral votes could be decisive—and, as it turned out, they were, because Wright carried the state by an overwhelming majority and saved New York for Polk.

Since Wright was nominated at the Syracuse Convention in September, it may seem strange that Whitman lost the editorship of the *Democrat*. But the fact was that many Democrats sabotaged their party by secretly working for the Whigs or one of the minor parties, such as the Native American, which was strongest in New York City. No copies of the New York *Democrat* for 1844 are known to exist, and we can only guess, therefore, at the exact circumstances of Whitman's removal from the editor's chair, but there can be little doubt that he was ousted by the "Old Hunker" politicians, the first of several defeats that he would suffer at their hands.

For two or three weeks in October, 1844, Whitman wrote for the *New Mirror*,[80] edited by George Pope Morris and N. P. Willis. He may have been substituting for someone on leave, but he was evidently employed for three or four months, because his name did not appear in the magazines again until the following March, 1845, when the *Aristidean*, edited by Thomas Dunn English, published two of his stories. In May he had still another story published in the *American Review* (later called *American Whig Review*), which was just then famous because of Poe's "The Raven" having appeared in the February number. To the April number he contributed "Richard Parker's Widow," [81] based on a recently published account of the British mutiny at Nore in 1797, the same event that Herman Melville was to use later as the background for *Billy Budd*. But whereas Melville was to write a great tragedy dealing with the philosophical and theological problem of natural depravity, Whitman was concerned only with the loyalty and suffering of the widow of Parker, the heroic leader of the mutineers. Though he depended largely on his source, he was able to appreciate the widow's agony and to write a simple, moving account. He would always be capable of sharing vicariously the emotions of mothers and older women.

From June to August the *Democratic Review*, in which none of Whitman's work had appeared for two years, printed a long story of his called "Revenge and Requital," [82] about a young man who, goaded by the cruelty and insults of his guardian to himself and his sister, got drunk and killed his tormentor. This was another crude piece of temperance fiction— no better or worse than *Franklin Evans*. None of Whitman's essays or stories of this period was in the least original. The magazines were filled with such accounts of virtue betrayed, fatal infatuations of the innocent for the wicked, romantic Indians, patriotic love for old sights, relics, traditions, and sentimental folk tales.

Walt Whitman was still writing from the surface of his mind. He had learned to play this artificial journalistic game with some skill, but nothing he had written so far had any genuine literary merit, and perhaps he had begun to become aware of that fact when he decided in August, 1845, to leave New York and return to Brooklyn. Certainly he would not have left New York if he had felt that his prospects there were still good. But with men like Rynders in control of Tammany Hall, there could be no future for Whitman in official Democratic journalism in the city. However, whatever the reasons, his four-year apprenticeship in New York journalism had come to an end.

⋙ III ⋘

THE SHAPES ARISE

The shapes arise!
Shapes of doors giving many exits and entrances,
. . . .
Shapes bracing the earth and braced with the whole earth.[1]

I

On that day in August, 1845, when the ferry pulled out of the New York
slip and headed for Brooklyn with Walt Whitman aboard, the young man
for the moment may have felt glad to be leaving the great city, though he
was not actually losing it, as he must have realized at the time. As in
his boyhood, he could still shuttle across the East River for amusement in
New York while living and working in Brooklyn. Now, more than ever,
he was a man of two cities, two loyalties. He might feel bitter toward certain Tammany politicians, but not toward the city that they misruled.
For Brooklyn he would always have a filial devotion, and for New York
a suburbanite's admiration.

Just how important the experience of these years in New York would be
to the future poet he himself could not appreciate until he had become a
real poet, some years hence. But at the time he could be grateful that he
had actually edited several metropolitan dailies, a record that perhaps no
one in Brooklyn could match. Probably it was the reason that Edwin B.
Spooner, who had inherited the *Long Island Star* from his father, was
willing to employ the former apprentice of the *Star*. That he had followed
Whitman's movements with some interest is revealed by the fact that in
1841, when Walt was making political speeches in New York, Edwin
Spooner advised him to forget politics and complete his journalistic apprenticeship.[2] This indicates that the Whig editor was a little annoyed by
Walt's political activities for the Democrats, though he may honestly have
thought of the young man as still immature—which of course he was, de-

spite the fact that he had already acquired a wider range of journalistic experience than Edwin Spooner. Spooner's distrust, whether personal or political, might explain why it is difficult to discover Whitman's exact position on the *Star*. He was never referred to as editor, and he appears not to have had a voice in determining policy. He was later said to have been paid only four or five dollars a week,[3] low even for the time. Perhaps he was employed as a sort of special reporter, though many of the articles that can be identified as his were more like the work of what today would be called a "columnist" or special correspondent—personal, informal, at times rather opinionated.

Walt Whitman's return to Brooklyn may have been influenced by his father's decision to move back there from Dix Hills, where the Whitman family had lived since May of 1840,[4] for them a long stay in one place. The Brooklyn Hall of Records shows that in October, 1844, Walter Whitman, Sr., bought a large lot on Prince Street at the northeast corner of Willoughby. There he built a house, though it was apparently not finished when the family moved in 1845, for they lived first on Gold Street, then a few months later at 71 Prince Street.[5] It is likely that Walt joined them immediately after they moved in, or very soon afterward—he could hardly have afforded a boardinghouse if he was making only four or five dollars a week.[6] Naturally he had kept in close touch with his family during his residence in New York and had doubtless visited them at Dix Hills. Mary was of course with her husband at Greenport, but Hannah, always Walt's favorite sister, and now a grown woman (aged twenty-two), was still with her parents. The two older boys, Jesse and Andrew, were probably away from home, though we have no information whatever about them for this period. George, now sixteen, was old enough to hold a job in Brooklyn.

Jeff, Walt's favorite brother, was still in school. Within a few years he would study civil engineering and surveying, but this would not have begun at the age of twelve. Furthermore, Walt first tried to make a printer of him[7] before Jeff discovered his vocation in land surveying and civil engineering. When this brother died in 1890, Walt wrote in his obituary: "As he grew a big boy he liked out-door and water sports, especially boating. We would often go down summers to Peconic Bay, east end of Long Island, and over to Shelter Island. I loved long rambles, and he carried his fowling-piece." [8] Quite likely the two brothers made such a trip in the summer of 1845, either before or after the move to Brooklyn. They were to be closely associated for the next few years, and would always be devoted to each other. Walt, slow, introspective, reticent, and serious, found special delight in his vivacious, fun-loving, extroverted younger brother. Edward, the feeble-minded cripple, now ten, required constant attention, but his mother was still able to care for him and Walt had not yet begun to feel the responsibility. In his notebook Walt recorded that "J.W. died at Dix Hills Sept. 8th 1845." [9] In a later notebook[10] he used these initials for his first cousin, Jacob Whitman, who had taught his father the carpentry trade. Doubtless Walt's father attended the funeral at Dix Hills, and Walt may have accompanied him.

In September Whitman began to write articles for the *Star* that can be identified.[11] On the fifteenth the *Star* printed an article on "Brooklyn Schools and Teachers" that was almost certainly his,[12] though it was unsigned. It contained ideas that Whitman was to express repeatedly during the next two years: criticism of the "miserable slovenliness in the plan of appointing teachers" in the Brooklyn schools, the assertion that the primary function of the teacher is "stimulating the pupil's *mind*," and a vigorous condemnation of "flogging or any kind of corporal chastisement" in schools.[13] On the subject of corporal punishment he became absolutely fanatical, and probably annoyed some of the Brooklyn teachers, for he several times referred to the fact that the majority of teachers still thought that whipping was sometimes necessary, and one wrote him a letter of protest.[14] After hearing Horace Mann lecture in Brooklyn, Whitman printed an article on October 22, signed "W.," in which he quoted the great educator as saying, "They who expel wrong doing by means of physical chastisement cast out devils, through Beelzebub, the prince of devils." Whitman asked rhetorically, "Are not some of our Brooklyn teachers a little too profuse of this satanic power?" He then declared that "the instructor who uses the lash in his school at all, is unworthy to hold the power he does hold" and has confessed by his action that he has no other means of holding it.[15]

Two or three times a week from September 22 to the following March Whitman contributed articles on his favorite subjects: education (his major topic), music, advice to apprentices, temperance, and manners.[16] Either by agreement with Mr. Spooner, or through discretion unusual for him, he avoided political topics. The style and opinions were forerunners of his more mature literary theory. For example, on October 27 this former devotee of the New York stage condemned the contemporary theater for its failure to inculcate sound moral principles and good manners: "until some great reform takes place in plays, acting and actors, nothing can be done in this country with the theatre, to make it deserve well at the hands of good men. . . . It must be made fresher, more natural, more fitted to modern tastes—and, above all, it must be Americanised . . ." [17] The "stuff" presented at the Chatham and Bowery theaters in New York, he declared, was nauseating. Even the more famous Park was but "a bringer out of English plays imbued with anti-republican incident and feeling," with "second-rate foreign performers, and the castings-off of London and Liverpool." He would prefer to see "no theatre in Brooklyn until the drama is pulled down and built over again."

Whitman fancied himself an experienced critic of dramatic performances, and early in December he announced that he had been invited to attend an amateur performance of *Hamlet*.[18] He was insultingly sarcastic even in this announcement, and hardly went to the performance in a frame of mind to enjoy it. On December 13 he reviewed it under the quotation "Hark! the Murder's Doing!" [19] He found all the male characters in this production of the great tragedy extremely comical—for some reason, chivalric or otherwise, he did not mention the Queen or Ophelia. Hamlet "was a long-necked, shambling fellow, with a walk such as never before was seen in Christian, Jew or Pagan . . . Then such monstrous spasms as passed over his face, at times—the token whereof was certainly never seen except in a cholera hospital!" The "character of the King must certainly have been a wag—or else a profound republican, who wished to make monarchy ridiculous—or else tipsy—or else foolish—which latter perhaps is the nighest truth." The Ghost "was totally unlike any *living* thing we ever saw." But, "The most ridiculous character, (if we may use such a phrase where there was hardly anything but a monotony of the ridiculous) seemed, by general consent, to be awarded to Polonius. It was lucky for us that he died in the third act . . ." Quite likely the performance was "a monotony of the ridiculous," but one cannot avoid the suspicion that the critic, proud of his familiarity with professional performances in New York, was a bit too condescending toward amateurs in Brooklyn. Certainly his hilarious sarcasm would not encourage further efforts. And there are implications of a feud between the critic and the Brooklyn teachers who directed the production.

Though he continued to hold a low opinion of the average teacher's competence and to denounce the cruelty of the profession in the classroom, the one thing that Whitman did find in Brooklyn schools which he especially approved was the teaching of singing. He warmly praised the local teachers of this subject, though he would have liked to see music given as much prominence in the curriculum as reading or arithmetic. Early in November he heard a quartet, composed of three brothers and a sister from Vermont, who called themselves the Cheyneys, sing in country style at Niblo's Saloon in New York, and he declared in the *Star* on the fifth, "For the first time we, on Monday night, heard something in the way of American music, which overpowered us with delightful amazement." In the flush of this delight Whitman submitted a short essay on "Art-Music and Heart-Music" to the *Broadway Journal*, which Poe was then editing, and which he published on November 29, with an editorial endorsement.[20] Some time later Whitman called on Poe—probably to collect for the article—and he found the poet "very cordial, in a quiet way . . . I have a distinct and pleasing remembrance of his looks, voice, manner and matter; very kindly and human, but subdued, perhaps a little jaded." [21]

By this time Whitman had acquired some familiarity with Italian opera,[22] but he thought the simple, unaffected country-style singing of the Cheyneys superior to any foreign music. "The subtlest spirit of a nation is expressed through its music—and the music acts reciprocally on the nation's very soul." Therefore, each nation has its own natural music, and European music, however good in and for Europe, can not take the place of American music. The Cheyneys, he thought, presented "something original and beautiful in the way of American musical execution . . . This, we said in our heart, is the true method which must become popular in the United States—which must supplant the stale, second-hand, foreign method, with its flourishes, its ridiculous sentimentality, its anti-republican spirit, and its sycophantic influence, tainting the young taste of the republic." [23]

Later in the month Whitman heard "The Oratorio of St. Paul" sung in the New York Tabernacle; and he was apparently even more deeply affected than he had been by the Cheyneys, and could only think of inadequate metaphors to describe the experience. "Who," he wondered, "shall sound the depths of that hidden sea [the soul], and tell its extent from a few dim and dull reverberations aneath its surface?" [24] Such music had become a mystic and religious experience to him. He was particularly responsive to vocal music, and for this reason continued to advocate the teaching of singing in the schools. But he also advocated it because he was convinced that music, and especially singing, influenced manners and conduct, and Americans needed this refining influence. "In musical Italy and musical France," he declared, on what could only have been second-hand knowledge, "the commonest man, the most ordinary grisette has an ease, grace and elegance, which are not too often found in what we call good society here." [25]

In these articles in the *Star* we have many hints of Whitman's life in the fall and winter of 1845–1846: his trips to New York,[26] his visits to the schools in Brooklyn,[27] his fluctuating enthusiasms and opinions. But sometimes it is not easy to separate his fanciful irony from his reporting. For example, in November, after discussing Mrs. Anna C. Mowatt's current play *Fashion*, a satire on the aping of European manners in the United States, he knowingly approved the recent French influence in the most fashionable circles of New York society:

The coming season promises to be one of considerable stir in the fashionable world . . . Parties, concerts, balls, and lectures are announced at a great rate.—The Polka increases in popularity. As for manners, we are assimilating [sic] to the Parisian, more and more—and I must confess I like it so. Stiffness and reserve are banished—dignified silence laughed at—all kinds of keeping one's state, sent to Coventry. A dash of familiarity even with the strangers, (either sex to either sex) you meet at parties, &c., is good breeding now; and the man or woman ("lady" and "gentleman" is counterjumperish)— who should play haughty as a general thing, would be quizzed most mortally. We are now speaking of the *true* fashion—the heart of hearts—of New York society.[28]

There is no evidence that the Brooklyn journalist was accepted in the "fashionable world" of New York, but he did attend the concerts and lectures there, and the theater too, despite his low opinion of its present condition, and thus knew something of the mores and manners in the city.

The young columnist was frequently generous with moral and practical advice. He often called his article "Hints to the Young," [29] "Hints to Apprentices," or "Some Hints to Apprentices and Youth." [30] Under the latter heading he warned against the habit of loafing, and asked, "What vulgar habits of smoking cigars, chewing tobacco, or making frequent use of blasphemous or obscene language have you begun to form?" [31] At another time he warned "young working people" against trying to dress fashionably and advised them: "Swear not! Smoke not! and rough-and-tumble not!" [32] Most of this advice was entirely lacking in originality, and at times was surprisingly prissy. Whitman was apparently unwilling to extend the new freedom of the society world to young apprentices. Sometimes he sounded a bit snobbish in warning against the artificial manners of "counterjumpers" [33] (clerks in stores), a class to which he always referred sarcastically—and he had a patrician scorn for vulgar display of any kind.

Although in these articles for the *Star* Whitman paid little attention to national affairs, there was one exception. The dispute between England and the United States over the Oregon boundary had become acute in 1845, and many editors were shrill in their denunciation of England. When the *Democratic Review,* which had previously been in favor of peace, began urging war unless England gave in, Whitman felt that he must speak out in protest. He had thought, he said, that the tension between the two countries was lessening and he was afraid the *Democratic Review* would revive the danger. He still approved Bryant's firm but reasonable stand in the New York *Post.* He believed in a "high and glorious destiny for this republic," but asked "what crying outrage have we now to avenge?" He was so opposed to war that he would even sacrifice the nation's "destiny" if it "were to be achieved through blood and rapine—if our fame and honor could come in no other path except the path of the cannon balls . . . and the groans of dying men—we could turn our face aside and almost say, let us never be a great nation!" [34]

While with the *Star* Whitman also began to pay a good deal of attention to books recently published, but almost invariably they were books that could be used in the schools, or books suitable for self-education. None of his brief reviews was literary. At that time he seemed to be unconcerned with any esthetic values except in music, and even in music he always found means for moral improvement. This trait led him, however, to espouse many good causes, such as night and technical schools in Brooklyn. The School Board was interested in a night school, but dallied, and Whitman repeatedly tried to stir it to action. [35]

II

In the midst of Whitman's editorial battles for these causes, the much-loved editor of the rival Brooklyn *Eagle,* William B. Marsh, died on February 26, 1846. He left a wife and several children almost destitute, and on March 3 Whitman published in the *Star* a signed appeal for financial aid for the Marsh family. The following week he succeeded William Marsh as editor of the Brooklyn *Eagle.*

The *Eagle* was only five years old and had had only one editor before Whitman. [36] Marsh, like Whitman, had worked as a printer in New York, and Horace Greeley was a friend of his. He had come to Brooklyn when the city had a population of about forty thousand, and during his editorship the *Eagle* had become not only the outstanding paper in Brooklyn but one respected in New York and the surrounding country. The owner was Isaac Van Anden, prominent in the Democratic party, and of course the paper was partisan. Henry C. Murphy, whom Whitman had known and admired in the *Patriot* office,[37] was a local Democratic "boss" and an arbiter of *Eagle* policy, and he may have had something to do with Whitman's appointment.

Whitman was nearly twenty-seven when he assumed editorship of the *Eagle*, and his escape from the restrictions of the Whig paper enabled him to assume almost overnight a sense of responsibility he had not been able to show in his writing for the *Star*. He dressed and conducted himself in a conventional manner, took a more active part in community affairs, and his support of the Democratic party resulted in his being elected for a year or two to the position of secretary of the General Committee of Queens County.[38]

One person who did not approve Whitman's new position was the owner of the *Star*. Whether he was piqued because he had lost an inexpensive reporter and special writer, or thought Whitman unequal to editing a daily, or—more likely—resented the political opposition the new *Eagle* editor would give him, Edwin Spooner published editorials ridiculing Whitman's "weakness." [39] This unkindness irritated Whitman, and he replied with heavy sarcasm, though carefully refraining from reflecting on the character or ability of the older Spooner:

Wouldst thou behold a newspaper which is the incarnation of nervelessness? the mere dry bones of a paper, with all the marrow long withered up?—Behold that paper in our venerable contemporary . . . the *Evening Star!* Conducted for years by one of the worthiest, best-hearted, most respected, and now [one] of the most venerable citizens—we mean that veteran editor and excellent man, Colonel Spooner—the *Star* was an interesting weekly budget of news, well digested, and making a readable family companion. But heaven bless us! it is fallen now into the sere and yellow leaf. . . . It is of the olden time—respectable enough perhaps;—but, great powers! for a paper like that to talk of "weakness." Why, one little drop more of "weakness" in its already full cup of that article, and it would have to get somebody's assistance before it could even lean against the wall and die! [40]

In the same editorial Whitman replied in abusive language to the editor of the Brooklyn *Advertizer*, another Whig, who had made fun of his grammar. Whitman's main point was that this paper was edited by English cockneys who did not know good English and were "really unacquainted with American institutions." Whitman confessed that he never sacrificed "at the shrine of formal construction," but insisted: "As to the style, we simply endeavor to be clearly understood: as to our 'grammar,' it is of course perfectly correct, or we shouldn't presume to write for an intelligent community." [41] But whether Whitman knew it or not, his syntax was often erratic.

The most detailed reminiscence of Whitman's personality and habits during his editorship of the *Eagle* comes again, as with the *Aurora* period, from a young printer who worked on the paper. He was Henry Sutton, a fifteen-year-old apprentice at the time Whitman took over the *Eagle*.[42] Walt soon became fond of Henry, or "Hen," and sent him on personal errands. Many years later Sutton described the editor as "A nice, kind man," who wore a short beard, dressed neatly and inconspicuously, and carried himself with becoming dignity. He did not live with his parents at 71 Prince Street but boarded on Adams, near Myrtle. Sutton was sure of this because Whitman did some of his writing in his room and occasionally sent Henry there for manuscripts.

The editor's sanctum was upstairs, and there he wrote most of his editorials, coming to work early and tending strictly to business. The few visitors he had were "mostly politicians," and Sutton did not remember ever having seen the owner, Van Anden, who occupied the business office, climb the stairs to Whitman's office. After completing his editorials in the morning, Whitman would send them down to the composing room and take a walk while they were being set up. Sometimes the young apprentice set them, and he remembered how insistent Whitman was that the printers follow his "copy" exactly, especially in spelling and punctuation. Having returned from his walk, Whitman read proof. That finished, he would go to Gray's Swimming Bath at the foot of Fulton Street, where he swam for exactly twenty minutes, then took a shower, with Sutton working the pump. Finally, he usually boarded the ferry for New York, where Sutton often saw him riding a Broadway omnibus, sitting beside the driver.

The picture we get is of a serious, energetic, hard-working young man, healthy, contented, and sure of himself—though a fifteen-year-old boy might not be the best judge of the latter. But we also see a certain stubborn independence in Whitman's daily ritual, the walk, the bath, and the trip on the ferry. He will live his life in his own way, regardless of what anyone thinks or says. This trait his brother George always remembered of him. His mother would say, "What will people think?" and Walt would reply,

"Never mind what they think." He would not be hurried, or swerved from the course of his own choice.

Except for the portions of the day and night that he systematically reserved for recreation and pleasure, Whitman gave his whole time and energy to editing the *Eagle*. He had neither time nor inclination to write more immature stories and poems for the magazines. He did reprint in the *Eagle* two of his poems and a number of his stories,[43] including the whole of *Franklin Evans* under a new title, "The Fortunes of a Country Boy, by J.R.S.," [44] but he probably did this more to fill space than to contribute to literature.

Like most newspapers of the time, the size of the *Eagle* was four pages, six columns wide, three-fourths of which was filled with advertising. When Whitman first took charge, he apparently was the whole editorial staff; later he may have had one reporter, though that is not certain.[45] Before he became editor, the whole front page was filled with advertisements, but he claimed two columns for literary material, poems, stories, and so on, and a note calling attention to the contents of the second, or editorial, page. The latter was filled with one or two editorials and summaries of the news, clipped, quoted or condensed from other papers. The actual daily "copy" produced by Whitman was at least two columns. This plus the reading of exchanges, the clipping and summarizing from other papers, and then reading proof on the whole paper, probably took six or seven hours a day—not overly strenuous, but not a sinecure either.

Sometimes Whitman also picked up news items or impressions in New York that he passed on to his readers. On April 28, 1846, P. T. Barnum arrived from Europe on the *Great Western*, having made the passage in seventeen days and six hours, bringing with him Tom Thumb, the dwarf, and "Mlle Jane, the only living Orang Outang in either England or America." The New York papers reported all of these marvelous facts next day. Whitman did not rush over to see Barnum, but on May 21 he had a chance to talk with the great showman, and two days later he printed an account of the interview. He asked Barnum if seeing Europe had made him love "Yankeedom" less. "My God!" said he, "no! not a bit of it! Why, sir, you can't imagine the difference.—There everything is frozen—kings and *things*—formal, but absolutely *frozen*: here it is *life*." [46]

Whitman appreciated his position as editor of the *Eagle*, and he believed himself fully adequate for it. He made little attempt to conceal his own personality behind the editorial "we"—often, in fact, parading it—but he had grown in sympathy and tolerance since editing the *Aurora*. Of course, he still railed at editors of opposition newspapers, but that was part of the game. He dared not forget that the *Eagle* was a party newspaper, but what he especially liked was simply his feeling of contact with the people through the medium of ink and paper. On June 1, 1846, proud of the new steam-propelled press that the management had just installed, and boasting playfully of the new format and appearance of his journal, he used the occasion to chat informally with his readers about his relationship with them. "There is a curious kind of sympathy (haven't you ever thought of it before?) that arises in the mind of a newspaper conductor with the public he serves. He gets to *love* them. Daily communion creates a sort of brotherhood and sisterhood between the two parties. As for us, we like this. We like it better than the more 'dignified' part of editorial labors—the grave political disquisition, the contests of faction, and so on." [47]

Whitman did not forget his duty to comment on political and national affairs, and the majority of his editorials looked beyond himself, or even his community, but he obviously enjoyed the times when he felt like writing about what he had just experienced, or the kind of city he wanted Brooklyn to be. At the end of June he made a trip to Greenport on the Long Island Railroad,[48] leaving Brooklyn at seven-thirty in the morning and arriving back at nine that evening, having left Greenport at five. He praised the town, the fishing there, the farmers of Suffolk county, and the L.I.R.R., whose dining car he patronized on the way back. Like most Americans, Whitman marveled at the mechanical achievements that enabled him to take "a flying picnic" a hundred miles away and return the same day.

Whitman had been to Montauk Point, some twenty-five or thirty miles southeast by boat from Greenport, and that was as far as he had ever traveled, in that year when American troops were crossing the Rio Grande, marching down the Santa Fe Trail to the Southwest country, or sailing around South America to California; while the Mormons trudged to Salt Lake Valley and other emigrants to Oregon, which had been United States territory for barely two years. These adventures Whitman shared vicariously and often discussed in his editorials, but the world of his senses was still bounded by the shores of Long Island and the New Jersey bank of the Hudson.

On the evening of July 7 the twice-postponed Independence Day celebration was held at Fort Greene,[49] the place that Whitman was continually urging the city to make into a park—which it is today. Across the river New York was holding a similar celebration in City Park, bigger and noisier, but in every other respect, the editor of the *Eagle* thought, inferior to Brooklyn's. He himself, by invitation, had written an ode for the occasion, to be sung to the tune of "The Star-Spangled Banner." This had been printed in the *Eagle* on July 2, presumably so that the crowd would be able to sing it. The poem itself was as bad as such productions usually are, but it shows that Whitman was taking an active part in the life of his city.

III

An editorial published on November 19, 1846, especially reveals Whitman's dual life in the two cities, his typical interests and amusements, and his half personal, half didactic attitude toward his readers. He called it "Matters which Were Seen and Done in An Afternoon's Ramble," [50] but it turned out to be a surprisingly long and circuitous ramble. Possibly he started from his parents' home on Prince Street, for he first observed the great number of new houses going up in East and South Brooklyn and pointed out to his readers the need for more churches in that region, which had only a small church on Prince Street and a new Methodist church going up on Bridge Street. Then he crossed to New York on the ferry. As he stood in Battery Park and gazed at the scenery, he thought that a park on the site of Fort Greene would have as fine a view. Here the Brooklyn editor was still speaking, but as he strolled up Broadway he forgot his editorial cares and simply enjoyed himself. "What a fascinating chaos is Broadway," he exclaimed, ". . . the bustle, the show, the glitter, and even the gaudiness." This was the real Walt Whitman, undiscriminating, easily stimulated by noise, color, and movement, happy to lose himself in the ceaseless flux of people going and coming.

Sauntering contentedly uptown, Whitman stopped in at the Art Union, where he admired "Brown's Statuary"—perhaps partly for the benefit of his Brooklyn readers, for the artist was a Brooklynite, the same Henry Kirke Brown who had helped Samuel Clements disinter the body of Elias Hicks in order to make a plaster cast of his face.[51] The pieces of sculpture described by Whitman were entirely classical, though a life-sized Adonis did not quite come up to his expectations. He had probably met Brown, but had not yet become intimate with him.

From the Art Union Whitman strolled into "Barks's," where he stared with interest but without comprehension at some rare Persian vases. He responded emotionally to almost all kinds of art, and the Oriental always fascinated him, but he had no one to guide him or interpret its symbolism in order that he might have an esthetic understanding of it. So, without loitering very long at Barks's he proceeded directly to the Park Theater, where he saw Mr. and Mrs. Charles Kean in a spectacular performance of *King John*, which Whitman thought "probably more Marlowe's play than Shakespeare's after all." Though he had become prejudiced against British actors, and confessed that he was no admirer of Kean, Whitman had to admit that this performance completely satisfied him, the acting, costumes, scenery, properties—everything. He was deeply moved by Mrs. Kean's portrayal of the "widowed and crownless Queen." The harrowing close of the third act was marked by the tears of half the audience, men as well as women. This performance so impressed Whitman that *King John* remained one of his two favorite Shakespeare plays, the other being *Richard III*, that perennial favorite with Bowery Theater audiences. This particular Kean production had opened November 16 after the papers had widely advertised its cost at nearly $12,000, regarded at the time as an extraordinary sum.[52] The program called attention to the 15,000 square feet of canvas painted by Hillyard and Grain, the 176 costly armours, the jewels, the historically authentic costumes, and other lavish wonders. The critics' reactions were the same as Whitman's and particularly, as with him, regarding Mrs. Kean. One critic wrote: "The intensity of maternal grief poured forth in tones that actually harrow[ed] up the soul . . . the vehemence of woe, the shrieks of despair, the impassioned action, not overdone, nor exaggerated, . . . could not be paralleled on the modern stage."[53] Despite the rave reviews, however, the performance drew only moderate houses and closed in three weeks.

Why did Kean's *King John* so strongly affect Whitman? The accounts leave little doubt that it was gaudy and rhetorical—as certainly the play itself is. It seems strange that Whitman was never so deeply moved by either the acting or the poetry of *Hamlet*, *Macbeth*, or *Lear*. Possibly they were not so well acted in his day. But there seems little doubt that he liked a spectacle and oratory on the stage, and *Richard III* and *King John* affected him much as Italian opera did.

There may have been one other reason for his liking *King John*. As we have seen, he was particularly stirred by Mrs. Kean's acting of the Queen's role. Whitman had a truly profound sympathy for mothers, and he could suffer emotionally with this mother in her grief for her murdered children. It is significant that on December 5 he published an editorial on Queen Victoria,[54] whom he continued to admire all his life. Democratically protesting against kings and queens, he nevertheless thought that "a gentle-hearted woman" at the head of a government would be a "benignant and kindly . . . influence," and he confessed that if he were "forced to live in a monarchy" he would "by all means prefer to be ruled by a Queen!"

Aside from his sympathy with mothers and matriarchs, Whitman's editorials contained few references to women. The preceding April 1, in a classification of the various kinds of "fools," he had included "single fools, the bachelors and maids who are old enough to be married." He advised them: "Buy candles and double beds; make yourself a reality in life—and do the state some service."[55] On other occasions he also urged marriage for the sake of progeny, and frequently wrote tenderly of children—including his perennial campaign against the cruelty of teachers in the classroom. But he never felt inclined to take his own advice about marriage, and when he happened to mention young women in a personal way it was nearly always with a tone of artificial sentimentality. One June morning he described himself as staring through his second-story window at the "bevies of our Brooklyn belles on their way to the ferry."[56] He noticed their "lithe graceful shapes such as the American women only have," and then continued: "the very sight of you is a mute prayer for peace" (an allusion to the war with Mexico), adding with intended facetiousness, "their refining presence" even made "the late sulky fit of weather" bearable.

During the following year (1847) Whitman had much to say about the degradation of female labor. He frequently called attention to the low wages of "sewing-women"[57] and of female workers in the factories,[58] though he confessed he had no solution. Just at that time labor unions were making considerable progress in New York City, but Whitman took no part in them, and had nothing to say about male labor except to condemn Negro slavery as unfair competition. We must, therefore, regard his concern over the plight of female servants, seamstresses, and women operatives in factories as another phase of his emerging mother-religion, later to produce some of his major literary themes and symbols.

Occasionally the mother-worship also appeared in Whitman's book reviews, which were one of his innovations and most important contributions as editor of the Eagle. Unlike Poe, whose critical judgment vanished when he reviewed one of the third-rate women poets so popular in the 1840's, Whitman did not "puff" female writers, yet he appreciated a book with a maternal point of view, such as Frederika Bremer's novels; he knew nothing, he said, "more likely to melt and refine the human character." [59]

Another side of Whitman's emerging view of women may be seen in a notice he wrote of Dr. Edward H. Dixon's *Woman and Her Diseases*,[60] in which he scored "the mock delicacy that condemns the widest diffusion among females of such knowledge as is contained in this book." He also exclaimed in this review on the rarity of "the sight of a well-developed, healthy *naturally* beautiful woman." As the "equal rights for women" movement gained momentum in this decade, Whitman began to envision a new race of muscular, athletic mothers; strong, fearless, and as able to endure hardships as their husbands.

Many of the authors whose direct influence can be traced in his later poetry Whitman reviewed in the *Eagle*, among them Carlyle, Emerson, Margaret Fuller (*Papers on Literature and Art*), Michelet, George Sand (*The Journeyman Joiner*), Goethe (*Autobiography*),[61] and the writings of some of the contemporary faddists, popular for two or three decades, such as O. S. Fowler, the phrenologist (*Physiology, Animal and Mental*, and *Memory and Intellectual Development*), and Mary S. Gove, the "water cure" quack, who was helping to make Americans conscious of their bodies.[62] To judge by the later results on Whitman's thinking and writing, some of these authors were subtly emancipating him from the puritanism and asceticism he had been taught in public school and Sunday school, but his reviews show little evidence of a mental revolution. His comments on books were still largely moral, didactic, and superficial.

Whitman's many book notices and short reviews and his personal chats with his readers revealed one side of his mind and personality. Another side was revealed in his demands for social reform, including women's rights, abolishing capital punishment, humanizing education, and civic improvements in Brooklyn. One of the most important reforms beginning to take shape in his mind was religious. He observed that "the comfortable pews, the exquisite arrangements, and the very character of the architecture of modern churches . . . lead a man into a complacent kind of self-satisfaction with himself and his doings." He particularly scorned the fashionable churches in New York. Like Frances Wright, he thought religion should liberate rather than restrain. He regarded Christianity as "incomparably superior to all other religions—though it cannot make man essentially different. All reforms tend to the great result of freeing man's body and his mind from the dark tyranny . . . that has been accumulating on them for centuries." [63]

IV

Whitman took over the editorship of the Brooklyn *Eagle* in one of the most momentous years in the history of the United States. Bernard De Voto has aptly called it "The Year of Decision," [64] and the "decisions" of 1846 changed the nation from a small aggregate of states on the Eastern seaboard to a continental power. The year began in crisis. The dispute with England over the Oregon territory had caused ominous threats of war. The Democratic party had recently won the election with the slogan "Fifty-four forty or fight." But most Americans had only the haziest notion of the vast stretch of land extending to 54° 40', which included what is now the states of Oregon, Washington, Idaho, part of Montana, part of Wyoming, and all of British Columbia, clear up to Alaska (then in the possession of Russia).

And before the Oregon dispute could be settled a Mexican crisis developed. In 1845 the ten-year-old Republic of Texas had asked to be annexed to the United States, but the Senate had dallied. Early in 1846, negotiations having broken down and Mexico even refusing to receive the American minister, President Polk ordered General Zachary Taylor to march with an army (or what passed for one) to the Rio Grande, and he finally arrived there in March.

As a third less acute problem, there was also California, and the intervening territory comprising not only the present state of California but also New Mexico, Utah, Arizona, Nevada, and parts of Wyoming and Colorado. President Polk and the American "expansionists" coveted these lands, most of which were unsettled except for some nomadic Indians, a few Mexicans in New Mexico, and a polyglot population (including some Americans) in California. For a long time historians regarded our methods of acquiring these lands as an ignoble grab, but they are beginning to justify Polk and to rationalize the action.[65] For one thing, they point out, the Mexican government was so weak internally that its control over these outlying territories was extremely precarious, and England or France, or possibly Russia, was eagerly waiting for the opportunity to seize them if the United States did not. The truth is that the rapidly expanding nation would inevitably absorb these lands sooner or later; that was a foregone conclusion biologically and psychologically—a brute fact, as inescapable as the ultimate doom of the Indian nations after European colonists had gained a foothold on the Atlantic coast. New England moralists, like Emerson and Thoreau, would condemn their government for seizing Texas and California (almost everyone wanted Oregon), but even they felt the magic attraction of the "West" and were unconsciously expansionists in their dreams and thinking. These unexploited lands had become a part of the American myth.

It was not until several weeks after Whitman began writing editorials for the *Eagle* that he showed any marked concern for the great problems facing President Polk and the nation. On March 18 he did print a strong condemnation of the laws that permitted Negro slaves to be imported by way of Brazil,[66] but he had not yet connected slavery and Western expansion. Nor had he given much thought to expansion itself. We may remember that as late as the previous December he seemed to doubt that the Oregon lands were worth risking war with Great Britain. But as General Taylor marched toward the Rio Grande, Whitman's patriotic fervor grew. On April 3 he crowed loudly over the American victory at Buena Vista and began to hero-worship General Taylor.[67] He was exactly the kind of man Whitman might be expected to admire: rugged, tenacious, careless in dress, and with no regard whatever for conventions or protocol. Historians agree that he was absolutely honest and fearless, but deficient in military science and imagination—and some say in intelligence.[68] More than one bright young officer (whose name would become famous later in the Civil War) staved off defeat by supplying the leadership he lacked, or won victories by improvised tactics not thought of by the general. But he captured the loyalty of his backwoods troops and the imagination of the newspaper correspondents. The Whigs were quick to see his possibilities as a candidate for the Presidency in the next election, and it was not difficult for them to suggest this idea to "Old Rough and Ready" himself. Thus he waged the war with half his attention on the Mexicans and the other half on the next Whig convention, and co-operated very willingly with the newspapermen. President Polk knew what was going on, and the prospect of having a hero-general oppose the Democrats in 1848 worried him about as much as the Mexicans did. But Whitman took the newspaper stories at face value and worshiped the general.

On the evening of April 15 the front of the *Eagle* building was covered by a "transparency" which showed the illuminated names of the places which American soldiers had made glorious in the newspapers: "Palo Alto, Resaca de la Palma, Monterey, Buena Vista, Vera Cruz . . ." Next day in the editorial column of the *Eagle* Whitman expressed his continued hopes for peace, but warned that "the desire on the part of our government for peace with Mexico must be met with a willingness for peace on the part of Mexico herself." [69] The difficulty was that the Mexican government was so unstable that it was impossible for the United States government to find anyone with whom to negotiate. By May most Americans, outside New England, were convinced that the Texas problem could only be solved by military force. On May 11 Whitman called for a declaration of war, [70] only four days before President Polk signed a resolution stating that a state of war existed.

On June 7 the great orator and radical clergyman in Boston, Theodore Parker, thundered from Melodeon Hall that "aggressive war is a sin . . . a denial of Christianity and of God . . . Treason against the people . . ." [71] But the editor of the *Eagle* not only supported the war, he had unlimited faith in the benefits that the American government could bestow upon the peoples of any territory conquered. On the day preceding Parker's anathema Whitman read a report that the province of Yucatan wished to be annexed by the United States, and he declared in his editorial: "The scope of our government . . . is such that it can readily fit itself, and extend itself, to almost any extent, and to interests and circumstances the most widely different." [72] He looked forward to seeing California and Santa Fe (New Mexico) "shine as two new stars in our mighty firmament." But he warned that "the mere physical grandeur of this Republic . . . is only desirable as an aid to reach the truer good, the good of the whole body of the people."

Some days later (June 23) Whitman thought the expansion of the United States natural and inevitable: "And for our part, we look on that increase of territory and power . . . with the faith which the Christian has in God's mystery." [73] Since the early days of their Republic most Americans had had the idealistic faith that their democratic form of government could not only be a beacon of freedom to other nations—an example and an influence—but that its success would hasten the day when oppressed people of all the world would throw off their shackles. It was a revolutionary doctrine, and as such feared by most European governments. In that very same "year of decision" William Cullen Bryant, recently returned from Europe, expressed these convictions in a poem, "Oh Mother of a Mighty Race":

Oh mother of a mighty race,
Yet lovely in thy youthful grace!
The elder dames, thy haughty peers,
Admire and hate thy blooming years.

.   .   .   .

They know not, in their hate and pride,
What virtues with thy children bide;

.   .   .   .

There's freedom at thy gates and rest
For Earth's down-trodden and opprest,
A shelter for the hunted head,
For the starved laborer toil and bread.
Power, at thy bounds,
Stops and calls back his baffled hounds.

To Bryant and Whitman this was both a political and a religious conviction. "Over the rest of the world," continued Whitman in his editorial,
"the swelling impulse of freedom struggles, too; though *we* are ages ahead
of them." [74] On July 7, discussing the prospect of annexing California,
he asked in all sincerity: "What has miserable, inefficient Mexico— . . .
with . . . her actual tyranny by the few over the many—what has she to do
with the great mission of peopling the New World with a noble race?" [75]
And on July 28, almost as if paraphrasing Bryant's yet unpublished poem,
Whitman wrote: "The old and moth-eaten systems of Europe have had
their day, and that evening of their existence which is nigh at hand, will
be the token of a glorious dawn for the down-trodden people." [76] This anti-
Europeanism was one aspect of American social idealism. On October 8
Whitman reiterated: "Long enough have priestcraft and kingcraft
stalked over those [European] lands, clothed in robes of darkness and
wielding the instruments of subjection." [77]

These editorials were preliminary drafts of what was to become the famous 1855 preface of *Leaves of Grass*, but the sentiments represented the
feelings of a great many Americans in 1846. And Bryant had considerable
influence on their formation and growth in Whitman's mind. On the occasion of Bryant's death Whitman recalled that he had known him over
thirty years, "and he had been markedly kind to me . . . We were both
walkers, and when I work'd in Brooklyn he several times came over, middle of afternoons, and we took rambles, miles long, till dark, out towards
Bedford or Flatbush, in company. On these occasions he gave me clear accounts of scenes in Europe—the cities, looks, architecture, art, especially
Italy—where he had travel'd a good deal." [78]

Meanwhile, after much bluster and some shrewd bargaining on both sides, England had agreed to settle the Oregon dispute with a boundary line on the 49th parallel, and on June 12 Congress voted to accept this agreement, much to Whitman's relief. Now he could turn his whole attention to Mexico. Whitman felt confident that General Taylor would soon bring the Mexicans to their senses, and he continued to idolize the hero of the press. On October 14th he exclaimed, "The more we hear and read of this man, the more we think he in many respects resembles Washington." [79] And Whitman was infuriated by the means some editors were using to oppose the Mexican War. On November 16 he accused Horace Greeley of the *Tribune* of aiding and abetting the enemy in his "open advocacy of the Mexican cause" and his "sneers at our officers and men." [80] On December 5 he was indignant over the report that General Winfield Scott was to be placed in supreme command.[81]

General Scott was another Whig who aspired to the Presidency, and it galled the President to have to use him; moreover, President Polk distrusted him because he was a West Point graduate and thought in terms of military science. General Scott's political enemies also regarded him as an exhibitionist, and at times he did seem to be conspicuously theatrical. He delighted in splendid uniforms and military ceremony, whereas General Taylor did not care what he wore and his speech and manners were as "common" as an old shoe. The hordes of half-wild backwoodsmen from Tennessee and Missouri under his command, who fought each other if no Mexicans were available, adored him, and though Whitman had never been near the backwoods or the frontier, he had a good deal of the frontier point of view.

General Scott had a plan for ending the war by an invasion through Vera Cruz, and after much urging by the military experts in Washington President Polk finally appointed him supreme commander and sent him off on the expedition. Although Polk consistently placed the good of his country ahead of the good of his party, he never forgot he was a Democrat, and it hurt him not to be able to find a Democratic general who could win the war for him. The Whigs, too, were in a dilemma, for they liked to oppose "Jimmie Polk's" war, despite the fact that their own extremely political-minded generals were conducting it.

Whitman, however, though editor of a party newspaper, did not think of Texas, Oregon, or California expansion in terms of politics, but as the means of extending the benefits of democracy to more people. For this reason he continued to oppose the "Native American" faction because he wanted to rescue as many people as possible from European despotism. "There is too much mankind and too little earth" in other parts of the world, but "The mind becomes almost lost in tracing in imagination those hidden and boundless tracts of our territory . . ." [82] How then can "any man with a heart in his breast, begrudge the coming of Europe's needy ones, to the plentiful storehouse of the New World?"

V

Though the question of how to use the Western and Southwestern lands gave rise to various political views, only the "Native American" splinter party opposed immigration outright in 1846. But in August another question arose that was destined to split the Democratic party—as it was already split in New York State—and eventually the nation. President Polk had asked Congress for an appropriation of two million dollars to be used as an advance payment for any territory that might be acquired from Mexico by treaty, and David Wilmot of Pennsylvania introduced an amendment to the bill forbidding the introduction of slavery into any new territory. This amendment, which became known as the Wilmot Proviso, was approved by the House and Senate—though the House later reversed its approval. All along the abolitionists, especially those of New England, had insisted that Southern politicians were fostering the war with Mexico in order to extend slavery and the political power of slavocracy. President Polk had not regarded the Mexican question as concerned with slavery one way or the other, but after the adoption of the Wilmot Proviso slavery was definitely involved, because it had become a major political issue.

In New York State this new dispute was to become a decisive factor in the next election. Walt Whitman's beloved Silas Wright had not been a very successful governor, and to a large extent because of the very honesty and political integrity that Whitman so much admired in him[83]—though it was also a fact that he drank too much. Having been compelled against his desire to become governor, he felt justified in remaining aloof from all patronage distribution and political conniving. To the idealist or political amateur this might seem like admirable conduct, but the practical result was that the Hunker faction seized the opportunity to press their recommendations, and President Polk inadvertently filled most of the important government positions in New York with appointees who opposed Wright and his friends. Thus as a result of Governor Wright's refusal to

make recommendations, he contributed through inaction, and President
Polk through incomplete knowledge of the situation, to a breach in the
Democratic party that lost the election in New York State in 1846 and
the national election in 1848. Yet despite Silas Wright's failure as a state
politician and his expressed desire to retire from politics altogether, he was
persuaded, during the summer of 1846, to become a candidate to succeed
himself as governor, and leading national politicians of both parties regarded him as the best candidate the Democratic party could run for the
Presidency in 1848.

During the summer of 1846 Whitman eagerly supported Wright for the
governorship, as he had done in the *Democrat* in 1844,[84] and, as with the
earlier newspaper, against the wishes of the owner, for Van Anden was a
"Hunker." The party had not, however, yet split into two irreconcilable
camps, and the editor of the *Eagle* was permitted to follow his independent course. The tragic split was to come later as a result of the Wilmot
Proviso. Governor Wright refused to make a political statement on the
subject, but to his friends he had indicated his sympathy with the Proviso
and he was generally thought to favor it. This was not openly an issue in
New York, though secretly it influenced voters, and indirectly encouraged
the gestation of a "free soil" political movement.

One of the open issues in the New York election was the anti-rent
movement. In several counties in New York the patroon system of the
Dutch still prevailed on many farms. Originally most of the land in the
central Hudson Valley had belonged to a few landlords, who had rented
it out to tenants on long-term leases. Usually the rent was nominal, and
could be paid in produce or money, but the land could not be bought. Collections of rent were often lax, and sometimes the rents were not paid for
many years. As a result some tenants got the idea that the land they, and
perhaps their fathers and grandfathers, had lived on ought rightly to belong to them without further payments of any kind. Following the death
in 1839 of one of the greatest of the "Old Patroons," Stephen Van Rensse-
laer, tenants began to protest, later to riot, and finally to form an
Anti-Rent party. This party was too small to win an election, but it possessed enough power to bargain with either major party. Governor Wright
tried to find legal means to solve the rent problem, but he refused to tolerate the flouting of law and order and once put down a rebellion with
troops. Whitman regarded his handling of the lawbreakers as highly ethical and commendable, and said so in an editorial on November 2.[85]

On the day after the election Whitman wished to find the reason for the defeat, rather than to abuse the "people" for voting as they did.[86] But he admitted that he could not find an explanation for the Democratic defeat (he apparently was unaware of the extent of the split in the party), and the best he could say on November 7 was that the Whigs were enjoying an upswing of popularity and that the Democrats should bide their time. For some months he had been developing a philosophical attitude toward elections. By April, 1847, he had evolved the rationalization that "the turbulence and destructiveness" of the democratic spirit at election times was an evidence of social vitality, an evidence "that the people act," even though the acts might not always be wise.[87]

This was not the rationalization of a party man, but of a social optimist, a man who had a Rousseauistic faith in the ultimate goodness of human nature and the political wisdom of the "people" in the long run. As Lincoln was to say later, "you can't fool all the people all the time." Whitman himself did not wait for a "party line" to formulate, or consult the Democratic "bosses" in Brooklyn for an expedient policy to advocate in the *Eagle*. He believed that the Wilmot Proviso was consistent with the basic Democratic doctrines of free trade, low tariff, and territorial expansion for the good of humanity. On December 21, 1846, he urged the Democratic party to come out for "free soil." [88] The following February he stated: "We believe the Brooklyn *Eagle* was the very first Democratic paper which alluded to this subject in a decisive manner," [89] and he thought, mistakenly, that all Democratic papers had since followed suit. He condemned the fanaticism of the abolitionists, and began to fear that the extremists on both sides might endanger the Union. This fear made him take a stand that has since been misunderstood; he would not sacrifice the Union to abolish slavery; slavery was bad but the preservation of the Union came before everything else—the very stand Lincoln was to take. Nevertheless, he stuck by the Wilmot Proviso and continued to urge the Democrats to endorse it. In April, 1847, when Calhoun charged the Northern states with trying to "appropriate all the territories of the United States now possessed, or hereafter to be acquired, to themselves, *to the entire exclusion of the slaveholding states*," Whitman replied that with the possible exception of South Carolina the majority of the freemen of the South did not own slaves, and that the only persons excluded would be the slaveholders themselves.[90] He was now thinking of slavery as a threat to free labor, North or South. And his desire to keep the new territories "free soil" for the protection of free labor intensified his idealistic enthusiasm for the "boundless democratic free West! . . . The slave States are confessedly either stationary, or on a very slow progress, or in an actual decline. The Atlantic States, with a rush after wealth, and the spread among them of effeminating luxuries, need a balance wheel like that furnished by the agricultural sections of the West." [91]

Throughout 1847 Whitman continued to support "free soil" in the *Eagle*, but meanwhile anti-Wilmot-Proviso Democrats gained control of the party in New York State, and the sudden death of Silas Wright in the summer worked to their advantage. At the time of his death he was in retirement on his farm at Canton and wished to remain there, but his name had continued to be frequently mentioned as a likely presidential candidate in 1848, and this possibility had helped to counteract the influence of the "Old Hunkers." But with Wright out of the way, they took over the party machine in New York, and this included the owner of the *Eagle*, who was treasurer of the local Democratic General Committee. Through their efforts the Democratic Convention at Syracuse ignored the Wilmot Proviso, and the party was defeated in the local elections in November. In the *Eagle* Whitman blamed the defeat on the cowardice of the New York Democrats.[92] The anti-Wilmot-Proviso faction then held a convention in Albany and tried to persuade the "free soil" faction to re-join them, but the latter could not be pacified and they were then read out of the party. Thereupon they held a convention at Utica and made plans to send delegates to the National Convention in the summer of 1848.

It is surprising that under these circumstances Whitman could remain editor of the Brooklyn *Eagle* throughout 1847. But at the end of the year a new development arose that completed his break with Van Anden and the "regular" Democratic party in New York. Late in December General Lewis Cass of Michigan, whose previous efforts had resulted in the House of Representatives' reversal of its support of the Wilmot Proviso, wrote a friend of his in Tennessee his reasons for opposing the Proviso, and this was circulated for publication in the Democratic press. Without printing the text, Whitman answered General Cass's arguments point by point on January 3, 1848.[93] Two days later nearly a column of extracts from General Cass's letter appeared in the *Eagle* without comment. It is not known whether Whitman was still editor on January 5, though he may have printed the extracts to prove his fairness. On the same day the *Eagle* also reprinted the second installment of his story "The Boy Lover," [94] signed "Walter Whitman," though this might have already been in type. However, his editorship probably did not definitely teminate until some days later. In his notebook he merely recorded that he edited the *Eagle* "till the last of January '48,"[95] which might mean any time near the last of the month. Probably the new editor, S. G. Arnold, had taken over by January 21, for on that day the *Eagle* replied to some satirical comments in the New York *Globe* on the Whitman affair: "The publisher, in the course of his business arrangements, has found it necessary to dispense with one of its editors [a fanciful exaggeration, for there was only one, the whole editorial staff], and although he did not see fit to consult the *Globe* in regard to the matter, yet he claims that it has no right to misrepresent his motives, or in any way meddle in his affairs."[96]

The same day the New York *Tribune* also printed a paragraph which showed that the row in Brooklyn had been going on for some time, and that Whitman's own political friends were working for him. The *Tribune* item was captioned "A Barnburner Paper"—using the Hunker's nickname for the radical faction in the Democratic party (the name alluding to the farmer who burned down his barn to get rid of the rats):

We are informed from the best authority that the Barnburners of Brooklyn are about starting a new daily paper, as, it is said, The Eagle has returned to Old Hunkerism again. Mr. Walter Whitman, late of The Eagle, is to have charge of the new enterprise. The split in the Loco-foco Party rages with all its bitterness in Kings County—a place where a clique of office-loving Locos[97] ["Loco-foco" faction] has for years bidden defiance to principle and public interest, too, for the sake of the drippings.[98]

VI

Some eight months later Whitman did found and edit a "Barnburner" paper in Brooklyn, but a lucky encounter on February 9 enabled him to escape from these bitter controversies for three months. On Wednesday evening he attended a performance at the Broadway Theater in New York, and between acts while strolling in the lobby he happened to meet J. E. McClure, who was planning to start a newspaper in New Orleans with A. H. Hayes. As Whitman later told the story, "after fifteen minutes' talk (and a drink) we made a formal bargain, and he paid me two hundred dollars down to bind the contract and bear my expenses to New Orleans."[99] Possibly McClure knew more about the recent editor of the Brooklyn *Eagle* than the account indicates, but it seems, nevertheless, to have been an impulsive bargain on both sides. For Whitman, however, it was a chance to travel, and though the Mexican War had just ended, New Orleans was still an exciting place, with troops and generals coming and going and newspaper correspondents using it as headquarters. Doubt-less, too, Whitman was disillusioned with the Democrats of Kings County, and his actual prospects of support for a "Barnburner" paper were prob-ably not very encouraging.

The first issue of the new paper was to appear on March 5, and the trip would require two weeks, with good luck. So, hastily making a few prep-arations for himself and his fourteen-year-old brother,[100] Jeff, whom Walt decided to take with him (whether by agreement with McClure is not known), the two Whitmans left Brooklyn by train on Friday, spent the night in Baltimore, and on Saturday morning at 7:00 A.M. boarded a train that would carry them to Cumberland, where they would take a stage-coach for the hard trip over the Alleghenies. They arrived at Cumberland about sunset, transferred almost immediately to a stage, which was jammed with passengers and baggage, and then jolted across the moun-tains all night and all next day, stopping only for meals and to change horses every ten miles, until they arrived at Wheeling, West Virginia, on Sunday night a little after ten o'clock. Here their Ohio River steamboat, the *St. Cloud*, was lying at the wharf waiting for them, and they stum-bled wearily aboard, found their comfortable stateroom, and sank imme-diately into heavy sleep. Walt was awakened next morning by the clang of the breakfast bell and was pleased to learn that they were already well on their way to Cincinnati.

After breakfast and a look around the boat, Walt sat down and re-corded his experiences since leaving Baltimore. During the remainder of the trip he continued to keep a diary, which he drew upon after his ar-rival in New Orleans for a series of three articles called "Excerpts from a Traveller's Notebook." [101] He recorded his trip to New Orleans,[102] his stay there, and the return trip,[103] and an unpublished fragment concerned with his actual experience on the *Crescent* staff was edited after his death.[104] Thus we have an abundance of documented details for this brief episode in Whitman's life.

Before this we have seen evidence of Whitman's tendency to idealize and romanticize. The New Orleans experience was, on the whole, pleas-ant and at times exhilarating, but it also afforded opportunity for con-trasting preconceived abstractions with reality, and some of these actu-alities were at least mildly shocking to him. Whitman's first shock was the appearance of the Ohio River. "In poetry and romance, these rivers are talked of as though they were cleanly streams; but it is astonishing what a difference is made by the simple fact that they are always and altogether excessively muddy—mud, indeed, being the prevailing character both afloat and ashore. . . . There is no romance in a mass of yellowish brown liquid." But he marveled at how soon he got used "to drinking it and washing in it." [105]

On the stagecoach Whitman had found his fellow passengers either unsociable or great bores, though he continued to believe young men of the Eastern cities, "with all the advantages of a compact neighborhood, schools, etc., are not up to the men of the West. Among the latter, probably, attention is more turned to the *realities* of life, and a habit formed of thinking for one's self; in the cities, frippery and artificial fashion are too much the ruling powers." But on the steamboat he got a close-up view of Western character, and the few observations he did record confirmed some of Dickens's satirical comments. For example, the Whitmans were delighted with the quantity and quality of food served on the boat, though Walt was amazed "that everybody gulps down the victuals with railroad speed." He could not understand why, with the "distressing want of a pleasant means to pass away the time," they should bolt down breakfast or dinner in five minutes. We hear no more romanticizing of Western character. Walt preferred to watch the drama of stopping to pick up or discharge passengers and freight and continually marveled at the amount of commerce carried on by this river traffic. All the steamers on the river carried freight, and the *St. Cloud* seemed to Walt to be constantly loaded to the limit with barrels of pork, lard, and flour, bags of coffee, rolls of leather, groceries, dry goods, hardware, coops of live geese, turkeys, chickens, "that kept up a perpetual farmyard concert." Aboard were also "divers living hogs," a horse, and a "resident dog." [106] Sometimes Walt counted the amount of produce loaded or unloaded. He was greatly impressed by the productiveness of this country, and its enormous "buying and selling," which the people on the steamboat took as a matter of course. This was Whitman's first awakening to the tremendous size, capacity, variety, and fertility of the growing nation.

Towns and occasional cities en route did not particularly impress him; however, he realized that the muddy banks of the river did not afford the most imposing views of these places. Cincinnati he acknowledged as a "Queen City" in commerce, if nothing else, but he seriously advised the city papers to have the streets cleaned, and kept so, regardless of the expense. (He failed to say why this should be the responsibility of the "city papers.") Louisville he explored on foot while the boat was changing cargo, and found it quieter and more "substantial" than Cincinnati; he thought he would find the citizens hospitable, if he only had time to get acquainted with them. But Cairo, at the junction of the Mississippi, was hopeless. "It is doubtful," he observed, "whether Cairo will ever be any 'great shakes,' except in the way of ague." These frequent stops and delays stretched out the passage from Wheeling to New Orleans to twelve exhausting days and nights.

VII

Whitman and his younger brother arrived in New Orleans on Friday night, February 25, 1848, about 10:00 P.M.,[107] and stopped at a boarding-house on Tojdrass Street, corner of St. Charles, which turned out to be very dirty and uncomfortable.[108] Jeff was already homesick, and he wrote to his mother that he had never before so much wanted her cleanliness.[109] But in a few days they moved to the Tremont House, "next door to the the-atre and directly opposite the office" of the *Crescent*.[110] There the street noise was incessant, but Walt and Jeff had good beds and slept well—or at least Walt did. They approved, they wrote home, "the plan of going to dinner when we liked, and calling for what we wanted, out of a variety of dishes [which] was more convenient than the usual way of boarding-houses." [111]

Whitman at first found his "situation rather a pleasant one." He re-corded in his memoranda, apparently after the experience was over: "People seemed to treat me kindly, particularly H. and M'C. My health was most capital; I frequently thought indeed that I felt better than ever before in my life." [112] He was not editor, and evidently did not ex-pect to be. The *Crescent* had a large staff for a newspaper of the time, including, besides the owners and Whitman, a "Mr. Larue," who wrote the leading editorials; a "Mr. Reeder," "an amiable-hearted young man, but excessively intemperate," who was the "city news man"; "and a young fellow named Da Ponte" who translated the Mexican dispatches and for-eign items. Whitman's job was "overhauling the papers rec'd by mail, and 'making up the news,' as it is called, both with pen and scissors." This sounds like very unimportant work, but in those days before the press as-sociations and teletype dispatches the general news was clipped or con-densed from other newspapers, and the papers vigorously exchanged with each other. Walt went to work at nine o'clock in the morning, and got home much sooner than he thought he would, by eleven at night, so Jeff wrote his parents.[113] How much of this time he actually spent in the office is not stated, but it would seem that he had a full day. In addition to editing the general news he also wrote what would later have been called "feature stories" for the *Crescent*—for which he was possibly supposed to be paid extra.

Jeff was employed at five dollars a week as office boy in the *Crescent* office.[114] His special duties were taking care of the exchanges, which he was permitted to sell for twenty-five cents a hundred—some indication of the large number received. He also had to handle outgoing mail bags, which Walt thought too heavy for him. Jeff was afflicted intermittently with dysentery, and this of course made him still more unhappy and homesick. He frequently wrote letters home and begged the family to write, but at the end of two months he and Walt had not received a single letter from the family in Brooklyn,[115] though friends[116] in the *Eagle* office took exchange copies of the *Crescent* to the Whitmans' house and occasionally reported on the health of the family—another indication, incidentally, of the friendly relations Walt had had with the *Eagle* office staff.

The first issue of the Daily *Crescent* appeared on Sunday, March 5, as scheduled, but thereafter it was published only on weekdays. This first number contained Whitman's account of his "Crossing the Alleghenies," and the following day his impressions of Cincinnati and Louisville were published, the connecting installment on "Western Steamboats—The Ohio" being held over until March 10. The March 6 issue also carried a short editorial by Whitman defending the "Model Artists," [117] a theatrical troupe which at the time was being much criticized in the Northern papers for its semi-nude performances, consisting of statuesque poses in imitation of famous pieces of sculpture. Whitman declared, "It is a sickly prudishness that bars all appreciation of the divine beauty evidenced in Nature's cunningest work—the human frame, form and face." The Mobile *Herald* attacked this defense, and Whitman continued the argument in the March 14 *Crescent*. "The only objection that we conceive of the undraped figure," he wrote, "arises from an assumption of coarseness and grossness intended. Take away this, and there is no need (in the cases under discussion) of any objection at all. Eve in Paradise—or Adam either —would not be supposed to shock the mind." [118] Here the journalist was taking a stand that would later become part of his poetic program—in a group of poems to be called "Children of Adam."

On March 10 he published an article on "The Habitants of Hotels" [119] that contained the embryonic plan of a series of articles. In sketching rapidly some of the "habitants" at, presumably, a New Orleans hotel, he included a vain, showy, braggart sportsman (who was also a bully such as Mark Twain satirized—probably an authentic type in New Orleans or St. Louis) and a conceited would-be sophisticate from New York City. In succeeding issues,[120] most of them in March, Whitman caricatured other types in more detail, including a four-flusher, Peter Funk, who posed in barrooms as a young "gentleman about 'town'"; a Creole flower vendor, Miss Dusky Grisette, who, the informal essayist speculated, was perhaps a seductive *jolie-grisette* by night, and a prosaic coffee vendor or washerwoman by day; a swaggering "game cock," Dagger Bowie-knife, Esq.; a New Orleans dandy, John J. Jinglebrain; an Irish cotton bales drayman, Patrick McDray; and a sentimental lover, Samuel Sensitive. Though he had borrowed a good many tricks from Dickens, Whitman showed considerable nimbleness, whimsey, and even close observation in these sketches. The lightness of touch was new to him, and for almost the first time in his imaginative writing he forgot to moralize.

But all the most charming and original sketches were published in March. In April Whitman's extra "features" dwindled both in number and in quality—possibly the effect of the Southern spring; possibly lack of encouragement from the proprietors. The newspaper report of John Jacob Astor's death provoked a brief reminiscence of Whitman's glimpse at Astor Place. On another day he described a visit to the cathedral on Good Friday, and later "A Walk about Town," such as he had written for the *Aurora*.[121] In May his contributions declined still more, numbering only four. One was but a paragraph describing the sensation at the St. Charles Theater on the evening of May 8, when General Taylor unexpectedly attended.

On May 18 Whitman published an elaborate burlesque entitled "A Night at the Terpsichore Ball by You Know Who."[122] Of all these sketches this is one of the most artificial and least original, but a host of biographers have used it as evidence that Walt Whitman had a love affair in New Orleans, and the "You Know Who" by-line has even been taken as a secret message to the woman. In the burlesque-narrative the author, a "bachelor . . . from inclination," goes to the ball wondering half seriously if he will find "her" there. Of course he does, his perfect dream-woman, but just as he is about to propose to her, the man who had introduced her to the narrator comes up and says, "Wife ain't it time to go home?"

The whole tone of the sketch is satirical, and it is difficult to understand why it has ever been taken for anything more than a humorous skit. A man actually in love would have been as unlikely to write it as the mockery of romantic sentiment in "Samuel Sensitive" (May 2), in which the young man's every sentiment was a stock emotion in popular fiction: "He sits and sighs, while visions of blond lace and fancy ribbons, to say nothing of 'love darting eyes and tresses like the morn,' flit before his imagination, and render him very qualmish indeed." Of course Samuel tried to write poetry, "saw beauty in the moon and stars," and quoted Burns's "Ae Fond Kiss" to a bale of cotton.

The first biographer to invent a New Orleans romance was Henry Bryan Binns, whose book was published in 1905.[123] While in this country collecting material, an admirer of Whitman in California told Binns his theory of the poet's being the father of some children in New Orleans.[124] According to this theory the mother was happily married, but the husband was sterile. Both met Whitman, "fell under the spell of his magnificent, healthy, loving, magnetic personality," and they selected him for the father. Binns, however, improved on the hypothesis, making the woman a beautiful, wealthy Creole of a proud family into which Whitman could not marry and which out of pride would always keep secret the paternity of the woman's children. This combination of spring in the romantic South and proud Creole beauty has proved irresistible for almost every biographer since Binns. But not one concrete fact has ever been discovered to support this romantic fiction.

It is true that Whitman shed some of his inhibitions during this first stay away from his native Long Island and New York, but none of the emotions in his essays, his letters to Brooklyn, or his personal memoranda are those of a man in love—especially for the first time. He did comment, as we have seen, on the Creole flower girl, and several times on the black woman from whom he bought coffee in the morning (very bad coffee he recorded in one place,[125] possibly the thick bitter kind brewed by the Spanish people). Except for the flower girl, Whitman's most vivid sketches were, as in his previous writing, of men.

The letters that Walt and Jeff wrote home did not reveal any great infatuation for New Orleans. It was Jeff who was homesick, but Walt agreed with him about the discomforts: the dirt, the low elevation, and the high prices for everything. They visited some of the Catholic churches and never ceased to marvel at the baskets of flowers for sale on the streets. But they thought constantly of home and became almost frantic because no one wrote them. Finally Mother Whitman did write, and said it had been so cold that their father could not work.[126] They were in financial difficulties as usual, and twice Walt wrote instructions to draw thirty-one dollars out of his account at the bank to pay the interest on their mortgage, due the first of May. He also inquired about the trees he had set out.[127] Jeff wrote that he was turning over his wages to Walt to save for him, and that as soon as Walter had saved a thousand dollars they would return.[128] Obviously neither had any intention of remaining permanently in New Orleans. Mrs. Whitman worried over the possibility of her sons' catching yellow fever, but Jeff assured her that the epidemic came only every three or four years, "and last season it was very bad and killed a great many persons." Besides, only persons who drank a great deal were in special danger: "You know that Walter is averse to such habits, and you need not be afraid of our taking it." [129] As we have several times noticed, Walt occasionally took a drink with a friend, but there are no indications that he drank very much.

In 1887 Whitman was invited by the New Orleans *Picayune* to write his reminiscences of the city, and he did so with the aid of the diary notes he had jotted down in 1848.[130] What he remembered first of all was the military atmosphere, "the crowds of soldiers, the gay young officers, going or coming, the receipt of important news, the many discussions, the returning wounded, and so on." He was at the St. Charles Theater when General Taylor dropped in to see a performance of "Dr. Colyer's troupe of 'Model Artists'" and a splendid tableau was presented in honor of the general. He "was almost the only officer in civilian clothes . . . jovial, old, rather stout, plain man, with a wrinkled and dark-yellow face," showing no regard for "conventional ceremony or etiquette," laughing "unrestrainedly at everything comical."

On Sunday mornings especially, Whitman liked to go down to the French market, where he bought coffee (this time he called it delicious) from a Creole mulatto woman who weighed 230 pounds.[131] During the week he enjoyed spending a midday hour or two on the crowded levees watching the stevedores and boatmen—an amusement similar to his former visits to the Battery in New York. Some biographers have assumed that Whitman picked up in New Orleans his fondness for French and Spanish words, but he himself confessed, "I have deeply regretted since that I did not cultivate, while I had such a good opportunity, the chance of better knowledge of French and Spanish Creole New Orleans people." [132]

Despite all that has been written about Whitman's romantic sojourn in New Orleans, he actually remained there only slightly more than three months, or exactly ninety-two days. On May 25 he resigned, and two days later he and Jeff boarded a steamboat bound for St. Louis.[133] The cordiality of the owners of the *Crescent* toward Whitman had worn off, and he never knew exactly why, though it was probably a combination of circumstances. In his personal memoranda he recorded: "Through some unaccountable means . . . both H. and M'C after a while, exhibited a singular sort of coldness, toward me, and the latter an irritability toward Jeff, who had, at times, much harder work than I was willing he should do." Jeff's repeated illness and Walt's interference may have been the initial cause of Mr. McClure's irritability. But there was probably a general uncongeniality between the Northern journalist and these Southern newspapermen, whose customs and habits of thought differed from those of the New Yorker, who "had been accustomed to having frequent conferences, in my former situations with the proprietors of newspapers, on the subject of management"—the implication here is that Walt was something like a managing editor on the *Crescent* staff.

But when the coldness above alluded to broke out, H. seemed to be studiously silent upon all these matters.—My own pride was touched—and I met their conduct with equal haughtiness on my part.—On Wednesday May 24th I sent down a note requesting a small sum of money.—M'C returned me a bill of what money I had already drawn, and stated that they could not make "advances." I answered by reminding them of certain points which appeared to have been forgotten, making me *not* their debtor [possibly he had not been paid for the extra articles he had written for the paper], and told them in my reply I thought it would be better to dissolve the connection. They agreed to my plan (after some objections on the part of me); and I determined to leave on the succeeding Saturday.[134]

The return trip was made by way of the Mississippi and the Great Lakes, and, as on the trip down, Walt kept a detailed record.[135] They left New Orleans on the *Pride of the West* on Saturday morning, May 27. Jeff had a fever and Walt was alarmed, but by Sunday morning the fever had subsided. They reached St. Louis about noon the following Saturday, and after walking around the city for a few hours took the *Prairie Bird* to La Salle, where they arrived Monday morning, and transferred to a canal boat for the remaining journey to Chicago. This boat was overloaded with passengers and freight and Walt had to sleep on the floor, but they finally landed in Chicago at 10:00 A.M. on Tuesday. On Thursday, after two days of sightseeing and resting at a comfortable hotel, The American Temperance, they left in the morning on the *Griffith* bound for Milwaukee.

While anchored there, Walt took a good stroll around the town and was so favorably impressed that he recorded: "It seems to me that if we should ever remove from Long Island, Wisconsin would be the proper place to come to." Aboard again, they sailed to Mackinaw, past Detroit (Walt wanted to see this settlement, but the boat did not stop), and reached Cleveland on Sunday evening, pausing long enough for Walt to get a glimpse of the town near the harbor, and then on to Buffalo, where they arrived on Monday night, June 12. From there they caught a train for Niagara—"went under the fall—saw the whirlpool and all the other sights." Thence on by train to Albany, and a pleasant all-day trip by boat down the Hudson to New York. On Thursday afternoon, June 15, about five o'clock, the travelers arrived safely back in Brooklyn. Walt had seen more of America than he would see again until old age. The trip had given him a sense of space, natural resources, and potential strength in the fast-growing nation.

VIII

Although, so far as we know, Whitman had no regular employment during the summer of 1848, nevertheless it was not an uneventful season. In June his story of Archie Dean, "The Shadow and Light of a Young Man's Soul," was published in the *Union Magazine of Literature and Art*, but this story was undoubtedly written before—probably long before—Whitman went to New Orleans; it reflected his mood at the beginning of his school teaching, and gives no clues for the summer of 1848.

Possibly Whitman did some work for the Brooklyn *Advertizer*, though there is no definite proof. The editor, Henry A. Lees, continued to show special interest in Whitman's quarrels with Van Anden the previous February, and on July 19 he printed a bit of gossip:

The true secret of Whitman's rupture with the *Eagle* consisted in two facts. One was that he was determined that the paper, while he edited it, should not be the organ of old hunkerism;—and the other was, that on one occasion, when personally insulted by a certain prominent politician, Mr. Whitman kicked the individual down the editorial stairs.—These two solemn facts were the head and front of his "incompetency." [136]

Naturally Van Anden could not let these explanations go unanswered; so the *Eagle* replied:

Mr. W. came here from the *Star* office where he was getting four or five dollars a week; he was connected with the *Eagle* for about two years and we think we had a pretty fair opportunity to understand him. Slow, indolent, heavy, discourteous, and without steady principles, he was a clog upon our success, and reluctant as we were to make changes, we still found it absolutely necessary to do so. . . . Mr. W. has no political principles, nor, for that matter, principles of any sort; and all that the *Advertiser* says in the above paragraph is totally and unequivocally untrue. Whoever knows him will laugh at the idea of his *kicking any body*, much less a prominent politician. He is too indolent to kick a musketo [sic].[137]

The truth about Whitman's kicking a politician down the stairs we shall probably never know. But since there had obviously been a violent political disagreement, Van Anden's explanation is not very convincing. No longer an editor, Whitman remained silent, but he could escape temporarily from these unpleasant attacks and personal criticisms, for he had formed the habit of going out alone to Coney Island, "at that time a long, bare unfrequented shore."[138] There he threw off all cares and worries as he cast aside his clothes to bathe in the surf or to lie in the hot sun. When bored with resting he would race up and down the hard sand, with only the surf and the sea gulls for an audience, and declaim Homer (Pope's translation) or Shakespeare by the hour. Sometimes he carried with him chapters which he had torn out of a book and stuffed into his pocket. These he would read and ponder while he listened half attentively to the sound of the sea. He had also begun to experiment with a new poetic technique, and always carried with him a little notebook in which he jotted down subjects and ideas for poems, or even first drafts of verses he might be able to use. But the plan to fill a book with these revolutionary poems was still vague and tentative.

Whitman had not yet given much concentrated thought to the book of poems because his immediate concern was still with politics. The free-soil dispute had been agitating both parties with bitterness. By the time Whitman arrived home from New Orleans both parties had held their national conventions, the Democrats in late May in Baltimore and the Whigs in early June in Philadelphia. The Barnburners and the Old Hunkers had sent delegates from New York to the Baltimore Convention, but the Democratic majority had refused to take any stand on the free-soil question and both New York groups (after they had each won the right to be seated) walked out in disgust. The Democrats then nominated

General Cass, arch-opponent of the Wilmot Proviso, to head their national ticket. The Whigs simply nominated General Taylor and Millard Fillmore without bothering with a platform. Anti-slavery men in both parties were disgusted, but especially the "radical" Democrats of New York.

Consequently, not long after Whitman's return to Brooklyn, local supporters of free soil of both parties began to talk of joining forces in the formation of a Free-Soil party now being widely discussed in several Northern states. Finally, on Saturday evening, August 5, a meeting was held in Brooklyn to elect delegates to represent Kings County at a convention to be held in Buffalo on the 9th, and among the fifteen delegates elected were Walter Whitman (Jr.) and Alden J. Spooner, his former employer (one of the Whigs who could not support Cass). The New York *Evening Post* reported this Brooklyn meeting on Monday, August 7, and commented in an editorial:

Mr. W. Whitman made some remarks introducing a resolution instructing the delegates from Kings County to go unconditionally for the nomination of Martin Van Buren. At the particular desire, however, of some of the members of the meeting, he accepted an amendment preserving the spirit of the resolution [which simply condemned Cass for his anti-Wilmot stand and Taylor for not taking any stand], but leaving out the positive instructions, which was adopted—though many preferred it in its first form.[139]

At Buffalo Van Buren was nominated for the Presidency and Charles Francis Adams for the Vice Presidency. Soon after his return Whitman was appointed a member of the Free-Soil General Committee for Brooklyn. Meanwhile the local group had been making plans and arrangements for Whitman's Free-Soil paper, and finally, with the backing of Judge Samuel V. Johnson, he was able to publish the first issue of the Brooklyn *Weekly Freeman* on September 9 in a room rented at 110 Orange Street.[140] But disaster struck almost immediately, for on the following day a great fire destroyed a large section of that part of town, including the building containing the *Freeman* office. It was a great blow to Whitman, for he lost everything, equipment and supplies. Two months later he was able to renew publication, but meanwhile, of course, the election had taken place and the Democrats had lost.

Although the Free-Soil ticket drew some votes from General Taylor, it seems probable that the third party did more harm to the Democrats than to the Whigs and may have been responsible for the Democratic defeat. For some months the Free-Soil party organization continued to function in New York State, and Whitman was able in the following spring to change the weekly *Freeman* to a daily, but by the end of the summer the leaders of the Old Hunkers and the Barnburner faction had made peace and Whitman saw that he would no longer have political support for his paper. Consequently he resigned his editorship and published his last issue on September 11, 1849.

During the winter of 1848–1849 Whitman had other responsibilities besides the *Freeman* and free soil. His father's health was failing[141] and the family needed financial help. In the spring of 1847 he had bought with his parents a lot on Prince Street,[142] for which, as we have seen, he was keeping up the payments on the mortgage while he was in New Orleans.[143] On October 30, 1848, he bought a lot on Myrtle Avenue for one thousand dollars and during the winter erected a three-story frame house.[144] In April the family moved into the upper stories and Walt used the lower floor for a combined printing office and bookstore.[145]

IX

The summer of 1849 passed without any material change in Whitman's life or his prospects for the future. One thing did occur, however, that would later have considerable influence on his poetry. As early as 1846 he had become mildly interested in the books on phrenology which he reviewed in the *Eagle*,[146] and in the summer of 1849 he began visiting the Fowlers' Phrenological Cabinet at 131 Nassau Street in New York City, where charts and physiological exhibits were on display to advertise this pseudo-science. In July Lorenzo Fowler examined Whitman's cranium and drew up a very flattering "chart of bumps" for the young journalist. He was found to be amply endowed in all the desirable categories on the phrenological chart, and ranked at the very top of the scale in "Amativeness" (sexual love), "Philoprogenitiveness" (love of mankind), and "Adhesiveness" (male friendship). The first paragraph of Fowler's analysis contained some rather shrewd guesses (or maybe he knew Whitman so well by this time that they were not guesses):

This man has a grand physical constitution, and power to live to a good old age. He is undoubtedly descended from the soundest and hardiest stock. Size of head large. Leading traits of character appear to be Friendship, Sympathy, Sublimity, and Self-Esteem, and markedly among his combinations the dangerous faults of Indolence, a tendency to the pleasure of Voluptuousness and Alimentiveness and a certain reckless swing of animal will, too unmindful, probably, of the conviction of others.[147]

Although in each case there had been extenuating circumstances, Whitman's loss of editorial positions certainly could be attributed in part to his natural over-endowment of "Self-Esteem," or his "reckless swing of animal will." His slow movements were deceptive. His Dutch tenacity made him at times little short of arrogant, and in his loyalty to a cause or moral principle he could be as adamant as a Puritan.

In 1850 Whitman felt that the politicians in the Democratic party had betrayed not only a great cause but himself personally. On June 14 he published in the New York *Tribune* a free-verse poem (about halfway between blank verse and his later technique) entitled "The House of Friends," [148] based on the Biblical text "I was wounded in the house of my friends" (Zechariah XIII, 6).

> If thou art balked, O Freedom,
> The victory is not to thy manlier foes;
> From the house of friends comes the death stab.

The depths of his passion can be judged from the bitterness of his sarcasm:

> Virginia, mother of greatness,
> Blush not for being also mother of slaves.
> You might have borne deeper slaves—
> Doughfaces, Crawlers, Lice of Humanity—

The old-guard are hopeless; therefore his call is to the young men:

> Arise, young North!
> Our elder blood flows in the veins of cowards—
>
> .   .   .   .
>
> Fight on, band braver than warriors,
> Faithful and few as Spartans;
> But fear not most the angriest, loudest, malice—
> Fear most the still and forked fang
> That starts from the grass at your feet.

The editor of the Brooklyn *Advertizer* (who between May 18 and June 6, 1850, had printed sixteen "paragraph sketches of Brooklynites" by Whitman) quoted part of this poem with great delight, and commented editorially June 22: "Here, now, is a specimen of the way one of the young democracy, Master Walter Whitman, lays it on to the members of 'the party' whom he has had the pleasure of knowing—Master

Whitman has evidently a very poor opinion of his old cronies; but who can wonder at that, after he was editor of the Brooklyn *Eagle* so long, and saw the operations of the Brooklyn 'democracy'?" [149]

That Whitman had a "poor opinion of his old cronies" was a monstrous understatement, but despite the fact that he was angrily striking back at them, he was also trying in his poem to support the cause of Freedom as he saw it, and this support was not confined to local or national politics. He had been tremendously stirred by the revolutions of 1848 in Europe. In 1850 he knew that so far as any practical results were concerned, they had failed, but he believed that out of these defeats there would yet come victories for Freedom. This he attempted to express in a poem called "Resurgemus," which was published in the New York *Tribune* on June 21—and was later included in revised form in *Leaves of Grass*.[150] The revolt against tyranny had leapt forth like lightning:

> God 'twas delicious!
> That brief, tight, glorious grip
> Upon the throats of kings.
>
> . . . .
>
> Meanwhile, corpses lie in new-made graves,
> Bloody corpses of young men;
> The rope of the gibbet hangs heavily,
> The bullets of tyrants are flying,
> The creatures of power laugh aloud:
> And all these things bear fruits, and they are good.
>
> . . . .
>
> Liberty, let others despair of thee,
> But I will never despair of thee:
> Is the house shut? Is the master away?
> Nevertheless, be ready, be not weary of watching,
> He will surely return; his messengers come anon.[151]

These Biblical allusions are evidence not only of Whitman's familiarity with the New Testament at this time[152] but also of his feeling that the cause of Freedom was holy, and that its defenders were dedicated souls.

⊸§ IV §⊸

THE OUTSETTING BARD

The love in the heart pent, now loose, now at
last tumultuously bursting
. . . the outsetting bard of love.[1]

I

THE most important period in the life of Walt Whitman as a poet was the
years between 1850 and 1855. Outwardly it was undramatic, and judged
in terms of worldly success it was a failure. But intellectually and spiritually these were the most exciting and adventurous years that Whitman
had experienced, for during this half-decade he wrote and printed his
first edition of *Leaves of Grass* and thereby created a new epoch not only
in American but even in world literature.

During this period Whitman had the best opportunities he was ever to
have to make money,[2] for the nation was enjoying another wave of prosperity; the ports of both New York and Brooklyn were jammed with ships
arriving and departing for California, China, Liverpool, and the chief
ports of the world. Thousands of men were still migrating by land and sea
to the gold fields of California; trade with the Orient had become so profitable that political pressure was building up to force an entrance to Japanese harbors; and commerce with Europe was growing with each passing
year.

Brooklyn needed more docks to take care of the increased shipping,
and alert businessmen were making new land out of marsh and the tide-
swept shore on the south side of the region soon to be known as the Atlantic Basin. Real-estate values in South Brooklyn were shooting up as a
result, new factories were being erected, and the building trade was becoming feverishly active, thereby stimulating the whole economic life of
Brooklyn. In a letter to the New York *Post* dated March 21 [1851], Whitman described the rapid changes taking place on the south side and

declared: "All this part of Brooklyn will have, when settled, a look of newness and modern style. For every house will have been built within the last few years." [3] And the editor of the *Star* exclaimed with admiration and civic pride: "On Red Hook, but recently a desert sand hill and unwholesome marsh, we now behold long rows of buildings, and listen to the busy hum of improvement." [4] Less than twelve months ago "the tide ebbed and flowed where now are new streets, laid out, graded and paved, and hundreds of eligible building sites are ready for occupancy." Within four years Brooklyn would consolidate her separately incorporated towns (Williamsburg, Bushwick, Greenpoint, and Brooklyn) and thus become the seventh largest city in the nation, with a population well over 100,000.

Walt Whitman did profit to some extent from these "boom times," but he did not apply himself wholeheartedly to making a fortune. In 1851 he was operating a small printing office and bookstore on the first floor of the three-story house that he had built at 106 Myrtle Avenue. [5] He had bought the lot and built the house while he was still editor of the *Freeman*, and since April, 1849, he and his family had lived on the upper floors. The city directory for 1851 listed Walter Whitman, Sr., and two of his sons, Andrew and George, as carpenters, though probably by this time his health was failing and his sons were taking over the support of the family. For several years after this date Walt provided the house, and doubtless also contributed to the household expenses. But it is not likely that he earned much money with his printing office and bookstore, or the throwaway advertising sheets that he published intermittently, or the articles he occasionally wrote for the Brooklyn *Advertizer* [6] and the New York *Post*. [7] The variety of these activities implies that none was especially profitable. However, for several years he speculated in real estate and house building, and he could have made money on these transactions, though there is no tangible proof that he did. He recorded that in May, 1852, he sold the house on Myrtle Avenue and built another on Cumberland Street, into which the family moved the following September. In March, 1853, he sold two three-story houses on Cumberland, evidently including the one in which the Whitmans lived, for in April they moved into a smaller two-story house on the same street. [8] This was the way the family had lived during Walt's childhood in Brooklyn, and there is no evidence that Walt was a better businessman than his father.

II

There were two reasons for Walt Whitman's failure to share the mania for quick profits. The first was his own disposition; one of the few low ratings that the phrenologist had given him was on "Acquisitiveness," [9] a shrewd evaluation of his character. The other main reason was that by this time Whitman had formed habits, ambitions, and friendships that gave him far more satisfaction than economic success. On February 1, 1851, he wrote an article for the New York *Post*[10] about the Brooklyn Art Union which gives several clues to the influences that were soon to aid in the transformation of the indifferent journalist into a major poet.

A group of Brooklyn artists, mostly painters, had recently founded the Art Union for the main purpose of promoting the sale of their works, but the organization also enabled them to associate themselves in a common cause and mutual interests, and this especially appealed to Whitman. In his article he mentioned specifically two painters with whom he was evidently on friendly terms, William Sidney Mount, a genre painter born on Long Island, and Walter Libby, a young man nearer Walt's own age. Whitman praised Libby's "Boy Playing a Flute" for its naïveté, fidelity to life, and its composition, adding humorously that there was nothing to prevent the boy in the painting from "becoming president, or even an editor of a leading newspaper." The knowing comments on lighting, coloring, and texture showed how much Walt had profited from his conversations with the artists, possibly with Libby especially, for whom about this time he sat for his portrait.[11]

Although he did not mention them in his article, Whitman was also on familiar terms with several other artists in Brooklyn, among them Henry Kirke Brown, best known today for his bronze statue of Washington in Union Square, New York City. Only five years older than Whitman, he had worked as a railroad surveyor in the West and had studied in Italy before opening a studio in Brooklyn in 1849. On the recommendation of William Cullen Bryant he was elected to the National Academy of Design in 1851—and Whitman's friendship with Bryant was another link between him and Brown, perhaps even the reason for Whitman's writing about Brooklyn artists for the New York *Post*.

Many of Walt's happiest hours were spent in Brown's studio: "There I would meet all sorts—young fellows from abroad stopped here in their swoopings: they would tell us of students, studios, the teachers, they had just left in Paris, Rome, Florence . . ." [12] For some reason—perhaps the fact that his hair was already beginning to turn gray—Whitman was called "Béranger" by the men who gathered in Brown's studio, and he enjoyed the implied comparison between himself and the venerable and renowned French lyricist. One young man professed to have known Béranger, and Walt liked to hear him talk about the French poet. He was Brown's brilliant young apprentice, John Quincy Ward. While visiting his sister in Brooklyn in 1849, Ward had happened upon Brown's studio and had had the good fortune to be accepted as a pupil.[13] One of the painters of this group may have taught Walt the rudiments of crayon sketching, for in a notebook he left some competent portraits and caricatures of himself and others.[14]

There are no records of the ideas Whitman heard discussed in Brown's studio, but Horatio Greenough, one of America's most famous contemporary sculptors and her first critic of architecture, had been discussing his theories for the past decade in such magazines as the *Democratic Review*, and in 1851–1852 he was publishing these in books.[15] Greenough's ideas were so vital for Whitman's generation that they were sure to be debated wherever American artists gathered, and many were acutely aware of the fact that his perennial battle with prudery was their battle too. Greenough himself had studied in Europe and was deeply conscious of the modern artist's debt to Greece and Rome, but he believed the American people to be the "advance guard of humanity," [16] and that they must have an art which would be truly their own. Despite the repressive moralism of his countrymen, which made them cherish Longfellow's facile poems and admire the insipid Eves, Evangelines, and Psyches sculptured by Hiram Powers, Greenough believed that "there is at present no country where the development and growth of an artist is more free, healthful, and happy than it is in these United States." [17] He championed the nude in art because he thought the human body "the most beautiful organization of earth, the exponent and minister of the highest being we immediately know." [18] In architecture he condemned all embellishment as an end in itself, and he was utterly contemptuous of fashion. Famed Trinity Church he dubbed "the puny cathedral of Broadway." [19] In his admiration for "the roar of the Astor House" (New York's largest hotel) and "the mammoth vase of the great reservoir" (the Croton Water Reservoir on the site of the present New York Public Library at Forty-second Street), he showed his prophetic taste for "functional art." [20] He denounced the bastard classical architecture of the national capital because it did not conform to the

American climate, customs, and practicality. Like Whitman a few years later, he preached that new forms must arise to satisfy new needs.

That Whitman was already groping toward his own theory of art, in 1851, is shown in a lecture he gave before the Brooklyn Art Union on March 31.[21] He felt himself and his artist associates to be aligned with the idealists against the materialists. Some years later he would write a poem on the beauty of a locomotive, but on this occasion it was not with approval that he called the United States a "nation of whom the steam engine is no bad symbol." Therefore, "To the artist, I say, has been given the command to go forth into all the world and preach the gospel of beauty." He thought the subject of death, so prominent in his own juvenile poems of the previous decade and soon to become one of his most inspiring poetic themes, could "be shorn of many of its frightful and ghastly features" by the cultivation of "a more artistic feeling among the people." Instead of symbolizing death "by a grinning skeleton or a mouldering skull," Whitman preferred the statue in a Greek temple which depicted "Death and his brother Sleep . . . as beautiful youths reposing in the arms of Night."

This example, incidentally, was apparently borrowed from a passage in Longfellow's *Hyperion*,[22] and at the time when he addressed the Art Union Whitman probably agreed with the "gentle" poet's definition of art as

> All that embellishes and sweetens life,
> And lifts it from the level of low cares
> Into the purer atmosphere of beauty;
> The faith in the Ideal . . .[23]

In equating esthetic and moral beauty, however, Whitman was in conformity with the majority of his Victorian contemporaries both in England and in America. "I think," he said, "of few heroic actions which cannot be traced to the artistical impulse. He who does great deeds, does them from his sensitiveness to moral beauty." Here was a doctrine which was to grow into one of Whitman's lifelong ideals. Within a short time he would be trying to make his own life into a poem and declaring that heroic action is not so much the subject of a poem as a poem itself. He had already arrived at the belief that art not only expresses the life of a nation but in turn helps to form the pattern of a freer, richer, and more perfect life.

The future poet of companionship also saw in the Brooklyn Art Union a means of conserving and directing the energies of the "ten thousand so-called artists, young and old, in this country, many of whom are working in the dark, as it were, and without aim." Thus the Free-Soil Democrat who had become disillusioned with political parties now dreamed of a kind of party for American artists, "a close phalanx, ardent, radical and progressive." But it was not to be a party for the advancement of the exclusive interests of painters, sculptors, and poets; it was to be more like a religion based on an idealization of Greek traditions, which at that time Whitman thought the most perfect of any civilization. Recently he had listened to someone (probably Parke Godwin) lecture in New York on Greek art and life,[24] and this influenced him to declare that it refreshed his soul to contemplate "one of that glorious and manly and beautiful nation, with his sandals, his flowing drapery, his noble and natural attitudes and the serene composure of his features." [25] Such thoughts made Whitman long personally for an incorruptible integrity and a freedom from cant and convention that would enable him to develop his own artistic powers.

Already he dressed as he pleased, made no concessions to public opinion, and ignored the advice of his family on ways to get ahead in the practical world. Despite the fact that he owned the house the Whitmans lived in and generously "paid board" whenever he had money, his family regarded him as impractical, had not the slightest understanding of his intellectual interests, and thought he neglected his business affairs—as he doubtless did. Recalling this period, George said, "He made a living now —wrote a little, worked a little, loafed a little. He had an idea that money was of no consequence." [26]

One example of Walt's working a little and loafing more was his prolonged visit to Greenport, where his sister Mary lived, in June and probably July of the summer of 1851. The work consisted of his writing two articles about summer life on Long Island, in the region of Greenport, for the New York Post.[27] These articles were evidently intended in part to advertise the charms of Long Island summer resorts, but the journalist devoted a good deal of space to describing his own amusements, which consisted mainly of swimming, eating bluefish (his favorite dish), and talking and rambling with the country folk, especially unsophisticated ones.

The second of these newspaper articles from Greenport was dated June 28, and on the same day the Brooklyn Daily Advertizer printed an article by Whitman pleading for pure water in Brooklyn.[28] New York City was so proud of its abundant and wholesome water piped from the Croton watershed that crowds of people walked daily to see the marvelous reservoir on Fifth Avenue at Forty-second Street. In fact, Croton water had become so famous and much admired that new health fads had arisen for its use in plunge baths, sitz-baths, wrapping a patient in wet sheets, and the use of packs and douches in numerous ways for every imaginable ailment.[29] Brooklyn, however, still used "pump-water," which Whitman pungently described as contaminated by the "privies, cess-pools, sinks and gulches of abomination." He thought the Croton Aqueduct "a far nobler token for New York than even her steamships, with the Trinity Churches [sic] to boot." Many people in Brooklyn had become highly excited over "swill-milk," that is, milk from dairies where the cows were fed the swill from distilleries,[30] and prohibitionists were using this hysteria for its full propaganda value. Whitman wished these reformers success, but declared that "rum and bad milk are not as nasty as pump-water." No one could say that his hobnobbing with Bohemian artists during the previous winter had made him indifferent to the welfare of his city.

III

Early in August Whitman was back in Brooklyn, for in a letter to the New York *Post* dated August 11 he described attending the opera at Castle Garden, down at the Battery in New York.[31] At the end of a hot day that had seemed as if it would never end, he stood on Brooklyn Heights to enjoy the breeze, the view of the harbors of the two cities, and the changing colors of water and sky. His "craving" for colors reminded him of a parallel "desire for measureless sound" which he had experienced while listening to Max Maretzek's orchestra accompanying a "pure Tenor," such as Bettini singing the role of Fernando in Donizetti's *La Favorita*.[32] He had often been moved to tears by the "fresh vigorous tones of Bettini." We learn from this account that he had heard all the musical celebrities who had visited New York during the past fifteen years, including the overly advertised Jenny Lind, who had been introduced to the city the previous year under the management of the greatest showman of the age, P. T. Barnum himself. However, she did not impress Whitman: "The Swedish Swan, with all her blandishments, never touched my heart in the least." [33]

Whitman's enjoyment of music was always primarily emotional, and up to this date he had never heard a female voice that had stirred him deeply. In fact, before hearing Bettini he had never realized "what an indescribable volume of delight the recesses of the soul can bear from the sound of the honied perfection of the human voice," adding, "The *manly* voice it must be, too." As he listened to Bettini in the role of Fernando, Whitman wondered how anyone would hesitate to assign Donizetti to the highest rank of composers. "Pure and vast, that voice now rises, as on clouds, to the heaven where it claims audience. Now, firm and unbroken, it spreads like an ocean around us. Ah, welcome that I know not the mere language of the earthly words in which the melody is embodied [Whitman of course knew no Italian]; as all words are mean before the language of true music."

Whitman had been hearing opera of all kinds, English, light, and Italian for a decade—sung in English, German, French, and Italian by artists from all these countries—but it was the Italian opera that especially appealed to him.[34] He enjoyed the acting, the spectacle, and the excitement shared with the crowd, and to help him follow the story he made a practice of studying the libretto before going to the theater; but it was the music that ravished his senses and made him at times almost swoon with delight. The Italian opera had been given at the Park Theater, one of Whitman's favorites, since 1841–1842. There in 1845 the French company had performed the same *La Favorita*. Since then the conventional pieces of Verdi, Bellini, Donizetti and other standard composers had been given regularly at Palmo's in Chambers Street, at Astor Place, the Broadway Theater, Niblo's Garden, and recently at Castle Garden—all frequented by Whitman. New York actually heard far more opera then than now, and some of the greatest singers of all time.[35]

Under the direction of Maretzek the 1851–1852 season at the Astor Place was particularly distinguished, with performances by Bettini, Bosio, Badaili, Marini, and Steffanone, all stars of the day as well known in Europe as in America. The very greatest of these singers, and some authorities still think the greatest coloratura soprano in the history of opera, was Marietta Alboni. During the summer of 1852 she was introduced to New York in a concert of arias from the more famous operas, making her greatest hit with a selection from *La Cenerentola*, which, we are told, "singers of today can no longer encompass" and do not attempt. During the winter season of 1852–1853 Alboni appeared in ten operas, each given four times, in addition to several concerts. She gave her last performance on May 26, and then departed for Europe, never to return. We have

Whitman's own word that he attended every one of her performances.[36] She had come to America at the height of her power, and he had now heard a female voice that eclipsed all others he had ever heard. In old age he still felt so indebted to her and Verdi, the composer, and Bettini, the tenor, that he wished they could know "how much noble pleasure and happiness" they had given him.[37] On another occasion he remarked of her singing in *Lucia*, "She used to sweep me away as with whirlwinds."[38]

Whitman continued to attend the opera until he left New York during the Civil War, and there were other good seasons, though none quite so remarkable as 1852–1853.[39] In 1854 the Academy of Music opened, and thereafter dominated the operatic field in New York, but the variety declined. In 1858 Whitman recorded that he did "not think much of [Marietta] Piccolomini, the present 'rage,'" and in memory he returned immediately to Alboni, especially to the pathetic scene in which Norma planned the death of her children, "with real tears, like rain, coursing . . . down her cheeks."[40] On another occasion, recalling this scene in *Norma* once more, he said, "Such are the things, indeed, I lay away with my life's rare and blessed bits of hours."[41] Whitman himself came to believe that "But for the opera I could never have written *Leaves of Grass*." And he also testified: "My younger life was so saturated with the emotions, raptures, up-lifts, of such musical experiences that it would be surprising indeed if all my future work had not been colored by them."[42]

Perhaps some of the characteristics of the Italian operatic performances that Whitman heard may give us a few clues to specific influences on his development as a poet. We are told that the "so-called arias were ordinarily decorated with florid passages"[43] designed to "give the singer an opportunity to display the resources of his voice." Before Rossini, singers had been permitted freely to improvise solo ornamentations, but "he carefully composed all the notes he wished his interpreters to perform and attempted to give musical and dramatic significance to even the most coloratura passages." Donizetti, Bellini, and Verdi, followers of Rossini, whose works Whitman admired,[44] made extensive use of the flowing melody. The *bel canto* style of Bellini, especially, made the voice a wind instrument, so that, as one critic declared: "Its perfect practitioners make sounds of quite unearthly beauty and move the listener quite as a miracle would, so well do they do something it seems superhuman, or inhuman, to do at all."[45] Certainly this was the effect Whitman sometimes experienced.

We are also told that Bellini and other composers made use of a note that produced "a kind of hushed, neurotic ecstasy, a kind of gently languorous orgasm, in moonlit, bloom pervaded gardens." [46] Perhaps Walt Whitman, therefore, was not unique in the "neurotic ecstasy" which time and again he described in trying to find words for the effect of Bettini's or Alboni's singing on him. Hearing them also gave him almost an obsession for the "perfect human voice," and he frequently speculated on the physiology of the vocal organ.[47] He came to believe that some sort of supreme wisdom could be conveyed not through words but through the musical tones of the words in the mouths of inspired speakers or singers.[48]

But of all these "perfect users" of the voice, Alboni was paramount, and in one of his major poems Whitman was later to make her a goddess of love and maternity.

> The teeming lady comes,
> The lustrous orb, Venus contralto, the blooming mother,
> Sister of loftiest Gods, Alboni's self I hear.[49]

The fact that he could not understand the language in which the operas were sung, but yet enjoyed the singing to the point of ecstasy, accounts in part for his literary ambition to convey more than the meanings of the words themselves; somehow by manner, tone, feeling, and implication to write so that he could say "The words of my book nothing, the drift of it everything." [50]

As with nearly all his other intellectual and esthetic pleasures, Walt usually had to enjoy the opera alone, although Jeff sometimes accompanied him. Jeff had taken music lessons[51] and could share at least part of Walt's enthusiasm. George remembered that Walt invited him to go, "but there was nothing in opera for me." [52] Hannah was always closest to Walt in temperament and affection, yet we find no reference to her ever having gone with him. And if Andrew or Jesse ever had any congenial relationship with Walt, the fact went unrecorded.

IV

The Whitman family was perhaps momentarily drawn closer together by the marriage of Hannah in the spring of 1852 to Charles L. Heyde, a French-born Brooklyn artist whom Walt had invited to the Whitman home and introduced to his sister, an act of hospitality he was to regret for the remainder of his life.[53] Before the marriage Walt and Heyde were apparently on good terms, and William Cullen Bryant, friend of both young men, is said to have accompanied Heyde in at least one of his visits to the Whitmans.

The couple departed almost immediately for Vermont, where Heyde hoped to establish himself as a landscape painter—at a time when portrait work was practically the only kind of painting that offered any chance of a livelihood. This was merely one example of Heyde's impracticality, poor judgment, and stubborn persistence—a trait he shared with Walt. Almost from the beginning the marriage proved uncongenial to both Hannah and Charley, as she called him, and Hannah's letters to her mother became increasingly neurotic.[54] Probably the fault was not entirely on one side, though the Whitman family would always blame Charley. Undoubtedly he was proud, irritable, erratic, and difficult to live with, but Hannah could not cook and was a disgracefully careless housekeeper.

It was in the May following Hannah's departure that Walt sold the house at 106 Myrtle Avenue. Probably his father and his two carpenter brothers, Andrew and George, helped him build the house on the corner of Cumberland Street and Atlantic Avenue into which the family moved on September 1, 1852. Walt himself worked as a carpenter during the summer, but in July and August he was employed at journeyman wages.[55] Possibly he hired himself out while his own house was under construction because he needed funds to buy building materials, though this is not an entirely satisfactory explanation. All we really know is that on August 21 a Mr. Scofield owed him $26.42 for twenty-three and a half days' work— probably not counting the eleven days he had worked in July. He was still listed in the city directory as "printer," but evidently he was not doing very much printing at this time, and in a biographical note written in 1856 he stated without details, "'51, '53, occupied in house-building in Brooklyn." [56] "House-building" could mean either speculative building or actually working as a carpenter, but part of the time, at least, he was working for daily wages as a carpenter.

But why did Walt Whitman, an experienced printer, editor, and journalist, become a carpenter at all, and what effect did the experience have on him? One can only guess at the answer. Despite his disappointments in journalism, he still had friends like the editors of the New York *Post* and the Brooklyn *Advertizer*. Although they may not have been able to give him full-time employment, they might have helped him to secure another editorial position. It appears, therefore, that for several years he did not desire another editorship. George later stated that during this time Walt "got offers of literary work [George would be likely to regard newspaper work as literary]—good offers: and we thought he had chances to make money. Yet he would refuse to do anything except at his own notion . . ." [57]

It is unlikely that Walt Whitman put on the carpenter's apron for any ideological reason, though two or three years later, after his role as a poet had become clear to him, he was pleased to recall that Christ Himself had been a carpenter and he began to regard his workman's costume as symbolical. He had also been reading George Sand's *Consuelo* and the sequel, *The Countess of Rudolstadt*,[58] in which a poet worked as a journeyman carpenter and wore the costume of a day laborer as a symbol of his proletarian sympathy. George Sand's poet-carpenter may have given Whitman some suggestions for the poet-prophet role he was constructing in fancy and gradually adopting in practice. While working as a carpenter (though actually he must have earned most of his income during these years in speculative building) he did become increasingly conscious of the symbolical possibilities of his life.

It appears that Whitman became a carpenter for purely economic reasons, and that he dropped the work within two or three years because it bored him, as farming, schoolteaching, and printing had done. Actually he was too slow ever to have been an expert carpenter, but the experience of dressing in jeans and workshirt and laboring beside common workmen liberated him entirely from his former dignified sartorial habits and conventional manners. His association with the artists had encouraged his natural desire for personal freedom, and the carpenter's trade completed his emancipation.

V

Meanwhile Whitman's almost daily contact with the great city across the river continued. If he spent the day in house building, he caught the ferry in the evening—and he did not always wait until evening. Most of the ferry-boat pilots were good friends of his and he always enjoyed the trip for their companionship.[59] Sometimes he would ride back and forth with them, but more often he would disembark on the New York side. One favorite amusement during those years, especially in the summer, was riding up and down Broadway on top of an omnibus beside the driver. Broadway from City Hall up to Union Square, a distance of about two miles, was still the main thoroughfare, and perhaps the busiest, most crowded, noisiest street in the world—or at least so New Yorkers thought.

Fifth Avenue had been laid out some distance beyond Forty-second Street, but most of it was little more than an unpaved country road, despite the fact that the millionaires were beginning to decorate it with their mansions. Only a few years earlier Broadway too had been a fine residential street,[60] but now it was lined with business houses, its sidewalks thronged with pedestrians, and the cobblestone avenue filled from curb to curb with vehicular traffic. As one historian says, "To cross from the 'shilling side' to the 'dollar side'—from east to west—sometimes took half an hour, and you attempted it at the peril of life and limb. So hazardous was the crossing that John W. Genin, the fashionable hatter whose shop was at the corner of Fulton Street, petitioned the Common Council for permission to build an iron foot bridge to protect his customers from accident." [61]

Walt Whitman loved the noise, the movement, the multitudes of people, but especially the hardy bus drivers, whom he later characterized as "a strange, natural, quick-eyed and wondrous race . . . They had immense qualities, largely animal—eating, drinking, women—great personal pride, in their way—perhaps a few slouches here and there, but I should have trusted the general run of them, in their simple good-will and honor, under all circumstances." [62] These were the kind of men—simple, "largely animal"—that Whitman had enjoyed associating with since childhood, when the fishermen took him on their boats around Long Island. Few if any of them could have understood or shared his enjoyment of music and literature, yet he sought them out for companionship, and they accepted him. Once when a driver was ill Walt took his place until he was able to resume work, turning the wages over to the driver's family.[63] Naturally such generous acts increased the devotion of these men to Whitman and explain their readiness to share the driver's seat with him.

Did Whitman also share the hearty indulgences of the omnibus drivers, such as their drinking and women? There is no evidence one way or another. He probably had an occasional beer or cobbler with them, but whether in the company of these rough men he visited any of the numerous brothels in the city—this was one of the lushest periods in New York history for that business—no one knows. In an editorial written only a few years later Whitman declared:

. . . the plain truth is that nineteen out of twenty of the mass of American young men who live in or visit the great cities, are more or less familiar with houses of prostitution and are customers to them . . .

Especially of the best classes of men under forty years of age, living in New York and Brooklyn, the mechanics, apprentices, sea-faring men, drivers of horses, butchers, machinists . . . the custom is to go among prostitutes as an ordinary thing. Nothing is thought of it—or rather the wonder is, how there can be any "fun" without it.[64]

But he lamented the prevalence of "the bad disorder" among these young men, and pointed out the consequent shame, concealment, and degradation. If prostitution continued, he said, the result would be a generation of scrofulous children: "What dropsies, feebleness, premature deaths, suffering in infancy to come!" There is no evidence that Whitman himself ever had the "bad disorder"; he seems always to have guarded his health so jealously that he seldom if ever took any chances of injuring it. But Whitman was well aware that "New York is one of the most crime-haunted and dangerous cities in Christendom," [65] for he knew his city. He did not have to conduct personal experiments, however, or be unusually acute to observe this unpleasant truth; it was only too apparent. It is significant, nevertheless, that before Walt Whitman took upon himself the task of celebrating in song the glories of his native land, he had acquired a sound factual understanding of the seamy side of life in the great metropolis.

We may assume that Whitman continued to attend the theater during these years, though opera now interested him more. Possibly it was about this time that he was associated with a group of amateur actors in New York. In reminiscing of the theater in one of his later prose works he added the comment that "there was a small but well-appointed amateur-theatre up Broadway, with the usual stage, orchestra, pit, boxes, &c., and that I was myself a member for some time, and acted parts in it several times—'second parts' as they were call'd. Perhaps it too was a lesson, or help'd that way; at any rate it was full of fun and enjoyment." [66] But all these productions which he attended or took part in seemed extremely transitory and evanescent. "O so much passion . . . over and over again, the season through—walking, gesticulating, singing, reciting his or her part —But then sooner or later . . . vanishing to sight and ear—and never materializing on this earth's stage again!"

More substantial, less evanescent, was the World's Fair that opened in New York on the Fourth of July, 1853, behind the Croton Reservoir between Fortieth and Forty-second streets (now Bryant Park, behind the Public Library). The building was modeled on the much-publicized Crystal Palace in London, which with great royal pomp and British chest-thumping had been opened two years previously. The United States, not to be outdone, quickly organized what some called "World's Fair Number Two," an "Exposition of the Industry of the Nations." The American Crystal Palace was not an exact duplicate of the British wonder, but native patriots thought it rivaled its prototype in beauty.[67]

American newspapers were filled with statistics on the size of their own Crystal Palace. Constructed of iron and glass, in the form of a Greek cross, with over 1200 tons of iron and 39,000 square feet of glass, it covered nearly four acres, and was surmounted by a dome that towered 148 feet—though this was not as tall as a conical observatory and ice-cream parlor that an entrepreneur erected in the background.[68] Financially this Exhibition was a failure, perhaps in part because the location was then out in the country and an inconvenient spot to reach.[69] Nevertheless, the Fair was opened by President Franklin Pierce with impressive military ceremony before 10,000 supposedly select guests and the city was greatly excited. It is hardly likely that Walt Whitman had been invited, but he probably attended the second day if not the first, though in his own account he dwells on the length of his attendance rather than his first experience there.

I went a long time (nearly a year)—days and nights—especially the latter—as it was finely lighted, and had a very large and copious exhibition gallery of paintings (shown at best at night, I tho't)—hundreds of pictures from Europe, many masterpieces—all an exhaustless study—and, scatter'd thro' the building, sculptures, single figures or groups—among the rest, Thorwaldsen's *Apostles*, colossal in size—and very many fine bronzes, pieces of plate from English silversmiths, and curios from everywhere abroad—with woods from all lands of the earth—all sorts of fabrics and products and handiwork from the workers of all nations.[70]

Whitman's enthusiasm is sufficient evidence that he shared Horace Greeley's opinion that the Crystal Palace Exhibition was "a thing to be seen once in a lifetime." [71] And he found character as well as art on exhibit. In some notes dated March 20, 1854, evidently jotted down after a visit to the hospital where sick omnibus drivers were treated, Whitman mentioned one young man who had attended the Exhibition with him: "Bill Guess—aged 22. A thoughtless, strong, generous animal nature, fond of direct pleasures, eating, drinking, women, fun, etc. Taken sick with the small-pox, had the bad disorder and was furious with the delirium tremens. Was with me in the Crystal Palace, a large, broad fellow, weighed over 200. Was a thoughtless good fellow." [72]

Here we have one of the many paradoxes in Whitman's own character. A man who loved Italian opera, carried Homer and Shakespeare in his pocket to read at the beach on his jaunts to Coney Island by himself, or packed Emerson's essays in his lunch pail to read during the noon hour respite from carpentering,[73] such a man habitually chose young men like Bill Guess for companionship. Or "Peter—," described in this same hospital memorandum. Though Whitman did not take the trouble to learn the surname, he recorded: "I never met a man that seemed to me, so far as I could tell in forty minutes, more open, coarse, self-willed, strong," and free of social conventions. There was also George Fitch, "Yankee boy," who was a bus driver, "Fine nature, amiable, sensitive feelings, a natural gentleman, of quite a reflective turn." He had left home because his father was always "down on him," but, like Walt, he loved his mother. He was good looking, twenty-three or -four, slender, smiling, and, again like Walt, wore his trousers tucked in his boots.

VI

Though emotionally Whitman was drawn to uneducated, "coarse" (he often used this adjective to describe them) fellows like these, they occupied only a small part of his daily life. There were also, we should remember, the artists in Brooklyn studios. And by this time Whitman had met a learned and distinguished man in New York who was to have a deep and lasting influence on his mind. This was the owner and curator of the Egyptian Museum at 659 Broadway.[74] Whitman got acquainted "with Dr. Abbott, the proprietor—paid many visits there, and had long talks with him, in connection with my readings of many books and reports on Egypt—its antiquities, history, and how things and the scenes really look, and what the old relics stand for, as near as we can now get."

By 1855 Dr. Abbott had found his Museum such a burden that he was trying desperately to sell it to the city, and to help the cause Whitman wrote an article about it for a magazine called *Life Illustrated*.[75] This article reveals not only an intimate knowledge of the collection, but also a surprising familiarity with the literature about Egyptology, including books recently published abroad. Undoubtedly Dr. Abbott had called Whitman's attention to some or all of these publications—perhaps loaned him books in English—and the echoes, allusions, and references to Egyptology in *Leaves of Grass* are so numerous that one must conclude that Whitman read the works closely and took notes on them. In fact, some of the notes have survived.

He began his article by saying, "Many lessons are to be learned along Broadway . . .", and then he made it clear that what he himself had learned above all else was an appreciation of the antiquity of civilization. Later critics of Whitman, especially European critics, were to say that he was an ignorant barbarian with no sense of the past. But aside from specialists like Dr. Abbott, few men of the period stood more in admiration of the great age of mankind. From Dr. Abbott and the Egyptian Museum Whitman received not only an imaginative feeling for the antiquity of the human race but also a sense of the continuity of life and human culture. He was able to anticipate twentieth century anthropologists in his realization that no one nation is superior (except for a temporary possession of physical power) and that any pattern of culture is good that works effectively in its own time and place. Probably even before he knew Dr. Abbott, Whitman's attention had been caught by a statement in a magazine article on "The Slavonians and Eastern Europe" [76] that "up to the present moment, the destinies of the species appear to have been carried forward almost exclusively by its Caucasian variety." Whitman underscored these words and wrote in the margin: "Yes, of late centuries, but how about those of 5 or 10 or twenty thousand years ago?" This comparative judgment included, of course, religion as well as language and mores. As a young man, under the influence of Tom Paine, Frances Wright, and Count Volney, Whitman had regarded religion as superstitious and socially reactionary, but he now understood that the religious sense is universal and that there is something good in every religion, even the most primitive types. In a footnote commentary on a statue in the Museum which he thought to be Horus, the son of Osiris, Whitman stated: "The theology of Egypt was vast and profound. It respected the principle of life in all things—even in animals. It respected truth and justice above all other attributes of man. It recognized immortality." [77] This was a religion he could admire and accept in principle himself.

Whitman now became fascinated with history and ethnology, and he filled pages and pages with notes, dates, facts, and speculations on the age and experiences of ancient peoples. Though never in doubt about the existence of God or a Supreme Power of some kind, he had begun to think of how the great human leaders had made such lasting contributions that succeeding generations had deified them. In a note which he may have written after the publication of the first edition of Leaves of Grass but which certainly reflected the influence of his study of Egyptology before 1855 he recorded the thought that "Back to ten thousand years before These States, all nations had, and some yet have, and perhaps always will have, tradition of coming men, great benefactors, of divine origin, capable of deeds of might, blessings, poems, enlightenment. From time to time these have arisen, and yet arise and will always arise. Some are called gods and deified—enter into the succeeding religions." [78] The myth of the fertility god Osiris interested him particularly, and influenced the development of his own poetic role.[79]

VII

Whitman's fascination with the development of the human race and man's place in the scheme of existence was broadened and made more philosophical by his becoming acquainted in the early 1850's with lectures and books on astronomy,[80] though unfortunately the actual names of authorities he heard or read must be supplied from internal evidence in his notebooks and the first *Leaves of Grass*. However, the internal evidence is so abundant, and at times verbal echoes so clear, that we can at least be sure of one source. This was the astronomer O. M. Mitchel, whose book *A Course of Six Lectures on Astronomy* (1848) Whitman unmistakably drew upon for facts, ideas, and figures of speech in many passages of "Song of Myself" and later poems. Mitchel lectured at the Broadway Temple in New York in 1847, and the chances are that Whitman heard him. Aside from the fact that he frequently attended such lectures, Whitman wrote a long editorial on Mitchel in March of that year.[81] Brooklyn was at that time trying to raise funds for an astronomical observatory, and Whitman cited as an example of what could be done Mitchel's success in raising funds for an observatory in Cincinnati by his lecturing tours. If Whitman had not already made the personal acquaintance of Mitchel by this time, it is likely that he did so subsequently.

The *Six Lectures* must have served Whitman for some time as a textbook, and presumably he also read Denison Olmstead's *Letters on Astronomy*, first published in 1840, which he reviewed in the Brooklyn *Eagle* during his editorship.[82] He may have earlier read C. S. Rafinesque's *Celestial Wonders of Philosophy* (1838), for in several passages in "Song of Myself" he was to make use of some of the figurative language of this book. For example, Rafinesque wrote: "Even the Heavens are not stable,

the orbs are ripening or growing or congregating in social clusters." [83]
Compare:

> I visit the orchards of spheres and look at the product,
> And look at quintillions ripen'd and look at quintillions green.[84]

In one of his lectures Mitchel described "the space annihilating tele-
scope" and invited his audience to take an imaginary trip with him into
the heavens.[85] They travel past Orion and continue for a radius of 500
times the distance between our sun and the nearest star, and yet, "All the
vast limits in the entire circuit . . . are filled with suns and systems that
burn, and roll, and shine as do our own." They were still, Mitchel told his
audience, "barely at the outskirts of one little island of the Universe." In
the future Whitman's poetic fancy would often take such a flight, sometimes as an imaginary comet, advancing "a moment only to wheel and
hurry back in the darkness"; [86] sometimes as a disembodied consciousness,
traveling with the speed of a meteor:

> Speeding through space, speeding through heaven and the stars,
> Speeding amid the seven satellites and the broad ring and the diameter
>   of eighty thousand miles,
> Speeding with tail'd meteors, throwing fire-balls like the rest, . . .[87]

Mitchel had given a particularly vivid description of the beautiful rings
of Saturn, "no less than seven subordinate worlds sweeping around the
great central orb and with it rolling through Space." [88] Various estimates
had been made of the diameter of the planet, but he gave it as 79,000
miles, closest of all the estimates to Whitman's rounder 80,000. It would
seem that from this popular lecturer Whitman gained not only such details as these, but also a poetic appreciation of the tremendous distances,
movement, and speed of all parts of the known universe. Perhaps more
important, however, was the influence of astronomical time on the nas-
cent poet, enabling him to see his own experience, and even the history of
the human race, as but a pin-point in comparison to the ages of the worlds
and constellations. These thoughts enabled him later imaginatively to
"transcend" time and space and to search intuitively in his poetry for eternal duration.

Moreover, astronomy was always to be the one branch of science that
Whitman knew best, and most accurately. For the next thirty-five or forty
years he would sprinkle his writings, poetry and prose, with references to
and observations of the planets, stars, and constellations, recorded with

surprising accuracy.[89] But he was never to know any other branch of science so well. Geology interested him, though what he got primarily from it was a sense of the vast age of the earth—another influence in his imaginative and emotional liberation from clock time. His pre-Darwinian concepts of biological evolution might have come from any number of sources, but evolution to him meant principally cosmic evolution, and this of course he got through astronomy. La Place's "nebular hypothesis" (later rejected by most astronomers) particularly appealed to him,[90] and along with it he derived a belief in the cyclic processes of creation, disintegration, and re-creation, something like Kant's concept of a universe perpetually winding up and unwinding itself.

Whitman's notebooks show that whenever he met someone who had traveled abroad, or possessed unusual knowledge,[91] he made a practice of soliciting all the information he could. But he also read with astonishing application for a man so sociable, so leisurely in his habits, so deceptively indolent. Even members of his own family were deceived by what appeared to them to be just plain loafing. George knew that Walt spent "a good many hours in the libraries of New York," [92] but he did not know, and was incapable of understanding, that Walt had any purpose in his reading.

VIII

In the late 1840's and throughout the 1850's Whitman made a practice of cutting out of certain books and magazines selections that he wanted to keep. As he read and studied these he underscored or bracketed passages that he thought especially important or that he wanted to re-read, and often he wrote comments in the margins. Many fine examples of these annotated clippings have survived,[93] neat and clean and the ink only slightly faded a century after Whitman pored over them. Also in the Library of Congress, as well as in a few private collections of his manuscripts, are summaries and critiques of books and outlines of biographical and historical data, such as notes on Lucretius's *De Rerum Natura*, Rousseau's *Social Contract*, synopses of medieval romances, and comparisons of the *Iliad* and the *Odyssey*.[94] The value of these summaries and annotations is not so much that they enable us to ferret out Whitman's literary sources, for any writer who reads as widely as Whitman did weaves hundreds of sources, and partial sources, into his own patterns, and no amount of painstaking research can ever unerringly pick out all the threads that went into the finished product. The value of these manuscripts and annotated clippings is that they enable us to follow the path of Whitman's thoughts at this critical period in his literary development. The passages he underscored and glossed may sometimes have given him a fact or an idea for the first time, but often they merely confirmed his own convictions, or clarified a thought which he had not yet entirely worked out to his own satisfaction.

Like Emerson, Whitman regarded reading as a creative activity, and in an article on this subject entitled "Thoughts on Reading," which he had torn out of the May, 1845, issue of the *American Whig Review*,[95] he underscored, "An author enriches us, not so much by giving us his ideas, as by unfolding in us the same powers that originated them." Then in the margin Whitman commented that even light reading could fertilize the mind. As for more solid reading, "The thousands of common poets, romancers, essayists and attempters exist because some twenty or fifty geniuses at intervals led the way long before."

In another part of the article the author had asserted that men of talent can only impart knowledge, not power (evidently he had read De Quincey), and Whitman underscored, "But the man of genius transforms us, for the time, into what he is himself . . ." At the bottom of the page he wrote "read once more." The fact that he carefully preserved these extracts from books and magazines indicates that he often did read them again, and therefore the date of the magazine is no sure clue to the time Whitman profited most from the selection. In fact, sometimes his marginal comments have been made with different pens, and occasionally a note is even dated years after the publication, proving that he re-read the item on several occasions. A good example of this is an article from an 1846 copy of the *Western Review* on "Early Roman History."[96] First Whitman underscored a passage on the practical energy of the Romans and wrote in the margin: "America now of all lands has the greatest practical energy—(But has it not also the highest infusion of pure intellect?)." Later, with a different pen, he showed that he had progressed toward his anti-intellectualism of the 1850's by adding: "Well, if it has, does it not want something *besides* intellect? What are you after in people? merely their intellect?"

"Thoughts on Reading," mentioned above, illustrates another problem in the study of sources. In a passage on the power of the older poets, especially the Elizabethans, Whitman underscored: "If they were wild and irregular, it was because nature is so . . ." This was precisely the analogy he was to use for many years to justify the apparent irregularity of *Leaves of Grass*.[97] His early biographers and friendly critics argued that he got this idea straight from Nature herself,[98] but actually by 1845 it was often expressed in the magazines Whitman was reading. What he did was to take it literally and find means of applying it in an original way.

Before 1850 Whitman had read a number of the Greek and Roman classics[99] in translation, and many of the standard British and American authors, such as Shakespeare, Milton—whom he never liked—Johnson, Burns, Scott, Dickens, Bulwer-Lytton, Carlyle, and among the Americans, particularly Cooper, Irving, Hawthorne—not a favorite though respected—Longfellow, and of course Bryant. Emerson's essays he had probably read at least in part, though the evidence is contradictory, and before publishing the first *Leaves of Grass* he had read Carlyle extensively.[100]

Some time around 1850 or a year to two later, Whitman's reading became more systematic, and two popular anthologies gave him suggestions and guidance. One of these was a four-volume collection edited by Charles Knight, called *Half-Hours with the Best Authors* (1847–1849).[101] It contained samples of early English literature, poems by well-known poets, and some prose selections that Whitman annotated, such as Johnson's essay on Shakespeare and sketches of the life and works of Crabbe and Spenser. One of the poems that Whitman clipped out was Shelley's "Hymn to Intellectual Beauty."[102] This anthology also contained some foreign literature that he extracted, such as an essay on Froissart and Guizot's "Civilization." Often these selections aroused Whitman's curiosity and caused him to look up other books and jot down more complete data on the lives of the authors and their principal works.

Out of another book, called *Memoria Technica,* Whitman clipped "One Thousand Historical Events, with the Dates," and to these leaves he attached various clippings on the history and literature of foreign countries, for example: "The Golden Verses of Pythagoras," Siamese proverbs, and the "Absurd Chronology of the Hindoos."[103] He also used a geography text for a scrapbook[104] of information on places, peoples, and ways of life in various parts of the world. However crude these methods of self-instruction may seem, they gave Walt Whitman a general knowledge of history, science, ethnology, and literary history.

IX

All during Whitman's reading and thinking in the 1840's he was almost constantly influenced by a literary group whom he later seldom mentioned, and whose importance to himself he failed to appreciate because the influence extended over many years. This was the "Young America" movement, started in 1837 with the founding of the *Democratic Review* by John L. O'Sullivan and Samuel D. Langtree.[105] As we have already seen,[106] Whitman contributed to the *Democratic Review* in the early 1840's and was encouraged by O'Sullivan. And as late as 1858, after the magazine had become defunct, he spoke of it as "of a profounder quality of talent than any since," adding that in the early 1840's it greatly impressed the public, "especially the young men." [107]

This opinion was well founded. O'Sullivan had not only attracted much of the best literary talent of the time, but his attempt to launch a movement to encourage a more intense literary nationalism had not been without success. Some of the best critics of the decade had joined him as contributors to the *Democratic Review* and as defenders of O'Sullivan's ideas in other periodicals. Among these were Evert A. Duyckinck, William A. Jones, Cornelius Mathews, William Gilmore Simms, the Southern poet, romancer and nationalist, and Parke Godwin, Fourierist and son-in-law of Bryant. All of these were radical Jacksonian Democrats, or Locofocos, like Whitman before he gave up the *Freeman*. They wanted not only to liberate American literature from its British heritage but to make it genuinely democratic and a living force in achieving the social and political ideals of Jefferson and Jackson.

Naturally they were opposed by the Whigs, and even by the "Old Hunker" Democrats whom Whitman defied, for both groups believed that literature should be kept aristocratic and not lowered by the taste or prejudices of the masses. The Whig critics attacked the Young America group as ignorant, noisy disturbers of the peace. The battle was raucous and bitter on both sides. It raged over the acceptance or rejection of American authors, especially Emerson, whom Young America critics consistently defended, though they regretted his aloofness to Locofocoism, and whom the Whigs denounced as subversive to religion and morality. Hawthorne was praised by both sides, but the Whigs thought he had simply fallen into bad company, though they did not know how ardently he supported Young America ideas in his correspondence and wished to help start a democratic revolution in Europe.[108] Melville became partially associated with the movement through his friend Evert Duyckinck, and while Duyckinck and Mathews were visiting him at Pittsfield in August, 1850, he wrote his exuberant and nationalistic review of "Hawthorne and His Mosses," in which he found the smell of native beeches and hemlocks and "the far roar of . . . Niagara." [109]

"It is not strange," says the historian of the movement, "that Young America often wrote about 'literature for the people' and 'poetry for the mass,' and that it felt called upon to explain rather self-consciously the function of criticism and otherwise to educate the new audience." These critics also called prophetically for a "great Poet of the people," a "Homer of the mass," who would become a "world-renowned bard." [110] As much as they admired Emerson, they found him too cold to the masses—a criticism Whitman was to repeat many times later. Emerson was, therefore, not the great poet expected; that person had not yet appeared. William A. Jones predicted that "this poet of the people" would write about the necessity and dignity of labor, the "native nobility of an honest and brave heart," the uselessness of "conventional distinctions of rank and wealth," the cultivation of liberality and generosity, an "honorable poverty and a contented spirit," and "the brotherhood and equality of men." [111] All of these general themes Whitman was to treat—though he undoubtedly fulfilled the prophecy in some ways not called for or expected by Jones.

In their theory of literature the Young America critics went little beyond the Romantic idealism of their British cousins—not all of whom, by the way, they denounced, for they recognized in Burns, Crabbe, and even at times Wordsworth (for all his old-age Toryism), friends and poets of the people. But "They shifted the approach to poetry from the text of the poem to the 'maker' or 'creator' of the poem" [112]—precisely the theory that Whitman was to make the keystone of his poetics.

All of these theories, in fact, Walt Whitman absorbed, along with others that fitted into the ambitions and patterns of thought slowly taking form in his consciousness—and doubtless his unconscious too. But he was never on intimate social terms with the group as a whole. He had not yet done anything to attract the notice of men like Jones and Mathews, and he was never to know either Hawthorne or Melville personally. It is not surprising that Melville did not invite Whitman to his house party in the Berkshires, when Duyckinck and Mathews drove up in August, 1850. He was simply not in their social orbit, and it is doubtful that Whitman realized how much he was of their intellectual orbit. Soon after this date various circumstances resulted in the dispersal of the group, and when a few years later Walt Whitman appeared on the literary scene in partial answer to their manifestoes and prophecies, it was not they but other critics who welcomed him.

Another influence contemporary with the Young America movement, and as pervasive, was the social reform and idealism of the 1840's. Whitman was not particularly attracted to Fourierism, but one of its most ardent American advocates, Albert Brisbane, expressed a social optimism that Whitman's democratic idealism was greatly to resemble, and in language as well as ideas. The following passage from *Social Destiny of Man* (1840) contains basic ideas and imagery used fifteen years later in the first *Leaves of Grass:*

Far away in the distant future I saw a globe resplendently cultivated and embellished, transformed into the grandest and most beautiful work of art by the combined efforts of all humanity. I saw a race developed, perfected by the continued influence, generation after generation, of true social institutions; a humanity worthy of that Cosmic Soul of which I instinctively felt it to be a part. I saw this resplendent humanity as a child of God, a god itself upon its planet; and the old intuition which had led me to combat the cold atheism of my father was now becoming clearer.[113]

X

Perhaps one reason for Whitman's not remembering, or being fully conscious of, his indebtedness to the "Young America" advocates and sponsors of literary nationalism was that about the same time he had become interested in the theories and opinions being expressed in several British reviews, particularly the *North British Review,* the *Edinburgh Review,* Blackwood's *Edinburgh Magazine,* and the *Westminster Review,* a liberal Benthamite journal that the critics and editors of the *Democratic Review* often praised. Whitman's early enthusiasm for John Stuart Mill could have been stimulated either by the *Westminster* or by the *Democratic Review,* for he was much admired in both.[114]

These British magazines were so popular in the United States that they were pirated in American editions. Since in most cases these were the editions that Whitman used,[115] he may have received them for review while he was still in newspaper work, for most of his clippings that have survived are from the 1848 and 1849 (mostly the latter) numbers; and in 1857–1859, when he was editing the Brooklyn *Times,* he was again reading these British reviews and giving critical summaries of them on his editorial page. Many of his annotations show that ideas which scholars have thought he got from Emerson or some other American source could actually have come from these British reviews. But still more important, these clippings demonstrate that British and American literary theory around 1850 were far more alike than is generally realized. It is worth repeating, however, that what Whitman marked or annotated may have been only statements that confirmed ideas he had derived from other sources or had arrived at independently.

One of the most important of these articles was a long review-essay on "R. M. Milnes' Life of Keats" in the November, 1848, *North British Review*.[116] In the earlier part of this essay Whitman found much to disapprove or question, such as: "Extraordinary poetical genius, notwithstanding its resemblance to exuberant health, has not unfrequently been found to be connected with deeply seated disease. In most cases, the poetical power seems to have been the result of an abnormal habit of sensation." Whitman felt too sure of his own robust health to be able to accept such a doctrine, for to accept it would have cast doubt on his own ability to be a poet. Nor could he entirely agree with a quotation in which Keats said, "A poet is the most unpoetical of anything in existence, because he has no identity; he is continually in for and filling some other body." In the margin Whitman wrote: "The great poet absorbs the identity of others, and the exp[erience] of others, and they are definite in him or from him; but he p[erceives] them all through the powerful press of himself . . ."

In a long review of [Sir Henry] "Taylor's Eve of the Conquest" in the April, 1849, *Edinburgh Review*[117] Whitman underscored the critic's belief that "individual robustness—and therefore character,—like intellectual greatness, is rarer than it was in ruder times." Whitman headed the column "Character," and drew the sign of a hand pointing the forefinger to indicate the reviewer's main arguments for the decline of character, such as standardization, increasing self-consciousness, and the stagnating effect of conventionality. Whitman did not object to the diagnosis, but he wrote in the lower margin that he would "take all these things that produce this condition and make them produce as great characters as any"—an idea that he would polish up and re-state in his 1855 preface.

On another page, when the critic argued for the use of concrete detail in poetry, Whitman wrote, "Materialism as the foundation of poetry," and underlined every word in one column and some sentences in the other.[118] The critic had anticipated his own increasing conviction that every part of the material universe and all forms of life are equally miraculous and divine in origin.

The following page Whitman headed "Cramming Poetry with too many thoughts," and underscored the opinion that gravity and not number of thoughts was important, and that poetry must be drawn from actual experience. On another page, after much applauding and underlining, he copied in the margin, "Without reality, poetic passion must ever be insincere." All this dated theorizing doubtless fitted into Whitman's emerging poetic "materialism," by which he hoped to express "truth" with a fidelity to "reality" never before attained in poetry. And these thoughts also directed his attention to the critic's meditations on style, especially the belief that "With the merely technical rules of style poetry has indeed little concern," and that "a superabundance of figures" is bad ("A metaphor tells us what things are like, not what they are"). The critic was merely cautioning against the over-use of figures, but his words may have encouraged Whitman in his resolve to refrain from using any comparisons or allusions in his poetry (though he would never be able quite to live up to it). These thoughts on style led both the critic and reader to think of language, and Whitman studiously underscored information about the origin of English and the superiority of concrete Saxon. Summing up many of these thoughts, with his own additions, Whitman wrote at the bottom of one of the final pages: "The perfect poem is simple, healthy, natural—no griffins, angels, centaurs—no hysterics or blue fire—no dyspepsia, no suicidal intentions."

We find other anticipations of Whitman's own poetic theory in some final underscored passages, to the effect that poetry is "the offspring and exponent of the poet's total being," and that "Every portion of it, as it grows, must be a true reflection from his own mind, or from nature as contemplated by that mind . . ." This noble process also necessitated such "unshaken self-possession in the midst of the marvels around him" as Dante exemplified, because "every first-rate poet is . . . the regent of a separate sphere, and the master of a complete poetic world of his own."

In an article in the October, 1849, number of *Blackwood's* called "Modern Poetry and Poets," [119] Whitman followed with interest a discussion of nationalism, and with great care underscored this sentence: "As a thousand rivulets are blended in one broad river, so the countless instincts, energies, and faculties, as well as associations, traditions, and other social influences which constitute national life, are reconciled in him whom future ages are to recognize as the poet of the nation." Whether the paradox involved in creating a poetic world of his own and at the same time being "the poet of the nation" had occurred to Whitman, his annotation does not show. So far he had not yet achieved a poetic individuality of his own, and he underscored this Emersonian statement, which probably expressed his own wish: "True genius will soon cast aside whatever is alien to its individual nature . . ." In the margin he wrote: "The poets are the divine mediums—through them come spirits and materials to all the people, men and women."

A critic of "Tennyson's Poems" in *Blackwood's* for the preceding April[120] had reproved this increasingly fashionable poet for his mannerisms, over-refined style, and dainty sentiments. These criticisms Whitman not only shared then, as his underlining pencil recorded, but he was always to hold such views regarding Tennyson's poetry, though in old age he came to admire the man. But two other ideas in this review particularly impressed him. One was the theory that the highest art depends upon "suggestion" for its effect, and along with this the additional doctrine that "self-exertion in the reader" (as Whitman summarized it in the margin) is necessary for the appreciation of the highest art. Both points were to be incorporated into Whitman's own poetics.

The other idea that impressed Whitman was that great poetry must be religious: "the soul of art is gone, when religion has finally taken her departure." This thought was reinforced by another critic of "Tennyson's Poems—The Princess" in the May, 1848, *North British Review*,[121] who asserted that "the great artist" externalizes and disseminates "the life of religion." Once again Whitman had encountered and approved—even as the Young America group had done—this Victorian doctrine of the interdependence of art, character, and religion. To judge by his wavy lines and pointing hands in the margin, he was delighted with the idea that "A work of art is the externalization of the artist's character."

It will be noticed that Whitman was fond of passages in which the critic spoke of what the "great artist" or "great poet" should be or do, or of the power of "genius" (that ambiguous word so dear to the critics of his generation). There can be little doubt that as Whitman read and marked these words, his own ambition for literary greatness soared. Exactly how high it had soared by 1851 no one can say, but it is perhaps significant that an article in the *American Whig Review* of that year (one of several literary articles he had clipped from this review in 1851) called his attention to his immediate problem. In a review on "The 'Hyperion' of John Keats"[122] the author pointed out that the greatest problem of a young writer is the right choice of subject, and Whitman marked: "If his genius is epical, but one theme will occur to him in the entire course of his life . . . The conjunction of four planets is hardly more rare than the fortunate conjunction of time, subject, circumstance, preparation, and ability for the work."

Whether Whitman's genius was epical he did not yet know, and to judge by his notebooks he did not discover until later that he had but one subject—*himself*—or the *self*. But he had already marked in an extract from William Gilmore Simms's *Views and Reviews* (in a discussion, incidentally, of the writings of Cornelius Mathews): [123] "To continue striving at numerous kinds of composition, only proves continued immaturity, or a prurient vanity, which baffles concentration, and, though it may provoke the passing wonder of contemporaries, will scarcely ever be able to command the lasting honours of posterity." After 1851 Whitman began to follow this advice. He had long ago given up his sentimental stories and his "graveyard" poetry. Now for several years he would give up journalism, and while supporting himself by house building he would read and seek the bent of his own "genius." His purpose in this reading was well expressed in another clipping which he had kept from the *Edinburgh Review* (April, 1849), on "The Vanity and Glory of Literature," [124] in which he had been told that "It is the privilege of genius . . . to extract their gold dust out of the most worthless books . . ." And he had emphatically marked: "In this way minute portions of the past are constantly entering by new combinations into fresh forms of life, and out of these old materials, continually decomposed but continually recombined, scope is afforded for an everlasting succession of imaginative literature." To use the same figure, Whitman's reading was the compost in which his "leaves of grass" were beginning to sprout.

XI

Though the actual writing of the poems in the 1855 *Leaves of Grass* certainly came later, Whitman probably started accumulating ideas for the book in the late 1840's before he had either the title or even a general plan in mind. In little notebooks,[125] small enough to carry around in his pocket, he jotted down tentative thoughts, themes, and trial workings of what was to become the 1855 preface and some of the poems in the first edition. The earliest of these notebooks[126] contains the date 1847 in Whitman's hand and the addresses 71 Prince Street and 30 Fulton Street (the latter the Brooklyn *Eagle* office), but these have been crossed out and 106 Myrtle Avenue substituted. Since he did not move from Myrtle Avenue until September 1, 1852,[127] he might have used this book at any time between 1847 and 1852—or even later. But one clue to the date is that a few of these notes seem to echo Lucretius, whom Whitman read in an 1851 translation.[128]

The first entry is: "Be simple and clear.—Be not occult." [129] Since there are no other specific thoughts on style in the first notebook, Whitman had probably not yet got very far in evolving his new versification. Thus he began on the most rudimentary level possible. He was concerned with ideas long before he had thought of literary form as a problem.

True noble expanded American Character is raised on a far more lasting and universal basis than that of any of the characters of the "gentlemen" of aristocratic life, or of novels, or under the European or Asian forms of society or government.—It is to be illimitably proud, independent, self-possessed, generous and gentle. It is to accept nothing except what is equally free and eligible to any body else. It is to be poor, rather than rich—but to prefer death sooner than any mean dependence.—Prudence is part of it, because prudence is the right arm of independence. [130]

Notice that the "American Character" is defined in the language of the Young America group. Walt Whitman would have to personify it in his own self and personality before he would be able to express the idea poetically, although most of these attributes had been his personal ideals since his apprentice days, when he had had those long talks with the old patriot, [131] the foreman printer William Hartshorne, who had known Washington and Jefferson. The rather odd use of "prudence" probably had some literary source, and there are several possibilities. The most obvious would be Emerson's essay called "Prudence" (First Series, 1841), and it is likely that Whitman had read it. But the concept was originally Epicurean, and as we shall see a little later, Whitman got his Epicureanism mainly from Frances Wright and Lucretius. "Prudence" meant the long range rather than the expedient view of conduct, or in Whitman's later words, "All that a person does or thinks is of consequence." What a person does may influence not only the remainder of his life but all eternity—a kind of moralistic determinism.

A little later in the notebook we find that Whitman's own patriotic sense of American character and his Hicksite religion were beginning to coalesce into a symbolical pride: "I never yet knew how it felt to think I stood in the presence of my superior.—If the presence of God were made visible immediately before me, I could not abase myself." [132] It was, in fact, more than a symbolical pride; Whitman's whole nature and past experience were pushing him into the philosophical realm of pantheism. By this time pantheism had spread from Spinoza through the whole German romantic school and then to Shelley, Carlyle, and Emerson. It reached

Whitman in a thousand ways and forms, but Heine's formulation of it was typical. "God," he declared, "is identical with the world," and He manifests Himself in all life, but supremely in man, who alone of all creatures has self-consciousness. "God, therefore, is the real hero of world history, the latter is His perpetual thought, His perpetual act, His word, His deed, and of all humanity, one may rightly say: It is the incarnation of God." [133]

Whitman, however, went beyond Heine. Believing more literally in the divinity of man, he made not God but Man the hero of world history, and as poet he was to make himself a symbol of that hero, and to give this symbolical self God-like powers and potentialities. But Whitman did not yet clearly conceive of God as Personality—that was to come many years later. Like Emerson in his "Over Soul" doctrine, Whitman conceived of the Supreme Power as "soul" or "spirit," which manifested itself in a pantheistic fashion through matter. In his notebook he wrote: "The soul or spirit transmits itself into all matter—into rocks, and can live the life of a rock—into the sea, and can feel itself the sea—into the oak, or other tree—into an animal, and feel itself a horse, a fish, or bird—into the earth—into the motions of the suns and stars . . ." To understand this process a man must imagine himself speeding with the planets, crashing with the thunder in the sky, or "growing fragrantly in the air, like the locust blossoms." [134] Soon Whitman would change "man" to "poet," and let him symbolize the processes of the "soul" at work. It was exactly this concept of the "soul" that Whitman was trying to think through, and he was probably not aware that he was attempting to do so in a neo-Platonic fashion; but the soul "makes itself visible only through matter—a perfect head, and bowels and bones to match is the easy gate through which it comes from its embowered garden, and pleasantly appears to the sight of the world.—A twisted skull, and blood watery or rotten by ancestry or gluttony, or rum or bad disorders,—they are the darkness toward which the plant will not grow, although its seed lies waiting for ages." [135] Heine had also stated that, "The aim of modern life is the rehabilitation of matter, its moral recognition, its religious sanctification, its reconciliation with the spirit." [136]

It is interesting to observe how each of these philosophical ideas merged with, or was modified by, Whitman's own personality and self-consciousness. He had always, as we have seen, had great regard for his own health, avoiding harmful food or drink in his youth, and now in his manhood he often enjoyed a mystical ecstasy of physical well-being. It was Thoreau who confessed in his *Journal*, "In youth, before I lost any of my senses, I can remember that I was all alive, and inhabited my body with inexpressible satisfaction . . ." [137] Whitman had enjoyed his youth, but without the intense awareness and self-consciousness of Thoreau. Now, during the gestation of his first edition, his health and physical sensations gave him a mystical joy, for he was evidently describing this period when he wrote the little essay on "Health (Old Style)," in which he declared that in the condition of health "the whole body is elevated to a state by others unknown—inwardly and outwardly illuminated, purified, made solid, strong yet buoyant." In this condition "Sorrows and disappoint-ments cease."

A man realizes the venerable myth—he is a god walking the earth, he sees new eligibilities, powers and beauties everywhere; he himself has a new eyesight and hearing. The play of the body in motion takes a previously un-known grace. Merely *to move* is then a happiness, a pleasure—to breathe, to see, is also. All the beforehand gratifications, drink, spirits, coffee, grease, stim-ulants, mixtures, late hours, luxuries, deeds of the night, seem as vexatious dreams, and now the awakening;—many [healthful gratifications] fall into their natural places, wholesome, conveying diviner joys.[138]

Perhaps we should make some allowance for the fact that this was written by an old man in very poor health, who longed for the physical vigor he had once enjoyed. But the early notebooks and the first *Leaves of Grass* are filled with an almost indescribable ecstasy of pure sensation. Then it was not only a joy merely to be alive, but merely being alive made Whit-man feel immortal.

Whitman's sense of physical well-being was doubtless the result in large part of his inherited nervous system and a body in which for many years all glands functioned properly. But at the same time his reading and thinking also influenced his organic life. In his notebook he recorded the thought that, "Wickedness is most likely the absence of Freedom and health in the soul." [139] And he made it part of his life-purpose to keep both his body and soul free and healthy. He would always regard evil as sickness.

Whitman nowhere attempted an exposition or treatise on his theory of the soul, as Emerson did in his "Spiritual Laws" or "The Over Soul," both of which doubtless influenced Whitman in his concepts; but this early notebook for his poems leaves no doubt that thoughts and convic-tions as to the nature of the "soul" and its powers were at the root of his first poems in *Leaves of Grass*. Under the head of "Dilation" he wrote:

When I walked at night by the sea shore and looked up at the countless stars, I asked of my soul whether it would be filled and satisfied when it should become god enfolding all these, and open to the life and delight and knowledge of everything in them or of them; and the answer was plain to me as the breaking water on the sands at my feet; and the answer was, No, when I reach there, I shall want to go further still.[140]

Here Whitman's soul becomes simply "I"—"I shall want to go further still." A few paragraphs below he records what does not seem to be a borrowed idea from his reading but a truly autobiographical confession: "I cannot understand the mystery, but I am always conscious of myself as two—as my soul and I: and I reckon it is the same with all men and women." [141] There is no biographical proof that Whitman was a divided personality. One psychoanalyst has said that this longing for identity, this insatiable desire for ever more and larger existence, knowledge, experience, was an unconscious expression of self-doubt, inner mal-ease, probably the result of insufficient parental love in his childhood.[142] The historian of ideas, on the other hand, would say that the mind of this writer was profoundly influenced by the Faust tradition in Western civilization.[143] But whatever the explanation, it was no mere literary or philosophical convention that gave Whitman these convictions as to the nature and destiny of his "soul." He actually walked the seashore at night alone, actually looked at the stars, genuinely believed that nature spoke the answer to him, and such experiences were to provide much of the primary imagery and symbolism of his future poems. Reading and his cultural heritage undoubtedly fertilized and stimulated his mind, but his words, images, and ideas were ultimately stamped by his own physical and emotional life.

XII

During the period of his early notebooks, Whitman was influenced by a book that he had been reading for some years, and was later to call one of his favorites. This was Frances Wright's *A Few Days in Athens* (1822),[144] passages of which were later silently quoted, paraphrased, or echoed in the pages of *Leaves of Grass*.[145] The purpose of this book was to popularize the Epicurean philosophy, though the Scotch authoress unconsciously mingled a good deal of Lockean empiricism, Humean skepticism, and Scottish "Common Sense" philosophy with her neo-Epicureanism.

The setting of *A Few Days* is supposed to be ancient Athens at the time of its greatest philosophy and art. Theon talks with a stranger about Zeno and Stoicism. He visits the garden of Epicurus, and is embraced by a young man, follower of Epicurus, who pronounces himself in love with Theon—a passion similar to Whitman's future "manly love" in his "Calamus" poems. "Prudence" is also found in this book. In Chapter X Theon is told, "And now Prudence shall bring you to the lovely train of virtues," and in the context the word has the meaning that Whitman was to attach to it. Epicurus likewise teaches that friendship is "the purest delight of earth"; however, he adds stoically, "yet if fate deprive us of it, though we grieve, we do not sink."

Metrodorus teaches that "everything is eternal," a very important idea in *Leaves of Grass*. It is "the different disposition of these eternal and unchangeable atoms that produces all the varieties in the substances constituting the great material whole, of which we form a part. Those particles, whose peculiar agglomeration or arrangement we call a vegetable today, then pass into, and form a part of, an animal tomorrow . . ." But only matter can be observed; what creates matter must be imagined, and mind is only a quality of matter. In matter itself exist all causes and effects. Nevertheless, life is a glorious thing, and all existences are equally wonderful.

Religion is "the bane of human happiness, perverter of human virtue." The Epicurean command is, "Enjoy, and be happy!" The "source of every enjoyment is within yourself. Good and evil lie before you. The good is—all which can yield you pleasure: The evil—what must bring pain. Here is no paradox, no dark saying, no moral hid in fables." What has perverted man? Religion! "Other animals . . . exercise the faculties they possess . . . Man alone . . . doubts the evidence of his superior senses, . . . and turns to poison all the sources of his happiness." [146] This idea Whitman was to express in his fashion in "Song of Myself" (Sec. 32), when he thought he "could turn and live with animals" because they were "so placid and self-contained."

> They do not sweat and whine about their condition,
> They do not lie awake in the dark and weep for their sins,
> They do not make me sick discussing their duty to God, . . .

Having heard of Lucretius from Frances Wright's little book, Whitman secured the translation of *De Rerum Natura, or The Nature of Things*, by the Reverend J. S. Watson, published in this country in 1851. He not only read it, but wrote out a summary.[147] Although this summary does

not show a very profound understanding of the poem, it does demonstrate that Whitman was well aware of Lucretius's major ideas. He first
noted that "The work is largely aimed at calming the fears of the Romans
against suffering after death—it seeks to convince the reader that Death
is cessation, annihilating, 'an eternal sleep.' " And, "It teaches a good,
mild, benevolent, contented life." He outlined the six books as follows:
"1st Book—Apostrophe to Venus as the reproductive power—invective
against superstition—'nothing can be produced from nothing.' 2d Book
—Atomic theory [.] 3rd Book—Body and Soul are one—the latter ceases
with the former—the folly of fearing death [.] 4th Book—The senses, &c.
—Love [.] 5th Book—The Origin of the World—the seasons, progress of
man [.] 6th Book—Extraordinary natural phenomenon [.]" Then going
back to Book IV, Whitman added: "Love—Desire &c [:] latter part of
Book IV treats of amativeness, procreation, conception, &c—describes the
heat of amorous appetite &c [—] tells the female how to act to conceive
best—enters into minute details &c—the lesson & general influence of this
latter part of Book IV is however sane and good."

Obviously Book IV impressed Whitman most, and these notes make it
impossible to rule out the likely influence of Lucretius on his poetic
theory of sex and his actual writing of the "Children of Adam" poems.
And the ideas in this translation, moreover, probably strengthened other
sources already at work in Whitman's mind. For example, his anti-clerical-
ism was in part the product of his father's experiences and reading and of
Whitman's own reading of Tom Paine, Volney's *Ruins*, and Frances
Wright's *A Few Days in Athens*. These sources might have made him
receptive to Lucretius's naturalism, rather than his discovering something
new in the Roman poet's arguments against the gods and religion. At any
rate, like Lucretius, he also wished to "argue not concerning God," believed the body and soul to be one, and regarded death as natural and
therefore unterrifying. All of these attitudes he could have found in *A
Few Days in Athens*. When he delivered his Art Union[148] speech he had
not read *De Rerum Natura*, though he probably had read Frances
Wright.[149]

Finally, it should be noted that certain aspects of the Stoic philosophy
also appealed to Whitman, and had at least as far back as the
"Thanatopsis" period in his juvenile poetry. According to his own testimony, he first read Epictetus, who was to remain one of his lifelong
favorites, when he was sixteen.[150] And in middle age he was fond of
Marcus Aurelius.[151] The phrenologists found him long on "caution,"

yet this was only another term for "Prudence," which could be interpreted in an Epicurean sense, that is, enjoy life, but act in such a way as to prolong the enjoyment, and not endanger it by a foolish surfeit of sense-gratification; or it could be regarded as Stoic self-restraint.

In his notebook Whitman also wrote that "The ignorant man is demented with the madness of owning things—of having by warranty deeds [and] court clerk's records, the right to mortgage, sell, give away or raise money on certain possessions.—But the wisest soul knows that no object can really be owned by one man or woman any more than another." [152] These sentiments could have been inspired by the doctrine of "Prudence," or Emerson's poem "Hamatreya," or the *Vishnu Purana* from which Emerson got the idea for his poem, or even by reading the *Dial* magazine. But Whitman had also expressed such thoughts as early as his editorship of the *Aurora*,[153] and at the very time he was keeping this notebook he was disappointing his own family by his indifference to raising money on possessions.

Whether Whitman had read any Oriental literature by this time the most diligent search of scholars has not yet determined. When Thoreau met him after the publication of the first *Leaves of Grass* he remarked that the book was "Wonderfully like the Orientals," and asked Whitman if he had read them. The reply was, "No: tell me about them." [154] But this may have been disingenuous, or it could have been modesty before a man who obviously knew a great deal about Oriental scriptures. In fact, in old age Whitman claimed to have read the "ancient Hindoo poems" [155] in preparation for *Leaves of Grass*, but he did not specify which poems. In possible corroboration of this claim, Hindu scholars and mystics have frequently professed to recognize the Vedantic teachings in *Leaves of Grass*.[156] As a recent scholar says, "Whitman's soul, like the self of *Bhagavad Gita*, is the unifying energy." [157] This self "is a passive spectator; it is Brahma incarnate in the body; and it is permanent, indestructible, eternal, all-pervading, unmanifest." Whitman believed that evil was mere sickness of the soul, therefore temporary and remedial. The Vedanta teaches that good and evil are *maya*, mere appearances. And as with all mystics, love unifies all existence, and knowledge is attained through intuition. These doctrines were basic in Whitman's early notebooks.

Whitman also resembled the Oriental mystics—and most of the mystics of all ages and lands—in his attitude toward *time*. Of all the concepts recorded in his notebooks, this is undoubtedly the most remarkable, most far-reaching in its shaping of his mind and art, and, perhaps most surprising of all, a link between him and twentieth century literature.[158] The way in which he had become interested in time is easily explained. The lectures he heard on astronomy and the geological theories on the age of the world that he managed to pick up here and there had convinced him that man was a comparative newcomer to the scene of existence. In his notebook he wrote: ". . . imagine the world in its formation —the long rolling, heaving cycles—Can man appear here?—Can the beautiful vegetable and animal life appear here?" [159] When he thought of how he himself had finally arrived on the scene, he realized his indebtedness to the whole past not only of mankind but of the very universe itself. This thought carried him both emotionally and intellectually almost the whole distance to his emancipation from both human and finite time, for he assumed that the creative process in the universe (or plurality of universes) is eternal: ". . . My right hand is time, and my left hand is space—both are ample—a few quintillions of cycles, a few sextillions of cubic leagues, are not of importance to me—what I shall attain to I can never tell, for there is something that underlies me, of whom I am a part and instrument." [160]

"My right hand is time, and my left hand is space . . ." Whitman had made not only an important philosophical but also a very important psychological and esthetic discovery. Let him now create a cosmic "I" that can travel through time and space like a Greek god—or a soul freed of all finite limitations—and he will have found a new literary technique. Mitchel, in his imaginary trips through the starry heavens, had suggested to him a non-terrestrial point of view, and Whitman used this in a trial poetic flight:

> Afar in the sky was a nest,
> And my soul flew thither and squat[ted], and looked out
> And saw the journeywork of suns and systems of suns, . . .[161]

Or he could explore the earth:

> I have split the earth and the hard coal and rocks and the solid bed
>   of the sea
> And went down to reconnoitre there a long time,
> And bring back a report, . . .[162]

Also while listening to music Whitman had experienced other sensations of flight into space, and of flight from everyday reality. These he described in a very revealing notebook passage in which musical, astronomical, and sexual imagery mingle—"dilating" him "beyond time":

I want that tenor, large and fresh as the creation, the orbed parting of whose mouth shall lift over my head the sluices of all the delight yet discovered for our race.—I want the soprano that lithely overleaps the stars, and convulses me like the love-grips of her in whose arms I lay last night . . . dilating me beyond time and air . . . calmly sailing me all day on a bright river with lazy slapping waves—stabbing my heart with myriads of forked distractions more furious than hail or lightning—lulling me drowsily with honeyed morphine—tightening the fakes of death about my throat, and awakening me again to know by that comparison, the most positive wonder in the world, and that's what we call life.[163]

Numerous passages in these notebooks reveal the sexual emotions stimulating Whitman's poetic fancy: "One touch of a tug of me has unhaltered all my senses . . ." [164] Some of these passages are esoteric or incoherent. Many are plainly autoerotic, and a few show a sense of guilt:

> I roam about drunk and stagger
> I am given up by traitors,
> I talk wildly I am surely out of my head,
> I am myself the greatest traitor.
> I went myself first to the headland[165]

These ecstasies and sexual urges enabled the poet to imagine himself in many situations, to give himself and of himself freely to anyone, to share his dream-power with men and women everywhere. Thus he and his "soul" travel up and down the highways of the world like a beneficent god bringing strength to the weak, hope to the discouraged, health and happiness to the sick or unfortunate. This gave the "outsetting bard" vicarious pleasure, expressed the "love" pent up in his own heart; and there are numerous indications in his notes that to some extent at least the expression was a compensation. For example: "I am not glad tonight. Gloom has gathered round me like a mantle, tightly folded." [166] Or, "The oppression of my heart is not fitful and has no pangs; but a torpor like that of some stagnant pool." [167] And again:

> Thus it comes that I am not glad tonight.—
> I feel cramped here in these coarse walls of flesh.
> The soul disdains its [unfinished]
> O Mystery of Death, I pant for the time when I shall solve you!

It seems evident, therefore, that there were intimate, personal associations for Whitman between the imaginary flights into space, the sexual imagery aroused by great vocal or instrumental music, the vicarious sympathy with all men and women past and present (and later he would include the future also), and the desire to attain perfect and eternal happiness—beyond the limits of mortal life, even beyond time and space. Tentatively he played with the esthetic use of suspended or frozen time: "If the light of a half day dawn were arrested, and held so for a thousand years" [unfinished].[168]

Whatever the origins of these wish-fulfillments, they did give Walt Whitman the intuitive knowledge of what he regarded as spiritual truths: that each human identity has a definite place in an eternal scheme and purpose; that the body and soul are equally important, though the body goes back to compost and thence into other forms of life while the soul advances infinitely through higher forms of existence; that every soul is eternally becoming something better, more complete, more god-like, so that in ultimate reality there is only one time, an everlasting present. What Walt Whitman wanted most in his life of the imagination was to immerse, to bathe, to float (these were to become key images in his poems) in the eternal stream of existence. Having attained these mystical insights and intellectual concepts, Whitman was emotionally and mentally equipped to write the great book he had been dreaming of since his "Sundown Papers" from his schoolmaster's desk.[169]

What he needed now was an adequate form, a literary vehicle. In his early free verse experiments he may have used several literary sources (certainly including the King James Bible), but, more important, he had discovered that his memory had already stored up an abundance of poetic imagery waiting to be released. At some time, probably not more than two or three years before the first *Leaves of Grass*, he set down, revised, and neatly copied out his first long poem. He called it simply and ineptly "Pictures," [170] because his memory seemed to him to be a picture gallery:

In a little house pictures I keep,
Many pictures hang suspended—
It is not a fixed house,
It is round—it is but a few inches from one side of it to the other side,
But behold! it has room enough—in it, hundreds and thousands, all the varieties;
Here! do you know this? this is cicerone himself;

And here, see you, my own States—and here the world itself rolling through
    the air;
And there, on the walls hanging, portraits of women and men, carefully kept,
This is the portrait of my dear mother—and this of my father—and these of my
    brothers and sisters;
This, (I name every thing as it comes,) This is a beautiful statue, long lost,
    dark buried, but never destroyed—now found by me, and restored to the
    light; . . .[171]

The contents of this poem are the remembered images from the poet's
own life and the scenes he had accumulated from his reading in such
diverse sources as A Few Days in Athens, Felton's History of Greece,
the Bible, Homer, the geography and history of his own nation,
Egyptology, and world history. The subjects range back and forth in time
and space. The only thing that provides a unity for the poem is that all
these images hang suspended in the poet's own "picture house." In the
handling of images and the treatment of time Whitman had advanced
far toward his mature technique, but his rhythms were simply those of
prose, with only a slight hint of the parallelism and reiteration which
would give his poems in Leaves of Grass their characteristic primitive
rhythm. But he realized how awkward this production was, for he put it
aside without publishing it. Nevertheless, "Pictures" was an embryo of
Leaves of Grass.

XIII

Throughout 1853–1854 Walt Whitman's mind was not solely preoc-
cupied with literary projects. In the spring of 1853 or 1854 he accompanied his father on a hasty trip back to the old homestead at West Hills.
Apparently the enfeebled old man realized that he did not have long
to live and he wished to see once more the rolling hills the Whitmans
had owned and the house he had built for his bride. He was either too
weak or did not have the opportunity to go on to Huntington.[172] Just
why Walt instead of one of the other sons took the trip with him is not
certain—though perhaps the other boys were hard at work and felt they
could not spare the time. In Walt's own old-age sickness he would become increasingly sympathetic with the memory of his father,[173] and it
is probable that the two men were drawn somewhat closer together by
this trip, though it was simply not possible for the father to understand
the literary plans that were beginning to agitate his son's mind.

At this time Whitman might even have taken up politics again if there had been any prospect of success in that field. But the political situation had not changed since the collapse of the Free-Soil party. At the Baltimore convention of 1852 the Democratic party was still being dominated by the slave-holders and those sympathetic to slavery, and as a consequence the delegates agreed upon a platform with a very strong foreign policy to cover up their inability to agree on domestic issues. With this strategy they elected the nonentity Franklin Pierce to the Presidency. Thus the conditions that Whitman had denounced in 1849–1850 continued. And we may be sure that he was deeply pained by the repeal of the Missouri Compromise early in 1854 and the passage of the Kansas-Nebraska bill in May, for in his sympathies he was still strongly anti-slavery. Then close on the heels of these events, and partly as a consequence, a fugitive slave, Anthony Burns, was seized in Boston by the United States Marshal and tried in court. Abolitionists from all New England rushed to the rescue and there was rioting and bloodshed, yet early in June the slave was returned to his owner in Virginia.[174] Whitman's indignation burst forth in a satirical poem, later to be called "A Boston Ballad" (though printed in the first *Leaves of Grass* without a title). Ironically he shouted:

Clear the way there Jonathan!
Way for the President's marshal! Way for the government cannon!
Way for the federal foot and dragoons . . . . and the phantoms afterward.

Troops had been called out from the near-by Marine base in Boston, and the Federal Government was said to have used various pressures to secure the conviction and return of the defendant. Therefore, the poet tells his countrymen bitterly that they might as well dig King George out of his coffin, "fetch home the roarers from Congress," and bury American liberty. Though written in long lines resembling the new free-verse rhythms with which Whitman was experimenting, the versification of this poem is actually a sort of jigging doggerel. Whitman was too angry and bitter to control his rhythms. And he almost certainly composed it in June, while the public indignation and excitement were at their height.

Whitman's intense concern with social and political problems is also revealed in a strongly worded "Memorial in Behalf of a Freer Municipal Government, and Against Sunday Restrictions," [175] which he addressed in October to the City Council. He was mainly protesting against recently adopted blue-laws that forbade streetcars and railroads to run on Sunday,

thus depriving many working people, as Whitman pointed out, of healthful outings and recreation on the only day when they could enjoy such
innocent pleasures. But he was also protesting the right of elected officials
to set themselves up as censors of morals and social conduct instead of
obeying the will of the people who had elected them. On October 16,
1854, an Alderman presented Whitman's letter to the Common Council
and the Mayor of Brooklyn, but no action was taken. The *Evening Star*
printed it on October 20, and apparently this, too, produced no results.

The intense feeling displayed in both the "Boston Ballad" and this
protest to the City Council indicates that Whitman was now experiencing
the emotional pressure that produced the first *Leaves of Grass*. Later his
friend in Washington during the Civil War, Mrs. Ellen O'Connor, was to
report: "In discussing the manner in which his book was written, *Leaves
of Grass*, he said that very much of it was written under great pressure,
pressure from within, he felt that he must do it." [176] This pressure had
been accumulating for several years—psychological pressure, personal ambition to be the poet the literary nationalists had been calling for, and
the desire to share with the public exciting ideas and convictions. Finally
this "pressure from within" became so strong that Whitman gave up his
house building and began to devote his whole attention to the preparation of his book of poems. This was probably late in 1854 or early 1855.
In old age he recalled half humorously: "I was working at carpentering
and making money when this *Leaves of Grass* bee came to me. I stopped
working and from that time my ruin commenced." [177] George's testimony was: "He would lie abed late, and after getting up would write a
few hours if he took the notion—perhaps would go off the rest of the day.
We were all at work—all except Walt." [178] But Walt had never let the
opinion of his family—or anyone else—influence him, and he certainly
made no concessions to it now.

Whitman probably attempted to secure a commercial publisher for his
book, but considering the kind of poetry that was being published and
read at the time, it is not surprising that no commercial house would
consider it. However, he was not to be balked. The two Rome brothers,
James and Thomas, who ran a good printing shop on the corner of Fulton
and Cranberry, were friends of his, and they printed books, though mainly
legal works. They were not only willing to print the book but would let
Walt supervise the work, even set some of the type himself—and he did
set about ten pages.[179] There at the Rome Brothers' printing office nearly
every morning during the spring of 1855 the poet sat in his special chair

in the corner. First he would read the morning *Tribune* and then he would correct proofs for a few hours.[180] The engraving of the frontispiece, and probably the binding, had to be done elsewhere, but the printing was the big job, and that was completed in time for bound copies to be placed on sale by July 6.[181]

How Whitman paid for the printing is not known. It may or may not be significant that his mother bought a house in her own name on May 24, 1855, on Ryerson Street.[182] Mrs. Whitman was given legal permission to sign the papers herself without "concurrence of her husband at any time during the present or future coverature by deeds or any instrument in writing to grant mortgages or devise the said premises . . ." This unusual permission had been granted because her husband was lying in bed helplessly paralyzed. The deed contains no mention of Walter Junior. He may have helped pay for the house, which was purchased for $1,840, without any mention of a mortgage—most unusual for a Whitman transaction. But we do not know, any more than we know where Mrs. Whitman got that much money. Of course, her other sons were working, and they may have helped. Possibly Walt did not, and this might account for some of the resentment implied in George's testimony. According to Walt's chronological record, the family moved to Ryerson Street in May, 1855,[183] so they could not have lost much time after the purchase of the new house. In view of the father's illness, the move must have been urgently necessary.

Perhaps under the circumstances Walt's family was not in a particularly sympathetic frame of mind when he carried home some copies of the freshly printed book. But it would have been a puzzle to them under any circumstances, as Walt himself was. George's words were: "I saw the book —didn't read it all—didn't think it worth reading—fingered it a little. Mother thought as I did—did not know what to make of it." [184] In this opinion, however, they were more typical than they could have realized themselves. For many years it was to remain one of the greatest puzzles in American literature.

◦§ V §◦

IN PATHS UNTRODDEN

In paths untrodden,

.   .   .   .   .

Escaped from the life that exhibits itself,
From all the standards hitherto published,
    from the pleasures, profits, conformities,
Which too long I was offering to feed my soul, . . .[1]

I

IMAGINATIVE critics have speculated that *Leaves of Grass* first went on sale
July 4, 1855,[2] but it is unlikely that the bookstores were open on that day.
On July 6 the following brief advertisement appeared in the New York
Tribune:

> WALT WHITMAN'S POEMS, "LEAVES OF
> GRASS," 1 vol. small quarto, $2, for sale by
> SWAYNE, No. 210 Fulton st., Brooklyn, and by
> FOWLER & WELLS, No. 308 Broadway, N.Y.

Four days later the name of Swayne was withdrawn from the advertisement, but Fowler & Wells continued to run the notice for a month. In
his old age Whitman recalled vaguely that some copies were displayed by
Dion Thomas on Nassau Street, near Spruce, in New York.[3] But evidently the phrenologists who had found poetic ability in their analysis of
Whitman's cranium were his main distributors. They also had a bookstore
in Boston and supplied it with copies too.[4]

In physical appearance the book was a thin quarto bound in green
cloth, with the title and border stamped in gold leaf. The back and front
covers were further ornamented with elaborate designs of leaves, buds,
and small flowers. The title itself sprouted fine roots and dangled leaves
in all directions. This ornate cover, however, was the most conventional

aspect of the book, for such fanciful bindings were common at the time.

If anyone opened the volume, and evidently only a few did, he encountered a steel engraved frontispiece portrait of a young man with good features and a short beard, standing in a nonchalant posture, right hand on hip and left in his trouser pocket, in shirt sleeves, collar unbuttoned, work jeans wrinkled, and on his head a felt hat cocked at a rakish angle. The engraving had been made by Samuel Hollyer from a daguerreotype taken one hot day in July of the previous year by Gabriel Harrison, a Brooklyn artist and friend of Whitman who had recently given up painting for the new art, photography. Whitman had placed the order for the engraving with Macrae in New York, but he was a mezzotint engraver, and this being a stipple job, he gave it to Hollyer, a stipple expert, to execute. Many years later, in a letter to a publisher, Herbert Small, Hollyer described his chance meeting with Whitman soon after the engraving had been finished:

. . . How I got the presentation copy of Leaves of Grass (1855) is this—shortly after the plate was out of my hands I was taking my frugal evening repast in a Fulton Street restaurant[;] it was not of a Delmonican order. Walt Whitman was taking his at the same table, somehow we entered into conversation—he was in his red flannel shirt—minus coat & vest and wore his broad brimmed felt hat with a rakish kind of slant like the mast of a schooner—I asked him how he liked his portrait[.] He smiled and asked me what I knew about it—I told him—he said it was all right but he would like one or two trifling alterations if they could be made[.] The next morning he brought the plate to my Studio in Trinity Buildings B[roa]d[wa]y, I made them to his entire satisfaction[.] One morning soon after he called on me with a package of Books, some dozen or so just from the Binders—and presented me with the first copy issued[.] [5]

On the title page, opposite the engraving, no author's name appeared, though on the verso one could see that the book had been copyrighted by "Walter Whitman." Then followed the preface, without title or heading of any kind, set double column in small type (eight-point, well spaced). This closely printed essay ran from pages iii to xii, and at a glance was formidable and unappealing. The poems, also untitled, covered pages 13 to 95. They were set in a more readable type (ten point, English), but the long irregular lines running clear across the wide page must have looked odd to anyone who took the trouble to read them in 1855.

Not very many, however, made the attempt—possibly as few as two or three dozen. Whitman had approximately one thousand copies printed,[6] but not all of these were immediately bound. Probably two or three hundred were bound in cloth, as described above, but some copies were bound in paper covers and were being advertised by Fowler & Wells several months later at the reduced price of $0.75.[7] Possibly the cloth-bound copies had been sold, but more likely Whitman and his distributors hoped that cheaper copies might sell better. Exactly what became of the first edition is still a mystery. A year later Whitman was to boast in a moment of self-advertising that the book "readily sold,"[8] yet in his old age he insisted that not a single copy was bought and that he himself kept only one copy.[9] The latter statements, however, seem about as exaggerated as the former, and the truth probably lies somewhere between. Indeed, the whole edition may have been disposed of in one way or another within a year, by sale in New York and Boston, by gifts of the author, and by free distribution by Fowler & Wells to critics and prominent authors. One complimentary copy was sent either by Whitman or his agents to Ralph Waldo Emerson, and this was to be the luckiest gift of all. But there was other disguised luck in the distribution of this first edition, for some of the copies sent to England for sale there found receptive readers, and thereby prepared the way for Whitman's British reception a little over a decade later.[10]

While Whitman anxiously waited for the verdict of the critics, his attention was distracted from his book by the death of his father on July 11. Walt, George, and Jeff were away when the crisis came. Exactly where we are not told, but they were near enough to be summoned to the bedside of their dying father, though George arrived only an hour before the end. Mary, farthest away, did not arrive in time. Hannah, still moving from boardinghouse to boardinghouse in Vermont, did not hear the news until about a week later when her mother wrote her a long letter full of details of the sickness and death, expressed in her own uneducated manner:

i sent for jeffy and sent for laura and walter came   they felt very much to blame themselves for not being home but they had no idea of any change your father had been [ill] so long and so many bad spells . . . mary took it very hard that she could not see her father   she was very sick coming from the evergreens where poor father was laid in a quiet spot . . .[11]

By "evergreens" Mrs. Whitman meant the Cemetery of the Evergreens, the principal cemetery in Brooklyn.[12] She also stated that the "babtist" minister presided at the funeral and prayed that the absent daughter might

receive the news of her father's death "with calmness and resignation."
Hannah's immediate response was a letter filled with self-pity and assurances of how much she loved her mother—they all leaned on the mother; none of the children ever expressed, so far as is known, a sense of dependence on their father. "I myself feel the need of comfort and sympathy," Hannah wrote. "It is hard, very hard, for me. I have more to regret than any of you, I feel it deeply." [13] But in her letter she actually did not mention her father in any way. She was so conscious of her own miseries resulting from her unhappy marriage that there was scarcely room in her thoughts for anything else. We may be sure that Walt read the letter and felt more sympathy than ever for his unhappy sister. She wanted to return to Brooklyn, and Heyde was quite willing for her to go; the implication was that he did not want her to return to him. But for some reason she did not go, either because her brothers did not send her money for railroad fare or because she secretly enjoyed her misery—subsequent letters were to reveal an unmistakable masochistic tendency.

The death of Walter Whitman, Sr., actually had very little effect, outwardly at least, on the life of his family. They continued living as they had for several years. Mary returned to Greenport, and George and Jeff to their jobs. What Jesse and Andrew were doing at this time is not known. Walt's attention returned, of course, to his recently printed book.

Meanwhile Emerson had received his copy of *Leaves of Grass* and he promptly read it through. On July 21 he wrote the author that he found it "the most extraordinary piece of wit and wisdom that America has yet contributed." [14] Here was the poet he had called for and predicted in his lectures and essays, and he impulsively sent Whitman his congratulations, in which he said among other flattering things:

I greet you at the beginning of a great career, which yet must have had a long foreground somewhere, for such a start. I rubbed my eyes a little to see if this sunbeam were no illusion; but the solid sense of the book is a sober certainty. . . .
I did not know until I, last night, saw the book advertised in a newspaper, that I could trust the name as real & available for a post office. I wish to see my benefactor, & have felt much like striking my tasks, & visiting New York to pay you my respects.

The visit was not to take place for some months, but Walt Whitman carried this remarkable letter around in his pocket all summer.[15] With such an endorsement, from so eminent a man of letters, he was thus armored against the most brutal onslaughts of the critics.

II

To understand Emerson's spontaneous and generous gesture we need to examine the actual contents of the book he had just read. His attention would have been caught first by the untitled preface, which contained much that he himself had been saying though expressed in new ways, and a good deal too that he had not said. At a glance Whitman's paragraphs resembled Emerson's own, deficient in transitions and logical order but strong in positive assertion, the logic implied in the grouping of concrete details and arrangement of imagery rather than in the correlation of ideas. Actually, this preface had more coherence and unity than the poems that followed it.

The preface began, "America does not repel the past or what it has produced under its forms or amid other politics or the idea of castes or the old religions." These were all to be accepted, assimilated, and then surpassed. Whitman was actually being more respectful toward the past than Emerson had been, but like Emerson he argued that cultural inheritances are good only for practical use, as the means of surpassing the achievements of all other nations in history. With this inheritance, and the advantages of the new land and opportunities, the possibilities for future development were unlimited. Hence, "The Americans of all nations at any time upon the earth have probably the fullest poetical nature." All human achievements of the past seem tame and orderly in comparison to the "largeness and stir" of this new land. "Here are the roughs and beards and space and ruggedness and nonchalance that the soul loves." But the "genius of the United States" resides most in its common people. In the half legendary, half mythical backwoodsman Davy Crockett, American folklore had already fused this theory of the influence of "space and ruggedness" on character with the myth of the "Common Man." To Whitman, of course, it was not myth but truth, and he wanted it expressed on the highest levels of art; not for the sake of art, however, but as a vital influence in forming a citizenry worthy of the land and natural resources: "The largeness of nature or the nation were monstrous without a corresponding largeness and generosity of the spirit of the citizen."

Whitman's own special contribution was his myth of the American poet, or poets, and he himself hoped to be the first example: "The American poets are to enclose old and new for America is the race of races. Of them a bard is to be commensurate with a people. To him the other continents arrive as contributions . . . he gives them reception for their sake and his own sake. His spirit responds to his country's spirit. . . . He incarnates its geography and natural life and rivers and lakes." [16]

This poet is properly called mythical because the expansiveness demanded is superhuman. Not only on him "rise solid growths" that correspond to the inventory of topographical and biological riches of the continent, but he will be capable of expanding with the growth of the nation, whether in its acquisition of new territory or in meeting new situations in the unforeseeable future, thus transcending the bounds of his own finite mind and experience. In fact, this poet is to be a sort of demi-god formed in part from America's vision of herself in all her wished-for power and moral perfection and in part from Whitman's memory of the virtues attributed to gods and heroes of other peoples and cultures. Whatever is most needed by his nation, this mythical poet will supply it, in peace or war, sickness or health, in national triumph or defeat. "If he breathes into any thing that was before thought small it dilates with the grandeur and life of the universe." [17] Paradoxically, "the others are as good as he, only he sees it and they do not."

The themes of this poet are to be "The land and sea, the animals fishes and birds, the sky of heaven and the orbs, the forests mountains and rivers," but he will not be satisfied with expressing the beauty and dignity of physical objects; his followers may depend upon him "to indicate the path between reality and their souls." Not only does he use language to mediate between matter and spirit, but he is a mediator in another way: he is a *time-binder*. (Whitman did not use this phrase, but it accurately describes his theory.) Quite literally the poet conserves the wisdom of the race and brings it to bear on the present and future: "Without effort and without exposing in the least how it is done the greatest poet brings the spirit of any or all events and passions and scenes and persons some more and some less to bear on your individual character as you hear or read. To do this well is to compete with the laws that pursue and follow time." [18] Time is all of a piece: "Past and present and future are not disjoined but joined." The poet must be able to intuit the real nature of time, and thus live emotionally and imaginatively in an eternal present. Then he can drag "the dead out of their coffins," stand them on their feet again, and say to the past, "Rise and walk before me that I may realize you"; he can place himself "where the future becomes the present." [19] Thus he "advances through all interpositions and coverings and turmoils and stratagems to first principles."

This concept of flowing time, and the ability of the greatest poet to immerse himself intuitively in it, had a profound effect on Whitman's style, even in his preface. In this prose (whole passages of which were later to be transferred to poems [20]) the images flow in almost uninterrupted procession, and even the cadences have a fluxional pulsation. In a series the "and" is repeated over and over again, or the comma is omitted (as in "animals fishes" and "forests mountains" in the preceding paragraph). The end of a given cadence is usually marked by dots (. . . .), which serve both as a caesura and to suggest a continuation of the thought: "The fruition of beauty is no chance of hit or miss . . . . it is inevitable as life . . . . it is exact and plumb as gravitation." [21]

Along with this concept of the unity of time, we also find a metaphysical equalitarianism that William James would later call "Pluralism." [22] "Did you suppose there could be only one Supreme? We affirm there can be unnumbered Supremes, and that one does not countervail another any more than one eyesight countervails another." The primary stress, however, is on the unity of the kosmos (Whitman's spelling), the oneness of time, nature, and of soul and body. The poet himself shall be a kosmos, symbolically harmonizing the diversity of forms and experiences, exemplifying by his every word and act the vital laws underlying and enclosing all existence. The cosmic poet, by his art and the harmony of his own life, must bring the body politic back to health. Out "of the float of the brain of the world" he will draw and use this integrating power.

At this point it is interesting to observe, as always with Whitman, the merging of his own self-consciousness, his literary ambitions, and his philosophical abstractions. Having turned his back on money-grubbing, he looked as disapprovingly as Thoreau on the prudential values cherished by most of his fellow citizens. But his own philosophy of "prudence" [23] consoled him in the belief that every event is linked to others, past and future, and no good action will ever be lost. Thus out of each of his failures will eventually come success.

Many of the basic doctrines in this preface could have come straight out of Emerson's own essay on "The Poet," and possibly they did. Emerson's poet also writes from experience and from intimate contact with physical things, and he too reveals the hidden truth that "the fountains whence all this river of Time and its creatures floweth are intrinsically ideal and beautiful." [24] Emerson's poet is likewise "representative" and "stands among partial men for the complete man, and apprises us not of his

wealth, but of the common wealth." His impressions of nature are theoretically as vivid as those of Whitman's poet: "Every touch should thrill."
And his form, too, is organic and analogous, for "things admit of being
used as symbols because nature is a symbol, in the whole, and in every
part." Even bare lists of words can be poetic to the excited imagination.
Perhaps most important of all, Emerson declares, "All that we call sacred
history attests that the birth of a poet is the principal event in chronology."
He describes the poets as "liberating gods." And he calls for a new poet
capable of celebrating the life of America and her "incomparable materials."

Whitman almost certainly read this appeal, but he had also read many
other romantic expressions of the same theory. Shelley in his *Defense of
Poetry*, for example, had elevated the poet to the dual position of legislator
and prophet. He too believed that, "A poet participates in the eternal, the
infinite, and the one; as far as relates to his conceptions, time and place
and number are not." And "Poetry, . . ." he said, "is at once the center
and circumference of knowledge; it is that which comprehends all science,
and that to which all science must be referred."

Much as his ideas resembled Emerson's, Whitman's temperament and
expression were basically different. Emerson, like Jonathan Edwards before
him,[25] saw nature always as a symbol of spirit, and even his most sensuous
descriptions remained somewhat abstract and intellectual. He was the lover
not so much of the universe as of the hidden soul of the universe, whereas
Whitman not only *felt* but *thought* sensuously. Emerson said, "We must
be warmed by the fire of sympathy to be brought into the right conditions
and angles of vision." [26] Whitman did not need to be warmed, and his
mind did not perform geometrically. During the months in which he
wrote the first edition of *Leaves of Grass* his imagination was constantly
super-heated by a secret volcano that threatened at any moment to burst
forth and overflow. In the preface this inner pressure was under control,
and as a consequence the literary form was disciplined to a much greater
degree than in the long dithyrambic, and unrepressed poems that followed. Emerson firmly believed that man and nature had become alien-
ated, and one of his fondest dreams was to recapture and to bring back to
a new generation the full vigor of that lost sensibility which man had enjoyed before the alienation. This same doctrine underlay Whitman's preface, but in the long poem that followed, later called "Song of Myself,"
Emerson found much of the sensibility which his inherited Puritan reserve
had never permitted him fully to experience himself.

III

Whitman's preface was undoubtedly hard going for most of his contemporary readers, but it must have been crystal clear in comparison to the first poem in the book, untitled, like the other eleven poems that followed. When it was later given the title "Song of Myself," that helped a little, though not much. It began intelligibly enough:

> I celebrate myself,
> And what I assume you shall assume,
> For every atom belonging to me as good belongs to you.[27]

But even this was misunderstood, and the poet himself was partly to blame, for despite his announced intention to celebrate himself as a representative man, the "I" of the poem is sometimes Walt Whitman blurting out personal confessions; sometimes a symbol of man, either modern or universal; and more often a personification of an animistic life-force, such as primitive minds before the dawn of history worshiped in the stallion, the bull, or some other god of fertility. The latter motif was entirely conscious and deliberate, for the poet declares,

> The bull and the bug [Egyptian scarab] never worshipped half enough,[28]

and in writing his poem he drew heavily on his accumulated knowledge of Egyptology and comparative religion.

But later in the poem the poet names himself and states what he regards as his personal attributes:

Walt Whitman, an American, one of the roughs, a kosmos,
Disorderly fleshy and sensual . . . . eating drinking and breeding,
No sentimentalist . . . . no stander above men and women or apart from them
    . . . . no more modest than immodest.[29]

Some of these characteristics the man actually possessed, though as we shall see on many a page of this biography, he often was a sentimentalist, his "breeding" was mainly if not wholly vicarious, and the balance between modesty and immodesty is open to grave doubt. Modesty was a crucial issue with his contemporary readers, for what appeared to them to be his immodesty was exactly what shocked them. Even Emerson had his second thoughts and consequent reservations.[30] And there was much in the poems to create doubt and confusion in the mind of the reader.

Friendly critics later tried to excuse the personal egotism, arrogance, and crudity by making for Whitman the same claim that Thoreau had made in *Walden,* that he boasted not of himself but for humanity; and throughout the remainder of his life Whitman was to claim that his first intention in *Leaves of Grass* had been to present himself as a representative American in the nineteenth century.

When he wrote "Divine am I inside and out" and "I dote on myself" [31] Whitman was, it is true, giving expression to actual characteristics of the American people during their great period of territorial expansion and material growth. In the 1855 *Leaves of Grass,* however, his personification of his country was not a major theme. "Song of Myself" might have been easier to understand if it had been. What was especially misunderstood was the use of sexual imagery to symbolize the doctrine of the equality and interdependence of body and soul, as when the poet "invites" his soul to come

Loafe with me on the grass . . . . loose the stop from your throat,
Not words, not music or rhyme I want . . . . not custom or lecture, not even
    the best,
Only the lull I like, the hum of your valved voice.

I mind how we lay in June, such a transparent summer morning;
You settled your head athwart my hips and gently turned over upon me,
And parted the shirt from my bosom-bone, and plunged your tongue to my
    barestript heart,
And reached till you felt my beard, and reached till you held my feet.[32]

Readers—both then and later—were disturbed not only by the sexual imagery, but the implication that the episode was somehow autoerotic, and many critics down to the present day have made biographical deductions from this passage.[33] What they have usually missed is that two problems are involved. One of these is what made Walt Whitman symbolize his concept of the union of body and soul in sexual terms. This is a problem for the psychoanalyst. The other problem is what the passage means in the context of the poem, and this the critic can answer: Whitman was dramatizing his doctrine that "a kelson of the creation is love," which the succeeding lines elaborate as the consequence of the mystical union:

Swiftly arose and spread around me the peace and joy and knowledge that pass
    all the art and argument of the earth;
And I know that the hand of God is the elderhand of my own,

And I know that the spirit of God is the eldest brother of my own,
And that all the men ever born are also my brothers . . . . and the women my
    sisters and lovers,
And that a kelson of the creation is love;
And limitless are leaves stiff or drooping in the fields,
And brown ants in the little wells beneath them,
And mossy scabs of the wormfence, and heaped stones, and elder and mullen
    and pokeweed.

This is one of the most magnificent passages in the literature of mysticism, conveying a sense of union with God, brotherhood with men and women, and sympathy with all living things, however small, lowly, or common. The whole passage has often been assumed to be an esoteric description of some physical experience, but there is no evidence that it was more than a fantasy creation—though to the poet Whitman had now become, that was real enough to have a life of its own. The term *mystic* has a variety of meanings. If by it one means a person who experiences hallucinations, hears voices, or goes into trances, then it does not apply to Whitman. But he was a mystic in the sense that intellectually and spiritually he believed *love* to be the creating, unifying, and life-giving principle of the universe, and as a poet he tried to illustrate this principle in visible analogies.

One of Whitman's major symbols was the grass, which he used both as imagery, for poetic structure, and as symbolism, for meaning.

A child said, What is the grass? fetching it to me with full hands;
How could I answer the child? . . . . I do not know what it is any more than
    he.[34]

As Epicurus had taught (according to Frances Wright in A *Few Days in Athens*), the *what* is unanswerable.[35] The mystic, too, finds his intuitions ineffable, but though Whitman does not know *what* the grass is, he can find poetic metaphors for it. Thus it is the "flag" of his disposition, "out of hopeful green stuff woven"; "it is the handkerchief of the Lord," with His signature in the corner; or is "itself a child . . . . the produced babe of the vegetation"; or "it is a uniform hieroglyphic," sprouting in all climates and zones—global, universal, cosmic. What above all it signifies is the eternal cycle of life, death and resurrection.

Homer had called the grass "the uncut hair of graves," and Whitman now expands this metaphor into some of the finest lines in his poem:

And now it seems to me the beautiful uncut hair of graves.

Tenderly will I use you curling grass,
It may be you transpire from the breasts of young men,
It may be if I had known them I would have loved them;
It may be you are from old people and from women, and from offspring taken
    soon out of their mothers' laps,
And here you are the mothers' laps.

This grass is very dark to be from the white heads of old mothers,
Darker than the colorless beards of old men,
Dark to come from under the faint red roofs of mouths.

Here the identity of the perceiver is less important than the truth perceived, which is that death is a human illusion:

What do you think has become of the young and old men?
And what do you think has become of the women and children?

They are alive and well somewhere;
The smallest sprout shows there is really no death,
And if ever there was it led forward life, and does not wait at the end to arrest it,
And ceased the moment life appeared.

All goes onward and outward . . . . and nothing collapses,
And to die is different from what any one supposed, and luckier.

These thoughts lead the poet to his desire to "merge," with all kinds of people in their varied experiences, with multiform reality of every sort, with the eternal stream of life itself, and thereby taste vicariously life, death, and immortality. On this level "Song of Myself" is one of the great lyrics in world literature.

But when the poet descends to the confidential tone, it is difficult to know whether the "I" is personal or symbolical, and this ambiguity has puzzled many of his readers from 1855 to the present:

> This hour I tell things in confidence,
> I might not tell everybody but I will tell you [the reader].[36]

And this ambiguity is still more disconcerting when the poet's lyric feeling for "the tender and growing night," the voluptuous "coolbreathed earth," and the amorous sea becomes increasingly urgent, sensuous, and orgiastic:

Prodigal! you have given me love! . . . . therefore I to you give love!
O unspeakable passionate love!

Thruster holding me tight and that I hold tight!
We hurt each other as the bridegroom and bride hurt each other.

You sea! I resign myself to you also . . . . I guess what you mean,
I behold from the beach your crooked inviting fingers,
I believe you refuse to go back without feeling of me;
We must have a turn together . . . . I undress . . . . hurry me out of sight of
    the land,
Cushion me soft . . . . rock me in billowy drowse,
Dash me with amorous wet . . . . I can repay you.[37]

One result of this "prodigal" and prodigious expenditure of vicarious
sexual emotion is the poet's defiant desire that through him the "forbid-
den voices" shall find expression:

Voices of sexes and lusts . . . . voices veiled, and I remove the veil,
Voices indecent by me clarified and transfigured.[38]

Throughout most of the nineteenth century this was the crux of most disapproval of Whitman and his poems. He insisted on removing the veil
from subjects outlawed by polite society from public sight or hearing.
Most twentieth century readers are in sympathy with his frankness and
honesty, but even they may find some confusion in the poet's treatment
of the most acute of his senses—touch. When he writes, "Is this then a
touch? . . . . quivering me to a new identity . . . ," [39] he evidently means
"the procreant urge of the world," mentioned earlier in the poem.[40] Whitman reveals a sense of guilt, however, when he cries out that he is "given
up by traitors" (that is, his senses), and that "on all sides prurient provok-
ers [are] stiffening my limbs."

I talk wildly . . . . I have lost my wits . . . . I and nobody else am the great-
    est traitor,
I went myself first to the headland . . . . my own hands carried me there.[41]

Many of these impassioned confessions and outcries of self-betrayal have
lyric power and beauty, but the general effect of them in the poem is to
give the reader the impression that the poet vacillates between sublimity
and pathos, between self-control and abandon, and consequent order and
disorder in his esthetic form. Another way to say this is that Whitman's

symbolical "I" is usually esthetically successful; his personal "I" less frequently successful—though he was never to attain this knowledge of his own poetry. Fortunately, he returned to the symbolical level toward the end of "Song of Myself," and was thereby able to end his poem triumphantly.

In his notebooks Whitman's thoughts about the soul were in the main abstract and impersonal: soul was equal but not superior to matter, yet it permeated all matter, and was eternal.[42] At times his thinking about the soul seems clearly, as implied in the previous chapter, to anticipate Bergson's *élan vital*, the life impulse that propels each generation of plant or animal through the cycles of existence, from the first crude germs to the most complex organism. Beginning especially with the portion of "Song of Myself" later numbered Section 31, the lyric "I" becomes this fluid and circling soul. The same "I" re-appears here and there in earlier parts of the poem, and overtones of the personal "I" persist to the end. But on the whole the last half of the poem gains tremendously in unity and power because the cosmic "I" predominates.

The cosmic "I" personifies the evolutionary process, the long journey of the forms of life which have finally culminated in man—and Walt Whitman specifically as a representative of man. (Here, and in this sense, the poet does become truly representative.) But what gives particular vividness to "Song of Myself" is the ability of the fanciful "I" to speed back and forth in time and space and view at will any stage of mankind on the spiral journey. This is notably effective in Section 33, in which the "I" flies "the flight of the fluid and swallowing soul." In this supernatural role the poet's "ties and ballasts leave him," his "elbows rest in sea-gaps," he skirts "the sierras," his palms "cover continents." With ease he looks down on the revolving globe with all its varied life and topography. He can also reverse the sequence of historical time and visualize dramatic scenes in the history of the nation, or in the history of the race, or the origins and stages of development of the forms of life. The time-binding function is performed with increasing success toward the end of the poem:

I am an acme of things accomplished, and I [am] an encloser of things to be.

My feet strike an apex of the apices of the stairs,
On every step bunches of ages, and larger bunches between the steps,
All below duly traveled—and still I mount and mount.[43]

Thus viewing life in its entirety, convinced of its purpose, unity, and perpetuity, the poet has no more fear of death than Lucretius had:

And as to you corpse I think you are good manure, but that does not offend me,
I smell the white roses sweetscented and growing,
I reach to the leafy lips . . . . I reach to the polished breasts of melons.

And as to you life, I reckon you are the leavings of many deaths,
No doubt I have died myself ten thousand times before.[44]

The "perpetual transfers and promotions" are the dominant theme as the poem nears its climax:

The past and present wilt . . . . I have filled them and emptied them,
And proceed to fill my next fold of the future.[45]

By the time he reaches the final lines the poet has outgrown the confused and crude ego exhibited earlier in the poem and he now becomes all soul:

I depart as air . . . . I shake my white locks at the runaway sun,
I effuse my flesh in eddies and drift it in lacy jags.

I bequeath myself to the dirt to grow from the grass I love,
If you want me again look for me under your bootsoles.

If he had stopped here, this would be "physical" (as opposed to "spiritual") pantheism, that is, the chemicals of the body going into plants and thus continuing to be a part of life. But the process involves more than this, for the beneficent soul or spirit of the departed still lives and influences or enters other persons.

You will hardly know who I am or what I mean,
But I shall be good health to you nevertheless,
And filter and fibre your blood.

Failing to fetch me at first keep encouraged,
Missing me one place search another,
I stop some where waiting for you.[46]

The "I" finally created in this poem resembles in many respects the god of primitive myth, such as in Egypt or Mesopotamia,[47] where the divine was comprehended as immanent and the gods were *in* nature—unlike the one God of the Old Testament who controls nature. Of course, Whitman did not literally create a myth, because that is a product of many minds, and probably can be formed only by primitive minds, which personify all abstractions because that is the only way they can comprehend them. True myth is a dramatization of nature. It is a form of poetry, yet it transcends poetry by proclaiming a truth. "Song of Myself" in its more successful aspects is also mythopoeic, for Whitman's imagery is a cloak for what he regards as profound truths about life and eternity. His myth is personal, however, in a more literal sense than in primitive myth, for it is the dramatized thought, experience, and wish-fulfillment of one ego. The final effect of "Song of Myself," therefore, is lyrical, and as a lyric it should be judged. It has passages which present dramatic scenes, but it has no plot; such narration as it has is episodic, and this only in a few spots. Yet despite its unevenness in structure and its ambiguities, "Song of Myself" will always remain one of Whitman's greatest lyrical achievements.

IV

None of the eleven untitled poems that followed the long poem in the 1855 *Leaves of Grass* was comparable to it in literary quality, but they are not without biographical and critical interest. In the second poem (later called "A Song for Occupations") the desire of the poet to make love to his readers is now expressed with undisguised clarity:

Come closer to me,
Push close my lovers and take the best I possess,
Yield closer and closer and give me the best you possess.

This is unfinished business with me . . . . how is it with you?
I was chilled with the cold types and cylinder and wet paper between us.

I pass so poorly with paper and types . . . . I must pass with the contact of
    bodies and souls.

I do not thank you for liking me as I am, and liking the touch of me I
    know that it is good for you to do so.

This sentimental impulse appears to result in the vicarious expression of emotions that had found insufficient or unsatisfactory outlets in physical reality. However, it also broadens into humanitarian sympathy, which is the "occupation" motif of the poem:

If you are a workman or workwoman I stand as nigh as the nighest that works
    in the same shop,
If you bestow gifts on your brother or dearest friend, I demand as good as your
    brother or dearest friend,
If your lover or husband or wife is welcome by day or night, I must be person-
    ally as welcome;
If you have become degraded or ill, then I will become so for your sake; . . .

    The poet's sympathy for men and women likewise extends to their en-
vironments, and thence to the whole cosmos:

There is something that comes home to one now and perpetually,
.   .   .   .
The sun and stars that float in the open air . . . . the appleshaped earth and
    we upon it . . . . surely the drift of them is something grand;
I do not know what it is except that it is grand, and that it is happiness, . . .

What is existence, and what is it for? The poet knows no more what it is
than he knew what the grass is, but he is intuitively certain that it is perfect, and that happiness is found in loving men and women:

In folks nearest to you finding also the sweetest and strongest and lovingest,
Happiness not in another place, but this place . . . . not for another hour, but
    this hour,
Man in the first you see or touch . . . . always in your friend or brother or
    nighest neighbor . . . . Woman in your mother or lover or wife,
And all else thus far known giving place to men and women.

This is neither philosophy nor religion—though the doctrine of love is
shared by all mystics. It is the lyric feeling of Walt Whitman, who could
think of no greater happiness than loving and being loved; that was the
totality of heaven to him.

    The third poem, later called "To Think of Time," comes nearer being
philosophical, though it has its basis in personal fact. The major theme is
fear of death. "Have you dreaded those earth-beetles?" Are you afraid that
after your death there will be nothing? Like Emily Dickinson a few
years later, Whitman feels deeply the pathos of losing his wonderful sense-
consciousness while nature goes on oblivious of the loss:

To think that the rivers will come to flow, and the snow fall, and fruits ripen
    . . and act upon others as upon us now . . yet not act upon us;
To think of all these wonders of city and country . . and others taking great
    interest in them . . and we taking small interest in them.

But unlike Emily Dickinson's lines (for example, "Safe in their alabaster chambers, . . . Ah, what sagacity perished here!"), there is no irony —or perceptibly little—in Whitman's lines. He can contemplate as cheerfully and stoically as Bryant in "Thanatopsis" the "Slowmoving and black lines [that] creep over the whole earth." Irony results from self-pity or loss of faith. The poet of this poem has complete faith that underlying birth and death is a process grander than life itself:

It is not to diffuse you that you were born of your mother and father—it is to
    identify you,
It is not that you should be undecided, but that you should be decided;
Something long preparing and formless is arrived and formed in you,
You are thenceforth secure, whatever comes or goes.

This cosmic process might be called "spiritual determinism":

The threads that were spun are gathered . . . . the weft crosses the warp
    . . . . The pattern is systematic.

"The guest [soul] that was coming . . . is now housed" in a body, and by the eternal laws as unalterable and dependable as gravitation will progress to other habitations. These are the spiritual and physical laws of a universe eternally in motion; everything must change, but the change is orderly, evolutionary. "We cannot be stopped at a given point," and death will be no final halt. But the immortality indicated here is more like the indestructible atoms of Leibniz than the survival of a personal identity, for "every thing has an eternal soul," even the trees "rooted in the ground," the weeds of the sea, and the animals.

In the fourth poem (later to be called "The Sleepers") the poet wanders all night in his vision, traveling around the globe with the ease of his cosmic flights in "Song of Myself." Here, more definitely than in any of the preceding poems, the imagery is unified by association of ideas, and the lyric "I" can enter the body of man or woman and experience their sensations and emotions. The experiences pictured in the flowing imagery are mainly those of dreams or the subconscious. A woman imagines that the dark is her truant lover coming to her and being passively received. An adolescent's clothes are stolen while he is asleep, and his sexual dreams make him feel ashamed and naked.

O hotcheeked and blushing! O foolish hectic!
O for pity's sake, no one must see me now! . . . . my clothes were stolen while
    I was abed,
Now I am thrust forth, where shall I run?

.   .   .   .

I feel ashamed to go naked about the world,
And am curious to know where my feet stand . . . . and what is this flooding
  me, childhood or manhood . . . . and the hunger that crosses the bridge
  between.

This is one of the most vivid passages in the whole poem, but when it was
that Whitman himself experienced "the hunger that crosses the bridge between" we can only guess. Nor need we assume that his clothes had actually been stolen while he was abed, though in the 1850's this was a common
experience of unsophisticates who visited the brothels of New York City.
Certain of these places were notorious for their sliding panels, behind
which hid pickpockets who worked with the co-operation of the "girls." [48]
It is of significance, however, that the sensations are symbolized in biological metaphors, "life-swelling yolks," milky juice of "rose-corn," [49] and
the phallic "tooth." These anticipate the leaves and roots of the later "Calamus" poems, and perhaps subtly imply an additional personal meaning
in the title of the book: the poet feels in himself the generative impulses
of nature seeking an outlet.

As the poem nears its climax the theme of "the sleepers" ascends, as
"Song of Myself" had done, toward the sublime. The poet finds the soul
"always beautiful" and the universe "duly in order." (The irony is entirely
unconscious and unintentional.) The "sleepers," too, are "very beautiful
as they lie unclothed" and "flow hand in hand over the whole earth," as if
in an apocalyptic painting by Blake or a drawing by the twentieth century mystic Kahlil Gibran. In the final lines the "I" becomes a soul migrating through the cycles of birth, death, and resurrection:

I will stop only a time with the night . . . . and rise betimes.

I will duly pass the day O my mother and duly return to you;
Not you will yield forth the dawn again more surely than you will yield forth
  me again,
Not the womb yields the babe in its time more surely than I shall be yielded
  from you in my time.

In the next poem ("I Sing the Body Electric") the poet is "en-
girthed" by the bodies of men and women and he engirths them. Like
Novalis, or the nineteenth century cult of the "Sacred Heart," [50] the main
doctrine here is:

If life and the soul are sacred the human body is sacred;
And the glory and sweet of a man is the token of manhood untainted,

And in man or woman a clean strong firmfibred body is beautiful as the most
    beautiful face.

If Walt Whitman could have kept to this lofty plane, his sex poems would
have been, as he hoped to make them, truly sane, wholesome, and religious. And he very nearly succeeds in this ambition in the following poem
on "Faces," though from a literary point of view it is not one of his best.
Here the poet has the magical power to see the soul behind the human
form. Even concealed by the face of the "slobbering idiot" in the asylum
he knows there is a soul unblemished by the faulty vessel, its temporary
abode:

> Spots or cracks at the windows do not disturb me,
> Tall and sufficient stand behind and make signs to me;
> I read the promise and patiently wait.

The "Song of the Answerer" (again using the later title) is a weak
treatment of one of the themes in the preface, the Messianic role of the
"great poet." He is the "answerer" who sends these miraculous "Signs":

Him all wait for . . . . him all yield up to . . . . his word is decisive and final,
Him they accept . . . . in him lave . . . . in him perceive themselves as amid
    light,
Him they immerse, and he immerses them.

The religiosity of this role has grown since the preface; at least this is the
effect of reading the book seriatim—whether it was composed before or
after the preface is anyone's guess. But this poem is more mystical than the
preface, and the next poem ("Resurgemus") ends with lines that almost
paraphrase the New Testament:

> Is the house shut? Is the master away?
> Nevertheless be ready . . . . be not weary of watching,
> He will soon return . . . . his messengers come anon.[51]

The remaining poems in the book may be dismissed briefly. "There
Was a Child Went Forth" is a neat lyric on the "incarnation" theme applied in both a psychological and a mystical manner. Every object the
child has seen or touched has become a part of him, not only momentarily
but "for many years or stretching cycles of years." Of special interest
is the picture of the mother as mild, loving, sympathetic; and the father
as "strong, selfsufficient, manly, mean, angered, unjust,/ The blow, the

quick loud word, the tight bargain, the crafty lure . . ." The poet desires that these things which have become a part of him shall in turn be absorbed by the readers of his poems, thus sharing once more his personal life with his unseen, symbolic "lovers." And in the following poem, "Who Learns My Lesson Complete," he announces to his reader that "my soul embraces you this hour," that is, as you read these lines.

The final poem in the first edition, "Great Are the Myths," is perhaps the weakest of all in composition, but it does underscore the pervading optimism of the 1855 *Leaves*. This optimism is emotional rather than intellectual, because the poet still insists that he does not know why the earth, nature, life, and death, good and evil, and everything else in existence, are "great"; he only knows intuitively that they are.

V

The first review of the 1855 *Leaves of Grass* appeared in the New York *Tribune* on July 23, possibly the day before Whitman received Emerson's letter (dated July 21). At that time Horace Greeley, editor of the *Tribune*, was in Washington, and Charles A. Dana wrote the review.[52] Whether he was personally acquainted with Whitman is not known, but the review was friendly and sympathetic. It contained generous quotations from both the preface and the poems, though neither the book nor the author was unqualifiedly praised. Whitman was called an "odd genius," anticipated by Emerson, and the critic added: "His language is too frequently reckless and indecent, though this appears to arise from a naïve unconsciousness rather than from an impure mind. His words might have passed between Adam and Eve in Paradise before the want of fig leaves brought no [sic] shame." But the poems were declared to be "certainly original in their external form, have been shaped on no pre-existent model out of the author's own brain," and "no impartial reader can fail to be impressed with the vigor and quaint beauty of isolated portions." Walt could hardly have claimed more for the poems himself, and indeed he was soon to admit some of the same faults mentioned by this *Tribune* reviewer— and possibly under his influence.

If Whitman had never before thought of his indebtedness to Emerson, this review and the almost simultaneous receipt of the letter from Concord might have been enough to convince him that he was indeed a true disciple—a relationship he actually did claim a year later. It is significant, too, that throughout the remainder of the summer the book attracted no further public attention, though in Concord Emerson continued to glow with approval and to recommend *Leaves of Grass* to his neighbors, Alcott, Thoreau, Frank Sanborn, and others; to his Boston friends; and to all and sundry who visited him. Probably Whitman did not know this at the time, but about the middle of September he was visited by an emissary straight from the sage himself. Moncure D. Conway, a former Methodist minister turned author, had spent an evening with Emerson in his home and had there heard of the marvelous book called *Leaves of Grass*.

On his return to Boston, Conway bought a copy of *Leaves of Grass* at the shop of Fowler & Wells, read it aboard the steamer to New York, and decided to visit the author, which he promptly did, and reported the experience to Emerson in a long letter dated September 17, 1855.

I found by the directory that one Walter Whitman lived fearfully far (out of Brooklyn, nearly), on Ryerton [Ryerson] Street a short way from Myrtle Avenue. The way to reach the house is to go down to Fulton Street Ferry [in New York], after crossing take the Fulton and Myrtle Avenue car, and get out at Ryerton Street. It is one of a row of small wooden houses with porches, which all seem occupied by mechanics. I didn't find him there, however. His mother directed me to Rome's Printing Office (corner Fulton and Cranberry Streets), which is much nearer, and where he often is.

I found him revising some proof. A man you would not have marked in a thousand [This opinion would not have pleased Walt!]; blue striped shirt, opening from a red throat; and sitting on a chair without a back, which, being the only one, he offered me, and sat down on a round of the printer's desk himself. His manner was blunt enough also, without being disagreeably so.

I told him that I had spent the evening before with you, and that what you had said of him, and the perusal of his book had resulted in my call. He seemed very eager to hear from you and about you, and what you thought of his book. He had once seen you and heard you in the lecture-room, and was anxious to know all he could of your life, yet not with any vulgar curiosity but entire frankness. I told him of the occasions in which Mr. Bartol and others had attempted to read it in company and failed, at which he seemed much amused.[53]

Conway wrote that Whitman looked much like the picture in his book: "His beard and hair are greyer than is usual with a man of thirty-six. His face and eye are interesting, and his head rather narrow behind the eyes; but a thick brow looks as if it might have absorbed much." The poet accompanied Conway back across the ferry to New York and seemed "hail fellow" to every man he met, at least of the laboring class. He said he was "personally dear to some thousands" of such men in New York, who "love him but cannot make head or tail of his book." Conway suspected

Whitman was guilty of "playing Providence a little with the baser sort," but he was delighted with the man, and thought him "clearly his Book."

Despite his nonchalance, Whitman by this time had decided that if his book was to receive further critical attention, he would have to provide the reviews himself, and the ethics of book reviewing were so vague or corrupt at the time that he had no difficulty in publishing three critical notices in September; in fact, he was probably encouraged by the editors to write the reviews. The *United States Review* (formerly the *Democratic Review*) printed a fairly long article on "Walt Whitman and His Poems," and the *American Phrenological Journal,* published by Fowler & Wells, printed a joint review of Tennyson's *Maud and Other Poems* and *Leaves of Grass.*[54] Then, on September 29, the Brooklyn *Times* printed a journalistic account of the poet and his book. All of these Whitman later admitted having written himself.[54a]

Since the poet thus put his own interpretations on record, they are worth examining for the light they may throw on his life—or at least the light he wanted thrown on it—and what he thought he had accomplished in his book. It is not surprising that the professional journalist would present himself in the Brooklyn *Times* as "Walt Whitman, A Brooklyn Boy," [55] and above all else stress the personality of the author who was already well known in his home town. In a very self-conscious way he tries to give a picture of himself as he would like to believe he is, though the result is practically a caricature of the intended self-portrait in "Song of Myself":

Very devilish to some, and very divine to some, will appear these new poems, the Leaves of Grass; an attempt as they are, of a live, naieve [*sic*], masculine, tenderly affectionate, rowdyish, contemplative, sensual, moral, susceptible and imperious person, to cast into literature not only his own grit and arrogance, but his own flesh and form, undraped, regardless of foreign models, regardless of modesty or law, and ignorant or silently scornful, as at first appears, of all except his own presence and experience, and all outside the fiercely loved land of his birth, and the birth of his parents and their parents for several generations before him.

The critical appraisal in the *United States Review* was written with a little more subtlety, but again the stress was mainly on the person: "An American bard at last! one of the roughs, large, proud, affectionate, eating, drinking, and breeding, . . . his postures strong and erect, his voice bringing hope and prophecy to the generous races of young and old." The lesson of this book: "We shall cease shamming and be what we really are." As for form: "The style of these poems . . . is simply their own style, new-born and red. Nature may have given the hint to the author of the 'Leaves of Grass,' but there exists no book or fragment of a book which can have given the hint to them."

As a matter of plain fact, this book was strewn with hints taken from other books—what book is not? It was astonishingly original in many respects, and despite the later attempts of numerous critics to find *the* source for *Leaves of Grass*, it was not based on one or a dozen sources; but it was Whitman's great achievement to fuse "hints" from hundreds of books with the authentic product of his own fantasy. In his preface he had acknowledged his and his country's indebtedness to the past; yet he now assumes a nationalistic contempt for all experiences except his own and the "land of his birth."

Although these self-created interpretations fairly represent many passages in the poems—indeed, paraphrase them—they do not do justice to the virtues of the first *Leaves of Grass*, its depth of thought, its religious mysticism, the beauty of much of its imagery, and the musical effects of many of the lines. As a whole the poems were often crude, more formless at first glance, and more genuinely naïve than the author could possibly have realized. Yet at the same time they were not produced by a semi-literate "child of nature," as Whitman liked to pretend. They had, as Emerson guessed, a vast foreground of reading and study and stylistic experimentation. Much of this naïveté is simply a pose, and such parading of the poet's "roughness" and sensuality cannot help arousing our suspicions. Was he really so sure of his masculinity? But be that as it may, this was the image that Walt Whitman wanted above all else to create of himself. And it was the image that most of his critics—friends and foes alike—were to accept for many years.

Of these three reviews, the most judicial and least personal was the one in the *American Phrenological Journal*. The main contrast made here between Tennyson as the representative poet of a decadent civilization and Whitman as the poet of a new, more vital civilization, was an overly simplified generalization; yet Whitman did show a genuine appreciation of Tennyson's merits. He seemed aware also of his own daring in assuming that he, the author of this first book of poems, could be compared at all with Tennyson—"Do you think the best honors of the earth are won so easily Walt Whitman?"—and anticipated the shudders that his egotism would cause. Still more perceptive, he foresaw the difficulties that readers would have with his structure, in "which every sentence and every passage tells of an interior not always seen." It is, he thinks, a truly new technique and a subtler one than had ever before been used in poetry, and he predicts that this poet will "prove either the most lamentable of failures or the most glorious of triumphs, in the known history of literature." Perhaps there were no more sincere words in this self-review than the confession of its author's "inability to decide which . . . it is likely to be."

But other critics were not slow in making up their minds. An anonymous reviewer in the September *Putnam's Magazine* called the book "a mixture of Yankee transcendentalism and New York rowdyism." [56] (Nearly everyone saw in it the influence of Emerson or transcendentalism, or both.) This reviewer did admit "an original perception of nature, a manly brawn, and an epic directness." But he was shocked by the mixture of slang, original coinage, and literary vocabulary, the confusion of the levels of usage often rendering "an otherwise striking passage altogether laughable." And concerning the self-portrait in "Song of Myself": "That he was one of the roughs was . . . tolerably plain; but that he was a kosmos is a piece of news we were hardly prepared for."

Considering the fact that the first *Leaves of Grass* was privately printed and was being distributed by a firm more interested in a pseudo-science than in literature, it is surprising that it so quickly received this much attention—even allowing for the three self-written reviews. Had Whitman not been an experienced journalist with many friends and acquaintances in the field and an intimate knowledge of the inside of an editorial office, he could not have "worked the angles" so shrewdly. But perhaps in some ways he worked them too shrewdly, as when his publicity sense caused him to permit Dana to print Emerson's letter, without permission, in the *Tribune* on October 10. Later he wanted to blame Dana for over-persuading him,[57] but this was a feeble excuse. More plausible was Whitman's statement on another occasion that he supposed the letter was intended for him to use as an endorsement of the book. Perhaps it was really a question of etiquette rather than of ethics, and the indiscretion could be regarded as a consequence of Whitman's indifference to the social amenities. One confirmation of this interpretation is the fact that he clipped the printed letter out of the newspaper and inserted it in copies of his book which he sent to other prominent literary men, including Longfellow.[58] Had he realized what a *faux pas* he was committing he would hardly have perpetrated it in Cambridge, so near Concord. Nevertheless, however interpreted, the printing of Emerson's letter was shrewd publicity tactics, and Emerson did not protest directly, though to Samuel Longfellow he remarked that Whitman had "done a strange rude thing in printing in the Tribune . . . my letter of thanks for his book." [59] But Emerson was not too angry to visit Whitman several times, probably for the first time on December 11, scarcely two months after the indiscretion. Apparently it was Whitman's subsequent use of the letter and protests that continued to pour in on Emerson from friends, relatives, and strangers that finally made him regret having written so impulsively.

Some of the reviewers also gave Emerson cause for reflection on his endorsement. On November 10 the *Criterion* announced that it would have ignored the book except for Emerson's letter. "An unconsidered letter of introduction has often-times procured the admittance of a scurvy fellow into good society," but the *Criterion* reviewer (probably R. W. Griswold) [60] seemed determined not to let this happen with Whitman, because he declared that the book "strongly fortifies the doctrines of Metempsychosis, for it is impossible to imagine how any man's fancy could have conceived such a mass of stupid filth, unless he were possessed of the soul of a sentimental donkey that had died of disappointed love." Nearer home to Emerson, the Boston *Christian Examiner* labeled the poems "impious libidinousness." [61] But on the other hand, Edward Everett Hale praised *Leaves of Grass* in the *North American Review*, at that time published in Boston, for its "freshness, simplicity, and reality," and gave the opinion that "there is not a word in it meant to attract readers by its grossness." [62] The more genteel poets, like Longfellow, Holmes, and Lowell, were never to find anything to admire in *Leaves of Grass*. Whittier is said to have thrown into the fire the complimentary copy that he received—probably with the *Tribune* clipping in it. Yet on the whole Boston and New England were actually more receptive to the book than was New York. Of course, Whitman did not know that Charles Eliot Norton of Harvard had written the *Putnam's* review,[63] though it is doubtful whether he could have appreciated the praise which was so nicely balanced by shocked condemnation. And it was still more impossible for the poet to know of even warmer praise—though also modified by as serious reservations—in a letter that Professor Norton had written to his colleague, James Russell Lowell, on September 23, 1855, saying "there are things in it that you will admire." Norton, however, egregiously misjudged what Lowell was capable of admiring.[64]

Reviewers were also stimulated by Whitman's odd manner of publication and the publicity resulting from his printing of Emerson's letter. For example, the *National Intelligencer* (Washington, D.C.) gave Whit-

BROOKLYN VILLAGE IN 1817: FRONT AND FULTON STREETS

From an oil painting by Francis Guy, courtesy of the Brooklyn Museum

WALTER WHITMAN, SENIOR
From a daguerreotype

LOUISA VAN VELSOR WHITMAN
From a daguerreotype

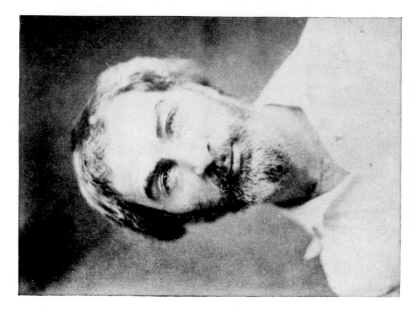

WALT WHITMAN, c. 1854
Courtesy of Walt Whitman House, Camden, N.J.

WALT WHITMAN, c. 1841
Courtesy of Walt Whitman House, Camden, N.J.

WALT WHITMAN, 1880
From a photograph by Gutekunst, Philadelphia

WALT WHITMAN, 1863
From a photograph by Gardener, Washington, D.C.

man's book a long review on February 18, 1856, although the paper had not received a review copy. This critic found *Leaves of Grass* "in every way a singular volume," but he was better prepared than most reviewers to comment on its singularity. "Holy Writ informs us that 'all flesh is grass,' which according to quaint old Sir Thomas Browne, is just as true literally as metaphorically. . . . Hence, it will be seen that 'grass' is what Mr. Whitman calls a 'uniform hieroglyphic' of the whole human family, and as such deserves to be scanned by the minute philosopher." The critic doubted that the poet had read either Spinoza or Plato, but he was sure that Whitman was both a pantheist and a Platonist "in the rough," who believed in the "immanence of all in each."

One of the most interesting of all the admirers of the first *Leaves of Grass* Whitman could not have known about at the time, and probably never knew, though some years later he heard that this man, Abraham Lincoln himself, had read his poems. Henry B. Rankin, a law student in the office of Lincoln and Herndon in Springfield, Illinois, recounts these details:

When Walt Whitman's *Leaves of Grass* was first published it was placed on the office table by Herndon. It had been read by several of us and, one day, discussions hot and extreme had sprung up between office students and Mr. Herndon concerning its poetic merit, in which Dr. Bateman engaged with us, having entered from his adjoining office. Later, quite a surprise occurred when we found that the Whitman poetry and our discussions had been engaging Lincoln's silent attention. After the rest of us had finished our criticism of some peculiar verses and of Whitman in general, as well as of each other's literary taste and morals in particular, and had resumed our usual duties or had departed, Lincoln, who during the criticisms had been apparently in the unapproachable depths of one of his glum moods of meditative silence . . . took up *Leaves of Grass* for his first reading of it. After half an hour or more devoted to it he turned back to the first pages, and to our general surprise, began to read aloud . . . His rendering revealed a charm of new life in Whitman's versification. Save for a few comments on some broad allusions that Lincoln suggested could have been veiled, or left out, he commended the new poet's verses, for their virility, freshness, unconventional sentiments, and unique forms of expression, and claimed that Whitman gave promise of a new school of poetry.[65]

One evening Lincoln took the book home with him, and when he returned it next morning he remarked that he "had barely saved it from being purified by fire by the women." (Probably Whittier's copy was not the only one that did perish in that fashion.) At Lincoln's request the book was left on a table in the office, and we are told that he frequently picked it up and read aloud from it.

This is only one of many stories which indicate that some of the first *Leaves of Grass* did get widely distributed. Some were even circulated in England, through Horsell and Company, Oxford Street, London, representatives of Fowler & Wells. Horsell sent review copies to London newspapers and magazines, and during the winter of 1856–1857 *Leaves of Grass* received almost as much critical attention in England as it had in America, with about the same proportion of motley praise and scorn. How many copies Horsell received we do not know, but apparently far more than he could sell, for after a few months they were remaindered to an itinerant peddler, through whose efforts copies reached persons who later were to champion the cause of the book and spread sympathy for the author in Great Britain.[66]

VI

Whitman's association with Fowler & Wells in the distribution of the 1855 *Leaves of Grass* also resulted in his becoming active in journalism again for nearly a year. The phrenologists published a weekly magazine in New York called *Life Illustrated*, and between November 1, 1855, and August 30, 1856, Whitman contributed to it frequently, on a wide variety of subjects, ranging from the opera, the Egyptian Museum, the hypocrisy of Grace Church, the poor architecture of workingmen's houses, and the slave trade operating out of New York and Brooklyn harbors, to the English language ("America's Mightiest Inheritance") and the life of Voltaire.[67]

Perhaps the chief importance of Whitman's connection with *Life Illustrated*, however, was the support and publicity that it gave to his book. On April 12, 1856, for example, he was praised as "more a DEMOCRAT than any man we have ever met," and his poems as expressing "the very soul of democracy." [68] A week later this magazine reprinted a review by William Howitt from the London *Dispatch*, which the editor of *Life Illustrated* introduced with the incorrect statement that, "Walt Whitman's 'Leaves of Grass' have been republished in England." [69]

In Howitt's review we can see once again the effect of Whitman's use of Emerson's letter: "What Emerson has pronounced to be good must not be treated lightly . . ." Howitt did have some reservations about the

style and versification, but he ended with the bold prophecy that Whitman's "poems in time will become a pregnant textbook, out of which quotations as sterling as the minted gold will be taken and applied to every
form and phase of the 'inner' or the 'outer' life . . ." (One wonders what
kind of critic would so mix his figures.) This prophecy, which was to be
amply fulfilled after the poet's death, was so exactly what Whitman would
have liked that one cannot help being a little suspicious, and this suspicion is increased by the comments a few months later in the *Saturday Review* (London, March 15, 1856): "We have received a volume, bound in
green, bearing the title *Leaves of Grass*, under rather singular circumstances. Not only does the donor send us the book, but he favors us with
hints—pretty broad hints—toward a favorable review of it." [70] Did the author, or someone through his agency, drop similar hints to the *Dispatch?*

Whatever the source, the reprinting of the London *Dispatch* review impressed one of the most popular American journalists of the time, the highest paid purveyor of sentimental pap, the incomparable Fanny Fern, cur-
rently writing for the New York *Ledger*. Her real name was Sarah Payson
Willis Parton, sister of N. P. Willis, a well-known critic and third-rate poet.
In 1856 she was living in Brooklyn with her third husband, James Parton, who had recently published a *Life of Horace Greeley*,[71] the first of a
series of excellent biographies. In the *Ledger* on May 10 Fanny Fern
gushed:

. . . Walt Whitman, the effeminate world needed thee . . . It were a spectacle worth seeing, this glorious Native American, who, when the daily labor of
chisel and plane was over, himself, with toil-hardened fingers, handled the types
to print the pages which wise and good men have since delighted to endorse
and to honor . . . Where an Emerson and a Howitt have commended, my
woman's voice of praise may not avail . . . I confess that I extract no poison
from these "Leaves"—to me they have brought only healing. Let him who can
do so shroud the eyes of the nursing babe lest it should see its mother's
breast.[72]

This review, at least, was not written by Whitman himself. It was promptly
reprinted in *Life Illustrated*, which continued throughout the summer to
publish and re-print notices favorable to him.

For nearly a year Whitman had been preparing a new edition of his
poems—he was reading proof when Conway met him in the printing office, in September, 1855. Some time during the intervening months

Fowler & Wells had agreed to finance the new edition, and on August 16, 1856, *Life Illustrated* announced that it would be ready by September 1. In view of the many uncertainties as to what happened to the first edition, perhaps this announcement deserves quotation in full:

It is evident that the American people will give a hearing to any man who has it in him to reward attention. Walt Whitman's poems, the now famous "Leaves of Grass," would scarcely have been thought likely to become speedily popular. They came before the public unheralded, anonymous, and without the imprint of a publisher. The volume was clumsy, and uninviting, the style most peculiar, the matter (some of it at least) calculated to repel the class whose favorable verdict is supposed to be necessary to literary success. Yet the "Leaves of Grass" found purchasers, appreciators, and admirers. The first edition of a thousand copies rapidly disappeared, and we now have the pleasure of announcing that a second edition, with amendments and additions, is about to be issued. The author is still his own publisher, and the Messrs. Fowler and Wells will again be his agents for the sale of the work. The new edition will be a neat pocket volume of four hundred pages, price, as before, $1. It has been stereotyped. Copies will be ready about the first of September.

Walt Whitman has thus become a fixed fact. His message has been found worthy of regard. The emphatic commendation of America's greatest critic has been ratified by the public, and henceforth the "Leaves of Grass" must receive respectful mention, wherever Americans are reckoning up those of their country's productions which could have sprung into existence nowhere but in America.[73]

Several of these statements must certainly be taken with the traditional grain of salt. Perhaps the various Fowler & Wells bookstores did manage by one means or another to dispose of the copies they had in stock; a considerable number seem to have been given away, though this may have been good advertising. But certainly "the public" had not "ratified" Emerson's "commendation," and only a handful of Americans—most of these friends of Emerson—would have counted *Leaves of Grass* among "their country's productions."

Even the statement about the improvement of the second edition over the first in physical make-up and appearance is open to question. The second, a thick little volume about four by six and a quarter inches in size, was more compact and portable. Perhaps the paper was also a little better in quality, but the cover, green like the first, was similarly decorated with floral designs and was no more attractive. The wide page of the first edition was particularly appropriate for the long lines of Whitman's poems, and even with the smaller type in the new edition the majority of the lines had to be run over—as was to be done in all subsequent editions in the poet's lifetime.

Whitman conspicuously flaunted Emerson's letter in the 1856 edition. On the backstrip, in bold gold-leaf letters, were the words: "I Greet you at the/ Beginning of A Great Career/ R. W. Emerson." At the end of the poems, under the heading of "Correspondence," was the text of Emerson's now famous letter, followed by a reply addressed to the poet's "Master." It began: "Here are thirty-two Poems, which I send you, dear Friend and Master, not having found how I could satisfy myself with sending any usual acknowledgment of your letter." This professed devotion was not necessarily insincere. After all, Emerson had been the main encouragement of the new poet, and the cause of most of his other encouragement; without that letter there might not have been a second edition.

With more questionable veracity Whitman continued: "The first edition, on which you mailed me that till now unanswered letter, was twelve poems—I printed a thousand copies, and they readily sold; these thirty-two Poems I stereotype, to print several thousand copies of." By whatever means the first edition was disposed of, it did not "readily sell," nor is it likely that "several" thousand copies were being printed of the second— though Whitman may have expected a demand for additional printings from the stereotype plates. In fact, he was probably not so much deliberately distorting the facts as letting his exuberance and wishful dreams outrun his judgment. "Other work I have set for myself to do," he continued, "to meet people and The States face to face, to confront them with an American rude tongue . . ." This was another of Whitman's illusions; for many years he continued to cherish the plan of carrying his message by word of mouth to the American people, but he was no orator, and would never become one. He was right when he added, "but the work of my life is making poems"; however, he continued to defy the gods with his pride and fateful optimism: "I keep on till I make a hundred, and then several hundred—perhaps a thousand. The way is clear to me. A few years, and the average annual call for my Poems is ten or twenty thousand copies—more, quite likely." Not even Emerson's poems ever sold like that, though Longfellow's and Whittier's did, and the audience for their poems would never be interested in Whitman's.

The remainder of the open letter to Emerson was taken up with a restatement of Whitman's theory of the American poet, who was to found a native literature, and a defense of his subject matter. American greatness is still not actual, but latent, he declares. "Up to the present . . . the people, like a lot of large boys, have no determined tastes, are quite unaware of the grandeur of themselves, and of their destiny, and of their immense strides . . ." America is still only a "divine true sketch."

Walt Whitman feels himself divinely called to fill out and help complete this "sketch." One of his methods is to be an honest, truthful expression of sex—"the eternal decency of the amativeness of Nature"—which he thinks "is so far quite unexpressed in poems." There was unintended irony in this bold intention of the professed disciple of Emerson, for if there was one subject on which Emerson was reticent, it was sex.

The erratic judgment displayed in this "answer" to the Master is also visible in many parts of the second *Leaves of Grass*. Most of the revisions in the twelve old poems are improvements in diction, rhythm, and imagery, and among the new poems is one of Whitman's finest, "Sun-Down Poem" (better known as "Crossing Brooklyn Ferry"). As a whole the new collection shows growth in lyric power and literary technique. But the expansive mood of the poet causes him to choose titles so pretentious and cumbersome as to be ludicrous. For example: "Poem of the Daily Work of the Workmen and Workwomen of These States" (later called "Song for Occupations"), "Poem of Wonder at the Resurrection of Wheat" ("This Compost"), and the prize title of the book—"Liberty Poem for Asia, Africa, Europe, America, Australia, Cuba, and the Archipelagoes of the Sea"!

Some of the new poems are little more than prose statements of general ideas. One of the most deficient in rhythm and imagery is the second of the new edition, "Poem of Women" (later "Unfolded Out of the Folds").

Unfolded only out of the folds of the woman, man comes unfolded, and is always to come unfolded,
.   .   .   .
A man is a great thing upon the earth, and through eternity—but every jot of the greatness of man is unfolded out of woman.
First the man is shaped in the woman, he can then be shaped in himself.

Obviously this composition was one of Whitman's efforts to justify his claims to being the poet of procreation, but it was a surface attempt to poetize an idea.

Although in his 1855 preface Whitman had called for a poet capable of "incarnating" the North American continent and the life of everything on it, his nationalism had not been jingoistic. In the past few months, however, he had been "promoting" himself as a uniquely American poet. These claims, combined with his expansive and overconfident mood of 1856 resulted in a blatant and arrogant nationalism in this second edition. A major example of this is "Poem of Many in One" (later "By Blue Ontario's Shore"). The title has two meanings: (1) one nation composed of many states, and (2) this composite to be symbolized by the poet who identifies his life with the multiform life of his nation so that the one "I" speaks for all the people of the nation.

Of course, the United States in the mid-1850's was itself a paradox. The young nation was already a house divided, with the tragic split only a few years ahead, but the patriotism generated by the "manifest destiny" sentiment of the previous decade still survived. William Gilmore Simms in South Carolina was no less nationalistic than James Fenimore Cooper in the North. The Democratic party, still in power, was unable or unwilling to take any steps toward solving the problem of slavery, but it hoped, as did most Americans, to export its democratic idealism to Europe and other continents. A further complication was that the defenders of slavery in the South were angling for foreign support—especially from Great Britain—and this increased the anti-European sentiment of Free-Soilers like Whitman. So furious was the ideological and sectional hatred that some members of Congress carried revolvers and loaded canes, and Charles Sumner, Senator from Massachusetts, was almost beaten to death in the Senate chamber by a Congressman from South Carolina. If at this period Whitman's nationalism was especially hectic, we should remember that he was afflicted by pressures from without and within, political and psychological.

"Poem of Many in One" is also a confused poem because Whitman attempted in it to unify his thoughts and moods of two different periods— though separated from each other by little more than a year. Many passages of the 1855 preface he carried over intact into this poem, but he attempted to fill them out and link them together by new passages. The preface began, "America does not repel the past or what it has produced. . . ." These products were to be absorbed, used, and improved upon. Whitman had no doubt that the destiny of his nation was to be more glorious in achievement than anything history had ever known before. But in that national dream he was not so provincial, fatuously self-sufficient, or isolationist as in his new nationalism of 1856:

A nation announcing itself,
I myself make the only growth by which I can be appreciated,
I reject none, accept all, reproduce all in my own forms.

A breed whose testimony is behaviour,
What we are, we are—nativity is answer enough to objections;
.   .   .   .
How dare a sick man, or an obedient man, write poems?

America shall make her own standards; if these are only "native," that
will be good enough. It must be admitted, however, that recklessness,
lawlessness, and violence were all too obvious in American character—
perhaps a product of the Revolution, frontier life, and the phenomenal
expansion of the young nation. American literature from the folk tales of
Davy Crockett, the stories of Mark Twain, and the characters in the
novels of Hemingway and Faulkner all bear testimony to these national
traits. Even in his delusion that space made the nation impregnable,
Whitman was realistically expressing the psychology of his countrymen,
then and later:

America, curious toward foreign characters, stands sternly by its own,
Stands removed, spacious, composite, sound . . . .

Yet despite her own spaciousness and the distance separating her from
the older nations, America was already sick from the canker gnawing
her vitals. Whitman was becoming aware of this fact, but he believed
there was health-restoring power in his own natural passions, which tallied
the basic forces of Nature herself:

I swear I have had enough of mean and impotent modes of expressing love for
    men and women,
After this day I take my own modes of expressing love for men and women.

I swear I will have each quality of my race in myself,
Talk as you like, he only suits These States whose manners favor the audacity
    and sublime turbulence of These States.

This does not contradict the sentiment and imagery found so abun-
dantly in the 1855 "Song of Myself," now repeated here:

I match my spirit against yours, you orbs, growths, mountains, brutes,
I will learn why the earth is gross, tantalizing, wicked,
I take you to be mine, you beautiful, terrible, rude forms.

Thus arrogant nationalism, audacity of style, and a rudeness symbolizing nature blend and finally characterize the new verses in this poem. The unity of the poem as a whole remains sadly deficient, but the additions plainly reveal the dominant state of mind of the poet and his nation in 1856. The mood is so similar to the boasting in the open letter to Emerson that we may guess "Poem of Many in One" to have been composed (or patched together) in the spring or even early summer of 1856.

The most successful poems in the second edition are those in which Whitman escaped from the confining themes of his personal life and the American nation into the freedom of time and space on the cosmic scale. The first of these is "Poem of Salutation" ("Salut au Monde"). The motif makes no advance over similar flights of the poetic "I" in the first edition, but the poem is notably successful in its empathy:

What widens within you, Walt Whitman?
.   .   .   .
Within me latitude widens, longitude lengthens,
.   .   .   .
What do you see, Walt Whitman?
.   .   .   .
I see a great round wonder rolling through the air,
I see diminute farms, hamlets, ruins, grave-yards, jails, factories, palaces, hovels,
        huts of barbarians, tents of nomads, upon the surface,
I see the shaded part on one side where the sleepers are sleeping, and the sunlit part on the other side,
I see the curious silent change of the light and shade,
I see distant lands, as real and near to the inhabitants of them as my land is
        to me, . . .

Here the incarnation of geography is no longer a theory but an esthetic fact. In these flights the poet visualizes the steamships, railroads, harbors, canals, and highways around the globe. The history of the race comes alive on the projection screen of his fantasy as he evokes the forms of worship, the shrines, temples, sacrificial grounds, and the ancient gods themselves walking in human form. He sees each being, custom, habitation, and activity as inevitable—limitless—eternally supported by the earth —one no less divine than the other. All are equal in the poet's universal democracy: Hottentot "with clicking palate," outcast "koboo," peon of Mexico, Russian serf, and American dweller on farm or in the city. No nationalism here.

Shifting from the photomontage, the poet imagines himself turned to vapor and carried by the winds to distant continents, where he falls as rain. Thus in vision he traverses the rivers of the globe, stands on the bases of peninsulas, and seeps down to imbedded rocks. He longs to penetrate and be absorbed by all parts of nature, all people, all experience, to become, as it were, a disembodied soul:

> What cities the light or warmth penetrates, I penetrate those cities myself,
> All islands to which birds wing their way, I wing my way myself,
> I find my home wherever there are any homes of men.

But powerful and sustained as the "Poem of Salutation" is, it is far surpassed by "Sun-Down Poem" ("Crossing Brooklyn Ferry"), the masterpiece of the first two editions. Here the poet transmutes his own dream life and personal experience into esthetic form. The imagery is real, rising vividly out of the poet's own memory, but the sentiment and the intuition transcend the actual. For the first time Whitman has everything under control—theme, imagery, rhythm, and symbolism—a feat which he would be able to repeat in major poems only two or three times during the remainder of his life. How or why this miracle suddenly took place, who can say? But it is significant that for once he was able to discipline his emotions; the poem is, in fact, a masterly demonstration of self-control, and shows what Whitman might have done if self-control had not been so difficult for him. Some time between the printing of the two editions he must have attained a momentary emotional and spiritual equipoise. We do not know precisely when this happened; we have only the poem to prove that it did.

Like Emerson in his mystical experience on a bare common in winter time on a cloudy day, the setting of this poem would seem at first glance to be unpromising: a ferry crossing the East River, with the grimy docks lining both shores and the turbid waves slapping against barges and ships of all descriptions—not to mention the floating garbage and refuse from two careless cities. But Walt Whitman's eyes did not rest on these realistic details. One of his most enjoyable diversions was crossing by ferry from his native city to fabulous, exciting Manhattan. Whitman loved both cities, the water surrounding them, and the hordes of people who shuttled back and forth each day on the ferry, like souls journeying from one eternity into another. (He was undoubtedly acquainted with Thomas Cole's allegorical paintings, "Voyage of Life," and may have received unconscious hints from them.) The trip, the water, the sunlight, time and place yielded him the symbolism he needed for his work of art. The time of day is particularly important: flood-tide, half an hour before sunset, the ferry freighted with humanity. As the poet crosses and recrosses in memory and imagination the mystic truth comes to him that:

It avails not, neither time nor place—distance avails not,
I am with you, you men and women of a generation, or ever so many generations
     hence,
I project myself, also I return—I am with you, and know how it is.

The imagery of the crossing shifts with the seasons: in December, the sea-gulls floating high in the air; in summer, the rays of the sun on the waves; and in all seasons the ships arriving and departing, and sailors at work in the rigging of other ships at anchor. Always change, always activity, going and coming; like the eternal cycle of life, death, and birth again.

The scallop-edged waves in the twilight, the ladled cups, the frolicsome crests
    and glistening,
The stretch afar growing dimmer and dimmer, the gray walls of the granite
    store-houses by the docks,
.   .   .   .
I too had been struck from the float forever held in solution,
I too had received identity by my body,
That I was, I knew was of my body, and what I should be, I knew I should be of
    my body.

The shadows that fall on the waters have their counterpart in the poet. For a moment only the poet of the ebullient second edition confesses the doubts that he has secretly harbored about his poems:

The best I had done seemed to me blank and suspicious,
My great thoughts, as I supposed them, were they not in reality meagre? Would
    not people laugh at me?

Whether vicariously or through experiences of which we have no record, or more likely in a sudden intuition of his inner nature, the poet feels sure he knows what it is to be evil: "The wolf, the snake, the hog, not wanting in me"; whatever guilty thoughts or sly intentions others have had, he has had the same.

The esthetic marvel is the balance of tensions in the poem, both the subjective and objective forces which the poet employs and controls to the last line: the distant sky and the sun and the nearby water, the tall masts of Mannahatta and the beautiful hills of Brooklyn; far and near, up and down, past and future, beginning and end, body and soul, life and death—and resurrection. The poet enjoys so much the experience of crossing on the ferry that he would like it to last forever, and time to stand still: "Suspend here and everywhere, eternal float of solution!" But he also wants to complete the experience and the cycle, to join the men and women who shall come after him, both those who shall make the ferry trip (and the allegorical journey) as he is doing, and those who will share the experience esthetically through his poem. Thus the river of time must flow on, and the poet invokes it to flow. The paradox is resolved by the thought that life is always in solution, souls forever crossing and recrossing from mortality to immortality and back again; and esthetically by the work of art itself. The poem is a ferry—as the poet, the "time-binder" is also—shuttling across time, carrying the poet and his reader side by side. This was the final satisfaction to Walt Whitman, the psychological motive of his best lyrics.

No other new poem in the second edition was as successful as the "Brooklyn Ferry" lyric, but the "great companions" theme of "Poem of the Road" ("Song of the Open Road") deserves mention. Here the poet feels himself charged with a magnetic force—"the fluid and attaching character"—that flows out to strangers, or even to inanimate objects, drawing and attaching him to them, and them to him:

The efflux of the soul comes through beautiful gates of laws, provoking questions,
These yearnings, why are they? these thoughts in the darkness, why are they?
Why are there men and women that while they are nigh me the sun-light expands my blood?

Why are there trees I never walk under but large and melodious thoughts descend upon me?

What is it I interchange so suddenly with strangers?
What with some driver as I ride on the seat by his side?
What with some fisherman, drawing his seine by the shore, as I walk by and pause?

The efflux of the soul is happiness—here is happiness,
I think it pervades the air, waiting at all times,
Now it flows into us—we are rightly charged.

Here rises the fluid and attaching character;

. . . .

Toward it heaves the shuddering longing ache of contact.

Allons! Whoever you are, come travel with me!

This is plainly the beginning of the "Calamus" or homoerotic motif of the next edition of the *Leaves*, but the yearning and "longing ache" for contact is not yet pathological, and the poet can rationalize it as a natural force like electricity (or more accurately "animal magnetism," so much discussed at the time)[74] that charges not only himself but all things, sunlight and trees as well as people. The pathetic tone is entirely absent in this poem. "The efflux of the soul is happiness," and the poet is overflowing with this efflux.

Although "Clef Poem" (No. 15) is a minor lyric in this edition, it is quite literally the "key" poem to Whitman's characteristic mood in the 1856 poems. He calls it, with his typical hyperbole, a philosophical intuition of the nature and meaning of the cosmos. But as usual, it is really a clue to his emotional state at the time of writing the poem. Because he feels that no happiness could surpass the life he now enjoys—and this is very significant—he asserts that a "vast similitude" spans and interlocks all "identities" [that is, beings] that have existed or may exist in any part of the universe. Walt Whitman's optimism can reach no greater height. With Pope he believes that this is the best of all possible worlds, and "Whatever is, is right."

In another minor but nevertheless very important poem in the second edition, "Poem of the Last Explanation of Prudence" (taken over in part from the 1855 preface), we have a still more effective treatment of the poet's teleology—a kind of mystic determinism. As noted in an earlier chapter,[75] Whitman's "prudence" was long-range, Epicurean in the true sense of the term: a sacrifice today may bring more lasting happiness tomorrow; or to paraphrase Whitman (and the New Testament) he who loses his life may gain eternal life; or a defeat may be a victory in disguise.

All day I have walked the city and talked with my friends, and thought of
    prudence,
Of time, space, reality—of such as these, and abreast with them, prudence.

After all, the last explanation remains to be made about prudence,
Little and large alike drop quietly aside from the prudence that suits
    immortality.

The soul is of itself,
All verges to it, all has reference to what ensues,
All that a person does, says, thinks, is of consequence,
Not a move can a man or woman make, that affects him or her in a day, month,
    any part of the direct life-time, or the hour of death, but the same affects
    him or her onward afterward through the indirect life-time.

The indirect is more than the direct,
The spirit receives from the body just as much as it gives to the body, if not
    more.

Not one word or deed—not venereal sore, discoloration, privacy of the onanist,
    putridity of gluttons or rum-drinkers, peculation, cunning, betrayal, mur-
    der, seduction, prostitution, but has results beyond death, as really as before
    death.

Critics were later to say that Whitman made no allowance for evil in his philosophy, yet he showed in this poem that he was well aware of the cumulative effect of good or bad deeds. The doctrine of prudence was as inexorable as the predestination and eternal justice of his Puritan ancestors.

With this doctrine of prudence as a philosophical background, it is interesting and revealing to examine Whitman's handling of sex themes in the second edition. As we have noticed in his letter to Emerson, he had emphasized the honest treatment of sex as necessary in a vital, democratic literature. Actually, however, sex is not as prominent in this edition as it had been in some of the poems of the first edition. Of the 1856 poems, the first on a sex theme is "Poem of Women," which merely asserts the obvious truism that the body of man is first shaped in the body of woman, and that he must then shape his character for himself. It is in no sense an erotic poem. And even the "Poem of Procreation" merely teaches that "Sex contains all" and celebrates the procreative instincts and acts as necessary in the cycle of "birth, life, death, immortality." The poet as a symbol of "robust husband" engrafts on tanned women— supple, strong, athletic—"a thousand onward years" (the law of prudence again). As D. H. Lawrence has said of Whitman's women, they are "muscles and wombs. They needn't have faces at all." They certainly have no faces in this poem, which images an idea, not a sensuous experience.

The remaining poem on a sexual theme in the second edition, with the bizarre title "Bunch Poem," is also rather programmatic. In the opening lines the sex of the "friend I am happy with," arm hanging idly over the shoulders of the poet, is not stated. But there is not the slightest suggestion that the companion is a woman, or for that matter, a lover, except for the sexual imagery that follows. In this imagery the emotions are more autoerotic than anything else. The poet calls his phallus "a poem," and all nature is sexual, from the hairy bee that curves on "the full-grown lady-flower" to the "wet of the woods." Other images vividly suggest "The torment—the irritable tide that will not be at rest," but this is simply blind instinct. The poet warns himself, in fact, against the "meanness of me should I skulk or find myself indecent, while birds and animals never skulk or find themselves indecent . . ." The poem ends with these lines:

The oath of procreation I have sworn,
The greed that eats in me day and night with hungry gnaw, till I saturate what
    shall produce boys to fill my place when I am through,
The wholesome relief, repose, content,
And this bunch plucked at random from myself,
It has done its work—I toss it carelessly to fall where it may.

The ending explains to some extent the odd metaphor for semen, but the random plucking of the "bunch" and tossing it "carelessly to fall where it may" seems very strange for a poet who believes in the eternal laws of "prudence." Whitman might have explained this by posing his other doctrine of the goodness of all life, and since the poet in his god-like way assumes that his semen is not only sound but endowed with a mystic potency, what difference does it make so long as the women are "fit for conception"? Still, the two attitudes do not seem altogether reconcilable and they constitute a paradox in the author of the first two editions: that is, the poet of "prudence" versus the poet of untamed nature, whose behavior shall be as lawless as animals in the rutting season. He had not made up his mind or did not know whether sex meant to him primarily an instinctive hunger or responsible paternity, and the confusion was to be even more pronounced in the third edition. If he had aspired to be only a lyric poet this confusion would not be so important as it is for a poet who longs to be a moral and social leader, as Whitman had announced in his 1855 preface.

To end the second edition Whitman chose one of his 1855 poems, "To Think of Time," which he now called "Burial Poem." As the final poem in the volume, it now has special significance, for the poet intends not to suggest death and burial but immortality:

I swear I think there is nothing but immortality!
That the exquisite scheme is for it, and the nebulous float is for it, and the
    cohering is for it!
And all preparation is for it! and identity is for it! and life and death are for it!

Not all poems in this second edition, as we have seen, accord with this resurrection theme, but his best poems and his strongest lyrical passages are those in which he displays his cosmic feeling for time, space, and eternity. He chose his most appropriate poem, therefore, for the end of his book. However, it had not been written for this purpose, and the choice was an improvisation, as indeed his whole arrangement was.

With this 1856 edition *Leaves of Grass* had proved itself a hardy perennial, but many seasons of growth would yet be necessary before it could reach maturity.

◦§ VI §◦

EMBLEMATIC BLADES

Come, I am determined to unbare this broad breast
    of mine—I have long enough stifled and choked;
Emblematic and capricious blades . . . you hide in
    these shifting forms of life, for reasons . . .[1]

I

WHILE the second edition of *Leaves of Grass* was going through the press during the summer of 1856 momentous events were taking place in the nation, and Walt Whitman was acutely aware of them. Perhaps, in fact, he had never been more deeply concerned for the fate of "These States," though in many of his new poems his exaggerated nationalism disguised the anxiety. This was a presidential election year, and even before the political conventions met in June public excitement and emotional tension had already reached an almost tragic intensity and bitterness.

This tension had been rapidly increasing since the Democrats had won the presidential election of 1852, to Whitman's intense disgust, by their coalition with the slavery interests of the South. In that election the Whigs had avoided a definite stand on slavery and had been so utterly crushed that their party was now dead. In the same election a new party, the local American or Native American, though generally called "The Know Nothing" party, had put up a national ticket. They had not won wide support, but they were still on the scene in 1856. Their primary objectives were to oppose the Roman Catholic Church in the United States and to elect only native-born Americans to office. Their political aims, however, were supposed to be secret, and to all questions from outsiders they replied that they knew nothing; hence the name. They were not concerned over the issue of slavery. The Republican party had been organized in 1854, but it had not yet become effective on a national scale, and thus no strong political group had appeared to oppose the pro-slavery Democrats.

The result of the election of Franklin Pierce in 1852 had been in effect to permit the South to dominate both Congress and the Presidency. Despite the fact that the free states in the North and West were potentially stronger in votes and financial resources than the slave states, the latter still managed by intimidation and political intrigue to control the National Assembly and a weak President. But they realized how precarious their hold on the nation was, and Southern politicians were extremely aggressive in trying to find some means to check and offset the Northern power. They talked of, and even tried to start, revolutions in Central America, and twice attempted to purchase Cuba in order to gain slave territory.

Meanwhile the pro-slavery Democrats managed in 1853 to pass the Kansas-Nebraska bill, and President Pierce signed it. This bill abolished the recent Compromise of 1850, which had sanctioned slavery in those states where it already existed but forever outlawed its extension to the new territory. It created two new territories out of the Nebraska territory and declared that the "Compromise" did not apply to them. Senator Stephen A. Douglas of Illinois, one of the sponsors of the Kansas-Nebraska bill, also promulgated at this time the doctrine of "squatter sovereignty," which held that settlers in the two territories must decide for themselves whether they would be slave or free. As a consequence both the slave states and the Northern states in which abolition sentiment was strongest began desperately rushing settlers into Kansas and Nebraska. Missouri, a slave state, tried forcibly to prevent the Northern emigrants from crossing, but they simply detoured through Iowa. When elections were held in the new territories the slave interests sent in bands of armed voters from Missouri and Arkansas, and of course bloodshed resulted. In fact, by 1856 Kansas was already practically in a state of civil war. Federal troops had been sent in supposedly to keep order but actually, under President Pierce's encouragement, to aid the pro-slavery forces. These, in brief, were the circumstances that created the highly charged atmosphere that the whole nation breathed when the parties met in 1856 to nominate their choices for the Presidency.

The Democrats held their convention on June 2 in Cincinnati and adopted as their platform: (1) a strict construction of the Constitution (this meant "states rights" and the return of fugitive slaves to their owners), (2) support of the Kansas-Nebraska bill, and (3) "squatter sovereignty." For their Presidential candidate they nominated James Buchanan, who as Secretary of State under Polk had made the first attempt to purchase Cuba, and as minister to Great Britain under Pierce had failed in the second attempt.

When the Know-Nothing or Native American party held their convention, they nominated Millard Fillmore. Elected Vice President by the Whigs in 1848, he had filled out Zachary Taylor's term after his death in office and had signed the Fugitive Slave Act of 1850. As in 1852, this party took no stand one way or the other on slavery.

To oppose the pro-slavery and the Know-Nothing parties, many of the former Whigs and a remnant of the Free-Soil Democrats had formed in 1854 a new party which they called the Republican. On June 17 the Republicans held their convention in Philadelphia and adopted a platform consisting mainly of the prohibition of slavery in the territories (the principles of the Wilmot Proviso, the support of which had cost Walt Whitman his editorship of the Brooklyn *Eagle* in 1848). The Republicans nominated for the Presidency John C. Frémont, the much-publicized Western explorer and colorful abolitionist. The slavery question would now be carried directly to the American voters.

We shall see how deeply concerned Walt Whitman was with the problems raised by these political conventions. Only one poem in the new edition of *Leaves of Grass* directly reflected the political climate of 1856, and that was probably already in type before June, but it plainly revealed Whitman's detestation of the political outlook of this period. With sarcasm very rare for him he declared in the poem which he first (1856) called "Poem of the Proposition of Nakedness," later "Respondez!," and finally discarded:

Let all the men of These States stand aside for a few smouchers! Let the few
    seize on what they choose! Let the rest gawk, giggle, starve, obey!
Let shadows be furnished with genitals! Let substances be deprived of their
    genitals!
Let there be wealthy and immense cities—but through any of them, not a single
    poet, saviour, knower, lover!
Let the infidels of These States laugh all faith away! If one man be found who
    has faith, let the rest set upon him! Let them affright faith! Let them
    destroy the power of breeding faith!
Let the she-harlots and the he-harlots be prudent! Let them dance on, while
    seeming lasts! (O seeming! seeming! seeming!)
Let the preachers recite creeds! Let them teach only what they have been taught!
Let the preachers of creeds never dare to go meditate candidly upon the hills,
    alone, by day or by night! (If one ever once dare, he is lost!)
Let insanity have charge of sanity!

In his journalistic writing during the spring and early summer Whitman avoided politics, and even for some weeks after the convention he seems to have cogitated in secret. The article which he wrote for *Life Illustrated* on how New York celebrated the Fourth of July (published July 12) [2] revealed indirect social criticism, though it contained no specific allusions to politics. Here he described with great vigor and clarity the unthinking and indifferent manner in which New Yorkers observed the anniversary of American Independence. Several days before the Fourth small boys began igniting firecrackers, and the noise steadily increased until, "On the evening of the Third, the nuisance is terrific; and for that night hardly anybody but an experienced old commodore or brigadier can sleep . . . This bombardment lasts in an intermittent state for some time after Independence Day, and dies off when the young artillerists can no longer replenish the military chest."

On the Fourth in 1856 there was a showy but confused parade in the mud produced by heavy rain in the early morning, a speech at Union Square dedicating Henry Kirke Brown's equestrian statue of Washington, a carnival atmosphere on the wet streets, large boys recklessly shooting pistols into the air, fireworks at night, and a huge consumption of lager beer, until finally "the blaze and sputter and whirl and fizz and whizz and bang is over," and the tired laborers prepare for another day's hard work. "The anniversary has fallen to . . . an occasion of aimless parades and noise and tumult; of tiresome, empty ceremony, and wasteful expenditure. The value and pleasure of the day, at least in this city, is hopelessly gone, unless its observance be reformed."

As for reform, Whitman would abolish the silly parades, have addresses "by the best speakers—not the poorest, as now," have fireworks, perhaps, for those who want them, "and let the remainder of the community 'celebrate' for themselves, as on a great day of hereditary national thanksgiving and pride, with rustic festivals and friendly hospitality, with public triumphs, if spontaneous, but not by chilly management of squabbling civic authorities . . ."

Two days after this article was published, the New York *Herald* printed an editorial that apparently re-aroused Whitman's interest in the slavery problem. The title of the editorial was "The Slave Trade—Fitting Out Vessels in the Port of New York," [3] and it listed the names of eighteen ships engaged in the slave trade that had sailed from New York in the past three years. This trade had been illegal since 1808, with death as the penalty for violation, but not one person had been executed and the

Herald pointed out that from 1845 to 1854 only five arrests had been made—with no convictions. During this period the slave trade had become more profitable than ever because of the increased demands for slaves on the Cuban sugar plantations, where the average life of a Negro was five years.

One of the vessels mentioned by the *Herald* was the *Braman*, then tied up in the Brooklyn Navy Yard while its owners awaited trial. Whitman promptly got permission from the United States Marshal to visit the ship; and it was probably from the deputy marshals, whose names he courteously mentioned in his article, that he obtained the essential facts for his exposé, which he labeled simply "The Slave Trade." This was published in *Life Illustrated* on August 2 as the third in the "New York Dissected" series." [4]

Whitman began his article with this italicized statement: "*It is safe to say that two or three slavers per month have fitted out and sailed from New York for the last ten years.*" After a few sentences he added: "Until the official term of the present faithful and energetic United States District Attorney, Hon. John McKeon, there seems to have been hardly any attempt to interfere with it . . . Within a few days last past, two more slavers have succeeded in leaving New York for Africa, and all along they have been slipping off at the rate of a dozen or twenty for every one caught." Most of the owners, Whitman stated, were Spanish or Portuguese, but Americans were guilty of assisting in fitting out the ships and indirectly sharing in the profits. He then gave explicit details of exactly how these operations were carried on, how much they cost, what the profits were—about nine hundred per cent—and how the Federal Court in New York permitted the culprits to escape with very light penalties or none at all. The main remedy, he explained, was the appointing of honest and competent officials and holding them responsible for the discharge of their duties. The implication was that corrupt judges were mainly to blame.

About this time Whitman probably also wrote a more ambitious treatise on the political aspects of contemporary slavery and the attempts of 350,000 slaveowners in the South to inflict their selfish will on thirty million American citizens. He called this essay "The Eighteenth Presidency!" subtitled "Voice of Walt Whitman to Each Young Man in the Nation, North, South, East and West." Exactly what Whitman intended to do with it is not altogether clear, for it exists only in a set of proof sheets now preserved in the Library of Congress, and so far as known it was never published during the poet's lifetime.[5] It did not endorse Frémont, and though Whitman's position was much nearer that of the Republicans than of the Democrats or Native Americans, his words show that he regarded himself as independent of all parties, and it was doubtless this very independence that prevented his getting this work circulated.

Read today without regard to the political situation in the summer of 1856, the language of "The Eighteenth Presidency!" seems violent and overly emotional. But the better one knows the period, the more pertinent and just he will find Whitman's words. In fact, if the audience Whitman hoped to reach could have read this pamphlet—which was apparently the mode of publication he intended—they might have found it a very useful primer on the theory of democratic government, how that theory was being frustrated and perverted, and how they might yet achieve the democratic government envisioned by the Founding Fathers. But Whitman was trying to reach this audience over the heads of all party organizations, and this was impractical and naïve. Thus he not only failed to convince; he failed to get any hearing whatever.

"First, Who Are the Nation?" Whitman asked. After effectively contrasting the total population of the nation with the small number of slaveowners who managed to control the political party still in power, he declared: "At present, the personnel of the government of these thirty millions, in executives and elsewhere, is drawn from limber-tongued lawyers, very fluent but empty, feeble old men, professional politicians, dandies, dyspeptics, and so forth, and rarely drawn from the solid body of the people." He believed that these conditions could be corrected only by electing a different class of men to office: "I expect to see the day when the like of the present personnel of the governments, federal, state, municipal, military and naval, will be looked upon with derision, and when qualified mechanics and young men will reach Congress and other official stations, sent in their working costumes, fresh from their benches and tools, and returning to them again with dignity."

As Whitman looked around he could not observe anywhere in politics "a single bold, muscular, young, well-informed, well-beloved, resolute American man, bound to do a man's duty, aloof from all parties, and with a manly scorn of all parties." Although this indictment may have been deserved, the naïve assumptions in this theory are obvious. First of all, Whitman had oversimplified the functions of government. He did not understand that training and experience were necessary for the holder of an executive office (though throughout their history the American people have often failed to realize this fact, too). He assumed that any honest, intelligent carpenter or farmer could step into the governorship or Presidency and discharge his duties with efficiency. But granting that such a genius and moral paragon existed, how could he be found and brought to the attention of the voters without a political organization? However admirable Whitman's idealism, he still did not have even a rudimentary understanding of practical politics.

He was, looking back with the perspective of a century later, entirely justified in his contempt for the sixteenth and seventeenth terms of the Presidency, and he was absolutely right that there was something wrong with a political system that could nominate Buchanan and Fillmore. He addressed himself to "Butchers, Sailors, Stevedores, and Drivers of Horses—to Ploughmen, Wood-Cutters, Marketmen, Carpenters, Masons, and Laborers—to Workmen in Factories—and to all in These States Who Live by Their Daily Toil"—it sounds like the title of one of his 1856 poems!—and warned that "What the so-called democracy are now sworn to perform would eat the faces off the succeeding generations of common people worse than the most horrible disease. The others are contributing to the like performance, and are using the great word Americanism without yet feeling the first aspiration of it . . ."

Perhaps Whitman had hopes for Frémont, for he condemned only two of the three parties, but instead of begging the working people to vote for the Republican candidate, he directed a plea to Frémont to rise to the occasion and become "the Redeemer President." Earlier in the treatise Whitman had described his ideal candidate:

I would be much pleased to see some heroic, shrewd, fully-informed, healthy-bodied, middle-aged, beard-faced American blacksmith or boatman come down from the West across the Alleghanies, and walk into the Presidency, dressed in a clean suit of working attire, and with the tan all over his face, breast, and arms; I would certainly vote for that sort of man, possessing the due requirements, before any other candidate.

Although Frémont might have claimed some of these characteristics, this hardly seems a description of him, and if Whitman had so intended it he would very likely have so labeled it. It came nearer being a prophecy of the candidate of the Republican party four years later, but at the time it was doubtless a product of Walt Whitman's imagination.

Although in the summer of 1856 Whitman must have favored the Republican candidate more than any of the others, some of his views were still Democratic. For example, to the question "Must Runaway Slaves Be Turned Back?" Whitman answered, "They must." A section in the fourth article of the federal Constitution specifically stated that "any person held to service or labor in one State under its law, and escaping into another State, shall not be absolved from service by any law of that other State, but shall be delivered up to the persons to whom such service or labor is due." To Whitman the Constitution was sacred and every section must be observed "in spirit and in letter." He regarded slavery as wrong, but until abolished by the action or consent of the states, the Constitution must not be violated even to combat slavery. He was as strict a constructionist as Senator Douglas himself—whom in fact he did continue to admire for several years.

Despite Whitman's political impracticality, he was a true prophet in these words addressed "To the Three Hundred and Fifty Thousand Owners of Slaves":

Suppose you get Kansas, do you think it would be ended? Suppose you and the politicians put Buchanan into the Eighteenth Presidency, or Fillmore into the Presidency, do you think it would be ended? I know nothing more desirable for those who contend against you than that you should get Kansas. Then would the melt begin in These States that would not cool till Kansas should be redeemed, as of course it would be . . . not one square mile of continental territory shall henceforward be given to slavery, to slaves, or to the masters of slaves—not one square foot. If any laws are passed giving up such territory, those laws will be repealed. . . . what laws are good enough for the American freeman must be good enough for you . . .

Here Whitman sided wholly with none of the party platforms of 1856—or at least with none of the Presidential candidates, for Frémont not only wanted to keep the territories free but he was also an outright abolitionist. Curiously, however, Whitman drew the line precisely where Lincoln was to draw it four years later.

Toward the end of his pamphlet Whitman extended this invitation "To Editors of the Independent Press and to Rich Persons":

Circulate and reprint this Voice of mine for the workingmen's sake. I hereby permit and invite any rich person, anywhere, to stereotype it, or re-produce it in any form, to deluge the cities of The States with it, North, South, East and West. It is those millions of mechanics you want; the writers, thinkers, learned and benevolent persons, merchants are already secured almost to a man. But the great masses of the mechanics, and a large portion of the farmers, are unsettled, hardly know whom to vote for, or whom to believe. I am not afraid to say that among them I seek to initiate my name, Walt Whitman, and that I shall in future have much to say to them. I perceive that the best thoughts they have wait unspoken, impatient to be put in shape; also that the character, power, pride, friendship, conscience of America have yet to be proved to the remainder of the world.

But no "wealthy person" answered this invitation. Did Whitman not know that the wealthy, like the merchants, were "already secured almost to a man"? And no editor of an independent newspaper was likely to adopt this private platform of Walt Whitman, the new poet—if he was a poet; the question had not yet been settled. This is one of the most revealing documents that Whitman ever wrote—one of the most eloquent and yet also pathetic in its naïveté. His treatise did not clearly enough endorse Frémont to appeal to the Republicans, there was no leader of the "independent vote," Whitman had no newspaper or magazine of his own to use for such a purpose, and no miracle produced a wealthy friend to subsidize his pamphlet.

II

One of Walt's mother's most devoted Brooklyn friends was Mrs. Abby Price, who moved to Brooklyn with her husband, Edmund Price, and their four children in 1856, living first at 31 Hicks Street, lower Fulton.[6] Mr. Price operated a pickle factory at 314 Front Street, the street on which the Whitmans had first lived in Brooklyn. It is not known how Mrs. Price and Mrs. Whitman became acquainted, though it may have been through Walt, who could have been attracted to Mrs. Price through her speaking and writing, for she had been very active during the past decade in several reform movements, including Anti-Slavery, Woman's Rights, and Dress Reform. Walt became a frequent visitor at the Prices', and henceforth counted Mrs. Price and her daughter Helen as two of his best friends.

According to Helen Price a "Mr. A." [John Arnold] was "living with his daughter's family [name not given], who occupied with us the same house . . . He was a Swedenborgian, not formally belonging to the church of that name, but accepting in the main the doctrines of the Swedish seer as revealed in his works." He and Whitman often discussed and argued Swedenborgianism, without "the slightest irritation between them." [7] They also frequently discussed democracy, Arnold believing that "among the masses are to be found only here and there individuals capa-

ble of rightly governing themselves," while of course Walt, despite current
political failures, stoutly maintained his faith in the ability of the masses
to govern themselves. Whitman, Miss Price says, was not "a smooth, glib,
or even a very fluent talker." He hesitated, chose his words slowly, and
listened more than he talked, but this family group liked him so much they
encouraged him to express his ideas. Although Walt's own mother was devoted to him, one gets the impression that the Prices gave Whitman a
substitute home, an affectionate circle in which, unlike his own family,
he was made to feel that he honored them by reading one of his poems
aloud.

The Prices, simple folk themselves, did not regard Whitman's manner
of dress as an affectation or especially eccentric. "We all thought that his
costume suited him, and liked every part of it except his hat. He wore a
soft French beaver, with rather a wide brim and a towering crown, which
was always pushed up high. My sister would sometimes take it slyly just
before he was ready to go, flatten the crown, and fix it more in accordance
with the shape worn by others. All in vain; invariably on taking it up his
fist would be thrust inside, and it would speedily assume its original
dimensions."

The report of one of Whitman's conversations with the Prices reveals a
reserve in him that throws light on the friendship sentiments in some of
his poems in the first two editions of *Leaves of Grass*:

He once (I forget what we were talking about—friendship, I think) said
there was a wonderful depth of meaning ("at second or third removes," as he
called it) in the old tales of mythology. In that of Cupid and Psyche, for instance; it meant to him that the ardent expression in words of affection often
tended to destroy affection. It was like the golden fruit which turned to ashes
upon being grasped, or even touched. As an illustration, he mentioned the
case of a young man he was in the habit of meeting every morning where he
went to work. He said there had grown up between them a delightful silent
friendship and sympathy. But one morning when he went as usual to the office,
the young man came forward, shook him violently by the hand, and expressed
in heated language the affection he felt for him. Mr. Whitman said that all
the subtle charm of their unspoken friendship was from that time gone.

The incident with the "young man" could have taken place at any of several printing or newspaper offices, but may have been at the *Eagle*
office.

Whitman discussed music with Mrs. Price, books with Helen, and politics with "Mr. A.," but, according to Helen, "it was in talking with my

mother on the spiritual nature of man, and on the reforms of the age and kindred themes, that he took special delight." Both mother and daughter thought that Whitman's "leading characteristic" was his "religious sentiment," and many years later Helen Price said that he was basically the most religious person she had ever known.

Whitman disliked being lionized, and Mrs. Price had difficulty in persuading him to come to her house when he thought she might be trying to show him off. But sometimes he did consent to meet strangers, and there made the acquaintance of Hector Tyndale (brigadier general during the Civil War), who became a loyal friend. On another occasion he met at Mrs. Price's a person about whom he had heard a great deal from surprising sources:

Some months after our first meeting with Mr. Whitman, my mother invited Mrs. Eliza A. Farnum (former matron of Sing Sing prison) to meet him at our house. In the beginning of conversation he said to her, "I know more about you, Mrs. Farnum, than you think I do; I have heard you spoken of often by friends of mine at Sing Sing at the time you were there." Then turning to Mr. A., who sat near by, he added in a lower tone, half seriously, half quizzically, "Some of the prisoners." This was said solely for Mr. A.'s benefit, as a kind of supplement to their talks on Democracy.

The "friends" to whom Whitman referred could have been former inmates of Sing Sing, though he had already begun visiting men in prison.[8]

Meanwhile Whitman was of course making frequent trips to New York, to engage in such amusements as we have already observed. One of the ferry-boat employees on the East River, Thomas A. Gere, remembered having "seen a youth swabbing a steamboat's deck with Walt's Homer in his monkey-jacket pocket." [9] Whether the youth ever read the book he did not say. And we may wonder about what these uneducated men thought of Walt's singing airs from the operas or reciting passages from Shakespeare, which he enjoyed doing late at night when few passengers were on board. Passengers who did not know him were curious about his odd appearance, and would ask: "Is he a retired captain . . . an actor? a military officer? a clergyman? Had he been a smuggler, or in the slave trade?" Walt laughed heartily when Gere repeated these inquiries to him. The ferrymen knew something of his literary activities, but they liked him for personal reasons: "What enjoyable nights they were," Gere declared in reminiscing, "when Walt would come to us after a long study at home or in some prominent New York library! He would, indeed, 'loaf' and unbend to our great delight with rich, witty anecdotes and pleasant sarcasms upon some events and men of the day. At times he would be joined by some literary acquaintance, generally to our disgust, or perhaps I should say jealousy, for we fancied that in some way we rather owned Walt . . ."

Among the literary personages who crossed the East River in the autumn of 1856 were two of Emerson's neighbors, Bronson Alcott and Henry D. Thoreau. Both were spending several weeks in New York and the vicinity, and they made not one but several pilgrimages to Brooklyn to see and talk with the poet whom Emerson was urging his friends to read and visit. On the afternoon of October 4 Alcott made his first trip alone and spent two hours with Whitman, finding him "an extraordinary person, full of brute power, certainly of genius and audacity, and likely to make his mark on Young America." Walt gave him a copy of the second edition of his book, and that night Alcott wrote in his *Journal*:

A nondescript, he is not so easily described, nor seen to be described. Broad-shouldered, rouge-fleshed, Bacchus-browed, bearded like a satyr, and rank, he wears his man-Bloomer in defiance of everybody, having these as everything else after his own fashion, and for example to all men hereafter. Red flannel under-shirt, open-breasted, exposing his brawny neck; striped calico jacket over this, the collar Byroneal, with coarse cloth overalls buttoned to it; cowhide boots; a heavy round-about, with huge outside pockets and buttons to match; and a slouched hat, for house and street alike. Eyes gray, unimaginative, cautious yet sagacious; his voice deep, sharp, tender sometimes and almost melting. When talking will recline upon the couch at length, pillowing his head upon his bended arm, and informing you naïvely how lazy he is, and slow. Listens well; asks you to repeat what he has failed to catch at once, yet hesitates in speaking often, or gives over as if fearing to come short of the sharp, full, concrete meaning of his thought. Inquisitive, very; over-curious even; inviting criticisms on himself, on his poems—pronouncing it "pomes."—In fine, an egotist, incapable of omitting, or suffering any one long to omit, noting Walt Whitman in discourse. Swaggy in his walk, burying both hands in his outside pockets. Has never been sick, he says, nor taken medicine, nor sinned; and so is quite innocent of repentance and man's fall. A bachelor, he professes great respect for women.[10]

On Sunday, November 9, Alcott and Thoreau went over to Brooklyn in the morning to hear famous Henry Ward Beecher preach, and in the afternoon they called at the Whitman home, but Walt was out. However, they got "something from his mother—a stately sensible matron believing in Walter absolutely and telling us how good he was and wise as a boy, how his four brothers and two sisters loved him, and how they take counsel of the great man he is grown to be now." On Alcott's first visit Walt had told him that he was a "house-builder," but Mrs. Whitman said "that his brother was the house-builder, and not Walt, who . . . had no business but going out and coming in to eat, drink, write, and sleep." [11]

Next morning Alcott and Thoreau called again, with a recruit, Mrs. Sarah Tyndale, abolitionist from Philadelphia and mother of Hector Tyndale, whom Walt had recently met—or would soon meet—at Mrs. Price's. This time they found Walt at home: "He receives us kindly, yet awkwardly, and takes us up two narrow flights of stairs to sit or stand as we might in his attic study—also the bed-chamber of himself and his feeble brother [Edward], the pressure of whose bodies was still apparent in the unmade bed standing in one corner, and the vessel scarcely hidden underneath." A few books lay on the mantel, and unframed pictures of "a Hercules, a Bacchus, and a satyr" were pasted on the rough walls. When Alcott asked which of these three was the new poet, Whitman "begged me not to put my questions too close, meaning to take, as I inferred, the virtues of the three to himself unreservedly." Encouraged by the flattering interest of his visitors, Walt told them that he bathed daily even in midwinter, that "he rode sometimes a-top of an omnibus up and down Broadway from morning till night beside the driver, and dined afterwards with the whipsters, frequented the opera during the season, and 'lived to make pomes,' and for nothing else particularly."

Despite Mrs. Whitman's loyal defense of Walt to the visitors, probably at times he tried even her patience. According to George's recollection: "If we had dinner at one, like as not he would come at three; always late. Just as we were fixing things on the table he would get up and go round the block. He was always so. He would come to breakfast when he got ready. If he wished to go out he would go—go where he was of a mind to —and come back in his own time." [12] In a family in which most of the men worked at day labor, these erratic habits must have been a constant irritation. Of course, Walt worked at his own literary tasks, but his family did not know what he was writing, or understand it when it was in print.

After the confidential revelations in his bedroom, Walt escorted his guests downstairs to the parlor. Alcott tried to start a conversation between him and Thoreau, "but each seemed planted fast in reserves . . . and it came to no more than cold compliments between them." In a short time the two men took their departure, leaving "the voluminous Mrs.

Tyndale—with the savage sovereign of the flesh." He made an appointment to meet Alcott next day at the International House, "if the mood favored." [13]

Perhaps the mood did not favor, for Alcott made no further reference in his *Journals* to such a meeting. But he held no resentment, for on November 20 he and Thoreau with still another recruit, John Swinton, dined with Whitman in Brooklyn and Alcott greatly enjoyed the experience.[14] Swinton himself was a colorful person, a Scotchman, educated in Canada and trained there as a printer, who had recently returned from Kansas, where he had managed a free-soil newspaper despite the violent opposition of the pro-slavery mobs.[15]

Alcott and Walt met again on December 12 in New York, and the poet was in such an expansive mood that Alcott could not resist some good-natured satire in his *Journal* entry:

. . . Walt Whitman comes, and we dine at Taylor's Saloon, discussing America, its men and institutions. Walt thinks the best thing it has done is the growing of Emerson, the only man there is in it—unless it be himself. Alcott, he fancies, may be somebody, perhaps, to be named by way of courtesy in a country so crude and so pregnant with coming great men and women. He tells me he is going presently to Washington City to see and smell of, or at, the pigmies assembled there at the Capitol, whom he will show up in his letters from there in some of the newspapers, and will send me samples of his work . . . If a broader and finer intercourse with men serves to cure something of his arrogance and take out his egotism, good may come, and great things, of him.[16]

This is the only hint we have that Whitman had planned to write articles from Washington for the newspapers—very similar to the unsuccessful experiment that Henry Adams was to try a few years later. How serious the plan was is anyone's guess.

The reserve that Alcott noted in Thoreau's attitude toward Whitman was less outright antipathy than uncertainty. In a letter to his friend Harrison Blake, dated November 19, 1856, Thoreau confessed himself "much interested and provoked" in the poet. "He is apparently the greatest democrat the world has seen." [17] This statement has often been quoted as Thoreau's profound observation of Whitman, but in the letter it was obviously partly satirical. He had not yet made up his mind about this great "democrat": "I am still somewhat in quandary about him,—feel that he is essentially strange to me, . . . He said that I misapprehend him. I am not quite sure that I do."

However, after reading the second edition of *Leaves of Grass*, Thoreau's opinion suddenly clarified, and he wrote to Blake on December 7: "That Walt Whitman, of whom I wrote you, is the most interesting fact to me at present." [18] He is especially impressed by the poem called "Walt Whitman" (later "Song of Myself") and "Sun-Down Poem" ("Crossing Brooklyn Ferry"). He admits that there are "two or three pieces in the book which are disagreeable, to say the least; simply sensual. He does not celebrate love at all. It is as if the beasts spoke." Yet Thoreau finds the poems "exhilarating, encouraging. As for its sensuality,—and it may turn out to be less sensual than it appears,—I do not so much wish that those parts were not written, as that men and women were so pure, that they could read them without harm, that is, without understanding them." He thinks the book as a whole "very brave and American," and better than all the sermons ever preached in the land. "We ought to rejoice greatly in him. He occasionally suggests something a little more than human." Yet at times Thoreau feels imposed on: "By his heartiness and broad generalities he puts me into a liberal frame of mind prepared to see wonders,—as it were, sets me upon a hill or in the midst of a plain,—stirs me well up, and then— throws in a thousand of brick." Nevertheless, "Since I have seen him, I find that I am not disturbed by any brag or egoism in his book. He may turn out the least of a braggart of all, having a better right to be confident."

Thoreau and Whitman were temperamentally so different that it is surprising they got along as well as they did. But despite Alcott's impression that they did not trust each other, each had a simplicity and frankness that the other respected. Whitman told Traubel that once Thoreau "got to the house while I was out—went straight to the kitchen where my dear mother was baking some cakes—took the cakes hot from the oven. He was always doing things of the plain sort—without fuss." [19] Whitman also remembered that "several times" (perhaps there were more visits than those recorded) Thoreau walked with him the two miles from the Whitman home to the ferry and this made a favorable impression on Walt. Thoreau, however, was outspoken and caustic. On his first visit to the poet he called the unfavorable critics of *Leaves of Grass* "reprobates," and Walt thought this too severe.[20] Another incident was reported by Herbert Gilchrist in Whitman's words:

"I liked Thoreau, though he was morbid. I do not think it was so much a love of woods, streams, and hills that made him live in the country, as from a morbid dislike of humanity. I remember Thoreau saying once, when walking with him in my favorite Brooklyn—'What is there in the people? Pshaw! What do you (a man who sees as well as anybody) see in all this cheating political corruption?' I did not like my Brooklyn spoken of in this way." [21]

It is curious that a man who had recently written "The Eighteenth Presidency!" should have resented Thoreau's remark, though perhaps the national corruption was an abstraction to him, while Brooklyn was personal; it was home and family. There always was, however, an opaque wall separating Whitman's journalistic comprehension of reality from the cheerful optimism of his daily life, which also carried over into the lofty idealism of his poetry.

Alcott's *Journal* gives us a final glimpse of Whitman's behavior at the house of Samuel Longfellow (brother of Henry Wadsworth Longfellow), where he and Thoreau were guests on December 28, just before returning to New England: "there is company in the evening and a Conversation, Walt Whitman being the observed—he coming in his Bloomers and behaving very becomingly, though not at home, very plainly, in parlours, and as hard to tame as Thoreau or any Sylvanus, or train in good keeping with the rest." [22]

Unfortunately, we have no exact information about the visits of the man who had been responsible for the pilgrimages of Conway, Alcott, and Thoreau to Brooklyn. Emerson must have made at least one trip to Brooklyn, for Whitman was later to tell Traubel that he would never forget Emerson's first call: "I can hear his gentle knock still . . . and the slow sweet voice, as my mother stood there by the door: and the words, 'I came to see Mr. Whitman . . .' " [23] But probably most of Emerson's meetings with Whitman took place in New York, as on the occasion when he invited the Brooklyn poet to dinner at a New York hotel, after which Whitman took the reserved New Englander to "a noisy fire-engine society," [24] which annoyed if it did not shock him. Various guesses have been made about exactly where Whitman took his guest, one suggestion being that it was to Pfaff's restaurant. But it could hardly have been anywhere except Firemen's Hall, a handsome brick and stone building opened in 1854 on Mercer Street as a social club for New York firemen, in which they took great pride. Emerson was not too offended to continue recommending *Leaves of Grass* by letter and word of mouth and to invite his "wild genius" to dinner whenever he passed through New York.

Whitman himself was too individualistic, too set in his stubborn Dutch ways, to be intellectually affected by these visits of the admirers of his poetry—or influenced one iota by their reservations or kindly suggestions. Nevertheless, they doubtless encouraged him to continue with the literary ambitions. Perhaps he was as vain as Alcott thought him, but what author —especially if he is not yet established—does not want assurance that what he is trying to do is worth doing? And he would hardly have been human if he had not also taken secret pleasure in the effects of these visits on his family. George says only that they "aroused curiosity," [25] but at least this is some indication that his family began to wonder if there might not after all be more than they had suspected in the book which George and his mother had not thought worth reading. It was not likely that they would ever understand it, but even a small degree of uncomprehending respect was worth something.

III

Both Walt himself and his mother told everyone during the fall of 1856 that he had no occupation except "making pomes," and so far as known, this was literally true. His last identifiable contribution to *Life Illustrated* appeared in August. Possibly he had such great expectations for his second *Leaves of Grass* that he thought he could live on its sale. But if so, he was once more speedily disillusioned. Despite the flattering visits of Emerson's friends, this edition was almost entirely ignored by the rest of the world. It did not even stir up adverse criticism. And after a few months Fowler & Wells made no further effort to advertise it. If any edition of *Leaves of Grass* was a complete failure, it was the second.

By New Year's 1857 even the sanguine Whitman could hardly have avoided realizing the seriousness of his failures. No one had shown interest in his "Eighteenth Presidency!" His poems were known only to a few dozen readers. And for some reason he was no longer on the contributing staff of *Life Illustrated*. Whether or not he had seriously considered going to Washington as a correspondent for the newspapers, even that was out of the question, for he was hardly well enough known to sell his letters to newspapers. Besides, he would have needed money for the trip and for living expenses until he could begin to sell his letters. Some time during this discouraging winter he borrowed $200 from his friend and neighbor James Parton,[26] the husband (since January, 1856) of Fanny Fern, who had praised his poems so lavishly the previous spring. Before many months this debt would cause him great embarrassment, but meanwhile the borrowed money helped him through the black winter.

In the spring of 1857 Whitman became once more the editor of a daily newspaper. This was the Brooklyn *Daily Times*, formerly the Williamsburg *Daily Times*, owned by George C. Bennett and published at 145 Grand Street in nearby Williamsburg[27]—the Whitmans lived near the dividing line between the two towns, consolidated since January 1, 1855. Although nominally an independent newspaper, the *Times* had supported Frémont in the 1856 election. Whitman would surely have sent proofs of "The Eighteenth Presidency!" to Bennett, and this work may have attracted his attention, even though he did not see fit to make use of it. At any rate, Whitman's political attitudes were right for the *Times*, and for this or some other reason he was employed when Charles Gaylor refused to read proof on the job printing and was discharged.[28] During 1856 and 1857 Gaylor had two plays produced in New York; so perhaps he was feeling independent in the spring of 1857. His duties on the *Times* may have also become heavier by then, for Bennett was buying new equipment and apparently expanding his business. Although the newspaper was only four pages in size—like the others Whitman had edited—writing the editorials (ranging in space from half a column to three columns), filling up the remainder of the page with summaries or clippings of news items in other newspapers, editing the correspondence to the editor, and selecting the fiction for the first page—all these must have taken considerable time. The *Times* did have a reporter to gather the local news, but his copy also had to be edited, and this, added to proofreading, would have made a busy day for the editor in charge of the paper.

The exact date of Whitman's beginning his new editorship has been a subject of conjecture.[29] He himself remembered in old age that he worked as an editorial writer in the Brooklyn *Times* office "in 1856, or just before," [30] though he was not sure of the date. One of the Brooklyn directories, dated May 1, 1857, listed Whitman as an editor. On March 14th the *Times* published an editorial signed "W.W.", advocating the running of streetcars on Sunday. If Whitman was editor, it seems rather odd that he would have initialed the editorial.[31] But the campaign for "Sunday Rail Cars" started with an editorial on February 19, and the writer of the initialed editorial on March 14 stated that he intended "to recur to this subject again, and to have something to say on the Company's payment of liberal wages to the drivers and conductors of the cars and one or two little improvements . . ." This sounds like the announcement of a writer who has the means of pursuing his campaign. The February editorial had stirred up the Reverend E. S. Porter, pastor of the Dutch Reformed

Church, to preach a sermon on March 8 opposing Sunday cars. A *Times* reporter took it down and it was printed the next day with an editorial reply. This was the beginning of a hot exchange of newspaper letters between the Reverend Porter and an alderman who agreed with the *Times*. On March 30 the Common Council approved the running of the cars on Sunday, and the *Times* next day claimed much of the credit.

On March 30 the editor also commented on the fact that the ministers (for others had jumped into the controversy) were opposing the will of the majority of the people, an indication, he pointed out, of the ever-widening gulf between the pulpit and the masses. This attitude toward the clergy and the churches was frequently shown by the *Times* during the next two years and gives another clue to the identity of the editor. Perhaps a stronger clue is that beginning with the issue of February 16 the *Times* began to print reviews and editorial comment on articles in British magazines, a practice continued each month through July, 1859. As we have already seen,[32] Whitman was particularly interested in these magazines. About the middle of February the editorials also began to increase in length and number, as if a new editor were in charge. Throughout the spring he wrote with vigor and gusto, evidently enjoying his work.

An interesting sidelight on Whitman's optimism is provided in the editorial he published on May 26, entitled "Croaking a Crash." This was a reply to an editorial in the New York *Herald* warning of an impending financial crash. The editor of the *Times* saw no cause for alarm and pointed to the vast resources of the country. This optimism was pathetically at variance with Whitman's own financial situation at the time, for he was being sued by James Parton for the $200 he had borrowed on a short-term note (probably six months).[33] Still unable to make a cash settlement in June, he offered books and an oil painting by Jesse Talbot in payment, and these were accepted on June 17, 1857, by Mr. Parton's lawyer, though he gave a receipt for only $181.00. Whitman also turned over to the lawyer other goods (not specified) which were carried away from the Whitman residence on Classon Avenue, but no receipt was given for them on the account—a mistake the poet would hear about in the future.

The full details of this episode will probably never be known. Whitman seems always to have felt loyal and sympathetic toward Parton, but a sentence in an editorial on July 9 may hold a clue. In discussing "Free Academies at Public Cost" the editor seemed to go out of his way to remark that "One genuine woman is worth a dozen Fanny Ferns . . ."[34] Many years later Whitman said that he did not blame Parton for the lawsuit:

"there were other elements in the story—venom, jealousies, opacities: they played a big part: and if I may say it, women: a woman certainly—maybe women: they kept alive what I felt James Parton would have let die, [had in fact,] left dead." [35] This is too mysterious to elucidate now. The sarcastic reference to Mrs. Parton may have been motivated by personal resentment, though in all honesty he probably was contemptuous of her sentimental journalism, and might have felt the same way had there been no lawsuit. The "kept alive" probably referred to the malicious gossip that continued for years afterward rather than to the suit itself.

On June 11 sympathizers with General William Walker, leader of the recent unsuccessful attempts to take Nicaragua by promoting a revolution there headed by Southern troops, gave a reception for him in Canal Street, New York City. The editor of the Brooklyn *Times* attended and made wry comments next day. He detested Fernando Wood, the notorious mayor of New York City, who had been elected with the help of the Dead Rabbit Gangsters of the Sixth Ward (Five Points region). The municipal police force had become so corrupt that the Legislature passed an act abolishing it and creating a Metropolitan Police under the control of the governor. In June the two police forces fought a pitched battle for two days around City Hall and state troops had to be called out. Throughout this whole sorry incident Whitman had much to say about the "Dead Rabbit Democracy." On June 29 he also analyzed the prostitution problem under the heading, "A Bad Subject for a Newspaper Article." New York police, he said, were driving prostitutes over to Brooklyn by their inconsistent policy of prolonged toleration followed by unexpected raids. Readers were urged to consider Dr. Sanger's recommendation of a system of licensing and medical inspection. But what Whitman particularly objected to was the alternation of tolerance and persecution; this, he thought, simply made the prostitutes a greater menace to society, and especially to Brooklyn, where they took refuge after the New York raids. Probably few readers of the *Times* were willing to do anything about this problem, but considering the frequent and realistic reports which they read in this and other newspapers on rape, seduction, incest, and other sex crimes, at least one of which was almost constantly before the city courts, it is difficult to imagine that many readers were shocked by this editorial. Contemporary literature was prudish and inhibited, but every unsavory fact of contemporary life in New York and Brooklyn was reported without reserve in the newspapers.

On June 3 Whitman devoted a two-column editorial to Henry C. Murphy, recently appointed ambassador to The Hague. Although this local "Old Hunker" Democrat had probably been partly responsible for Whitman's difficulties on the *Eagle*, the editor of the *Times* now fondly recalled their experiences together on the Long Island *Patriot*. In subsequent editorials he praised Mr. Murphy's translation of *The Voyages of D. P. de Vries*, endorsed the plans for a banquet in his honor, and finally sent him on his way with good wishes.

In midsummer the *Times* editor began to smell corruption in the Health Board. But when the Council finally investigated and expelled one alderman who admitted accepting a gift from someone who hoped to influence the Board, Whitman became sympathetic and suggested that the public ought to show compassion and understanding for human frailty. But he could not forgive the policeman who arrested boys for bathing in the river, and denounced the city ordinance against public bathing.[36]

In August the engineer in charge of the Water Works development, J. P. Kirkwood, issued a gloomy report on an unexpected difficulty in the grade of the canal beyond Jamaica Creek, which would have to pass below the waterline of the gravel plain and thus permit water to seep in so fast that the clay lining the walls could not set. The editor could not understand why this difficulty had not been foreseen, but thought Mr. Kirkwood would be able to find a solution.

During the fall of 1857 the crash predicted by the *Herald* took place, and Whitman was forced to admit that it was the worst since 1837. On September 29 he published an editorial on "The Gloomiest Day" and sadly called attention to the long list of business failures printed in that day's paper. He tried to head off a run on the Williamsburg Savings Bank and declared poetically that "long as grass grows and water runs" it would remain secure. The run continued for several days, but though numerous other banks did fail, this one justified the editor's confidence. Throughout the fall Whitman searched for remedies but found none. The ministers urged prayer and a return to spiritual faith, but on October 13 Whitman expressed the opinion that more material remedies would be necessary, and ten days later he called for public works, such as New York City was planning.

Of course, hard times increased the dissatisfaction of the poor and mob violence became more common in New York. Clashes between "Native American" hoodlums and Irish immigrants were particularly violent. On November 12 Whitman stated the only remedy he knew, though he admitted it offered no immediate solution: "Educate, Educate,—it is the only true remedy for mobs, emeutes, wild communistic theories, and red-republican [that is, French Revolution] ravings . . ."

Some of the reviewers of *Leaves of Grass* had interpreted literally the poet's claim to being "one of the roughs." But despite Whitman's hob-nobbing with omnibus drivers and ferry pilots and introducing Emerson to the society of firemen, Alcott and Thoreau had found him mild and gentle in manners. Throughout his editorship of the *Times* he frequently denounced "Rowdyism," just as he had done while editor of the *Eagle*, or earlier in his moral advice to apprentices while he was with the *Star*.[37] Prize fights, which were still illegal and had to be fought in Canada or in secret, Whitman opposed [38] both because of the brutality of the sport and the encouragement they gave to rowdy and vicious conduct among the spectators. He liked men who worked with their hands, but he had no use for sportsmen, carousers, or troublemakers. His costume was still practi-cally the same that Alcott had observed the previous year. Charles Skin-ner, a Brooklyn journalist who gathered information from Whitman's associates of this period, described his appearance thus: "His dress was heavy, coarse, but clean, and seemed to belong to a farmer or a miner rather than to an editor . . . flannel trousers, belted and tucked into boots that reached to the knee [what Alcott called the 'man-bloomer'], a pea jacket never buttoned, a blue shirt open at the throat, a red kerchief at the neck, and a broad-brimmed hat! Even Horace Greeley, who affected a rus-tic make-up, was more conventional in his costume." [39]

During 1858 Whitman's editorials followed the general pattern of those he had published the previous year, though of course new subjects emerged. One of these was the extremely bitter controversy stirred up in the spring by the expulsion of Judge E. D. Culver from the First Baptist Church because he stood up in the congregation one Sunday to challenge a defense of slavery on Biblical texts made by the pastor from the pulpit.[40] Whitman printed letters on both sides of the quarrel, but he repeatedly supported the judge in his editorials, and vigorously pointed out the arbi-trary and unfair conduct of the minister and his supporters.

The second topic that most excited Whitman in 1858 was the laying of the Atlantic cable. During the spring he was consistently optimistic, while others, such as the editor of the *Eagle*, were predicting that the cable would never be successful, and he never lost hope throughout the summer despite the numerous delays and rumors of failure. When the first message—a greeting from the Queen of England to the President of the United States—was actually sent on August 17, he gave editorial whoops of joy. Brooklyn celebrated the event the next day, and Whitman declared this was the biggest celebration in the history of the city. On August 26 the cable carried the news of the peace concluded by England and France with China, and by September 4 Whitman was pointing out the need for a second cable to take care of the great demand for its services. Of course, after this it broke again, but Whitman's faith in eventual success did not falter. Previously, on July 17, he had also discussed the need for "A Northern Pacific Railroad" and predicted its construction. Some years later he would be able to celebrate these two engineering feats in one of his great poems, "Passage to India."

In the summer of 1858 the reformers and Utopian planners were publicizing many radical schemes for re-making society. On all these the *Times* editor cast his withering scorn. After reading a news report of a suicide in the Free Love community at Berlin Heights, Ohio, he declared: "A feeble and diseased physical condition predisposes a weak mind to all sorts of mental eccentricities. The *mens sana in corpore sano* is the best safeguard against the mania of the 'modern lights.' " [41] And on September 14 he commented on "The Finale of the Free Love Convention" at Utica: "All the mental deformities and intellectual monstrosities of the union were collected . . ."

A letter from George C. Bennett to the New York *Tribune*, dated October 21, and reprinted in the *Times*, indicated that he was a member of the "Conference Committee" of the Republican party in Brooklyn but stated that he would support any good candidate to represent the Fifth Congressional District. Despite this Republican affiliation, Bennett let his editor be as independent in politics as the paper claimed to be. After the election in November Whitman noted that Douglas had won in Illinois and suggested that he could now organize "a great middle conservative party," neither "proscribing slavery, like Seward, nor fostering it, like Buchanan." This was evidently the kind of party Whitman wanted, and he would continue to admire Senator Douglas until Lincoln's nomination, in 1860.

Early in 1859 some local politicians began making attacks on the Water Commissioners, charging that they had deviated from the original plans. Probably the real motive of these attacks was to influence the action on a bill then pending in the State Legislature which, unless killed or amended, would give more power to the Water Commissioners. Several Brooklyn aldermen wanted control of the Water Works transferred from the Commissioners to the Common Council. The *Times* consistently supported the Commissioners throughout this argument, and late in April the Legislature passed the kind of bill the *Times* had been advocating.

That Whitman was still in charge of the paper during the Water Works debate is clearly indicated in one paragraph of a long survey of progress which was printed on March 15, with the Whitmanian title, "Our Brooklyn Water Works—The Two or Three Final Facts, After All":

The water itself has a character of its own. It is deliciously sweet—it almost has a flavor. Many a time in passing along the line, and at Baisley's Pond, or at some of the springs, have we realized the sweet character of this water. We have drank [sic] in all parts of North America, at Niagara, at the Straits of Mackinaw, the Missouri, the Mississippi, the Ohio water—and we say there is none to equal this product of the Long Island ponds, fed from their myriads of natural springs, filtered through the sands and rocks that underlie our island surface. It is far, far better than the Croton.

Whitman had not by any means been in "all parts of North America," but on his round trip to New Orleans he had gone down the Ohio and Mississippi rivers, and had returned by way of the Mississippi and Great Lakes, stopping briefly at St. Louis (where he tasted Missouri water), Chicago, Milwaukee, Mackinaw, Cleveland, and Niagara.[42]

In view of this evidence that Whitman was still editing the *Times* in the spring of 1859, the editorial comments on Brooklyn's most famous minister, the Reverend Henry Ward Beecher, are particularly interesting. Beecher is said to have admired *Leaves of Grass*,[43] but by this time Walt seems to have lost patience with the renowned minister. The January 25th *Times* contained a sarcastic comment on Beecher's having been well enough to lecture at Cooper Institute in New York, but too ill to preach in his own Brooklyn church. Then, on May 4, under the title "Beecherolatry," the editor discussed at length the minister's encouragement of worship of himself, especially among his women parishioners. Some of the blame might be placed on the women, but the writer of the editorial quoted an extract from Beecher's own writings to show that he encouraged such idolatry: "Women, who have much need of love, *ought not* to find it hard to come to Jesus Christ, and put their arms about his neck, and tell him with gushing love, that they give themselves, body and soul into his keeping." Whitman's comment was:

We have only to say . . . that ladies who cannot entertain a belief of a doctrine without acquiring so intense a personal interest in the utterer, had better join some church where the organization absorbs the identity of the individual minister, than remain in one where the minister stands forth so prominently as the recipient of so lavish and profuse an idolatry.

A young German printer and poet, Frederick Huene, employed in the *Times* office, said that, "Mr. Whitman resigned his place in consequence of articles which were very unfavorably criticized by ministers and church people, and about which he had quite a philosophical debate with Mr. Bennett." [44] The Culver dispute had taken place the previous year, but many of Whitman's editorials during the past two years had contained jibes both at the clergy and at institutional religion that might have irritated churchgoing readers. It is likely that Bennett had received many complaints, and there may not have been any single incident that provoked his discharging Whitman. Actually, it is an assumption that he was discharged at all; he may have resigned simply because he and Bennett could not agree on an editorial policy. Skinner, in the first study made of "Whitman as an Editor," declared that "he resigned" in consequence of the objections of "certain orthodox deacons of what was then a smug, conventional town . . . , yet he never showed the least impatience toward his critics, carrying himself with a large, bland dignity to the last." [45]

The subject matter and the treatment of a considerable number of the editorials published in the *Times* during June suggest Whitman's authorship, though we have no conclusive evidence. On June 20 an editorial on "A Delicate Subject" revived the discussion of the problem that was being created by the New York police's driving prostitutes over to Brooklyn, and once more the author endorsed Dr. Sanger's solution. Since similar views had been presented in the *Times* on several occasions before,[46] the editorial probably did not create an immediate crisis. But an editorial in the next day's paper may well have caused repercussions. Under the title "Unsound Churches" appeared a list of the churches in the Eastern District (that is, Williamsburg) recently condemned as unsafe by fire inspectors, and the editor's comments amounted to a peremptory command that they be repaired immediately. The list included nine churches representing almost as many denominations, and the editor guessed that as many or more in other parts of Brooklyn were in as bad condition. It is not difficult to imagine that this publicity of neglect on the part of so many church officials irritated a considerable number of people—perhaps all the more because no effective reply could be made. The following day, under the title "Can All Marry?," there was a guarded discussion of sex repression. This could have caused trouble, but it was so ambiguously worded that it probably did not. Another indication that Whitman was still editor was the continued appearance of the reviews of the British magazines. Also an article in the July *Atlantic Monthly* stimulated the editor to print on June 28 a long, sympathetic editorial on Paine, in which the statement was made that so far he had received "no biography worth mentioning." This sounds very much like Whitman, who admired Paine all his life.[47] Thus there is a strong probability that Whitman was with the *Times* until about the end of June.

The only difficulty in accepting this conclusion is provided by a notation that Whitman entered in his notebook under the date of June 26, 1859: "It is now time to *stir* first for *Money* enough, *to live and provide for* M——. *To Stir*—first write stories and get out of this Slough." [48] This notation has led most Whitman students to assume that the poet had been unemployed for some weeks or months. But it is unlikely that he had been able to save much money during the two years on the *Times*, and the immediate prospect of unemployment might have been sufficient to put him in a mental "Slough." "M——" could hardly have been any one except his mother. Walt's younger brother, Jeff, had married the previous February.[49] He was employed as a surveyor on the Water Works development, and according to Lain's Directory for 1858–1859 had established a home of his own on 5th Avenue near 12th Street. What the other brothers were doing is not known, but at the moment Walt may have had the complete responsibility for the support of his mother.[50]

On May 1, 1859, the Whitman family moved to North Portland Avenue, corner of Myrtle.[51] Whether this had any connection with Walt's impending unemployment there seems no way of determining. Lain's Directory for 1859–1860, however, indicates one of the means by which Walt was trying to earn a living, for it lists him as "copyist." This, of course, would not be likely to provide steady employment and probably left him abundant time for other activities, such as revising his poems.

IV

While Whitman was writing editorials for the *Times* on municipal problems, trying to keep the Water Works out of local politics, commenting on the wickedness and corruption of New York, or speculating on the political strategy of the Democrats, Republicans, and Native Americans, he did not publish any poems. But he had by no means abandoned *Leaves of Grass*, and his notes, letters, and manuscripts show that he was planning a third edition. On February 25, 1857, probably soon after he had taken over the editorship of the *Times*, he dined with Hector Tyndale, and recorded afterward: "Asked H. T. where he thought I needed particular attention to be directed for my improvement—where I could especially be bettered in my poems. He said: 'In massiveness, breadth, large, sweeping effects, without regard to detail.—As in the Cathedral at York I came away with great impressions of its largeness, solidity and spaciousness, without troubling myself with its parts." [52] This advice impressed Walt, and in later years he would claim that *Leaves of Grass* had been long abuilding, like a great cathedral.[53]

Meanwhile Whitman had been working away at his poems, as a long letter to Hector's mother, dated June 20, 1857, reveals. After much news and gossip about Mrs. Sarah Tyndale's friends and acquaintances, Whitman confided his plans for a new edition:

Fowler & Wells are bad persons for me.—They retard my book very much.—It is worse than ever.—I wish now to bring out a third edition—I have now *a hundred* poems ready (the last edition had thirty-two.)—and shall endeavor to make an arrangement with some publisher here to take the plates from F. & W. and make the additions needed, and so bring out the third edition.—F. & W. are very willing to give up the plates—they want the thing off their hands.—In the forthcoming Vol. I shall have, as I said, a hundred poems, and no other matter but poems—(no letters to or from Emerson—no Notices or any thing of that sort.)—It is, I know well enough, that *that* must be the true *Leaves of Grass*—and I think it (the new Vol.) has an aspect of completeness, and makes its case clearer.—The old poems are all retained.—The difference is in the new character given to the mass, by additions.[54]

Whitman did not succeed in making an arrangement with a publisher, but in 1858 the Rome Brothers began setting up the new poems and furnishing him proofs of them.[55] This does not indicate that Whitman intended to have them print the book, as they had the first edition. For many years after this date he continued to have the Romes set his poems in type merely to secure copies in proof, which he kept instead of the holographs; the typewriter had not been invented, and besides the ex-printer liked to see his poems in type. Fortunately the Rome Brothers carefully preserved the manuscripts,[56] and these enable us to trace the poet's growth.

Most of the sixty-eight new poems that Whitman planned to add to the thirty-two of the 1856 edition were fairly short, and none of them show any appreciable increase in his literary stature. But they give interesting clues to Whitman's moods and emotions during the years between his second and third editions (1856–1860). For example, both in the 1855 version of "Song of Myself" and the 1856 "Sun-Down Poem" ("Crossing Brooklyn Ferry"), the poet had felt within himself evil as well as good, but he now intended to emphasize this motif in what was to be poem No. 42, "Confession and Warning":

I go no farther till I confess myself in the open air, in the hearing of this time
    and future times,
Also till I make a leaf of fair warning.—

I am he who has been sly, thievish, mean, a prevaricator, greedy,
And I am he who remains so yet.—
.   .   .   .
Beneath this impassive face the hot fires of hell continually burn—within me
    the lurid smutch and the smoke;
Not a crime can be named but I have it in me waiting to break forth,
Lusts and wickedness are acceptable to me,
I walk with delinquents with passionate love,
And I say I am of them—I belong to them myself,
And henceforth I will not deny them—For how can I deny myself?

—This leaf I specially sign with my name, to signify to anyone concerned;
Let no man complain but I have given him his fair warning,
Let no woman complain but I have given her hers.[57]

The poet does not say, even in fantasy, that he has committed any wickedness, only that he feels within himself every potential crime. Did he actually at this period have a sense of guilt because of something he had either done or desired to do? The only clue that his sixty-eight new poems offers is that they contained thirteen of a group which in 1860 Whitman would call "Calamus," on the theme of male friendship, but some lines are plainly homoerotic. Perhaps it is significant, too, that the list contained only two poems later to appear in "Children of Adam," whose ostensible theme was to be procreation—and neither of these two were specifically concerned with procreation. It is obvious, therefore, that the sex theme that most interested Whitman in 1857 was homoeroticism, though it is by no means certain that he yet realized this fact.

Another poem, numbered 51 and entitled "Wander-Teachers," gave a sketch of what was evidently a real ambition of Whitman's around 1856–1858: to travel over America as a wandering orator, or teacher by word of mouth—not as a substitute for his role as poet but as a complement to it. For many years he was to cherish this idea, and he may have dreamed most intensely of it during his unemployment in the winter of 1856–1857, but he was still planning it in 1858.

Now we start hence, I with the rest, on our journeys through The States,
We willing learners from all[,] teachers of all, and lovers of all.—

I have watched the seasons dispensing themselves and passing on—and I have
     said, Why should not a man or woman do as much as the seasons, and
     effuse as much?

We dwell awhile in every city and town,
We pass through Kanada, the north-east, the vast valley of the Mississippi,
     and the Southern States,
We confer on equal terms with each of The States,
We make trial of ourselves, and invite men and women to hear[,]
We say to ourselves, Remember, fear not, be candid, promulge the body and
     the soul,
Promulge real things,—never forget the equality of humankind, and never
     forget immortality,
Dwell awhile and pass on—Be copious, temperate, chaste, magnetic—And what
     you effuse may then return as the seasons return, and may be as much as
     the seasons.—[58]

In 1858 Whitman's plan to give lectures had become sufficiently definite for him to draw up a circular,[59] which he evidently intended to print and distribute ahead of his tours, and to use also as a cover for his printed lectures. His manuscript clearly states his objective:

WALT WHITMAN'S LECTURES

     I desire to go by degrees through all These States, especially West and South, and through Kanada: Lecturing, (my own way,) henceforth my employment, my means of earning my living—subject to the work elsewhere alluded to that takes precedence.—[on the back of the sheet he had a long note on *Leaves of Grass*.]
     Of this, or through the list present and to come, (see last page of cover,) any [lecture] will be recited before any society or association of friends, or at the defrayment of some special person.—

AMERICA
A Programme, &c.

     Some plan I seek to have the vocal delivery of my Lectures free, but at present a low price of admission, One Dime—Or my fee for reciting, ["a Lecture" deleted] here, $10, (when any distance expenses in addition.)
     Each lecture will be printed, with its recitation, needing to be carefully perused afterward to be understood. I personally sell the printed copies.

At the top Whitman had written "15 cents," probably intended as the price of each printed lecture, and at the bottom, "trade supplied by De Witt, 162 Nassau St., New York." One of the most curious aspects of this plan is the date 1858 on the circular, when Whitman was certainly editing the Brooklyn *Daily Times*. It would not be surprising if he had planned to go on a lecture tour after the loss of his position in 1859, but the date on the circular cover is plainly 1858.

So far as is known neither the circular nor the lectures were ever printed, though the manuscript of one lecture, apparently written about this time, has survived. Whitman gave it the descriptive title, "Slavery—The Slaveholders—The Constitution—the true America and Americans, the laboring persons," [60] and internal evidence dates it not earlier than 1858. This lecture may have been delivered at Groton, Connecticut, for in one place the author addressed some place that is almost illegible in the manuscript but looks like "Groton." That was just across the Sound from Long Island, and Whitman may have secured an engagement there. But if so, it was evidently one of the few places where he attempted to carry out his lecture scheme.

The last three poems in this first stage of the third edition also give evidence of Whitman's desire to secure financial backing. In No. 99, "To Rich Givers," we have what reads like gratitude for material gifts received, but was surely only another wishful dream, like the appeal for some rich person to subsidize "The Eighteenth Presidency!" or the "Wander-Teachers" fantasy.

To Rich Givers

What you give me I cheerfully accept,
A little sustenance, a hut and garden, a little money—these as I rendezvous
    with my poems,
A traveler's lodging and breakfast as I journey through The States—Why need
    I be ashamed to own such gifts? Why to advertise for them?
For I myself am not one who will bestow nothing upon man and woman,
For I know that what I bestow upon any man or woman is no less than the
    entrance to all the gifts of the universe.—[61]

That Whitman did by this time firmly believe that he himself had precious gifts to bestow upon his readers, and the nation, there can be no doubt; but not until extreme old age would he be able to find "rich givers" to bestow upon him needed "sustenance." [62]

V

The manuscripts that Whitman left with the Rome Brothers also enable us to trace a second stage in the growth of the third edition. Indeed, it is possible to subdivide this second stage into three chronological layers, for in his preliminary versions Whitman wrote on different kinds of paper—first pink, then blue, and finally white.[63] This interesting story of the growth of the poems is far too long and complicated to be told here, but some phases of it are too important biographically not to be mentioned.

The series of drafts for the longest poem in these manuscripts, at the time called "Premonition" ("Proto-Leaf" in 1860; finally "Starting from Paumanok"), bear evidence of a great emotional and intellectual conflict that took place in both the life and art of Walt Whitman around 1858–59. "Premonition" was a program poem, serving the same function as the 1855 preface. Approximately the first third of the poem, written on pink paper, announces and develops the poet's intention to compose "a song for These States," which are welded by an "organic" compact. In the first twenty-one sections (copied on pink paper) we have the poet who had wished to "incarnate" his native soil, to "strike up for a new world," to lead his nation to the creation of a grander art and culture; but then the theme of "lovers" and "companions," or "adhesiveness," [64] enters (on inserted blue paper), and thereafter the poet's desire to make personal confessions battles logically and esthetically with the broader prophet-leader motif (the retained earlier passages on pink paper).

For example, Section 22 is on blue paper.

I will make the song of companionship,
I will show what alone can compact These States,
I believe the main purport of America is to found a new ideal of manly friendship, more ardent, more general,
I will therefore let appear these burning fires that were threatening to consume me,
I will lift what has too long kept down those smouldering fires—I will now expose them and use them.

I will make the new evangel-poem of lovers and comrades,
(For who but I should understand love, with all its sorrow and joy?
And who but I should be the poet of comrades?)[65]

What were these "smouldering fires"? By the time Whitman wrote this passage he had passed through an experience—or a series of experiences—that had, he felt, threatened to destroy him. Now he will "show what alone can compact These States." But the history of the emotional turmoil through which he had passed is only hinted in the blue-paper versions of "Premonition." He had revealed it with much greater clarity in a separate group of poems which he had first thought to call "Live Oak, with Moss" and later "Calamus-Leaves" (to be changed in 1860 simply to "Calamus").

"Calamus-Leaves" consisted of twelve poems[66]—but not the twelve (or thirteen) mentioned above[67] as having in 1857 constituted part of the projected one hundred poems. The 1857 "Calamus" poems had treated the theme of "manly affection" and friendship in a general way; this new group tells such a story as might have been found in an Elizabethan sonnet sequence, which was perhaps its archetype. These poems are scattered in Whitman's manuscripts and were probably not composed consecutively, but the fact that Whitman went through his pages and carefully numbered these poems with ornamental Roman numerals (he used Arabic numbers for all other numbering) proves that he considered gathering them into a single cluster. Arranged in this numbered series these twelve poems tell a story and carry a clearer meaning than do the forty-five poems finally printed in 1860 as "Calamus," [68] among which Whitman scattered these twelve, after slight revisions. The theme and imagery of No. I are the same as in the passage in "Premonition" (Section 22) quoted above: "Not the heat flames up and consumes—more than the flames of me, consuming, burning for his love whom I love . . ."

The second poem contains the symbol which Whitman had first intended to use as his title, "Live Oak, with Moss":

I saw in Louisiana a live-oak growing,
All alone stood it, and the moss hung down from the branches,
Without any companion it grew there, glistening out joyous leaves of dark
    green,
And its look, rude, unbending, lusty, made me think of myself;
But I wondered how it could utter joyous leaves, standing alone there without
    its friend, its lover—For I knew I could not;
And I plucked a twig with a certain number of leaves upon it, and twined
    around it a little moss, and brought it away—And I have placed it in
    sight in my room,
It is not needed to remind me as of my friends, (for I believe lately I think of
    little else than of them,)

Yet it remains to me a curious token—it makes me think of manly love,
For all that, and though the live-oak glistens there in Louisiana, solitary in a
   wide flat space, uttering joyous leaves all its life, without a friend, a lover,
   near—I know very well I could not.[69]

The live-oak of Louisiana could have been remembered as a poetic
symbol some years after 1848, when Whitman actually saw this tree, and
probably was, for the implications of this poem are almost entirely lacking
in the first two editions of *Leaves of Grass*. In the third poem, in which
the poet has found his "friend" and "lover," the imagery suggests Long
Island; but since no one knows whether the poem is based on experience or fantasy, it is idle to try to locate the place or assign a precise date.

When I heard at the close of the day how I had been praised in the Capitol, still
   it was not a happy night for me that followed;
Nor when I caroused—Nor when my favorite plans were accomplished—was I
   really happy,
But that day I rose at dawn from the bed of perfect health, electric, inhaling
   sweet breath,
When I saw the full moon in the west grow pale and disappear in the morning
   light,
When I wandered alone over the beach, and undressing, bathed, laughing with
   the waters, and saw the sun rise,
And when I thought how my friend, my lover, was coming, then O I was
   happy;
Each breath tasted sweeter—and all that day my food nourished me more—
   And the beautiful day passed well,
And the next came with equal joy—And with the next, at evening, came my
   friend,
And that night, while all was still, I heard the waters roll slowly continually
   up the shores[,]
I heard the hissing rustle of the liquid and sands, as directed to me, whispering,
   to congratulate me,—For the friend I love lay sleeping by my side,
In the stillness his face was inclined towards me, while the moon's clear beams
   shone,
And his arm lay lightly over my breast—And that night I was happy.

In No. IV the poet sits "alone, yearning and pensive," and his thoughts
go out to "other men, in other lands," who may be equally lonely, and he
thinks that "if I could know those men I should love them." One might
guess from this poem that the happy mood of III was pure fantasy, but V
seems to elaborate the situation in III:

Long I thought that knowledge alone would suffice me—O if I could but obtain
knowledge!
Then the Land of the Prairies engrossed me—the south savannas engrossed
me—For them I would live—I would be their orator;
Then I met the examples of old and new heroes—I heard of warriors, sailors,
and all dauntless persons—And it seemed to me I too had it in me to be
as dauntless as any, and would be so;
And then to finish all, it came to me to strike up the songs of the New World
—And then I believed my life must be spent in singing;
But now take notice, Land of the prairies, Land of the south savannas, Ohio's
land,
Take notice, you Kanuck woods—and you, Lake Huron—and all that with you
roll toward Niagara—and you Niagara also,
And you, Californian mountains—that you all find some one else that he be
your singer of songs,
For I can be your singer no longer—I have ceased to enjoy them,
I have found him who loves me, as I him, in perfect love,
With the rest I dispense—I sever from all that I thought would suffice me, for
it does not—it is now empty and tasteless to me,
I heed knowledge, and the grandeur of The States, and the examples of heroes,
no more,
I am indifferent to my own songs—I am to go with him I love, and he is to go
with me,
It is to be enough for each of us that we are together—We never separate
again.—[70]

The poet's indifference to his own poems did not long continue, but
the effect of the satisfying relationship with the friend-lover (whether real
or imaginary) was to make him shift, momentarily, his poetic program to
the expression of such relationships. In VI the greatest subject he can
hope to record is that of "two men I saw to-day on the pier, parting the
parting of dear friends,/ The one to remain hung on the other's neck
and passionately kissed him—while the one to depart tightly prest the
one to remain in his arms." And in VII the poet requests:

You bards of ages hence! when you refer to me, mind not so much my poems,
Nor speak of me that I prophesied of The States and led them the way of their
glories,
But come, I will inform you who I was underneath that impassive exterior—I
will tell you what to say of me,
Publish my name and hang up my picture as that of the tenderest
lover . . .[71]

What makes this sound completely authentic is the poet's confession that he "often lay sleepless and dissatisfied at night . . . dreading lest the one he loved might after all be indifferent to him,"

> Whose happiest days were those, far away through fields, in woods, on hills, he and another, wandering hand in hand, they twain, apart from other men.

In VIII the poet is so lonely and miserable that he wonders if he is different from other men:

> Hours continuing long, sore and heavy-hearted,
> Hours of the dusk, when I withdraw to a lonesome and unfrequented spot, seating myself, leaning my face in my hands,
> Hours sleepless, deep in the night, when I go forth, speeding swiftly the country roads, or through the city streets, or pacing miles and miles, stifling plaintive cries,
> Hours discouraged, distracted,—For he, the one I cannot content myself without —soon I saw him content himself without me,
> Hours when I am forgotten—(O weeks and months are passing, but I believe I am never to forget!)
> Sullen and suffering hours—(I am ashamed—but it is useless—I am what I am;)
> Hours of my torment—I wonder if other men ever have the like, out of the like feelings?
> Is there even one other like me—distracted—his friend, his lover, lost to him?
> Is he too as I am now? Does he still rise in the morning, dejected, thinking who is lost to him? And at night, awaking, think who is lost?
> Does he too harbor his friendship silent and endless? Harbor his anguish and passion?
> Does some stray reminder, or the casual mention of a name, bring the fit back upon him, taciturn and deprest?
> Does he see himself reflected in me? In these hours does he see the face of his hours reflected? [72]

This, surely, was neither imaginary nor symbolical, but written out of shame and remorse: "it is useless—I am what I am."

The redeeming feature of these poems motivated by unsatisfied homoerotic yearnings is that the poet was able to transcend his personal suffering. He would never be able to escape the torment of his emotions, but he could generalize them, as in poem No. IX, in which he "dreamed in a dream of a city where all the men were like brothers." And in XI he now suspects that what he feels within himself is analogous to some terrible force in the Earth, "ready to break forth." Finally, he will become a teacher of "friendship," though the last poem in the group has some of the esoteric frenzy of the earlier, more obviously homoerotic lyrics.

However, the best resolution to the crisis recorded in "Calamus-Leaves" is not in this group itself, but in the later revisions of "Premonition." Many of the blue-paper insertions in this poem were evidently written while the poet was enduring the "flames" which threatened to consume him and which made him consider giving up the poetic role that he had announced in the first part of "Premonitions" (the pink-paper version). One of the strongest objective evidences of the relation between "Calamus-Leaves" and the "adhesiveness" theme in "Premonition" is the fact that one leaf of the latter was written on the back of a "Calamus" poem manuscript—on white paper, the latest version. Sections 35–36 show how the poet rationalized his emotions in this part of "Premonition":

The unseen something in all life,
The prophetic spirit of materials shifting and flickering around me,
The wondrous interplay between the divinity of the future and the divinity of
    the present,
This extasy touching and thrilling me,
This contact daily and hourly that will not release me.
How effective at last it all has become upon me!

Not he whom I love, kissing me so long with his daily kiss, has winded and
    twisted around me that which holds me to him forever,
Any more than I am become welded to the heavens, to the spiritual world, and
    to the identities of the Gods, my unseen lovers, after what they have done
    to me.[73]

Note that the "extasy touching and thrilling me" suggests to the poet some relationship beyond him "whom I love . . . I am become welded to the heavens, to the spiritual world," and so on. Many primitive cultures have made sex a symbol of divinity or the potency of Nature. To the primitive mind the mysterious generative power of sex was a perpetual miracle, and by its proper ritual use man could share and wield the potency of God or Nature. Even the Christian mystics have symbolized Divine Love by human affections, and the cult of the Virgin was such a personification. Henry Adams pointed out that Diana and Venus were worshiped not for their beauty but for their "force," yet when he tried to think of an American artist "who had ever insisted on the power of sex, as every classic has always done . . . he could think only of Walt Whitman." Thus in using his emotional urges and yearnings as symbols of what he regarded as universal and spiritual truths, Whitman was only doing what both primitive men and Christian mystics have done throughout the ages.

> States!
> You do not need maternity only,
> You do not need to be born and matured only,
> There is a subtler influence still to go with your conformation.[74]

This influence was "love"—sexual love on the physical level, but that symbolized a principle underlying all life, all creation. Other creatures besides man feel and express this "subtle influence." The poet had observed the "she-bird" on her nest in the orchard and the "he-bird" sitting nearby, "inflating his throat and joyfully singing."

> And I have perceived that what he really sang for must be something beyond
> the she-bird.[75]

By analogy, Whitman inflates his throat to sing for Democracy "and something beyond." In Section 42 (the end of the white paper insertions) Democracy or the nation becomes, by extension of this analogy, "Ma femme," and the poet declares to her:

> Our offspring shall be provided for,
> None could come to what was wanted till I have come,
> For you, and something beyond you, I will send forth strong and haughty
> chants different from those of all the rest of the earth.[76]

At this point Whitman returns to his early or pink-paper versions. He has traveled round the cycle to his 1855–1856 role of poet of Democracy and moral leader. He will "make the true poem of riches, namely to earn for the body and the mind what adheres and goes forward, and is not dropt by death"—the "prudence" theme of the first edition. He will effuse egotism, be the Bard of Democracy, show the equality of male and female, teach that no one thing is inferior to another, and that all things in the universe are perfect miracles. He envisions

> A world primal again—Vistas of glory incessant and branching,
> A new race, dominating previous ones, and grander far,
> New politics—New literatures and religions—New inventions and arts.[77]

But the new age will not come into existence calmly and peacefully. The poet feels within himself prophetic tides:

You oceans that have been calm within me! how I feel you, fathomless,
    stirring, preparing unprecedented waves and storms.[78]

It is not clear whether the poet was actually prophesying about himself or the nation. If himself, he perhaps anticipated a period of great creative activity; if the nation, he was indeed a true prophet, since this must have been written before 1860. But it is significant that his mood so closely paralleled the actual condition of "The States" between 1856 and 1860.

Finally, with a mighty rhetorical flourish, Whitman brought his poem to an end with a rather forced symbolization of his reader as his fancied "lover":

O rendezvous at last! O us two only!
.   .   .   .
O hand in hand—O wholesome pleasure—O one more desirer and lover!
O to haste, firm-holding—to haste, haste on with me.

Before publishing this poem in 1860, Whitman would be able to fuse the diverse elements into a more artistic whole, but it is fortunate that these manuscripts have survived, for they give us a glimpse not only into his literary workshop, but also into his most private emotions and psychological problems.

VI

During the period of the final preparation and actual publication of the third edition of *Leaves of Grass* Whitman spent much time at Pfaff's restaurant, on Broadway just above Bleecker Street. The proprietor of this restaurant was a German-Swiss named Charles Pfaff, who had begun about 1854 to build up a clientele of writers, artists, and would-be Bohemians. In the 1850's this restaurant was situated in a basement, and consisted of a bar at which Herr Pfaff himself presided and a dining room that extended out under the pavement. The bar became famous for the excellence of its wines and liquors, Charlie Pfaff being regarded by many of his admirers as the best judge of wine in New York, and his good food at reasonable prices became equally famous. Furthermore, the "Bohemians" who gathered there created an atmosphere and acquired a somewhat scandalous reputation that attracted the curious, so that this was one of the busiest, noisiest, and most-sought-out by visitors to the city of any restaurant in New York.[79]

Exactly when Whitman became one of the Pfaff habitués is not clear, but he was certainly a frequenter of the place soon after he ceased to edit the Brooklyn *Times*, and perhaps as a consequence of his new leisure. By this time Henry Clapp, editor of the recently founded (1858) *Saturday Press*, had made Pfaff's his informal club and had gathered around him a coterie of writers and wits reputed to be very sophisticated, irreverent, and "Bohemian." Even this term was alien to America and had been self-consciously transported from Paris, which Clapp and several others had visited, returning to their native land with contempt for its puritanism and a mania for shocking it.

Clapp was a former New Englander who had been a sailor, had educated himself to be a freethinker and skeptic, had acquired a varied experience in journalism, had worked for a while with Horace Greeley and Albert Brisbane in trying to popularize the doctrines of Fourier and socialism, and was now attempting to edit a smart and sprightly literary and critical journal, which did manage to achieve considerable prestige but could seldom pay its contributors.

The notoriety both of the restaurant and of the *Saturday Press* received a powerful stimulus when Jane McElheney, better known as "Ada Clare," returned from Paris, where she had gone to bear her illegitimate son. It was an open secret that the father was Louis Moreau Gottschalk, a well known American pianist and composer.[80] Ada Clare, a cousin of the distinguished Southern poet Paul Hamilton Hayne, came to New York from Charleston, South Carolina, in 1855 at the age of twenty-three. She tried without success to act, but gained considerable temporary renown for her wit, good looks, and her newspaper poems, in which she paraded her private life. After her return from Paris she wrote a weekly column for the *Saturday Press* and was known as the "Queen of Bohemia." She and Walt Whitman became friends, and when she died in 1874, supposedly of rabies, he defended her character.[81]

Pfaff reserved a large table against the far wall for his literary customers, who included besides Clapp and Ada Clare, Fitz-James O'Brien, a clever short-story writer; George Arnold, a satirical poet; William Winter, sentimental poet and later dramatic critic; E. C. Stedman, Thomas Bailey Aldrich (who later went to Boston and became "respectable"), John Swinton, R. H. Stoddard, Adah Isaacs Menken (who arrived early in

1860), and several others. Arnold, especially, was quarrelsome, but nearly everyone argued freely and sometimes violently. The exception was Walt Whitman, who, according to all witnesses, sipped his beer with the rest but said little. One witness says also that of the whole Pfaff group, "Whitman was the only one who was never tipsy and never 'broke' . . . he was an easy borrower, though it does not appear that he asked for large amounts or made needless delays in his repayments." [82]

In the summer of 1860 the young Ohio journalist and poet William Dean Howells, who had contributed to the *Saturday Press* and felt honored to have his work appear in such a distinguished journal, visited both the *Press* office and Pfaff's, and later described the experience.[83] He had just arrived in New York for the first time after a delightful visit to New England, where he had talked with his literary idols Lowell, Emerson, and Hawthorne, with whom he had been completely charmed. Perhaps under the circumstances he could hardly have been expected to be favorably impressed by the New York Bohemians, but the very fact that he was an unsympathetic outsider made him more observant.

When Howells arrived at the *Press* office early in the morning, only the office boy was there, but the editor finally drifted in. With some of his contributors and assistants forming an appreciative audience, "He walked up and down his room saying what lurid things he would directly do if any one accused him of respectability . . ." [84] Boston and all the New England writers he classified as respectable and therefore had nothing but scorn and sarcasm for them. Howells innocently remarked that he had visited Hawthorne, and when Clapp asked "how I got on with Hawthorne, and I began to say that he was very shy and I was rather shy . . . the king of Bohemia took his pipe out to break in upon me with, 'Oh, a couple of shysters!'" Howells was abashed and disgusted, until someone else in the office said "the thought of Boston made him as ugly as sin," and then the young man from Ohio felt that "men who took themselves so seriously as that need not be taken very seriously by me."

Nevertheless, Howells, who neither smoked nor drank, visited Pfaff's that night, and was as little impressed as he had been at the *Saturday Press* office. But as he was leaving someone whispered that Walt Whitman was there and promptly took him over to the poet's table. Howells remembered "how he leaned back in his chair, and reached out his great hand to me, as if he were going to give it me for good and all. He had a fine head, with a cloud of Jovian hair upon it, and a branching beard and mustache, and gentle eyes that looked most kindly into mine, and seemed to wish the liking which I instantly gave him, though we hardly passed a word, and our acquaintance was summed up in that glance and the grasp of his mighty fist upon my hand." [85]

In the Pfaff group as a whole there probably was much pretension of unconventionality. Several of the members, however, such as Aldrich and Stoddard, were as innately "respectable" as Howells himself, and doubtless none of them were as wicked as they tried to appear. And Clapp must have had more character and ability than Howells thought. In Whitman's later opinion he had "abilities way out of the common," which in a different environment and with financial resources, "might have loomed up as a central influence" on American literature. Howells may have been partly right in thinking that Clapp had taken Whitman up because he was so obnoxious to respectable society, and Whitman's gratitude may have led him to exaggerate Clapp's importance. But the editor of the *Saturday Press*, along with Ada Clare, Ned Wilkins, and several others, did render a service to the history of American literature by giving Whitman companionship and encouragement when he greatly needed them. In his old age Whitman told Traubel that his "own history could not be written with Henry left out." [86] Since no complete file of the *Saturday Press* has survived, it is not possible to trace every detail of Henry Clapp's editorial support of Whitman, but it seems not to have developed until late in 1859.[87]

Aside from his friendship and personal encouragement, Clapp earned Whitman's gratitude by printing on the front page of the *Saturday Press* in the special Christmas number of December 27, 1859, "A Child's Reminiscence" ("Out of the Cradle Endlessly Rocking"), which was to be the finest poem in the new edition of the *Leaves*. On the editorial page appeared this notice:

WALT WHITMAN'S POEM

Our readers may, if they choose, consider as our Christmas or New Year's present to them, the curious warble, by Walt Whitman, of "A Child's Reminiscence," on our First Page. Like the "Leaves of Grass," the purport of this wild and plaintive song, well-enveloped, and eluding definition, is positive and unquestionable, like the effect of music.

The piece will bear reading many times—perhaps, indeed, only comes forth, as from recesses, by many repetitions.[88]

The suggestion that the song eludes definition and has the effect of music almost certainly indicates that Whitman himself wrote this notice, as he just as surely did the defense of the poem, called inanely "All About a Mocking-Bird," in the January 7, 1860, issue of the *Press*, in reply to a fierce attack on it in the Cincinnati *Daily Commercial*. Despite Whitman's self-promotion of his first edition, he had not attempted to reply to any of the attacks on *Leaves of Grass*, and he probably defended this poem only because the Cincinnati critic had so egregiously misunderstood its form and intention. The essay contained many of the gaucheries of diction that were always to mar Whitman's attempts at self-criticism, but it also included several statements of purpose that throw light on the development of Whitman's mind and art. First of all, he promised that, "His songs, . . . will . . . after this date, profusely appear," and announced the forthcoming edition:

We are able to declare that there will also soon crop out the true "Leaves of Grass," the fuller-grown work of which the former two issues were the inchoates —this forthcoming one, far, very far ahead of them in quality, quantity, and in supple lyric exuberance.

Those former issues, published by the author himself in little pittance-editions, on trial, have just dropped the book enough to ripple the inner first-circles of literary agitation, in immediate contact with it. The outer, vast, extending, and ever-wider-extending circles, of the general supply, perusal, and discussion of such a work, have still to come. The market needs to-day to be supplied—the great West especially—with copious thousands of copies.

Indeed, "Leaves of Grass" has not yet been really published at all. Walt Whitman, for his own purposes, slowly trying his hand at the edifice, the structure he has undertaken, has lazily loafed on, letting each part have time to set,—evidently building not so much with reference to any part itself, considered alone, but more with reference to the ensemble,—always bearing in mind the combination of the whole, to fully justify the parts when finished.[89]

These paragraphs show how seriously Whitman had taken Tyndale's advice.[90] That he actually had a structural plan in mind seems very doubtful, though he may have believed that he was intuitively working toward such a plan. In fact, he was relying very heavily on intuition. The Cincinnati critic had insisted that no meaning whatever could be found in "A Child's Reminiscence." To this Whitman replied that it must be tested by the ear, and that he had never "addressed one single word in the whole course of his writings" to the intellect. This would be obscurantism of the rankest sort except for his further advice that the reader should look for the same kind of music found in the Italian opera. The flat assertion that "Walt Whitman's method in the construction of his songs is strictly the method of the Italian Opera" was certainly an exaggeration. But the musical analogy was pertinent, and may still lead readers to a clearer understanding and appreciation of the poem.[91]

Whitman gave no clues, however, to the possible origin of this poem in some personal experience. The reader today will see at once a similarity in tone, theme, and some of the imagery to "Calamus-Leaves," but of course in the 1860 edition those twelve poems were scattered. Miss Helen Price remembered that Whitman read this poem to her family in 1858,[92] and it probably was composed in that year. Nearly all critics have thought it a veiled allegory of a personal experience,[93] though no one has ever discovered what experience. "All About a Mocking-Bird" contained not the faintest hint that the poem should be so interpreted. Whitman told the Prices that his poem "about a mocking bird" was "founded on a real incident," but this could suggest the reality of the bird-story rather than a human incident of love and death.

In this first published version Whitman divided "A Child's Reminiscence" into two parts (though it really had three parts).[94] The first he called "Pre-Verse,"[95] evidently intending by this something like an overture—similar to the function of "Premonition," with which he was planning to introduce the third edition. In these opening lines (the first later greatly improved in rhythm) he created especially the illusion of space and motion, in a setting of moonlit seashore in the foreground and a mockingbird singing in a blackberry thicket in the background:

PRE-VERSE

Out of the rocked cradle,
Out of the mocking-bird's throat, the musical shuttle,
Out of the boy's mother's womb, and from the nipples of her breasts,
Out of the Ninth-Month midnight,
Over the sterile sea-sands, and the fields beyond, where the child, leaving his
    bed, wandered alone, bareheaded, barefoot,
Down from the showered halo and the moonbeams,
Up from the mystic play of shadows twining and twisting as if they were alive,
Out from the patches of briars and blackberries,
From the memories of the bird that chanted to me,
From your memories, sad brother—from the fitful risings and fallings I heard,
From that night, infantile, under the yellow half-moon, late-risen, and swollen
    as if with tears,
From those beginning notes of sickness and love, there in the mist,
From the thousand responses in my heart, never to cease,
From the myriad thence-aroused words,
From the word stronger and more delicious than any,
From such, as now they start, the scene revisiting,

As a flock, twittering, rising, or overhead passing,
Borne hither—ere all eludes me, hurriedly,
A man—yet by these tears a little boy again,
Throwing myself on the sand, I,
Confronting the waves, sing.[96]

The empathy of "Out of . . . , Over . . . , Down from . . . , Out
from . . . ," then the reiteration of "From . . . From . . . From . . ."
is marvelously effective and suggestive. Even the long sentence, with its
writhing syntax, gives the reader a sense of covering uneven ground in the
shadowy moonlight.[97] The skillful blending of sound and images sets the
mood for the major theme of the poem: the bird's "notes of sickness and
love" which awaken in the boy a sense of his mission as a poet.

In the 1859 version the remainder of the poem was called "Reminiscence," and was composed of narration and words intended to translate
the song of the bird, composed apparently on the analogy of recitative and
aria in the Italian opera, as Whitman had indicated. The story was simply
this: In the spring the little boy (the future poet) observed a pair of
mockingbirds, "two guests from Alabama" (and ornithologists say that
mockingbirds were fairly common on Long Island in Whitman's youth).[98]
They built a nest, sat on the eggs, and sang to each other their song of
"Two together!" But one forenoon the she-bird did not return, and
throughout the remainder of the spring and summer the little boy heard
the he-bird calling for his lost mate. The boy understood this song of the
bird, his "brother," and treasured up in his memory every note. The bird
caroled symbolically of the waves and the night:

> O *madly the sea pushes upon the land,*
> *With love—with love.*

But the mate did not come back, and the boy pondered the meaning of
these events until finally, "the aria sinking," he identified himself with the
bird and received the gift of song (or prophecy of it) himself, and "A
thousand warbling echoes" started to life within him.

O you demon,[99] singing by yourself! Projecting me!
O solitary me, listening—never more shall I cease imitating, perpetrating you,
Never more shall I escape,
Never more shall the reverberations,
Never more the cries of unsatisfied love be absent from me . . .

Now he would have a sign, some intimation of his own fate:

O give me some clue!
O if I am to have so much, let me have more!
O a word! O what is my destination?
O I fear it is henceforth chaos!

The answer comes not from the bird, but from the sea, which whispers as it creeps steadily up to the poet's feet, "Death, Death . . ." And this answer the poet will never forget, "But fuse the song of *Two Together* . . ."

My own songs, awaked from that hour,
And with them the key, the word of the sweetest song, and all songs,
That strong and delicious word which, creeping to my feet,
The sea whispered me.

There is, undoubtedly, allegory of a kind in this poem. The poet feels himself to be also solitary; from him "the cries of unsatisfied love" will never be absent, and he must therefore sing as the bird sang out of its own grief. But the poet is more than a creature of nature; to him comes a higher understanding of death—for it is to him, not the bird, that the sea whispers the answer.

If this were a real elegy, the hypothetical basis would be the loss by death of someone whom the poet loved passionately and the consequent reconciliation to the fact of death. But so far as known, Whitman had not experienced such a loss—and if he had had such an experience, it seems strange that he never afterward mentioned it to any of his friends, a dozen of whom wrote biographies or reminiscences of him. The poet of the "Calamus-Leaves" had lamented his lover's treatment of him, and this poem could be a symbolical treatment of that experience, though the sublimity of the poem seems out of proportion to such a motivation.

A more universal interpretation gives the poem greater depth of meaning and therefore seems more tenable. Subjectively, the poet had, in one way or another, experienced such loneliness as he had observed in the bird. And the fear that his own "destination" might be emotional and spiritual "chaos" probably also echoed a period of doubt through which he had passed between the writing of the poems of the second edition and the composition of this poem (1858?). But these need not be the sum total of the intention and achieved expression of "A Child's Reminiscence," which has been admired by critics as one of Whitman's two greatest artistic achievements. In abstract summary, the poet says there is something beyond and more important than personal grief and longing for a lost mate or lover, however great that may be. Out of the chaos of physical stimuli and lacerated emotions emerges the poet's intuitive realization of the ultimate meaning of death, which is that it is the absorption of the individual into the soul of nature or the universe. This spiritual truth not only reconciles the poet to the cruel facts of life but enables him to accept them joyously, and thus to transcend the pathos of his own private emotions. Whatever the possible motivation in personal experience, Whitman managed in this poem to attain a consistency of imagery on a plane sufficiently objective for the work to be intelligible and coherent without knowledge of the poet's biography.

Thus this poem stands as evidence (an esthetic artifact) that in life and in art Walt Whitman gained an emotional equilibrium and spiritual poise after the interlude of despair intimated in "Calamus-Leaves" and the bifurcated purpose still visible in the ending of "Premonition." The victory may have been temporary—all we know is that it lasted until the completion of the poem. But only in such rare moments of equipoise could Whitman fashion a masterpiece. When his self-control wavered, he wrote such passages as the flawed ending of "Premonition." Therefore, "A Child's Reminiscence" stands not as a cenotaph to a private grief but as a great poet's intuition of the victory of the soul over chaos and death.

VII

Near the middle of February, 1860, Whitman received a letter from a new publishing firm in Boston that electrified him almost as much as Emerson's letter had five years previously. This was the exciting letter:

BOSTON FEB 10/60.

WALT WHITMAN

DR SIR. We want to be the publishers of Walt. Whitman's Poems—Leaves of Grass.—When the book was first issued we were clerks in the establishment we now own. We read the book with profit and pleasure. It is a true poem and writ by a *true* man.

When a man dares to speak his thought in this day of refinement—so called —it is difficult to find his mates to act amen to it. Now *we* want to be known as the publishers of Walt. Whitman's books, and put our name as such under his, on title pages.—If you will allow it we can and will put your books into good form, and style attractive to the eye; we can and will sell a large number of copies; we have great facilities by and through numberless Agents in selling. We can dispose of more books than most publishing houses (we do not "puff" here but speak *truth*).

We are young men. We "celebrate" ourselves by acts. Try us. You can do us good. We can do you good—pecuniarily.

Now Sir, if you wish to make acquaintance with us, and accept us as your publishers, we will offer to either buy the stereotype plates of Leaves of Grass, or pay you for the use of them, in addition to regular copyright.

Are you writing other poems? Are they ready for the press? Will you let us read them? Will you write us? Please give us your residence

Yours Fraternally
THAYER & ELDRIDGE.[100]

As soon as the basic agreement had been reached, Thayer and Eldridge were ready to proceed with the printing of the book, and Whitman arrived in Boston scarcely more than a month after he had received the first letter from the publishers. Twenty-one years later, when Whitman was again staying in Boston for the same purpose of getting out a new edition with another Boston publisher, the sight of the big elms on Tremont and Beacon streets recalled to his mind a memorable two-hour stroll and discussion there with Emerson "of a bright sharp February midday twenty-one years ago,"[101] but perhaps the "sharp" weather caused his memory to deceive him as to the month, for the letters he wrote during the spring of 1860 indicate that he arrived on March 15.

The talk with Emerson was apparently Whitman's first important experience in Boston, for he wrote to his friend Mrs. Abby H. Price[102] that Emerson called upon him immediately after his arrival. In his old-age reminiscence of this event Whitman revealed that Emerson attempted on that memorable day to persuade him not to publish his "Children of Adam" poems, and this may have been one of the reasons for Emerson's prompt hospitality, for he probably hoped to prevent Whitman from sending these poems to the printer. Actually the "Enfans d'Adam" (later changed to "Children of Adam") poems were still in manuscript, and Emerson could only have read them if Whitman had sent them to him in manuscript (or proof sheets supplied by Rome Brothers). There seems a strong probability, too, that Emerson had been consulted by Thayer and Eldridge about publishing Leaves of Grass, and if so this would have given him a personal interest in the contents of the book.

For two hours, Whitman recalled, Emerson advanced every argument he could command against publishing these poems, though the main one (perhaps he thought the most strategic) was that their inclusion might endanger the financial success of the book. After he had finished, Emerson asked, "What have you to say then to such things?" And Whitman replied, "Only that while I can't answer at all, I feel more settled than ever to adhere to my own theory, and exemplify it." Against this Dutch stubbornness Emerson was helpless, but he accepted the reply calmly, "Where-upon," Whitman adds, "we went and had a good dinner at the American House." It is interesting, too, that Emerson objected to the "Enfans d'Adam" group but apparently said nothing against the "Calamus" po-ems. One reason for this may have been that he himself had often used "friend" and "lover" interchangeably,[103] and had therefore regarded what later critics were to find homoerotic in Whitman's poems as merely sym-bolical or metaphorical.

Whitman's refusal to take his friend's advice did not diminish Emerson's cordiality. The records of the famous old library in Boston, the Athe-naeum, show that on March 17 Emerson introduced "W. Whitman [of] Brooklyn, N.Y.," [104] and presumably secured reading privileges for him. Emerson also, according to his neighbor F. B. Sanborn, wanted to take Whitman as his guest to the exclusive Saturday Club, but Longfellow, Lowell, and Holmes all insisted that they had no desire to meet the Brook-lyn poet, and consequently Emerson did not extend the contemplated in-vitation.[105] In view of the fact that Lowell, editor of the *Atlantic Monthly*, was printing Whitman's "Bardic Symbols" ("As I Ebb'd with the Ocean of Life"), in the April *Atlantic*, his indifference seems a little strange; but possibly he already regretted having promised Emerson to print the poem.

Two weeks after the memorable discussion under the Boston elms, Whitman wrote to Mrs. Price about the progress on his book and his impressions of Boston.[106] The publishers had not asked him what he "was going to put into the book—just took me to the stereotype foundry and gave orders to follow my directions." Walt was pleased with Boston, and glad he had come, "if only to rub out of me the deficient notions I had of New England character." (Mrs. Price herself was a New Englander, and part of this may have been written to please her.) Proofreading re-quired only three hours a day, and he spent much time walking the streets and strolling in the Common: "I create an immense sensation in Wash-ington Street. Everybody here is so like everybody else—and I am Walt Whitman!—Yankee curiosity and cuteness—for once is thoroughly stumped, confounded, petrified, made desperate."

Aside from his publishers, Whitman knew very few people in Boston, though R. J. Hinton was there at least part of the time,[107] and he made the acquaintance of a sculptor, T. H. Bartlett,[108] and of James Redpath,[109] au-thor of *John Brown*. His Concord friends, Emerson, Thoreau, and Alcott, wanted to invite him over to their homes, but their wives and sisters ob-jected so vehemently that they did not dare to do so.[110] This, of course,

Whitman probably did not know at the time, but it indicates with what difficulty these men maintained their friendship and loyalty to the author of *Leaves of Grass*. Meanwhile he found amusement in going to hear "Father Taylor" (Edward Thompson Taylor), the Methodist minister who preached in Seamen's Chapel and whose nautical language Melville had recently reproduced in *Moby-Dick*. This minister's oratory made such a profound impression on the poet that in his old age he would publish an essay on "Father Taylor (and Oratory)," in which he would describe these experiences:

. . . quiet Sunday forenoons, I liked to go down early to the quaint ship-cabin-looking church where the old man minister'd—to enter and leisurely scan the building, the low ceiling, everything strongly timber'd (polish'd and rubb'd apparently), the dark rich colors, the gallery, all in half-light—and smell the aroma of old wood—to watch the auditors, sailors, mates, "matlows," officers, singly or in groups, as they came in—their physiognomies, forms, dress, gait, as they walk'd along the aisles—their postures, seating themselves in the rude, roomy, undoor'd, uncushion'd pews—and the evident effect upon them of the place, occasion, and atmosphere.[111]

As in New Orleans twelve years earlier, Whitman's family did not write to him and he became anxious for news. On April 1 he wrote to Jeff, begging him to write, and giving him an account of the printing of his book.

. . . The young men that are publishing it treat me in a way I could not wish to have better. They are go-ahead fellows, and don't seem to have the least doubt they are bound to make a good spec. out of my book.—It is quite curious, all this should spring up so suddenly, aint it?

. . . I am very well, and hold my own, about as usual. I am stopping at a lodging house, have a very nice room, gas, water, good American folks keep it —I pay $2—eat at restaurant. I get up in the morning, give myself a good wash all over, and currying,—then take a walk often in the Common—then nothing but a cup of coffee generally for my breakfast—then to the stereotype foundry.—About 12 I take a walk and at 2 a good dinner. Not much else, in the way of eating, except that meal.[112]

Probably Walt had scarcely mailed this letter to Jeff before he received a letter from his mother written March 30, telling him that Andrew had almost died of pleurisy, but had been "blistered and cupped" and was now a little better; that Jesse had returned to work at the Navy Yard; and that she had rented another house, half of which she had sublet to "one of mr Beechers church members by the uncommon name of John Brown." [113]

Jeff also answered Walt's letter promptly. On April 3 Jeff wrote in high good humor, anticipating the joyful times he and Walt would have reading the reviews of the Boston edition: "you must expect the 'Yam yam yam writers to give you a dig as often as possible but I don't suppose you will mind it any more than you did in the days of your editorship of the B. Eagle when the Advertiser Lees used to go at you so roughly . . ." [114]

Next day Mrs. Whitman wrote again, repeating much of her previous letter, fearing, for some reason, that it had miscarried. Evidently her chief motive was to ask Walt for five dollars. George had told her that Jesse wanted to "come home," but "I told him I had hired so much of the house out he would have to hire his board." [115]

On April 16 Jeff wrote once more, conveying the information that "Mother wants me to be sure and tell you that you must bring her one of the books by the author of 'Consuelo,' also Redpath's 'John Brown'!" [116] The latter had recently been published by Walt's new publisher, and perhaps Walt had mentioned it in one of his letters. On May 3 Mrs. Whitman wrote:

. . . we thought you would be through this week and should begin to look for you home but your letter says you are not . . . Eddy is some lame yet   he cant do much   I think its the rheumattics   Andrew has got quite well he has been here three days in succession . . . [The Brown family consisted of a man and wife, a son 17 and a son 9] all but the 9 years one belongs to mr beechers church . . . they have the back basement and the next floor through and one bedroom in the attic . . . we are a little crampt in the basement . . . Hector Tindale was here last week   he looks very fat and well and behaved very friendly indeed   talked much of his mother   says she died of gout in the stomach . . . he thought you had forgotten him or you would have sent him a few lines . . . [117]

By this time Walt had met William Douglas O'Connor, whose abolition novel *Harrington* was also in the process of being published by Thayer and Eldridge. [118] O'Connor had already read with approval the earlier editions of *Leaves of Grass* and he was delighted to make the personal acquaintance of the author in the publishers' office. Mrs. O'Connor had known *Leaves of Grass* since the summer of 1855, when her brother-in-law, Dr. William F. Channing, had secured a copy from the Corner Book Store in Boston, on Emerson's recommendation, and since then she had heard of Whitman through Moncure Conway and Hector Tyndale; but she did not meet the poet until December 1862.

Toward the end of his stay in Boston Walt met another unknown admirer of the first edition, proving again that the 1855 *Leaves* had sunk deeper roots than its author knew, or was later willing to admit. John Townsend Trowbridge was a self-educated journalist and novelist who had begun his career in New York in the early 1840's, but he and Whitman had not chanced to meet, and since he wrote under several pen names Whitman could not have known much about him from his stories. In 1848 he had moved to Boston, and had become a successful editor and popular novelist. He was in Paris when the 1855 *Leaves of Grass* came out, but a newspaper notice reached him (probably Dana's review in the New York *Tribune*): "It was the most exhilarating piece of news I had received from America during the six months of my absence abroad." [119] As soon as he returned home he bought a copy. He found in both this volume and the 1856 edition much that impressed him as "formless and needlessly offensive," yet he recognized "the tremendous original power of this new bard," and he had an "intense curiosity as to the man."

One day in late April or early May a friend of Trowbridge stopped him on Washington Street and startled him with the announcement: "Walt Whitman is in town; I have just seen him!" They hurried around the corner and found "a gray-bearded, plainly dressed man, reading proof-sheets at a desk in a little dingy office, with a lank unwholesome-looking lad at his elbow, listlessly watching him." The lad was a friendless boy whom Whitman had found at his boardinghouse and was trying to cheer up and strengthen by imparting to him some of his "magnetism," as the poet remarked to his visitors.

After the boy's departure the three men stood awkwardly talking. Trowbridge had imagined the poet to be "proud, alert, grandiose, defiant of the usages of society," but he "found him the quietest of men." Trowbridge remembered distinctly only one comment: "The talk turning upon his proof-sheets, I asked how the first poems impressed him, at this rereading; to which he replied, 'I am astonished to find myself capable of feeling so much.'" Whitman talked very quietly, in a low tone, and Trowbridge went away somewhat disappointed. But it was different the following Sunday morning when Whitman visited him in his new home, to which he had recently brought his new bride, on Prospect Hill in Somerville, a suburb of Cambridge.

It was early May, and the weather was perfect. Whitman felt at ease and talked with animation, and Trowbridge was delighted with him, recalling afterward: "He was not a loud laugher, and rarely made a joke, but he greatly enjoyed the pleasantries of others. He liked especially any allusion, serious or jocular, to his poems." On this occasion Whitman told his host a great deal about his life, from boyhood to his publication of *Leaves of Grass.* The two greatest influences on his mind and poetry, he said, had been the Italian opera and reading Emerson. "He freely admitted that he could never have written his poems if he had not first 'come to himself,' and that Emerson helped him to 'find himself.'" His words were: "I was simmering, simmering, simmering; Emerson brought me to a boil." [120]

Toward the end of April Thayer and Eldridge sent out an announcement that *Leaves of Grass* would be published within a few days, and Henry Clapp gave the forthcoming book a nice puff in the April 28th issue of *Saturday Press,* in which he stated that "large orders" had been received already.[121] On the same day the newsstands carried the first issue of a new comic magazine called *Momus,* and it contained some verses in which *Leaves of Grass* was called "pestilent . . . rotten and foul" and the author the "dirtiest beast of the age." That this was a grudge attack is plainly indicated by the fact that the editor of *Momus* was the Charles Gaylor whom Whitman had replaced as editor of the Brooklyn *Times.*[122] Gaylor was living on Myrtle Avenue, only a short distance from the Whitmans, and apparently he had never forgiven Walt for having succeeded him on the *Times.* Whitman may well have wondered if he would ever escape from the personal abuse to which journalism had subjected him ever since he had edited the *Tattler.*

During this spring in Boston Whitman earned the life-long friendship of another resident of Concord, Frank B. Sanborn, who was on trial in Boston for aiding some of John Brown's followers. Sanborn saw Whitman sitting in the court room wearing his gray or blue (he was not quite sure which) carpenter's jacket, and felt encouraged by his presence. Some years later Whitman told Sanborn that he had attended in order to see that justice was done him and that he was ready to help rescue him if necessary.

On May 10 Whitman was still in Boston, but he wrote to Jeff [123] that the book was finished and two days later Henry Clapp acknowledged receiving copies—[124] though they must not have been entirely complete, for the frontispiece, an engraving from the portrait of the author by Charles Hine of New York, was still unfinished, and then there remained the binding. Thayer and Eldridge had printed 1,000 copies, and both Whitman and the publishers expected enough demand for additional printings. Whitman was highly pleased with the appearance of the book, but he was now impatient to get the job over and return home, partly because he found "hiring a room, and eating at restaurants" a drain on his finances: "7 cents for a cup of coffee, and 19 cents for a beefsteak—*and me so fond of* coffee and beefsteak." [125] He was still an interested observer of "the Yanks," enjoying with great naïve amusement the impression he made on them: "Of course I cannot walk through Washington Street, (the Broadway here,) without creating an immense sensation," he confided to Jeff. Perhaps for this reason he was thinking of visiting Hannah during the following summer and touring, "partly business and partly for edification, through all the N.E. states . . ." What the business was to be we can only guess, but quite likely this was another of those futile dreams of becoming a "wander-teacher" or orator. Now, however, after nearly two months away from home, he was becoming very eager to return, and planned to do so the following week:

Should you write to me, in response to this, you must write so that I would get the letter not later than Wednesday morning next—as I feel the fit growing upon me stronger and stronger to move—And the fare is only $3 now from here to New York, cabin passage, in the boat,—Besides I could go deadhead if I was to apply.

—Jeff, I feel as if things had taken a turn with me, at last.—Give my love to Mat, and all my dear brothers, especially Georgie.

On the same day that Walt wrote Jeff this homesick letter, Henry Clapp sent him a letter filled with practical advice on advertising his book and listed persons to whom he should have review copies sent.[126] These included a Mrs. Juliette H. Beach, of Albion, New York, who, Clapp said, would do Whitman "great justice in the Saturday Press." Perhaps Mr. Clapp's motives were not entirely altruistic, for he also wondered if his friend could induce his publishers to advance the *Press* one hundred dollars, just then greatly needed, for future advertising. How much advance the poet wangled we do not know, but in June *Leaves of Grass* was twice advertised in the *Saturday Press*. With review copies dispatched and advertising arranged for, Whitman completed his work in Boston, and probably sailed for New York on Sunday, May 13, as he had planned.

Just before his departure Walt may have received Henry Clapp's letter of May 12, which Henry said was to be delivered personally by his brother George, who was going to Boston. Clapp was still so gravely concerned over his financial struggle to keep the *Saturday Press* alive that he could think of little else, though he did assure Whitman that his success was certain: "It is written all over the book. There is an aroma about it that goes right to the soul." He also promised: "What I can do for it, in the way of bringing it before the public, over and over again, I shall do, and do thoroughly—if the S.P. is kept alive another month. We have more literary influence than any other paper in the land, and as your poems are not new to me, I can say it will all be used for the book—in the interest of poetry." [127]

VIII

The third edition of *Leaves of Grass* was a thick duodecimo volume, bound in heavy boards with beveled edges, running to 456 pages, with the date of 1860–61 on the title page, though as indicated in Whitman's letter to his brother, it was actually printed in May, 1860. Copies with various bindings still exist, but the first issue was probably bound in orange cloth, heavily blind-embossed with wavy vertical lines and decorative designs. The spine was embossed with the figure of a hand with a butterfly perched on outstretched forefinger. On the front cover was the design of a globe floating on clouds, showing the Western Hemisphere. This book was fully as ornate as the first edition had been, though of a decidedly different format; and like the first, this one was also typical of the period. Later in the year other issues (as many as twelve have been counted)[128] were bound in different colors, including one in green and one in brown cloth, with minor variations in the ornamentation and blind-embossing. Though Walt wrote Jeff that the first issue was to be one thousand copies, whether they were all immediately bound is not known, or how many copies were printed in all before Thayer and Eldridge failed soon after the beginning of the Civil War. Small batches could have been bound up on twelve or more occasions, and probably two or three thousand copies were printed before the publishers' bankruptcy.

For the frontispiece Whitman used an engraving made from an oil painting by his friend in New York, Charles Hine. This picture showed a bust of Whitman in a Victor Hugo pose, with curly hair, short beard, a Byronic collar, and a dark silk scarf tied loosely in a huge bow knot. It was the most artificial and uncharacteristic portrait that Whitman was ever to use in any of his books.

The typography of this third edition was clear and readable, and the paper of good quality. For the titles of section headings Whitman used a variety of sizes and styles of type. Though unconventional, they did give each section a character of its own. Whitman himself may have drawn the emblems used wherever the end of a section would have left half a page or more blank. There were three: the globe design from the cover, the hand and butterfly from the spine, and a sun either rising or setting behind the waves of an ocean. If these were intended as symbols, they could have stood for the poet's national and cosmic themes and his romantic feelings for nature. Although artistically somewhat rococo, this edition was expertly printed and bound.

And in this edition Whitman began the experimentation in revision and rearrangement of his poems that he was to continue for the next twenty years. If his projected 1857 edition had been printed it would have been merely a reissue of the 1856 edition with sixty-eight new poems annexed. But the freedom that Thayer and Eldridge gave Whitman enabled him to start building the kind of poetic structure that he hoped would satisfy such criticism as his friend Hector Tyndale had made. For his keystone he used the newly completed "Proto-Leaf," revised only slightly from the manuscript of "Premonition." [129] This served as a preface in verse, indicating the poet's origin in time and place and his national and personal intentions in his poems. It was followed by the long "Walt Whitman" ("Song of Myself").

Then came the first group called "Chants Democratic and Native American." This included several poems from the earlier editions and began with a fortissimo "Apostroph" as prelude:

> O mater! O fils!
> O brood continental!
> O flowers of the prairies!
> O space boundless! O hum of mighty products! etc., etc.

This was the most forced and unpoetic piece of the whole book, and was dropped in the next edition.

The poems in "Chants Democratic" had no titles, only arabic numbers. Number 1 was the 1856 "Poem of Many in One" ("By Blue Ontario's Shore"), itself a poetic preface and actually composed to a large extent of passages from the 1855 preface. Then came the "Broad-Axe" poem and others from the '55 and '56 editions. Among the new poems, Number 9 advanced the idea that America in her growth must pass through convulsive pains and parturitions, illustrating "evil as well as good," and correlatively the poet's song must illustrate the same stages of birth, growth, and death.

In Number 21, the final poem of the group, the poet declares that as he walks "solitary, unattended" he hears the world praising material things, ships, factories, inventions. He admits that they are real and have their place, but he brings realities too—liberty and freedom—the most permanent realities. Democracy, he says, rests upon such poets, whose vision shall "sweep through eternity."

On the whole, "Chants Democratic" was perhaps the weakest group in the book, too loosely held together by vague themes, containing no new poems of major significance, and indicative more of the poet's good intentions than of any positive achievements. Whitman evidently placed this group early in his book to emphasize the nationalism announced in "Premonition." But aside from this prelude to the group, he had not given much constructive thought or effort to this aspect of his program since 1855–56. As we survey subsequent groups in this edition we may catch hints of why this was so.

The next group Whitman called "Leaves of Grass," a puzzling title. Since it was the same as the title of the book, did he mean to imply that it contained the essence of the book—as the author of a collection of short stories or essays sometimes gives his book the title of his major piece? The poet himself gave no clues, but "Leaves of Grass" did contain some very important poems, both old and new.[130] Of special importance among the new poems was "Bardic Symbols" [131] ("Leaves of Grass" Number 1 in 1860), later called "As I Ebbed with the Ocean of Life." This is not in the holographs kept by Rome Brothers and presumably had not been completed when Whitman turned over his manuscripts to them to set up. This indicates 1859 as the year of probable composition, and in mood it conforms to the "slough" that Whitman felt himself to be in during the early summer of 1859, though the imagery is autumnal. It is quite likely that in September or October of that year, before he knew of the possibility of Thayer and Eldridge's publishing his third edition, he did walk the beach at Coney Island and muse on the "ebb" which he felt his life had entered.

I, musing, late in the autumn day, gazing off southward,
Alone, held by the eternal self of me that threatens to get the better of me,
    and stifle me,
Was seized by the spirit that trails in the lines underfoot,
In the rim, the sediment, that stands for all the water and all the land of the
    globe.

As the poet walked the shore of Paumanok (Long Island), which he knew in all its reality, the "old thought of likenesses" (the Transcendental doctrine of "correspondence") suggested to him that some actual, physical experience (or experiences) through which he had been and possibly was still passing, threatening "to get the better" of him, was symbolized by these sea-shore objects:

As I wend the shores I know not,
As I listen to the dirge, the voices of men and women wrecked,
As I inhale the impalpable breezes that set in upon me,
As the ocean so mysterious rolls toward me closer and closer,
At once I find, the least thing that belongs to me, or that I see or touch, I know
  not;
I, too, but signify, at the utmost, a little washed-up drift,
A few sands and dead leaves to gather,
Gather, and merge myself as part of the sands and drift.

Whether the poet felt himself to be physically, emotionally, or morally wrecked the reader can only guess, and the biographer has no objective evidence. Whitman's recent loss of his editorship, and his inability to provide for his mother as he felt he should, may have been partly responsible for this vicarious sympathy with debris and human wrecks. But the poetic failure was evidently a major factor:

O baffled, balked,
Bent to the very earth, here preceding what follows,
Oppressed with myself that I have dared to open my mouth,
Aware now, that, amid all the blab whose echoes recoil upon me, I have not
  once had the least idea who or what I am,
But that before all my insolent poems the real ME still stands untouched,
  untold, altogether unreached,
Withdrawn far, mocking me with mock-congratulatory signs and bows,
With peals of distant ironical laughter at every word I have written or shall
  write,
Striking me with insults till I fall helpless upon the sand.

O I perceive I have not understood anything—not a single object—and that no
  man ever can.

This is not a protest against neglect or misunderstanding. Nor is it merely self-doubt, but doubt of the human mind's ability to pierce the opaque wall separating appearances and reality. Out of such doubt Melville had written *Moby-Dick*, but the tragic tone of this passage had never before been sounded by Walt Whitman, and was not to be characteristic of him in the future. The contrast between this poem and the arrogant boasting in the open letter to Emerson in 1856 measures the whole distance between the crest and depths of Whitman's emotional nature. Now he is bowed by the weight of his *hybris*, and in his humility we see not blank despair or useless nihilism but a stoic acceptance that shows new depth of character.

Now for the first time, too, the father-symbol emerges clearly in his poetry:

You friable shore, with trails of debris!
You fish-shaped island! I take what is underfoot;
What is yours is mine, my father.

I too Paumanok,
I too have bubbled up, floated the measureless float, and been washed on your
    shores;
I too am but a trail of drift and debris,
I too leave little wrecks upon you, you fish-shaped island!

I throw myself upon your breast, my father,
I cling to you so that you cannot unloose me,
I hold you so firm, till you answer me something.

Kiss me, my father,
Touch me with your lips, as I touch those I love,
Breathe to me, while I hold you close, the secret of the wondrous murmuring I
    envy,
For I fear I shall become crazed, if I cannot emulate it, and utter myself as well
    as it.

Despite the fact that the poet feels his life and poetry to have been a failure (like the life of his real father, Walter Whitman, Sr.), he still has hope that he "will yet sing, some day" the meaning of the "Crooked-tongued waves." [132] He has confidence, too, that just as in nature the *ebb* finally gives way to the *flow*, so will his ebb recede and the flow return. Yet he retains his new self-knowledge; his humility is genuine, and he now knows that both his life and his poems, "Me and mine," are but "loose winrows, little corpses,"

> Buoyed hither from many moods, one contradicting another,
> From the storm, the long calm, the darkness, the swell,

and he casts himself and all he has accomplished at the feet of his readers:

We, capricious, brought hither, we know not whence, spread out before You,
    up there, walking or sitting,
Whoever you are—we too lie in drifts at your feet.

Whitman may not have intended his imagery as actual allegory. By
"Bardic Symbols" [133] he could have meant only "poetic symbols"; but
whether consciously or intuitively, he shows in these symbols penetrating
comprehension of the origin and nature of his poems. They had indeed
been "Buoyed hither from many moods, one contradicting another," and
he was right that "the storm, the long calm, the darkness," would be followed by "the swell," and he would again be able to "float the measureless float" as in "Crossing Brooklyn Ferry."
As if in answer to this prophecy, he recorded in "Leaves of Grass"
Number 10 what sounds like a moral resolution based on this new self-
knowledge:

It is ended—I dally no more,
After to-day I inure myself to run, leap, swim, wrestle, fight,
.   .   .   .
Let others deny the evil their enemies charge against them—but how can I
    the like?
Nothing ever has been, or ever can be, charged against me, half as bad as the
    evil I really am; . . .

He warns against those who would expound him, or attempt to found any
theory or school on his teachings; he prefers to "leave all free as I have
left all free." Purged and resolute, he feels himself once more capable of
being a seminal influence.

I henceforth tread the world, chaste, temperate, an early riser, a gymnast, a
    steady grower,
Every hour the semen of centuries—and still of centuries.

I will follow up these continual lessons of the air, water, earth,
I perceive I have no time to lose.

In Number 20 the poet anticipates the publication of his third edition, but he thinks there is a strong possibility that it will be his last—
though that depends not upon himself but upon what happens to his nation:

So far, and so far, and on toward the end,
Singing what is sung in this book, from the irresistible impulses of me;

But whether I continue beyond this book, to maturity,
Whether I shall dart forth the true rays, the ones that wait unfired,
(Did you think the sun was shining its brightest?
No—it has not yet fully risen;)
Whether I shall complete what is here started,
Whether I shall attain my own height, to justify these, yet unfinished,
Whether I shall make THE POEM OF THE NEW WORLD, transcending all others
    —depends, rich persons, upon you,
Depends, whoever you are now filling the current Presidentiad, upon you,
Upon you, Governor, Mayor, Congressman,
And you, contemporary America.

The closing poem of this section was a short piece, apparently composed after the manuscript had gone to Rome Brothers, which sounds like an early fragmentary draft of the longer poem that was to end the whole book.

Lift me close to your face till I whisper,
What you are holding is in reality no book, nor part of a book,
It is a man, flushed and full-blooded—it is I—*So long!*
We must separate—Here! take from my lips this kiss,
Whoever you are, I give it especially to you;
So long—and I hope we shall meet again.

This dream of intimate personal contact with the reader, and the fantasy that the book was really the poet's own flesh and blood (by the miracle of poetic consubstantiation) has been noted in the first and second editions, and need not be commented upon further. But the hope that "we shall meet again" was undoubtedly real, and showed Whitman's desire to carry his work through to future editions.

After some intervening poems following the "Leaves of Grass" section came the group that Emerson had tried so hard to persuade Whitman to leave out, "Enfans d'Adam." Doubtless Whitman had ideological reasons for placing these poems here between "Leaves of Grass" and "Calamus," but he left convincing evidence in his notebooks that the group was an after-thought, growing not from an inner compulsion but used for the strategic purpose of balancing "Calamus"—or more accurately the cluster of twelve poems first called "Live-Oak Leaves," before Whitman had thought of his calamus plant symbol. The first idea of "Enfans d'Adam" was "A string of Poems, (short etc.) embodying the amative love of woman —the same as Live-Oak Leaves do the passion of friendship for men." [184]

("Amative" was a phrenological term meaning heterosexual attraction.) [135] Later Whitman jotted down this plan:

Theory of a Cluster of Poems the same *to the passion of Woman-Love* as the *Calamus-Leaves* are to adhesiveness, manly love.

Full of animal-fire, tender, burning,—the tremulous ache, delicious, yet such a torment.

The swelling elate and vehement, that will not be denied.
Adam, as a central figure and type.
One piece presenting a vivid picture (in connection with the spirit) of a fully complete, well-developed, man, eld, bearded, swart, fiery,—as a more than rival of the youthful type-hero of novels and love poems.[136]

In the first of these poems Whitman neatly set forth his main symbols: the beginning of human existence in the Garden of Eden, the necessity of sex in the cycles of life, the innocence and naturalness of the "quivering fire" that attracted Adam to Eve and man to woman ever since.

In Number 2 the theme of sex has become a program, to be vehemently adhered to regardless of consequences—Whitman expected opposition:

From that of myself, without which I were nothing,
From what I am determined to make illustrious, even if I stand sole among
    men,
From my own voice resonant—singing the phallus,
Singing the song of procreation, . . .

The song of "the phallus" is consistent with the program, but a few lines later the poet is "Singing the song of prostitutes," and he wants to be "free and lawless" like "Two hawks in the air—two fishes swimming in the sea." Here the reader may be pardoned for wondering whether the poet really wants to celebrate "procreation" or to be free of restraints and inhibitions. Once more, as in the second edition, the poet's intention seems to be confused, as in the 1856 "Spontaneous Me," now incorporated into "Enfans d'Adam," Number 5. And in Number 6 the poet wonders what his "shouts amid lightnings and raging winds mean." In Number 8 also he believes in "loose delights" and shares "the midnight orgies of young men," or

I take for my love some prostitute—I pick out some low person for my dearest
    friend,
He shall be lawless, rude, illiterate—he shall be one condemned by others for
    deeds done;
I will play a part no longer—Why should I exile myself from my companions?
O you shunned persons! I at least do not shun you,
I come forthwith in your midst—I will be your poet,
I will be more to you than to any of the rest.

That the poet is giving expression to strong emotional urges there can
be no doubt, but they seem to cover an astonishingly wide range, and
he and the reader lose sight of the procreation theme.

    Further doubts are raised by Number 9, which read in the manuscript
version:

Once I passed through a populous celebrated city imprinting on my brain for
    future use, its shows, with its shows, architecture, customs and traditions,
But now of all that city I remember only the man who wandered with me, there,
    for love of me,
Day by day, and night by night, we were together,
All else has long been forgotten by me—I remember, I say, only one rude
    and ignorant man who, when I departed, long and long held me by the
    hand, with silent lip, sad and tremulous.—[137]

This Whitman transformed into an "Enfans d'Adam" poem not only by
changing "man" to "woman" but also, in conformity with his theory, by
inserting the "animal fire" he had decided upon in his notebook plan:

> I remember I say only that woman who passionately clung to me,
> Again we wander—we love—we separate again,
> Again she holds me by the hand—I must not go!
> I see her close beside me, with silent lips, sad and tremulous.

    Certainly the poet had the right to make any revisions he wished to
achieve his artistic purpose. Either of these versions fits neatly into the
"Calamus" or "Enfans d'Adam" groups respectively. And the male-
friendship motif is not necessarily erotic, though that is the way it will
usually be taken. But, more important, the poet seems to have difficulty in
writing enough "Enfans d'Adam" poems to fill out his cluster and has to
resort to such transformations as the above.

    In Number 10 he elevates his sex theme to embrace the history of the
race—one of the most impressive motifs in the 1855 edition:

I, a child, very old, over waves, toward the house of maternity, the land of migrations, look afar . . .

This is continued successfully through Number 12:

Ages and ages, returning at intervals . . .

In Number 14 love-aching is equated with gravitation, and the "I" of the poem is attracted to "all I meet." The final poem of the series in 1860 (Number 15) is merely the injunction, "Be not afraid of my body," though the Adamic motif has mythopoeic implications of resurrection and transmigration:

> Early in the morning,
> Walking forth from the bower, refreshed with sleep,
> Behold me where I pass—hear my voice—approach,
> Touch me—touch the palm of your hand to my body as I pass,
> Be not afraid of my body.

The "Enfans d'Adam" group thus ends artistically on the theme of the sacredness of the human body, but this theme has had little development in the preceding poems, so that this final poem seems like an after-thought, an artificial epilogue.

One might expect the "woman-love" poems to be followed immediately by the "man-love" poems, which the former were written to counter-balance. But Whitman inserted three 1855 pieces between these groups: "Poem of the Road" ("Song of the Open Road"), "To the Sayers of Words," and "A Boston Ballad."

The "Calamus" poems number forty-five, including all those formerly planned for the "Live-Oak, with Moss" cluster or "Calamus-Leaves." The key symbol is never fully explained, but it may have grown out of the "leaves" and "root" imagery of "Scented Herbage of My Breast" (now Number 2). The appropriateness of the calamus plant, an aromatic sweet-flag, with phallic-shaped bloom and stiff slender leaves, growing in swampy ground, is suggested in Number 1:

In paths untrodden,
In the growth by margins of pond-waters,
Escaped from the life that exhibits itself,
From all the standards hitherto published—from the pleasures, profits, con-
formities,

Which too long I was offering to feed to my Soul;
Clear to me now, standards not yet published—clear to me that my Soul,
That the Soul of the man I speak for [myself], feeds, rejoices only in comrades;
Here, by myself, away from the clank of the world,
Tallying and talked to here by tongues aromatic,
No longer abashed—for in this secluded spot I can respond as I would not
    dare elsewhere,
Strong upon me the life that does not exhibit itself, yet contains all the rest,
Resolved to sing no songs to-day but those of manly attachment,
Projecting them along that substantial life,
Bequeathing, hence, types of athletic love,
Afternoon, this delicious Ninth Month, in my forty-first year,
I proceed, for all who are, or have been, young men,
To tell the secret of my nights and days,
To celebrate the need of comrades.

This geographical and botanical symbolism is highly significant. The poet is no longer the frequenter of city streets, crowded ferry boats, and public places. He now desires to withdraw to a secret, unfrequented place, where he can escape from "all standards hitherto published"—not sexual alone, but other conventionalities as well. Though these "Calamus" poems or "leaves" originated in the poet's desire to exhibit the sexual nature he believes contemporary society has forced him to conceal, the impulses symbolized in the poems are extremely complex and involve the total personality, character, and future ambitions of the poet.

In the arrangement of the 1860 edition the "Calamus" poems do not delineate personal history, except by implication. To judge by the title Whitman first gave the group in his manuscripts, Number 20, "I Saw in Louisiana a Live-Oak Growing," the original impulse was a sense of loneliness and the poet's doubt that he could "utter leaves" (write poems) "without a friend, a lover, near." But Number 26, "We two boys together clinging," seems to have been a fantasy wish-fulfillment rather than the record of an actual experience, for in a manuscript version[138] called "Razzia" (Algerian pronunciation of an Arabic word meaning "raid" or "foray"), the friendship motif was entirely lacking:

Up and down the roads going—North and South excursions making,
Power enjoying—elbows stretching—fingers clutching,
Armed and fearless—eating, drinking, sleeping, loving,
No law less than myself owning—Sailing, soldiering, thieving, threatening,
Misers, menials, priests, alarming—Air breathing, water drinking, on the turf
    or the sea-beach dancing,

With birds singing—With fishes swimming—With trees branching and leafing,
Cities wrenching, ease scorning, statutes mocking, feebleness chasing,
Fulfilling my foray.

Thus the desire for adventure, excitement, breaking free of all artificial restraint, acting as naturally as birds, fish, and trees, was the basic impulse in the genesis of this and doubtless other "Calamus" poems. Although these desires could have had a sexual origin, in the poems they are
often generalized and fused with various other motifs.

In Number 27 the poet feels that he has sloughed off his old life like a
snake its skin, and he is glad that what he was for years is now dead:

O love!
O dying—always dying!
O the burials of me, past and present,
O me, while I stride ahead, material, visible, imperious as ever!
O me, what I was for years, now dead, (I lament not—I am content;)
O to disengage myself from those corpses of me, which I turn and look at,
    where I cast them!
To pass on, (O living! always living!) and leave the corpses behind!

But this new self has not found the lover-friend sought and dreamed of
in the poems. In Number 28 the poet is not envious of the great heroes
he reads about in biography and history:

But when I read of the brotherhood of lovers, how it was with them,
How through life, through dangers, odium, unchanging, long and long,
Through youth, and through middle and old age, how unfaltering, how affec-
    tionate and faithful they were,
Then I am pensive—I hastily put down the book, and walk away, filled with
    the bitterest envy.

The kind of relationship the poet desires is described in Number 29:

One flitting glimpse, caught through an interstice,
Of a crowd of workmen and drivers in a bar-room, around the stove, late of a
    winter night—And I unremarked, seated in a corner,
Of a youth who loves me, and whom I love, silently approaching, and seating
    himself near, that he may hold me by the hand;
A long while, amid the noises of coming and going—of drinking and oath
    and smutty jest,
There we two, content, happy in being together, speaking little, perhaps not
    a word.

Such a relationship of trust and affection Whitman would like to extend to society, and in Number 34 he has dreamed of "a city invincible" in which "robust love" dominates every thought and action:

> It was seen every hour in the actions of the men of that city,
> And in all their looks and words.

Like the ancient Greeks, the "Calamus" poet believes in two kinds of love, a "primeval" type "for the woman I love" (though there was no one woman so far as we know), and a higher, more unphysical ("disembodied"), satisfying love for a man:

Primeval my love for the woman I love,
O bride! O wife! more resistless, more enduring than I can tell, the thought
    of you!
Then separate, as disembodied, the purest born,
The ethereal, the last athletic reality, my consolation,
I ascend—I float in the regions of your love, O man,
O sharer of my roving life.

Number 43 indicates the "subtle electric fire" that the poet feels for someone (whether specific or general is not entirely clear), but he apparently conceals his emotion, for "Little you know . . ."

O you whom I often and silently come where you are, that I may be with you,
As I walk by your side, or sit near, or remain in the same room with you,
Little you know the subtle electric fire that for your sake is playing within me.

This is very revealing, and corroborates many other implications in these poems and in the reminiscences of Whitman's friends that he gave expression to such emotions in his poems rather than in actual physical relationships—compare the story of the young man in the printing office told to Helen Price.[139] Indeed, it seems highly probable that the poems were a vicarious substitute for physical experience.

Probably the psychology involved in the writing of these poems was not clear to Whitman himself. One of his strongest motives appears to have been his desire to confess, "To tell the secret of my night and days," and yet in these poems we find more esoteric symbols than in any other group in the book. Whitman was not, however, unaware of this paradox, as Number 44 shows:

Here my last words, and the most baffling,
Here the frailest leaves of me, and yet my strongest-lasting,
Here I shade down and hide my thoughts—I do not expose them,
And yet they expose me more than all my other poems.

The same impulse that caused Whitman's fantasy to create symbols of a higher, more "ethereal," and more consoling love than heterosexual attraction also caused him to dream of establishing a spiritual rapport with readers long after his death. In fact, the idea of becoming disembodied, all spirit, was a powerful stimulus to his poetic faculties, as we have already seen in the masterpiece "Crossing Brooklyn Ferry" [140]—which in the 1860 edition immediately followed "Calamus"—and doubtless explains why the poet of "A Word Out of the Sea" ("Out of the Cradle Endlessly Rocking") found the "delicious word" *death* to be "The word of the sweetest song, and all songs."

In the final "Calamus" poem (Number 45), as in the "So Long!" at the end of the book, the poet is again a "time-binder":

Full of life, sweet-blooded, compact, visible,
I, forty years old the Eighty-third Year of The States,
To one a century hence, or any number of centuries hence,
To you, yet unborn, these, seeking you.

When you read these, I, that was visible, am become invisible;
Now it is you, compact, visible, realizing my poems, seeking me,
Fancying how happy you were, if I could be with you, and become your lover;
Be it as if I were with you. Be not too certain but I am now with you.

In the manuscript version [141] the age of the poet is thirty-eight, and Whitman may have written this poem on his birthday in 1857. Other poems in the "Calamus" group were probably written in 1859 (they are on white paper), so that this is by no means a record of the climax of Whitman's "Calamus" emotions; but esthetically it transcends the whole complex of these emotions.

After another sandwich-layer of miscellaneous poems, fragments, "Says," "Debris," and so on, the third edition ended, as remarked above, with "So Long!", preceded by "To My Soul," in which the poet anticipates his death. In "So Long!" he announces "what comes after me," but this is not the arrogant prophecy of 1855–1856 of his nation's greatness and his own success as its spokesman and poet-leader. Rather, he now announces "that all I know at any time suffices for that time only," and greater poets and orators must take care of the future. Neither in his 1855 preface nor in his 1856 open letter to Emerson was he so humble as this. He had begun his career with the intention of being the poet of "consummations":

I remember I said to myself at the winter-close, before my leaves sprang at all,
    that I would become a candid and unloosed summer-poet,
I said I would raise my voice jocund and strong, with reference to consum-
    mations.

He still believes that America can consummate the great ideals promised, but neither he nor the nation has yet achieved them. He himself has
only been a forerunner:

Yet not me, after all—let none be content with me,
I myself seek a man better than I am, or a woman better than I am,
I invite defiance, and to make myself superseded
All I have done, I would cheerfully give to be trod under foot, if it might only
    be the soil of superior poems.

Whitman is nowhere more typically American than in his pragmatic belief that the old must be destroyed to make way for the new:

I demand the choicest edifices to destroy them,
Room! room! for new far-planning draughtsmen and engineers!
Clear that rubbish from the building-spots and the paths!
.   .   .   .
So long!
I announce a life that shall be copious, vehement, spiritual, bold,
And I announce an old age that shall lightly and joyfully meet its translation.

And now he takes the stage in person:

My songs cease—I abandon them,
From behind the screen where I hid, I advance personally.

This is no book,
Who touches this, touches a man,
.   .   .   .
I spring from the pages into your arms—decease calls me forth.

As in "Premonition," [142] Whitman ends with a sentimental appeal to the
reader:

Dear friend, whoever you are, here, take this kiss,
I give it especially to you—Do not forget me,
I feel like one who has done his work—I progress on,
The unknown sphere, more real than I dreamed, more direct, darts awakening
    rays about me—*So Long!*
Remember my words—I love you—I depart from materials,
I am as one disembodied, triumphant, dead.

Thus Walt Whitman the poet has attained his ultimate goal: he is "disembodied, triumphant, dead." But in his book he hopes to live as long as Americans shall read his poems.

⋖ VII ⋗

LOVING COMRADE

Long, long I muse, then on my way go wandering;
Many a changeful season to follow, and many a scene of life;
Yet at times through changeful season and scene, abrupt, alone, or in the
    crowded street,
Comes before me the unknown soldier's grave, comes the inscription rude in
    Virginia's woods,
Bold, cautious, true, and my loving comrade.[1]

I

OF ALL editions of *Leaves of Grass* published (or privately printed during
Whitman's lifetime), the third made the most promising beginning.
Thayer and Eldridge handsomely advertised it,[2] and Henry Clapp kept his
promise of May 12 to publicize the book. On May 19, 1860, the *Saturday
Press* carried a long article on "Walt Whitman/ Leaves of Grass," which
began, "We announce a great Philosopher—perhaps a great Poet—in every
way an original man." The critic, probably Clapp himself,[3] admitted that
the book contained some passages "which should never have been published at all." But he also declared that the poems evinced "the philosophic mind, deeply seeking, reasoning, feeling its way toward a clear
knowledge of the system of the universe," and praised the "felicity of
style" in such phrases as "bare-bosomed Night," "slumbering and liquid
trees," and "Earth of the vitreous pour of the full moon, just tinged with
blue!"[4]

However, the review that Clapp received a few days later from Albion,
New York, certainly did not do Whitman the "great justice" that the editor of the *Saturday Press* had led him to expect.[5] It was not signed by Mrs.
Beach, but Clapp thought that a mistake and published it on June 2 as
by Juliette H. Beach. The reviewer began by saying that he had read only
a few of the poems, but apparently he could instinctively sniff out the
most offensive passages:

Walt Whitman assumes to regard woman only as an instrument for the gratification of his desires, and the propagation of the species. To him all women are the same, with but this difference; the more sensual have the preference, as they promise greater indulgence. His exposition of his thoughts shows conclusively that with him the congress of the sexes is a purely animal affair, and with his ridiculous egotism he vaunts his prowess as a stock-breeder might that of the pick of his herd.[6]

The reviewer finally ended by advising the poet to commit suicide, but begged him not to use any of the usual methods, "because some full man, to whom life has become a grievous burden, may at a later day be compelled to choose between death by the same means and a hateful life, and with the pride of noble manhood turn shuddering to live on, rather than admit so much of oneness as would be implied by going to death as did Walt Whitman."

Clapp commented editorially on this "unfavorable view" of *Leaves of Grass* but added, "It always gives us pleasure to print every variety of opinion upon such subjects. . . ." The following week, however, the *Saturday Press* printed this "Correction":

A *note from* MRS. JULIETTE H. BEACH *informs us that the article in our last issue, on* Walt Whitman's 'LEAVES OF GRASS,' *was written, not by her, but by Mr. Beach, whose initials were, indeed, appended to it. The error arose from the fact that we were expecting an article from Mrs. Beach on the book (it having been forwarded to her by the publishers at our particular request), and that when the looked-for MS. arrived we sent it directly to the printer, with the usual instructions to sign the name of the author—concerning which we had not the slightest doubt—in full.*

Two weeks later someone who signed herself simply "A Woman" contributed a defense of Whitman and his book that seemed designed to counteract Mr. Beach's attack, and this may have been Mrs. Beach's belated review—not signed to avoid further advertising of a family quarrel. In this essay Whitman was hailed as an embodiment of the new "National Genius," who ennobled every subject he touched. Only a few readers, said the correspondent, were able to "fathom the deep spiritual significance" of these poems, but she predicted: "These bold and truthful pages will inevitably form the standard book of poems in the future of America. . . . It is all good, the sudden transition, the obscure connection, the grand sublimity and boldness, but better far the spirit of the writer, so raised beyond everything else, sometimes even beyond himself, grasping at ideas too great for words. God bless him. I know that through 'Leaves of Grass,' Walt Whitman on earth is immortal as well as beyond it."

There may have been more than mere literary disagreement in the Beach family. We have Ellen O'Connor's word that Whitman wrote the poem "Out of the Rolling Ocean" for "a certain lady" who incurred her husband's wrath by corresponding with the poet,[7] and Clara Barrus stated that "Miss Juliette H. Beach" (the "Miss" obviously a mistake), was the woman "to whom Whitman wrote 'Out of the rolling ocean.' She wrote many beautiful letters to Walt which J.B. [John Burroughs] tried in vain to get her consent to publish."[8] This statement does not say that these were love letters, though that seems to be the implication; and we know nothing about Whitman's replies—he must have written some that encouraged Mrs. Beach to continue writing. We do not know whether the attraction was physical or mainly appreciative and sympathetic, but it appears that the review copy sent to Mrs. Beach did cause a quarrel between her and her husband, and there may have been an emotional sequel.

The third Leaves of Grass was likewise the cause of Whitman's gaining another loyal woman friend, who admired his poems so much that she tried to become a disciple and to adopt some traits of his versification. This was the colorful actress and poet Adah Isaacs Menken, who had been introduced to the Pfaff circle about the time Whitman went to Boston.[9] She and Ada Clare became great friends, and this may also have influenced her hero-worship of Whitman. She had been married twice, the last time to the famous prize fighter John Heenan, who deserted her when he went to England to fight the British champion in the spring of 1860. Meanwhile the editor of the New York Sunday Mercury, Robert Henry Newell, had been attracted by this vivacious woman and had begun early in 1860 to print her poems. Newell strongly disliked Whitman's poems, but Adah Menken charmed him into printing her highly eulogistic review of the new Leaves of Grass on June 3. Like the anonymous reviewer in the Saturday Press, she regarded Whitman as a great philosopher, "centuries ahead of his contemporaries. . . . He hears the Divine voice calling him to caution mankind against this or that evil; and wields his pen, exerts his energies, for the cause of liberty and humanity!"[10]

One of the most surprising aspects of the critical reception of the 1860 Leaves was the number of women who spoke out in defense of the poems that many of the male critics found indecent and shocking. On June 5 Mary A. Chilton of Islip, Long Island, sent to the Saturday Press a strong endorsement of the sex poems and her letter was printed June 9. After reading Whitman's poems many times, she testified, "the simple grandeur of his expressed soul, filled mine with awe and reverence for the pages he had the genius to inspire." She defended his poetic treatment of the human body and its natural functions with the philosophical and ethical argument that "In childhood there is no blush of shame at sight of a nude form, and the serene wisdom of maturity covers this innocence with a halo of glory, by recognizing the divinity of humanity, and perceiving the unity of all the functions of the human body . . . and those functions which have been deemed the most brutal and degrading, will be found to be first in rank when nature's hierarchy shall be established and observed. . . ."

In his old age, speaking of Ada Clare, Whitman remarked that "it is very curious that the girls have been my sturdiest defenders, upholders," [11] and he certainly had good cause to be grateful, for these women of New York State were not the last to come to his aid.[12] Possibly the current campaigns for women's rights had something to do with their broadmindedness toward his treatment of their sex, but they also found in the poet's character and personality traits that they especially admired. Women like Mrs. Price,[13] who knew him in his own home and community, liked him, and other women such as Mrs. Beach who apparently knew him only (or mainly) through his poems, found him equally attractive and admirable.

After Whitman's death his friend and publisher, C. W. Eldridge, remembered that when the third edition was published "the tone of the Press was universally contemptuous, when not abusive." [14] Abuse there was unmistakably, but Eldridge's recollections about the reception of the 1860 edition were not entirely accurate. Perhaps they were unconsciously colored by the events of his bankruptcy in the following year and Whitman's subsequent difficulties in finding a publisher. Statistically the abuse may have been more abundant than the praise, but there was praise too, and even the abuse made Whitman's name known. In addition to the continued support of the *Saturday Press*, the 1860 *Leaves* was widely reviewed and commented upon, not only in New York but as far away as the New Orleans *Weekly Mirror* (June 9), the *Southern Field and Fireside* (June 9) of Augusta, Georgia, the London *Leader* (June 30) and London *Spectator* (July 14).[15]

Even more numerous were the parodies, both serious and satirical, that began to appear in newspapers and magazines by late summer and early fall. This was another indication that Walt Whitman was gaining notoriety, and the editor of the *Saturday Press*, apparently thinking that the publicity would help his friend, reprinted as many of these parodies as he could.[16] But probably such fame gave Whitman little satisfaction. In his home town the *Eagle* reprinted and gloated over an attack on the poems published in the October *Westminster Review*. This was a double blow because the *Westminster Review* was one of Whitman's favorite magazines during the 1850's, as we have noticed.[17] That these attacks hurt the poet deeply is indicated by his once again writing anonymous reviews of his work. A defense of *Leaves of Grass* in the Brooklyn *City News* on October 10 was almost certainly written by him. He had still not received the hearing he longed for, and he continued to feel misunderstood and to be impatient because the new edition had not changed the situation and brought him the recognition he believed rightly to be his. The bankruptcy of Thayer and Eldridge a few months later must have completely shattered his dream of success which he had confided to his brother while the book was being printed.

II

During the summer of 1860 the subject of greatest interest to Whitman was probably the critical reception and actual sale of his book, but it was not in his nature to be indifferent to local and national affairs. The prize fight that finally took place in England on April 17 between Heenan and Sawyers, the British champion, was of little interest to him. But this event was quickly superseded by the more exciting political rivalry at the presidential conventions. Previous to the two major conventions, the Party of the Union and Constitution had met at Baltimore and on May 9 nominated John Bell of Tennessee for the Presidency and Edward Everett of Massachusetts for the Vice Presidency.

Late in April the Democrats met at Charleston and nominated Stephen A. Douglas, whom Whitman had praised in his Brooklyn *Times* editorials. Around the middle of May the Republicans met in Chicago, in the convention hall they called the "Wigwam." For several days the New York *Tribune* printed lengthy reports from the Wigwam predicting the certain nomination of William Henry Seward, former governor of New York and now a United States senator, who two years previously had warned the nation of the "irrepressible conflict" between North and South. But on May 18 Abraham Lincoln was nominated on the third ballot, and New Yorkers were stunned and shocked by the news. In the near future Whitman would become a staunch admirer of Lincoln, but what he thought at the time of his nomination is not known.

Although Lincoln, like Whitman himself, was not an actual abolitionist, nevertheless his nomination, as events were to prove, made the "irrepressible conflict" really inevitable. Yet despite Whitman's foreboding "Eighteenth Presidency!" [18] and his bitter satire on recent "Presidentiads" [19] in his new edition, there is no evidence that in the summer of 1860 he regarded war as imminent. Actually, the only record of his thoughts during this fateful summer is to be found in a poem in which he greeted the beginning of what he believed to be a new era of peace and international harmony. Seven years previously Admiral Perry had brought an end to Japan's "closed door" policy, and since then diplomatic and commercial negotiations had been under way.[20] Before Whitman left Boston a group of Japanese "ambassadors" (that is, envoys) had arrived in Washington to discuss a treaty with the United States, and for weeks the newspapers had been filled with details of their appearance, manners, customs, and the official receptions given in their honor. The nation had not been so excited since Barnum had brought Jenny Lind to American shores.

Late in May the Japanese visitors started North, stopping in Baltimore and Philadelphia for parades and more receptions. For the moment even the campaign for the Presidency was almost forgotten. On June 16 the Japanese "ambassadors" arrived in New York and were greeted by a mammoth parade up Broadway,[21] which Whitman personally witnessed. He was so deeply moved that almost immediately he wrote a poem on the occasion, and on June 27 the New York *Times* printed it. In this newspaper version Whitman called his poem "The Errand-Bearers," but after the war he changed the title to "A Broadway Pageant," thus shifting the emphasis from prophecy to public spectacle. Reading the lines today, one can still catch the excited curiosity of the crowd and the eagerness of the poet to see in the pageantry omens of progress and happiness for the whole civilized world:

Over sea, hither from Niphon,
Courteous, the Princes of Asia, swart-cheek'd princes,
First-comers, guests, two-sworded princes,
Lesson-giving princes, leaning back in their open barouches, bare-headed, impassive,
This day they ride through Manhattan.

.   .   .   .

When million-footed Manhattan, unpent, descends to its pavements,
When the thunder-cracking guns arouse me with the proud roar I love,

．．．．．．．．．．．．．．．．

When every ship is richly drest, and carrying her flag at the peak,
When pennants trail, and festoons hang from the windows,
When Broadway is entirely given up to foot-passers and foot-standers—
    When the mass is densest,
When the facades of the houses are alive with people . . .

                      . . . When the answer
    that waited thousands of years, answers,
I too, arising, answering, descend to the pavements, merge with the crowd, and
    gaze with them.[22]

In this poem Whitman is less concerned with the Japanese envoys and the actual purpose of the trip than with the symbolism of the coming of the representatives of the Orient to the young Western nation. He calls the event the "murky night-morning of wonder and fable." The circle is complete: past and present, East and West are now joined; their cultures and people mingle. The poet foresees American commerce and political influence threading the islands and archipelagoes of the globe. The Western Republic "shall sit in the middle thousands and thousands of years." However, he begs his nation for once to bend its "proud neck to the long-off mother now sending messages over the archipelagoes to you," because this magnificent future which he envisions will not be the simple product of innate superiority—though that perhaps he takes for granted—but will be the result of the divine plan, followed unconsciously by mankind in its upward journey throughout the centuries.

—Were the children straying westward so long? So wide the tramping?
Were the precedent dim ages debouching westward from Paradise so long?
Were the centuries steadily footing it that way, all the while, unknown, for you,
    for reasons?
—They are justified—they are accomplished—They shall now be turned the
    other way also, to travel toward you thence,
They shall now also march obediently eastward, for your sake, Libertad.

This is the final stage of "manifest destiny," refined and "spiritualized" since Whitman's crude editorials in the 1840's, but no less unboundedly optimistic. The irony is that the marvelous destiny that Whitman's fancy projected for his nation would be rudely interrupted in less than a year from the date of this parade. For ages to come the vision might yet be a true prophecy, but in the short-term practical world "Libertad" would soon be locked in the bloodiest civil war in history.

Aside from Whitman's witnessing the parade for the Japanese envoys,

there is little concrete information about his life from the time of his return from Boston in late May until the following spring. This is not because he in any way concealed his activities during those months, but more
likely because he was not doing much of anything. He may have done
some free-lance writing for the newspapers, but if so he did not sign his
articles, or think any of them worth preserving. Possibly Thayer and
Eldridge gave him an advance on his anticipated royalties,[23] and this may
have enabled him to support himself and his mother. Since the records of
Thayer and Eldridge have been lost, it is not known how many copies of
the 1860 *Leaves of Grass* were sold, though John Burroughs, who became
an intimate friend of the poet three years later, estimated the number at
between 4,000 and 5,000 copies.[24] If Whitman received twenty-five cents
for each copy sold (the royalty he demanded from his later Boston publisher), he could have earned a thousand dollars or more, though the
chances are that he lost some of this as a consequence of the firm's bankruptcy in 1861.

Whitman's principal income, therefore, probably came from Thayer and
Eldridge during the second half of 1860 and early 1861. This deduction is
supported by the fact that in an advertisement inserted in O'Connor's
Harrington these publishers announced a second book by Whitman as "in
preparation." It was to be called *Banner At Day-Break*, and was to contain
besides the title poem, "Washington's First Battle," "Errand-Bearers,"
"Pictures," "Quadrel," "The Ox-Tamer," "Poemet," "Mannahatta," "Sonnets," and other poems, making a book of about two hundred pages.
Thayer and Eldridge failed before this book was published, but Whitman
was probably working on it during the summer and fall of 1860. The inclusion of "Errand-Bearers" proves that the contents were announced some
time after June 16, when the parade took place. Several of these titles can
be recognized in poems that Whitman later printed in *Drum-Taps*.[25]

But if Whitman's writing lagged, his habitual activities and amusements
did not. He continued to visit the sick stage drivers in the hospital, and
fortunately a witness of these visits in 1860, Dr. D. B. St. John Roosa, has
left a record with circumstantial details.[26] Dr. Roosa was resident physician
of New York Hospital on Broadway at the head of Pearl Street, where ailing stage drivers, injured firemen, victims of traffic accidents and other
daily metropolitan mishaps were taken. Like thousands of other New
Yorkers, Dr. Roosa had seen Whitman perched beside the driver on the
Broadway stages (no one then called them buses) before he became acquainted with the poet in the hospital. After giving a description of these

drivers that corroborates Whitman's own accounts, he says, "I often watched the poet and driver, as probably did many another New Yorker of those days":

In the intervals of collecting fares, in which Whitman assisted—for a New York stage, in the memory of the present and preceding generation, never had a conductor—there always seemed to be a great deal of spirited talk between the driver and his passenger. Whitman appeared to be about forty years of age at that time. He was always dressed in a blue flannel coat and vest, with gray and baggy trousers. He wore a woolen shirt, with a Byronic collar, low in the neck, without a cravat, as I remember, and a large felt hat. His hair was iron gray, and he had a full beard and mustache of the same color. His face and neck were bronzed by exposure to the sun and air. He was large, and gave the impression of being a vigorous man. He was scrupulously careful of his simple attire, and his hands were soft and hairy. . . .

. . . Whatever might be the truth about the literary merit and good taste of his poems, his personality was extremely pleasing. Why this was so it would be hard to say. It must have been from the gentle and refined caste of his features, which were rather rude, but noble. No one could see him sitting by the bed-side of a suffering stage driver without soon learning that he had a sincere and profound sympathy for this order of men. Close observation of their lives at that time would convince one that they endured hardships, which natu-rally invited the sympathy of a great nature. When we found that Walt Whit-man was anxious to visit sick stage drivers, the house staff gave him the largest liberty of entrance. . . .

Soon this liberty extended to the room at the front of the hospital, which was the combined office and living quarters of the house physician himself. There all sorts of people passed in and out every day. Recently a former President of the United States, Franklin Pierce, had been received, and not long before that a famous novelist, Anthony Trollope, had called to inspect the wards but had been "so overcome by one of the sights that he grew faint by the side of the superintendent, as he was tak-ing him around the wards." After Whitman had made his rounds, without any of the symptoms manifested by Trollope, he got into the habit of stopping in Dr. Roosa's office, and he was so well liked that other young physicians gathered there whenever they could to talk with him: "We young men were often very tired, for our labor was arduous, day and night, and Walt Whitman interested us, and his presence was always rest-ful. . . . I do not remember—and I saw him at least fifty times—ever hav-ing heard him laugh aloud, although he smiled with benignancy. He did not make jokes or tell funny stories. We always wondered why he was interested in the class of men whom he visited."

In later years, however, Dr. Roosa thought he could understand the attraction, for he came to recognize the character, endurance, and virility of those mid-century stage drivers. Usually they had grown up in the country and there learned to manage horses. "The London bus driver is nothing if not a cockney, while the Broadway Jehu was a pure and simple countryman, with more than ordinary intelligence, who, after two or three years, summer and winter, from 4 o'clock in the morning until 12 midnight, up and down Broadway, with all kinds of passengers, and always in imminent danger of collision at certain parts of his trip, had become thoroughly conversant with the outdoor aspect of New York society. . . ."

Sometimes the house staff would go in the afternoon with Whitman to Pfaff's famous cellar restaurant, to smoke (though Whitman did not), drink beer, perhaps eat a frankfurter wurst, and continue their conversation. They had Pfaff's almost entirely to themselves at that time of day. They never met the *Saturday Press* crowd, and knew nothing of Whitman's friendship with Henry Clapp, in fact thought the poet "had no intimate acquaintance with the literary New Yorkers of that time," for he "was not generally considered a literary man."

Despite the misinformation here, Dr. Roosa's impression was in the main correct. Though Whitman was a frequent visitor to Pfaff's at more fashionable hours, only a few considered him a literary man. This testimony also demonstrates how successfully Whitman kept his friends in separate compartments, and how wisely he refrained from trying to introduce one set to the other. The young doctors, of course, knew something of his stage-driver friends, with whom they had no more in common than they had with the literary Bohemians. But only Whitman could be congenial and at ease with all three groups.

Of the three, however, Whitman was most at ease with the stage drivers. He was probably far more widely read than the young doctors, and certainly his interests were more extensive. With Dr. Roosa and his associates he could discuss ideas beyond the comprehension of the uneducated drivers, but it was the latter he chose for his boon companions and with whom he spent whole days. In their ancestry, social backgrounds, experiences, habits, speech, and simple good nature they were like Walt's grandfather Van Velsor or even his own brothers. With them he could relax and be himself. They were not critical like the Bohemians; did not feel superior to the laboring class, as did the doctors, for they themselves were average members of the laboring class. To such men Whitman had tried to address "The Eighteenth Presidency!" [27] and he would have liked nothing better than to write poems for them to read, but here he showed himself as blind to their true mentality as he was familiar with their character and habits.

Actually the stage drivers gave Whitman a greater emotional satisfaction than did his literary associates at Pfaff's, for both he and all contemporary observers agree that he took no part in the battles of wit and the spirited debates over art and literature that raged almost every night in the famous restaurant. Whitman was always a slow thinker and deliberate in his speech. He was no match for the mercurial Fitz-James O'Brien, satirical George Arnold, or perhaps even his sardonic friend Henry Clapp. Looking back on these experiences, he summed them up for Traubel in this sentence: "My own greatest pleasure at Pfaff's was to look on—to see, talk little, absorb." [28] But after a while all this noise and jest and desperate effort to be lighthearted seemed unreal to him and in his notebook he wrote down a rough draft of a poem to be called "The Two Vaults," [29] which he never completed.

The vault at Pfaffs where the drinkers and laughers meet to eat and drink and carouse,
While on the walk immediately overhead, pass the myriad feet of Broadway
As the dead in their graves, are underfoot hidden
And the living pass over them, recking not of them, . . .

The "drinkers and laughers" in the brightly lighted vault seemed as unreal to him as those other phantoms in the vault "entirely dark." The poet evidently intended to carry the comparison of the two vaults further, but he never did. Maybe the phantoms were too insubstantial to grasp with words. Perhaps, too, his own macabre fantasy was the product, to some extent at least, of his half-conscious sense of guilt and frustration as a result of his literary idleness. A poet needs to absorb life, but his greatest satisfaction comes from his struggle to express it creatively. However much Whitman may have been absorbing, in the last half of 1860 and the early part of 1861 he created little.

III

For some months after the election of Lincoln in November, 1860, events seemed to confirm the growing conviction Whitman had had for several years that incompetence and misrule were as possible in a democracy as in any other form of government. Senator Douglas ran a strong second in the popular vote, but Lincoln was strong in the states which had the largest electoral votes and thus attained the Presidency of a precariously united nation. As soon as the results were known, the South at once began taking steps to carry out its threat to secede, though the North was inclined to interpret these actions as more of the South's sound and fury. But in New York City, especially, anti-Lincoln feeling was very strong. Fernando Wood, the extremely corrupt mayor whom Whitman had often vigorously denounced in the Brooklyn *Times*, had managed to crawl back into office at the November election, and he courted the support of the numerous Southern sympathizers in the city by threatening to carry the metropolis into a secession from the Union and form a new state, composed of Manhattan, Long Island, and Staten Island, to be called, Tri-Insula.[30]

In the midst of these threats and uncertainties, the President-elect passed through New York City on February 18 on his way to his inauguration, and by chance Whitman saw him for the first time.[31] Despite—or perhaps because of—Lincoln's unpopularity in the city, many people gathered to see him alight from his barouche at the Astor House. The general fear of violence was so great that a hush descended upon the crowd as the tall figure climbed out of his conveyance. On the same spot Whitman had seen noisy demonstrations for Jackson, Clay, Webster, Kossuth of Hungary, "Filibuster" Walker, and the Prince of Wales.

But on this occasion, not a voice—not a sound. From the top of an omnibus, (driven up one side, close by, and block'd by the curbstone and the crowds,) I had, . . . a capital view of it all, and especially of Mr. Lincoln, his look and gait—his perfect composure and coolness—his unusual and uncouth height, his dress of complete black, stovepipe hat push'd back on the head, dark-brown complexion, seam'd and wrinkled yet canny-looking face, black, bushy head of hair, disproportionately long neck, and his hands held behind as he stood observing the people. He look'd with curiosity upon that immense sea of faces, and the sea of faces return'd the look with similar curiosity. In both there was a dash of comedy, almost farce, such as Shakspere [sic] puts in his blackest tragedies. The crowd that hemm'd around consisted I should think of thirty to forty thousand men, not a single one his personal friend—while I have no doubt (so frenzied were the ferments of the time), many an assassin's knife and pistol lurk'd in hip or breast-pocket there, ready, soon as break and riot came.

But no break or riot came. The tall figure gave another relieving stretch or two of arms and legs; then with moderate pace, and accompanied by a few unknown-looking persons, ascended the portico-steps of the Astor House, disappear'd through its broad entrance—and the dumb-show ended.[32]

Though this "dumb-show" made a deep and lasting impression on Whitman's mind, outwardly his life showed no change since the fateful election. While he rode up and down Broadway with his favorite stage drivers, or visited New York Hospital, or sat moodily observing the Pfaff crowd, Lincoln slipped quietly and unobserved into Washington without mishap, and was peacefully inaugurated. But the clamor from the South and the newly organized Confederacy increased in violence, and the capital itself was a house divided; yet most people still did not expect outright war.

On April 13, however, the whole nation was electrified by the news that Fort Sumter had been fired upon the previous evening by Confederate batteries. Whitman himself has left one of the most vivid accounts of this event:

News of the attack on Fort Sumter and *the flag* at Charleston harbor, S.C., was receiv'd in New York City late at night (13th April, 1861,) and was immediately sent out in extras of the newspapers. [The early morning papers would have been dated the 13th; the bombardment started on April 12 and the fort held out until the next day.] I had been to the opera in Fourteenth Street that night, and after the performance was walking down Broadway toward twelve o'clock, on my way to Brooklyn, when I heard in the distance the loud cries of the newsboys, who came presently tearing and yelling up the street, rushing from side to side even more furiously than usual. I bought an extra and cross'd to the Metropolitan hotel (Niblo's) where the great lamps were still brightly blazing, and, with a crowd of others, who gather'd impromptu, read the news, which was evidently authentic. For the benefit of some who had no papers, one of us read the telegram aloud, while all listened silently and attentively. No remark was made by any of the crowd, which had increas'd to thirty or forty, but all stood a minute or two, I remember, before they dispers'd.[33]

It is not likely that Whitman felt like talking to his friends on the ferry boat crossing the East River that night. Whether he was able to sleep when he got home we can only guess, but it is certain that the news profoundly affected him, for three days later, under the recorded date of April 16, 1861, he wrote in his notebook: "I have this day, this hour, resolved to inaugurate for myself a pure, perfect, sweet, clean-blooded robust body, by ignoring all drinks but water and pure milk, and all fat meats, late suppers —a great body, a purged, cleansed, spiritualized, invigorated body." [34]

There is a story that Whitman left Pfaff's in anger when someone offered a toast to the Confederacy,[35] but as late as September he dined there with Fred Gray, who had recently taken part in the battle at Antietam, Maryland.[36] And John Burroughs wrote a friend of his in the fall of 1862 that Whitman frequently attended Pfaff's.[37] Burroughs, who had been a constant reader of the *Saturday Press*, and had even contributed to it, had already become acquainted with *Leaves of Grass*, and he had gone to New York for the specific purpose of meeting Whitman. The *Saturday Press* was then defunct, but Henry Clapp was employed on the *Leader*, for which Ada Clare and others of the Bohemian group were writing as they had for the *Press*. Burroughs called at the *Leader* office, and Clapp told him that Whitman was at Pfaff's almost every night.

In the days immediately following the attack on Fort Sumter the President began mobilizing an army, and in the popular mood of the moment even Mayor Wood began issuing patriotic statements for the press. But almost no one in the North had any real understanding of the magnitude of the war that had just begun. Whitman recalled later that, "Nine-tenths of the people of the free States look'd upon the rebellion, as started in South Carolina, from a feeling one-half of contempt, and the other half composed of anger and incredulity." [38] Senator Seward predicted that it would blow over in "sixty days." Whitman remembered talking about it on a Fulton ferry boat with the Brooklyn mayor, who said he only "hoped the Southern fire-eaters would commit some overt act of resistance, as they would then be at once so effectually squelch'd, we would never hear of secession again—but he was afraid they would never have the pluck to really do anything." Two companies of the Thirteenth Regiment marched out of the city "all provided with pieces of rope, conspicuously tied to their musket barrels, with which to bring back each man a prisoner from the audacious South, to be led on a noose, on our men's early and triumphant return!"

Among the sanguinary recruits of the Thirteenth Regiment was George Whitman, who had enlisted for a hundred days after Federal troops on their way to Washington were attacked by secessionist mobs in Baltimore on April 19. He received his training in and near the capital, which he also helped to guard throughout the summer of 1861,[39] for both government officials and citizens in Washington feared and expected an imminent attack from Confederate troops massed in Virginia. On July 12 Walt wrote George that the whole family was glad he was coming home (evidently anticipating the expiration of George's first period of enlistment) because they were afraid there was "something in" the accounts they had been reading in the papers about the shameful negligence of the commissariat in his regiment, though George had denied these reports in his letters, and Walt realized that the *Eagle* was playing up the charges "to stop men from enlisting." But Walt himself showed how little he understood the military situation by adding: "All of us here think the rebellion as good as broke—no matter if the war does continue for months yet." [40]

Soon, however, "All this sort of feeling was destin'd to be arrested and revers'd by a terrible shock—the battle of first Bull Run. . . ." [41] On Monday, July 22, the routed Union troops began pouring into Washington, coated with mud, soaked to the skin by a steadily falling rain, and often without their weapons, which had become too burdensome to carry. Some thoughtful people hastily improvised kettles of hot soup and coffee. Many of the men, too exhausted to eat or move a step further, dropped on the sidewalk and slept in the rain. Washington was thrown into "a mixture of awful consternation, uncertainty, rage, shame, helplessness, and stupefying disappointment." [42] Southern troops could probably have taken the city with ease if they had arrived promptly. Whitman was to look back on this as the bitterest hour in the history of the Union. But the President immediately set about "reorganizing his forces, and placing himself in position for future and surer work." From this day on Whitman's admiration for Lincoln steadily increased.

Then the great New York papers at once appear'd, (commencing that evening, and following it up the next morning, and incessantly through many days afterwards,) with leaders that rang out over the land with the loudest, most reverberating ring of clearest bugles, full of encouragement, hope, inspiration, unfaltering defiance. Those magnificent editorials! they never flagg'd for a fortnight. The *Herald* commenced them—I remember the articles well. The *Tribune* was equally cogent and inspiriting—and the *Times, Evening Post,* and other principal papers, were not a whit behind. They came in good time, for they were needed. For in the humiliation of Bull Run, the popular feeling North, from its extreme superciliousness, recoil'd to the depth of gloom and apprehension. [43]

It was soon after Bull Run that Whitman wrote "Beat! Beat! Drums!", and the poem was permeated by the spirit of those editorials. It was, indeed, Whitman's own editorial contribution.

Beat! beat! drums!—Blow! bugles! blow!
Through the windows—through doors—burst like a force of ruthless men,
Into the solemn church, and scatter the congregation;
Into the school where the scholar is studying:

Leave not the bridegroom quiet—no happiness must he have now with his
    bride;
Nor the peaceful farmer any peace, plowing his field or gathering his grain;
So fierce you whirr and pound, you drums—so shrill you bugles blow.

.   .   .   .

Beat! beat! drums!—Blow! bugles! blow!
Make no parley—stop for no expostulation;
Mind not the timid—mind not the weeper or prayer;
Mind not the old man beseeching the young man;
Let not the child's voice be heard, nor the mother's entreaties;
Make even the trestles to shake the dead, where they lie awaiting the hearses,
So strong you thump, O terrible drums—so loud you bugles blow.[44]

This poem was published simultaneously in *Harper's Weekly* and the
New York *Leader* on September 28. The fact that it appeared in so popular a magazine as *Harper's Weekly* shows how timely it was. Though there
were still many "Copperheads" in New York City the North as a whole
was now determined to get on with the war and wipe out the disgrace of
Bull Run.

Walt was not the only member of the family who felt the strong emotions that engendered this poem. Not long after its publication George
re-enlisted in the Fifty-first New York Volunteers for three years or the
duration of the war, and departed for training camp on October 30.[45]
Andrew may also have enlisted,[46] even though he was married and the
father of two children, but his record is not clear; and if he did enlist, it
was evidently for a short term—or he may have been quickly discharged
because of ill health. Later critics were to question Walt's patriotism because he did not offer himself immediately for military service,[47] but one
good reason was his age. He was forty-two, and looked much older. Both
James Russell Lowell and Herman Melville, for example, were the same
age as Whitman, and though both felt very strongly about the Southern
rebellion, neither made any effort to volunteer for military service. Another complication was that, with George's long-term enlistment, Walt
probably felt himself to be the main support of his mother and sub-normal
brother, Edward. Jeff was employed and lived with his mother, but he
also had a wife and a year-old child to support, and, as we shall see later,[48]
could not be entirely depended upon by his mother either then or later.
During the summer Jesse had been employed at the Navy Yard,[49] loading
provisions onto the naval vessels, and presumably he was still so employed
in the autumn, but he had always been emotionally and mentally unstable. George was undoubtedly the strongest, most practical and com-

pletely normal of all Mrs. Whitman's sons. His eagerness to defend his country was greatly to his credit, but his leaving home increased Walt's responsibilities.

Besides "Beat! Beat! Drums!" Whitman published only two other poems in 1861. One of these was "Little Bells Last Night" (later title: "I Heard You Solemn-Sweet Pipes of the Organ"), printed in the New York *Leader* on October 12, 1861:

War-suggesting trumpets, I heard you;
And you I heard beating, you chorus of small and large drums;
You round-lipp'd cannons!—you I heard, thunder-cracking, saluting the frigate from France;
I heard you, solemn-sweet pipes of the organ, as last Sunday morn I pass'd the church;
Winds of Autumn!—as I walk'd the woods at dusk, I heard your long-stretch'd sighs, up above, so mournful;
I heard the perfect Italian tenor, singing at the opera; I heard the soprano, in the midst of the quartet singing;
Lady! you, too, I heard, as with white arms in your parlor, you play'd for me delicious music on the harp;
Heart of my love!—you, too, I heard, murmuring low, through one of the wrists around my head—
Heard the pulse of you, when all was still, ringing little bells last night under my ear.[50]

In this first (newspaper) version the love theme was incidental, though distinctly present, and without any suggestion of "Calamus" emotions whatever. When he later included the poem in *Leaves of Grass* Whitman omitted the first three lines and the seventh, and placed it in his "Children of Adam" group, thus suggesting that for him the sexual associations were the strongest of the remembered experiences alluded to in the imagery; but in the autumn of 1861 the themes of war and sex mingled in the poet's consciousness.

Meanwhile Whitman had also become active again in journalism. Since June he had been contributing, with some interruptions, a series of articles called "Brooklyniana" to the Brooklyn *Standard*.[51] These were primarily concerned with the social history of Long Island and Brooklyn, with a considerable amount of personal reminiscences, ending with an account of a trip to Greenport and an impromptu picnic excursion to Montauk Point that Whitman took in the fall of 1861—though not described until a year later.[52] The first number was published on June 8, 1861, and the last on November 1, 1862. Whitman had long been interested in the history of his native town and island, and it may have been partly a coincidence that he now became a recorder of local history just at the time when the national events threatened to change the course of the nation's history. However, his faith in the future of his country was unshaken, and he firmly believed that "there will come a time, here in Brooklyn, and all over America, when nothing will be of more interest than authentic reminiscences of the past. Much of it will be made up of subordinate 'memoirs,' and of personal chronicles and gossip—but we think every portion of it will always meet a welcome from a large mass of American readers." [53]

During the winter of 1861–1862 Whitman continued to visit the hospital on Broadway, which had begun to receive soldiers after Bull Run and steadily increased its services to military men as the war continued. By the spring of 1862 this hospital was taking care of several hundred sick and wounded soldiers, and Whitman was regularly spending his Sunday afternoons and evenings visiting them and trying to cheer them up. [54] Though this was a remote contact with the war, it gave him an intimate sense of its reality. Like the stage drivers, these veterans were often unsophisticated country boys, surprisingly youthful, and Whitman found them wonderfully congenial and interesting: "One Sunday night, in a ward in the South Building, I spent one of the most agreeable evenings of my life amid such a group of seven convalescent young soldiers of a Maine regiment." They were happy over leaving next morning to rejoin their regiment. "I shook hands with them all around at parting, and I know we all felt as if it were the separation of old friends." [55]

This report Whitman gave in a new series of articles which he called "City Photographs," published in the New York *Leader*. Ever since his personal sketches of Broadway in the New York *Aurora* this had been one of his favorite types of journalism. And it is not surprising that he made "The Broadway Hospital," which he had been visiting for several years, the subject of his first four sketches. [56]

In his second article, written from notes gathered in the "middle of March, 1862," Whitman gave statistics on the number of patients admitted annually, explained how the hospital was supported (fees, State help, and payments by the United States Government for the soldiers), and mentioned various members of the staff, praising especially "Aunty Robinson," a colored nurse. Obviously the hospital authorities were being as co-operative as possible in supplying information; in fact, part of Whitman's purpose in writing the articles was evidently to bid for wider financial support for the hospital. This purpose became even more apparent in the third article, which listed and praised the men and women who had promoted the work of this institution, either by personal service or donations of money, since its founding in 1770. In both the third and fourth installments Whitman cited examples of important contributions to medical history made in famous operations or new techniques perfected in this hospital. For example, here in 1817 Dr. Wright Post "tied the right subclavian artery, for a brachial aneurism, above the clavicle." [57] And in October, 1845, Dr. John Kearney Rodgers "performed the operation in which the left subclavian artery was tied for aneurism, on the inner side of the scaleni muscles." Of course the surgeons themselves had supplied these technical details, and Whitman publicly thanked them "for the opportunity of seeing several very fine operations, and for their interesting explanations of them to me, before and after." Thus once more we have evidence of Whitman's deep interest in science and his eagerness to learn by observation and interview, which he always valued more than books. And although he could not have known it at the time, he was also storing up information that would soon be of great use to him in army hospitals in Washington.

At New York Hospital Whitman also made another observation that was to have a profound influence on his own life during the following three or four years. He reported that a lady who wished to remain anonymous had been doing much good among the soldiers by going quietly through the wards distributing papers, books, delicacies to eat or drink, and other comforts or conveniences not provided by army or hospital. When Walt made his rounds the soldiers delightedly exhibited to him what this kind woman had left, and thus he witnessed the effects of her simple but valued donations.[58]

The remaining articles in this series were devoted to "The Bowery," its stores, hotels, places of amusement, and its polyglot life. Whitman very graphically revealed the crudity and vulgarity of this part of the city, but without condescension or satire. In a vivid sketch he described "A Popular Lager-Beer Hall," and in another a nearby dance hall, which he visited May 9: "Here, too, on one side, is a shooting gallery. A placard annexed informs patriots who wish to join the army, and desire first to perfect themselves in the art and mystery of hitting the mark, that they will be taught free by an accomplished professor." [59]

During the spring of 1862, when Whitman was roaming the Bowery and writing "feature" articles for the *Leader*, he may have had an affair

with a woman who signed herself mysteriously "Ellen Eyre." After Whitman's death Traubel showed to his friends a love letter that she wrote the
poet, and copies were made of this interesting epistle.[60] Though the authenticity of the copy quoted below cannot be guaranteed, it nevertheless
seems worth quoting:

Tuesday, Mar 25 1862

My dear Mr. Whitman:

I fear you took me last night for a female privateer. It is time I was sailing
under my true colors.—but then today I assume you cared nothing piratical
though I would joyfully have made your heart a captive. Women have an unequal chance in the world. Men are its monarchs, and "full many a rose is born
to blush unseen and waste its sweetness on the desert air." Such I was resolved
would not be the fate of the fancy I had long nourished for you. A gold mine
may be found by the divining rod, but there is no such instrument for detect-
ing in the crowded streets of a great city the unknown mine of latent affection
a man may have unconsciously inspired in a woman's breast. I make these explanations in extenuation not by way of apology. My social position enjoins
precaution and mystery and perhaps the enjoyment of my friends [friend's?]
society is heightened while yielding to its fascination. I preserve my incognito,
yet mystery lends an effable charm to love and when a woman is bent upon
the gratification of her inclination she is pardonable if she still spreads the veil of
decorum over her actions.

Hypocrisy is said to be the homage that sin pays to virtue, and yet *I* can see no
vice in that generous sympathy in which we share our caprices with those who
inspired us with tenderness. I trust you will think well enough of me soon
to renew the pleasure you afforded me last p.m. and I therefore write to remind
you that this is a sensible head as well as a sympathetic heart, both of which
would gladly evolve with warmth for your diversion and comfort. You have
already my whereabouts and hours. It shall only depend on you to make them
yours and me the happiest of women.

I am always yours sincerely,
Ellen Eyre.

Whatever may have taken place between Walt Whitman and "Ellen
Eyre" during the spring of 1862, the relationship had probably come to
an end by midsummer. In a little notebook that he carried in his pocket
Whitman recorded of an acquaintance he had made: "Frank Sweeney
(July 8 '62) 5th Ave. Brown face, large features, black moustache (is the
one I told the whole story to about Ellen Eyre)—talks very little." [61] Of
course "whole story" is ambiguous, but it implies something that had happened in the past, and a history that Walt Whitman himself regarded as in

some way remarkable. If he ever told it to anyone besides Frank Sweeney, that person evidently talked as little as Frank did.

Only a few details of Whitman's life during the fall of 1862 have survived. Clapp told Burroughs that Whitman managed to exist on his earnings of six or seven dollars "per week writing for the papers." [62] He did not say for the *Leader*, but "papers," and since the *Leader's* finances were extremely precarious[63] it is likely that Whitman was not solely dependent on it for support. Possibly, he also did odd jobs of copying or other work to bring in needed money. And he was probably working on some of the poems that he was later to publish in *Drum-Taps*,[64] such as "Rise O Days from Your Fathomless Deeps," which was a call to Democracy, in the midst of a rising sea and darkening clouds, to "Thunder on! stride on . . . strike with vengeful stroke!," or "City of Ships":

> In peace I chanted peace, but now the drum of war is mine;
> War, red war is my song through your streets, O city!

Whitman had not yet seen war at first hand, and George was so anxious to keep his mother from worrying that in his letters he minimized the dangers and horrors which he was experiencing. It would be difficult to imagine a more compassionate man than Walt Whitman, but far away from the actual slaughter, safe from immediate danger, he felt impatient, and perhaps secretly a little guilty because he was safe while so many of his countrymen were fighting and dying. Therefore he wanted the Union armies to strike hard, and personally longed for "an intense life, full to repletion and varied!" He was excited by patriotic crowds, "the torchlight procession," the "dense brigade bound for the war," and the noise, bustle, and nervous activity of a great city mobilizing.

IV

During the early months of the war Whitman had jotted down in his notebook the first lines of another poem, which began, "Quicksand years that whirl me I know not whither." [65] He could hardly have realized in the fall of 1862 how prophetic these words were, for events were shaping up to whirl him into a new emotional and geographical orbit.

Naturally the whole Whitman family was continually uneasy about George, despite the fact that he seemed to lead a charmed life in the Army, going through battle after battle without a scratch and winning promotion after promotion. The day after he re-enlisted in the fall of 1861

he was promoted to sergeant-major.[66] He distinguished himself during the
storming of the Confederate forts at Roanoke, North Carolina, in February, 1862, and was promoted to the rank of second lieutenant. For valor
displayed in the second engagement at Bull Run he was made a first lieutenant. But despite his success, he constantly longed, like any other soldier, for news from home, and often amused himself by trying to imagine
what each member of the family was doing. On September 30, near Antietam, Maryland, he wrote:

. . . I often think that I can imagine just what you are all doing at home and ile
bet now, that Mother is making pies. I think Mat is putting up shirt bosoms like
the deuce so as to get through before dinner [.] I guess Sis [Manahatta, usually called Hattie] is downstairs helping Mother mix the dough, Walt is upstairs writing, Jeff is down town at the office, Jess is pealing Potatoes for dinner,
and Tobias [Edward] has gone down cellar for a scuttle of coal. Bunkum
[Andrew] I guess is around somewhere looking for a good chance to go sogering.[67]

Why it was so difficult for Andrew to go soldiering is not easy to guess.
Actually his health was unequal to military life, but the physical standards
of the recruiting officers were far from rigid. Who was to support his wife
and two children while he was away is also a mystery, though he may have
expected his mother to do so from George's salary, which George regularly
sent to his mother to bank for him or use whenever she needed funds.

The Whitmans knew in December that George was camped near Fredericksburg; consequently, when the newspapers announced that a great battle had taken place there on December 13 they were even more than
usually apprehensive, and the headlines on the 14th and 15th reporting continued skirmishes increased their fears. Then on Tuesday, December 16,
the New York *Herald* printed in a supposedly final and complete list of
the wounded in the Fifty-first New York Volunteers the name of "First
Lieutenant G. W. Whitmore, Company D." Exactly how the Whitman
family knew that this name was a misprint for G. W. Whitman we can
only guess, but they had no doubt that George was intended; perhaps in
his letters he had mentioned all the officers in his company and they knew
it did not contain a Whitmore. At any rate, they were filled with consternation. No details were given in the bare list and they had no way of finding out how serious the wound was. The casualty lists[68] in the New York
Times and *Tribune* did not include any name resembling George's.[69]
Mother Whitman was almost frantic. The excitable Jeff, we may be sure,
had an idea a minute as to what to do, none of them practicable. Martha

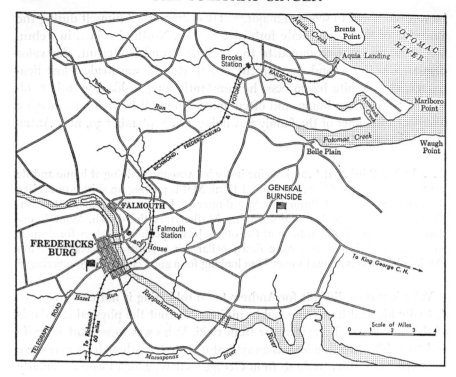

FREDERICKSBURG BATTLEFIELD

Redrawn from "Topographical Map of the Seat of War on the Rappahannock,"
printed in the New York *Herald*, December 16, 1862.

wanted to go down to Virginia to find and nurse her brother-in-law,[70] but
Walt dissuaded her from this rash plan by announcing that he would go
himself—immediately.[71]

They had evidently not seen the *Herald* until late in the morning; probably Walt discovered it on his way to the ferry and rushed home with the
bad news. These surmises are based on Walt's statement that he left
Brooklyn on an hour's notice and that he started on the trip early Tuesday afternoon.[72] He also set out carrying a purse of $50 (probably drawn
from the bank by Mrs. Whitman out of the funds she had been deposit-
ing for George). In those days there was no direct train connection between New York and Washington. Walt had first to take a ferry over the
East River, then cross Manhattan, and take another ferry across the Hudson to Jersey City, where he could catch a train to Philadelphia, at which
point he had to change again for the Washington train.

In the confusion of the hurrying, crushing throng in Philadelphia a pickpocket got all the money Walt carried.[73] As a result of this misfortune and his anxiety over George, he "put in," as he wrote his mother, "about three days of the greatest suffering I ever experienced in my life." For two days he searched the hospitals of Washington, "walking day and night, unable to ride, trying to get information—trying to get access to big people" who would not see him.[74] There were nearly forty military hospitals in and around the city[75] and the only means of locating a patient was by use of the incomplete and inaccurate lists published in the Washington newspapers, none of which contained the name of George Whitman. Finally Walt had the good luck to run across one of the friends he had made in Boston, William D. O'Connor, who was employed in the capital as a clerk in the Treasury Department.[76] O'Connor loaned him some money, but was not able to help him locate George.

On Thursday, however, Walt decided that his brother might still be with his regiment near Falmouth, across the river from Fredericksburg, and in the afternoon he discovered that he could go there on a government boat that ran to Aquia Creek, where he could take a train (under Army control) to Falmouth.[77] After a wearisome trip he arrived at the camp Friday afternoon and without much difficulty traced the Fifty-first Volunteers. But before he actually found George he had to pass a huge pile of amputated arms and legs lying under a tree in front of an army hospital. This would have been a shocking encounter at any time, but at the moment the thought that some of George's own limbs might be in that horrible heap almost overcame him.[78] He went on, however, and soon found George whole and in good spirits. A shell fragment had pierced one cheek, but the wound was healing nicely and George was on active duty.

Since George's wound had not been serious enough to confine him to a hospital, he had not expected his family to hear of it. In fact, he tried to make sure that his name was not on the official list of wounded; thus he was surprised to learn from Walt that they had been alarmed.[79] Walt immediately dispatched the good news to his mother by messenger to Washington, where it could be telegraphed, and wrote letters both to her and to Hannah. Despite his exhaustion, now that he had found his brother alive and well, all his difficulties of the past four days seemed of no importance, and he was delighted to accept George's invitation to share his tent for a few days. That evening and the next day he proudly observed how universally his brother was liked and admired by the soldiers and of-

ficers who knew him. For his conduct in the recent battle he was promoted to captain, and Walt had the pleasure of being present when the
commission arrived.[80]

Walt remained at the camp for eight or nine days, living as he described
in a letter to his mother:

While I was there George still lived in Capt. Francis's tent—there were five of
us altogether, to eat, sleep, write, etc., in a space twelve feet square, but we got
along very well—the weather all along was very fine—and would have got
along to perfection, but Capt. Francis is not a man I could like much—I had
very little to say to him. George is about building a place, half hut and half
tent, for himself, (he is probably about it this very day [December 29,
1862],) and then he will be better off, I think. Every captain has a tent, in
which he lives, transacts company business, etc., has a cook, (or a man of all
work,) and in the same tent mess and sleep his lieutenants, and perhaps the
first sergeant. They have a kind of fireplace—and the cook's fire is outside on
the open ground.[81]

Though Walt readily adapted himself to this life, that revolting sight of
amputated human limbs in front of the hospital which he had seen on the
day of his arrival was hard to get out of his mind. The hospital had been set
up in a large brick mansion, the "Lacy house," on the banks of the Rappahannock. On December 21 Walt visited the men confined there, and
then began systematically making the rounds of all the hospitals in the
region. But it was at the Lacy house that he "struck up a tremendous
friendship with a young Mississippi captain (about 19)" who had been
badly wounded at Fredericksburg and taken prisoner. Walt met him soon
after one of his legs had been amputated—perhaps he had contributed to
that pile under the tree. In a short time he was sent to a Washington hospital, where Walt continued to visit him, and wrote two of his young friends
in New York, "our affection is an affair quite romantic." [82]

While at Camp Falmouth Whitman also went out under a flag of truce
to help direct the burial of the dead still lying on the field of battle.[83] One
morning at daybreak he had an experience that he later elaborated in a
poem, "A Sight in Camp in the Day-Break Grey and Dim." Emerging
from his tent, early in the morning, into the cool, fresh air, the poet be-
held three stretchers covered with heavy army blankets. Lifting one corner
of the nearest blanket, he saw the corpse of an elderly man, "gaunt and
grim, with well-grey'd hair, and flesh all sunken about the eyes." Under
the second was a "sweet boy, with cheeks yet blooming."

Then to the third—a face nor child, nor old, very calm, as of beautiful yellow-
    white ivory;
Young man, I think I know you—I think this face of yours is the face of the
    Christ himself;
Dead and divine, and brother of all, and here again he lies.[84]

Christmas day at the front impressed Whitman particularly. In the afternoon he walked out to a large deserted camp ground, still littered with the debris of the departed soldiers. From this point of observation he began to realize the enormity and bitter irony of the war. On a road nearby passed interminable caravans of six-mule teams carrying military supplies. As far as he could see was open ground, not a fence standing; the trees had been cut down for fuel and building purposes. In the distance were several teamsters' camps, and in the middle-distance carcasses of horses and mules. Sitting on a pine log and facing southeast, Whitman could see "the depression in the landscape, where the Rappahannock runs, and one or two signs of Fredericksburgh, (a battery could easily shell it from where I sit.) I hear the sound of bugle calls, very martial, at this distance—a fine large troop of cavalry is just passing, the hoofs of the horses shake the ground, and I hear the clatter of sabres. Amid all this pleasant scene, under the sweet sky and warm sun, I sit and think over the battle of last Saturday week." [85]

But interested as he was in every detail of these unfamiliar scenes, Whitman's thoughts were principally occupied by the suffering of the sick and wounded in the "division hospitals":

These are merely tents, and sometimes very poor ones, the wounded lying on the ground, lucky if their blankets are spread on layers of pine or hemlock twigs, or small leaves. No cots; seldom even a mattress. It is pretty cold. The ground is frozen hard, and there is occasional snow. I go around from one case to another. I do not see that I do much good to these wounded and dying; but I cannot leave them. Once in a while some youngster holds on to me convulsively, and I do what I can for him; at any rate, stop with him and sit near him for hours, if he wishes it.[86]

When not in the hospitals, Whitman frequently toured the camps, especially at night, when he sat with the men around the fires in their "she-bangs." Sometimes he went out with them on picket duty. Everyone seemed to like him, officers and enlisted men. In less than two weeks he accumulated impressions that would influence the remainder of his life, and literary material for two or three dozen poems, a number of news-paper articles, and a considerable portion of a book of essays.

On Sunday, December 28, Whitman left the camp at Falmouth before sunrise in charge of a trainload of wounded bound for Washington. The wounded were loaded on flat-top cars and thus transported ten or twelve miles to Aquia Creek, where they were transferred to a steamer for the journey up the Potomac.[87] At the creek landing were many more wounded men also waiting for the steamer to arrive, and Walt went among the stretchers, talking to the men and taking messages to be sent next day (Monday) by mail to some member of their families. No provisions had been made for this sort of personal aid, and Whitman could see how much the sufferers were helped by his sympathy and promises to send the messages. During the boat trip he had his hands full trying to wait on all his patients, and despite his efforts one man died on the steamer.

After delivering his charges to the hospital authorities, Whitman went early in the afternoon to call on the O'Connors at 394 L Street, near 14th, to ask William to help him find a room.[88] Although Mrs. O'Connor had heard a great deal about Whitman from her husband, this was the first time she had seen him. Fortunately, she instantly liked him as much as William did. Whitman told them that he was planning to stay in Wash-ington only a week or ten days in order to visit the soldiers from Brooklyn who were in various hospitals in and near the capital. In Virginia he had heard about these men from members of the Fifty-first Volunteers.

After searching for an hour or two for an inexpensive room, Walt and William returned without success to the O'Connors' place, where Walt rented a small bedroom on the second floor from the Irish landlord. The O'Connors rented larger rooms on the third floor, and they urged Whit-man for the present to take his meals with them without charge. This ar-rangement he agreed to, thinking it would be temporary. But in the next day or two he met another friend, his recent publisher, Charles W. Eldridge, who was now assistant to the Army Paymaster, Major Lyman Hapgood, and through Eldridge Whitman secured an appointment as copyist in the Paymaster's office.[89] This work kept him occupied for only two or three hours a day, but it paid enough to meet his immediate ex-penses and left him much time for visiting the boys in the hospitals. It was so satisfactory an arrangement, in fact, that his intended stay of a week or ten days stretched into months and finally into years.

Each day after he had completed his secretarial work Walt had the freedom of the Paymaster's office for his own correspondence or other writing. On January 2, near the end of his first week with Major Hapgood, he described his office in a letter to his sister-in-law. It was on the top floor of a large building on the corner of 15th and F Street, with a grand view of the Potomac and Georgetown. But Walt could not enjoy the view for the misery he daily witnessed among the soldiers coming from the hospitals to collect their pay, which many needed for their fare home. "They climb up here, quite exhausted, and then find it is no good, for there is no money to pay them; there are two or three paymasters' desks in this room, and the scenes of disappointment are quite affecting. Here they wait in Washington, perhaps week after week, wretched and heart-sick—this is the greatest place of delays and puttings off, and no finding the clue to anything." [90]

Although Whitman himself did not know it, this sympathy for the sick and discouraged would make it impossible for him to leave Washington, except temporarily, so long as the war continued to take its toll in human suffering. On the same day that he began his letter to Martha (quoted above) he visited two Brooklyn boys in Campbell Hospital. One had had a forearm amputated and the other was recovering from frozen feet. Both were recuperating rapidly and were in good spirits. Of course, they were glad to see someone from Brooklyn, but they did not especially need Walt's help. As he passed through the wards, however, other cases deeply stirred his emotions. One young man, John Holmes, half dead with diarrhea and bronchitis, had been overlooked by the nurses and doctors and had received no medical attention whatever. Walt sent for the doctor, who made a thorough examination and said the young man would recover. Walt wrote a letter to his family, gave him some money to buy a glass of milk, and thus gave him the will to live, which he had lost.[91]

This work of bolstering the morale of the sick and discouraged was the one thing that Walt Whitman seemed especially created to do. The poet who in "Song of Myself," vicariously imagined "I am the man, I suffered, I was there," [92] had accurately divined his own nature and unconsciously forecast his later conduct in the Washington hospitals:

Agonies are one of my changes of garments,
. . . .
To any one dying, thither I speed and twist the knob of the door,
Turn the bed-clothes toward the foot of the bed,
Let the physician and priest go home.

I seize the descending man and raise him with resistless will,
O despairer, here is my neck,
By God, you shall not go down! hang your whole weight upon me.[93]

John Holmes was only one of many similar cases that Whitman recorded
in his notebooks and newspaper articles. In one of the articles which he
contributed to the New York *Times* he expressed this observation: "To
many of the wounded and sick, especially the youngsters, there is something in personal love, caresses, and the magnetic flood of sympathy and
friendship, that does more good than all the medicines in the world." [94]

In his description of his preparation for these visits later published in
Specimen Days, Whitman showed how well he understood the psychology
of his hospital work:

> In my visits to the hospitals I found it was in the simple matter of personal
> presence, and emanating ordinary cheer and magnetism, that I succeeded and
> help'd more than by medical nursing, or delicacies, or gifts of money, or any-
> thing else. During the war I possess'd the perfection of physical health. My
> habit, when practicable, was to prepare for starting out on one of those daily
> or nightly tours of from a couple to four or five hours, by fortifying myself
> with previous rest, the bath, clean clothes, a good meal, and as cheerful an ap-
> pearance as possible.[95]

The Army provided a fairly adequate staff of physicians and nurses,
whom Whitman found, with a few notable exceptions, to be competent
and efficient. But with hundreds of cases to take care of, they had no time
for individual attention, and many of them soon became callous and indifferent to the mass suffering which they had to witness day and night.
The Government had also been entirely unprepared for the casualties of
the first battles, and both hospital facilities and staffs had had to be improvised, with consequent confusion, bungling, and sacrifice of human
lives. Some months before Whitman arrived in Washington many citizens
had become aroused by the conditions in the military hospitals. Patients
were not supplied with adequate clothing, and the food was often poorly
prepared, or too coarse for a sick man to eat. A few hospitals became notorious for their inefficiency or brutality, such as Judiciary Square, where the
dead were dumped naked on a vacant lot to await burial.

Even in the better hospitals asepsis was little understood. The surgeon
wore no gloves, sharpened his knife on his bootsole, and mopped the
wound with a sponge that had only been rinsed in water since the last operation. All wounds were expected to suppurate. It is no wonder that, as

one authority says, "Blood poisoning, tetanus, secondary hemorrhage and gangrene were familiar visitors in the finest of shining, whitewashed new pavilions of which Washington was so proud, and helped to fill the pine coffins which went jouncing in the dead carts to the cemetery." [96]

Early in the war Dr. Henry Bellows, a Unitarian minister in New York City, began agitating for a commission to study the discoveries made by the physicians and nurses in the Crimean War and to use this and other scientific information in saving the lives of Union soldiers. Finally a United States Sanitary Commission was set up, with Dr. Bellows as president, and by the end of 1862 this organization had effected many reforms and improvements, but medical science was still very primitive. Consequently, the most appalling losses were still, as Whitman quickly observed, not from battle wounds but diarrhea, "camp fever" (probably typhoid), and other infectious diseases.[97]

A civilian organization called the Christian Commission had also been formed by the churches to provide much the same kind of aid that Whitman was to render, and some biographers[98] have thought that perhaps he may have begun his ministrations as delegate of this organization, but he repeatedly stated in letters and newspaper articles that he was working entirely by himself and on his own initiative. He wrote his mother that he had a high opinion of the Christian Commissioners—"they go everywhere and receive no pay"—but he thought the Sanitary Commissioners "incompetent and disagreeable." He reported that the men lying helpless in bed always "turn their faces from the sight of these agents, chaplains, etc. (hirelings, as Elias Hicks would call them—they seem to me always a set of foxes and wolves.)" [99] But he was favorably impressed by the Catholic priests, and was on more friendly terms with them than with the clergymen of any other denomination—whom he habitually distrusted. Years later he said: "When I was in Washington it was surprising how many Catholic priests I came to know—how many took the trouble to get acquainted with me—on what good terms we kept with each other." [100]

As he had done in New York Hospital, Whitman at first merely talked with the soldiers, took messages to send to their relatives, and performed little personal services for them. But gradually he began using his own meager funds to buy stamps, fruit, reading matter, or other inexpensive items that he saw they especially needed or wanted. Although he himself did not use tobacco in any form and most hospital authorities strongly disapproved of its use by their patients, Whitman noticed the solace that it gave to some of the men, and began carrying parcels of tobacco to distribute to anyone who wanted it. In each case he fitted the gift to the recipient. He was careful to overlook no one, not even the Confederate soldiers confined in these Union hospitals. Some needed special nursing care, and after he had become experienced, Whitman sometimes dressed a wound, or sat up all night with a man at a time of crisis.[101] But this was exceptional. He was primarily a nurse of the soul (in its psychological sense), not the body. The physicians soon observed that his judgment and tact were not only reliable but nearly infallible, and most of them—especially at Armory Square, which he frequented more than any other hospital—gave him the same freedom that he had enjoyed in the Broadway hospital.[102] One physician, Dr. D. W. Bliss, became a loyal friend and admirer,[103] much as Dr. Roosa had in New York.

Walt's descriptions in his letters of the conditions in the hospitals and the good he was doing aroused an immediate sympathetic response from his mother, Jeff, and Martha. Jeff began enclosing small sums of money in his letters and solicited the help of his friends and the staff of the Brooklyn Water Works, where he was employed. His superintendent, Moses Lane, contributed $10, and everyone else on the staff seems to have contributed something, and continued to do so throughout the remaining months of the war. Whitman wrote to Emerson and other friends in Concord and Boston about his work, and they also began to send contributions.[104] In February he published two articles in the New York *Times* vividly describing the need for his "missionary" work and citing case histories. In the first of these (February 16) he clearly stated, "I am not connected with any society, but go on my own individual account, and to the work that appears called for." [105] This was an indirect appeal for funds, but it had some effect, especially in Brooklyn, for besides being best known there, Whitman attracted local support by mentioning the names of Brooklyn soldiers in the hospitals and giving specific details about their condition, a fact that undoubtedly influenced the Brooklyn *Eagle* to reprint the article.[106] His friend John Swinton was now managing editor of the *Times*,[107] and he aided not only by printing and paying for these articles but also by sending cash contributions of his own.

Despite this help from his friends, however, Whitman very quickly felt the inadequacy of his income from his work in the Paymaster's office and began trying to find more lucrative employment with the Government. He urgently needed more money not only for his hospital work but also to help his mother. Jeff was paying the rent, and apparently providing some of her food, but she was constantly in need of funds for incidental expenses for which she called on Walt. Although George had written her to use his bank account, she wanted to keep this intact, partly because George had expressed a desire to save enough money to buy her and Edward a small house and grounds in the country, and Walt had planned to return and help build the house.[108] Emerson had already written two letters of recommendation for Whitman to use,[109] and early in February Jeff was trying to secure other recommendations from prominent men in Brooklyn. In a letter to Jeff dated February 13, 1863, Walt reported that he had talked with Secretary of State Seward, Preston King, Senator for New York, and Charles Sumner, Senator for Massachusetts. Walt was planning to apply also to Salmon P. Chase, the Secretary of the Treasury, and wanted the backing of as many prominent men as possible. Preston King teased Walt by telling him he looked like a Southern planter, but he gave him an endorsement both to Chase and to General Meigs, head of the Quartermaster Department. Walt opined that he was "getting better and better acquainted with office-hunting wisdom and Washington peculiarities generally." [110] He was not discouraged, and assured Jeff that he made "about enough to pay my expenses by hacking on the press here, and copying in the paymasters' office, a couple of hours a day."

Whitman needed to acquire "office-hunting wisdom," or at least patience, for he would have to continue for two more years to support himself and carry on his hospital philanthropy as he had begun doing. Although he did not keep a ledger record of all his hospital expenditures, the contributions he acknowledged in his letters were scarcely adequate for all the implied expenses noted in his private diaries. He no doubt often drew upon his own slim purse for the purchase of stationery, tobacco, sweets, an occasional ice-cream treat for a large ward, and other gifts. So far as known he was never employed on the Washington papers; thus "hacking on the press here" must have meant writing those occasional articles for the New York and Brooklyn papers. The O'Connors were also generously contributing to the hospital work by giving Walt his two meals a day—all he usually ate—breakfasts at eight-thirty and dinner at four-thirty.[111]

Despite his discouraging experiences in office-hunting and his fatiguing trips to the hospitals, Walt found time to look over the new building going up on the Capitol grounds in the midst of the war. In the early 1860's Washington was in a half finished stage.[112] Architects had mapped the plans for the wide-radiating streets—though even Pennsylvania Avenue was still unpaved—and the white marble buildings with Italian domes and Greek columns were in the process of construction. Herman Melville laughed ironically at "the rust on the iron dome," [113] and many people wondered whether the grand design of the French engineer Major Pierre L'Enfant would ever become an American reality. Some patriots thought that the construction should be halted until the nation had survived its death struggle, but the President insisted that the work must continue as a symbol of the vitality and future permanency of the Union. Consequently, the carpenters and masons and sculptors and painters labored on hopefully while the guns roared on the other side of the Potomac, sometimes audible even to these workmen and artists.

A few days after his return from Virginia, Whitman strolled through the half finished rooms and found them incredibly gorgeous "beyond one's flightiest dreams." [114] He could not think of anything to compare these sights to except the interior of Taylor's saloon on Broadway, or the window displays of Tiffany's. He advised Jeff to think of Tiffany's when he imagined "the paintings of Cupids and goddesses . . . spread recklessly over the arched ceiling and broad panels of a big room—the whole floor underneath paved with tesselated pavement, which is a sort of cross between marble and china, with little figures, drab, blue, cream color, etc." But the many colored marble columns, the bronze and gold chandeliers, and the ornate clocks in every room seemed to him needlessly extravagant, lacking in strength and simplicity, and un-American. The nation itself was now, though still in its youth, "feeble, bandaged, and bloody," like those poor men in the hospitals whom he could never forget even for a few hours. On his first visit Walt found the sight of the fine interiors more than he could bear and he hastened away from the Capitol grounds.

V

Meanwhile Whitman was harassed by many family worries. Hannah, still in Vermont, was ailing as usual, and all the Whitmans were concerned about her at the time that Walt left home. Heyde's response to Walt's letter about finding George and seeing the pitiful sights near the battlefield was that he ought to reserve some of his pity for the suffering of his own family.[115] He complained that Hannah was a burden to him, making it impossible for him to paint, and he suggested that Walt come and take her back to Brooklyn. Jeff called Heyde hard names, Walt urged his sister Mary to undertake the rescue, and George was in complete agreement with the plan.[116] But then Heyde changed his mind, and apparently

Hannah did not really want to desert her husband, despite her grievances. She remained in Burlington and her family continued to worry about her, though in the spring she wrote one or two cheerful letters.

In January Mrs. Whitman was also ill from a prolonged cold, and complained more than usual of "rheumatism." The noise of the Browns, who occupied part of the house she rented, often annoyed her and she thought of moving on May 1. Jeff bought a lot and was considering borrowing money to build a house of his own.[117] This would have created an additional problem for Mrs. Whitman, because although Jeff was willing to have his mother live with him, he did not want Eddie. He wrote Walt that he and Martha frequently invited his mother to take meals with them,[118] but she seldom did—doubtless because she knew Eddie was not welcome at their table. Although Martha was six months pregnant, she often left Hattie with her mother-in-law while she went with Jeff to the opera or visited friends. It was very far from a happy household, and Mrs. Whitman could not resist ruminating on her troubles in her letters to Walt. But she did not move on May 1 because Jeff decided not to build a house and he and Martha wished to continue the present arrangement; so Walt urged his mother to overlook the friction with the Browns and try to make the best of the situation.[119] His mother may have been the peacemaker in the family during his youth, but it was now he who patched up quarrels and persuaded various members of the family to forgive and forget petty annoyances. In March Mrs. Whitman was cheered by a brief visit from George, but he spent so much time in New York or with his friends in Brooklyn that it seemed to her he had come and gone before she was scarcely aware of it. Before leaving he drew all of his money out of the bank to buy a new uniform and accessories in New York.[120] However, in April he sent his mother $350, though she wrote Walt she was only able to bank $200 of it because she had to pay a large grocery bill, and she kept some of it for Mary to use in going for "Han" (though she did not go). Mrs. Whitman was also having difficulty protecting the money from Jeff and Martha:

i will tell you walt all about it   before i got it mat and jeff began to hint about their having it   i would not mind lending jeff but it seems as if martha had no thought whatever   jeff is very much in debt and it will go in short order for things they could be just as well of[f] without   i told mat the other day she knowed what expence it would be when she was sick [she was expecting her second child in June] and i would not get more than i needed but its not [no] use . . .[121]

By this time Walt was having trouble with his hearing and his mother advised him to put drops of sweet oil in his ears to soften the wax, which she thought had hardened.[122] Almost the only sickness Walt had ever experienced before this spring was a "sun-stroke" about five years previously and he was depressed by the change in his health; it was, in fact, the beginning of a decline. Probably he was overtaxing his strength, and though he insisted he ate well, his diet may have been too starchy, for he was steadily gaining weight. He was already up to two hundred pounds,[123] and in succeeding months he began to suffer from what was probably hypertension, though he blamed his pains in the head and dizziness on colds. Of course, he was constantly exposed to infections in the hospitals, and his habit of greeting some of his most afflicted patients with a kiss endangered his health more than he could have realized.

As soon as George had returned to Virginia, Mrs. Whitman began worrying about him again. Walt watched the papers, sifted rumors circulated by the soldiers, and deduced most of the movements of the Fifty-first Volunteers, trying always to find consoling reassurances for his mother. But Andrew was now becoming a greater worry to the family than either Hannah's precarious health and unhappy domestic life or George's fate in the war. In April his throat affliction became so severe that he lost his voice.[124] His disease was later diagnosed as tuberculosis of the throat.[125]

On April 15 Walt explained in a long letter to his mother,[126] which he intended for her to pass on to Andy, that the health of the mucous membrane of the throat and bronchia depends upon the health of the whole system, and that to get well Andrew must build up his body by rest, nourishing food, and—most important of all—"nary [a drop] of whiskey under any circumstances." This advice he repeated in subsequent letters, but his mother complained that every time she gave Andrew money he got drunk with some of his cronies. By this time he was unable to work, and Mrs. Whitman had to pay his rent and buy food for the family, of course with funds supplied by her sons, mainly George. As Andrew grew worse, he took most of his meals with his mother. Nancy, his wife, could not be trusted with money to buy necessities for herself and her two boys, "Georgey" and "Jimmy," and Andrew's life in his own home became a veritable hell. But in his letters Walt sent friendly greetings even to Nancy and tried to counteract the rising hatred of her in-laws in Brooklyn.

To his other sister-in-law Walt wrote sage advice on the proper bringing up of "Sis" (Mannahatta). Her grandmother had difficulty in controlling her and after his mother had quoted some "smart" remark of hers in a letter, Walt begged the family not to "notice her smartness" or make critical remarks about her in her hearing. He hoped, too, Jeff would "not make his lessons to her in music anyways strong or frequent on any account—two lessons a week, of ten minutes each, is enough. . . ." [127] But Walt's life was not completely weighed down by his sense of family responsibilities. He also wrote, with ponderous facetiousness, that he was "as much of a beauty as ever . . . Well, not only as much but more so—I believe I weigh about 200, and as to my face, (so scarlet,) and my beard and neck, they are terrible to behold. I fancy the reason I am able to do some good in the hospitals among the poor languishing and wounded boys, is, that I am so large and well—indeed like a great wild buffalo, with much hair."

The facetiousness scarcely concealed Whitman's serious concern with his appearance and its influence on others. In May he suddenly realized that his clothes were in rags—he had left Brooklyn hurriedly without baggage. But his mother sent him several shirts she had made for him, roomy and cut just as he liked them, and he bought "a nice plain suit of dark wine color." [128] He assured his mother that, attired in one of his new shirts and his new suit, he "cut quite a swell." He had not trimmed his beard since leaving home, but thought it had not grown much longer, only a little bushier. He may have looked shaggier than he realized, however, for the soldiers frequently addressed him as "old man." [129] Yet in late spring he was feeling almost robust again, though the doctors cautioned him against subjecting himself too steadily to "the air and influences of the hospitals," and sometimes he skipped a day or shortened his visits. [130]

Several times during the spring Walt asked his mother and Jeff about the *Drum-Taps* manuscripts he had left in Brooklyn. He wanted to be assured that they were safe because he planned to publish the book as soon as he could make arrangements with a publisher. And he also continued to toy with the idea of lecturing, now for the definite purpose of raising money for his hospital work. In June he wrote his mother, "I have quite made up my mind about the lecturing . . . project—I have no doubt it will succeed well enough the way I shall put it in operation." [131] Yet despite this confidence, he made no effort to carry out his plan. He may have been partly distracted by the unpleasantness of the Washington summer, which was beginning to annoy him. Toward the last of June he had another severe attack of sore throat and "distress" in his head, and throughout the summer he complained frequently of the heat. [132] The heat also increased the suffering of the sick and wounded, especially those in the improvised sheds, which was the only shelter that some of the hospitals had. Deaths were more frequent, and of course these depressed Whitman. On June 1 the O'Connors had moved, and Walt was now preparing his own breakfasts and taking his dinners at a restaurant.[133] Naturally his little bedroom was stifling on those hot, humid Washington nights.

In a letter to his mother dated June 22 Walt acknowledged Jeff's letter telling him of the birth of Martha's second child (first named California and later changed to Jessie Louisa). Walt expressed satisfaction over its being a girl, adding, "I am not sure but the Whitman breed gives better women than men." [134] The news made him long more than ever to see his family again, but it was no time for him to leave Washington. A battle was in progress over in Virginia: ". . . yesterday [there] was a fight to the southwest of here all day; we heard the cannons nearly all day." The wounded, mostly from the cavalry, were now arriving, and the least serious cases were being sent on to Philadelphia and New York, which looked as though the authorities expected soon to have very heavy casualties from a big battle. Even the capital itself was thought to be in danger of a raid by Lee. However, Whitman added, "I fancy I should take it very quietly if I found myself in the midst of a desperate conflict here in Washington." [135] For Walt Whitman this was not an unusual state of mind, or a thoughtless boast. He did not easily panic, nor was he naturally belligerent; thus he thought not of the resistance he would put up but fancied that he would "take it very quietly."

The raid did not come, though the residents of Washington continued to be apprehensive. On June 30 Walt wrote his mother about seeing the President drive past 14th Street every evening on his way to the Soldiers Home, outside the capital. He rode in a shabby barouche drawn by horses that "my friends the Broadway drivers would call *old plugs*," followed by about thirty cavalrymen. The President looked more careworn than usual, and Walt felt sorry for him, and wondered how anyone could feel vindictive toward such a man, adding: "I really think it would be safer for him just now to stop at the White House, but I expect he is too proud to abandon the former custom." [136]

About an hour after the President had passed on the day of Walt's letter, a large cavalry regiment, accoutered for the battlefields, went by. They were preceded by a mounted sixteen-piece band—mostly drums. "I tell you, mother, it made everything ring—made my heart leap." The men and officers were unshaved, roughly dressed, but mounted on prancing horses, making quite a clatter on the hard-packed turnpike. Walt was both elated and saddened by the martial scene. "They are off toward the region of Lee's (supposed) rendezvous, toward Susquehannah, for the great anticipated battle. Alas! how many of these healthy, handsome, rollicking young men will lie cold in death before the apples ripen in the orchard."

Walt formed intimate friendships with some of the soldiers he met, but always in the background was that foreboding of their possible destruction in the prime of life. In the spring of 1863 he became attached to a young man in the Armory Hospital named Lewis ("Lewy") Kirke Brown, who had received a severe leg wound the previous summer at Cedar Mountain.[137] The leg refused to heal and he had been in Armory Square Hospital for several months when Whitman became acquainted with him. He was a simple country boy from Maryland who had enlisted at the age of eighteen, and Whitman regarded him as a sort of adopted son, as he often did his young soldier friends of Lewy's age (he was twenty in October, 1863).

Whitman formed a still stronger emotional attachment, however, to a friend of Lewy's, Sergeant Thomas P. Sawyer of the Eleventh Massachusetts Volunteers. Whether he himself had been a patient at Armory Square or had only visited friends in this hospital is not certain, but he seemed to be acquainted with a number of the boys there, whose condition Whitman reported in his letters to him. Tom left Washington in April for a camp near the same place where Walt had found George, and during the succeeding months Walt wrote several letters to him.[138] The young man had evidently had meager schooling, though perhaps more than Lewy had had, and found writing letters awkward and unpleasant, so that he did not reply to all the letters he received from his older and more literary friend. Perhaps also he was puzzled by the ardent tone of some of these letters and hardly knew how to reply, though he insisted in his letters to Lewy that he wished to do so. These letters of Whitman to Sergeant Tom Sawyer are, indeed, not easy for a modern critic to interpret, for they were evidently motivated by a mixture of vicarious paternalism, longing for companionship, and some rather confused erotic impulses that perhaps Whitman himself did not clearly understand.

What sounds like Whitman's first letter was written on April 21, 1863.[139] Addressing the young man as Tom, he reports on the news of the Armory Square Hospital, but especially on Lewy Brown's condition and future plans. "Lew is so good, so affectionate—when I came away he reached up his face [and] I put my arm around him and we gave each other a long kiss half a minute long." Reporting on his own affairs, Whitman says he manages to pay his way by "writing letters for the New York papers" and doing clerical work. "I go around some, nights when the spirit moves me, sometimes to the gay places just to see the sights. Tom, I wish you was here—Somehow I don't find the comrade that suits me to a dot—and I won't have any other, not for good."

After a considerable amount of patriotic comment on the progress of the war and defiance of Jeff Davis, Whitman then writes somewhat incoherently: "Tom, you tell the boys of your company there is an old pirate up in Washington, with the white wool growing all down his neck—an old comrade who thinks about you & them every day, for all he don't know them, and will probably never see them, but thinks about them as comrades & younger brothers of his, just the same." A few lines later Whitman becomes still more emotional:

Dear comrade, you must not forget me, for I never shall you, My love you have in life or death, forever. I don't know how you feel about it, but it is the wish of my heart to have your friendship and also that if you should come safe out of this war, we should come together again in some place where we could make our living, and be true comrades and never be separated while life lasts —and take Lew Brown too, and never separate from him. Or if things are not so to be—if you get these lines, my dear darling comrade, and any thing should go wrong, so that we do not meet again, here on earth, it seems to me, (the way I feel now) that my soul could never be entirely happy, even in the world to come, without you, dear Comrade.[140]

A few days later (April 26) Whitman wrote again, saying that Lewy Brown had received two letters but Tom had not written to him "for some time." And here we learn of another disappointment:

I was sorry you did not come up to my room to get the shirt & other things you promised to accept from me and take when you went away. I got them all ready,—a good strong blue shirt & a pair of drawers and it would have been a satisfaction to me if you had accepted them. I should have often thought now Tom may be wearing around his body something from *me* & that it might contribute to your comfort down there in camp, on picket, or sleeping in your tent. . . . Now my dearest comrade, I will bid you so long, & hope God will put it in your heart to bear toward me a little at least of the feeling I have about you. If it is only a quarter as much I shall be satisfied. Your faithful friend & brother

WALT

A letter that Tom wrote to "Friend Lewis" on April 12 either had been delayed or Lewy had failed to show it to Whitman, for in that Tom had sent this erratically spelled message:

I want you to give my love to Walter Whitman and tell him I am very sorry that I could not live up to my Prommice because I came away so soon that it sliped my mind and I am very sorry for it   tell him also that I shall write to him myself in a few days . . . tell him I have got that little Book in [*sic*] witch he gave me. and I shall always keep it for old acquantence Sake.

On the very day that Whitman was writing his letter of April 26, however, Tom was writing to him. Though he used the salutation Walt had requested, he wrote in a neater and more flourishing hand than he had used in his more relaxed letters to Lewy, and his diction was self-consciously formal. Addressing Whitman as "Dear Brother," he said: "As you have given me permission, I have taken the liberty to address you as above. And I assure you I fully reciprocate your friendship as expressed in your letter and it will afford me great pleasure to meet you after the war will have terminated or sooner if circumstances will permit."

Walt received this letter only two days later (April 28), but he did not reply until May 27, when he again assured Tom of his love: "My dearest comrade, I cannot, though I attempt it, put in a letter the feelings of my heart—I suppose my letters sound strange to you as it is, but as I am only expressing the truth in them, I do not trouble myself on that account. As I intimated before, I do not expect you to return for me the same degree of love I have for you." The remainder of the letter was confined to comment on the war, praise of Lewy Brown (Walt hoped to share with him after the war whatever "means" he might have), and gossip about Armory Square Hospital.

In July Whitman wrote Tom a more restrained letter, in which he wondered why Tom had stopped writing. The following November, while visiting in Brooklyn, he wrote again, still wondering why Tom did not write. But apparently Tom's silence was not deliberate, for in January, 1864, he again took his pen in hand and indited another formal, painfully self-conscious note. The critics and biographers who have claimed that Whitman's dangerous "Calamus emotions" were sublimated and vanquished by his hospital sacrifices evidently did not make use of this correspondence with Sergeant Tom Sawyer.

One of the truly major friendships in Whitman's life also began during the momentous year of 1863. This was with John Burroughs, who had been reading *Leaves of Grass* for two or three years, and had already, as previously mentioned, made at least one unsuccessful attempt to meet the poet in New York.[141] He did not actually come to know him until October of this year, but meanwhile his friend E. M. Allen, who was now part owner of an army supply store in Washington, had been writing Burroughs about his friendship with Whitman, thus increasing Burroughs's eagerness to come to the capital. On May 5 Allen wrote, "Between Walt Whitman and me has passed the bond of beer, and we are friends." [142] He then described the appearance and dress with which we are familiar. We learn from Allen that Whitman had received letters from his friends in New York indicating the declining popularity of Pfaff's and the scattering of the "good fellows" who had gone there before the war. Later in the month Allen wrote:

Walt strolled in today as he frequently does. The whole front of our store is open and shaded with an awning, and is a cool pleasant place, coming in from the street. Sometimes when I am busy I'll see Walt's picturesque form in one of the many camp-chairs, a fan in his hand; and then, after a while, he is gone. When I am not busy I sit down and talk with him. He says he is going to give me a book of Thoreau's which the author sent him some years ago. I would prize it highly. We projected an excursion for Sunday up the Branch to the same woods where Florence and I went. I wish you could be with us.[143]

"Florence" was Elizabeth Akers, widow of the sculptor Paul Akers, who wrote under the pen name of "Florence Percy." She disliked Whitman because she disapproved of his poetry, and after Allen married her his friendship with the poet declined.[144]

On June 18 Allen wrote again: "Walt just passed with his arms full of bottles and lemons, going to some hospitals, he said, to give the boys a good time. He was sweating finely; his collar and shirt were thrown open, showing his great hairy throat and breast." [145] And in July: "Walt and I quaffed beer today from great goblets that would become the halls of Walhalla. Walt is much interested in you, and I sketched your history some to him. He would like to know you. He is a good fellow, and although over fifty [he was only forty-four], belongs to the present generation."

Toward the end of October Burroughs abandoned schoolteaching and went to Washington. On November 8, 1863, he wrote his wife, "I have seen Walt and think him glorious." [146] For several evenings he had visited Allen's store, hoping Whitman would come in, and finally on entering he saw the poet sitting in a canvas chair at the rear. Allen introduced them with, "Walt, here's the young man from the country I told you about," and they were immediately friends. Burroughs was invited to join the group that gathered frequently in the evening at the O'Connor home. The group included Charles W. Eldridge; J. J. Piatt, friend of W. D. Howells; Dr. Frank Baker of the Smithsonian Institution; Aaron Johns, a soldier; Arnold B. Johnson, private secretary to Senator Sumner; and several others. Although the talk had a wide range, it was often on literary topics.

For relaxation after his exhausting tours in the hospitals Walt often played his favorite game of "Twenty Questions" at the O'Connors'. He had used this game as a teaching device on Long Island and later with the soldiers in New York Hospital on Broadway. Mrs. O'Connor remembered that the friends who played this game at her home became quite expert at it. Once the subject was the white beard of Gideon Wells, the Secretary of the Navy, which they guessed in less than twenty questions. On another occasion a new Bible was placed on the mantel by Walt on his arrival, and they guessed it in about ten questions, after which the Bible was given to the O'Connors' daughter.[147]

One snowy New Year's Eve Walt arrived looking like a veritable Santa, with snowflakes glistening on his beard, hat, and shoulders. In his large pockets he carried a bottle of Scotch whisky, a lemon, and some lump sugar, and he announced he would make hot punch himself. Ellen O'Connor was amused at his meticulous precision. Everything must be exactly so: the water was taken off the stove just as it came to a boil, each slice of lemon was just so thick and no thicker, and each glass received a lump of sugar exactly the same size. Everyone praised Walt's skill, but the drinking was moderate, for at midnight enough punch remained for toasts to the New Year.

The O'Connor circle helped Whitman through the trying days which he was experiencing, but it is doubtful that he shared with any of them, unless the O'Connors themselves, the worst of his trials, which were concerned with family matters. He talked, of course, of George, and occasionally made loving references to his dear old mother in Brooklyn. He may also have occasionally mentioned Jeff, though we may be sure in a complimentary way. As a matter of fact, he was so fond of Jeff that it is doubtful whether he completely realized his brother's thoughtlessness and lack of consideration for others. Walt frequently had to beg and plead with Jeff to send him a copy of a Brooklyn newspaper containing an article Walt had written. Despite his apparent jolly, happy-go-lucky nature, Jeff was often moody, depressed, and negligent. Repeatedly Walt would try to persuade him not to be so "down in the mouth" over the failure of the Army of the Potomac, insisting that the "Rebs" were suffering more than the North was aware. Nor was Jeff impressed by Walt's defense of the

President. On June 13 he wrote: "Well, Walt, you and I cannot agree in regard to 'Uncle Abe.' I cannot think that he is the man for the place or he would have surrounded himself with men that could do something." [148]

As usual, Walt was tolerant of these differences of opinion. And early in the summer he began worrying about the possibility of Jeff's being drafted. Congress had passed a conscription act the preceding March, but no attempt to enforce it was made until summer. In New York City disorderly demonstrations, supposedly in protest against the draft, began on Saturday, July 11, which quickly developed into huge riots.[149] From Sunday until the following Wednesday mobs numbering from fifty to seventy thousand people terrorized the city, burning, looting, hanging Negroes to lamp posts, and murdering prominent officials. State troops finally restored order on Wednesday after some two thousand people had been killed, eight thousand wounded, and property damaged to an estimated loss of $5,000,000. Henry J. Raymond, publisher of the New York *Times*, insisted that the mob was "not the people," as the *World* and *Tribune* first stated, but "for the most part . . . the vilest elements of the city," [150] and historians were to agree with him. The participants were mainly the lawless gangs (particularly impoverished Irish immigrants) of the Bowery and the slums around Five Points. However, the Democratic mayor and alderman are said to have aided the rioters, by releasing them from jail as soon as the policemen had locked them up, in order to embarrass the national Republican administration. Of course, the city was notorious for its Southern sympathizers.

The reports that Whitman got in Washington were garbled, and when he wrote his mother on July 15 he was on the defensive against the condemnation of New York which he was hearing expressed all around him: "The feeling here is savage and hot as fire against New York (the mob— 'Copperhead mob' the papers here call it), and I hear nothing in all directions but threats of ordering up the gunboats, cannonading the city, shooting down the mob, hanging them in a body, etc., etc. Meantime I remain silent, partly amused, partly scornful, or occasionally put [in] a dry remark, which only adds fuel to the flame. I do not feel it in my heart to abuse the poor people, or call for a rope or bullets for them, but that is all the talk here, even in the hospitals." [151] He was not greatly worried that any member of his family would be injured in the riots across the river, but he was now much concerned over the possibility of Jeff's being drafted, which he said would be the "downfall of our whole family."

By August 18 Walt had learned the truth about the riots, and he wrote his mother: "Well, I thought when I first heard of the riot in N.Y. I had some feeling for them [the rioters], but soon as I found what it really was, I felt it was the devil's own work all through." [152] He was now as much in favor of Government firmness as the Washingtonians whose opinions he had earlier resented. But he was still worrying over Jeff. The regulations were that a draftee could get excused by paying a fee of $300 for a substitute. Walt's plan was to borrow this sum, possibly from Jeff's employer, Moses Lane, if Jeff were drafted, though Walt was also still planning to start his long-dreamed-of lecture tour, and he thought he might be able to raise enough money in that way to help his brother. Jeff, of course, had saved no money himself. However, he was not selected at this time, and so the problem did not arise until late in the summer of 1864.[153]

But even though Jeff was able to remain at home and hold his position with the Water Works (he did have his salary cut from $100 to $50 a month), the family relationships were becoming increasingly disagreeable and sordid. On August 4 Jeff wrote Walt:

I certainly think Mother is following a mistaken notion of economy. I think the only decent meals that any of them have had for three months is what they have eaten with Mat and I. As regards Mother I am perfectly willing she should live with us all the time (that is to eat, I mean) but Ed and Jess I cant stand entirely. Dont understand that they do eat with us, for they dont as much perhaps as they use to. Mother certainly does not, not as much as we wish her to, for we always call her. I notice however that when Jess does eat with us that he does not throw up his victuals. Somehow or another Mother seems to think that she ought to live without spending any money. Even today she has 25 or 30 dollars in the house and I will bet that all they have for dinner will be a quart of tomatoes and a few cucumbers. And then Mother wonders why Jess vomits up his meals. However Mother gets them just as good or better than she has for herself.[154]

As a result of this letter Walt tried tactfully to suggest to his mother the importance of a proper diet.[155] He described the substantial meals he ate and told her she should have as good ones. Probably she was not a good manager, but she also knew how difficult it would be to replace the dollars she spent. And life was certainly not easy for her, living with those two defective sons, one feeble-minded and the other bordering on violent insanity, and Jesse with a weak stomach. She also confided in her letters to Walt that Jeff and Mat continued to make frequent efforts to persuade her to "lend" George's money to them.

Conditions in Mrs. Whitman's home were, in fact, rapidly growing worse. On September 3 she wrote Walt about her difficulties with Andrew and Nancy.[156] He had been drinking again, and quarreling with Nancy. Jesse was also unwell, she said, apparently too sick to work, and he stayed home all the time, rocking the cradle for Martha "day in and day out." Writing again on October 26, she said she was by herself that evening; "Ed" had gone to church, as he did nearly every evening, and not one word had she received from Jeff or Mat or Han or Mary—"you are my whole dependence." Hannah and Mary were never good correspondents, and Jeff and Mat were apparently out of town and had been away for some days.

On November 1 Mrs. Whitman wrote that her difficulties were increasing. At the very time she was writing, Walt was preparing to leave Washington for a visit to Brooklyn, and the next day he made the trip while his mother's letter was on its way to Washington.[157] She was finding it hard to support Andrew and his family because of his and Nancy's extravagance, and Martha and Jeff resented her helping her incompetent son and daughter-in-law. Andrew was now spending most of the daytime with her, lying down much of the time, eating his dinner (midday) there, and then taking food home for his supper, with extra handouts for Nancy and the children.[158] Jimmy, however, was staying with his grandmother, too, and she found him a burden, as she did Hattie, whom she called very "obstropolus," and Hattie's uncle Andrew said that if she were his he'd break her neck. Nancy was so dirty, ugly, and lazy that Mrs. Whitman could hardly blame Andrew for drinking, she confessed to Walt.

This was the kind of bickering and squalid misery that Walt came back home to, but perhaps his cheerfulness helped to soothe the overwrought nerves. He had not been able to spare the railroad fare; so O'Connor had spoken to the President's secretary about Walt's need for a pass, and John Hay had provided it, ostensibly to enable him to vote in the November election.[159] In calling for the pass Whitman had obtained a close-up view of the President, which he described in his diary, along with the dates, events, and impressions of his trip to Brooklyn:

October 31. Called at the President's house, on John Hay—saw Mr. Lincoln standing, talking to a gentleman, apparently a dear friend.

November 1. [This seems to be a continuation of the above notation spilled over into the next printed date in the diary.] His face & manner have an expression & are inexpressibly sweet—one hand on his friend's shoulder, the other holds his hand. I love the President personally.

November 2. Came through to-day from Washington to Brooklyn. Got home about [8 or 9 o'clock] in the evening—very pleasant trip, weather fine, country looks good, the great cities & towns through which I passed looked wonderfully prosperous—it looks anything else but war—everybody well drest, plenty of money, markets boundless & of the best, factories all busy—I write this in Brooklyn.[160]

Whitman failed to record in his diary that he voted, but to Lewy Brown he wrote on November 8: ". . . I got home in the evening [of November 2] between 8 and 9—Next morning I went up to the polls bright and early—I suppose it is not necessary to tell you how I voted—we have gained a great victory in this city—it went union this time, though it went democratic strong only a year ago, and for many years past. . . ."[161] He attended the opera in New York, inspected the Water Works with Jeff, and wrote letters to soldiers and friends in Washington.[162] To Charles W. Eldridge he wrote:

BROOKLYN
Nov. 17, 1863.

DEAR FRIEND,
I suppose Nelly has received a letter from me posting you up on my doings, &c. Any letters that come to me, up to Saturday next, please send on here. After that, do not send any, as I shall return Monday or Tuesday next. The weather here the last three days is very unpleasant, sloppy and thick. I was at the opera last night, Trovatore—very, very good singing & acting.

I feel to devote myself more and more to the work of my life, which is making poems. I must bring out Drum Taps. I *must* be continually bringing out poems—now is the hey day—I shall range along the high plateau of my life and capacity for a few years now, & then swiftly descend. The life here in the cities, & the objects, &c of most, seem to me very flippant and shallow somehow since I returned this time—

—My New York boys are good, too good—if I staid here a month longer I should be killed with kindness—The great recompense of my journey here is to see my mother so well, & so bravely sailing on amid many troubles & discouragements like a noble old ship—My brother Andrew is bound for another world—he is here the greater part of the time—Charley I think sometimes to be a woman is greater than to be a man—is more eligible to greatness, not the ostensible article, but the real one. Dear Comrade I send you my love, & to William & Nelly & remember me to Major [Hapgood]

WALT—[163]

On November 25 Walt was back in New York, seeing the sights, as in the old days. In his diary he recorded: "Saw a large regiment of blacks, marching in from the country, all armed & accoutred with the U. S. uniform muskets &c. March up Broadway about 11 o'clock tonight." [164] On December 1 he told Andrew goodbye, fully realizing what the parting meant, and made a night trip back to Washington. Two days later he received a telegram from Jeff saying that Andrew was dead. On the same day Jeff wrote this letter:

BROOKLYN, N.Y. December 3rd 1863
Thursday 11 A.M.

DEAR BROTHER WALT,

I have just telegraphed to you that Andrew was dead. Poor boy he died much easier than one would have supposed. I do hope to God you will come on. I have been with him. Mary, Mother Mat and I, almost all the time since you left. Mary and I watched last night. He has been dying ever since Wednesday morning—fully 24 hours—Poor Nancy, she takes it woful hard   Mary has acted like the best of Women   It is very affecting to see Nancy and the children   Mattie did everything that she possibly could   She watched with us till near 3oclk this morning   Andrew was very desirous of having us all around him when he died. The poor boy seemed to think that that would take nearly all the horror of it away. If you will come on I will try and give you the passage money. Mother and the rest take it very hard. I hope to get an answer by telegraph.

JEFF.[165]

On December 6 Walt wrote to George: "I sent you a letter four days ago that Andrew was gone at last, poor fellow. I have written to Han. I did not go to Andrew's funeral. (I suppose it was yesterday—but I am very sorry now that I did not stay while I was home. . . .)" But for Walt this was not the end of the sordid drama of his brother's death. On December 4 his mother wrote him a long letter filled with graphic details of the events that took place during the days immediately following his departure.[166] Andrew began failing the very morning after Walt left. Mary was summoned, and members of the family and young men friends took turns sitting up with him. Wednesday morning his children were sent to their grandmother's house, and Andrew asked to have his mother's rocking chair sent over for him to spend his last hours in—he knew he was dying. Apparently he was unable to lie down, and he sat in the chair until the end came. Jeff and Martha sat with him on Wednesday night, and "they had to fan him all night and bathe him in brandy." Nancy went to bed, but "when she came out in the morning she brought such a smell that Jeffy got sick and had to come home . . ."[167]

Andrew's brothers and sister had considered moving him to his mother's, but Nancy objected, created a scene, and the idea was given up though Andrew wanted to go. A few hours later, surrounded by his family, he turned his head to get a good look at the photographs of Walt and George, drank some water without choking, and then quietly died "like any one going to sleep."

Thursday evening Martha sent Jesse to Andrew's house with tea for Nancy, and he was deeply affected by seeing his brother's corpse. His mother said he looked strange when he came back. But next day he returned to the house of mourning while Martha was there with her two children. Hattie did something that annoyed him and he threatened to whip her. Martha forbade him to touch her child, and Jesse "called her very bad names." Mrs. Whitman calmed him by reminding him that his brother lay dead upstairs. But she knew that Jeff intended to write Walt about the scene. Jeff seems not to have written until December 15, but he was still almost wild with resentment and threatened to kill Jesse if he ever touched his child, and then added this condemnation:

To think that the wretch should go off and live with an Irish whore, get in the condition he is in by her act and then come and be a source of shortening his mother's life by years   I feel a constant fear for Mother—she says he has these kind of things quite often with her. Calls her everything—and even swears he will keel her over &c.   —Ed I don't mind so much because he couldn't help being what he is—but Jess did to himself and made himself what he is—and I think is answerable for it.[168]

Despite these quarrels the funeral went off without any more scenes. Andrew's friend, James Cornell, provided two carriages, one for Nancy, one for himself, and the Whitmans rode in a third. There were ten carriages in the procession and Mrs. Whitman felt that they gave Andrew a decent funeral: "it done him no good i know but it was the last office we could perform." [169] The undertaker charged $52, which he called for a few days later, only an hour after Mrs. Whitman had received $150 from George, most of which she had to use to pay the undertaker and settle "a very large grocery bill." [170]

Mrs. Whitman's troubles may have been lessened slightly by Andrew's death, but she still had great burdens to bear. On Christmas day she wrote Walt that their dinner had been "not turkeys nor geese but pot pie made of mutton," and even that had been spoiled by the tantrums of Hattie, whom her grandmother called "the worst child I ever had anything to do with." [171] She reported, too, that Nancy "goes it yet in the street," and evidently Mrs. Whitman was not reporting idle gossip, for in subsequent letters both she and Jeff added details of Nancy's sending the children out to beg and of her own misconduct.[172] Very likely she had been a street-walker before Andrew's death. But Mrs. Whitman's greatest worry was even closer home. Jesse was becoming more violent and Jeff was evidently trying to force his mother to commit him to an asylum:

. . . Jeffy must have wrote very strong about him [Jesse] . . . well Walt Jessy is a very great trouble to me to be sure and dont apprecete [sic] what i doo for him but he is no more deranged than he has been for the last 3 years   i think it would be very bad for him to be put in the lunatic assilyim . . . he is very passionate almost to frenzy and always was but of course his brain is very weak   but at the time of his last blow out we had everything to confuse and irritate . . . i think Walt what a poor unfortunate creature he has been   what a life he has lived   that as long as i can get any thing for him to eat i would rather work and take care of him   that is as long as i see no danger of harm . . .[173]

VI

By the time New Year's, 1864, arrived Whitman had spent a whole year in Washington, minus his November weeks in Brooklyn. His one satisfaction was the help he had given many soldiers in the hospitals. His literary plans had so far led nowhere. Late in the fall he had tried to interest his Boston friend James Redpath in publishing his war diaries as *Memoranda of a Year*—perhaps the most important year, he declared in his prospectus, in the history of the American people. Redpath had responded that the book Whitman described might require an investment beyond his means, but he suggested that the manuscript be completed and sent to him: ". . . if I can't publish it, I will see if some other person won't." [174]

Whitman had already had enough experience with such promises to know that this was nothing he could count on, though he did not entirely abandon his plan for the book. He intended to give not only a factual account of his experiences and observations but also to attack certain conditions and practices which he thought should be reformed.[175] One of these was the present undemocratic tendency of the Army to depend upon West Point for its officers. Whitman thought meritorious men should be promoted from the ranks. In view of the fact that George, with only a common school education, had risen in two years from private to captain, Walt's prepossession with this idea seems not to have been entirely in accord with the facts, but he had cherished it since his editorship of the Brooklyn *Eagle*.[176]

The fact that Whitman had been wholly unsuccessful in his efforts to secure a Government position had, of course, increased his desire to publish a book that might bring in some income. His new friend John Burroughs had obtained a clerkship in the Treasury Department within a few weeks after his arrival.[177] This, incidentally, had not interfered with the growth of their friendship, for Whitman was not by nature either jealous or envious. Early in January, 1864, Burroughs wrote to his friend Benton: "The more I see of Walt, the more I like him. . . . There is nothing more to be said after he gives his views. It is as if Nature herself had spoken. And so kind, sympathetic, charitable, humane, tolerant a man I did not suppose was possible. He loves everything and everybody. I saw a soldier the other day stop on the street and kiss him. He kisses me as if I were a girl." [178]

Two weeks later Burroughs was proposing to arrange lecture engagements in Washington for Walt, and he asked Benton if he could not do the same at Poughkeepsie. Should the Washington lectures succeed, Whitman would try them in New York, Brooklyn, and Boston, but nothing came of these plans. In March Burroughs wrote again to Benton: "Walt is as glorious as ever and, as usual, looks like a god. He expects to bring out his 'Drum Taps' pretty soon. He discoursed with me an hour the other day on his plans and purposes. He anticipates a pecuniary success with his book. By and by he expects to make himself felt lecturing. He is quite ambitious. Allen calls him the Old Goat. I tell him I wish I was an Old Goat." [179]

Another friend who was trying at the same time to help Whitman in a different way was John T. Trowbridge, who had come down from Boston the previous November to gather material for a biography of Salmon P. Chase, Secretary of the Treasury.[180] He was a guest in Chase's fine house on Pennsylvania Avenue, and he was greatly surprised when he asked O'Connor about Walt Whitman to be told that he lived diagonally across the square from the Secretary, corner of Sixth Street, in a little garret room. O'Connor promised Trowbridge that if he would come to his house the following Sunday evening he would find Walt there. Trowbridge accepted this invitation, spent a stimulating evening at the O'Connors', and after ten o'clock he and William walked home with Whitman.

In the fine, large mansion, sumptuously furnished, cared for by sleek and silent colored servants, and thronged by distinguished guests, dwelt the great statesman; in the old tenement opposite, in a bare and desolate back room, up three flights of stairs, quite alone, lived the poet. Walt led the way up those dreary stairs, partly in darkness, found the keyhole of a door which he unlocked and opened, scratched a match, and welcomed us to his garret.

Garret it literally was, containing hardly any more furniture than a bed, a cheap pine table, and a little sheet-iron stove in which there was no fire. A window was open, and it was a December night. But Walt, clearing a chair or two of their litter of newspapers, invited us to sit down and stop awhile, with as simple and sweet hospitality as if he had been offering us the luxuries of the great mansion across the square.[181]

The three men sat in the cold room, with the window open, discussing Shakespeare and *Leaves of Grass* until late into the night. O'Connor was a "Baconian," and for the sake of argument Whitman joined Trowbridge in supporting Shakespeare's authorship of the plays. We have noticed many times before this that Whitman was not a ready speaker, and in describing this evening Trowbridge mentioned the fact again, but added that in talking of his "pomes" he glowed with enthusiasm and animation. O'Connor always maintained that *Leaves of Grass* was as great a literary work as any of those attributed to Shakespeare, but Trowbridge was more restrained in his admiration; some passages he regarded as great poetry, but he thought other passages could be spared without loss.[182]

Two mornings later Trowbridge called again at Walt's garret. He had been warned not to come before ten o'clock, and it was after ten. Walt was partly dressed and was preparing his breakfast on the sheet-iron stove. With his jackknife he cut slices of bread, which his guest kindly toasted for him on a sharpened stick. He made tea in a tin kettle, dipped sugar out of a brown paper bag, and used another piece of brown paper for a butter plate. For cupboard he used an oblong pine box standing against the wall. Breakfast over, he burned his butter plate. Besides the teakettle, his entire housekeeping equipment consisted of a tin cup, a bowl, and a spoon.

Breakfast out of the way, Walt took out of his trunk a package of manuscript poems. "These were his war pieces, the Drum-Taps, then nearly ready for publication. He read them unaffectedly, with force and feeling, and in a voice of rich but not resonant tones." [183] Trowbridge was interested not only in the poems, but in Whitman's interpretations of the irregular rhythms. He found the compositions more literary than Whitman's earlier poems, at times even conventional in diction. But they seemed to him often "fine, effective, patriotic, and pathetic"; moreover, they were "entirely free from the old offences against propriety." Trowbridge promised to do what he could to interest a Boston publisher in them—but this turned out to be more difficult than he had anticipated; the poet's reputation was too unsavory in Boston literary circles.

Trowbridge also made an immediate attempt to help Whitman in his search for a position. Learning that he had a letter from Emerson to Chase, which Whitman had never attempted to present, Trowbridge offered to act as intermediary. Whitman surrendered the Emerson letter and Trowbridge promptly carried it to the Secretary of the Treasury, with a personal endorsement of his own. The Secretary was impressed by Emerson's letter, but he had heard that Whitman had written a "notorious" book—he had not read it. Trowbridge tried to assure him that the poet had been misunderstood and misjudged. He was not a New York rowdy, but "as quiet a gentleman in his manners and conversations as any guest who enters your door." The reply was: "I am bound to believe what you say; but his writings have given him a bad repute, and I should not know what sort of place to give to such a man. . . ." [184]

Chase was a polished, dignified, and conventional New Englander, whose consuming ambition was to succeed Lincoln in the Presidency, and he was extremely fearful of appointing anyone to office who might be adversely criticized. Trowbridge, seeing that his case was hopeless, said he would withdraw his plea and relieve him of the letter; whereupon Chase replied, "I have nothing of Emerson's in his handwriting, and I shall be glad to keep this." Thus Whitman's friend had to report back that not only had he been unable to secure an appointment, but that the Secretary had kept Emerson's letter.

The irony of this situation was that Emerson's letter had probably deprived Whitman of the coveted position, because it called attention to his authorship of *Leaves of Grass*. Trowbridge was confident that he could have secured an appointment for an unknown Walter Whitman. "But I felt that the Secretary, if he was to appoint him, should know just whom he was appointing; and Whitman was the last person in the world to shirk the responsibility of having written an audacious book." [185] The fact that there had been scandals in the Department made Chase especially cautious, and Trowbridge pointed out to Whitman that he himself was partly to blame for misunderstandings about *Leaves of Grass*, for had he not there called himself " 'rowdyish,' 'disorderly,' and worse?" Whitman laughed and said, "I don't blame him; its about what I expected."

Perhaps such discouraging experiences as this account for the increasing homesickness that began to creep into Whitman's letters to his mother. In January George went home with his regiment for a thirty-day furlough before re-enlisting,[186] and the fact that George was at home naturally made Walt long more than ever to be there too. In his letters he inquired frequently whether George had re-enlisted (he did). But neither personal discouragement nor homesickness interfered with the continuation of Walt's visits to the hospitals. Dr. Bliss decided that Lewis Brown's leg would have to be amputated. At Lewy's request Walt was present when the operation was performed on January 5, and for several nights he slept in the hospital near the young man until the danger of a hemorrhage had passed. On January 29 Walt wrote his mother that Lewy was recovering and his condition was no longer critical. At the same time he mentioned having acquired a new friend, James A. Garfield, member of Congress from Ohio.[187]

Early in February Whitman became eager to visit the army at the front again, and on February 5 he wrote his mother that he was leaving the next day.[188] The following week he was in Culpeper, Virginia, where he found the troops more comfortably housed than they had been the previous winter. The wounded were also being better taken care of. Now they were usually sent promptly to Washington, though diarrhea cases were kept too long at the front, and fatalities were numerous. Walt traveled around freely and visited several camps. To his mother he wrote: ". . . I have no difficulty at all in making myself at home among the soldiers, teamsters, or any—I most always find they like to have me very much; it seems to do them good. No doubt they soon feel that my heart and sympathies are truly with them, and it is both a novelty and pleases them and touches their feelings, and so doubtless does them good—and I am sure it does that to me." [189]

While Whitman was at Culpeper he received a good-sized package of books from Trowbridge, which he distributed in a small hospital for teamsters that he found entirely lacking in reading matter.[190] Some skirmishes took place at Brandy Station, nine miles from headquarters, while he was there. One night Whitman stayed at the home of "a real secesh woman," who was having to billet a number of Union officers, and he was delighted that she talked with him in a friendly manner and gave him a good supper and bed. The country also impressed him: "Dilapidated, fenceless, and trodden with war as Virginia is, wherever I move across her surface, I find myself rous'd to surprise and admiration." [191]

On March 15, back in Washington after having spent about two weeks with the soldiers at the front, Walt was depressed by the thousands of diarrhea cases in the hospitals. He felt the need, he wrote his mother, of women like her and Mat to nurse the sick boys. "Every one is so unfeeling. . . . There is no good nursing. . . . Mother, I feel so sick when I see what kind of people there are among them, with charge over them." [192] Though these sentiments were certainly sincere, and typical of Whitman, who was always most sympathetic with the men whose need was greatest, and who did not spare himself from unpleasant or even sordid tasks in their behalf, nevertheless, his attitude toward the "unfeeling" nurses and doctors was partly the result of his own declining health. The symptoms had not yet become alarming, but they had been apparent for some time. He was depressed, too, by continued news of his mother's poor health during the late winter and early spring months. And as usual, there was the yearly uncertainty over re-renting the same house on Portland Avenue or moving. Mrs. Whitman reported that the Browns had been downright mean,[193] yet she was relieved when Mat and Jeff decided once more to remain with her, and thus the status quo was maintained. The news about Nancy continued to be depressing too. On April 5 Walt commented in a letter to his mother: "So Nance has had another child, poor little one . . ." [194]

In April Whitman began following closely the bitter debates in Congress between the Copperheads and the loyal Unionists. The Army of the Potomac was still ineffective, despite the huge supplies of men and matériel that the Government had poured into it, and some congressmen now began openly advocating that the war be ended by recognizing the Confederacy. Weary as he was of war, sickness, and death, Whitman had no doubt that the awful struggle must be continued until the rebellion was crushed. On April 10 he confided to his mother: "I could willingly go myself in the ranks if I thought it would profit more than [my hospital work] at present, and I don't know sometimes but I shall. . . ." [195] Yet despite these thoughts, he was planning two days later to return home in about a month to "try to print Drum-Taps." Actually, at this time he was torn by several conflicting desires, responsibilities, and ambitions. Toward the end of the month Congress was holding night sessions, and Whitman was going frequently to hear the debates. He was saddened to find that "the speaking and the ability of the members is nearly always on a low scale. It is . . . melancholy to see such a [low] rate of talent, there, such tremendous times as these." But he had discovered that the "Capitol grows upon one in time." [196]

On April 26 Walt wrote his mother that he had seen George. Burnside's army had passed through the previous day, and after watching for three hours Walt saw George and fell in step beside him. George was so excited over seeing him that he forgot to salute the President while passing the reviewing stand. Walt reported that George was looking well and in excellent spirits. It took four or five hours for the sunburnt men in soiled uniforms and loaded down with provisions and equipment to pass. To Walt it was "a great sight to see an army 25 or 30,000 on the march. They are all so gay, too. Poor fellows, nothing dampens their spirits." [197]

From this day until Whitman left Washington in June he followed daily reports and rumors of the movements of Burnside's army. In letters to his mother he conjectured that George would not be in General Grant's drive to take Richmond. Maybe he was merely trying to console his mother, though of course no one, not even the President, knew Grant's exact plans. Probably Whitman based his prediction on the fact that the Ninth Corps under General Burnside had been detached from the Army of the Potomac, but on May 5 his men were among those who crossed the Rapidan and entered the Virginia Wilderness. There for eight days some of the bloodiest fighting of the war took place, and on Friday, May 6, George was in a severe battle; but his luck held and he survived unscathed.

The fighting continued through Saturday and Sunday, while the North anxiously read the extras and waited for decisive news. Then on Monday night the wounded began to arrive in Washington. For three days and nights the ambulances rolled without ceasing from the docks on the Potomac to the hospitals scattered throughout the city, past the flowering shrubs and the magnolia trees in full bloom. The stench of wounds mingled with the sweet perfume of cape jasmine and running honeysuckle. In the midst of the suffering and death this bloody spring Walt Whitman began to think of what it would be like to fall in battle, and he decided that meeting death in this way would have no terror for him. "Of the many I have seen die," he wrote, "or known of, the past year, I have not seen or heard of *one*, who met death with any terror." [198] This was not written simply to prepare his mother for bad news, because he elaborated the observation in *Specimen Days*—and of course it also confirmed the doctrines of Lucretius which had impressed him before publishing his first *Leaves of Grass.*[199]

The house where Whitman had been living was sold, and on May 21 he moved to a third-story hall bedroom at 502 Pennsylvania Avenue, near Third Street.[200] This was a regular boardinghouse and he contracted to take his meals there too, but in a short time he was calling both room and meals "miserable." Probably they were, but he did not usually complain of personal hardships. The truth was that he had become quite ill. On June 3 he said he was staying in Washington only to wait the outcome of Grant's attempt to take Richmond.[201] He now felt the strain of the hospital sights to be almost unbearable, and he admitted to his mother that he was homesick. Of course, everyone felt the tension of the prolonged war. On June 7 Walt commented on the number of insane men now found in the hospitals.[202] His own faintness, dizziness, head pains, and sore throat were becoming steadily worse, but he hung on for a few days hoping to hear from or about George. His last letter to his mother was dated June 17,[203] and on June 25 he wrote George from Brooklyn.[204] He arrived in Brooklyn a sick man, suffering in part from a painfully infected throat, and his condition grew much worse after his arrival. He was unable to leave the house until July 8, when he went riding with Jeff and felt much better.

In a letter dated July 9 Walt told Eldridge that if his strength improved he would "probably go down the island." [205] Since he did not suffer a relapse, it is safe to assume that he made the trip, certainly as far as Greenport, where Mary lived. Not long after he left Washington, a Confederate raid was made on the city and it seemed for a time that the capital might be taken. Trenches were hastily dug and manned by troops in the neighborhood, volunteers from the hospitals, and able-bodied citizens. Lewis Brown hobbled out on his crutches and was indignant that no one would give him a gun.[206] On August 2 Burroughs wrote: "I was out at the front during the siege of Washington and lay in the rifle pits with the soldiers. I got quite a taste of war and learned the song of those modern minstrels —the minie bullets—by heart." [207] And on August 13 O'Connor wrote about drilling every afternoon, and finding the weight of a sixteen-pound rifle and accoutrements a strain in the torrid heat.[208] Perhaps Walt himself missed such experiences by only two or three weeks.

On September 11 Walt wrote O'Connor that his health was "quite reestablished" and that he went "two or three times a week among the soldiers here." Particularly interesting was his description of his amusements:

I go out quite regularly, sometimes out on the bay, or to Coney Island—& occasionally a tour through New York life, as of old—last night I was with some of my friends of Fred Gray association, till late wandering the east side of the city first in the lager beer saloons & then elsewhere—one crowded, low, most degraded place we went, a poor blear eyed girl bringing beer. I saw her with her McClellan medal on her breast—I called her & asked her if the other girls there were for McClellan too—she said yes every one of them, & that they wouldn't tolerate a girl in the place who was not, & the *fellows* were too (there must have been twenty girls, sad sad ruins)—it was one of those places where the air is full of the scent of low thieves, druggies, foul play, & prostitution gangrened.

Walt was evidently revolted by the place, but one wonders about the friends who accompanied him on such expeditions, "as of old." He probably told O'Connor the story because of the General McClellan association; Walt himself detested "Little Mac." [209]

Early in October the war was brought home to the Whitman family in Brooklyn, first by lack of news of George after a battle on September 30, and later by confirmation of their suspicions that he had been captured. On October 8 Walt wrote Eldridge:

. . . I am perhaps not so unconsciously hearty as before my sickness. We are deprest in spirits here about my brother George—if not killed, he is a prisoner —he was in the engagement Sept. 30—on the extreme left—

My book is not yet being printed. I still wish to stereotype it myself. I could easily still put it in the hands of a proper publisher then and make better terms with him.

If you write to William I wish you to enclose him this letter—I wish him to receive again my faithful friendship—while health and sense remain I cannot forget what he has been to me. I love him dearly—

. . . The political meetings in New York and Brooklyn immense. I go to them as to shows—fireworks, cannon, clusters of gas lights, countless torches, banners and mottoes. 15, 20, 50,000 people—Per contra I occasionally go riding off in the country, in quiet lanes, or a sail on the water, and many times to . . . Coney Island.

All the signs are that Grant is going to strike farther, perhaps risk all. One feels solemn when one sees what depends. The military success though first class of war, is the least that depends.

Good bye, dearest comrade . . .

WALT [210]

During the autumn Whitman began writing for the newspapers again, no doubt partly to earn some money, but also because he was stirred up over George's capture. On October 29 the New York *Times* printed an unsigned article on George's regiment, entitled "Fifty-First New York City Veterans," [211] and on December 11 the *Times* printed another article signed "W.W." on "Our Wounded and Sick Soldiers—Visits Among the Hospitals." [212] In the latter article he estimated that the Union hospitals had treated "near four hundred thousand cases," and that half that many soldiers were still receiving medical attention. After sketching many of his observations, especially those of his two visits to the troops in Virginia, Whitman tried to tell his readers some of the realistic facts of this little known side of the war:

Whatever pleasant accounts there may be in the papers of the North, this is the actual fact. No thorough previous preparation, no system, no foresight, no genius. Always plenty of stores, no doubt, but always miles away; never where they are needed, and never the proper application. Of all harrowing experiences, none is greater than that of the days following a heavy battle. Scores, hundreds, of the noblest young men on earth, uncomplaining, lie helpless, mangled, faint, alone, and so bleed to death, or die from exhaustion, either actually untouched at all, or with merely the laying of them down and leaving them, when there ought to be means provided to save them.[213]

Later in his article Whitman pointed out that such neglect and inefficiency was not something far away and invisible to his readers. They existed in New York and Brooklyn. In fact, of the dozens of hospitals he had visited, the worst of all was Brooklyn City Hospital, where soldiers were taken on contract: "This Brooklyn hospital is a bad place for soldiers, or anybody else. Cleanliness, proper nursing, watching, etc., are more deficient than in any hospital I know." [214] He did not blame the physicians, who did the best they could, but the management.

In contrast, Whitman had found (November 27) the Central Park Hospital in New York, near 104th Street, "a well-managed institution." He also praised several hospitals in Brooklyn and Flatbush which treated local patients (not soldiers). Among these he included (under the date of December 7) "the extensive lunatic asylum [in Brooklyn], under charge of Drs. Chapin and Reynolds. Of the latter [institution] . . . I have deliberately to put on record about the profoundest satisfaction with professional capacity, completeness of house arrangements to ends required, and the right vital spirit animating all, that I have found in any public curative institution among civilians." These cheerful though somewhat incoherent words concealed a painful experience through which the author had just passed. The surviving records of the Brooklyn State Hospital show that on December 5, 1864, Walt Whitman committed his brother Jesse to the Kings County Lunatic Asylum.[215] The record of admission reads:

JESSE WHITMAN

Admitted December 5th 1864. Born in New York [should read: West Hills, New York], aged 48 years. Single. A seafaring man. Temperate. About sixteen years ago had a fall from the mast which injured his head. He remained in City Hosp. N.Y. about six months, and went out apparently well. He has been considered somewhat insane by his friends for the last four years. For the last year he had been worse, at times violent, usually in the night on awaking from sleep.[216]
[Near bottom of page]
Walter Whitman (brother)
    122 Portland St. Brooklyn

It is evident from this record that Walt had had to take the initiative and responsibility for committing his brother. Presumably Jesse had become so violent that even his mother had to give her consent. The struggles that the family had been having with him "in the night on awaking from sleep" we can imagine, but we have no authentic details.[217] If Walt had been in Washington during this time his mother would undoubtedly have written some of her experiences, but, fortunately for her, Walt had gone through them with her.

However, the satisfaction of having Walt with her was one of the few pleasures that Mrs. Whitman had on Christmas, 1864, for aside from her sadness over the absence of Jesse, she still had not heard from George. And on the day after Christmas she was, if possible, even more saddened by the sight of his trunk. Walt described the experience in a memorandum:

Monday night December 26, 1864. I am writing this in the front basement in Portland Avenue, Brooklyn, at home. It is after 9 o'clock at night. We have had a wet day with fog, mud, slush, and the yet unmelted hard polished ice liberally left in the streets. All sluggish and damp, with a prevailing leaden vapor. Yesterday, Christmas, about the same. George's trunk came by express today early in the forenoon from City Point, Virginia. Lt. Babcock, of the 51st was kind enough to search it out & send it home. It stood some hours before we felt inclined to open it. Towards evening Mother and Eddy looked over the things. One could not help feeling depressed. There were his uniform coat, pants, sash, &c. There were many things reminded us of him. Papers, memoranda, books, nick-nacks, a revolver, a small diary, roll of his company, a case of photographs of his comrades (several of them I knew as killed in battle) with other stuff such as a soldier accumulates. Mother looked everything over[,] laid out the shirts to be washed, the coats and pants to hang up, & all the rest were carefully put back. It made us feel pretty solemn. We have not heard from him since October 3rd; whether living or dead we know not. I am aware of the condition of the union prisoners south, through seeing them when brought up, & from lately talking with a friend just returned from taking part in the exchange at Savannah and Charleston by which we have received 12,-000 of our sick. Their situation, as of all men in prison, is indescribably horrible. Hard, ghastly starvation is the rule. Rags, filth, despair in large open stockades, no shelter, no cooking—such the condition of masses of men, in some places two or three thousand, & in the largest prison as high as thirty thousand confined. The guards are insufficient in numbers, & they make it up by treble severity, shooting the prisoners literally just to keep them under terrorism. I cannot get any reliable trace of the 51st officers at all. I supposed they were at Columbia, South Carolina, but my friend has brought a list purporting to be complete record of all in confinement there, & I cannot find any of the 51st among them.[218]

Among George's effects was a diary. Walt examined it, and though it contained merely a skeleton of dates and events (George had no gift for literary detail), it fascinated the mind of the poet, who called it "a perfect poem of the war," comprehending its passions and the endurance and courage of "a newer, larger race of human giants."

The following day, December 27, Walt had a long letter on the exchange of prisoners published simultaneously in the New York Times and the Brooklyn Daily Eagle.[219] He could have written it immediately after the arrival of George's trunk, but more likely he had submitted it several days before. Although a few exchanges of prisoners (especially officers) had taken place, by this time exchanging had nearly ceased, and Walt was convinced that high officials in his own Government were chiefly to blame, either because of indifference or unwillingness to exchange able-bodied Southern prisoners for sick and feeble Union men.

While these events were taking place, Whitman's friends in Washington were doing their best to help him obtain a Government position. On December 30 O'Connor had written him[220] to send an application to W. T. Otto, Assistant Secretary of the Department of the Interior, and a duplicate to J. Hubley Ashton, Assistant Attorney General. O'Connor had been working through their mutual friend Ashton, who had in turn talked to Otto. Ashton, reported O'Connor in this same letter, had "secured me some little time ago a place in the Post Office for you, but I declined it, because I thought it was not the proper place for you. I think a desk in the Interior would be first-rate."

On January 6 Whitman replied to O'Connor that he had followed instructions, saying he was "most desirous to get the appointment." [221] It would enable him to continue his attentions to the soldiers and perhaps help him to get *Drum-Taps* published. Given new hope by these letters from Washington, Whitman now thought he might still be able to publish his book during the winter, printing and stereotyping it himself; hence one of his needs for income. The manuscript, he said, was now in perfect condition for the printer, and he felt satisfied with the book, believing it to be "superior to Leaves of Grass—certainly more perfect as a work of art." He added that "Drum-Taps has none of the perturbations of Leaves of Grass," and this is an interesting confession, for "perturbations" is an astronomical term used in the books and lectures on astronomy with which Whitman had been acquainted in the 1850's. It meant the "deviation in the principal motion of a planet or satellite caused by the gravitational power of some object less than that of the body about which the planet or satellite revolves." [222] Thus the poet believed that in his war poems he had gained an emotional poise and a mastery of his art which he had not had in writing at least some of the poems in the first three editions of *Leaves of Grass*. However, he quickly added that he was not rejecting his *Leaves*, his "first-born." Though he saw some things in it he would not now write, "yet I shall certainly let them stand, even if but for proofs of phases passed away." [223]

Whitman's eagerness to get away from Brooklyn and return to Washington was almost pathetic. "I am well, but need to leave here—need a change," he wrote O'Connor. Doubtless he felt stifled by some of the responsibilities he had had to shoulder in the past two months, and he also needed the stimulation of his friends in Washington, contact with soldiers, and perhaps the feeling that he was near the pulse of the Union. He was now more at home in the capital than in Brooklyn and New York. The suspense of waiting was not at an end yet, but he continued to receive assurances that this time his application was really being considered. Finally, on January 12, 1865, Otto wrote him that upon reporting to the Department of the Interior "and passing a satisfactory examination you will be appointed to a First Class [that is, lowest grade] Clerkship at a compensation of twelve hundred dollars per annum." [224]

Apparently Whitman knew that the "examination" was a mere formality, for he remained in Brooklyn for at least a week after receiving this letter. On January 20 he recorded, "We have just heard from George after a blank of four months." [225] The letter was dated November 27, 1864, and had been written in the Confederate Military Prison at Danville, Virginia. George said that after being captured he had been taken to Libby Prison in Richmond, then to Salisbury, North Carolina, and back to Danville. Typically, he insisted that he was well and hearty and asked his mother not to worry, though of course she did, for she knew George's habit of making light of his hardships; besides, many things could have happened to him since November. This delayed letter made Walt more impatient than ever to get back to Washington, where he might be able to get more recent news of George, or maybe even find a way to expedite his exchange.

One of the last things that Walt did in preparation for his imminent departure was to visit Jesse in Kings County Lunatic Asylum and notify the authorities there of his expected change of address. [226] In his letter to O'Connor two days earlier Whitman had stated that he planned to leave Brooklyn on Monday morning, January 23, taking the eight o'clock train in Jersey City, which would get him to Washington by seven that evening. [227] Evidently he stuck to his schedule and reported next morning for the "examination," whatever that was, for he received by hand his official letter of appointment, dated January 24, 1865. [228] At last he was a government clerk, in the first salaried position he had occupied since his editorship of the Brooklyn *Times*. If now he could only locate George and get him released from whatever Confederate prison he was confined in, life in Washington would be good again, with daily or nightly visits to the O'Connors, frequent trips to the boys in the hospitals, and light employment that left him sufficient time and energy for his literary plans and activities. Soon he might even be able to print *Drum-Taps*.

OVER THE CARNAGE

Over the carnage rose prophetic a voice,
Be not dishearten'd—Affection shall solve the problems of Freedom yet;
Those who love each other shall become invincible—they shall yet make Columbia victorious.[1]

I

THE branch of the Department of the Interior to which Whitman was assigned on January 24, 1865, was the Indian Bureau, which had charge of the administration of the Indian lands and funds. He was assigned to this office only because there happened to be a vacancy there, but his imagination was stirred by the sight of the aboriginal chieftains and delegates who sometimes called at the office on tribal business.[2] He was mainly delighted with his position, however, because the work was light and he had abundant time for his hospital visits and the composition and revision of his poems. Probably the incumbent Secretary of the Interior, John Usher,[3] was running his department somewhat perfunctorily anyway, for he expected to resign after President Lincoln's second inauguration in order to make way for a new appointee.

As soon as Walt was settled he wrote his mother about his position, and of course shared with her the family anxiety over George. Before leaving home he had left instructions for sending food and clothing to George, and on January 26 Jeff enclosed two letters addressed to Walt and reported that he had shipped a box, reinforced by iron hoops, containing a ham, smoked beef, condensed milk, coffee, canned peaches, and the clothes George had requested.[4] The family was elated, Jeff said, over yesterday's news in the papers that prisoners would be exchanged, though of course they were all still apprehensive. He wanted to know "What the devil is the Indian dept.?" He had teased his mother by telling her that undoubtedly

Walt's first duty "would be to calculate just exactly how many little indians [*sic*] John Brown did have." Jeff suggested to Walt that he "should not go it too strong in the Hospital way, for a while—I would draw it mild for a month or so. . . ." In a postscript he added: "Mother, Mat and the babies send their love [;] the baby calls *Walt*—and asks if he is gone—Hat wants to be remembered to Uncle Walt."

Walt did not receive this letter until January 30, when he answered it immediately. The two letters Jeff had enclosed were from officers who had heard indirectly from Danville about George's being there, though unfortunately they did not mention the date of their information. Walt had arranged to send another box of food to George through a Captain Mason. In his letter to Jeff he also told about his own life in Washington. The weather had been cold, but he had a comfortable room in the home of "a very friendly old Secesh landlady, whose husband and son are off in the Southern army." But he had to get his meals, "poor and expensive," wherever he could.

You speak of the Indian Office—it is a Bureau in the Department of the Interior, which has charge of quite a large mass of business relating to the numerous Indian tribes in West and Northwest, large numbers of whom are under annuities, supplies, &c. from the government. All I have hitherto employed myself about has been making copies of reports and bids &c. for the office to send up to the Congressional Committee on Indian Affairs.—It is easy enough—I take things very easy—the rule is to come at 9, and go at 4—but I don't come at 9, and only stay till 4 when I want, as at present to finish a letter for the mail—I am treated with great courtesy . . .[5]

Jeff received this letter the next afternoon, and sat down at once to answer it,[6] partly because he felt "very sad and downhearted," and partly because he had a new plan for bringing about George's release. He had decided correctly[7] that "Gen Grant is the one that does not want to give an exchange." But he had read of some "special exchanges," and he believed that if the "right influence" could be brought to bear an exchange might be arranged for George. He proposed to work through Dr. Ruggles,[8] an eccentric physician and painter in Brooklyn who was a friend of the Whitman family, and John Swinton, managing editor of the New York *Times*. Swinton had been the first editor to "blow" for Grant, as Jeff put it, and Jeff thought the general would be glad to do a favor for his supporter, out of gratitude and perhaps fear too: "Gen Grant is just now in the position when a few words of censure in a print like the *Times* would do him great injury—I know he is in no danger of getting it from the Times [.] Yet he would—I should think like to make it sure by doing a supposed favor to its editor."

Probably Walt had not yet received this letter when he wrote his mother on February 1 that he had received a week's pay on Monday (January 30), and gave his new address as 468 M Street, near 12th. He sent her some money and enclosed one dollar for Nancy.⁹ Two days later (February 3) Jeff wrote again, more depressed than ever, and again urging Walt to try appealing to Gen Grant through Swinton. He still thought "it perhaps might work." ¹⁰ He now missed Walt more than ever, and apparently felt guilty over not having gone to see Jesse, "but they are taking such quantities of small pox patients out to that hospital (even out in the cars they take them) that I am almost afraid to [go]."

The Whitman family had other worries too. The landlord had sent word that he would raise their rent, though he did not say how much. Jeff was again thinking of borrowing money to build a house on his Flatbush Avenue lot, but materials were high and he would have to pay 10 per cent interest, almost as much as the rent for a year. Maybe prices would come down in another year. "Mat has been over to New York 'looking for work' as usual to-day with partial success . . . and as a matter of course bought a new carpet and some other things." (She did piece work at home for the garment industry.) Then in a more cheerful vein: "Just now in looking over the Evening Post I saw among the musical gossip a notion [notation] that our old friend Bettini ¹¹ was winning great success in Warsaw—tis the first time I have seen his name in 10 or 12 years—I've no doubt the mention of his name will call to you many pleasant thoughts—those were very pleasant times Walt."

A letter from Jeff dated February 7 reveals that Walt had responded to his brother's plan to appeal to Grant through Swinton, though he had adopted a more diplomatic approach than Jeff had so crudely and forthrightly suggested: "We are all very joyful over what you wrote in regard to George—It seemed to put new life in mother—I went to see the Dr to-day —He said immediately that he would go and see Swinton and talk with him about the matter and urge him to write to Gen Grant—The Dr. thinks that Swinton will do it and that Grant will grant the request. . . ." ¹² Whitman had evidently also got directly in touch with Swinton himself without telling Jeff, because on February 3 Swinton had sent Walt a short note, with which he enclosed a letter addressed "To the Lieutenant General/ Commanding Armies United States," ¹³ for Walt to send if he thought it would do any good, though Swinton pointed out that the state-ment had just been published "that Grant has made the arrangements for a general exchange which is to begin immediately." Walt did not take chances on the "general exchange" but sent the letter on as soon as he got it.

News of the failure of the President's secret peace mission to Hampton Roads on February 3 had leaked out, and Jeff declared (in his February 7 letter) that if the President showed the Confederate officials that the pres-ervation of the Union was all he demanded, he displayed "more states-manship than I ever gave him credit for." Walt, of course, had a more fa-vorable view of the President, but he had also consistently regarded the Union rather than abolition as the main issue. And as he indicated on the previous day (February 6) in a letter to J. T. Trowbridge, he was not at all sure that the peace conference had been a failure: the "shrewd ones" in Washington were saying that the President and Seward were withholding the results "to avoid at present the tempest of rage which would beat about their heads, if it were known among the Radicals that Peace, Am-nesty, *every thing*, were given up to the Rebels on the single price of re-assuming their place in the Union. . . ." [14] Walt confessed that he himself knew nothing on the subject, yet he was inclined to accept this theory of the "shrewd ones."

Though Walt and Jeff were almost entirely in agreement on acceptable peace terms, on a more personal level there were contrasts in their atti-tudes. Further on in his February 7 letter Jeff commented: "Well Walt so you have gone to keeping house have you [?] You must be careful or you will get sick again—I fear you do not live well—I think the great cause of good health is good eating—Keep up the supply of good things . . ." Walt liked to eat too, but he was not as self-indulgent as his younger brother, and he would continue to scrimp and prepare makeshift meals in his drab little room in order that he might have funds for his hospital trips and donations for his mother's personal expenses. He had now begun to enclose paper currency in nearly every letter he mailed to his mother, vary-ing in denomination from "shinplasters" to five- or ten-dollar bills. He still hoped to receive some financial help in the hospital work,[15] as he had previously, but of course as the peace talk increased such aid dwindled.

For some days the thought uppermost in Walt's mind remained the wel-fare of his imprisoned brother. Although Swinton's letter to General Grant, combined with Walt's own efforts, very soon produced a definite promise that a special exchange would be arranged, Walt continued to fear that something had happened to George since November 27, when he had written the letter that his family eventually received. Even the weather was gloomy and foreboding when Walt brooded over the situation on the night of February 17, 1865: "I write this in my room in Washington. A heavy sulky night, & beating snow storm. I have just opened the window and looked out. It is bleak and silent and dim. Off in a distant camp the drums beat tattoos, and in a neighboring hospital the long-drawn bugle notes give the same signal." [16] He had learned that day from the Headquarters of the Armies at City Point that General Grant had ordered the exchange of George and Lieutenant Pooley. But no one had heard from George since last November, and in a printed list of prisoners in Danville on February 1, 1865, George's name had not been included. Then, too, the newspapers had reported a huge fire in Danville "about a week ago." Yet John Swinton's letter, forwarded by Walt, had resulted in Grant's ordering the exchange on February 13. Thus Walt continued to live in suspense.

Two days after Walt confided these agonizing thoughts to his diary, George was released from the Danville prison, but Walt was not to know this fact for almost three weeks. Meanwhile he continued copying documents for the Indian Bureau, visiting hospitals, and meeting his friends in the evening. As soon as the weather improved, he spent many hours on the street, especially Pennsylvania Avenue, the highway for all military traffic. One could stand in front of Willard's Hotel and sooner or later nearly every soldier in the Union Army would pass by. Toward the end of February large groups of Confederate prisoners were being conducted through the city, and on the 23rd a procession of these ragged men held the attention of the poet: ". . . deserters they are call'd, but the usual meaning of the word does not apply to them . . ." [17] Some, "divining pity and fatherliness" in the face of the bearded man beside the Avenue, nodded to him. "Several of the couples trudg'd along with their arms about each other, some probably brothers, as if they were afraid they might somehow get separated. . . . Some of them here and there had fine faces, still it was a procession of misery."

February 27 was a pleasant day, after a long spell of bad weather, and Walt wandered about "a good deal, without other object than to be outdoors." [18] Several hundred more escapees from the Confederate army passed, and he was able to talk with a number of them. The following day a crowd of these men stopped near the White House, and Whitman had a good talk with two brothers from North Carolina. "The elder had been in the rebel service four years . . . the younger had been soldiering about a year. . . ." [19] The latter had made some money on the boat selling tobacco, but the elder had nothing, and Walt gave him "a trifle," just as he would have treated a Union soldier, and advised both to go to one of the nearest Northern states and get farm work until the war was over. He regarded these men as victims of Southern tyranny and felt no trace of resentment against them.

Walt had still heard nothing whatever from or about George, and on the evening following his talk with the North Carolina brothers he wrote in his diary that the past four days had put him "through all the changes of hope and dismay." [20] He had been thinking for a fortnight that George "was at last as good as within our lines." But two or three days ago he had been told that "although all the Danville prisoners had indeed come up . . . neither George nor any other 51st officers had come." Yet one of the returned men had brought a note from George, dated February 14 at Danville. A talk with "Gen. H." on February 28 relieved Walt's mind "a good deal," but he was still worried: "What exaltations and depressions this war consists of, full of hope one day and all despair and heart sick the next and so on for weeks."

February 28 fell on Tuesday, and the following day Walt should have received a joyful letter from his mother, written Sunday afternoon,[21] containing a brief note which George had given to Captain William Cook (being exchanged) on February 14 to be delivered to his mother.[22] George's note said only that he was a "Prisoner of war at Danville Va. in tip top health and spirits." [23] However, this news did not elate Walt as it had his mother, for he had already (as mentioned above) received such a slip the preceding Sunday night (that is, February 26). And on February 28 Captain Cook wrote Walt a note (probably received March 1 or 2) in which he admitted that he did not know George[24]—a strange contradiction of his message to Mrs. Whitman. Thus Walt's state of mind recorded in his diary on February 28 continued for several days. And his mother unintentionally prolonged his suspense. Early in the week she received a letter from George himself, written February 24 at Annapolis, telling her of his freedom and his expected visit to her, but she assumed that Walt had seen George's name in the New York *Times*, and in her excitement did not think of the precaution of informing him. But about March 1 (Wednesday), learning from Walt's anxious inquiry that he did not yet know of George's release, she sent him George's letter and added a hasty explanation (undated):

Walter i should have sent you this letter from George but thought of course you knew all about his arrival at Anapolis   i saw his name in the times with 5008 others arrived   my not hearing from you we thought you had gone there to see him the letter was missent to boston so it was some days before i got it i expect him home every hour   i am very sorry indeed you did not know he was exchanged   jeffy has gone to Wheeling . . . matty had a letter from him yesterday . . .[25]

This satisfying news should have reached Walt before the Inauguration, and the interest he took in the occasion indicates that he had been relieved of the chief anxiety which had oppressed his mind and nerves for the past five months. The day began with a freakish storm that made him wonder if the very elements were not conveying supernatural signs and portents. The House of Representatives had stayed in session all Friday night, and in the early dawn of Saturday morning the congressmen were weary and exhausted from loss of sleep and the pages stumbling on their errands; a terrific thunderstorm, accompanied by fierce and deafening hail, had suddenly burst upon the drowsy assembly.

For a moment, (and no wonder,) the nervous and sleeping Representatives were thrown into confusion. The slumberers awaked with fear, some started for the doors, some look'd up with blanch'd cheeks and lips to the roof, and the little pages began to cry; it was a scene. But it was over almost as soon as the drowsied men were actually awake. They recover'd themselves; the storm raged on, beating, dashing, and with loud noises at times. But the House went ahead with its business then, I think, as calmly and with as much deliberation as at any time in its career. Perhaps the shock did it good.[26]

Later in the day the weather cleared and the afternoon was bright, sunny, and pleasantly warm. A monstrous parade, with elaborate floats and military splendor, had been planned, and doubtless Whitman witnessed this spectacle, though he was not present at any of the formal ceremonies. About noon he saw the incumbent President ride down to the Capitol in his own simple carriage, perhaps, Whitman thought, to escape "marching in line with the absurd procession, [with] the muslin temple of liberty and pasteboard monitor." [27] And from the same sidewalk observation post he saw the President return at three o'clock, after the parade was over, looking very worn and tired, the "demands of life and death, cut deeper than ever upon his dark brown face; yet all the old goodness, tenderness, sadness, and canny shrewdness, underneath the furrows." [28] Whitman felt more strongly devoted to him than ever.

In the evening the President held a public reception (or levee) at the White House, and Whitman attended that too:

Never before was such a compact jam in front of the White House—all the grounds fill'd, and away out to the spacious sidewalks. I was there, as I took a notion to go—was in the rush inside with the crowd—surged along the passage-ways, the blue and other rooms, and through the great east room. Crowds of country people, some very funny. Fine music from the Marine Band, off in a side place. I saw Mr. Lincoln, drest all in black, with white kid gloves and a claw-hammer coat, receiving, as in duty bound, shaking hands, looking very disconsolate, and as if he would give anything to be somewhere else.[29]

Whitman did not report the destruction wrought by the souvenir hunt-ers, though he implied it in the "rush" and the crowd surging through the historic rooms. Many in that crowd tore up the curtains, cut designs out of the wall paper, and made off with nearly everything readily portable. It was probably the crudest and most disorderly throng that had visited the White House since the inaugural reception for Andrew Jackson.[30] The "rush" was so frantic that many people were injured, and only a small fraction of the huge crowd were able to shake the President's aching hand. Probably Whitman did not try, for as usual he seems to have been content merely to look on and admire Lincoln from a distance. Apparently the President knew him by sight, and had often nodded to the picturesque poet in passing him on Pennsylvania Avenue,[31] but Whitman never per-sonally met him.

The excitement and fatigue of this memorable day left Whitman in a highly emotional state. Three times he had a close-range view of the man whom he loved almost as fervently as his own mother. At intervals throughout the day he probably thought of George and wondered whether he had yet reached Brooklyn. The paradoxical weather, too, remained a never ceasing marvel. It had been almost as theatrical as one of those prophetic scenes in *Julius Caesar*. Probably he was not the only one who thought of possible symbolism in the stormy night and sunny afternoon. Whether from actual observation or hearsay, he was later to report that "as the President came out on the Capitol portico [after his inauguration], a curious little white cloud, the only one in that part of the sky, appear'd like a hovering bird, right over him." [32]

This seemed to be a good omen, if one were superstitious, and for the moment Whitman was half inclined to be. Indeed, for days rumors of plots to abduct or assassinate the President had circulated in Washington, and nearly everyone was apprehensive. Lincoln himself had dreamed of lying in state in the East Room on a catafalque, though he was unwilling to take extra precautions for his safety. The very atmosphere seemed charged with fear and suspicion. And yet, like the contrasting weather, or Whitman's own changing emotions, the crowds were hopefully expecting news at any moment that the Confederate states had surrendered or Grant had captured Richmond, which, it was generally believed, would inevitably force a speedy capitulation. In the clear sky the night after the Inauguration, and for several succeeding nights, the evening star glowed with what seemed to Whitman portentous splendor. A few days later he made a literary record of this apparent phenomenon:

Nor earth nor sky ever knew spectacles of superber beauty than some of the nights lately here. The western star, Venus, in the earlier hours of evening, has never been so large, so clear; it seems as if it told something, as if it held rapport indulgent with humanity, with us Americans. Five or six nights since, it hung close by the moon, then a little past its first quarter. The star was wonderful, the moon like a young mother. The sky, dark blue, the transparent night, the planets, the moderate west wind, the elastic temperature, the miracle of that great star, and the young and swelling moon swimming in the west, suffused the soul. Then I heard, slow and clear, the deliberate notes of a bugle come up out of the silence, sounding so good through the night's mystery, no hurry, but firm and faithful, floating along, rising, falling leisurely, with here and there a long-drawn note; the bugle, well play'd, sounding tattoo, in one of the army hospitals near here, where the wounded (some of them personally so dear to me,) are lying in their cots, and many a sick boy come down to the war from Illinois, Michigan, Wisconsin, Iowa, and the rest.[33]

With the continuation of this almost miraculously good weather also came more welcome news about George—mingled with distressing details of his recent suffering. On Sunday night following the Inauguration Mrs. Whitman wrote that George had arrived home that morning, looking thin and showing the effects of his prison life.[34] In January he had been so near death that an official had started to rifle his pocket but desisted when George showed signs of life. George also told his mother that twenty famished men had died the day before at Annapolis from over-eating. Walt should have received this letter Tuesday, March 7. His joy over George's actual return home, after so many heartbreaking delays, was of course mingled with new anxiety over his health. Naturally Walt was now more eager than ever to see and talk with him. Consequently he promptly applied for and obtained a two-weeks leave, and probably arrived home during the week end of March 18–19.[35]

II

After Walt had been at home for a few days he wrote the O'Connors on March 26, 1865, that George was bothered so much by rheumatism in his legs that he was unable to get much sleep at night. Walt had been trying to persuade him to ask for an extension of his furlough, but George did not wish it. Walt himself was feeling fine, and "never enjoyed a visit home more. . . ." Earlier in the month O'Connor had offered to help Jeff secure a position with the Government as an engineer, but Jeff had replied that he was totally deficient as a draughtsman and was therefore unqualified for such a position. Through Walt he thanked O'Connor for his kindness.

Walt himself was deeply concerned over a problem of his own. "I find myself perplexed," he wrote, "about printing my book. All the printers tell me I could not pick a more inopportune time—that in ten days prices of paper, composition &c will all be very much lower . . . I shall decide tomorrow." [36] Despite this discouragement, he decided to go ahead with the printing of *Drum-Taps,* and obtained extension of his leave until April 17[37] in order to get the work well under way before his return to Washington. On April 7 he wrote O'Connor that his book would be small and thin but well printed.[38] Ordinarily this would have been the subject of greatest interest to him, but during the past few days the war news had been so exciting that the events in Virginia were now uppermost in his mind. On March 26 General Sheridan had joined forces with General Grant before Petersburg, which they assaulted and took on April 2, and the following day Richmond fell to them.

These were the events that Whitman had in mind when he wrote: "The grand culminations of last week [he doubtless meant the preceding Sunday and Monday, April 2 and 3] impress me profoundly of course. I feel, more than ever how America has been entirely re-stated by them—and they will shape the destinies of the future of the whole of mankind." [39] Like nearly everyone else in the North, he expected any hour to hear of the end of the war, and two days later Lee did surrender to Grant at Appomattox Courthouse—though Montgomery, capitol of the Confederacy, held out until April 12.

During this historic week George finally agreed to ask for a lengthened furlough and received a twenty-day extension. Thus except for ailing Hannah in Vermont, demented Jesse in the nearby asylum, and perhaps Mary out at Greenport, the Whitman family would spend Easter together. With the war finally at an end and George safely at home—though he would have to return to the army until his regiment was mustered out—they were looking forward to the happiest Easter they had enjoyed since the war began. Daffodils, hyacinths, and early tulips were in bloom on Good Friday (April 14), and the air was faintly tinged with their delicate perfume. But Saturday morning the Whitman family read the staggering news that the President had been assassinated the night before. As Walt later recalled: "Mother prepared breakfast—and other meals afterwards—as usual; but not a mouthful was eaten all day by either of us. We each drank half a cup of coffee; that was all. Little was said. We got every newspaper morning and evening, and the frequent extras of that period, and pass'd them silently to each other." [40]

Toward noon the sky darkened and it began to rain, not hard but steadily, and the moisture-saturated atmosphere seemed oppressively heavy and gloomy.[41] Late in the afternoon Walt crossed the East River by ferry and walked up Broadway, where often in the past he had watched from the curb or the top of an omnibus the great parades and spectacles exhibited with pride and lavish opulence of color, noise, and pomp. There jubilant crowds had cheered the many bands playing marches or opera airs. Whitman remembered the transparencies at night celebrating American victories in the Mexican War, and the political rallies on many occasions with the long processions bearing countless torches and banners.

But now the stores were closed, and nearly all commercial and pleasure vehicles had disappeared from the streets. Hardly even a cart was left, though there remained the rumbling of the heavy Broadway stages incessantly rolling on the wet cobbles. And instead of the colorful flags and bunting of those gala occasions of the past, now everything was dead black: the façades of buildings festooned with black; the plate-glass windows empty and draped in black, and on the streets the steady drip, drip of the rain and subdued conversation of the few people—mostly men dressed in black—passing by. Whitman felt the "strange mixture of horror, fury, tenderness, & a stirring wonder brewing." The assassin had escaped and many rumors circulated freely both in the newspapers and by word of mouth on the streets. It was generally thought that the defeated Confederacy had instigated the crime and in the North there were furious cries for revenge.

Concerning the revolting deed, Walt Whitman had no theories, and he was not by nature vengeful. No one felt the loss more deeply than he, but he was aware only of emptiness, dread for the future, and that ubiquitous blackness. Even when he looked up at the sky he saw "long broad black [clouds] like great serpents slowly undulating in every direction." And yet he felt a strong desire to mingle with the crowd, which increased to a densely packed throng around six o'clock, especially near the bulletin boards in front of the *Herald*, the *Tribune*, and the *Times* offices. "When a great event happens, or the news of some great solemn thing spreads out among the people, it is curious to go forth and wander a while in the public ways."

How Whitman spent Easter Sunday we do not know. He may, indeed, have taken the morning train back to Washington, though more likely he waited until that night, and arrived back in the capital early Monday morning. But of course, as he might have expected, the Government offices were closed, and the capital was also draped in mourning. Yet the city to which Whitman had come back was different from the New York he had left, for here was bustling activity in the midst of the mourning and crepe and flags at half-mast. "Andy" Johnson had been promptly inducted into office. Seward, whose assassination had also been attempted, lay near death. But Stanton, the Secretary of War, was still in power, and he had agents and troops scouring Maryland and Virginia in search of the killer and the men believed to have assisted him.

At the same time feverish preparations for the funeral had begun. Large supplies of mourning draperies had been shipped down from New York, possibly on the same train that Whitman had ridden.[42] By Monday afternoon the embalmers had finished their work and Lincoln was returned to the White House, where throughout Tuesday he lay in state on the catafalque in the East Room exactly as he had dreamed. All day the public was admitted and a steady procession tramped slowly past the bier, but Whitman did not join it. That night every hotel and boardinghouse in the city was jammed with out-of-town visitors who had come to attend the public funeral on Wednesday. Although Whitman appears not to have heard the funeral sermon, we may be sure that he witnessed the solemn procession through the streets, with the military bands playing the dead march that had so deeply impressed his small-boy mind when he heard it for the first time after the naval explosion near his school in 1829.[43] Regiments and battalions, accompanied by hundreds of officers of the Army, Navy, and Marines, marched slowly past with arms reversed and banners furled. Behind the hearse came Lincoln's favorite horse with his master's boots in the stirrups, followed by thirty thousand participants in the funeral pageant.[44] It was one of the most solemn and impressive sights in

American history. Whitman immediately commemorated the occasion by writing a short poem, "Hush'd Be the Camps To-Day," but the date, April 19, was the symbolical burial in Washington; the funeral train would not leave for two more days.

During the day following the funeral service in the capital the body of the recent President lay on view in a catafalque under the Capitol dome; then on Friday morning, after a brief service in the Rotunda, the funeral train started north on the first lap of the circuitous journey through Baltimore, Philadelphia, New York, Buffalo, Cleveland, Chicago, and thence finally to Springfield, Illinois. Whitman was acutely aware of these events, and his great elegy was already forming in his mind. The lilacs were in full bloom, for in Washington the vegetation was nearly a month earlier than on Long Island. The newspapers commented on the profusion of lilac sprays that banked the coffin, and this flower became intertwined in Whitman's memory with the death of the President.

III

Despite President Lincoln's death, Whitman found this spring in Washington in many ways pleasant and exciting. In addition to the satisfying companionship of the O'Connors and their common friends whom he continued to meet at their home, he now experienced almost as much enjoyment at the quaint red-brick house that John Burroughs and his wife had rented on Capitol Hill, where the Senate Office Building was later erected. "There," as Burroughs's biographer says, "on an acre of ground, after office hours, the Treasury clerk hoed his potatoes, looked after his chickens, and turned Chloe the cow out to grass on the common near the Capitol, for in those days cows had the freedom of the city, goats cropped rosebushes through fence pickets, and pigs dreamed dreams under many a garden fence." [45] Whitman, of course, did not participate in the gardening, but he liked the rural atmosphere of the Burroughs home and listened appreciatively to John's talk about the growth of his vegetables.

Although practical Mrs. Burroughs had little use for poets, and regarded Walt's poems as worthless if not disgraceful, as many people thought, she liked the man and gave him a standing invitation to Sunday morning breakfast. The fact that she bore with his tardiness in silence shows how really fond of him she was, for she had a sharp tongue. Burroughs himself gave a contemporary description of a typical Sunday morning:

Walt was usually late for breakfast, and Ursula, who was as punctual as the clock, would get in a pucker. The coffee would boil, the griddle would smoke, and car after car would go jingling by, but no Walt. The situation at times verged on the tragic. But at last a car would stop, and Walt would roll off it and saunter up to the door—so cheery, and so unaware of the annoyance he had caused, that we soon forgot our ill-humor. He always said Ursula's pancakes and coffee couldn't be beat.[46]

Frequently Walt also took long, leisurely strolls through the woods with John Burroughs, often tossing a large stone from hand to hand for exercise as he walked. Burroughs was now seriously applying himself to becoming an amateur naturalist, and at the moment was particularly interested in ornithology. Whitman's "Cradle" poem, with its accurate description of the mocking bird, proves that he had not been unobservant of birds; [47] yet he had made no close study of ornithology before meeting John Burroughs, and to this young naturalist must go the credit of supplying the poet with a key symbol—and motif—in the threnody on which he was working during the spring and early summer following President Lincoln's death. In Burroughs's enthusiastic description of the song of the hermit thrush Whitman recognized the symbolical serenity and harmony which he hoped to convey in his funeral hymn.[48] Probably John's description also brought back to Walt memories of his childhood on Long Island when he had heard the sweet, lyrical notes of this lovely songbird.

But at the same time that Whitman enjoyed the soothing beauty of that Southern spring—for in April Washington is unmistakably Southern—he felt a sadness persistently mingling with his deep happiness in natural things. The main cause of this sadness is obvious in the rough skeleton of an uncompleted poem which he jotted down in one of his hospital notebooks:

APRIL 1865

I heard
        The blue birds singing
I saw the yellowish green where it covered the willows
I saw the eternal grass springing up
The light of the sun on the bay—the ships, dressed with
I saw in the distant city the gala flags flying
I saw on the ships the profusion of colors
I knew of the fete, the feasting
—Then I turned aside & mused on the unknown dead
I thought of the unrecorded, the heroes so sweet & tender
The young men

The returned—but where are the unreturned
I thought of the unreturned, the sons of the mothers.[49]

The thought of "the unreturned, the sons of the mothers," and that great man mouldering in the tomb in Springfield echoed with sweet-sadness in the poet's mind like the liquid notes of the hermit thrush. But he had also seen "the eternal grass springing up" and the yellowish green color return to the willows. Out of these perennial symbols a great poem was germinating in his mind and emotions.

However, Whitman was not living in an enchanted land of pure poesy and abstract thought. Ordinary personal experiences and family problems continued to jostle his esthetic concentration. On May 11 he was promoted to a second-class clerkship in the Office of Indian Affairs,[50] and this of course pleased and reassured him. George had meanwhile been promoted to major and was stationed at nearby Alexandria, Virginia, where Walt could visit him. Three days later Jeff wrote Walt that George would like to stay in the regular army if he could retain the rank of captain. As usual Jeff was busily scheming ways of using "influence" to accomplish this purpose and begged for Walt's co-operation.[51] Whether Walt followed any of Jeff's suggestions is not known, but he probably felt that he could not call on John Swinton again (Jeff planned to use him), and with the exception of the physicians in the hospitals, his military friends were mainly enlisted men.

The greatest spectacle in Washington during May was the Grand Review of the Union armies, which took place on the twenty-third and twenty-fourth.[52] Jeff had not been able to come down to see this much publicized show, as he had hoped to do, and next day Walt wrote his mother about it, though he warned her that it had been too immense and impressive to be described. He asked her to imagine "a great wide avenue like Flatbush avenue, quite flat, & stretching as far as you can see with a great white building half as big as Fort Greene on a hill at the commencement of the avenue, and then through this avenue marching solid ranks of soldiers, 20 or 25 abreast, just marching steady all day long for two days without intermission, one regiment after another, real war-worn soldiers, that have been marching & fighting for years. . . ." [53]

Several times, Walt told his mother, he had seen President Johnson, "stood close by him, & took a good look at him . . . he is very plain & substantial—it seemed wonderful that just that plain middling-sized ordinary man, dressed in black, without the least badge or ornament, should be the master of all these myriads of soldiers, the best that ever trod the earth, with forty or fifty Major-Generals, around him or riding by with their broad yellow-satin belts around their waists . . ."

The 51st Regiment marched on the first day of the review, and Walt saw George but did not get a chance to speak to him. Lest Jeff should feel left out, Walt added a paragraph for him:

Dear brother Jeff, I was very sorry you wasnt able to come on to see the Review—we had perfect weather & everything just as it should be—the streets now are full of soldiers scattered around loose, as the armies are in camp near here getting ready to be mustered out.—I am quite well & visit the Hospitals the same.—Mother you didn't write whether you got the package of 5 Drum-Taps—I keep thinking about you every few minutes all day—I wish I was home a couple of days—Jeff, you will take this acc't of the Review, same as if it were written to you.

Now that the Grand Review had been held, Whitman could feel that the war was really over—though the mustering out might continue into the summer. And the printing of Drum-Taps doubtless seemed to him a fitting climax, for he regarded the book as itself a poetic review of the whole war and its earliest aftermath. A few days later Mrs. Whitman wrote that the printer had brought two stereotype plates and five copies of the book.[54] She had apparently not yet tried to read the poems, and Jeff did not mention them in his letters. But at last the book was printed, though Whitman had not been able to make any satisfactory arrangement for its distribution.

IV

The printing of Drum-Taps in May, 1865,[55] was a very important event to Whitman because he had put much of his own life into the book; furthermore, getting it printed had been perhaps his greatest personal ambition for the past two years. If he had only waited a few months longer, he might have made it a more complete reflection of the war years and his own emotional and imaginative life during the period; but he was so keenly conscious of the hiatus in his poetic career which the outbreak of the war had caused that his most urgent desire had become his re-assuming the role of national poet which he had so bravely and perhaps rashly begun almost exactly a decade earlier. Nothing else meant so much to him as to be accepted by the American people as a poet, and preferably as the American poet.

Drum-Taps, as we have already observed,[56] was not, despite the title, exclusively filled with Civil War poems. Of the fifty-three poems, several had been written before the outbreak of the war, and a few, such as "Pioneers! O Pioneers!", were not obviously connected with the war. Yet even this poem had something in common with the other pieces in *Drum-Taps*. It celebrated the march of the pioneers of civilization—the explorers, inventors, and adventurers on the frontiers of knowledge—through the many obstacles and delays. Whitman regarded the war to preserve the Union as one of the unavoidable delays in the "Years of the Unperformed" before America, and eventually the whole world, could fulfill his dream of a new era in which tyrants would fall and "crowns grow dim" and there would be "but one heart to the globe."

Thus the *Drum-Taps* collection as a whole had at least a suggestive organic structure and unity. In fact, in Whitman's persistent ambition to produce a book of poems with such unity, he succeeded better in this work than in any single edition of *Leaves of Grass*. He was to continue striving in each edition to arrange his poems in an ideal symbolical or dramatic sequence, without ever being able to achieve more than a prologue and epilogue with allegorical section titles in between. In *Drum-Taps* he also refused, characteristically, to arrange his poems in an historical or genetic chronology, but his "prelude" struck an authentic note of pride in Manhattan's prompt and vigorous response to the Confederate attack on Fort Sumter. This and succeeding poems recorded the rise and fall of Whitman's own militant emotions during the course of the war. While Mannahatta was "a-march" and George was enlisting, he was thinking and singing "It's O for a manly life in the camp!" After the defeat of the Union Army at Bull Run, he wrote "Beat! Beat! Drums!" and George re-enlisted. The poem entitled "1861" stated his revised literary theory that the poet for the "arm'd year . . . of struggle" must be "a strong man, erect, clothed in blue clothes, advancing, carrying a rifle on the shoulder." But for some reason—probably both his age and his temperament—Whitman could not bring himself to a literal application of this theory.

Of course, he did finally go to the battle front, but only to find his wounded brother. However, some of his poetic intuitions had been correct. His responses to the needs of the young soldiers for the sympathy, affection, and tender aid of an older man like himself was instantaneous—and instinctive. From this time forth he acted like a man with a sacred mission. And the poems which he wrote from notes taken in camp or hospital had none of the pose or affectation of many of his earlier com-

positions. War was now an observed reality to him, and he did not romanticize or glorify it or the cause for which it was being fought.

Death had been a favorite theme in the first three editions of *Leaves of
Grass,* but now it was no longer theoretical or mythical. Whitman had
seen death at firsthand, and it had brought out the great mother-soul concealed by his huge lumbering body and bearded face. The sight of death
did not drive him to protective cynicism or bitter irony, as it often does a
man physically or morally weak. Whitman did become angry on hearing of
atrocities committed on prisoners[57] or on observing the needless suffering
of the wounded caused by the callousness or inefficiency of military officials and medical personnel.[58] But the sight of the dead and wounded did
not stir up his hatred for the enemy; his compassion embraced the stricken
of both armies and led him to advocate through his poems, even before
the end of hostilities, a reconciliation of North and South.

Whitman thought, as we have noticed,[59] that *Drum-Taps* contained
none of the "perturbations" of the earlier *Leaves.* He was right, though
this was not because his innate nature had changed, but rather because he
had found a calming satisfaction in his activities as "The Dresser" ("The
Wound-Dresser") :

> The hurt and the wounded I pacify with soothing hand,
> I sit by the restless all the dark night—some are so young;
> Some suffer so much—I recall the experience sweet and sad;
> (Many a soldier's loving arms about this neck have cross'd and rested,
> Many a soldier's kiss dwells on these bearded lips.)

Later Whitman added three lines to recapitulate the stages of his self-
discovery:

> (Arous'd and angry, I'd thought to beat the alarum, and urge relentless war,
> But soon my fingers fail'd me, my face droop'd and I resign'd myself,
> To sit by the wounded and soothe them, or silently watch the dead;) . . . [60]

Whitman had not conquered all his inner "perturbations"; he was, in
fact, engaged in a life-time struggle with them. But one means by which
he controlled them in his *Drum-Taps* poems was through the transmuta-
tion of his private yearnings for affection into a universal philosophy of
love as a social force. (He had attempted that, too, in the "Calamus"
poems, but sporadically and inconsistently.) The burden of "Over the Carnage Rose Prophetic a Voice" is that military power may win the war, but

something stronger must preserve Liberty, guarantee Equality, and compact the states:

> It shall be customary in the houses and streets to see manly affection;
> The most dauntless and rude shall touch face to face lightly;
> The dependence of Liberty shall be lovers,
> The continuance of Equality shall be comrades.

Here the awkward inversions, found more often in *Drum-Taps* than in the earlier poems, obscure the thought. The poet is trying to say: Liberty depends upon the existence of lovers; only comrades can maintain Equality.

> Were you looking to be held together by the lawyers?
> Or by an agreement on a paper? or by arms?
> —Nay—nor the world, nor any living thing, will so cohere.[61]

In the "Hymn of Dead Soldiers" the poet also finds consolation in the thought that not even death can conquer love, a theme continued in the climactic poem of the book, "Pensive on Her Dead Gazing, I Heard the Mother of All." This is not a patriotic poem. The "Mother of All" is not the Nation, or symbolical mother of the states, but Nature:

Pensive, on her dead gazing, I heard the Mother of All,
Desperate, on the torn bodies, on the forms covering the battle-fields gazing;
As she call'd to her earth with mournful voice while she stalk'd:
Absorb them well, O my earth, she cried—I charge you, lose not my sons! lose not an atom;
.   .   .   .
Exhale me them centuries hence—breathe me their breath—let not an atom be lost;
O years and graves! O air and soil! O my dead, an aroma sweet!
Exhale them perennial, sweet death, years, centuries hence.

The poet capable of taking this long-range view of death was also capable of making so impersonal a response to a lover that he must have seemed well-nigh inhuman to the person concerned. On first thought, *Drum-Taps* seems a strange place to publish "Out of the Rolling Ocean," the poem said to have been written to Mrs. Juliette Beach.[62] But presumably it was written during the war years, and the sentiment is in perfect harmony with "Hymn of Dead Soldiers" and "Pensive on Her Dead Gazing . . ."

Out of the rolling ocean, the crowd, came a drop gently to me,
Whispering, *I love you, before long I die,*
I have travel'd a long way, merely to look on you, to touch you,
For I could not die till I once look'd on you,
For I fear'd I might afterward lose you.

(Now we have met, we have look'd, we are safe;
Return in peace to the ocean my love;
I too am part of that ocean, my love—we are not so much separated;
Behold the great rondure—the cohesion of all, how perfect!
But as for me, for you, the irresistible sea is to separate us,
As for an hour carrying us diverse—yet cannot carry us diverse for ever;
Be not impatient—a little space—know you, I salute the air, the ocean and
    the land,
Every day, at sundown, for your dear sake, my love.)

Whether Mrs. Beach actually made a pilgrimage to Washington has not
been determined, and of course we need not take the separation by "sea"
literally. But if she was actually aggressive in her love for the poet—like
Mrs. Gilchrist a few years later[63]—this poem probably made her feel that
she might as well have been in love with a monk. Indeed, there is a positive
religious connotation in the absolute renunciation and advised resignation of this response. In effect the poet says, "Return, my love, to the
ocean of humanity, and lose your identity again in that ocean." The
"Over-Soul" doctrine is also implied, so that the poet is also saying, "Return to the ocean of eternal spirit, where we as disembodied souls, pure
spirits, shall some day dwell together." It is the argument of all great pantheistic elegies, such as Shelley's "Adonais," Emerson's "Threnody," and
Whitman's own "When Lilacs Last in the Dooryard Bloom'd." Yet the
poet, in effect, condemns the physical love to death. To the woman he
says that earthly life is of short duration; but, "Be not impatient—a little
space," and we shall be absorbed into "the air, the ocean and the land"
forever. The solution is, in fact, a symbolical death—the path to eternal
happiness.

Perhaps further light may be thrown upon this poem by considering
the origin of a later poem, "A Noiseless Patient Spider," not included in
Drum-Taps but trial lines of which may be found in a hospital notebook
of 1862–1863.[64] After a notation that did contain the germ of a *Drum-
Taps* poem ("A Sight in Camp in the Day-Break Grey and Dim," in which
the poet thought the face of the young man "the face of my dead
Christ" [65]) are these experimental lines:

The Soul, reaching, throwing out for love,
As the spider, from some little promontory, throwing out filament after fila-
    ment, tirelessly out of itself, that one at least may catch and form a link,
    a bridge, a connection
O I saw one passing alone, saying hardly a word—yet full of love I detected
    him, by certain signs
O eyes wishfully turning! O silent eyes!
For then I thought of you oer the world
O latent oceans, fathomless oceans of love!
O waiting oceans of love! yearning and fervid! and of you sweet souls perhaps
    in the future, delicious and long:
But Dead, unknown on the earth—ungiven, dark here, unspoken, never born:
You fathomless latent souls of love—you pent and unknown oceans of love!

The chief theme of these verses is the poet's sense of loneliness—almost
cosmic in scale. His soul, like the spider throwing out filaments, is trying
to form a bridge through empty space to another soul, or some spiritual
anchor. Then in his fantasy the poet recognizes by familiar signs a man
who is searching as he is searching, but the thought comes to him that this
person is also but a drop out of a vast ocean of "sweet souls . . . yearning
and fervid" like the poet. The situation is strangely reminiscent of Whitman's juvenile fantasy "Eris; a Spirit Record," in which Dai is condemned
for eternity to go "wandering in the confines of the earth, or amid the
streets of the beautiful land . . . earnestly calling on one he loves.
'Wherefore is there no response?' " [66]

This poem fragment is roughly contemporary with the letters to Sergeant Tom Sawyer.[67] The poet, like Dai, had still found no response. He
had recognized, too, that the love he had glimpsed in his fantasy was supernal, and therefore not humanly attainable—a surprising restatement of
Poe's theory of Beauty, which as a literary theory Whitman did not respect.[68] When he jotted down these lines of the spider poem, Whitman
had not yet attained the philosophic resignation which he was to com-
mend to the woman, the "drop," who came to him "out of the ocean, the
crowd." His "Soul" was still "throwing out filament after filament," and
had found no anchor.

Unfortunately we do not know which of these poems was composed
later: probably the one supposedly written for Mrs. Beach, but this is only
conjecture. It is significant, however, that the notebook poem has an unmistakable "Calamus" motif (though Whitman finally placed the revised
version in "Whispers of Heavenly Death," [69] another indication that the vision was supernal); but he added "Out of the Rolling Ocean, the Crowd"

to his "Children of Adam" group.[70] Perhaps these assignments explain the difference between the poet's unsatisfied yearning and his serene renunciation during the period when these poems were being composed. It cost little effort to advise renunciation to the woman, but the "Calamus" sentiment made the poet feel like a lost soul.

V

In the same letter (June 3, 1865) in which Mrs. Whitman reported that the printer had delivered the copies of *Drum-Taps*, she confided to Walt her increasing annoyance with the Brown family, with whom she was still having to share her house. They quarreled constantly with Hattie, or with the Whitmans about one thing or another. She did not mention Edward, but he may have been another cause of friction. In her vexation she wrote that "the old brown has gone to work at Harrisburg" and she wished "they were all gone." She had other worries, too, for apparently Jeff had stopped paying her rent, either because he was now often away from home on business trips to make surveys for water works projects in other cities or because he was trying to shift the responsibility to Walt, now that he was on a regular salary. Probably his neglect of his mother was not deliberate, for he was obviously as thoughtless and careless as he was impulsively kind and affectionate. At any rate, on June 3 Walt's mother begged him to send her enough money to pay her rent.

The following day Jeff wrote a very revealing letter[71] on a major cause of Mrs. Whitman's unhappiness. His letter was doubtless more illuminating than he was aware, for now he wanted to get rid of his feeble-minded brother—ostensibly for his mother's sake, but his own hatred for Edward was unconcealed:

When I got home last night Mat told me that during the afternoon Mother came up stairs crying as if her heart would break all on account of that lazy baggage Ed—Mother cant do anything with him—he wont wait on himself hardly and wont do the least thing for her—I think he is the most infernal lazy and the most ugly human being I ever met—unless something can be done he certainly will shorten Mothers life by years. . . .

Jeff promised his mother that if she would part with Edward he would take care of her and help pay Ed's board—undoubtedly at some place where he would be out of sight—but Mrs. Whitman had already complained to Walt of the undependability and wastefulness of both Jeff and

Mattie, and it was not likely that she would agree to Jeff's suggestions. These letters, therefore, emphasize the importance of Walt's holding his present Government clerkship. In addition to his own needs and ambitions, he was now acutely aware of the financial dependence of his mother and Edward upon him. Later she was to confide, "they none of them want edd," [72] but Walt knew this already.

Probably Whitman's promotion to a second-class clerkship had made him feel that his position and his needed income were safe, despite the change in the head of the Department of the Interior. But the promotion was dated May 11,[73] and four days later James Harlan was sworn in as Secretary of the Interior. Whitman must also have heard rumors, which he was to record a few months later,[74] about the bitter contest between Colonel Jesse K. Dubois and Senator Harlan of Iowa for this position. Senator Harlan had won the appointment, according to Whitman's notation the following September, only because he had had the powerful support of the Methodist Church, and especially of an influential bishop in Philadelphia. Perhaps Whitman did not know, or by September did not wish to recall, that the Iowa Senator, former college president, and former Methodist minister, was also a personal friend of President Lincoln and his family. It seems unlikely, too, that Whitman would not have known of an action of the new Secretary reported in the New York *Herald* (and doubtless other newspapers) under a Washington date line of May 30, 1865 (printed May 31): "The Secretary of the Interior has issued a circular to the heads of bureaus in the department, to report as to the loyalty of each of the employés under him, and also whether there are any whose fidelity to duty or moral character is such as to justify an immediate dispensation of their services."

It is significant that the check was on "loyalty," "fidelity to duty," and "moral character." Nothing was said of forced economy, though this was the excuse given later. At that time there was, of course, no Civil Service for the protection of Government employees, and heads of departments were free to discharge their subordinates for any or no reason whatever. "Loyalty" probably meant political support or sympathy, and Harlan belonged to the "Radical Republicans," who were intent on harsh terms for the South, an issue which was to bring him into conflict with the new President and force his resignation a little over a year later. Whitman's sympathies were with President Johnson, though it is not likely that his views were known to Secretary Harlan.

Regarding the second criterion, no charge was ever made against Whitman's "fidelity to duty." But he was vulnerable on a narrow and conventional interpretation of "moral character." We have already seen[75] the inability of Trowbridge to secure an appointment for Whitman in the Treasury Department after Secretary Chase learned that the applicant was the author of *Leaves of Grass*. It should not be surprising, therefore, that this Methodist from Iowa should have been equally shocked by Whitman's authorship of the book. He had probably never read a line of *Leaves of Grass*, but could hardly have avoided hearing of it, and it so happened that the poet himself unintentionally brought the book to Harlan's attention. He was revising a copy of the Thayer and Eldridge text in preparation for a new edition and had left this paper-bound copy in his office desk. Whether one of Harlan's "stool pigeons" found the copy and carried it to him, or the Secretary himself snooped around after office hours and found it, as Whitman later believed,[76] the book did come to Harlan's attention and he examined it. Possibly the fact that nearly every page contained markings, cancellations, emendations, and additions made him read it with special care. One fact beyond dispute is that without warning Whitman received an official notice dated June 30, 1865, informing him that his services would be "dispensed with from and after this date." [77]

In dazed consternation Whitman carried this note to his friend William O'Connor. He did not know at the time about Harlan's having seen his desk copy of *Leaves of Grass*. But simply losing his position was disaster enough for him, and it was natural that he should turn immediately to William, probably the most intimate friend he had and the one who had exerted himself most to secure his appointment. Many accounts have been given of the events following O'Connor's reading this message, but the man in the position to know more of the facts than anyone else was the Assistant Attorney General, J. Hubley Ashton, for it was he who had interviews with all parties concerned. Moreover his legal mind was capable of recalling the facts with less distortion and obvious bias than any other witness. This was his version:

I remember as if it were yesterday the day in the summer of '65, on which O'Connor came down to my office from his room above in the Treasury Building, where the Attorney General's department was then located, with Secretary Harlan's letter to Walt in his hand, and his terrific outburst against the Secretary for his act of infamy, as he described it, when he put the letter on my table.

Everybody who knew William O'Connor and has read "The Good Gray Poet" can imagine the scene in my office. I fancy that there never was before such an outpouring of impassioned eloquence in the presence of an audience of one,

The wrong committed, as O'Connor said, was the ignominious dismissal from the public service of the greatest poet America has produced, an offence against the honor and dignity of American letters, and against humanity itself as consecrated in "Leaves of Grass." I agreed that the wrong was a great one, and it seemed to me of the highest importance that the Government of the United States, through the Secretary of the Interior, should not range itself among the enemies of Walt Whitman by dismissing him from its service as an unworthy person.[78]

Of course at this point neither O'Connor nor Ashton knew exactly why Whitman had been dismissed, though apparently Ashton did not think it was for reasons of economy. In his reminiscences he went on to state that the same day, as he recalled, he obtained an interview with Secretary Harlan. It was then, as Ashton testified elsewhere,[79] that he learned about Harlan's having seen the copy of *Leaves of Grass*. Ashton admired Whitman's poetry, but he was immediately concerned with the practical question of either getting him reinstated in his position or having him transferred to another department. Harlan stubbornly insisted that even the President could not force him to reinstate Whitman, and it was with great difficulty that Ashton persuaded him not to oppose Whitman's appointment to another position in Government service.[80]

Ashton's plan was to secure the transfer of Whitman to his own department. "The Attorney General, Mr. James Speed, gave his ready assent to my plan, and the result of it all was that the Government finally became the friend and protector, instead of the enemy and persecutor, of our poet." This transfer took place immediately, on July 1, which was the day of the momentous interview, according to notes which Whitman made several days later after talking with Ashton about his interview with Secretary Harlan. It was not, therefore, until around July 5 that Whitman knew exactly why he had been dismissed. Probably his indignation would have receded with the passage of time had not his Irish friend's mercurial temperament and imagination become more and more heated as the hot Washington summer wore on.

Jeff learned of Walt's dismissal both from the newspapers and his brother's letters. On July 16 he wrote Walt:

We of course all felt very indignant at the way you had been treated—but when I came to the statement that Harlan was a parson of course his conduct was to be expected[.] From that class you can never get anything but lying and meanness—I hope you do not allow it to have any effect on you   you must not—The poor mean-minded man—If Christ come [*sic*] to earth again and didn't behave different from what he did when he was here he would have a mighty poor show with Harlan would'nt he—

The most outrageous thing was published in the Eagle   If you have any curiosity abt it I will send it to you   It was perfectly in keeping with the paper and I've no doubt was considered a very good thing by little Van [Van Anden, the owner who had discharged Whitman from his editorship of the *Eagle* in 1848]. . . .[81]

It is not known whether Walt had enough curiosity to ask for the clipping from the *Eagle,* but the editorial published July 12 shows how readily his old antagonists seized this opportunity to express their disapproval of his whole poetic program and career. It was called "Morality in Washington," and began:

Our eccentric fellow citizen Walt Whitman has lost his position in the Interior Department at Washington under the general order discharging immoral persons, his "Leaves of Grass" being produced as evidence of his immorality. Most of our readers probably know Whitman by sight; he used, in his own language to "celebrate himself" so conspicuously along the streets of Brooklyn. Walt is personally a good-hearted fellow, with some ability, but he was bitten with the mania of transcendentalism, which broke out in New England some years ago, and still flourishes in that region. . . .

The editor claimed that Whitman was "rather too much a 'child of nature' " even for Emerson. "He wrote of things no rightminded person is supposed ever to think of, and used language shocking to polite ears."

During the war Whitman went to Washington and did humane service in tending the sick and wounded soldiers in the hospitals; he was rewarded with a clerkship in the Interior Department from which he has just been discharged. Walt, however, has been provided for elsewhere. He now occupies a desk in the Attorney General's office, where we suppose they are not so particular about morals.

Probably the staff of the *Eagle* first learned of Whitman's dismissal on July 3, when the New York *Herald* printed, in its Washington letter of July 2, this report:

Quite a commotion has been kicked up in a quiet way by a portion of the clerks in the Interior Department in consequence of the dismissal of some of their number by Secretary Harlan. Walter Whitman, A. L. Stevens and Judge Jesse Connard of Indiana (rep.) are reported among those with whose services Mr. Harlan has concluded to dispense.

By coincidence the *Herald* printed a sarcastic comment on the Harlan dismissals (though without mentioning personal names) on the very day that the *Eagle* editorial appeared. The Washington letter of July 11 (printed in the *Herald* next day) contained this paragraph:

Secretary Harlan seems disposed to make very extensive changes in the Interior Department. The Superintendent of the Census has been followed into retirement by the Commissioner of Indian Affairs, and other changes in the heads of the bureaus are spoken of. Many removals of clerks have been made, and a large proportion of those who remain feel anything but secure in their places. The Secretary evidently regards the Interior Department as a sort of Augean stable, which it is his herculean task to clean out. Of course this cannot be effected without exciting much complaint and remonstrance among the victims and their friends; but the Secretary calmly pursues his task, and doubtless has good reason for the belief that new men, even though lacking in experience, can better administer the affairs of the department than those who have grown gray and rusty in the service.

Although there seems no reason to doubt that Whitman's authorship of *Leaves of Grass* was the main cause of his dismissal—at least for his inclusion in the first group dropped—it seems rather unlikely that he could have long escaped if he had been passed over on the first round of "stable cleaning." Had Secretary Harlan not found this convenient excuse, he would probably have found some other, and Whitman was doubtless more fortunate than most of the other discharged clerks, who did not have an Assistant Attorney General to secure a transfer for them.

Except for the personal annoyance, Whitman's life and career had not been seriously affected by this episode. Had he not been promptly reemployed, his future would have been seriously jeopardized, and he might not have been able to print what became the fourth and fifth editions of *Leaves of Grass* (at his own expense, as usual). But, as sometimes happens with seeming misfortune, the poet had discovered that he had several loyal and influential friends, and he was shifted to a department in which his service and his literary talents were far more appreciated than they ever would have been in the Department of the Interior. Consequently, after only a slight interruption he continued earning his salary, visiting the hospitals, writing new poems for a *Sequel to Drum-Taps*, and revising that copy of *Leaves of Grass* that had shocked Secretary Harlan.

Fortunately, this unique copy still exists,[82] and it is worth studying for the light it throws on the growth of *Leaves of Grass*. Practically all biographers have been content to generalize from Whitman's own comments about this book, and several have interpreted his words to mean that he had marked some of the most offensive passages for deletion, and that these deletion marks therefore called Harlan's attention to lines that he might otherwise not have read. But Whitman did not actually say this, and the inference is wholly incorrect.

What this copy does show is that Whitman was mainly revising for strictly literary purposes, improving the rhythms, straightening out the syntax, strengthening the imagery, and deleting merely rhetorical passages or even a whole poem, like "Apostroph," the original introduction to "Chants Democratic," which he marked: "take this piece out altogether." In fact it was this group rather than any of the sex poems that he was revising most, because he had decided to eliminate the group and redistribute the poems, with whatever alterations seemed needed—and they were extensive. Several of these poems he was combining for what would soon become "As I Sat Alone by Blue Ontario's Shore" (later "By Blue Ontario's Shore"—based primarily on the 1855 Preface and the 1856 "Poem of Many in One").

Something else that Whitman was doing, which would not have interested Harlan, was inserting many new lines and phrases alluding to the Civil War. This he was doing in many places throughout the book—one example of how even the early poems were affected by the poet's war experiences. In "Song of Myself," usually associated with the poet's 1855 period, he inserted such lines as this (page 90 in the 1860 edition): "The black ship mail'd with iron, her mighty guns in her turrets." [83] Or this long insertion in "Poem of Many in One" (page 115):

Lo! High toward heaven, this day,
Libertad! from the conqueress' field return'd,
I mark the new aureola around your head,
No more of soft astral—but dazzling & fierce,
With war's flames, & the lambent lightnings playing,
And your port immovable where you stand;
With still the inextinguishable glance, & the clench'd and lifted fist;
And your foot on the neck of the one, the last great Scorner, utterly crush'd
    beneath you;
The menacing, arrogant one, that strode & advanced with his senseless scorn,
    bearing the murderous knife;
Lo! the wide swelling one, the braggart that would yesterday do so much!
Already a carrion dead, & despised of all the earth—an offal rank,
This day to the dunghill maggots spurned, . . .[84]

But Whitman knew that the revision of this poem would not soon be finished, and he wrote in the margin: "take out & finish for future volume." He left it out of the 1866-67 *Leaves of Grass*, though he included it in the Annex, and restored it to the *Leaves* in 1872.

The one part of the book in which Whitman's revisions were in the direction of discretion was the "Calamus" group. He marked Number 12 ("Are You the New Person Drawn Toward Me"): "out without fail." And Number 32 (about the two men on the pier, who clung to each other, reluctant to separate), he marked boldly "Out." However, both of these poems were retained in 1866. Also in Number 18 ("City of My Walks and Joys") he marked for deletion the last three words in this line:

Not those [literary or fashionable people]—but, as I pass O Manhattan! your
    frequent and swift flash of eyes offering me love . . .[85]

But these words he also retained in 1866. In the first line of this poem he inserted "orgies," so that it read, City of orgies, walks, and joys!

Perhaps in the later retention of these "Calamus" poems which Whitman had probably marked for deletion before Harlan saw them, and in the strengthening of some of the lines, we have some evidence of the Secretary's influence on *Leaves of Grass*. If so, the effect of the Harlan episode on Whitman was to make him more stubborn than ever about giving in to prudish critics. And subsequent events will bear out this conclusion.

VI

In spite of the excitement over Whitman's peremptory dismissal from the Department of the Interior, the summer of 1865 was in many respects the most enjoyable he had spent in Washington. His illness of the previous summer did not return, nor did he complain of the heat as he had during both of the preceding summers. Apparently his health had definitely improved, though he continued to frequent the hospitals and subject himself to the influences which the doctors had warned him against. Now that the war had been over for several months, few of the men still in the hospitals were recuperating from wounds, though in some ways the patients who remained were more pathetic than those Whitman had visited during the war, for they were mainly incurable or those suffering from the most persistent and malignant diseases, or wounds that would not heal. Whitman's visitations were therefore fully as much needed as they had been during the progress of the war.

But George's army life was nearly over. On July 14 he wrote from Camp Augur, near Alexandria, Virginia: "I have been over to Washington two or three times since I saw you, but it was always in the afternoon (after C. M. hours) so that I could not get up to your place in time to see you. Walt come over and see us, the stage leaves Willards [hotel] twice every day, and brings you right to Camp, so jump in and come over. . . ." [86] Walt promptly responded to this invitation and went over twice. George took him to dinner at the Arlington House and Walt enjoyed the trips, though of course he was also glad when his brother could go home to stay. On the morning of July 27 George's regiment broke camp in Virginia, crossed the Potomac by the Long Bridge, and marched the five miles to the Washington railroad station. There Walt saw the 51st and other regiments climb onto a long train bound for Baltimore and New York. The twenty cars were inadequate and the men covered the roofs like so many bees. [87]

A few days after George's departure Walt received a letter from New York, written partly in response to the publicity given to his dismissal, that greatly delighted him. [88] The correspondent, who signed himself A. Van Rensellaer, wrote: "I saw a paragraph about your dismissal from the Interior Department, and as I once read your book, I am moved to express my feelings in the matter. The act strikes me as pretty mean but quite of a piece with Harlan's character." He then hinted very strongly that he knew something about Harlan's character that was quite in keeping with his treatment of Whitman. He said he would tell it to Whitman in confidence when he visited Washington a few days later. Whether he did so is not known. But in his letter he also proceeded to narrate an incident that obviously pleased the poet very much, both then, while he was working on his Lincoln elegy, and later in his old age, when he needed balm for his ego. Van Rensellaer said that once while calling on President Lincoln in the company of a member of Congress, Whitman had strolled past the White House, and Lincoln had asked who he was.

I spoke up and said, mentioning your name, that you had written Leaves of Grass, etc. Mr. Lincoln didn't say anything but took a good long look till you were quite gone by. Then he says (I can't give you his way of saying it, but it was quite emphatic, and odd), "Well," he says, "*he* looks like a *man.*" He said it pretty loud but in a sort of absent way and with the emphasis on the words I have underscored.

On August 8 Walt's mother wrote him that George was home but having difficulty in settling down:

. . . george is here . . . I guess they are all sorry   i don't know as they are
sorry the war is over but i guess they would much rather staid in camp . . .
[George] is very restless   i tell him to not be worried   i dont think it is because he is uneasy about getting a living but such a change   he is much stouter
than when he was home before . . . i tell him not to be in a hurry but rest but
i can see he is very uneasy   he got a very honorable discharge . . . write walt
what you think about georges going into the building line [89]

By the end of the month Mrs. Whitman had decided to visit Hannah,
perhaps after she had seen George would not, and on August 29 she asked
Walt to notify Hannah that she would make the trip the following Monday (September 4). Apparently George had not supported Jeff in his objections to her going. Nor had George taken any interest in his brother in
the asylum, for Mrs. Whitman complained that she had "heard nothing
from poor jess." Probably, too, no one could do very much for Andrew's
children so long as Nancy had charge of them. Mrs. Whitman wrote that
"jimmy brings them up here sometimes," adding, "poor little objects of
misery they are." [90] She was now worried, too, about George. Despite his
restlessness, he had not yet decided on what to do. Mrs. Whitman felt perhaps he wanted to use what money he had for some business venture; she
hated to ask him for anything, and she was finding the situation very awkward. She did wish, she said, they could find a more pleasant house to live
in. George thought they could rent a small house, which they could have
entirely to themselves, but she knew that rents were very high. In view of
this situation she needed more help from Walt and asked him to send her
small sums while she was visiting Hannah.[91]

The day after she arrived in Burlington (September 5), Mrs. Whitman
reported that she had found Hannah in better health than she expected.
A girl came in every day to do the housework, and the Heydes seemed "to
have any quantity of eatables but the same Charley is here. . . ." [92] On
the 10th "there was quite a blow out" between Charley and Hannah, and
next day Mrs. Whitman wrote Walt about it. She said she had not participated, but she wondered how much longer she would be able to stay.
She was also worrying about Mat, fearing that Ed was causing her much
trouble. Letters from Mat, however, assured her that he was not, and Mrs.
Whitman remained with Hannah for nearly a month. Hannah was dreaming of Walt's buying a place in nearby Birmingham and settling down
with his mother near her. How Walt could earn a living there neither she
nor her mother seemed to consider, but they continued to make plans.
They found a house for sale, and both wished Walt would come up and

look at it. Part of the time Mrs. Whitman seemed to think of it as a summer home; perhaps that was what she was really dreaming of. On September 21 she wrote:

. . . i have had a letter from Jeffy and one from Matty but none from George i suppose he is very busy   Jeff says he [George] has got a job to new york rather a big job i should think   Jeffy says he is not going to doo anything in the way of building his house this winter   i was very sorry to hear that as i was in hopes he would have a place of his own   he says brick is so very high i dont know but what we shall all have to go to birmingham to live   every thing is so monstrous dear   i have heard more about the place today it certainly is quite a desirable place   people that has lived here at burlington . . . likes it there much better   there is many well-off farmers and provisions is low so a person could live if they had a small income . . . i wish walter you would write to the doctor at flatlands and see how Jessee is and let me know   i cant help but think so much about him [93]

Mrs. Whitman returned to Brooklyn about the middle of October, and during the month Walt took a short vacation too. He had had the *Sequel to Drum-Taps* printed in Washington, and he probably took copies of the, pamphlet to New York to have them bound in with the original *Drum-Taps* for a new book. The latter deductions are supported by a letter which his mother wrote him on November 14, 1865, after his departure, asking "where is all the Drum taps?" She thought he had left some copies upstairs but she had been unable to find a single copy: "i had one of the first ones on the table here and i cant find it   i used to read some in it almost every night before i went to Bed." [94] She also complained of having "waited and waited" to hear from him and feared something had happened. Her uneasiness suggests that Walt had left some days before, probably around the last of October. And her letter also indicates that the second edition of *Drum-Taps* was bound before he left, for her reference to "one of the first ones" implies that she has seen *later ones*.

VII

Sequel to Drum-Taps[95] was a very thin pamphlet of twenty-four pages, printed by Gibson Brothers, a prominent printing house in Washington.[96] "When Lilacs Last in the Dooryard Bloom'd," which most critics now recognize as Whitman's masterpiece, appropriately headed this new collection. Here, for the third time in his whole career, Whitman was able to harmonize his theme and his poetic form in a unified work of art. He obviously wrote the poem with sustained attention and controlled emotion. When one examines it against the historical background and the poet's recent experience, many subjective elements become apparent; but emotional and romantic as the poem is, Whitman did not let his private problems, or his usual idiosyncrasies of language or gesture or poetic theory intrude. He expressed his own personal attitudes indirectly through a consistent set of symbols and modulated his music in conformity to a symphonic structure. He permitted none of his usual pride in his size or appearance or fancied strength to show through his imagery. The poem is completely intelligible without reference to the biography of the poet, and can stand alone as a work of art without any support from biography.

However, the lilac poem was not anonymous, and it does have Walt Whitman's stamp on it. In many ways it tells us much about the poet; and the history of its growth in his mind can show at least how and why he found the symbols and structure he did. Much of this personal background has already been implied in the preceding account of Whitman's life during the spring of President Lincoln's death. The circumstances of George's imprisonment and his family's almost frantic worry about him, Walt's emotion-filled visits to the sick and wounded in the hospitals, and the general excitement and tension throughout the Union as the war drew to a close, all combined to strain the poet's nerves and heighten his sensitivity to physical and mental stimuli. The sight of the unusually brilliant evening star, which appeared to hang suspended for several nights in March, gave the poet, at the actual time of observation, a sense of receiving some esoteric message, perhaps some supernatural omen of good fortune for the nation—a wish-fulfillment, for he was at the moment hoping for the end of the war. The clear, lyric notes of the bugle floating on the balmy air seemed also to convey a wordless message, and as he listened the poet felt both the pathos of the wounded soldiers in the hospitals scattered over the half sleeping city and at the same time a warm glow of love for the men in the hospitals whom he knew personally. He was conscious particularly of a strong admiration for the Western boys from "Illinois, Michigan, Wisconsin, Iowa," and those other Western states which he knew little about but perhaps for that very reason idealized. For many years he had romanticized the West, from which he expected some day a new and superior breed of men.

Soon after this experience with the evening star, Venus, bending low in the western sky, and the mystic notes of the bugle floating across the moonlit landscape, Whitman learned that George had already reached

Brooklyn, and as soon as he could he hastened there to join the family circle. While at home the awful news of the President's death arrived, suddenly reversing the meaning of those omens of the weather, the star, and the music. Quite literally, too, the weather in Brooklyn and New York turned murky and depressing. Furthermore, the news that arrived before breakfast that Saturday morning came at a time when the attention of the Christian world was occupied with thoughts of the Saviour's death and resurrection, for it came between Good Friday and Easter.

When Whitman returned to Washington (by Easter Monday) the lilacs were in full bloom, and either then or the following Wednesday, when the funeral service was held in Washington and the casket was banked with lilacs, this flower became everlastingly associated in the poet's memory with the death of Lincoln: "I remember where I was stopping at the time, the season being advanced, there were many lilacs in full bloom. By one of those caprices that enter and give tinge to events without being at all a part of them, I find myself always reminded of the great tragedy of that day by the sight and odor of these blossoms. It never fails." [97]

Thus Whitman already had his three basic symbols before he had scarcely thought of writing an elegy.

> When lilacs last in the door-yard bloom'd,
> And the great star early droop'd in the western sky in the night,
> I mourn'd . . . and yet shall mourn with ever-returning spring.
>
> O ever-returning spring! trinity sure to me you bring;
> Lilac blooming perennial, and drooping star in the west,
> And thought of him I love.

In Washington the great star "droop'd," but just before Easter it had "fallen" (Section 2), and in his grief on that dark Saturday morning in Brooklyn and later in the day on Broadway in New York, "black murk" hid the star, now an allegorical symbol:

> O powerful, western fallen star!
> O shades of night! O moody, tearful night!
> O great star disappear'd! O the black murk that hides the star!
> O cruel hands that hold me powerless! O helpless soul of me!
> O harsh surrounding cloud that will not free my soul.

After this aria of emotional grief, the poet remembers "an old farm-house near the white-wash'd palings," such as his grandparents had lived in, and the lilac-bush "with heart-shaped leaves of rich green," and "every leaf a miracle." This association of objects experienced in the poet's youth brings more controlled emotions, and he seizes a sprig of blooming lilac as his token funeral bouquet. From now on he manipulates his symbols with multiple meanings. The sprig is also the "golden bough" of myth, a symbol of "ever-returning" spring, Easter, and resurrection.

Then in Section 4 a new symbol enters, the hermit thrush, which likewise suggests spring and new life, but also, like the mocking bird in the earlier poem, "Out of the Cradle," the voice of Nature and the hidden meaning of life and existence. The poet and the thrush have much in common; they are both poets, and the human poet's "brother" sings a "Song of the bleeding throat,/Death's outlet song of life . . ." The pathos of death in spring, with Nature's promise of resurrection, is thus beautifully and poignantly suggested, but the dramatic structure of this elegy has not yet clearly emerged. In Section 5 Whitman once more demonstrates his ability to combine imagery and rhythm for the sake of empathy. Just as the actual historical train wound through cities and across farms where millions of Americans were mourning the death of their leader, so do the words, the rhythms of the syllables, and the very syntax give the reader the sensation of traveling.

Over the breast of the spring, the land, amid cities, through the woods, along the lanes, and across the wheat fields with "every grain from its shroud in the dark-brown fields uprising," passing through blooming orchards,

> Carrying a corpse to where it shall rest in the grave,
> Night and day journeys a coffin.

Even in the first edition of *Leaves of Grass* Whitman showed himself a master of montage, but he had never used this device quite so successfully as here. As the coffin passes, the poet throws on it his token of roses and early lilies, but mostly armfuls of lilacs.

At this point (Section 9) the *tension* which Walt Whitman had actually experienced begins to control the form of the poem, giving it a dramatic structure. The evening star which had given him a premonition, first of happiness, and then in retrospect of tragedy, now becomes the symbol of the poet's grief for the loved one who had died; and the burden of the hermit thrush's song is the necessity of death in the natural process of life. The dramatic conflict is in the attraction of both of these symbols. The poet is ready to follow the bird-sprite, but he is also detained by the star:

Sing on, there in the swamp!
O singer bashful and tender! I hear your notes—I hear your call;
I hear—I come presently—I understand you;
But a moment I linger—for the lustrous star has detain'd me;
The star, my comrade, departing, holds and detains me.

Before this conflict can be resolved, the poet must make his own contribution, and he asks himself what "picture" he shall hang on the walls of the tomb. The funeral of the President seems to him comparable in historical and tragic significance to the burial of one of those pharaohs of old whose hieroglyphic-decorated tombs (or at least fragments of them) he had seen so many times in the Egyptian Museum in New York City while he was writing the first *Leaves of Grass*.[98] But the "pictures" this democratic poet uses to decorate the fanciful tomb of the great President are those of simple American life, "of growing spring and farms and homes." They convey, too, not only the democratic way of life but the "body and soul" of America.

The remainder of the poem acquires its form and structure from a continuation and development of the dramatic conflict between the bird and the star: between philosophical acceptance of death and instinctive grief for the individual who has died. The minor symbol, the black cloud (that is, grief) also darkens the land, though by montaged imagery the poet shows that the life of the country goes on even while the coffin journeys to its final resting place—a fact that Whitman and his mother had found hard to accept on that terrible Saturday morning in April, but one to which he had probably become resigned by the time he attended the funeral in Washington. In the poem the song of the thrush continues, to the "tally" of the poet's soul, and eventually reconciles the poet to the fact of death: then with "the knowledge of death [the message of the thrush] as walking one side of me, / And the thought of death [the meaning of the star] close-walking the other side of me, / And I in the middle . . . holding the hands of companions," [99] he finally arrives, completely resigned, at the end of the coffin's journey, "in the fragrant pines, and the cedars dusk and dim." The poem, with "Lilac and star and bird, twined with the chant of my soul," will keep alive in the memory of the poet, and the minds of future readers of this poem, the true meaning of the President's death, and the inevitable death of every individual; but like the resurrection myths of all lands and people, this elegy ends on the note of hope and joyous acceptance.

After reading this masterful elegy, one finds the remaining poems in the

Sequel anti-climactic, though one, "O Captain! My Captain!," has become the most popular—and uncharacteristic—poem Whitman ever wrote. One other piece, "Dirge for Two Veterans," has often been set to music.[100] The final poem, "To the Leaven'd Soil They Trod," catches the rhythm of marching feet and the spirit of reconciliation which the poet shared with the post-war President, but it is really more concerned with Whitman's poetic program than with the war and its aftermath. Here, as in his 1855 Preface, Whitman is ambitious to embrace the continents in his songs. He calls to the Alleghanian hills, "the tireless Mississippi," the rocks, the forests, the prairies, the "far-off sea," and the elements:

> . . . And responding, they answer all, (but not in words,)
> The average earth, the witness of war and peace, acknowledges mutely;
> The prairie draws me close, as the father, to bosom broad, the son;
> The Northern ice and rain, that began me, nourish me to the end;
> But the hot sun of the South is to ripen my songs.

"The hot sun of the South" meant Washington, which actually was in many ways Southern, and which Whitman consistently regarded as the South. There are no indications in his letters that he had any intention of going farther south, but he did intend to remain in Washington and vigorously pursue his literary ambitions.

In between the elegy and the above "program poem," Whitman collected several pieces having little or nothing to do with the war, the most important of which was "Chanting the Square Deific." Whitman had been interested in comparative religion for at least fifteen years, and had been trying to evolve a new eclectic religion suitable for a democracy ever since the publication of his first edition.[101] In "Chanting the Square Deific" he substituted for the Christian Trinity a Quaternity, which was a One or Absolute embracing (1) the theological symbols of law and authority, (2) the Consolator or Christ, (3) resistance to the godhead or Satan, and (4) "Santa Spirita" or the life-principle,

> Including all life on earth—touching, including God—including Saviour or Satan;
> Ethereal, pervading all, (for without me, what were all? what were God?)
> Essence of forms—life of the real identities, permanent, positive, (namely the unseen,)
> Life of the great round world, the sun and stars, and of man—I, the general Soul,
> Here the square finishing, the solid, I the most solid,
> Breathe my breath also through these little songs.

"Santa Spirita" is not, as sometimes thought, the "Holy Ghost," but more like Emerson's Over-Soul, or Bergson's "l'élan vital." It is the godhead that the poet worships, whose spirit he hopes to convey somehow through his poems. This is a prophecy of Whitman's shift of emphasis in his poems from the body to the soul, with an increasing religious mysticism. But he had not progressed any further than this one poem when *Sequel to Drum-Taps* went to press.

In fact, even to fill up the twenty-four pages Whitman had to dig into his files and literary workshop. For the first time he printed in a book the 1861 "I Heard You, Solemn-Sweet Pipes of the Organ," [102] pruned of several contemporary allusions. Some of the war poems that he included border on the trite and conventional, such as the dream of the slain passing in review, or the fantasies in which the bayonets cannot pierce the immortal soul. Many of the *Drum-Taps* poems—both editions—have trochaic lilts, and "O Captain! My Captain!" has a near-regular meter, with rhyme and a stanza pattern. On the whole the prosodic form is still that of Whitman's long free-verse line, but his more frequent inversions, less realistic language, and more conventional diction should have reconciled many of his contemporary readers to his poetic form—though perhaps by this time his literary reputation was so bad that nothing could have reconciled the countless admirers of Longfellow and Lowell to anything published under the name of Walt Whitman.

This is the conclusion suggested by an examination of the reviews of *Drum-Taps* (which usually included the *Sequel* if it was noticed at all). Although many critics had attacked the first two editions of *Leaves of Grass*, Whitman's novelties of style and subject matter had at least attracted attention. The third edition was also, as we have observed,[103] widely commented upon, though the defenders were not usually the men or women of distinction in the literary world. Although *Drum-Taps* was actually more ignored than any of Whitman's previous editions, it was reviewed at length in several influential publications, and these reviews were to have great influence on Whitman's future, for he had definitely arrived at a crisis in his poetic career.

The first important review to appear was by William Dean Howells in the *Round Table*, November 11, 1865. Before the war Howells had himself published (in collaboration with J. J. Piatt, whom Whitman knew in Washington during the war)[104] a volume of romantic and conventional verse, and he had recently returned from Italy, where he had served as consul in Venice during Lincoln's administration. On that occasion in

1860 when he had met Whitman at Pfaff's[105] he had liked the man more than his poetry, and this was still his attitude in 1865. He began his review by complaining that Whitman's "artistic method" had not changed since the 1855 *Leaves of Grass*, and Howells was quite certain that it was an unacceptable method.

Howells could not help being a little impressed by the greater "purity" of subject matter and less crudity of expression in *Drum-Taps* than in *Leaves of Grass*, and he was likewise kindly disposed toward the poet because of his "burly tenderness" in the hospitals. In some of the poems he found "the same inarticulate feeling as that which dwells in music," and he admitted that "the poet conveys to the heart certain emotions which the brain cannot analyze, and only remotely perceives." But, "We must not mistake this fascination for a higher quality." Art must do more than suggest. Every man has tender emotions, but only the true poet can give them a lasting and perfect form. "So long, then, as Mr. Whitman chooses to stop at mere consciousness, he cannot be called a true poet. . . . There are such rich possibilities in the man that it is lamentable to contemplate his error of theory."

Thus Howells thought that real talent was being frustrated by a wrong theory. But Henry James, with all the assurance of his twenty-two years, could see nothing good whatever either in the man or in his poetry. Writing anonymously in the *Nation* (November 15, 1865),[106] he declared: "It has been a melancholy task to read this book; and it is a still more melancholy one to write about it." Though perhaps he had skimmed the contents of *Drum-Taps*, the main object of his attack was actually *Leaves of Grass*—or it might be more accurate to say the reputation of *Leaves of Grass*.

Like hundreds of other good patriots, during the last four years, Mr. Walt Whitman has imagined that a certain amount of violent sympathy with the great deeds and sufferings of our soldiers, and of admiration for our national energy, together with a ready command of picturesque language, are sufficient inspiration for a poet. If this were the case, we had been a nation of poets. . . . To become adopted as a national poet, it is not enough to discard everything in particular and to accept everything in general, to amass crudity upon crudity, to discharge the undigested contents of your blotting-book into the lap of the public. You must respect the public which you address; for it has taste, if you have not.

Perhaps if Whitman had known the youth and inexperience of this savage critic he might have made some allowance for the attack, but probably at the time nothing that anyone could have said against him hurt quite as much as this accusation of his having exploited his hospital experiences. It is unlikely that he took it quite as philosophically as his mother did on November 25 in comparing it with another attack in the Brooklyn *Union*:

. . . i have got a union with an article about your book . . . would you like to have it or dont you care about it   it is not so severe as the one in the nation of the 16th of november   tom Rome left it here for me to read   he is quite put out about it   i should like for mr oconnor to see that in the nation   it is a long piece with flourishes   the one in the union made me laugh[107]

VIII

While Mrs. Whitman was visiting with Hannah and urging Walt to come up to look at the place for sale in Birmingham, William O'Connor was absorbed in the writing of *The Good Gray Poet*. In view of Whitman's own critical activities in his own behalf and his avid interest in this monograph, at least one critic[108] has wondered if Whitman himself did not either write or collaborate in the writing of *The Good Gray Poet*. That he did contribute ideas, information, clippings, and perhaps some passages from his Civil War diaries seems more than likely. It is doubtful, however, as sometimes asserted, that he suggested the title,[109] and his private correspondence gives no clue to his actual authorship of the essay. Furthermore, there are many things in it that Whitman was incapable of writing, such as the analogues—and comments on them—from Latin, Greek, and Italian literature.

On October 19, 1865, while both men were on vacation, O'Connor wrote Whitman from New Ipswich, New Hampshire,[110] thanking him for a clipping from the London *Leader*, which was evidently a review of the 1856 *Leaves of Grass*.[111] Probably Whitman had run across it among his papers stored in Brooklyn. "I shall incorporate it," O'Connor promised. "Part of it is very fine." This is one example of Whitman's co-operation. And we also learn from this letter that O'Connor had finished a draft of his essay and was seeking a publisher for it. He had already solicited the advice and aid of G. W. Curtis, of Harper's, whose reply of September 30 William enclosed in his letter to Walt. Mr. Curtis wrote in part:

The task you undertake is not easy, as you know. The public sympathy will be with the Secretary for removing a man who will be considered an obscene author and a free lover. But your hearty vindication of free letters will not be less welcome to all liberal men.

Personally I do not know Whitman; and while his Leaves of Grass impressed me less than it impressed many better men than I, I have never heard anything of him but what was noble nor believed anything but what was honorable.

That a man should be expelled from office and held up to public contumely, because of an honest book which no candid mind can truly regard as hurtful to public morality, *is* an offence which demands exposure and censure.[112]

Curtis offered to do what he could "to redress the wrong" that O'Connor had undertaken to right. This naturally encouraged William and doubtless Walt too. Despite a very severe and prolonged cold, William hoped soon to be able to announce to Walt that the manuscript had a publisher. He added that Miss Jenny Bullard, at whose house he was staying, greatly admired *Leaves of Grass:* "The first thing she read in the book was Enfans d'Adam, which she cordially liked and wondered how anyone could mistake its atmosphere and purport."

Around the end of the month both William and Walt returned to Washington, without any real prospects of the publication of William's monograph. Then in November came the bad reviews of *Drum-Taps*. This autumn could not actually be called one of the low points in Whitman's life, but it was a dreary and discouraging time. And Mrs. Whitman's letters during December certainly did not cheer Walt up. On December 3 she wrote of her money worries. She had spent all her savings, and George had become strangely parsimonious. "George is good enough and gives me money when i ask him but Walt you know how i dislike to ask." [113] She knew she could be worse off, "but i get kind off [sic] down hearted sometimes living always in the basement and working so hard but i guess i wont say any more about it at present." However, a week later her relations with George had become so puzzling and difficult that she had to pour out her trouble to Walt:

at noon i hadent one cent and i asked george to give me 50 cents and after looking for a considerable time he laid me down 50 cents   well Walt i felt so bad and child like I cried because he dident give me more . . . george has been moody and would hardly speak only when i spoke to him . . . sometimes i would think maybe he is tired of having me and Edd and then i would think george is too noble a fellow for that to be the cause . . . i acted just the same as if i did not notice any change but i felt awful bad and what has made him act so god only knows but i believe it runs in the Whitman family to have such spells . . .[114]

Although there is some doubt about the exact month and year, it may have been during this same December of 1865 that Walt met a young man who was to become his most intimate friend during his remaining years in Washington.[115] This was Peter Doyle, an eighteen-year-old Irish lad from Alexandria, Virginia, who had served in the Confederate Army, been captured and brought to Washington and later paroled in the capital. He then became a horse-car conductor, and it was on the streetcar that Walt met him one cold, stormy night on his way to his room after spending the evening with John and Ursula Burroughs. Doyle later described this meeting:

. . . the storm was awful. Walt had his blanket—it was thrown round his shoulders—he seemed like an old sea-captain. He was the only passenger, it was a lonely night, so I thought I would go in and talk with him. Something in me made me do it and something in him drew me that way. He used to say there was something in me had the same effect on him. Anyway, I went into the car. We were familiar at once—I put my hand on his knee—we understood. He did not get out at the end of the trip—in fact went all the way back with me. . . . From that time on we were the biggest sort of friends.[116]

Young Doyle was uneducated and incapable of intellectual companionship, but his loneliness and youth appealed strongly to Whitman's affectionate nature. He filled an emotional need that neither the O'Connor nor the Burroughs families quite satisfied, dear as they were to Walt, especially O'Connor, nor any of Whitman's other friends, such as Ashton or Eldridge, who were nearer the poet's own age and intellectual level. It was precisely Doyle's youth, simplicity, and need for parental affection that aroused Whitman's latent paternalism—he often addressed Pete as "Son." And Peter Doyle responded as Tom Sawyer had not been able to. But this new comradeship did not interfere with Whitman's other friendships in Washington. None of the others except John Burroughs liked Doyle, but Whitman could still, as in New York during his Pfaffian and Broadway hospital days,[117] enjoy different levels and circles of friends simultaneously without feeling the need to integrate them.

William O'Connor was still Whitman's fiercest admirer and defender, and early in January Bunce & Huntington in New York published his *Good Gray Poet*.[118] This remarkable polemic had two purposes: to condemn Secretary Harlan for dismissing a worthy and virtuous man and to defend the general principle of freedom in literature. And this monograph is important in Whitman's biography for both of these purposes, though judged from a remote and impersonal point of view, the author was far more successful in the second than in the first intention.

In defending Whitman's innocence and attempting to brand Harlan as a villain, O'Connor not only created a mythical poet, ten times larger than life and as majestic as a Greek statue, but he also made him a veritable reincarnation of Christ; and not unconsciously, either, for two years later O'Connor underscored this interpretation in his short story "The Carpenter," [119] in which Whitman by his compassionate love performs a miracle on Christmas Eve. After describing the magnetic "nimbus" of the Good Gray Poet's personality, O'Connor declared: "We who have looked upon this figure, or listened to that clear, cheerful, vibrating voice, might thrill to think, could we but transcend our age, that we had been thus near to one of the greatest sons of men." Far from being a bad man or a free lover, as Harlan is said to have asserted, "His is the great goodness, the great chastity of spiritual strength and sanity."

He has been a visitor of prisons, a protector of fugitive slaves [though only vicariously], a constant voluntary nurse, night and day, at the hospitals, from the beginning of the war to the present time; a brother and friend through life to the neglected and the forgotten, the poor, the degraded, the criminal, the outcast, turning away from no man for his guilt, nor woman for her vileness. His is the strongest and truest compassion I have ever known.[120]

It is possible that Whitman himself objected to this fulsome eulogy—though most of the above statements were literally true—for O'Connor in his letter of the previous October[121] had promised that he would revise the essay, and "you will like it better by the excision of nearly all the personality." However, by "personality" he could have meant personal attack on Harlan; and it is difficult to imagine that his unrevised draft magnified and praised Whitman's personality more than the published version. Moreover, Whitman had himself dramatized and exploited his own personality for the past fifteen years, sometimes crassly in order to advertise his poems, but also consistently as a consequence of his theory that the greatness of a poem is determined by the strength of the character and personality that created it. He had honestly cultivated his own personality in order to create great poems; he could not believe in them without believing in himself. Thus O'Connor's hagiography was a faithful reproduction of the ideal image which had been shaping Whitman's life and work for many years; and the poet himself was one of the last persons able to detect discrepancies between the physical fact and his guiding ideal.

In O'Connor's mind the defense of Whitman had undoubtedly transcended his second purpose, but his defense of freedom in literature was not only good strategy in this controversy; it was also a principle in which this Irish idealist believed so strongly that he became truly eloquent in defending it, and for this reason much of *The Good Gray Poet* is as pertinent today as in the 1860's. He developed his argument on two planes. Those persons, such as Secretary Harlan, who had labeled *Leaves of Grass* immoral, always cited words and expressions which they declared to be indecent. O'Connor did not think that any of these in their context were indecent, but granting for the sake of argument that they were, he asked how many could be found in the entire book. He thought, by a liberal count, there might be eighty lines out of a total of nine thousand. How did this compare, he asked, with the writing of Shakespeare, Homer, Dante, Montaigne, or dozens of other literary masters from the Bible to Lord Byron. Many of these passages, he admitted, had been expurgated in nineteenth century editions, but this only proved, he declared, that the masterpieces themselves were less "pure" than *Leaves of Grass*.

This argument came dangerously close to being sophistical, but what O'Connor really wanted to demonstrate was not that *Leaves of Grass* was morally superior to *Job*, or the *Iliad*, or *Hamlet*; he was against all expurgation and censorship—and prudery: "Shakespeare is all good, Rabelais is all good, Montaigne is all good, not because all the thoughts, the words, the manifestations are so, but because at the core, and permeating all, is an ethic intention—a love which, though mysterious, indirect, subtle, seemingly absurd, often terrible and repulsive, means, seeks to uplift, and never to degrade." [122]

Even on such ground, however, some contemporary critics still maintained that *Leaves of Grass* was immoral. Many years later Howells believed that the coarseness of the sixteenth century or the frankness of the eighteenth were out of place in the nineteenth century literature because meanwhile people had grown more refined. "The manners of the novel have been improving with those of its readers. . . . Generally, people now call a spade an agricultural implement; they have not grown decent without having also grown a little squeamish, but they have grown comparatively decent. . . ." It was such critics whom O'Connor was attacking in his fight against neurotic prudery:

When I went to the hospital, I saw one of those pretty and good girls, who in muslin and ribbons ornament the wards, and are called "nurses," pick up her skirts and skurry away, flushing hectic, with averted face, because as she passed a cot the poor fellow who lay there happened, in his uneasy turnings, to thrust part of a manly leg from beneath the coverlet. I once heard Emerson severely censured in a private company, five or six persons present, and I the only dissenting voice, because in one of his essays he had used the word "spermatic." When Tennyson published the "Idyls of the King," some of the journals in both America and England, and several persons in my own hearing, censured the weird and magnificent "Vivien," one of his finest poems, as "immoral" and "vulgar. . . ."

A civilization in which such things as I have mentioned can be thought or done is guilty to the core. It is not purity, it is impurity, which calls clothes more decent than the naked body. . . . It is not innocent but guilty thought which attaches shame, secrecy, baseness, and horror to great and august parts and functions of humanity. . . .[123]

O'Connor found it difficult to believe that this morbidity would last, but he admitted: "It may be that the devotees of a castrated literature, the earthworms that call themselves authors, the confectioners that pass for poets, the flies that are recognized as critics, the bigots, the dilettanti, the prudes and the fools, are more potent than I dream to mar the fortunes of his [Whitman's] earthly hours . . ." He was confident, however, that some time in the future a healthier and saner civilization would arrive, "And Time will remember him." [124]

Whitman's influence on this monograph is obvious, for the essay brilliantly recapitulated all the theories and rationalizations that he had used, or was later to use, in defense of his subject matter and his frankness of expression. But what has not been so obvious to most critics of Whitman is the influence of the pamphlet on the poet. Henceforth he would be even more uncompromising in his belief in the sacredness of sex, and insist that he was only trying to give a healthy treatment to the wholeness of life and nature. Neither he nor O'Connor, nor any of his critics up to this time, had raised objections to the "Calamus" emotions. The contemporary sin was to mention sex organs and acts, and it is difficult for a twentieth century reader to appreciate the strength of the taboos that Whitman had violated.

But *The Good Gray Poet* probably affected Whitman most by giving him consolation for the increasing violence of American critical reaction to his poems: "And Time will remember him." As the hostility, or the conspiracy of silence, increased, this promise became Whitman's own stubborn conviction. And with the appearance of *The Good Gray Poet* the hostility began noticeably to stiffen. It is difficult today to determine whether Whitman's friends did him more harm than good, for *Drum-Taps* had been largely ignored by the critics before O'Connor's defense was published, and this work at least jarred some of them into noticing the book, though mostly to condemn it.

One example was the review of *The Good Gray Poet* in the *Round Table* on January 20, 1866, by Richard Henry Stoddard, whose critique was flippant, satirical, and abusive both of the poet and of his defender. Stoddard did admit, however, that Harlan "deserved and deserves to be pilloried in the contempt of thinking men for this wanton insult to literature in the person of Mr. Whitman." [125] This statement provoked a reply by Charles Lanman, a friend of Harlan's, that Whitman had been removed from his clerkship for "two satisfactory reasons: he was wholly unfit to perform the duties which were assigned to his desk; and a volume which he published and caused to be circulated through the public offices was so coarse, indecent, and corrupting in its thought and language, as to jeopardize the reputation of the Department." [126]

To this O'Connor spiritedly replied that Harlan had never accused Whitman of incompetence; the poet had never "circulated" his book in the office (the Secretary had surreptitiously examined a book published five years before); and that the principle he (O'Connor) was fighting for was "intellectual liberty and freedom of letters."

Meanwhile the *Saturday Press* published a review of *Drum-Taps* the same day that Stoddard's criticism of *The Good Gray Poet* appeared.[127] The reviewer began by calling Whitman both "much over-praised" and "greatly underrated," but admitted that, "It is impossible to sympathize heartily with the greatest thoughts that have found utterance in literature, and not to admire him." However, each bit of praise was fairly well canceled by a demurrer: "What is called his sanity, his tenacious grasp on realities is, after all, the monomania of a man whom a great thought has robbed of his self-possession. . . . His songs, though beautiful and inspiring, smack too strongly of the earth. His suggestions are sometimes vast, but himself is chaotic and fragmentary." The invocation to death in the elegy contained the "essence of poetry." But, "He shuts himself from hearty sympathy on all sides."

Both books received a few more notices. On February 3 the Boston *Commonwealth* published an editorial on "Secretary Harlan Playing Cato the Censor," which condemned Harlan without defending the poet:

For our own part, though we cannot share in all Mr. O'Connor's indignation or enthusiasm, we have no doubt that the Secretary has done a very ridiculous and indefensible thing. Considering the notorious immorality in Washington life, and the actual deeds of many officials higher in grade than Mr. Harlan's clerk, the squeamish virtue that could not endure an occasional coarseness in an unpopular author would seem to be too delicate for the atmosphere of Washington.

But Whitman was soon to receive a sympathetic review in the *Commonwealth*. On February 24, 1866, F. B. Sanborn, whose friendship Whitman had won in Boston in 1860 by attending his trial, contributed a long critique of *Drum-Taps*.[128] He had followed closely Whitman's hospital experiences and had collected and personally contributed funds to be used in his visits. Sanborn was therefore particularly sympathetic with the subject matter of *Drum-Taps*, and he made a special point of calling attention to the poet's labors and sacrifices for the sick and wounded soldiers. Then he gave some information for which there is no other authority:

Having served in his chosen work through the war, both before and after his appointment and dismissal from a clerkship at Washington, he sought in his native city [evidently New York intended] a publisher for his patriotic verses, but he found none willing to put his name to the volume. Messrs. Bunce & Huntington finally printed it, but without their name, and without taking any of the customary steps to introduce the book to the reading public. It is scarcely to be got at a bookstore, has hardly been noticed by a newspaper, and, though full of the noblest verses, is utterly unknown to the mass of readers.

Sanborn probably got this information directly from Whitman (no one corrected it in subsequent issues of the *Commonwealth*), and the fact that Bunce & Huntington published *The Good Gray Poet* adds to the probability of their having had something to do with *Drum-Taps*, though it seems strange that they would acknowledge the former and not the latter. But Sanborn made effective use of his information. He pointed out that at the same time this publisher was treating *Drum-Taps* and its patriotic author shabbily, they were extensively advertising a novel by a Virginia traitor, John Esten Cooke, who served in the Confederate Army, used his pen to support the rebellion, and whose "fourth-rate novel" published by Bunce & Huntington was "full of the rankest treason and laudation of traitors." This, declared the reviewer bitterly, "is the way we encourage poets and patriots; this is the way we reward them and make treason odious!"

Even Sanborn, however, was forced to admit that Whitman was "fitfully great," and pleased "only at intervals." He could be "as tiresome as

Wordsworth in his dull passages," and he had other faults springing from his willfulness and impatience with rules. But: "The complaints made of his earlier poems, that they were coarse and immoral in passages, will not apply to this little volume, which is as free from reproach on this score as Mr. Harlan's hymn-book. It will do much, we are confident, to remove the prejudice against Mr. Whitman in many minds, and to secure him that place in literature during his lifetime which he is sure to hold in the next age." Nevertheless, the established authors and recognized critics continued to ignore *Drum-Taps,* or to judge it with the prejudice that now clung tenaciously, both in the popular and the professional literary minds, to *Leaves of Grass.*

IX

After the flurry of excitement occasioned by the reviews of *The Good Gray Poet* and *Drum-Taps* in January and February, and a long letter which O'Connor directed to the Boston *Transcript* in protest against an unfavorable review of his book (the *Transcript* did not print the letter,[129] but of course Whitman read it in manuscript), Whitman's life settled back into the old groove. A minor annoyance throughout the spring was the frequent loss of money that he enclosed each week in his letters to his mother.[130] He reported the thefts to the Brooklyn postmaster and also to the Washington post office, but this did no good at the time—though some months later the Brooklyn postmaster was removed from office for irregularity in his accounts. Whitman solved this problem temporarily by sending money orders, and later he hit upon the plan of having his mother tip the mail carrier regularly, which greatly reduced the number of letters that went astray.

Toward the end of March Mrs. Whitman wrote:

. . . george is building his [carpentry] shop and he gets very tired   he had never ought to have commenced to work at his trade   he says he had ought to have staid in the army and if his money was not invested he would go south Jeff says he ought to have patience and wait   there will be work bye and bye george says i wanted him so much to buy that lot in putnam aven   so i did for i thought all his money would be gone and he would have nothing to show for it   i sometimes wish i was to birmingham or some other out of the way place but here i must stay on the account of edd as he must live i suppose for somebody to support . . .[131]

On May 1 the Whitman family moved to a house at 840 Pacific St., though it did not prove to be much more satisfactory than the place Mrs.

Whitman had hated so much. Walt of course took great interest in all the details. On May 7 he wrote Jeff that the Attorney General was in Kentucky and there was little work to be done in the office. Count Gurowski's funeral had attracted much attention in Washington. Walt was well acquainted with the count, "a strange old man, a great lord in his own country, Poland, owner 30,000 serfs & great estates—an exile for conspiracy against the government—he knew everything & growled & found fault with everybody—but was always very courteous to me, & spoke very highly of me in his book, his *Diary* printed last winter . . ." [132]

The reference to Count Gurowski reminds us again of the variety of minds and personalities in the old O'Connor circle. Eldridge later described Whitman as one of the most conservative of this argumentative group:

I was not only one of the Boston publishers of Walt's 3rd edition of "Leaves of Grass," but for ten years, from 1863 to 1873, was probably more intimate with him than any person now living, except perhaps Mrs. E. M. Calder, now of Providence, and then the wife of William D. O'Connor of blessed memory. During that period we met at O'Connor's house every night for months at a time with hardly a break, and we talked of everything that the human mind could conceive. . . .

It will surprise some of Walt's admirer's to learn that as revealed by his conversations he was one of the most conservative of men. He believed in the old ways; had no faith in any "reforms" as such, and thought that no change could be made in the condition of mankind except by the most gradual evolution . . . he did not believe that Woman's Suffrage would do any particular good. Susan B. Anthony was far from his ideal of a "fierce athletic girl." He delighted in the company of old fashioned women; mothers of large families preferred, who did not talk about literature or reforms. . . . Anything like free love was utterly repugnant to his mind, and he had no toleration for the Mormons. . . . He was likewise very hostile to anything like anarchy, communism or socialism. At one time after the War Albert Brisbane, perhaps the ablest exponent of Fourierism in this country, spent the winter in Washington, and was often a visitor at O'Connor's, and met Walt. They had many talks together which I listened to, but Walt never yielded an inch of ground to him. . . . He strenuously opposed the impeachment of President Johnson as an unwarranted attack on the independence of the Executive. In the headlong impetuosity of youth I was warmly in favor of it, but the lapse of time has convinced me that Walt was right.

For the abolitionists he had no sympathy. While opposed to slavery always, he thought that they considered the subject too all important and were incendiary in their methods. O'Connor and I who were always ardent abolitionists had many a "hot time" with him over this subject.[133]

These spirited sessions at the O'Connors' doubtless relieved what would otherwise have been a drab existence for Whitman during the spring of 1866. His mother was unhappy as usual.[134] The house which she had rented was inconvenient—no water except in the basement, and George had to walk too far to work. She suspected George was thinking of getting married: "he appears to be very much taken with someone." A week later she reported that Jeff looked bad, and added, "his salary has been put up to 200 dols a month but their expences is very great." Heyde was writing again that he was tired of Hannah and intended to leave her, but as usual nothing was done to bring her back to Brooklyn, and Heyde did not make good his threat. George and some of his friends were buying lots on Portland Avenue and planning to build brick houses on them. His mother was more convinced than ever that he was going to get married: "he thinks he is very sly but murder will out." [135]

On June 29 Walt wrote his mother that Hector Tyndale had been to see him again and "always talks about you." He had served as brigadier-general during the war and had received a serious head wound, from which it had taken him a year to recover. In the same letter Walt sent advice to George about the danger of overheating, and revealed some ominous symptoms in his own physical condition: "I find I have to maneuvre through the very hot days, like a general in fight—I carry an umbrella, and if the sun gets to fall on me good & strong, any of the real hot days, my head gets swimming & I have to stop in the street, or rather get inside some store or something, & sit down—I have had just that happen to me twenty times—so now I am very slow & careful. . . ." [136]

The new Attorney General was finally appointed on July 23. He was Henry Stanberry, recently a Senator from Ohio, though born in New York City. Walt found him fully as congenial as the other Attorney Generals he had served under, and a week later he began to think of asking for a leave. He had not heard from his old friend Abby Price in some time, but in a rapid exchange of letters[137] he made arrangements to room at her house during his vacation because "Mother's apartments in Pacific st. are very limited." On August 1 he wrote that he had obtained the leave, and "am coming up to New York, principally to bring out a new & much better edition of Leaves of Grass complete—that unkillable work!" [138] This arrangement worked out to everyone's satisfaction, and on August 25, from Mrs. Price's home at 279 East 55th Street, Whitman wrote Andrew Kerr, the young man who was substituting for him during his leave:

I am having good times here, rather quiet—My book is being printed—gets along rather slowly—I ride out on Long Island, & up New York, Central Park, &c. occasionally—the country is beautiful now—I take a walk on Broadway almost every afternoon—then sometimes a sail on the river or bay— so you see I am enjoying myself in my way—with three or four hours work every day reading my proofs. . . .[139]

Walt had intended to return to Washington on September 12, but he wrote Andy two days before this date that his book was "little more than half done" and he would have to remain to prevent its being "blotched and full of blunders." [140] The printing of *Leaves of Grass* continued to drag, and a second time Walt had to prolong his stay. Evidently he did not continue at Mrs. Price's for the entire period of his protracted leave, for on October 10 his mother wrote that on going to the bureau to get something she found that he had left his two new shirts and handkerchiefs and the sight made her "feel real bad." [141]

Probably Walt had to leave before his new *Leaves of Grass* was bound, but doubtless he had seen it through the printing stage. On October 30 he was rather excited over hearing that the distinguished *Fortnightly Review* in England had a long and favorable article about him and *Leaves of Grass*[142] (the work in general, for the new edition could hardly have yet reached England); but the article, written by Moncure D. Conway, the Brooklyn visitor of 1855, turned out to be full of minor errors and journalistic exaggerations, and on November 13 Walt wrote his mother that "it was meant well, but a good deal of it is most ridiculous." [143] He was especially annoyed by Conway's description of finding the poet on his first visit lying on a sandy common (probably Fort Green Hill), with the thermometer standing at one hundred degrees. When asked if he did not find the sun rather hot, he replied: "Not at all too hot," and confided that "this was one of his favorite places and attitudes for composing 'pomes.'"

Exactly how much of this actually took place it is now impossible to determine, but a decade after Conway's visit Whitman was fully aware of the absurdity of the scene. And in view of Harlan's action, Whitman probably also wished that Conway had not described his bedroom with the pictures of Bacchus and Silenus on the wall. He encouraged O'Connor to attribute these pictures to Conway's imagination,[144] but Alcott, we will recall,[145] also commented upon them in his *Journal* right after his visit of the same period. Doubtless what Whitman really objected to was this implied influence of Bacchus and Silenus on his early poetry. The article was to rankle in his mind for the remainder of his life, but this did not prevent his encouraging Conway to continue working for the recognition of *Leaves of Grass* in England.[146]

Three days after Whitman expressed to his mother his disappointment over the *Fortnightly Review* article he wrote again to share the good news[147] that the Attorney General had promoted him to a permanent third-class clerkship (the highest rank), at an annual salary of $1600. The appointment was retroactive to November 1.

By this time, at least some copies of the new *Leaves of Grass* must have been bound and ready for shipment, though it was not until two weeks later that Walt offered to give his mother an order on the New York binder if she wanted an extra copy.[148] The volume was octavo in size, printed on cheap paper by William S. Chapin and Company of 24 Beekman Street, New York,[149] and was unsubstantially bound in half-morocco (black), with marble board sides and leather corners.[150] Although Whitman had boasted to Mrs. Price that this was to be the most complete *Leaves of Grass*, its completeness consisted only in the revisions and rearrangement of the poems, and the addition of *Drum-Taps* and the *Sequel* as annexes, printed from the old plates. These annexes, with consequent separate pagination, were simply bound in with *Leaves of Grass*: they had not yet truly been integrated into it. A semblance of the eventual order of the poems was beginning to appear, but the process would continue for another quarter of a century.

The whole edition showed the impact of the recent war on the poet. The beginning of "Starting from Paumanok" now read:

Starting from fish-shape Paumanok, where I was born,
Well-begotten, and rais'd by a perfect mother;
After roaming many lands—lover of populous pavements;
Dweller in Mannahatta, city of ships, my city—or on southern savannas;
Or a soldier camp'd or carrying my knapsack and gun—or a miner in California;
Or rude in my home in Dakotah's woods, my diet meat, my drink from the spring;
. . . .
Having studied the mocking-bird's tones, and the mountain hawk's,
And heard at dusk the unrival'd one, the hermit thrush from the swamp-cedars,
Solitary, singing in the West, I strike up for a New World.[151]

Aside from the artistic improvements (and the new mannerism of writing past participles as 'd), the poet was now trying to give the impression that he had experienced—as in many ways he had—what in 1860 was still only a literary theory. He had not literally camped with miners in California or lived in the "Dakotah" woods (and in actuality he might have found more wooded regions!), but he *had* talked and lived with soldiers from many states and shared vicariously their experiences and diversity of character and personality. Consequently he now felt better qualified to sing his national songs. Yet in some ways the war had over-stimulated his nationalism—the result in part of the hostility of England and other European nations to the North during the Civil War, and in part of Whitman's sympathy for the men who had suffered that the Union might endure:

America isolated I sing;
I say that works made here in the spirit of other lands, are so much poison to
    These States.

How dare these insects assume to write poems for America?
For our armies, and the offspring following the armies.[152]

In 1860 Whitman had been aware that he had not yet arrived at his destination, and might never arrive; his role had changed from the 1855 poetic Messiah speaking for the ages, to the more modest role of poetic spokesman for his own time and place. In 1860 "So Long!" began:

To conclude—I announce what comes after me,
The thought must be promulged, that all I know at any time suffices for that
    time only—not subsequent time;
I announce greater offspring, orators, days, and then depart.[153]

But with the return of confidence, Whitman eliminated the second verse in 1866. He still announced "what comes after me," but he expected to exert a powerful influence on a "mightier offspring, orators, days . . ." In spite of his disappointment over the critical reception of *Drum-Taps* and the *Sequel* he had gained poise and confidence during the war years—not the bravado of his first two editions, or the confused assertion of his national and "Calamus" leadership in 1860, but real confidence. He had now begun in earnest to prepare his book for posterity.

This confidence Whitman's friends also shared to such a degree that the most articulate of them would henceforth be unwilling to leave his reputation in the hands of the professional critics and conventional authors. While he was in New York overseeing the printing of his new edition, John Burroughs wrote a lengthy review of *Drum-Taps*[154] and submitted it to a new magazine, the *Galaxy*, started in New York the previous spring. This article was accepted for publication in the issue of December 1, 1866, and around Thanksgiving Walt began reminding Jeff and George to be sure to buy a copy for their mother.[155] He had a right to be proud of this critique, for it was not only sympathetic—naturally—but it was also the most intelligent of any criticism he had received up to that time. This article likewise contained the first reliable biographical sketch of Whitman (O'Connor's hagiography hardly counted as biography). Of course, Burroughs had received the facts from Whitman himself, but he presented them without obvious bias. A few of his biographical statements contained minor inaccuracies, such as his saying Whitman went to New Orleans in 1850 instead of 1848, but Burroughs probably made these mistakes because he wrote the essay while Whitman was away and he had to depend on his memory of widely separated conversations.

Burroughs's critical interpretation of "When Lilacs Last . . ." was especially perceptive. He said the rhythms were "like intricate and involved music, with subtle, far-reaching harmonies." Possibly he got his cue from Whitman's own critical comments on "Out of the Cradle," but at any rate it was especially applicable to the elegy. In writing his poem on the analogy of music, the poet had wisely left out all realistic details of "the great man's death."

. . . the piece has little or none of the character of the usual productions on such occasions. It is dramatic, yet there is no procession of events or development of plot, but a constant interplay—a turning and re-turning of images and sentiments, so that the section in which is narrated how the great shadow fell upon the land occurs far along in the piece. It is a poem that may be slow in making admirers, yet it is well worth the careful study of every student of literature.[156]

No other critic until the twentieth century was to perceive that the poem was "dramatic" in structure, with "a constant interplay . . . of images." The review is still worth reading, though of course it contains some "dated" statements. Burroughs was also the first critic to realize fully how much books had meant to Whitman, an influence that the poet himself minimized. Since Burroughs was at that time almost completely unknown in the world of letters, his praise did not carry much weight; but he deserves credit for having lifted the criticism of Whitman's poems to the plane of reason and intellectual appreciation.

William O'Connor, however, presently achieved a more spectacular victory for the poet whose cause he was championing. On December 2 the owner of the New York *Times*, Henry J. Raymond, not only gave O'Connor four whole columns of the Sunday editorial page for a review of the new *Leaves of Grass* and a discussion of the poet, but he himself wrote another half-column of endorsement of the article, even though he still thought that the book was too indecent to be circulated freely. Not content to rank Whitman with Homer, Dante, and Shakespeare, O'Connor insisted that he could bring "to the States of America the cohesion and union Homer gave to the states of the Hellenic confederacy." But these over-statements sound more ridiculous in summary than in context. The article was persuasively written, so persuasive that Raymond considered giving O'Connor an editorial position on the *Times*.[157]

Whitman's delight in these two critical defenses by his friends can be judged by the frequency of his mentioning them in his letters to his mother. On December 10 he remarked to her: "It seems as if things were going to brighten up about *Leaves of Grass*," adding, "I rather think it is going to be republished in England." [158] Hence, despite a neuralgic condition that had plagued him since before Thanksgiving, he was in a hopeful frame of mind as the year neared its end. On Christmas Eve he was looking forward to a dinner which he had arranged for the soldiers in the hospital. But he was amazed—though half amused—by a sly trick Heyde had tried to play on him, which he reported in his letter to his mother:

Don't you believe that fool Heyde lately wrote a long letter to Mr. Raymond, editor of the N.Y. *Times*—in it he said "Walt was a good fellow *enough—but*"—&c then he went on to run down *Leaves of Grass*, like the rest of 'em—The way I know is Wm. O'Connor was invited by Raymond to come & see him—& he told O'Connor he had received a number of letters about that piece in the *Times* of Dec. 2, which I sent you. He said they all praised the piece, & thanked him (Raymond) for printing it, except one he got from a fellow in Vermont who called himself Walt Whitman's relation—a brother-in-law, he believed—quite a good deal of stuff. Raymond seemed to think the man was either crazy or a fool, & he treated the letter with contempt.—I don't want you to write any thing about it to Han, of course—only if she was here we would tell her. The puppy thought I suppose that he could get his letter printed, & injure me & my book.[159]

The Attorney General, Walt told his mother with pride, had given him "a beautiful knife, a real Rogers steel." This Christmas present from Stanberry assured Walt that his present employer was as much his friend as James Speed, the former Attorney General. And a few days later Ashton showed Walt a letter from Speed that proved he had not been forgotten. Writing from Louisville, Kentucky, on December 29, 1866, he sent the poet this message:

I have been appointed to make an address upon the inauguration of a beautiful marble bust of Mr. Lincoln in this city, and am so crowded with business that I have no time to prepare or to make such preparations as I should. Will you see our friend Walt Whitman and ask him whether he will take my rough draft of an address and revise & finish it for me—I have a notion that if he has the time & is in the mood he can do it better than any man I know—Please let me hear from you or Mr. Whitman soon as to this matter. . . . Say to Mr. Whitman that if he can comply with my request he will greatly oblige me. . . .[160]

≈§ IX ₴≈

SHIPS AT SEA

In cabin'd ships at sea,
The boundless blue on every side expanding,
. . . .
Speed on my book! spread your white sails my little bark athwart the imperious
waves, . . .[1]

I

At the beginning of 1867 Whitman was still living in an unheated room, and the winter was unusually severe, but the guards of the Treasury Building, in which the Attorney General had a suite of offices, would always admit him at any hour of day or night.[2] Consequently Walt spent a great deal of time in the evening and on holidays reading and writing at his desk in the office. There on New Year's Day he wrote his mother about the Christmas dinner he had arranged for the soldiers in one of the hospitals. They had feasted on turkey, four kinds of vegetables, and mince pie. Walt had taken a large supply of tobacco, navy plug and smoking tobacco, "and after dinner everybody that wanted to had a good smoke." [3] Walt himself had apples, oranges, and "a large sugar cake for supper." The O'Connors had invited him to New Year's dinner. It was snowing as he wrote, and some people were out sleigh riding. Several days ago, he told his mother, he had had a visit from Bayard Taylor. Walt had evidently enjoyed the holidays.

But this winter was very painful for Mrs. Whitman. She found her hilltop house almost impossible to keep warm, especially on the west side, and she was plagued with "rheumatism" during the cold months. Once she complained that "it has been almost as much as your life was worth to get to the privy" because the path to it was "so descending and slippery." [4] George, too, frequently felt discouraged in his speculative building, partly because labor was so high, carpenters getting four dollars a day and plasterers six. Jeff was often away on business trips, and Martha gadded more than ever, leaving her children with Mrs. Whitman. Although their grandmother was fond of them, she confessed to Walt that they "annoy me very much," and admitted that she felt her age "more this winter than i ever did before." [5]

Walt worried about his mother, but wrote her cheerful letters. Several times he mentioned attending the opera, and of course he continued his visits to the hospitals. The struggle between President Johnson and Congress was becoming increasingly bitter, and there was talk of impeachment. On January 29 Walt wrote his mother: "The debates in Congress now are quite exciting—sometimes they hold their sessions quite late in the night, & things get to be quite stormy." [6] Occasionally he sat in on these stormy sessions.

Late in January a bill providing an increase in salary for Government clerks was presented in Congress. Walt was skeptical about its passing, but it did and he received a raise of $25 a month.[7] Meanwhile he had finally decided that he could not endure his miserable room any longer and on February 12 he moved to 472 M Street, two doors west of 12th. There Jeff visited him a few days later—during the February thaw. The O'Connors were greatly pleased with Walt's jolly young brother, and of course this increased Walt's enjoyment of the visit. Walt also liked his new boardinghouse, even though his room was in the attic. And in his letters to his mother he frequently commented upon the congeniality of his associates in the office and his pleasant surroundings. On March 12 he wrote: "I go evenings up to the office frequently—I have got me a splendid astral lamp, to burn gas by a tube & it works to admiration, (all at the expense of the office,)—& there I can sit, & read &c. as nice as you please—then I am getting many books for the Library (our office Library) that I have long wanted to read at my leisure . . ." [8]

The wording of this message implies that Whitman had charge (perhaps by an informal arrangement with Mr. Stanberry) of building up the office library, or at least that someone was willing to order books that he wanted. For this and other reasons Walt was as well satisfied as he had ever been with a position. His relations with the present Attorney General, Henry Stanberry, were as congenial as they had been with Mr. Speed, and he did not find his duties burdensome. He assured his mother that he had a pocketful of money, on which she could draw at any time she wished—and he soon began sending her ten- instead of five-dollar bills in his letters. In fact, he felt able to offer George $500 to use on a real-estate investment.[9] Also, despite the rough winter, his health was better, and except for the fact that *Leaves of Grass* was about as much opposed, or ignored, as ever, he had no special cause for feeling dissatisfied. However, there were still personal griefs and worries. On March 15 his mother wrote that Jeff and Mat had attended the funeral of Dr. Ruggles, the special friend of the family to whom Walt had often sent greetings in his letters to his mother and Jeff. From the obituary of Dr. Edward Ruggles in the March 16, 1867, *Round Table*, we learn that this man was an artist, though he held an M.D. degree. His "cabinet pictures," popularly known as "Ruggles Gems," were greatly in demand at the time of his death, though apparently other artists were contemptuous of them. Many thought him eccentric, and apparently some found him unpleasant: "For the shams and phariseeisms of life he had no sympathy and not much charity; and he did not hesitate to say what he thought for fear of consequences. To say things which run counter to common prejudices is not to court popularity; and it may be that Dr. Ruggles sometimes gained disfavor by such a course without securing any compensating advantage." He sounds very much in some ways like Walt Whitman himself.

At this time Walt must have worried about the increasing friction between the two women he most adored, his sister-in-law and his mother. Mrs. Whitman wrote that Jeff and Martha went out nearly every night, returning late, and that she was exhausted from loss of sleep.[10] On March 21 she felt especially disgusted:

mr rice and masons sister is here   mat and she is going to philadelphia tomorrow   i hope when she comes back she will settle down and be a little like herself   i hardly see her   she is so engaged in company and dress   you know i wrote about sis [Hattie] swollowing the penny   the next day morning matty and her friend went out so i kept sis and wached her and the penny passed through her   when her mother came home she never asked any thing about it . . .[11]

Walt's reply on March 26 gave a number of interesting insights into his life in Washington during the spring of 1867. Surratt, one of the conspirators in the plot to assassinate Lincoln, was about to be tried. St. Marie, the man who had discovered Surratt in Rome, had come to Walt for advice and help—"wanted me to intercede for him with some members of Congress." [12] He was afraid of retaliation from Surratt's friends, and thought Government officials had not appreciated his help in finding one of the conspirators, but Walt declined "to mix in the matter." The half-melted snow in the streets had made walking so difficult that Walt had not been able to visit the hospital on Sunday. He had recently received one of Heyde's "damn fool's letters." Congress was about to adjourn, having "carried all their measures successfully over the President," a foreshadowing of the approaching impeachment proceedings against President Johnson.

Although Walt did not make a practice of trying to use his "influence," he had the previous year secured a pardon for Otis Parker, a postmaster in Monument, Massachusetts, who had been accused of robbing the mails.[13] His niece believed him innocent and through Mrs. Abby Price she had persuaded Whitman to investigate. He had examined the evidence, found that of seven charges he had been convicted on only one, and that a minor one. Whitman reported his findings to the Attorney General, and the pardon resulted. On March 27, 1867, Mrs. Price appealed to Walt again, this time to lobby against a proposed national tax on "ruffles." She supported herself and her family partly by dressmaking, and she was alarmed over the report of this impending tax. Walt promised her that he would lobby against the bill when it came up but warned her not to be hopeful. A year later he was able to write her that ruffles would be exempt, that apparently there had never been any intention to tax them.

On March 28, 1867, Mrs. Whitman wrote that Martha was still in Philadelphia. In fact, so many times during the winter she had been left alone except for Ed and Hattie that they had given her a whistle to blow if anyone tried to break in, but she thought she would be more afraid of the night watchman than of the burglars. Probably there was no danger, she admitted, but the cold winter nights were very dreary, so far from the center of town, on a lonesome hill, and she worried about the danger of fire.[14]

In April O'Connor visited New York to discuss with Raymond the possibility of his taking an editorial position on the *Times*, and he called on Mrs. Whitman, who was charmed by him. He brought back to Walt the news that Jeff had been offered the position of Superintendent of Water Works in St. Louis.[15] Walt immediately wrote Jeff advising him to accept, though he was worried about how Jeff's leaving would affect his mother's domestic arrangements. The consequence was that Martha decided to live with a friend in the country until Jeff could find suitable quarters in St. Louis, and Mrs. Whitman had to give up the house they had been renting. One of Jeff's professional associates, a Mr. Davis, rented the house, and he wanted Mrs. Whitman to vacate promptly.[16] Martha

sold most of her household possessions, and as Mrs. Whitman wrote Walt
on May 3, "spent the money as fast as it came in for clothes to go in the
country."

However, Martha evidently did not stay in the country very long. George
either bought or rented another house and Mrs. Whitman moved in
July,[17] and the following autumn Martha was living next door to her
mother-in-law, and imposing on her as usual: "matt brings all her callers
in here . . . tells them she only sleeps in next door   i think sometimes it is
pretty true." [18] Early in the new year Martha finally joined her husband in
St. Louis, and Mrs. Whitman discovered how much she missed her.[19]

II

While Mrs. Whitman worried about her erratic household and Walt
read in the office library or scribbled by the light of his astral lamp, *Leaves
of Grass* was quietly winning friends for the poet in Great Britain. Of
course, Whitman knew that Conway was working for him, and Walt appreciated his help in spite of his disappointment over the *Fortnightly Review* article the previous autumn, but he was greatly encouraged to learn
that more prominent writers and critics were beginning to take notice of
his poems. Perhaps he would have been even more delighted if he could
have known that two men of his own social class, the very kind he had
hoped from the beginning to impress, had been instrumental in bringing
Leaves of Grass to the attention of the Rossetti circle. The first of these
was James Grindrod, an itinerant book peddler and auctioneer, who later
came to America and fought in the Civil War.[20] Copies of the first edition
that Fowler & Wells had sent to Horsell and Company to sell in London were remaindered to this peddler, and one of the copies that he auc-
tioned off early in 1856 was purchased by Thomas Dixon, a cork cutter in
Sunderland, but an unusual artisan who had founded a School of Art
and a Free Library in his native town and to whom Ruskin was later to
dedicate his *Letters to an English Working Man*. Dixon was so delighted
with his purchase that he shared it with his friend William Bell Scott, a
minor poet of the period, and he in turn sent a copy to William Michael
Rossetti for a Christmas present in 1856.[21] By this circuitous route the
book finally reached the man who was to do most for it and its author in
Great Britain.

Although William Rossetti immediately recognized the originality of
Whitman's poems and sensed their literary value, he did nothing for sev-

eral years except recommend them to his friends. Most of them, however, like his brother Dante Gabriel, could see little in the poems except their crudity. For a decade William Rossetti knew almost nothing about the poet himself, but on April 26, 1866, Horace Scudder, a Boston author and editor, sent him a copy of *Drum-Taps* and O'Connor's pamphlet *The Good Gray Poet*. Though Scudder did not believe a new American poetry could be established "on a reckless disregard of natural laws of rhythm," he thought that "O Captain, My Captain!" expressed the grief "felt by all," and that no one had caught so accurately as Whitman "the most elusive elements of American civilization." [22]

About a year later Rossetti began to think of publishing something on Whitman. On April 30, 1867, he recorded in his diary: "Called on Conway to fetch the edition of Whitman [the 1866–1867 *Leaves of Grass*] which he had offered me. He lent me also the pamphlet (in proofs) which Burroughs has written on W . . ." [23] (In view of Rossetti's subsequent influence in spreading Whitman's fame and reputation, it is interesting that he was almost totally dependent on Whitman's American friends for information and initial enthusiasm.) What Rossetti called Burroughs's pamphlet was his *Notes on Walt Whitman as Poet and Person*, which had been written with considerable help both from O'Connor and from Whitman, O'Connor assisting him with the critical interpretation and Whitman with the biographical details. After failing to find a publisher, Burroughs printed it at his own expense during the following summer. But Rossetti's reading it in proof was to do the poet's cause more good than any influence it had after the book was printed. After he had examined these publications by and about Whitman, Rossetti wrote an article on him and his poetry which the London *Chronicle* printed on July 6, 1867. He called *Leaves of Grass* "incomparably the largest poetic work of our period." Accepting a cue from O'Connor, he declared that Whitman's work "may be expected to stand in a relation to future poetic efforts hardly less typical and monumental than the Homeric poems toward Grecian and epic work, or those of Shakespeare toward English and dramatic."

Conway clipped the article for Burroughs and sent it to him on July 13 with praise for the *Notes* and a good deal of gloating over the favorable turn in Whitman's reception.[24] He was now as ardent a partisan as either Burroughs or O'Connor, and he assured the former, "I am writing weekly for the [New York] 'Tribune,' and you will now and then see some sly mention of what we are interested in." Burroughs himself commented on

August 2, in a letter to his friend Benton, on the reception of his book and the effect of Rossetti's article. In New York City the *Citizen*, the *Leader*, and the *Evening Post* had published friendly reviews, and Rossetti had praised the book in the London *Chronicle*. The *Chronicle* article Burroughs called "magnificent," and said it had had a profound effect. "The editor of the 'Pall Mall Gazette' says 'Leaves of Grass' is the most wonderful work he has ever read, of any country or age. The victory is ours beyond all doubt." [25]

One of the most remarkable aspects of this "victory" and its aftermath was the way in which Whitman and his friends worked together to exploit it. Trowbridge made an effort to find a dealer who would sell *Leaves of Grass* in Boston,[26] and several friends clipped and distributed favorable publicity. But the "cause" was mainly promoted by a kind of "round-robin" correspondence between Whitman-O'Connor-Conway-Rossetti. On July 24 Whitman sent to Conway by a "Mr. Philp" a copy of the latest edition of *Leaves of Grass* and an introduction supposedly written by O'Connor, which he hoped might be used as "copy" for a British edition. The letter read in part:

DEAR FRIEND. I avail myself of an opportunity to send you by the hands of Mr. Philp, just starting for London, a copy of my Poems prepared with care for the printers, with reference to republication in England. The Introduction is written by William O'Connor. All is sent you, so that in case there comes any opening you may have a proper copy of latest date, prepared by me, to publish from. Of course I do not expect you, and would not permit you, to make yourself the job of running around and seeking after a publisher; only, please take charge of the copy—I hereby clothe you with power over it, and should any good chance befall, it is what I should wish a London edition set up from.

Mr. O'Connor has shown me your note of April 30th last to him. I wish to send you, as also to those other friends and well-wishers whom it seems I have in England, my true thanks and love.[27]

In the letter of April 30th, which Whitman said he had seen, Conway reported that he had been present at a conference between the publisher, John Camden Hotten, and Swinburne and Rossetti, at which they had agreed that printing *Leaves of Grass* in England unexpurgated "would bring legal prosecution on any publisher." [28] However, on July 13 Conway wrote Burroughs: "Rossetti tells me he was misquoted by Swinburne in thinking that there was anything in 'Leaves of Grass' that couldn't be published in England." [29] This sounds as though Conway had not been present at the conference and casts doubt on the accuracy of his reports. But of course Burroughs showed Whitman this letter, too, and he therefore knew that discussions with Hotten were going on. Perhaps also he feared that an expurgated edition would be suggested by Rossetti or Hotten, and that was why he wrote the ambiguous instructions to Conway.

On October 12 Conway wrote Whitman that "John Camden Hotten had already contracted with W. M. Rossetti to prepare and edit a volume of selections from your Poems. I found that Hotten is not yet ready to bring out the whole work as we would wish." [30] There was an advantage, Conway pointed out, in having a man so well known as William Rossetti edit the volume. Furthermore, since O'Connor is hardly known at all in England, his introduction would carry little weight (a bit ironical, since Whitman himself had in fact written the introduction), whereas Rossetti's recommendation of the poems would. Although of course Conway did not say so, actually Whitman's introduction, which he so deviously attributed to O'Connor, was wholly unsuited for the use he had intended. Written in the poet's most mannered style, it stressed the unique Americanism of the poems and asserted that, "It possesses, more than any other known book, the magnetism of living flesh & blood, sitting near the reader, & looking & talking." [31] Certainly this was the effect that Whitman most wanted to produce, and for a few readers it had had and was still to have this personal appeal, but for a reader versed in the great literature of another nation, Whitman's best poems were capable of making a universal literary appeal far more important than the illusion that

> This is no book,
> Who touches this, touches a man,
>
> .   .   .   .
> It is I you hold, and who holds you,
> I spring from the pages into your arms . . . [32]

But the literary value of his poems Walt Whitman never understood. As a critic of his own work he was always inept and totally unable to discriminate between his artistic achievements and failures. Even in the biographical sketch of this introduction supposedly written by O'Connor, Whitman was needlessly devious: "By report of an English gentleman and traveler, a believing reader of Walt Whitman, who sought & found him out in America, we have our latest direct account of the poet." [33] Rossetti wondered who this man could be, for it was obvious that Philip, the messenger, had not written it. Here Whitman seemed to be pretending that someone in England, such as Conway, was writing the introduction.

In his letter of October 12 Conway diplomatically asked permission for Rossetti to delete a few words, such as "father-stuff," "onanist," "veneralee," and so on, from the selections he had chosen to include—though Conway did not explain that one of the main principles of Rossetti's selection was to exclude those poems which contained the greatest number of passages likely to offend British readers. Rossetti, Conway reported,[34] was also curious to know the meaning of "Calamus." On November 1 Whitman replied, granting permission "to make verbal changes," and expressing doubt that his 1855 preface was worth reprinting—another example of his inability to recognize his own greatest achievements. Regarding the symbolical term:

"Calamus" is a common word here; it is the very large and aromatic grass, or root, spears three feet high—often called "sweet flag"—grows all over the Northern and Middle States . . . the recherché or ethereal sense, as used in my book, arises probably from it, Calamus presenting the biggest and hardiest kind of spears of grass, and from its fresh, aromatic, pungent bouquet.[35]

On November 17 Rossetti wrote directly to Whitman, thanking him for the liberties granted through Conway. He explained that the words he had seen fit to leave out were all in the 1855 preface. "As for the *poems*, I felt bound not to tamper with their integrity in any the slightest degree, and therefore any of them which appeared to contain matter startling to the length of British ears have been entirely excluded." [36] But then he went on to remark that now since Whitman had given him permission to omit a few words or lines from his poems, he thought perhaps a complete edition of *Leaves of Grass* could be published in England. Before this letter had quite had time to reach Whitman, Rossetti wrote in his diary on November 28 that O'Connor had written of his "great distaste" over the "concession to the outcry against W's indecencies." [37] In view of Whitman's close co-operation with William, we may be sure that he shared this "distaste" for Rossetti's book of selections.

Meanwhile Whitman had received Rossetti's suggestion of an expurgated *Leaves of Grass*, and on December 3 he wrote diplomatically but firmly that the omissions he had consented to were intended only for a book of selections, and he asked that in his introduction Rossetti "make no allusion to me as authorizing, or not prohibiting, &c." If *Leaves of Grass* should be reprinted it must be without any deletions whatever. But before he received this letter, Rossetti wrote again (December 8) that the publisher was interested only in a book of selections, and insisted that the one he was editing was not "an expurgated edition." [38] After receiving Whitman's letter of December 3, Rossetti wrote again on December 16, apologizing for any uneasiness he had caused, and assuring Whitman that of the poems reprinted, he had not altered a single syllable.[39] However, he admitted he had taken the liberty of changing some of the titles. Here the discussion rested, and Rossetti's *Poems of Walt Whitman* was published in February, 1868.[40]

Whitman remained grateful to his British editor for his good intentions —Rossetti had certainly acted with tact and patience—but Walt could not help feeling that his own principles had been compromised, and he was ever afterward unhappy over having consented to the publication of what, after all, was an expurgated book of his poems. He also still regretted not having succeeded in getting "O'Connor's" introduction used. And there were a few other aspects of the edition that probably contributed to his dissatisfaction.

Rossetti's introduction was mainly a reworking of his *Chronicle* article. Though very friendly to the poet, it was reserved and admitted some faults: "he speaks on occasions of gross things in gross, crude, and plain terms"; he uses "absurd or ill-constructed" words; his style is at times "obscure, fragmentary, and agglomerative"; "his self-assertion is boundless." But his virtues fully compensate for these faults: he has "originality and daring"; is "a master of words and sounds"; "the most sonorous poetic voice . . . of actual and prospective democracy"; "one of the huge . . . forces of our time." One of the minor details that probably rankled in Whitman's mind was Rossetti's drawing upon Conway's *Fortnightly Review* article for biography. He called this article, which had so disappointed Walt, "the best sketch that I know of Whitman as an accessible human individual. . . ." He even quoted the story of Conway's having found the poet in Brooklyn lying on the scorching sand, with the thermometer near 100°.

Whether Whitman objected to Rossetti's changing some of his titles, he never indicated. Here the editor's intention was only to shorten and avoid the cumbersomeness of the second edition. On the whole Rossetti exercised good judgment in this first publication of Whitman's poems in England, and as a consequence most of the reviews were favorable. The book actually won Whitman more prestige in Great Britain than he had yet received or was to enjoy for some time in his own country. After the *Poems* were published, Whitman concealed his disappointment and assured Rossetti that he was entirely satisfied.[41] He also encouraged Hotten's attempt to arrange for the sale of this book in America on a royalty basis for him, though this plan failed and the only material reward he ever received was three complimentary copies. However, this edition was a turning point in his career, for it won him the attention and later support of several writers who were to be of great help to him, personally, financially, and as promoters of his fame.

III

During 1867 Whitman also found a new market for his writings in his own country, partly as a result of Rossetti's article in the London *Chronicle* and partly through the intervention of O'Connor and Burroughs. This was the *Galaxy*, a magazine started in New York in the spring of 1866 as a competitor of the *Atlantic Monthly* in Boston and *Lippincott's Magazine* in Philadelphia. The owners and editors, William C. and Francis P. Church, invited a number of authors to contribute, among them William O'Connor, who was known for his abolitionist novel and journalistic writings. When first invited he did not have anything to contribute, but he began urging the Churches to publish Whitman,[42] and he probably influenced their accepting John Burroughs's review of *Drum-Taps*, which they published in December. However, they did not invite Whitman himself to contribute until the summer of 1867, then probably as a result of the publicity given to Rossetti's article. In any case, Walt had already mailed them his poem "A Carol of Harvest for 1867," by August 7, and exactly one month later he thanked the Churches for their check for $60.[43] Although the poem was five *Galaxy* pages in length, this was a good price, a little higher rate, in fact, than Longfellow received from the *Atlantic Monthly*, which was about $10 a page.[44] Whitman and his friends had a right to feel elated. When the poem was printed in the September number, an anonymous critic in the *Nation* was almost impressed by it, but finally decided that it was incoherent, expressed no ideas, and suggested mere emotion.[45] Considering the *Nation*'s previous hostility, this was a mild reaction. Actually, the poem did have an idea, and a good deal of lyric power. It might be called an amplification, or new application, of the theme of one of the *Drum-Taps* poems, "Pensive on Her Dead Gazing, I Heard the Mother of All," in which Nature ("Mother of All") charged the earth to absorb her young men's beautiful bodies and precious blood, and "let not an atom be lost." [46] Now, two years after the survivors of the war had returned to their fruitful pursuits, fertile America was "bathed, choked, swimming in plenty," and the heroes living and dead had been absorbed into the life of the nation.

The Church brothers promptly accepted another poem, "Ethiopia Commenting" (probably the poem later called "Ethiopia Saluting the Colors"), though they did not publish it and Whitman finally withdrew it the following year.[47] However, they encouraged the poet to write a reply to Carlyle's "Shooting Niagara: And After?" The extension of suffrage in England in 1867 had caused the dour Scot to prophesy that the rise of democracy would eventually destroy civilization, and in the course of the essay he savagely attacked American democracy. Horace Greeley reprinted the essay in the New York *Tribune* on August 16, and it aroused vehement protests,[48] with which "the poet of democracy" naturally sympathized.

In September Whitman took his annual vacation, and this gave him a chance, as he confided to O'Connor in a letter dated September 27, to talk over his plans with one of the editors of the *Galaxy*, Francis P. Church, whom he found to be

a sample of a New Yorker, a club man, (he pressingly invited me to a dinner at Atheneum [*sic*] Club—I declined,) young, cordial, refined, &c. He made no very decided impression on me, however—we will see how the acquaintance works & holds out in the future. The indirect & inferential of his tone & words in speaking to me would have satisfied your highest requirements—They evidently meant that in his opinion I was, or was soon to be, "one of the great powers." [49]

Whitman's disapproval of the editor's refinement did not diminish his enthusiasm for the article he had promised to write, and he wrote William that he would likely return to Washington the following Monday, September 30, in order to devote the remaining three weeks of his vacation to finishing it. This plan he carried out, and on October 19 mailed his essay to the *Galaxy*. It was promptly accepted and published in the December number. Whitman had started out to refute Carlyle, but the more closely he examined contemporary American society, the nearer he came to agreeing with its severe critic. He had to admit:

. . . Society, in these States, is canker'd, crude, superstitious, and rotten. . . . Never was there, perhaps, more hollowness at heart than at present . . . here in the United States. . . . The depravity of the business classes of our country is not less than has been supposed, but infinitely greater . . . our New World democracy . . . [despite its] materialistic development . . . is, so far, an almost complete failure in its social aspects. . . .

This was written in the autumn of 1867, during the confusion of "reconstruction" and Andrew Johnson's bitter struggle with Congress, on the very border of what Mark Twain was to name the "Gilded Age" and historians were to call one of the most corrupt periods in American history.

Even the people, Whitman found, were difficult to defend. As he looked around him he saw everywhere low morals, poor health, and bad manners. And yet he stubbornly believed that the mass of people were basically good. His experience in the war had justified this faith, for the "unnamed, unknown rank and file" had shown courage, sacrifice, and borne the "labor of death" in the face of "hopelessness, mismanagement, defeat." He did not resolve this dilemma by resorting to Rousseauism, blaming government and defending the innate goodness of human nature —though he did believe in the latter. Instead he pointed out that Democracy is not so much a political system as a "grand experiment" for the development of individuals. Before the war he had found "primarily thieves and scallawags arranging the nominations to offices, and sometimes filling the offices themselves" (compare "The Eighteenth Presidency!").[50] And now that the war had been fought and the Union preserved, conditions were not much better. Nevertheless, "Political democracy, as it exists and practically works in America, with all its threatening evils, supplies a training-school for making first-class men." Note the stress on *practical* and *working*—"pragmatic" was a word still to be used in America, but Whitman anticipated its basic meaning. He saw democracy not as a dated fact but as a dynamic process of becoming, whereby the society could progressively improve and purify itself; in which individuals were constantly tested, exercised, and stimulated to grow stronger and better in the struggle.

Whitman's language and his thinking were awkward, partly because he was pioneering and partly because he was not naturally facile with logic; but with sustained originality and insight he was exploring problems and presenting empirical answers that actually gave a preview of the main course of American philosophy for the next century, for what was this theory of "Democracy" but the forerunner of William James's "Pluralism" and John Dewey's "Pragmatism"? Whitman's doctrine of "Democracy" was also to be confirmed by a great twentieth century sociologist. After Dr. Gunnar Myrdal from Sweden had explored the Negro problem in the

United States in the late 1940's, he echoed Whitman by declaring that despite the failure of Americans to achieve the ideals which they professed to believe in, hardly any other nation in the world showed so much promise of improvement and future achievements, for "America believes in and aspires to something so much higher than its plane of actual living. The ideals are constantly pressing for their more perfect realization." [51] Whitman not only believed this, but he hoped to build up the pressure and to aid the process of improvement.

But the kind of contemporary society that Whitman described was not likely to understand or appreciate his thinking in "Democracy." And apparently only a few idealists like Bronson Alcott and his most devoted friends did. The *Round Table* called it "Walt Whitman's Utopia." The *Nation* found the article "without form and void." [52] Nevertheless, the editors of the *Galaxy* agreed in February to take a follow-up essay, which Whitman said he would call "Personalism," though they later declined a third, to be called "Literature," or perhaps "Orbic Literature."

At the beginning of the New Year Whitman had good cause for feeling that the tide had really turned. In the fall of 1867 Burroughs was still living on Capitol Hill (though he was building a house on the north edge of the city), and there in an attic room O'Connor finally got busy on a story based on Whitman's character.[53] Writing feverishly far into the night, under the stimulation of strong coffee and tobacco, he managed to finish it by early winter and it was quickly accepted and published in January, 1868, in *Putnam's Magazine*. O'Connor called it "The Carpenter," and presented Whitman in a thinly disguised allegory as a modern Christ, able to perform miracles by his charity and healing personality. It is difficult to account plausibly for O'Connor's intention. Was he trying to start a myth about the poet, or did he actually believe in Whitman to that extent? As fiction the story was certainly mawkishly sentimental, and to many men such homage would have been revolting. But Whitman was devoted to William, and he had not received enough homage to satisfy his craving for recognition or his need for being assured that he was a dynamo of love, which had long been his fondest ambition, personal and literary. Besides, he knew that he had done much good with his magnetic personality, and he had letters from soldiers to prove it.

By early January Burroughs had completed his brick house at 1332 Y Street and moved into it—and the O'Connors also, for they rented rooms from him. There Whitman took breakfast every Sunday morning, as he reported to his mother in a letter dated January 26, 1868. He also wrote her that he "had been applied to by an English magazine *The Broadway* to write something for them—Well I have lately sent them a piece of poetry —if they accept it I shall get pay for it." [54] The poem was "Whispers of Heavenly Death," for which Burroughs said he received fifty dollars in gold, and added, "His stock has gone up immensely." [55]

Distinguished visitors to the United States from the British Isles were also beginning to call on Whitman in Washington, giving him tangible assurance that his fame had spread across the ocean. One of these during the winter of 1867–1868 was the statesman and journalist (later Viscount) John Morley, editor of the *Fortnightly Review*, which had published Conway's article. Morley had "half a dozen saunters through the streets of Washington" with Whitman and "liked the kindly geniality of his ways," though he was not conquered by the poet's "doctrines of art without apparel." [56] Whitman would have liked, of course, to have won approval of his art, but Morley's searching him out half a dozen times for walks and chats was the kind of flattery that he especially appreciated.

Written approval also continued to arrive from across the Atlantic. Hotten was sending Whitman all the reviews and notices of Rossetti's edition of the *Poems* appearing in England. Early in the year he wrote that he had mailed Swinburne's *William Blake*, which he had just published, and when it finally arrived in March Whitman learned that Swinburne had ended his book with a flattering comparison of him and Blake. Among other things Swinburne said:

Whitman has seldom struck a note of thought and speech so just and so profound as Blake has now and then touched upon; but his work is generally more frank and fresh, smelling of sweeter air, and readier to expound or expose its message, than this of the "Prophetic Books." Nor is there among these any poem or passage of equal length so faultless and so noble as his "Voice out of the Sea" ["Out of the Cradle . . ."], or as his dirge over President Lincoln —the most sweet and sonorous nocturne ever chanted in the church of the world. But in breadth of outline and charm of colour, these poems recall the work of Blake; and to neither poet can a higher tribute of honest praise be paid than this.[57]

April was a busy month, with many things to distract as well as interest Whitman. He was hard at work on his third article for the *Galaxy*, while he waited for "Personalism" to appear in the May number, and the editors finally encouraged him to submit the article. By this time there was much talk in Washington about the political conventions to nominate the candidates for the Presidency. But the greatest excitement during March and April was provided by the impeachment proceedings against President Johnson. Attorney General Stanbery resigned on March 12 in order to direct the defense. However, he was ill during most of the trial and William M. Evarts had to take over, and it was he who gave the closing argument. Meanwhile, Orville H. Browning was appointed Attorney General and served until July 15.

While these exciting events were taking place, Bronson Alcott had read "Personalism" and was so pleased with it that he adopted the word to designate his own philosophy.[58] The curious thing is that Whitman was the first person in America to use this term which later became the name of a philosophy teaching that "the ultimate reality of the world is a Divine Person who sustains the universe by a continuous act of creative will." [59] Schleiermacher in Germany had used *Personalismus* in this sense, though it had not yet been used in any of the translations of his essays into English.[60] Immediately after reading Whitman's essay Alcott summarized the doctrine in his *Journal:* "We must grow into and become one with the Person dwelling in every breast, and thus come to apprehend the saying, 'I and my Father are one'—that is, perceive that all souls have a Personal identity with God and abide in him." [61] On April 28 he recorded: "Read 'Personalism' again after day's work. Verily, great grand doctrine, and great grand Walt, grown since I saw him in his Brooklyn garret in 185-. Greater, and grown more open-eyed, as perhaps ourself, since then. Another American beside Thoreau and Emerson." [62] Of course, Walt did not know about the *Journal* entries, but Alcott also wrote an approving letter.[63]

It is by no means certain, however, that Whitman actually intended to use his term in this theological sense. His essay can be so interpreted, but he was more immediately concerned with the practical aspects of the development of well-rounded, healthy personalities in order that a more perfect democracy might be possible. He foresaw that the greatest problem in a democratic society was to provide for the widest individual freedom while at the same time inculcating a sense of collective responsibility and maintaining social integration. He had begun as the poet of individualism, and he had not shifted ground, but he well knew that individualism like Thoreau's could become atomistic and socially destructive. His solution was to eliminate the repressions and frustrations that thwart the natural growth of personality (here he was almost pre-Freudian) and to aid the mind and character in reaching full maturity. Thus, "Produce great persons, the rest follows." He had never had any faith in the value of laws or artificial restraints to reform society. Nor was he so gullible as later sociologists who were to think and teach that moral reforms could be effected automatically by changing the physical environment. Whitman knew that the health of a society depended upon the combined physical and mental health and growth of each individual in it. Yet the conditions favorable to healthy growth must be maintained by group effort. He illustrated this interdependence by the analogy of the separate states and the Union:

This idea of perfect individualism it is indeed that deepest tinges and gives character to the idea of the aggregate. For it is mainly or altogether to serve independent separatism that we favor a strong generalization, consolidation. As it is to give the best vitality and freedom to the rights of the States (every bit as important as the right of Nationality, the union), that we insist on the identity of the Union at all hazards.[64]

Whitman's third essay on "Literature" was essential to the presentation of his philosophy of a true democratic society. Perhaps the inability of many readers of the *Galaxy* to understand or approve the arguments of "Democracy" and "Personalism" influenced the Church brothers to reject the final installment, and Whitman was thus forced to wait until the publication of *Democratic Vistas* two years later to complete his rationale. He had shown in his first essay that the genuinely democratic society had not yet been attained in America, and in his second essay he outlined a theory of education and psychological development to produce human beings who could live democratically. But what practical guides and examples could be used in the nurturing process? Here in his unpublished essay he applied the theory he had propounded in his 1855 preface. The archetypal models could only be provided by literature and the arts. Hence a democratic art must precede and prepare the way for a democratic society. Unlike the later realists, who were to dominate American literature soon after his death, Whitman regarded the function of literature not to report contemporary life objectively but to present an ideal model of what the culture and society should be. In these three essays, with all their stylistic faults, he contributed the most profound thinking on the theory and function of a democratic society that anyone had achieved in America up to that time—and *Democratic Vistas* has retained its vitality to the present day.

IV

May 1, 1868, was moving day in Brooklyn, but Mrs. Whitman was able to stay in the house on Atlantic Avenue without the upheaval she had experienced so many times since coming to Brooklyn twenty-five years before. However, a new family with five children moved in upstairs. She wrote Walt about them on May 5, along with other domestic happenings and her thoughts on the impeachment trial. She found the speeches in the trial too long and tedious to read, but she felt sorry for President Johnson: "poor old man i wonder how he feels   it will be rather sad if he is convicted for all i suppose he hasent done right   i see in the papers if he leaves he will be escorted through the citys. . . ." [65] In a postscript she added: "Mr Lane told george they had raised Jeffs salary to 6000 but i think it must be a mistake."

Two weeks later Mrs. Whitman began writing about Nancy's conduct and begging Walt to help get Andrew's children committed to an orphanage. Nancy's sister-in-law, Jenny Maguire, "tells me awful things of the wreched [*sic*] creature." [66] She had recently given birth to twins: "one is dead and the other is living and the children is sent out to beg by the day." Her brother wanted to have the three children taken away from her and placed in an orphanage. Walt's mother begged him to write to Justice Cornell, asking him to use his power to take the children away from their degraded mother: "she drinks and [does] everything else thats bad." On June 25 she was still urging that the children be rescued from Nancy. She said she could not begin to tell "half the worse that wreched woman does." At the orphanage in Flatbush the children would at least be clothed, fed and kept clean; much better Mrs. Whitman thought, than letting them be sent out in the street to beg and live in filth with their mother.[67] Walt's replies seem to have been lost, and his attitude on the subject is not known. However, apparently nothing was done, and it is possible that Walt did not write to Judge Cornell.

In June Walt's interest was absorbed by political developments and impending changes in the Attorney General's office. On June 7 he asked his mother how she liked the Republican ticket, Grant and Colfax. He confessed that he approved of it, and observed sardonically that Salmon P. Chase was "cutting up, trying to get somebody to nominate him, & doing his best to injure the Republican ticket—He is just the meanest & biggest kind of shyster." [68] Of course, Walt may not have been unprejudiced, in view of Trowbridge's experience in trying to secure an appointment for him in Chase's department during the war.

The summer of 1868 was extremely warm, and Walt suffered more from the heat than he had for several years—partly the result, no doubt, of his increasing hypertension, though he did not know this. On Friday afternoon, July 10, he began a letter which he did not finish until three days later. Each day he began by commenting on the heat, and on the 10th he was resolved not to spend another summer in Washington if he could help it. Both personal and national events were also depressing. The O'Connors had had "quite a falling out with Mrs. Burroughs," whom Walt called "a curious woman," though she had been kind to him.[69] Mrs. O'Connor was seriously ill with dysentery. The Democrats had nominated Seymour and Blair, "a regular old Copperhead Democratic ticket, of the rankest kind." Local Democrats were dissatisfied, though Walt supposed "the old Democrat bummers around New York and Brooklyn" would be pleased.

Despite the weather, which was apparently as bad in Brooklyn as in Washington, George had bought a lot and in July started to build a house.[70] The buying and selling of real estate was now so brisk he had difficulty in employing someone to survey it, and then he worried about having money to pay the workmen. He himself was now working for the city, supervising the laying of water mains. On July 15 Mrs. Whitman gave Walt a report on this and other local matters:

. . . we have got along so far all pretty well considering this awful weather we have had   these rooms is quite cool if there is any air at all but monday night we had to keep shut up all the front part of the house   on sunday there was one of the car horses died and he laid just acrost the street . . . till tuesday and the whole neighborhood was distressed with the smell   the horses drop[ped] from the cars in several rout[e]s . . . georges house is raised   was raised last saturday   three story and cellar with store under . . . walt the [Republican] nomination aint it great   i wish you could see the eagle   it is worse than ever   all the respectable radicals is in favor of Seymore   the eagle says they are nearly all copperheads around here but they are kindy put aback   if chase had only been the one they would have carried everything before them . . .[71]

On the same day that Mrs. Whitman wrote this letter William Maxwell Evarts,[72] who had so ably taken over the defense of President Johnson, was appointed Attorney General. He was a prominent New York lawyer, once known as a "Hunker Whig," though he had supported abolition and appears to have been a man of competence and integrity. But Walt was a bit apprehensive when he wrote his mother on July 17. The new Attorney General had not yet made his appearance, and Walt hoped he would "be as agreeable for a boss as the others have been—but somehow I don't believe he will." [73] Jeff had written that "Mat has some cough yet." She was already suffering from tuberculosis of the lungs, but she—and perhaps her physician—did not know at that time the cause of her persistent cough.

Evarts took over the Attorney General's office early in August, although for the remainder of the summer he let Ashton largely run it.[74] The weather also improved, and since the work at the office was light, Walt was able to spend a considerable amount of time out-of-doors. On August 15 he wrote his mother about a very delightful trip he had taken the day before on a boat to Alexandria and back.[75] Congress was in recess and life in the capital was rather dull. Many clerks in the Treasury and War departments were being dismissed and Walt was depressed over their misfortunes, but he assured his mother that "as far as appears at present, I expect to stay on as usual." [76] Later, on a hot Sunday afternoon, Walt wrote his mother: ". . . I have come around to the office to sit quiet awhile by my big open window—nice old window—I have spent so many quiet comfortable hours by it, I shall be sorry enough when I leave it—I never get tired looking out, there is rivers & hills & gardens & trees—can see ten or twelve miles—& boats sailing."

Whitman was leisurely editing his *Galaxy* articles, including the unpublished essay on "Literature," for book publication. Although the last issue of the 1867 *Leaves of Grass* was only a few months old, he had already prepared "copy" for the next printing: "the new edition of Leaves of Grass is all ready fixed—so I don't bother with it any more." At the end of August Walt described to his mother the eccentric people who had begun to visit him because they had read something about him in the newspapers.[77] Sometimes they wanted his help in securing Government positions. He got rid of them as kindly as he could. But he promised to sit for a Mrs. McKnight who asked to paint his portrait.

On September 7 Walt acknowledged his mother's sending him a newspaper account of the "accidental and sudden death of little Andrew." This was undoubtedly a clipping of the following item in the September 2, 1868, Brooklyn *Eagle*:

A CHILD RUN OVER AND KILLED.—About one o'clock, a little boy, named Andrew Whitman, while playing in Hudson Avenue, near Myrtle, was killed by being run over by a cart driven by Peter Webber. It appears that the children were so much engrossed in play that the deceased ran against the cart, and before the cart could be stopped the wheel passed over the little fellow's head. Webber immediately gave himself up to the Police authorities, and the deceased, who was only five years of age, was taken to the residence of his parents [sic], No. 151 Navy Street. The case will be investigated by the coroner.

Walt's comment was: "poor little child—I believe I have never seen him [he was born a few months after Andrew's death]—it was sad enough—but the poor young one is out of this world of sin and trouble— & I don't know as we have any cause to mourn him." One hardly knows whether to regard this as trite consolation for the boy's grandmother or callous indifference, though of course, considering the kind of woman the mother had become, the child had indeed been delivered from "a world of sin and trouble." Oddly, Mrs. Whitman did not begin renewed agitation to have the remaining children taken away from Nancy.

In the middle of September Walt took his annual vacation. He roomed at Mrs. Price's at 331 East 55th Street, in New York, as he had the previous year, but he spent the greater part of each day with his mother and always took his dinner with her.[78] His letters to Peter Doyle and William O'Connor (the latter largely unpublished) give a very complete account of his experiences and thoughts during this six-weeks-long vacation. Pete was mailing him copies of the Washington Star. On September 25 Walt thanked him for this kindness and reported that he was having printed a new edition of the 1867 Leaves of Grass with Drum-Taps and the Sequel added.[79] But he was mostly enjoying his vacation by spending much time with his mother, riding back and forth across the East River with his old friends who piloted the ferry boats, and sleeping and eating a great deal. Walt assured Pete, "I think of you very often, dearest comrade, and with more calmness than when I was there. I find it first rate to think of you, Pete, and to know that you are there all right and that I shall return and we will be together again." He was sending a copy of the Broadway magazine containing "Whispers of Heavenly Death," the poem for which, according to Burroughs,[80] Whitman had been paid $50. Walt told Pete it would not interest him much, "only as something coming from me." But it was important to the poet, because he planned to write a series, perhaps a book, on the subject of "Heavenly Death." He had treated the theme of death as birth many times before, but for some reason—possibly an intuition of his own physical decline—this subject now appealed to him more strongly than ever.

Of all the young men with whom Whitman corresponded, Peter Doyle's friendship was most lasting and most satisfying. But evidently there were times when he was emotionally disturbed even in his relations with Pete, though just why is not easy to determine. Both Whitman's and Doyle's letters contain allusions whose meanings can only be guessed at by the reader—the outsider—and it is quite easy to guess wrong or jump at conclusions for which there is no actual proof. For instance, why was it possible for Whitman in New York to think of his "dearest comrade . . . with more calmness than when I was there"? And in Peter's letter to Walt on September 27 he sent this message from one of the streetcar men: "Jim Sorrill sends his love & best respects, & says he is alive and kicking but the most thing he dont understand is that young Lady that said you make such a good bed fellow." [81] This obviously alludes to some private joke in one of Walt's letters that has not been preserved. It could refer to some actual experience Walt had had with a woman, or to some slight incident that had been exaggerated for the sake of the joke. The very fact that Pete and Jim Sorrill evidently enjoyed the joke hugely may indicate that Walt had made what seemed to them a preposterous insinuation.

Whitman's friendship with Doyle was almost entirely affectional. On one level of the relationship Peter was a substitute son, and while separated from him the older man planned for him and worried about his health as a mother might have. For intellectual companionship and mutual interest in promoting the reputation of Leaves of Grass, Whitman turned to O'Connor. Someone had recently brought to their attention an article on Whitman and his poems that Ferdinand Freiligrath had published in the Augsburg Allgemeinen Zeitung the previous spring. Freiligrath had written it while living in exile in Great Britain, where he had seen the articles by Conway and Rossetti and the edition of the selected Poems of Walt Whitman.[82] Both Whitman and O'Connor were eager to learn Freiligrath's address in order that they might send him other publications and thus, perhaps, encourage him to translate Leaves of Grass into German. O'Connor managed to get hold of Freiligrath's address in Cologne, to which he supposedly had returned, and Whitman wrote to William on September 27 that he would make up a package on his return to Washington[83]—which he did.[84]

In the same letter Whitman also reported on the surprising effect that

Swinburne's comparison of himself and Blake had had on his old friend
John Swinton, the managing editor of the New York *Times*:

I had quite an interview *tete-a-tete* with John Swinton a few nights ago. He is
much more deeply impressed with *Leaves of Grass* than I had supposed—said
that the more he read it, the more it impresst him with the meanness & super-
ficiality of all current literature & journalism—went on in a strain that would
have answered your and John Burroughs's extremest demands, &c.
    Swinton has lately been posting himself about William Blake his poems, has
the new London edition on W.B. in two vols. He, Swinton, gives me rather
new information in one respect—says that the formal resemblance between
several pieces of Blake, & my pieces is so marked that he, S. has with persons
that partially know me, passed them off temporarily for mine, & read them
aloud as such. He asked me pointedly whether I had not met with Blake's
productions in my youth, &c—said that Swinburne's idea of resemblance &c
was not so wild, after all. Quite funny isn't it? [85]

The talk with John Swinton also resulted in his insertion of a generous "puff" of Whitman and his work in the *Times* a few days later. On
October 1, 1868, the following notice, obviously either written by the poet
himself or paraphrased from notes supplied by him, was printed on the
editorial page:

With the bright, crispy Autumn weather, WALT WHITMAN again makes his
appearance on the sidewalks of Broadway. His large, massive personality,—his
grave and prophetic, yet free and manly, appearance,—his *insouciance* of manner and movement,—his easy and negligent, yet clean and wholesome dress,—
go to make up a figure and an individuality that attracts the attention and interest of every passer-by. . . .

The editorial then called attention to the growth of Whitman's reputation
abroad. Rossetti had classed him with Homer and "one or two other great
poetic geniuses of the world." Freiligrath was translating *Leaves of Grass*
—an exaggeration. The editorial ended by announcing the forthcoming
publication of a "small work" in prose, "Democratic Vistas."
    Besides riding on the ferries and omnibuses and the horse cars, Whit-
man also derived an immense amount of pleasure from the political rallies in New York. He was now a staunch Republican and the Democrats
were putting on the biggest shows in the city, but he enjoyed their spectacles anyway. On October 6 he wrote Peter Doyle that he had witnessed
"the greatest political show I ever saw even in New York—a grand Democratic meeting and torch light procession."

As I was on my way home in a 2nd Avenue car between 12 and 1 o'clock we got blocked in by a great part of the returning procession. Of course we had to just stand and take it. I enjoyed it hugely from the front platform. They were nearly an hour passing us, streaming both sides. In the procession were all sorts of objects, models of ships forty or fifty feet long, full manned, cars of liberty with women, etc., etc. The ranks spread across the street, and everybody carried a blazing torch. Fireworks were going off in every direction. The sky was full of big balloons letting off rockets and Roman candles 'way up among the stars. The excitement, the rush, and the endless torches gave me great pleasure. Ever and anon the cannon, some near some distant. I heard them long after I got to bed. . . .[86]

Three days later Walt wrote that he was having "about 225 copies of Leaves of Grass bound up, to supply orders." He was planning to have a "new and improved edition set up and stereotyped in Washington during the coming winter"—probably the edition that he had written his mother earlier was all ready for the printer. A few days later he wrote Pete again that he had had about 230 copies of his book "finished up and bound"— probably the final count—but "there is a hitch about the sale and I shall not be able to sell them at present." He did not say who had stopped the sale; no court order is known to have been issued. Perhaps the dealers had refused to carry the book in their shops, for he added:

There is a pretty strong enmity here toward me and *L. of G.* among certain classes—not only that it is a great mess of crazy talk and hard words all tangled up, without sense or meaning (which, by the way, is, I believe, your judgment about it)—but others sincerely think that it is a bad book, improper, and ought to be denounced and put down, and its author along with it. There are some venomous but laughable squibs occasionally in the papers. One said that I had received 25 guineas for a piece in an English magazine, but that it was worth all that for any one to read it. Another, the *World* said: "Walt Whitman was in town yesterday carrying the blue cotton umbrella of the future" (it had been a drizzly forenoon)—so they go it. When they get off a good squib however I laugh at it just as much as anyone.[87]

The October *North American Review* also contained some comments that left Whitman feeling that the opposition of leading American critics to him had not been seriously dented by the favorable British criticism.[88] Two years before in reviewing W. D. Howells's *Venetian Life* Lowell had praised it for being "as perfectly natural" as Whitman's style was "perfectly artificial." And now in reviewing the *Poems* of John James Piatt, Howells's Ohio friend, Lowell returned to his contrast, making at the same time an onslaught against the theory of nationalism which he himself had advocated twenty years earlier,[89] but had since renounced. "One of the dreams of our earlier horoscope-mongers was, that a poet should come out of the West, fashioned on a scale somewhat proportioned to our geographical pretensions." Lowell called this "a cheap vision . . . Life in its large sense, and not as it is temporarily modified by manners or politics, is the only subject of the poet. . . ." It did not matter whether the setting was India or Minnesota. Dante's "theme was Man, and the vision that inspired him was of an Italy that never was nor could be, his political theories as abstract as those of Plato or Spinoza." Whitman's theme was also man, and in his best poems, as even, too, in "Democracy" and "Personalism," his vision was likewise as abstract as Plato's or Spinoza's. But Lowell could not see the poetry for the man posturing in front of it, and indeed Whitman himself was never to realize that when he was truly inspired, as in his great elegy, he was impersonal, timeless, universal.

On October 15 Whitman interrupted his New York vacation for a week's visit to Providence, Rhode Island. Thomas Davis, a manufacturer and former member of Congress whom Whitman had known in Washington, invited him, and the fact that the poet's old friends Dr. and Mrs. William F. Channing were also living there made the invitation doubly attractive. As a further inducement William O'Connor, who was recuperating from a recent illness, was spending his vacation in Providence, and he encouraged Walt to come.[90] Two days after his arrival Walt wrote: "Pete, your old man is in clover." The Davises lived in "a sort of castle built of stone, on fine grounds, a mile and a half from the town," and the Channings also had an orchard, a vineyard, and pleasant surburban scenery. "At both places I stop we have plenty of ripe fresh fruit and lots of flowers. Pete, I could now send you a bouquet every morning far better than I used to—of much choicer flowers." (This last remark is another interesting revelation of Whitman's curious relationship with Doyle.)

It is quite a change here from my associations and surroundings either in Washington or New York. Evenings and meal times I find myself thrown amidst a mild, pleasant society, really intellectual, composed largely of educated women, some young, some not so young, everything refined and polite, *not* disposed to small talk, conversing in earnest on profound subjects, but with a moderate rather slow tone and in a kind of conciliatory manner—delighting in this sort of conversation and spending their evenings till late, in it. I take a hand in, for a change, I find it entertaining, as I say, for novelty's sake, for a week or two—but I know very well that would be enough for me. It is all first-rate, good and and smart but too constrained and bookish for a free old hawk like me.[91]

With the exception of the Samuel Longfellow gatherings in Brooklyn some fifteen years earlier at which he had felt ill at ease and said little,[92] Whitman had had little experience in drawing-room conversation. At times Eldridge, Trowbridge, and O'Connor had found him capable of holding up his end of an animated discussion, but these talks had taken place in small intimate groups, and at least at O'Connor's there had been no emphasis on salon manners. In this account written for the uneducated horse-car conductor Whitman's social inferiority, dimly realized and half resented, is quite apparent. And from such a description it is easier to understand the over-compensation which often led to the deliberate crudity of the "free old hawk." Even the myth of the barbaric yawp was part of the over-compensation, and often a falsification of a man instinctively and innately refined but accidentally unfamiliar with the superficial habits of polite society.

Whitman spent a week in Providence and obviously enjoyed it very much. The fact that he was an honored guest, mildly lionized, prevented his sense of social inferiority from being so conscious as to be painful. On October 18 he was so exhilarated that he bragged with elaborate facetiousness about his flirtations and conquests among the women, for he was, he confided to Pete, "at the present time mainly in the midst of female women, some of them young and jolly." [93] But he was glad to return to New York on October 22. Martha and her two children had arrived from St. Louis the very day he had left for Providence,[94] and of course he wanted to see them again before his leave was up on the following Monday, October 26. Walt considered asking for an extension so that he could vote in Brooklyn, but a Democrat whom he knew and trusted agreed to "pair" with him. This left him no excuse for not returning to the capital on schedule, thus ending his six weeks of vacation.

V

Walt apparently did not return to Washington with much enthusiasm, and perhaps there were several reasons. He was probably already beginning to experience vague symptoms of the illness that would afflict him within a few months. The incoming President was expected to appoint a new Attorney General, and this prospect made Whitman wonder about his own tenure. Then, despite his increasing reputation abroad and the loyalty of a few friends in America, the last issue of *Leaves of Grass*, with *Drum-Taps* and the *Sequel* added, did not seem likely to win a more favorable reception than the preceding editions had received. And on top of everything else the news from Brooklyn was depressing.

On November 11 Mrs. Whitman wrote that Mat had a bad throat and was under a physician's care; nevertheless, she talked so incessantly, thus aggravating her affliction, that her mother-in-law dreaded to see anyone come in.[95] Hannah, too, had an infected thumb and Heyde wrote frequent reports of her condition, though Mrs. Whitman thought it was "pretty hard to tell how she is by his letters." Furthermore, George was leaving Brooklyn for Camden, New Jersey, where he had been offered a position as inspector of pipes in a foundry. He still paid his mother's rent, and occasionally gave her $10 when she asked for it, but she hated to ask and she found it increasingly difficult to understand how he could have changed from the generous, carefree person he had been before and during the war. She was sure he was interested in some woman and agreed that he might have uses for his money she did not know about. Jeff and his wife also had grown more selfish and thoughtless: "so Walt you see folks changes and Walter i think you and your old mother is about as reliable and good as you can find." A week later she wrote:

. . . as to Jeff he is I suppose on his way to Brooklyn   will be here probably on saturday or sunday   I am glad he is coming   poor Jeff i feel sorry for him and sorry for matty and sorry for myself   i have my hands full i will assure you Walter dear   I feel sometimes almost done out then I get recreuited [96]

On his recent vacation in New York Walt had become acquainted with a young man named Jack Flood, who, like Peter Doyle, worked on a streetcar. Two or three weeks after Walt's return Jack wrote him, apparently just such a letter as Lewy Brown or Pete might have written, and on November 22 Walt replied in a letter that plainly indicated his present boredom:

You speak of coming here and paying me a visit. Dear boy, I hope you will come truly, for it would be a great comfort to me if we could be together again. I don't know whether it would be very pleasant to you here, Jack, for this is a stupid place compared to New York—but we would have each other's society, and that would be first rate.

There's not much excitement in Washington—at least none that I take any interest in. Politics and politicians carry the day here—but I meddle with them very little. In a couple of weeks more, Congress will meet, and then the city will be quite lively.[97]

Two days later Walt wrote his mother that he would be glad when Grant took office and appointed a new Attorney General; there was little possibility, he thought, for "Mr. Evarts remaining here after Grant comes in." [98] To Martha Walt sent word to "keep up good spirits—I have no doubt she will get all right again." He wanted to know what George had done about the Portland Avenue house. As for himself, he was being kept very busy in the office.

Despite his boredom Whitman continued to work at his literary plans. On November 30 he asked Emerson to do him a favor:

DEAR MR. EMERSON: On the eve of sending the enclosed piece abroad I have taken a notion to first offer it to the Atlantic and, if not too great a liberty, to solicit your services for that purpose. I would be obliged if you would take it in to Mr. Fields the first time you go to Boston. If available at all, I propose it for the February number of the magazine. The price is one hundred dollars; and thirty copies of the number in which it may be printed. Of course Mr. F. may read this letter.

I shall require an answer from Mr. Fields within a week from the time of the reception of the piece.

I scrupulously reserve the right to print the piece in the future in my book.[99]

Evidently Emerson took the poem to Boston immediately after receiving it, for three days later (December 5, 1868) Fields replied that, "Mr. Emerson has handed me the poem which you offer to the Atlantic Monthly; which I shall gladly publish in our February number, and enclose herewith, check for one hundred dollars, the sum named in your letter to Mr. Emerson." [100]

The poem was "Proud Music of the Storm," probably one of the compositions Whitman had worked on during his long vacation in New York. Although it occupied more than four pages in the February, 1869, *Atlantic Monthly*, nevertheless it would seem that Fields paid a good price for it, and the promptness with which both he and Emerson carried out Whitman's requests certainly indicated flattering respect for the poet. And his luck in England held. On December 17 Whitman wrote to John Morley, offering him a shorter poem, "Thou Vast Rondure, Swimming in Space" (later incorporated into "Passage to India" as Section 6), for four pounds, or $20.[101] This too was promptly accepted for publication in the April number of the *Fortnightly Review*—though for some reason it was never printed.

Meanwhile, Mrs. Whitman's letters did not become more cheerful. Hannah finally had to have her thumb amputated, and her mother worried more than ever about her and wished she could be taken away from her irascible husband, who had written a very ill-tempered letter about Walt, apparently because he had suggested that she should come home.[102] By this time Martha had decided that Brooklyn did not agree with her and she returned to St. Louis with Jeff and her children. Probably Mrs. Whitman had encouraged her to make this decision, for about the middle of December she wrote Walt about how much trouble they had given her:

o Walt haint i had a seige   they pretended to live up stairs but the provisions was prepared down   well Walter dear i have lived through it but some things i have thought rather hard of   they have never paid a cent of rent nor a cent of gass bill nor give me a dollar when they went away   they gave me an allapacca dress when they first came and Jeff bought me a little mite of a castor   that is all . . . and matty borrowed 50 dollars of george but Jeffy dident settle it   they had plenty of money . . . but let everything go but i would ask more than [$]100 to go through the same again   burn this letter[103]

Christmas came and went without anything of significance happening, and Walt found January, 1869, dreary and depressing except for his knowledge that the two prominent magazines were soon to publish his poems. The editor of the Washington *Star* was friendly to him, and he had begun to submit little squibs or short articles about himself and his poems which the *Star* printed from time to time.[104] On January 18, probably just before the February *Atlantic Monthly* was on the Washington news stands, the *Star* ran a comment on Whitman's recognition "by the literary set in Boston," evidenced by the publication of a poem of his in the February *Atlantic.* "Between *Blackwood's* and the *Atlantic* he is now pretty well endorsed on both continents—a circumstance that may be gratifying to his friends, but which, we suspect, matters very little to him." Whitman's conniving to get these notices inserted completely belied his pretended indifference, but this was part of the myth he was now striving to build up about himself as a poetic personality.

Yet despite his justifiable pride over his appearance in the *Atlantic* and his forthcoming appearance in the *Fortnightly Review* in England (or so he still thought), Walt was not feeling well at the time. On February 2 he wrote his mother that he was still troubled with a severe cold in his head: "I suppose it is that which causes me to have these bad spells, dizziness in the head—I have them a great deal lately, sometimes three or four in an hour." [105] These were more dangerous symptoms than he realized—almost certainly the result of increasing hypertension. Fortunately, at this time his work in the office had slackened, perhaps as a result of the uncertainty over the next Attorney General. The following day he commented in an addition to his letter: "Great excitement here among the politicians—Cant [*sic*] tell you who will be the new Attorney General under Grant—but don't think Mr. Evarts will continue on—still I don't know."

Mrs. Whitman had rejoiced over Grant's election, but as the time for the inauguration drew nearer she did not feel so confident about him: "you remember Walt i always said if Grant got to be president i hoped he wouldent disappoint his party but i dont know   i hope he wont but i suppose time will tell." [106] On March 4 she mused on the "stirring time, today at Washington." Just before going out of office President Johnson had pardoned a great many people and Mrs. Whitman thought perhaps "the old codger" had pardoned many who "ought not to have been." Walt himself took little interest in the inaugural ceremony. Of course it lacked the excitement and suspense of 1865, when he had written a vivid account for his mother, but by this time he was also weary and a bit jaded with life in the capital.

Although George was now working in Camden, he was trying to build a house on Portland Avenue and probably made frequent trips back and forth to Brooklyn to supervise the construction. On March 15 Mrs. Whitman asked Walt if he could lend George $600 until May to pay the plasterers[107]—why George himself did not make the request is not apparent. The workmen refused to apply the final coat until they were paid for the whole job, and George had been unable to borrow the money. Jeff was paying $200 a month as his share in the investment, but he could not advance more money or step up his payments. It is safe to assume that Walt sent the money, though the evidence seems not to have survived. Whether justifiably or not, Mrs. Whitman thought George extravagant. She said he was "saving enough" toward her, "but these gals and amusements takes the greenbacks." [108]

To judge by her letters, Mrs. Whitman had not worried for some time about her son in the institution for the insane at Flatlands, but on April 7 she wrote Walt about an encounter Eddie had had with Henry Rome (one of the printing family), who had escaped from the same hospital where Jesse was confined:

. . . two or three weeks ago edd was down town and encountered henry rome he talked a great deal about Jess   said it was too damned bad to keep him there   that he henry had broke out and got away   he is evidently deranged   i dident know but what he would induce Jess to leave and come with him but i dont know as they can get away very easy   i dont know what i should doo if such should happen   they must have much trouble with henry   smith told George he came running up the street the other day without hat or coat or shoes . . .[109]

But the spring of 1869 was not all worry and vexation for Mrs. Whitman. In April Walt sent her a generous money order, probably as an Easter present, and she bought "lots of things" for herself, including a new bonnet, "not quite so fashionable as the eagle advertises," but one that satisfied her.[110]

VI

With the spring weather Walt's spirits also rose, as they usually did at that time of year—to such an extent, in fact, that he began to think of printing a new edition of *Leaves of Grass* during the coming summer. And these plans led to a renewed desire for favorable publicity. By this time he had won the friendship of a second Washington editor, Alexander H. Shephard, of the *Chronicle*.[111] On May 9, 1869, this paper ran a long article on Whitman which anyone familiar with his vocabulary, style, and ideas of himself as poet and personality will immediately recognize as emanating from his own pen. It began with a reference to Whitman's approaching fiftieth birthday, and assured his friends in New York, Brooklyn, and elsewhere that "on the verge of becoming half a centenarian, he retains his accustomed health, eats his rations regularly, and keeps his weight well toward 190 pounds." The value of his poetry was still being hotly debated, but "a late German critic . . . characterizes him as 'the most radically *Christian* and *Socratic* poet of any modern writer.'" The article stated that the author of *Leaves of Grass* still considered his poems unfinished, but expected to publish "a final digest and edition" next summer, with special emphasis on "religious themes." Then followed a description of Whitman's employment under five Attorney Generals, his personal appearance and "magnetism," his indifference to the slanders and misrepresentations that had been circulated about him, and ended with instructions to the reader on where to find the best photographs of the poet; Gardiner, on Seventh Street was said to have a "capital photo," and

Messrs. Seybold and Tarisse, "on the Avenue, below Sixth, have a good head, just taken, very strong in shade and light."

In view of the fact that Whitman had printed his last issue of a revised edition of *Leaves of Grass* scarcely more than six months previously, it may seem strange that he was now eager to print still another edition during the summer of 1869. But the article in the Washington *Chronicle* indicates clearly that he was planning to do so—and perhaps would have if sickness had not prevented. This article also gives valuable clues as to the nature of the edition planned and the new personal and literary desires which Whitman was trying to satisfy. To some extent "religious themes" had been used in all previous editions of the *Leaves*, but for several months Whitman had been wishing to specialize in them. He had obviously had this desire before he had known about Freiligrath's review, but the German poet's finding in his poems (to use Whitman's summary of Freiligrath's interpretation)[112] "a treatment of the whole material frame of things . . . as but the gateway, through death and decay, to spiritual existence" evidently strengthened and intensified his ambition to write a whole collection of poems on life, death, and immortality. The poem which the *Atlantic Monthly* had published the preceding February was one contribution toward this new collection.

Actually "Proud Music of the Sea-Storm" ("Sea-" later omitted in the title) was not based entirely on a new theme, for what the poet was seeking was a "clew" to the meaning of physical existence, and this had been the theme of several previous poems, notably "Out of the Cradle Endlessly Rocking," in which he had even used a symbolical sea-storm. However, in the "Cradle" poem Whitman had explored the psychological origins of his poetic faculty as well as the cycle of life-death-resurrection, and now he was no longer concerned with the origin but with the ultimate use of his poetic gifts. "Proud Music" was not really, therefore, a reworking of old materials.

Like another earlier poem, "The Sleepers," the "Proud Music of the Sea-Storm," is almost medieval in its allegory, for it is a symbolical dream, from which the poet awakes and adds a *coda*. Although it has some visual imagery, it is primarily a symphony of sounds, though not a pure *tone-poem* because the allegory predominates. The many sounds made by the storm signify the seemingly chaotic experiences of life, "Blending with Nature's rhythms, all the tongues of the nations . . ."

The "Almighty Leader" of the orchestra of Nature signals with his baton and all the living instruments blend into a harmony of symphonic music. Once more, as in "Crossing Brooklyn Ferry," the poet becomes a time-binder:

> Now airs antique and mediaeval fill me!
> I see and hear old harpers with their harps, at Welsh festivals;
> I hear the minnesingers, and their lays of love,
> I hear the ministrels, gleemen, troubadours, of the feudal ages.

He hears the folk tunes of all nations, then the great operas and the voice of Alboni, "Sister of the loftiest gods . . ." He hears the Hebrew lyres, the Egyptian harp, the Hindu flutes, and the sacred music floating out of the cathedrals of Europe. In his trance he prays to the muse to fill him "with all the voices of the universe." Then, waking from his trance, he says to his "silent, curious Soul,"

> Come, for I have found the clew I sought so long,
> Let us go forth refresh'd amid the day,
> Cheerfully tallying life, walking the world, the real,
> Nourish'd henceforth by our celestial dream.

He tells his Soul that what she has heard was not the sounds of nature or of history, but

> . . . a new rhythmus fitted for thee,
> Poems, vaguely wafted in night air, uncaught, unwritten,
> Which, let us go forth in the bold day, and write.

This summary emphasizes the philosophical inconclusiveness of the poem. The poem does not answer the riddle of existence—except to suggest that a Divine conductor leads the orchestra. But this is only a prelude, a promise of compositions to come, in which the rededicated poet will attempt (as in 1871 he rephrased the next to the last line quoted above) "Poems bridging the way from Life to Death . . ." Thus the real subject of this poem turns out to be Whitman's announcement of his future poetic program.

The other poem accepted for publication, "Thou Vast Rondure, Swimming in Space," was completed late in 1868 and was to have appeared in the April, 1869, *Fortnightly Review*.[113] However, in subject matter and time of composition it is a companion piece to "Proud Music of the Sea-Storm" and should be examined here. It supplements the intention announced in the *Atlantic Monthly* poem and climaxes it, because here the poet attains his most lofty conception of his function and destiny as a poet. It now seems to him that his thoughts begin to span the "Vast Rondure, swimming in space,/ Cover'd all over with visible power and beauty"; and to understand the answer to the questions, "*Wherefore unsatisfied soul? and, Whither O mocking life?*"

Ah, who shall soothe these feverish children?
Who justify these restless explorations?
Who speak the secret of impassive Earth?
Who bind it to us? What is this separate Nature, so unnatural?
What is this Earth, to our affections? (unloving earth, without a throb to answer ours,
Cold earth, the place of graves.)

Yet soul, be sure the first intent [God's purpose] remains—and shall be carried out;
(Perhaps even now the time has arrived.)

After the seas are all cross'd, (as they seem already cross'd,)
After the great captains and engineers have accomplish'd their work,
After the noble inventors—after the scientists, the chemist, the geologist, ethnologist,
Finally shall come the Poet worthy that name;
The true Son of God shall come, singing his songs.

Then, not your deeds only, O voyagers, O scientists and inventors, shall be justified,
All these hearts, as of fretted children, shall be sooth'd,
All affection shall be fully responded to—the secret shall be told;
All these separations and gaps shall be taken up, and hook'd and link'd together;
The whole Earth—this cold, impassive, voiceless Earth, shall be completely justified;
Trinitas divine shall be gloriously accomplish'd and compacted by the true Son of God, the poet,
(He shall indeed pass the straits and conquer the mountains,
He shall double the Cape of Good Hope to some purpose;)
Nature and Man shall be disjoin'd and diffused no more,
The true Son of God shall absolutely fuse them.

To paraphrase, the poet "worthy that name" (whether Walt Whitman or his successor) shall be able to teach mankind—and lead it to accept— the proper application of the discoveries and inventions of the scientists and engineers. Only he shall have the power to heal the breach between man and nature and link all people into a loving confederation. A lofty vision indeed! Fatuous visionary, many would say, for how could a poet accomplish what the Son of God of the New Testament had not accomplished in nearly two thousand years? But the solution of both sons of God was the same—love. And the mind of man has never been able to conceive of a better solution, or cause him to accept and apply it. It should be noticed, too, that Whitman, despite his almost incredibly exalted conception of the function of the poet, was not setting himself up as a Messiah (though O'Connor seemed willing to go that far). This "true Son of God, the poet," need not compete with any churches or religions which teach that love can save mankind from destruction, and indeed he could support and reinforce their efforts. Perhaps Whitman's esthetic theory was vague, but he plainly believed that the poet's esthetic intuition and creations could have, ultimately, profound religious influence, in the deepest sense of religion and ethics.

The "Rondure" poem was to become Section 6 (later numbered 5) of one of Whitman's greatest compositions, "Passage to India," but the chronology of the parts of the "Passage" is difficult if not impossible to determine. The fact that Section 6 had been completed in December, 1868, possibly indicates that it preceded Whitman's larger plan (or may even have suggested it), because two of the three historical events that he was to celebrate in "Passage to India" did not take place until 1869. One of these was the completion of the Suez Canal. Although this engineering feat had been in progress for several years, water did not begin to flow into the canal from the Mediterranean until February, 1869, and not from the Red Sea until July; and the canal did not become navigable until the following October. The second event, the joining of the Union Pacific and the Central Pacific railroads at Promontory Point, Utah, took place on May 10, 1869. On that day Leland Stanford drove the last spike, made of California gold, and the electric telegraph (itself still a marvel) clicked the sound of the strokes of the hammer for all the nation to hear. Of course, the newspapers made a great display of the ceremony. The third event celebrated in the poem, the completion of the Atlantic cable, had taken place a decade earlier—and Whitman had commented excitedly on it in his editorials in the Brooklyn *Times*.

These dates of the completion of the Suez Canal and the American railroads suggest that Whitman's whole conception of his poem did not form until at least May, and possibly later in 1869. But he had already clearly perceived the need for balancing the great engineering and mechanical achievements of his age by a humane use of them. He saw in them the possibility of a social millennium, but he fully realized, as he said in *Democratic Vistas*—which he had prepared for publication in the summer of 1868—that this prospect was still shrouded in the hazy distance of the future. With his poetic vision he had only glimpsed an ideal vista, but a grand and inspiring one.

VII

Information about Whitman's life during June and July, 1869, is scanty, but whether this is because he was too busy working on his manuscripts to write many letters, or because he was unwell, is not apparent. His mother's letters do not show any apprehension regarding his health. Mrs. Whitman herself seemed to be feeling spryer than usual, and as critical of her daughter-in-law as ever. On June 23 she reported that Burroughs and a friend of his had called on her the day before. The house was in order, and she had a clean cap on, and they did not put her "aback in the least." [114] They talked of Walt, admired his picture, and everyone enjoyed the visit, but they were only able to stay an hour. This pleasant account given, Walt's mother then got down to her present feelings about Mat and Jeff. Mat had recently sent her two twenty-five-cent bills. Considering all that she had done for them she thought she "would not be indebted if they was to send me considerable," and fifty cents seemed almost insulting. Jeff, however, had loaned George $3,000 for which he apparently held mortgages. The transactions were very involved and Mrs. Whitman told Walt he might have to read her description several times to understand it. George had rented a house at 101 Portland Avenue for his mother and her references to him in her letters to Walt indicate that he was more often in Brooklyn than in Camden; apparently he was not yet working steadily in Camden. [115]

In August Walt obtained a month's leave and on the 18th he made a night trip to New York. Probably he had not been feeling well before leaving Washington, for the day after his arrival he became quite ill. He had left Peter Doyle in a morbid state of mind because of a painful eruption on his face, which a friend of Walt's, Dr. Charles Bowen, an Army physician, had diagnosed as "barber's itch" and had treated by lancing and cauterizing with nitrate of silver. [116] On August 21 Walt wrote from Brooklyn. He had had a pleasant trip home, but during the past three days he had been "prostrated and deadly weak." The weather had been extremely hot, but Walt had now begun to feel better, and his thoughts turned to Doyle:

Dear Pete, you must forgive me for being so cold the last day and evening. I was unspeakably shocked and repelled from you by that talk and proposition of yours—you know what—there by the fountain. It seemed indeed to me (for I will talk out plain to you, dearest comrade) that the one I loved, and who had always been so manly and sensible, was gone, and a fool and intentional suicide stood in his place. I spoke so sternly and cutting. (Though I see now that my words might have appeared to have a certain other meaning, which I didn't dream of—insulting to you, never for one moment in my thoughts.) But will say no more of this—for I know such thoughts must have come when you was not yourself but in a moment of derangement,—and have passed away like a bad dream. Dearest boy I have not a doubt but you will get well and entirely well . . .[117]

Walt assured Pete, "if you are not well when I come back I will get a good room or two in some quiet place, and we will live together and devote ourselves altogether to the job of curing you, and making you stronger and healthier than ever." Walt could go on working in the Attorney General's office, and they could send Pete's mother some money every week. He told Pete he was sending him some money by Adams Express, "and when it is gone you shall have some more, for I have plenty." Walt ended his letter by sending his love to "Johnny Lee, my dear darling boy." Although at this time Peter Doyle was Whitman's most beloved male friend, it should be noticed that the poet habitually used terms of endearment to other men, especially young men of the working class such as Johnny Lee, for whom he evidently felt a vicarious paternalism. His love was not exclusive. His affection for Doyle spread out to embrace all his friends too, who were mostly firemen and streetcar men.

The hot weather of August 19–21 aggravated Walt's physical debility, but it was evidently not the sole cause of his illness. In his present condition he envied George's vigor, as he confessed in a letter to O'Connor: "My brother George is remarkably well & robust this summer—he was out in all the excessive heat of the three latter days of last week, & came home every evening to his supper, unflagging, & full of strength & fun—I quite envied and admired him—especially as I felt deathly weak—indeed despicable. . . ."[118]

The first week of September was cool, dry, and pleasant in Brooklyn, but Walt's health did not improve as rapidly as he had hoped. On September 3 he wrote Pete, "I have those spells again, worse, last longer, sick enough, come sudden, dizzy and sudden sweat." [119] The doctor called it "hospital malaria, hospital poison absorbed in the system years ago"—a diagnosis that Whitman was to believe until the end of his life. Yet for some reason the Brooklyn doctor thought his patient was better off in Washington. After a few days Walt began to feel well enough to take a few rides on Broadway, which seemed to him to look finer, gayer, and more crowded than ever. But he did not feel like indulging in any of his other favorite amusements, such as attending the theater or going to Coney Island. However, on September 10 he had almost recovered his old enthusiasm for the city.[120] On this day the flags were at half-mast in honor of the funeral for General John Rawlins, recently Secretary of War under President Grant. Walt was feeling so much better, and so enjoyed the spectacle and mass excitement of any kind, that in his letter to Pete he seemed to regard the occasion as a festival: "All along Broadway hundreds of rich flags and streamers at half-mast . . . From the tall buildings they waved out in a stiff west wind all across Broadway—late in the afternoon I rode up from the Battery to look at them,—as the sun struck through them—I thought I had never seen anything so curious and beautiful. On all the shipping, ferry boats, public buildings, etc., flags at half-mast too. This is the style here. No black drapery for mourning . . ."

By mid-September Whitman was back in Washington, and the weather was hot and humid, but apparently he did not suffer a relapse of his sick spells. Actually, reliable details of his life are extremely meager, though doubtless he continued to take Sunday breakfasts with the Burroughs, to visit the O'Connors, and to work leisurely on his manuscripts. He evidently gave satisfaction in the Attorney General's office, for there are no indications that he ever had any difficulties with Hoar, the current Attorney General. Presumably Peter Doyle's face had healed, and Walt no longer worried about him.

Before Whitman went to Brooklyn, O'Connor had shown him a letter from William Rossetti accompanied by copies of some very flattering critical appreciations of his poems written by an anonymous English woman, identified only as a "wife and mother." [121] Since she was deeply responsive to the personal appeal that Whitman had always hoped to make to his readers, these extracts should have pleased him immensely; and probably they would have if he had not already been quite unwell and suffering from the tropical heat in the capital. But his actions indicate that for several months he forgot about his unidentified admirer. Perhaps at the

time not even the usually alert O'Connor fully realized the value of Rossetti's enclosures. But some time during the autumn he made copies for
Walt, and after re-reading them early in December the poet suddenly
awoke to the prize that had been dropped into his lap. On December 9,
1869, he wrote to Rossetti, intending his letter as much for the unknown
woman as for him, and in a separate package sent a photograph of himself to be passed on to her.[122] He said he was "deeply touched by these
sympathies and convictions, coming from a woman and from England,
and am sure that if the lady knew how much comfort it has been for me
to get them, she would not only pardon you for transmitting them to Mr.
O'Connor but approve that action. . . ."[123] He added that he planned
to print "new editions" of his works (that is, *Leaves of Grass* and *Democratic Vistas*) in the coming spring, and, "I shall forward you early copies." He ended by saying, "I want you to loan this letter to the lady, or
if she wishes it, give it to her to keep."

At this time Whitman had no intimations of romantic longings concealed in these appreciative criticisms of his poems, and he could hardly
have dreamed that by sending his photograph and suggesting that his letter be passed on to her he was encouraging this unknown admirer to fall
passionately in love with him—to respond literally to the appeal he had
made at the end of the 1860 edition. Yet such was the case. The woman
whose identity Rossetti had so discreetly shielded was Mrs. Anne Gilchrist, widow of the late biographer of William Blake, Alexander Gilchrist.
In fact, she had finished the Blake biography after her husband's unexpected death in 1860 and rightfully won for herself a reputation in literature and the friendship of some of England's great men of letters, the
Rossettis, Carlyle, Swinburne, Tennyson, and others.

The previous June she had written to William Rossetti that while calling on Madox Brown he had "put into my hands your edition of Walt
Whitman's Poems. I shall not cease to thank him for that. Since I have
had it, I can read no other book; it holds me entirely spell-bound, and I go
through it again and again with deepening delight and wonder."[124] To this
Rossetti replied: "Your letter has given me keen pleasure this morning.
That glorious man Whitman will one day be known as one of the greatest
sons of Earth, a few steps below Shakespeare on the throne of immortality." And he added: "Anybody who values Whitman as you do ought to
read the whole of him. . . . My own quite complete copy is already lent
out; but I have the unbound copy wh. Whitman himself sent over for
possible English publication, with his own last corrections—also the sep-

arate original editions." [125] Thus it came about that Mrs. Gilchrist first read the unexpurgated *Leaves* in the copy that Whitman had prepared for the printer with his own hands—and by this time such personal associations with the poems were becoming increasingly dear to her.

On July 11, Mrs. Gilchrist thanked Rossetti for making Whitman's complete poems available to her and gave him an account of her response to the book:

I had not dreamed that words could cease to be words, and become electric streams like these. I do assure you that, strong as I am, I feel sometimes as if I had not bodily strength to read many of these poems. In the series headed "Calamus," for instance, in some of the "Songs of Parting," the "Voice out of the Sea," the poem beginning "Tears, Tears," &c., there is such a weight of emotion, such a tension of the heart, that mine refuses to beat under it,—stands quite still,—and I am obliged to lay the book down for a while. [126]

Rossetti thought such critical interpretation as this too good not to be published, but he was afraid that Mrs. Gilchrist might expose herself to embarrassing publicity in the British press and the ridicule of people who knew her if she printed her true thoughts about Whitman's poems in England under her own name. Besides, he judged that such an article as she was able to write might do more good in America, and he also wished that Whitman himself could read her words; hence his sending copies of her letters to O'Connor. [127] He knew that O'Connor would show them to Whitman, and he hoped that the ardent friend of the poet would be able to suggest a way of publishing this criticism in America. Despite Whitman's silence for several months, Rossetti continued to encourage Mrs. Gilchrist to rework her letters into an article suitable for publication, and she had completed it by early fall. Rossetti then meticulously copied this essay in his own hand so that no one could identify the author from the handwriting, and this manuscript he finally sent to O'Connor late in November. It is improbable that Whitman could have seen it before he wrote his letter to Rossetti on December 9. [128]

Later in the month Rossetti, and through him Mrs. Gilchrist, received news of Whitman through W. J. Stillman, an American painter and art critic who had visited Rossetti in England. Writing on December 17, 1869, he declared:

I have just seen Whitman—had a ride with him in the horse-car up Pennsylvania Avenue (if you are any wiser for that), and a long talk principally about you, whose history (as far as I know it) and that of your family I gave him. He is employed in the Attorney-General's Office, and seems more well-to-do than when I saw him before. He is certainly a man of remarkable personal qualities—full and harmonious life. . . . He is grey as a badger—white, I should say. . . .[129]

Perhaps an improvement in Whitman's dress had led Stillman to think he was "more well-to-do" than formerly. Actually he was living much as he had been for several years. Another British visitor, the journalist and member of Parliament, Justin McCarthy, looked Whitman up in the winter of 1870, and he later gave a more detailed description of the conditions under which the American poet was living at this time. He found him "lodged in a room like a garret up several flights of stairs in a thickly populated building." [130] He had been told by some that the poet lived on the barest necessities, while others said he "went in for being a penniless poet" and acted the role. As he stood in Whitman's room for the first time, McCarthy hardly knew which interpretation to believe. "There was the humble bed, there was the poor washstand, there were the two or three rickety chairs, there was the shelf with the cut loaf of bread, there was the staggery writing-desk, and there were leaves of paper strewn over the desk and table." But then he looked into the poet's eyes, and, "If ever sincerity and candour shone from the face of a man, these qualities shone from the face of Walt Whitman. There was an unmistakable dignity about the man despite his poor garb and his utterly careless way of life."

Whitman asked his guest about English life and literary men. "He found good-natured fault with some of the friends who had gone too far, as he thought, in sounding his praises throughout England; and he altogether disclaimed the idea that he considered himself as a man with a grand mission to open a new era for the poetry of his country. He claimed no mission, he said, and he had only written poems because they came into his mind, and he wrote them in the form which they had worn when they presented themselves to his imagination. . . . I am not certain whether we should have talked of his poems or poetry at all if I had not directly brought up the subject and made it clear to him that I was anxious to hear something from his lips about it."

Whitman's modestly disclaiming his mission as a prophet and herald of a new epoch in American literature is rather surprising, but this might have been either Mr. McCarthy's own deduction or the role that Whitman at the moment happened to be in the mood to play. It is possible, too, that by this time he had begun to doubt his ability to fulfill his prophecy in the 1855 preface of the poet who was to inaugurate a new literature. In *Democratic Vistas*, soon to be published in book form, he still called for such a poet, or at least such a revitalized democratic literature, but he did not himself lay claim to any accomplishment of his ideal.

McCarthy might have been able to understand why Whitman lived the way he did if he could have known the many uses that the poet had for his money. As a third-class clerk (top-classification, to which Whitman had been promoted in 1866) he drew a salary of $1600 a year, on which he had to pay a small income tax. Although he occasionally sold a poem at a good price, it is doubtful that he broke even on the editions of *Leaves of Grass* that he continued to print at his own expense. Even so, if he had had only himself to support, he might have lived fairly comfortably on his modest salary. But his mother and Eddie were constantly in need of more income than George provided, and Jeff no longer contributed anything to his mother's living expenses. How much Walt gave away to others it is not possible to estimate, but he certainly helped Peter Doyle when he was sick or unemployed, and probably a few ex-soldiers and workingmen down on their luck.

On March 21, 1870, the authorities at Kings County Lunatic Asylum notified Walt that Jesse had died and was being buried in a potter's field.[131] Whether this was the day of the death is not clear. Perhaps Walt would have provided a funeral for his oldest brother if he had known in time, but this is only conjecture. Since the notice was sent to Walt in Washington, the only relative listed on Jesse's record, Mrs. Whitman did not know of the death of her oldest son until Walt wrote her. She replied pathetically on March 24, evidently immediately after receiving the news:

o Walt aint it sad to think the poor soul hadent a friend near him in his last moments   and to think he had a paupers grave   i know it makes no difference but if he could have been buried decently . . . i was thinking of him more lately than common   i wish Walter you would write to Jeff and hanna that he is dead   i will write to george   i feel very sad of course Walt if he has done ever so wrong he was my first born   but gods will be done   good bie Walter dear[132]

Four days later she asked Walt if the doctor had not said anything about how long Jesse was ill before he died, and on April 5 she was still wishing that "the doctor would write something about the poor unfortunate's death." She thought "it would be some consolation to hear." Presumably Walt inquired, but what the answer was, if any, is not on record.

Several weeks later Walt was cheered by the publication of Mrs. Gilchrist's article in the Boston *Radical*, a magazine edited and supported by the New England Transcendentalists. It appeared anonymously in the May number as "A Woman's Estimate of Walt Whitman." [133] The article was a complete justification of the poems in their totality—form, vocabulary, subject matter, ideas, emotions, effect, and so on. "I see that no counting of syllables will reveal the mechanism of the music. . . . But I know that the music is there. . . ." One of the poet's great sources of "vitalizing power . . . is the grasp laid upon the present." He shows that "there is nothing so great" as being capable of happiness. The "Children of Adam" poems do not trouble her in the least:

It was needed that this silence, this evil spell, should for once be broken, and the daylight let in, that the dark cloud underlying might be scattered to the winds. It was needed that one who could here indicate for us "the path between reality and the soul" should speak. That is what these beautiful, despised poems, the "Children of Adam," do, read by the light that glows out of the rest of the volume: light of a clear, strong faith in God, of an unfathomably deep and tender love for humanity—light shed out of a soul that is "possessed of itself."

This was a vindication on Whitman's own grounds, and more imaginatively expressed than his own defense in the open letter to Emerson in the second edition, or any of the self-written reviews in which he had struggled to rationalize his inclusion of physiological functions in his poems. But it was not the first time that a woman had attempted to defend Whitman's poetic use of sex. The two women contributors to the *Saturday Press* in the summer of 1860, one of them possibly Mrs. Juliette Beach, had used similar arguments and expressed as strong faith in the "sanity" and "purity" of these controversial poems.[134] Nevertheless, such eloquence as this from so impassioned a writer across the ocean seemed to Whitman and his loyal circle of friends to be a major victory for him and for *Leaves of Grass*.

VIII

Good fortune, however, seldom comes unalloyed. In May Whitman unluckily cut his thumb, and it became infected. Unable to perform his secretarial duties, he secured a two-weeks leave. On May 11, unable to hold a pen, he dictated a letter to O'Connor from Brooklyn, in which he said:

"My hand has been pretty bad, but looks more encouraging to-day. I don't think there is anything very serious, but it has caused me much suffering, since I have been here." [135] On June 1, after his return to Washington, his mother wrote that she felt "quite down hearted to hear your thumb is so bad yet." She could hardly bear not hearing from him, but she realized how difficult it was for him to write. Yet she begged him not to get discouraged, "for it certainly will get well." [136]

Of course his mother was right, but even after Walt was well enough to return to work he was still not happy. On or about June 17 he had been analyzing himself, was dissatisfied with his life for some time past, and he recorded these resolutions in his notebook:

cheating, childish abandonment of myself, fancying what does not really exist in another, but is all the time in myself alone—utterly deluded & cheated by *myself*, & my own weakness—REMEMBER WHERE I AM MOST WEAK, & most lacking. Yet always preserve a kind spirit & demeanor to 16. But PURSUE HER NO MORE.

A cool, gentle, (*less demonstrative*) *more* UNIFORM DEMEANOR—give to poor —help any,—be indulgent to the criminal & silly & to low persons generally & the ignorant—but SAY little—make no explanations—*give no confidences*—never attempt puns, or plays upon words, or utter sarcastic comments, or, (under ordinary circumstances) hold any discussions or arguments.
June 17   good! July 15[137]

Evidently his mind was still on this subject when he reread this resolution and pronounced it "good!" Probably work was slack on that hot Friday afternoon, July 15, because in his depressed state of mind Whitman probed further into his conscience and came to some very emphatic resolutions. The Franco-Prussian War had just begun, but his thoughts were mainly on himself:

It is IMPERATIVE, that I obviate & remove myself (& my orbit) *at all hazards* from this *incessant enormous* & PERTURBATION

Congress adjourned in great excitement   War is said to be declared in Europe   2½ P.M.——I am writing in the office, not feeling very well——opprest with the heat   July 15——1870

TO GIVE UP ABSOLUTELY & *for good, from this present hour,* this FEVERISH, FLUCTUATING, *useless undignified pursuit of 164——too long, (much too long)* persevered in, ——so humiliating——*It must come at last* & had better come now——(*It cannot possibly be a success*)   LET THERE FROM THIS HOUR BE NO FALTERING, NO GETTING————————————*at all henceforth,* (NOT ONCE, *under any circumstances*)——*avoid seeing her, or meeting her, or any talk or explanations*——*or* ANY MEETING WHATEVER, FROM THIS HOUR FORTH, FOR LIFE.

July 15, '70.[138]

Many biographers and critics have attempted to decipher the mysterious numbers "16" and "164" and have advanced theories about the love affair that Whitman had resolved to end immediately and irrevocably. It was about six years earlier that Whitman had told Mrs. O'Connor about the woman for whom he had written "Out of the Rolling Ocean the Crowd," and even then the events of which he spoke could have taken place still earlier. Of course, it is quite possible that Whitman could have been carrying on an affair with a woman about whom Mrs. O'Connor knew nothing. But if anyone in 1870 knew about it, Peter Doyle surely would have. In 1895 he told two of Whitman's literary executors, "I never knew a case of Walt's being bothered up by a woman." [139] However, if Doyle had possessed such knowledge he might have withheld it after Whitman's death, especially if he suspected his statements would be published. Yet this testimony is corroborated by another witness in just as good a position to know and under the circumstances that practically guarantee his candor. Writing confidentially to John Burroughs in 1896, Charles W. Eldridge said, "As you are aware, for ten or twelve years I was about as intimate with Walt as anybody ever was, and . . . there was nothing in his conduct which from a large and generous standpoint was discreditable to him. His relations with women, so far as I had any knowledge of them, were always noble and on the highest plane." [140]

Yet on July 15, 1870, Whitman was feverishly agitated about some experience, or relationship, which his judgment told him to end promptly and firmly. One critic has attempted to interpret "164" as a phrenological symbol standing for "Hope," which in some phrenological charts was personified as a woman.[141] Hope in this sense would have meant expectation of financial or professional success; with Whitman most probably literary success. But the extremely personal implications of Whitman's notations make it difficult for us to accept this abstract interpretation. Furthermore, there is no supporting evidence that Whitman's literary ambitions had abated in the slightest degree. And he had never pursued mere financial success; had, indeed, many times passed up opportunities to gain economic reward—though naturally he wanted a competence for himself and his mother and Eddie.

There remains the possibility that Whitman cautiously reversed the sex of the third-person pronouns in these notations to guard against a chance reader's understanding their implications. One critic has privately suggested[142] that Whitman did this and used a code familiar to every elementary school child, in which letters of the alphabet are simply numbered from 1 to 26. Thus 16 would stand for P and 4 for D. One objection to this theory is that Whitman did not break off his friendship with Peter Doyle. But, on the other hand, in the same notebook, following the passage quoted, Whitman wrote: "Depress the adhesive nature/ It is in excess—making life a torment/ All this diseased, feverish disproportionate *adhesiveness*." There can be no doubt that "adhesiveness," used over and over again in Whitman's writings, was a phrenological term for male-friendship ("manly love" Whitman often called it) or affection for a man as distinguished from "amativeness," or heterosexual attraction. Incidentally, even if Whitman had been indulging in a heterosexual affair, his "adhesive" nature might have interfered with his enjoyment of it, so that it could not "possibly be a success."

One more quotation may throw some light on these strange notebook passages. Whitman left Washington a little over a week after his notebook analyses of himself, and from Brooklyn he wrote to Peter Doyle on July 30:

DEAR PETE. Well here I am home again with my mother, writing to you from Brooklyn once more. We parted there, you know, at the corner of 7th St., Tuesday night. Pete there was something in that hour from 10 to 11 o'clock (parting though it was) that has left me pleasure and comfort for good—I never dreamed that you made so much of having me with you, nor that you could feel so downcast at losing me. I foolishly thought it was all on the other side. But all I will say further on the subject is, I now see clearly, that was all wrong.[143]

To recapitulate, on July 15 Whitman felt (as he had many times in his "Calamus" poems, his letters to Tom Sawyer, and so on) that he was "fancying what does not really exist in another, but is all the time in myself alone . . ." On July 26, an hour before leaving Washington, he was pleasantly surprised to discover his affection for Peter Doyle was reciprocated, though after three and a half years of knowing him Walt had "foolishly thought it was all on the other side." Incidentally, whatever the psychologist may think of this abnormally strong affection of the two men for each other, these dates make actual perversion seem unlikely. Incipiently the relationship may have been a dangerous one, but it does not appear actually to have been so. Many years later John Addington Symonds, whose own emotions gave him special insight into such relationships, placed a sinister construction on this friendship, to the horror and consternation of Charles Eldridge as shown in the same letter to Burroughs quoted above.

Had it been a physical rather than a psychological relationship, Whitman might not have been so torn by doubt and desire to end his self-deception as he had been on July 15, 1870. His "adhesive nature" had long made his "life a torment," but he struggled to "depress" it. The important fact is not his affection for men like Lewis Brown, Thomas Sawyer, and Peter Doyle, but his struggle for self-control and self-understanding. Out of that struggle had sprung many of his poems, and even some of his profoundest insights into human nature, such as love as the solvent of all social evils.

This observation also leads to another which has been neglected by the biographers and critics, and one that actually has more bearing on *Leaves of Grass* than any of the theories about the meaning of "164." Following Whitman's notation dated July 15, '70, he jotted down an "Outline sketch of a superb calm character":

his emotions &c are complete in himself irrespective (indifferent) of whether his love, friendship, &c are returned, or not

He grows, blooms, like some perfect tree or flower, in Nature, whether viewed by admiring eyes, or in some wild or wood entirely unknown

His analogy the earth complete in itself enfolding in itself all processes of growth effusing life and power for hidden purposes.[144]

After Whitman's self-instructions regarding "adhesiveness" he also wrote, apparently as an ideal: "Merlin strong & wise & beautiful at 100 years old." What he obviously wanted to do was so to order and control his life that he could become a Merlin. He realized only too well that he was not "complete in himself," but he intended to cultivate such inner repose that outwardly he would become an example of strength, wisdom, and beauty. This was really no new or sudden ambition with him; he had certainly had it as early as 1855, though he obviously did not feel in 1870 that he had yet become the strong poet-leader adumbrated in his 1855 preface.

In an undated manuscript entitled "The idea of reconciliation," he had outlined the kind of personality he wished to acquire:

The idea of personality, that which belongs to each person as himself, or herself, and that you [that is, anyone] may so heighten your personality by temperance, by a clean and powerful physique, by chastity [N.B.], by elevating the mind through lofty discussions and meditations and themes, and by self-esteem and divine love, that you can hardly go into a room—or along the street, but an atmosphere of command and fascination shall exhale out of you upon all you meet—[145]

This was probably written earlier than 1870, but Whitman still wished to exhale such an "atmosphere of command [that is, influence] and fascination" both in personality conveyed to the reader of his poems and in his physical presence that everyone he met in body or in print would find his life forever afterward charged and enriched. And it was not an idle dream, for an increasing number of readers were experiencing this rapport with the poet; from this time henceforth nearly everyone who met him in person and later wrote about him praised his impressive repose and his magnetic charm. In fact, many had become convinced that as between the man and *Leaves of Grass*, it was the man who was the greater success and the more inspiring to know. His more ardent admirers came to think that this remarkable personality was innately and instinctively calm, poised, and happy, but these secret notebooks tell another story and a more dramatic one: for Walt Whitman the struggle to acquire the strength, wisdom, and beauty of Merlin was a continuous and heroic battle with himself.

IX

Before leaving Washington on July 27, 1870, Whitman had made arrangements with John Rowland to substitute for him,[146] of course with the consent of the Attorney General, and this permitted him to take an extended leave. Aside from wishing to escape from the capital heat, he had planned to print a new edition of *Leaves of Grass*, along with paper-bound editions of *Democratic Vistas* and *Passage to India* to be issued as publications of J. S. Redfield of New York.[147]

During his ten-weeks leave Whitman's life and habits were much the same as they had been on other occasions when he had printed his books in New York and stayed with his mother in Brooklyn. Except for Eddie she was alone now, since Jeff and his family were in St. Louis and George in Camden; so it was not necessary for Walt to board with Mrs. Price. He spent four or five hours each day in reading proofs, then indulged in his usual amusements in New York and on the water surrounding Long Island.[148] On August 4 he wrote Pete about watching the yachts practice for the race scheduled to begin the following Monday. He thought the *America* "the handsomest little craft" he had ever laid eyes on. "I also saw Henry Ward Beecher and had some talk with him—I find myself going with the pilots muchly—there are several that were little boys, now grown up, and remember me well—fine hearty fellows—always around the water —sons of old pilots—they make much of me, and of course I am willing." [149]

The nation was experiencing a financial slump in the summer of 1870, and Peter Doyle worried about unemployment. Once he was suspended by the streetcar company for some infraction of the rules, and at least once Walt sent him money and promised more any time Pete needed it. Walt followed closely all the war news. At first he had sympathized with the Prussians, and on September 6 he still thought "Louis Napoleon . . . the meanest scoundrel (with all his smartness) that ever sat on a throne." [150] But a week later he had changed his mind: "I find myself now far more for the *French* than I ever was for the Prussians." Peter was nominally a Catholic, but not a very devout one. Walt promised to take his first drink with him after his return, "in celebration of the pegging out of the Pope and all his gang of Cardinals and priests—and entry of Victor Emmanuel into Rome, and making it the capital of the great independent Italian nation." [151]

On September 29 New York City had planned an impressive memorial funeral for Admiral Farragut, but the thousands who turned out to see the spectacle—and of course Walt was right there—got "soaked with rain and covered with mud." Walt saw "one crack battalion, all so spruce and handsome, with white pants, and silver gray coats, and everything so bright and trim when they marched down—and an hour and a half afterwards, they looked like draggled roosters that had been pumped on . . ." [152]

Before he left New York on October 15 Whitman had engaged his binder to finish two or three hundred copies of *Leaves of Grass*, without the "Passage to India" annex, thus giving Redfield a chance to sell that separately. By the time he left, or soon after, *Democratic Vistas* was also ready for distribution. About three weeks later (October 19, 1870) John Swinton wrote:

DEAR WALT—I delivered the book to Mr. [Whitelaw] Reid for the Tribune [he was managing editor]—and had some considerable talk with him about a review article. I was afraid of [George] Ripley [regular critic for the *Tribune*] but Reid confirmed my impression that Greeley is or has been favorable, and he agreed to speak to Greeley, and see what could be done in the premises. The conversation was exhaustive—that is to say, I exhausted the powers I for the time being possessed—and the upshot was the rather limited result above mentioned. In any event, if the matter goes to Ripley it will have gone to him by a friendly line.

I read the Vistas—not in the morning but at night. There are very good and striking ideas, with plenty of opportunity for difference of opinion and criticism.[153]

This letter does not state whether "the book" was the new *Leaves of Grass* or *Democratic Vistas*—perhaps the latter, since that is what Swinton commented on. Apparently, too, the "friendly line" did not sufficiently impress Ripley. But he was not an exception among the critics. There seemed to be almost a conspiracy of silence regarding Whitman's three latest publications. To some extent this is understandable so far as the *Leaves* was concerned, for despite much shifting around and regrouping of the poems, the first issue of the fifth edition was superior to the fourth edition mainly in the printing and format. But *Passage to India* deserved serious critical attention. To fill this little booklet of 120 pages Whitman had pulled out many short poems from *Leaves of Grass*, including his finest lyrics on death, but his title poem was one of the best he had written, and revealed, to anyone willing to read it attentively, very considerable intellectual and spiritual growth.

Around "Thou Vast Rondure, Swimming in Space," now placed in the center of the "Passage to India" poem, Whitman had skillfully constructed a philosophical lyric (perhaps better called an "ode") on a Miltonic theme—no less than justifying the ways of God to man. But it differed from *Paradise Lost* not only in length but also in conveying a more optimistic theology than Milton's Puritan predestination. Whitman's subject was not the fall of man but the human soul's triumph over Time, Space, and Death. The poem was truly cosmic in range of ideas and imagery, but lyric in form and structure.

Whitman was less concerned with celebrating the engineering feats which had linked the world and the peoples of the world together by physical means of transportation and communication than with the meaning of these achievements. That they might eventually result in an age of greater tyranny and barbarism he never for a moment considered. Rather he saw in them an unfolding of God's beneficent plan.

> Passage to India!
> Lo, soul! seest thou not God's purpose from the first?
> The earth to be spann'd, connected by net-work,
> The people to become brothers and sisters,
> The races, neighbors, to marry and be given in marriage,
> The oceans to be cross'd, the distant brought near,
> The lands to be welded together.
>
> (A worship new, I sing;
> You captains, voyagers, explorers, yours!
> You engineers! you architects, machinists, yours!
> You, not for trade or transportation only,
> But in God's name, and for thy sake, O soul.)

The poet's concept of "soul" is not easy to define; but it seems to include: the faculty of thought; the psyche or the unconscious, from which rises the poet's conscious imagery; and a belief in the survival or immortality of some sort of mental faculty—though the last may be only a poetic personification of the infinite character of mind as compared to the finite character of matter. Perhaps a good analogy would be Emerson's "Over-Soul," except for the fact that the Over-Soul was impersonal, whereas Whitman believed in the personality of God and the human personality as a fragment of God's personality.

The poet of *Leaves of Grass* had always been fascinated with the idea of the present as only "a growth out of the past" (Section 1), and in "Song of Myself" he had taken space- and time-annihilating flights with his fancy. This new subject gave him new opportunities for such flights, with dramatic contrasts between the physical achievements and the spiritual possibilities. Thus on his mental screen he projects the images of physical space which the engineers have conquered, the deserts, mountains, and oceans across which the trains and ships and telegraphic dispatches race with marvelous speed. Then before his inner eye rise visions of the great explorers of oceans and continents, who shall be followed by the greater explorer, the poet, who shall be able to discover the moral and spiritual laws for the use of the lands which the other explorers have claimed in the name of temporal kings and earthly powers. Next, projecting his intuition into the future, the poet evokes the millennium, when not only the continents shall be spanned and joined by physical means, but all peoples of the globe shall likewise be linked together by love and understanding.

Yet not even this is the end of the journey. "India" is not only a continent, the historical cradle of humanity and of religion and of all great dreams for the race; it is also a symbol of spirituality and the ultimate meaning of existence. At last the poet and his soul "take ship . . . on trackless seas . . . on waves of ecstasy to sail . . . singing our song of God . . ." Here Whitman's "Calamus" emotions and poetic motifs find a sublime application and resolution:

(O pensive soul of me! O thirst unsatisfied! waitest not there?
Waitest not haply for us, somewhere there, the Comrade perfect?)
Thou pulse! thou motive of the stars, suns, systems,
That, circling, move in order, safe, harmonious,
Athwart the shapeless vastnesses of space!
How should I think—how breathe a single breath—how speak—if, out of myself,
I could not launch, to those, superior universes?

The physical man shrivels "at the thought of God,"

At Nature, and its wonders, Time and Space and Death . . .

But then he turns to his soul, "thou actual Me,"

And lo! thou gently masterest the orbs,
Thou matest Time, smilest content at Death,
And fillest, swellest full, the vastnesses of Space.

There are no "perturbations" in this poem; "adhesiveness" is not mentioned or alluded to. The poet has truly found a companion in God, who (at least so far as the poem reveals) is completely satisfying; it is the ultimate reconciliation.

The poet asks his "soul" if her wings are "plumed indeed for such far flights." The soul never speaks in the poem, but the poet has abiding confidence in her power, and he is anxious to hoist anchor. It is highly significant that now in his fantasy Whitman sails boldly away from the land. In his earlier poems the imagery had always been of the sea-shore, the poet standing near the shore hearing or seeing the ocean.[154] But now he no longer walks along the shore and muses on the mystery of the beyond. He boldly sets forth on the unknown seas; he embraces, absorbs, becomes a part of the mystery.

X

Whitman was never again to experience so exalted a mood as "Passage to India" reveals. For him this was the absolute summit of his poetic life, and the time was near when he would begin the descent which he had anticipated not long before his appointment to a government clerkship. Throughout the winter of 1870–1871 his American reputation seemed to be in a decline also, despite the fact that his new editions were on sale in New York, Boston, Philadelphia, and Washington.[155] He was not under the sharp attacks to which he had several times been subjected after the distribution of a new edition; he was simply, for the most part, ignored in America.

In England and Europe, however, his fame was growing—as well as active opposition to him. Some of this he knew about through the letters of Rossetti and Conway, but most of it he did not know until later. He had perhaps learned that Adolf Strodtmann had included some translations of his poems, made under the encouragement of Freiligrath, in his *Amerikanische Antologie* in 1870. Of course, he could not have known that these translations would be almost entirely ignored in Germany.

But in the spring of 1871 Whitman received what was perhaps the most exciting recognition he had yet known when Swinburne addressed a long poem, or ode, to him in *Songs before Sunrise*. It was called "To Walt Whitman in America," and began:

> Send but a song oversea for us,
>   Heart of their hearts who are free,
> Heart of their singer, to be for us
>   More than our singing can be;
> Ours, in the tempest at error,
> With no light but the twilight of terror;
>   Send us a song oversea!
>
> Sweet-smelling of pine-leaves and grasses,
>   And blown as a tree through and through
> With the winds of the keen mountain-passes,
>   And tender as sun-smitten dew;

Sharp-tongued as the winter that shakes
The wastes of your limitless lakes,
  Wide-eyed as the sea-line's blue.

O strong-winged soul with prophetic
  Lips hot with the bloodbeats of song,
With tremor of heartstrings magnetic,
  With thoughts as thunders in throng,
With consonant ardors of chords
That pierce men's souls as with swords
  And hale them hearing along.

Whitman probably took this for more complete approval of his poetry
than Swinburne intended, for he apparently thought it was an absolute
endorsement, whereas Swinburne only used him as a symbol of democracy and freedom to contrast with decadent tyranny-ridden Europe.

Chains are here, and a prison,
  Kings, and subjects, and shame.
If the God upon you be arisen,
  How should our songs be the same?
How, in confusion of change,
How shall we sing, in a strange
  Land, songs praising his name?

This was not to be the last time that Whitman would be used in Europe for social and political propaganda, but the very fact that Swinburne's stereotyped conception of Europe as decadent and America as
youth and vigor so closely corresponded to the stereotype that Whitman
had inherited from the "Young America" [156] movement and had accepted
uncritically, led him to think that this radical young Englishman had
thoroughly understood him. In fact, this attitude that an English poet
was handicapped and must perforce sing a more constrained song than
the poet in the land of youth and freedom would almost inevitably have
to be renounced if Swinburne continued trying to be a poet. Possibly
Adah Menken, who looked upon Whitman as a sort of New Messiah,
may also have recently influenced Swinburne to see in Whitman a
prophet of the new social order.[157]

Yet despite this pleasing encouragement, Whitman did not immediately send his 1870 edition to Rossetti and the woman who had written
the Boston *Radical* article. If there was any reason other than procrastina-
tion for the delay, it may have been that he was waiting to have a special

edition of the *Leaves* bound up with "Passage to India" included as an annex. He probably made arrangements for such an edition (which seems to have been very small) during the vacation that he took the latter part of June and continued until August 1, 1871.[158] On August 28 Rossetti wrote Mrs. Gilchrist that Whitman was sending him a package with a double set of his recent publications and photographs,[159] one set and photograph evidently intended for her.

Meanwhile Edward Dowden, Professor of English Literature at the University of Dublin, had finally succeeded in publishing his article on "The Poetry of Democracy: Walt Whitman," in the July number of the *Westminster Review*, one of the same British magazines that Whitman had read and reviewed so often in the Brooklyn *Times* two decades earlier. It had taken Dowden over a year to get this article in print, during which time the manuscript had gone the rounds of the British reviews.[160] *Macmillan's* had rejected it because the editor would have nothing to do with Walt Whitman. Other editors said, "God save us from Whitmanism." The *Contemporary Review* accepted it and set it up in type, and then decided not to publish it. Possibly Whitman saw these rejected proof sheets, because on February 1, 1870, Dowden asked Rossetti for the poet's address, saying that he wanted him to have the article. While in Brooklyn, Whitman may have received a copy of the *Westminster Review* in which the article finally appeared, and if so, it provided one of the few excitements of this visit. His vacation in 1871 was unusually quiet and uneventful because his mother was ill.[161] Walt nursed her himself, and was thankful that he could stay with her, but as a consequence he did not see so much of New York or his old friends in either city as he had on former trips.

Soon after his return from his Brooklyn vacation, Whitman received an invitation that for a few weeks exhilarated him. On August 1 a committee representing the American Institute in New York invited him to deliver a poem celebrating the opening of the fortieth National Industrial Exhibition on September 7, 1871.[162] They offered to pay him $100 and his expenses, and requested the privilege of supplying copies of the poem to the metropolitan press "for publication with the other proceedings." Whitman lost no time in accepting these terms. Fairs and exhibitions had always fascinated him, and aside from the liberal honorarium, the publicity would be a real windfall.

Actually, the invitation carried less prestige than Whitman wanted to think. In all the forty years of this annual exhibition of the products of industry, no poet had ever graced it with his official presence.[163] However, the managers had grandiose plans for raising $2,000,000 for permanent buildings and the maintenance of museums, probably to be located in Central Park,[164] and Whitman's imagination glowed with visions of the great industrial palace that would house models of every American machine invented or in use with skilled men and women demonstrating their operations. There were also to be other sumptuous buildings for a large art gallery, a vast music conservatory, a huge lecture hall (of course everything must be on an unprecedented scale), a scientific library, an academy of arts, and so on. As a matter of fact, New York City today has several magnificent museums that fulfill much of this dream, though not under one management or conducted as the managers of the American Institute and their guest poet planned in 1871.

On the scheduled day Whitman appeared and delivered his poem "After All, Not to Create Only." Horace Greeley was usually the main attraction on opening day, but he was away on a lecture tour, and Walt Whitman attempted to put on a show in his place. He not only supplied some two dozen copies of his poem for the newspapers of New York and Brooklyn, but he also provided what would later have been called "press releases," [165] and he succeeded in getting publicity, though not much of it to his liking. Twelve out of seventeen metropolitan papers printed his poem next day, and a few printed his "handouts" either before or after the performance. But the papers were for the most part satirical or downright hostile after the event.[166]

On opening day of the exhibition the workmen were still noisily building or arranging the exhibits, and several papers reported that of the two or three hundred in the audience scarcely anyone could hear a word the poet said. The *World* commented that, "The vacancy caused by Mr. Greeley was regarded with painful emotion." [167] In the *Tribune* Bayard Taylor, recently a friend of Whitman, wrote a parody that began:

Who was it sang of the procreant urge, recounted sextillions of subjects?
Who but myself, the Kosmos, yawping abroad, concerned not at all about either
     the effect or the answer.[168]

Whitman replied to the slurs and attacks with anonymous articles in the Washington *Chronicle* and *Evening Star*. In the former a purported correspondent from New York reported that when the poet began reading, five or six hundred carpenters, machinists, and other workmen paused with their tools in their hands to listen, and that the audience of two or three thousand people several times interrupted with applause.

His gestures are few, but significant. Sometimes he stands with his hands in his breast pockets; once or twice he walked a few steps to & fro. He did not mind the distant noises & the litter & machinery, but doubtless rather enjoyed them. He was perfectly self-possessed. His apostrophe to the Stars and Stripes which floated above him, describing them in far different scenes in battle, was most impassioned. Also his "Away with War itself," & his scornful "Away with novels, plots, & plays of foreign courts!"

A few of his allusions were in a playful tone, but the main impression was markedly serious, animated, & earnest. He was applauded as he advanced to read, besides several times throughout, & at the close. He did not respond in the usual way by bowing. All the directors & officers of the Institute crowded around him & heartily thanked him. He extricated himself, regained his old Panama hat & stick, and, without waiting for the rest of the exercises, made a quiet exit by the steps at the back of the stand.[169]

The article in the *Star* stressed the fact that Roberts Brothers, one of the leading publishing firms of the time, would publish the poem—which it did—and that Roden Noel would soon have an article on Whitman in a new magazine at Oxford University, called *Dark Blue*.[170] "The truth about Whitman," the article stated, was that his contempt for the poets and poetry, and his "unprecedented novelty," made him a ready target for the "smart writers" and "verbal fops" on newspapers.

. . . Walt Whitman *is* a pretty hard nut to crack. His involved sentences, . . . his kangaroo leaps as if from one crag to another, his appalling catalogues, (enough to stagger the bravest heart,) his unheard of demand for brains in the reader as well as in the things read, and then his scornful silence, never explaining anything nor answering any attack, all lay him fairly open to be misunderstood, to slur, burlesque, and sometimes to spiteful innuendo; and will probably continue to do so.[171]

Today one can sympathize with Whitman in his attempt to surmount his very formidable difficulties without necessarily sharing his attitudes toward his critics. This is another example of the poet's total lack of critical judgment regarding his own poems. He had made himself extremely vulnerable to parody and satire by the kind of poem he had delivered at the exhibition—if it can be called a poem, for in style, subject matter, and tone it was more like an oration than a poem. Perhaps the basic theme, "not to create" only ploughs, locomotives, steamships, and so on, but,

"To fill the gross, the torpid bulk with vital religious fire," had some poetic possibilities. However, Whitman did not succeed in treating it poetically. His attempt at humor, as when he invited the Muse to migrate from the old countries to the new, was scarcely less bathetic than the spread-eagle peroration to the Flag at the end. It is difficult to understand how a poet who had recently written "Passage to India" could have composed so bad a poem as "After All, Not to Create Only." Yet this is what the desire to be topical and *popular* could bring him to.

So far as Whitman's life as a poet was concerned, this American Institute invitation was unfortunate in every respect. He made himself ridiculous with his poem and mannerisms, and the resulting travesties on him and his poetry left wounds that would continue to fester until the end of his life. How deeply hurt he was we can see in the defense in the *Star*, in which he claimed that he answered his tormentors by "scornful silence." He even stiffened the opposition by some of his advance publicity, such as the editorial in the New York *Globe*[172] (which contained specific details that must have come from Whitman himself). Here he paraded his popularity in England: "It would astonish Longfellow and Lowell to travel to England, and learn how highly Walt Whitman is regarded." America was still extremely sensitive over British criticism, and such gibes were sure to alienate many of his countrymen and lose some of the friends he had. Moreover, Whitman was using bad psychology for his own personal welfare. He was encouraging himself to feel persecuted—as well as inviting it in actuality—and forgetting his good resolutions of the previous year to cultivate "a superb calm character." When he had cautioned himself to "remember where I am most weak" he could not have meant this weakness, because he always seemed unaware of it, but his conduct during this whole pathetic episode did indeed reveal one of his major weaknesses both of character and of judgment, and especially judgment.

XI

The package of books that Whitman had sent to William Rossetti and the "Lady" was waiting for Rossetti on his return from his vacation the last of August,[173] and he immediately dispatched Mrs. Gilchrist's set to her, which included the second issue of Burroughs's *Notes* as well as Whitman's poems and *Democratic Vistas*. At last Rossetti assured Mrs. Gilchrist that, "I think you will be quite right in addressing Whitman:

the letters seem to have made their way in the right quarters without stirring up any noisy outcry—& the time for the latter may be supposed mainly gone by now." [174] She lost no time in acting upon his suggestion, for Rossetti wrote on September 3, 1871; Mrs. Gilchrist received his letter that day, and her first letter to Whitman was dated the same day. She began by thanking him for "the beloved books," then she explained why she had married Mr. Gilchrist without loving him; apparently she wanted to convey the impression that her heart was virginal. This was also a prologue to her real confession, which she had painfully harbored in secret for two years, "obeying the voice of conscience":

For, dear Friend, my soul was so passionately aspiring—it so thirsted & pined for light, it had not power to reach alone and he could not help me on my way. And a woman is so made that she cannot give the tender passionate devotion of her whole nature save to the great conquering soul, stronger in its powers, though not in its aspirations, than her own, that can lead her forever & forever up and on. It is for her soul exactly as it is for her body. The strong divine soul of the man embracing hers with passionate love—so alone the precious germs within her soul can be quickened into life. . . . This was what happened to me when I had read for a few days, nay, hours, in your books. It was the divine soul embracing mine. I never before dreamed what love meant: not what life meant. Never was alive before—no words but those of "new birth" can hint the meaning of what then happened to me.[175]

Apparently this "new birth" happened instantly, for the reading of the Rossetti selections had caused her to write those letters of appreciative criticism which Rossetti encouraged her to incorporate into the article "A Woman's Estimate of Walt Whitman." They were really disguised confessions of love (Rossetti did not understand this), which she probably hoped he would pass on to Whitman—as he did. This is the implication in her first letter to Whitman, in which she proposed to him about as plainly as any woman could:

In May, 1869, came the voice over the Atlantic to me—O, the voice of my Mate: it must be so—my love rises up out of the very depths of the grief & tramples upon despair. I can wait—any time, a lifetime, many lifetimes—I can suffer, I can dare, I can learn, grow, toil, but nothing in life or death can tear out of my heart the passionate belief that one day I shall hear that voice say to me, "My Mate. The one I so much want. Bride, Wife, indissoluble eternal!" It is not happiness I plead with God for—it is the very life of my Soul, my love is its life. Dear Walt. It is a sweet & precious thing, this love; it clings so close, so close to the Soul and Body, all so tenderly dear, so beautiful, so sacred; it yearns with such passion to soothe and comfort & fill thee with sweet tender joy; it aspires as grandly as gloriously as thy own soul. Strong to soar—soft & tender to nestle and caress. If God were to say to me, "See—he that you love you shall not be given to in this life—he is going to set sail on the unknown sea—will you go with him?" never yet has bride sprung into her husband's arms with the joy with which I would take thy hand & spring from the shore.[176]

She explained that she had consented to Rossetti's advice to remain anonymous in her article because she did not know how her "dear Boy" would take her words of praise. But she was evidently disappointed that he had not perceived the implications. "O dear Walt, did you not feel in every word the breath of a woman's love?" A year ago she had been so ill that she seemed dying, and she decided then to tell her children. "I told them of my love: told them all they could rightly understand. . . ." She also gave them her "earnest injunction" to go to America in case she died.[177] But she had recovered her health, she explained, and would soon move into her own home in Surrey, between Portsmouth and London. After finally bringing her long letter to a close, she added this postscript:

The new portrait also is a sweet joy & comfort to my longing, pining heart & eyes. How have I brooded & brooded with thankfulness on that one word in thy letter "the comfort it has been to me to get her words," for always day & night these two years has hovered on my lips & in my heart the one prayer: "Dear God, let me comfort him!" Let me comfort thee with my whole being, dear love. I feel much better and stronger now.[178]

Whitman made no reply, and Mrs. Gilchrist wrote again on October 15, but this letter is missing and its contents can only be surmised. On October 23 she wrote a third time, telling Whitman of her first letter (which she incorrectly remembered as having been written on September 6—the date of her postscript) and asking whether he had received it. Fearing he had not, she briefly summarized its contents, and added a new inducement: "I am yet young enough to bear thee children, my darling, if God should so bless me. And would yield my life for this cause with serene joy if it were so appointed, if that were the price for thy having a 'perfect child'—knowing my darlings would all be safe & happy in thy loving care—planted down in America." [179]

At last Whitman wrote a short letter on November 3, without salutation —no doubt, in his dilemma, not knowing how to address her:

(To A. G., Earl's Colne, Halsted, Essex, Eng.)

I have been waiting quite a while for time and the right mood, to answer your letter in a spirit as serious as its own, and in the same unmitigated trust and affection. But more daily work than ever has fallen to me to do the present season, and though I am well and contented, my best moods seem to shun me. I wish to give to it a day, a sort of Sabbath, or holy day, apart to itself, under serene and propitious influences, confident that I could then write you a letter which would do you good, and me too. But I must at least show without further delay that I am not insensible to your love. I too send you my love. And do you feel no disappointment because I now write so briefly. My book is my best letter, my response, my truest explanation of all. In it I have put my body and spirit. You understand this better and fuller and clearer than any one else. And I too fully and clearly understand the loving letter it has evoked. Enough that there surely exists so beautiful and a delicate relation, accepted by both of us with joy.[180]

This whole correspondence was destined to be extremely pathetic from beginning to end. Whitman fully appreciated the supreme compliment that this talented and large-hearted woman had paid him, and probably, for her sake if not for his own, he would have liked to make her happy. But he knew only too well where he was "most weak, most lacking." It was simply impossible for him to feel the emotions that would have satisfied her. He did say, "I send you my love," but the whole tone of his letter—and his obvious struggle to make his words say more than he honestly meant—conveyed all too clearly that it was not the "love" that Anne Gilchrist felt for him. It is ironic that the "Calamus" poems had seemed to her a plea for love such as she could give. Her woman's intuition was not able to fathom the meaning of those poems—precisely because she was a woman.

On November 27 she replied (in part): "Your long waited for letter brought me both joy & pain; but the pain was not of your giving." However, she assumed that her letter of September 6 had not reached him, "nor yet a shorter one which, tortured by anxiety & suspense about its predecessor, I wrote Oct. 15 . . ." She professed not to be disappointed by the brevity of his letter, and said, "Your book does indeed say all—book that is not a book . . ." But so long as she believed this of the book she could not accept it as Whitman wanted her to.

Do you know, dear Friend, what it means for a woman, what it means for me, to understand these poems? It means for her whole nature to be then first kindled; quickened into life through such love, such sympathy, such resistless attraction, that henceforth she cannot choose but live & die striving to become worthy to share this divine man's life—to be his dear companion, closer, nearer, dearer than any man can be—for ever so.[181]

She could not help protesting the cruelty of some of his words: "Ah, that word 'enough' was like a blow on the breast. . . . I thought you would say to yourself, 'Perhaps this is the voice of my mate,' and would seek me a little to make sure if it were not so. . . ."[182] When she lay dying, she thought he would one day seek her and refuse to lose her. She felt that her silence would kill her. Then came the book, "but with it no word for me alone," and there was such a storm in her heart that she could not read it for weeks. "I wrote that long letter out in the Autumn fields for dear life's sake. I knew I might, and must, speak then. Then I felt relieved, joyful buoyant once more. Then again months of heart-wearying disappointment as I looked in vain for a letter . . ."

Whitman was now driven into a corner. He realized that he must not let her delude herself any longer. Like Hamlet to his mother, he must be cruel to be kind. About two weeks after receiving Mrs. Gilchrist's last letter he wrote:

WASHINGTON, U.S.
Dec. 26, '71

DEAR FRIEND.
 Your late letter has just reached me—& I write at once to at least say specifically that both your letter of Sept. 6 and that of Oct. 15 safely reached me—this that comes today being the third.
 Again I will say that I am sure I appreciate & accept your letters, & all they stand for, as fully as even you, dear friend, could wish—& as lovingly & *bona fide*.

WALT WHITMAN [183]

This matter-of-fact brevity should have made his position clear, though he did equivocate by saying he accepted her letters and all they stood for as fully as she could wish, a statement that the whole tone of his letter belied. Perhaps it would have been kinder if he had been even more blunt, but maybe he did not quite know himself what he wanted to do in this situation. The adulation was pleasant, especially from a distinguished woman of letters from a foreign country. Yet all he really wished for was

for her to confine her love to his poetic personality in *Leaves of Grass*—
the disembodied spirit that he had longed to be in "So Long!" He could
not even bring himself to use a more affectionate term than "dear
friend." He wanted to dismiss her as he had the woman to whom he had
written "Out of the Rolling Ocean the Crowd"—"return to the ocean,
my love." [184]

On January 24, 1872, Mrs. Gilchrist wrote more calmly and imperson-
ally. She sent her photograph, or rather two photographs, chatted about
her children and domestic matters. After receiving it, Whitman replied
about a week later on the same level, to the mother of children. He would
like to see her and her children, he said. But he referred to an invitation
Tennyson had sent him, and this gave her a cue for another personal letter. She began it on April 12 with details of her friendship with Tennyson, her neighbor. Then she reported that a letter Whitman said he had
written on March 20 from Brooklyn had never arrived:

I can ill afford to lose the long & eagerly watched for pleasure of a letter. If it
seems to you there must needs be something unreal, illusive, in a love that
has grown up entirely without the basis of personal intercourse, dear Friend,
then you do not yourself realize your own power nor understand the full
meaning of your own words, "whoso touches this, touches a man"—"I have put
my Soul & Body into these Poems." Real effects imply real causes.[185]

In the letter of March 20 which Mrs. Gilchrist said she had not received, Whitman told her bluntly that she was deluding herself: "Let me
warn you about myself and yourself also. You must not construct such an
unauthorized and imaginary figure and call it W. W., and so devotedly
invest your loving nature in it. The actual W. W. is a very plain personage
and entirely unworthy such devotion." [186]

Now the strange thing is that in her letter of April 12 she replied to this
message which she denied having received: "please, dear Friend, do not
'warn' me any more—it hurts so, as seeming to distrust my love." Perhaps
unconsciously she tried to blot these words out—pretend they had never
been written. Her intelligence told her the hopelessness of her longing,
but her emotions would not let her give up hope: "O, I could not live if I
did not believe that sooner or later you will not be able to help stretching
out your arms towards me & saying, 'Come, my Darling.'" She felt that
she could not live without hearing from him, but she knew how precarious this one-sided correspondence was; so she pathetically suggested a simple compromise: "When you get this will you post me an American news-

paper (any one you have done with) as a token it [my letter] has reached you—& so on at intervals during your wanderings—it will serve as a token that you are well, & the postmark will tell me where you are." [187] This was a request that Whitman could grant, and henceforth he kept in touch with her—or perhaps kept her in touch with him—by sending newspapers, sometimes packages of books or clippings, and occasionally even a short note.

XII

In 1872 Whitman was on leave from his clerkship three times, totaling over three and a half months. On the first vacation he arrived in Brooklyn about the middle of February and stayed until mid-April. One excuse for the long stay was that he was supervising the printing of a final issue of the fifth edition of *Leaves of Grass*. But since the pages of this book and *Passage to India*, which he added as a separately paged annex, were already stereotyped, bringing out the new edition was not, as he confided to Peter Doyle on March 4, "much of a job." [188] The winter weather was either unusually rough or Whitman could not endure it as formerly, because he complained often of the cold and did not venture out very often. Part of the time he was ill with a sore throat, and his mother also had a siege of illness. On March 15 he wrote that his books "were beginning to do pretty well," [189] but no sales figures have survived. That afternoon, though it was still cold and windy, he planned to go "over to New York to have a lot of my books sent to England by tomorrow's steamer."

While he was at home he received a copy of the February number of a Danish magazine, *For Idea og Virkelighed* (For Idea and Reality), containing an article on him as the poet of American democracy by Rudolf Schmidt, with whom he had been corresponding for several months.[190] Schmidt was the leading editor and journalist for the socialist party in Denmark, and he was less interested in Whitman's poetry than in his ideas. Whitman knew only that he had won another warm friend in Europe, and this consoled him at the same time it increased his bitterness over his difficulty in gaining acceptance in his own country.

But Walt's friends in Washington did not forget him. Soon after his return from Brooklyn, Dr. Frank Baker, of the Smithsonian Institution, sent out an invitation to a May picnic to be held on High Island, in the Potomac, to be reached by canal boat. The invitation was elaborately fanciful and playful, listing the women invited under the heading of

"Floral Fragrance" and the men under "Lunch Consumers." [191] Then came quotations from Shakespeare, Emerson, and Walt Whitman. Such homage was sweet to the poet.

An invitation that pleased Whitman even more than Dr. Baker's, however, was the one he received in the spring of 1872 from the students of Dartmouth College asking him to deliver the commencement poem in June. What he did not know was that a group of students in the senior class had voted to invite him as a prank to annoy the faculty, which was quite conservative and orthodox.[192] Of course Whitman accepted, and he wrote a poem, which he called "As a Strong Bird on Pinions Free," and prepared to deliver it. The preparation consisted mainly of supplying copies of the poem and an account of its delivery to be "released" for publication in newspapers on the day following the commencement exercises on June 26—though the newspapers were completely unresponsive.[193]

Despite the fact that the students had succeeded in shocking the faculty by inviting the notorious Walt Whitman he was courteously entertained in the home of the college pastor. The minister himself was in Europe, but his wife found her guest well-mannered and considerate and she liked him personally. A witness of Whitman's performance on commencement day reported that his delivery was monotonous and without animation.[194] Scarcely anyone beyond the first or second row could hear him, and the audience was obviously relieved when the chairman rose to shake hands with the poet, thus indicating that the ordeal was over. That evening Whitman attended a concert in the auditorium and expressed his approval, and attracted attention, by shouting "Bravo!" just as if he were hearing an operatic performance in New York.

Whitman himself thought his performance had been a success, though in his letter to Peter Doyle next day he confessed that "since Sunday last I have been about half sick and am so yet, by spells." [195] He planned to go to Vermont in a couple of days to visit Hannah, and then return to Brooklyn. He wanted to know whether the Washington *Chronicle* or *Patriot* had printed his poem—they had not. He liked the rural appearance of Hanover:

It is a curious scene here, as I write, a beautiful old New England village, 150 years old, large houses and gardens, great elms, plenty of hills—every thing comfortable, but very Yankee—*not an African to be seen all day*—not a grain of dust—not a car to be seen or heard—green grass everywhere—no smell of coal tar.—As I write a party are playing base ball on a large green in front of the house—the weather suits me first rate—cloudy but no rain.

"As a Strong Bird on Pinions Free" was better than "After All Not to Create Only," but it was a reworking of old themes and ideas. The "strong bird" personified the nation, but the symbolism was rather mixed and trite, for the poet also personified Democracy as a ship. Here, too, as in many of his former poems, he regarded the United States as a culmination of past civilizations, and prophesied that the nation would surpass them all and eventually achieve the "destinies of the Soul," whatever those were.

The most important item in the pamphlet *As a Strong Bird on Pinions Free and Other Poems*, which Whitman had had set up and printed by S. W. Green in New York, was not the title poem nor the other six poems he included, but the Preface. This was dated May 31, 1872, from Washington. Here he said plainly that he had brought *Leaves of Grass* to an end and was starting a new book. Looking back, he felt confident (or at least he said he did) that in *Leaves of Grass* he had "fulfilled . . . an imperious conviction, and the commands of my nature as total and irresistible as those which make the sea flow, or the globe revolve." He also called the book "an epic of Democracy," and admitted that "any future pieces from me are really but the surplusage forming after that Volume, or the wake eddying behind it." He confessed that he felt uncertain about the new volume he had begun: "Having from early manhood abandoned the business pursuits and applications usual in my time and country, and obediently yielded myself up ever since to the impetus mentioned, and to the work of expressing those ideas, it may be that mere habit has got dominion of me, when there is no real need of saying any thing further. . . ."

What had happened to the plan to write a collection of poems around "Passage to India," on the theme of "heavenly death"? Whitman seems not only to have forgotten that but to feel now that he has written himself out. This was probably the result of his physical decline. The ideas were no longer bubbling to the surface; his emotions had cooled, and the images had lost their freshness. Yet out of habit he must keep on.

After returning to Brooklyn from Vermont, Whitman was too ill to make the trip to Washington, and on July 12 he wrote to Peter that he would remain in Brooklyn ten or twelve days.[196] At this time Mrs. Whitman was also greatly disturbed over an impending change in her life. George had finally married Louisa Orr Haslam the previous April and had established a home in Camden, New Jersey. Both George and his bride insisted that Mrs. Whitman and Edward should come to live with them and Walt reluctantly agreed, for now that George had a home of his own he would not feel that he could continue to provide a house for his mother in Brooklyn. Consequently it was agreed that she should move the following September—later changed to August. She dreaded leaving her friends and familiar surroundings in Brooklyn, and Eddie was greatly upset over leaving the church that he had been attending—one of his few pleasures in life. Yet there was nothing she could do about the arrangements her sons had decided upon.

Early in August Mrs. Whitman did move and on the 13th Walt, now back in Washington, was planning to visit her for a few days. He wrote: "I think as I am likely to come quite a good deal, I would like in future to pay Sister Lou $1 a day for what time I stop there—I should feel better satisfied & come oftener." [197] He had also agreed to pay for Eddie's board, and of course without agreement would continue to send money to his mother. Ten days later he was still planning the trip and added: "When you write again tell me whether Ed has recovered his spirits—Mother it is always disagreeable to make a great change, & especially for old folks, but a little time gets things working smoothly, & then one is glad of the change & better off. . . ." [198] Mrs. Whitman, however, continued to be extremely unhappy in her new home and frequently wrote Walt hypochondriacal letters.[199] She could not help resenting the fact that another woman was in charge of the household, and she complained of Lou's parsimony, did not sympathize with George's coddling his wife, and felt that they thought she and Eddie were in the way. All indications are that Lou was a devoted, unselfish wife and daughter-in-law, but Mrs. Whitman was in such poor health by this time that she was scarcely responsible for her attitudes or emotional states. Mrs. George Whitman was not very strong herself, and having her resentful mother-in-law and the defective Edward to care for must have taxed her strength unmercifully.

In November Jeff planned a visit to Camden, and Mat said she would accompany him if Mrs. Whitman would go back to St. Louis with her.[200] But Mrs. Whitman did not feel equal to the trip, and actually Martha herself was in no condition to travel. She deluded herself by believing that she was better.

Two quarrels in 1872 also increased Whitman's nervous tension, one personal and the other remote but involving the poet's pride in his rising English fame. Precisely when they most affected him is not definitely known, but it was probably toward the end of the year. The personal one was with his passionate friend William Douglas O'Connor, an uncompromising abolitionist. Whitman had never believed in slavery, but, like Lincoln, he had regarded the preservation of the Union as the central issue at stake in the Civil War, and during the "reconstruction" years he did not believe that the recently freed Negroes were yet ready to be intrusted with the franchise. He thought they should be taught to read and write and given a chance to gain some understanding of political problems before being permitted to vote.

O'Connor, on the other hand, was all for giving the Negroes the vote immediately, and he could not understand how there could be any doubt or delay. As John Burroughs reported the quarrel, O'Connor became enraged at Whitman's vehement declarations and taunted him.[201] Whitman, in turn, became "brutal and insulting"—certainly uncharacteristic of him —and "O'Connor fired up and turned on him." These ambiguous words do not tell us whether the violence was entirely verbal or threatened to become physical. But the climax of these disagreements was an angry dispute in O'Connor's home in which Walt felt so insulted that he "took his hat and went home in a pet." Next day when the two men met on the street, Walt put out his hand, but William ignored it and walked silently past. Walt now saw no way of restoring the friendship. Aside from losing the companionship of the most eloquent defender of his poetry, he also keenly regretted the interruption of his almost daily visits to the O'Connor home. Ellen O'Connor remained as friendly as ever, but it was now awkward and inconvenient for Walt to see her often.

The other quarrel that affected the poet in 1872 was a purely literary one in far-away London, and Whitman at the time knew very few of the details—never, in fact, knew many of them. But probably by the end of the year he had heard that Swinburne had retreated from his high praise of *Leaves of Grass* the previous year. One of Whitman's most ardent but eccentric admirers in England, a reformer and Owenite socialist, Robert Buchanan, was partly responsible.[202] He had highly praised Whitman in the *Broadway* magazine in 1868, and in 1871 he had published in the *Contemporary Review* an anonymous article, called "The Fleshly School of Poetry," in which he had fiercely attacked Swinburne and Dante Gabriel Rossetti for their alleged sensuality. Swinburne replied, also anonymously, in the *Examiner*, and asked Buchanan (for he knew his antagonist) why he "despised so much the Fleshly School of Poetry in England and admired so much the poetry which is widely considered unclean and animal in America." Buchanan was neatly trapped, and he was forced to admit that *Leaves of Grass* might contain as many as "fifty lines of a thoroughly indecent kind," but he insisted that the American poet was "a most mystic and least fleshly person." Then to goad his enemies anew he added:

It is in a thousand ways unfortunate for Walt Whitman that he has been introduced to the English public by Mr. William Rossetti, and been loudly praised by Mr. Swinburne. Doubtless these gentlemen admire the American poet for all that is best in him; but the British public, having heard that Whitman is immoral, and having already a dim guess that Messrs. Swinburne and Rossetti are not over-refined, has come to the conclusion that his nastiness alone has been his recommendation. . . .[203]

Perhaps these jibes made Swinburne take a closer look at Whitman—or maybe his poem "To Walt Whitman in America" had actually been misunderstood. At any rate, in a critical monograph called "Under the Microscope," published in 1872, Swinburne declared:

To me it seems that the truth for good and evil has never yet been spoken about Walt Whitman. There are in him two distinct men of most inharmonious kinds; a poet and a formalist. Of the poet I have before now done the best I could to express, whether in verse or prose, my ardent and sympathetic admiration. Of the formalist I shall here say what I think; showing why (for example) I cannot for my own part share in full the fiery partisanship of such thoughtful and eloquent disciples as Mr. Rossetti and Dr. [sic] Burroughs.[204]

By "formalist" Swinburne meant didactic theorist, or preacher—today we would say "propagandist":

What he says is well said when he speaks as of himself and because he cannot choose but speak; whether he speak of a small bird's loss or a great man's death, of a nation rising for battle or a child going forth in the morning. What he says is not well said when he speaks not as though he must but as though he ought; as though it behoved one who would be the poet of American democracy to do this thing or be that thing if the duties of that office were to be properly fulfilled, the tenets of that religion worthily delivered. Never before was high poetry so puddled and adulterated with mere doctrine in its crudest form.[205]

Since in his ode to Whitman he had seemed to praise him most as a symbol of political and social freedom, Swinburne was not entirely consistent. Yet, speaking now as a poet, and esthetic critic, there was logic in his pronouncement, and there was both logic and good sense in his finding fault with "Dr. Burroughs" and some other of Whitman's most ardent defenders for assuming that "if he is right all other poets must be wrong." Whitman himself in his growing petulance with all opposition had become almost fanatical in this doctrine, and it was so uncompromising a position—and one so automatically compromising to all other contemporary poets—that it must inevitably generate opposition on both sides. This doctrine would soon prey upon Whitman's mind and reputation like a fatal disease, and perhaps it was influenced to a large extent by the physical disease that was soon to strike him down.

Despite his cheerfulness, Walt's own illness had been steadily growing on him. Looking back on his life, it does not seem surprising that his poetry should have so markedly degenerated during the past two years. Those dizzy spells and long periods of lassitude had been warnings that none of the physicians who treated him had correctly diagnosed, nor had they warned him against the exertions that would bring disaster. So it was that during the closing months of 1872 and early weeks of 1873 he continued the life and habits acquired during ten years of living in Washington.

It was on the night of January 23, 1873, that Whitman suffered his first stroke. By some psychological quirk, he later remembered the date as February 22 or 23,[206] but it was a month earlier. Seven years later he gave his friend Dr. R. M. Bucke a circumstantial description of that night —with the mistake in date:

On the night of the 22d of February, 1873 I was in the Treasury building in Washington; outside it was raining, sleeting, and quite cold and dark. The office was comfortable, and I had a good fire. I was lazily reading Bulwer's "What Will He Do With It?" But I did not feel well, and put aside the book several times. I remained at the office until pretty late. My lodging-room was about a hundred yards down the street. At last I got up to go home. At the door of the Treasury one of the friendly group of guards asked me what ailed me, and said I looked quite ill. He proposed to let a man take his place while he would convoy me home. I said, No, I can go well enough. He again said he would go with me, but I again declined. Then he went down the steps and stood at the door with his lantern until I reached the house where I lived. I walked up to my room and went to bed and to sleep—woke up about three or four o'clock and found that I could not move my left arm or leg—did not feel particularly uneasy about it—was in no pain and even did not seem to be very ill—thought it would pass off—went to sleep again and slept until daylight. Then, however, I found that I could not get up—could not move. After several hours, some friends came in, and they immediately sent for a doctor —fortunately a very good one, Dr. W. B. Drinkard. He looked very grave— thought my condition markedly serious. I did not think so: I supposed the attack would pass off soon—but it did not.[207]

The friends who rallied around and nursed and waited on Whitman were Peter Doyle, Charles Eldridge, Mrs. Burroughs, Mrs. O'Connor (William was still estranged), and Mrs. Ashton, who wanted to move him to her home,[208] but he wished to remain in his own room. His first thought was of his mother, and as soon as he could be propped up, the third day after his attack, he scribbled an optimistic report to her in a shaky hand.[209]

Jan. 26, 1873
Sunday afternoon

DEAREST MOTHER,

I have been not well for two or three days, but am better to-day. I have had a slight stroke of paralysis, on my left side, and especially the leg—occurred Thursday night last, & I have been laid up since—I am writing this in my room, 535 15th st as I am not able to get out at present—but the doctor gives me good hopes of being out and at my work in a few days—He says it is nothing but what I shall recover from in a few days—Mother you must not feel uneasy —though I know you will—but I thought I would write & tell you the *exact truth—neither better nor worse—*

I have a first rate physician Dr. Drinkard—I have some very attentive friends, (& if I have occasion can & will telegraph to you or George—but do not expect to have any need) . . .[210]

EBBING TIDE

Last of ebb, and daylight waning,

. . . .

On, on, and do your part, ye burying, ebbing tide! [1]

I

In later years Walt Whitman and several of his most intimate friends often attributed his paralytic stroke on January 23, 1873, to the poison he had absorbed in the military hospitals during the war and the years immediately following. But once in discussing his "break-up" with Horace Traubel he reported a different opinion from his Washington physician: "Doctor Drinkard seemed to understand me well: he charged it [the first paralytic stroke] to the emotional disturbances to which I was subjected at that time. . . ." [2] Whitman did not say the emotional strain of the war years—though doubtless that did contribute—but "at that time."

What caused Whitman's debilitating nervous strain preceding his paralytic stroke is a matter for conjecture, but his notebooks leave no room for doubting that he did experience some great emotional crisis in the summer of 1870, about which we actually know no more than the soul-searching words that he wrote down. [3] This emotional upheaval might well have helped bring on the physical decline that became obvious in 1871–1872; or, on the other hand, his physical condition, which had not been good for several years, could have been mainly responsible for his emotional state a year earlier. Who can say which was cause and which effect? Whitman's poems show very plainly his loss of mental vigor, though they contain no suggestive clues such as his "Calamus" poems give to that earlier emotional and intellectual crisis around 1858–1859. Aside from the numerous vacations that he took in 1872 he also revealed his concern over his health by making a will in the autumn—leaving everything he owned to his mother to be used for the support of his defective brother.

Whitman, therefore, had not been unaware of the warnings nature had given him of his approaching collapse. But after it had occurred, the poet who had made his youthful health and strength a symbol of the goodness and beauty of Nature could not believe that his condition was permanent. Stubbornly he insisted in his letters to his mother that he would soon recover and return to work. Of course, he was trying to keep up her courage as well as his own, but hope was now the one thing left to him—except his friendships. He was permitted to hire a young man to substitute for him and was granted an indefinite leave of absence. Since he had to pay the substitute only $50 a month, he still had enough income left to pay $20 a month for Edward's board and to send his mother a little spending money after meeting his own expenses.

On Wednesday afternoon, January 29, Walt wrote his mother that he was still lying in bed and that any attempt to move caused dizziness and nausea, "But I am certainly over the worst of it."

. . . I still have many callers—only a few particular ones are admitted to see me—Mrs. O'Connor comes & a young woman named Mary Cole—Mrs. Ashton has sent for me to be brought to her house, to be taken care of—of course I do not accept her offer—they live in grand style & I should be more bothered than benefitted by their refinements & luxuries, servants, &c.

Mother I want you to know truly, that I do not want for any thing—as to all the *little extra fixings* and *superfluities,* I never did care for them in health, & they only annoy me in sickness—I have a good bed—a fire—as much grub as I wish & whatever I wish—& two or three good friends here. So I want you to not feel at all uneasy—as I write Peter Doyle is sitting by the window reading —he and Charles Eldridge regularly come in & do whatever I want & are both *very helpful* to me—one comes day time, & one evening. . . .[4]

But despite the devotion and attention of his friends, it appears that Whitman spent the nights, or at least most of them, quite alone in his attic room.

A week later Whitman reported to his mother that he was gradually regaining the use of his left limbs, "very, very slowly, but *certainly gaining.*" On February 8 he received a letter from Jeff telling him that Mat was "sinking." [5] He now knew that there was no hope for her recovery. Two days later Walt wrote his mother that George should not think of "coming on here for me." In fact, in a day or two more he thought he would be able to get out, or at least walk to the front door. Considering the fact that he was on the fourth floor, this really was optimism. However, a week later he did manage, with the assistance of Peter Doyle and another friend (unnamed), to go out as far as the street, though the stairs tired him so much that he may have been injured more than benefited by this exertion.[6] Next day he felt much worse. And then on February 19 came a telegram from Jeff saying that Martha had died that day. Two days later Walt wrote his mother that he was "much depressed about Mat's death," but he still thought he was "rather on the improve." [7] On the day of the funeral, Saturday, February 22, he hobbled up and down the four flights of stairs, but "I kept thinking all the time it was the day of Matty's funeral—Every few minutes all day it would come up in my mind. . . ." [8]

John Burroughs was now back in New York State, employed as a Government bank inspector. He was planning to buy some land and build a house near his old home in Roxbury. Walt missed him very much, but Mrs. Burroughs was still in Washington, having remained to dispose of their property. In every letter to her John asked about Walt, and as soon as Walt was able to get out she took him on drives around the city. The first was on February 26, after which Mrs. Burroughs wrote her husband that she had never seen anyone enjoy anything so much as Walt had that drive.[9] Dr. Drinkard was now using electrical shock (battery) therapy every day, but it did little if any good.[10]

Mrs. Whitman became even more unhappy at George's after the death of her daughter-in-law in St. Louis. In her dissatisfaction with Lou she often wished she could talk with Mattie, and now she worried about Jeff's children. On February 28 she wrote to Walt that Lou and George wanted her to write Jeff that they would take the children: "of course they expected jeff to pay a good board," and George thought Lou could manage the children, but she was sure "they would never be satisfied to live as we doo so its best as it is." [11] George had bought a lot, "and now if they only had money to build a house . . ." This constant talk of "money matters" annoyed Mrs. Whitman because it made her more self-conscious of her dependency.

Mary promised her mother to visit her when summer came, and she invited Walt to come to see her at Greenport. Mrs. Whitman wished that they could both go "when it comes hot weather," and suggested that "we must both get so we can walk without limping." In March Lou's aunt came to stay with them, and Mrs. Whitman felt more than ever that she was unwanted and neglected. She now remembered Mattie as the perfect daughter-in-law.

Walt tried to help his mother by writing her cheerful letters and suggesting that they would yet be able to live together again. On March 28 he wrote her about a rosebush blooming in his window and assured her that he would yet get well and "hire or buy or build a little place here, rooms enough to live in for you & Ed and me. . . ." [12] As Mrs. Whitman's dissatisfaction increased, this dream-house grew in her imagination. On April 8 she wrote that since Louisa's aunt had come to live with them the food had improved, but Lou and her aunt wanted "to be by themselves." They thought Lou was "in the family way," and George carried her up and down the stairs, while Mrs. Whitman did most of the housework—though George was now paying Lou's aunt a "salary," presumably to help around the house. [13] Mrs. Whitman's nervousness and what she regarded as "dispepsy" got worse. Probably her symptoms were caused by a heart condition rather than by stomach trouble. On May 16 Lou wrote Walt that his mother was a little better, and Mrs. Whitman herself added a postscript: "dear Walter dont be worried   i shall be better dont come till you can walk good and without injury to your getting fully recovered." [14] But in three or four days her condition became so alarming that he had to be summoned.

By this time he was able to spend a couple of hours a day at his desk, and therefore it was possible for him to make the trip to Camden by himself. He arrived on May 20, only three days before his mother's death. Before his arrival she had realized that she was near the end and had written out this message: "farewell my beloved sons farewell I have lived beyond all comfort in this world   dont mourn for me my beloved sons and daughters   farewell my dear beloved Walter." [15] After she was gone Walt wrote to Peter Doyle, "It is the great cloud of my life." [16]

The best account of Whitman's life during the weeks immediately following his mother's death was given by Eldridge in a letter which he wrote to Burroughs on June 26:

. . . Walt returned here about a week after the funeral in a very depressed condition and complaining more in regard to himself than I have ever heard him do since he got sick. He was not content to stay at his room so he availed himself of the invitation of the Ashtons and went up there and staid for ten or twelve days. . . . The change to Ashton's was good for him as there were women and a baby, and he had more agreeable surroundings. He thought he was decidedly improving before he went away, but I have had a letter from him this week which is not so encouraging. He still has those distressed spells in the head quite often, and his locomotion is no better. He has two months' leave of absence from June 15. Barfield behaved very handsomely.

The fact is, I begin to doubt whether Walt is going to recover, and I am very apprehensive of another attack. . . . He is a mere physical wreck to what he was. . . . It is a terrible misfortune, one of the saddest spectacles I have ever seen. His mental powers seem to be as vigorous as ever, which is the brightest part of his case, but to be stricken with such physical weakness that he cannot walk a block without resting—it is very pitiful. Such vigor, health, and endurance to be so changed, is a melancholy thing; and if it should continue for any length of time, I think it would prey upon his spirits and make him hypochondriacal. The doctor fears this, but hopes to restore him to a condition of comparative health. Walt himself believes that he is going to get well, and we all do as much as possible to encourage that belief—for it is his sheet anchor.[17]

Walt had no intention or expectation of remaining in Camden permanently. Doyle helped him pack his trunk and store his few possessions in Washington, to which he expected to return by the end of his two-month leave. After he had been in Camden a few days, he was terribly lonesome, and more depressed than he had yet been, but he kept in touch with Pete through frequent letters and pathetically planned for the future—both his and Pete's. He had thought he would feel better if he could take a vacation on Long Island, or even the New Jersey coast,[18] but this proved impossible.

At 322 Stevens Street Walt was only about 70 rods from the depot of the Camden and Amboy Railroad and he could hear "the bells and whistles and trains rumbling continually, night and day." [19] These sounds tantalized him, not because of the noise but because they reminded him of Pete, and of the "R.R. men living near, around here—if I only felt just a little better I should get acquainted with many of the men, which I could very easily do if I would." And these sounds also made him long to travel; if only he had Pete to convoy him, he could take a train almost from his own door to Cape May, or Long Branch, or ride the steamboat up and down the Delaware River, only about a quarter of a mile away. But such dreaming of the impossible only intensified his loneliness.

Some time during the summer Walt wrote Mrs. Gilchrist telling her of his illness and double bereavement, and begging her forgiveness for his long delay in writing her. He ended with this gesture: "The enclosed ring [possibly his mother's wedding ring] I have just taken from my finger, &

send to you, with my love." [20] Whether or not he intended this as a sort of token engagement, Mrs. Gilchrist could hardly be expected not to interpret it so. She promptly answered on September 1, 1873. Her letter began: "I am entirely satisfied & at peace, my Beloved—no words can say how divine a peace." And it ended: "Your silence is not dumb to me now—will never again cloud or pain, or be misconstrued by me. I can feast & feast, & still have wherewithal to satisfy myself with the sweet & precious words that have now come & with the feel of my ring, only send any old paper that comes to hand (never mind whether there is anything to read in it or not) just as a sign that the breath of love & hope these poor words try to bear to you, has reached you." [21]

On September 5 Whitman wrote Ellen O'Connor what he himself called a "perturbed sort of letter." [22] His condition had not improved, and Dr. Matthew Grier had diagnosed his "principal trouble" as cerebral anaemia, the result of long-continued emotional strain. "He thinks it has been coming on for many years, says I need rest, rest for a long time & social exhilaration." The latter was exactly what he missed most, though Charles Eldridge had visited him on his way back to Washington. Burroughs had written, but he was now planning to settle at Esopus on the Hudson and would not often be passing through. Sometimes Walt read in the Mercantile Library in Philadelphia, "though the atmosphere of a *reading room* soon weighs on me." Socially his life had become "an utter blank." He looked "long and long" at the miniatures of his mother and Martha and wished he could be with them.

Walt's brother and sister-in-law were apparently as kind to him as they knew how to be, and Walt never criticized them in his letters to Peter Doyle and his other friends, but they could offer no substitute for the companions the poet had left in Washington. George and Walt had never disliked each other, but neither had they had much in common except their blood relationship. As Walt once remarked, George was interested in pipes, not poems.[23] On Friday, September 26, Walt confided to Pete:

. . . . I don't know a soul here,—am entirely alone—sometimes sit alone and think, for two hours on a stretch—have not formed a single acquaintance here, any ways intimate—My sister-in-law is very kind in all housekeeping things, cooks what I want, has first rate coffee for me and something nice in the morning, and keeps me a good bed and room—all of which is very acceptable— (then, for a fellow of my size, the friendly presence and magnetism needed, somehow, is not here—I do not run afoul of any)—still I generally keep up very good heart. . . . I am finishing this by the open window—still in the room where my mother died, with all the old familiar things—but all drawing to a close, as the new house is done, and I shall move on Monday.[24]

The following week the family moved into the new house on the next block at 431 Stevens Street. Perhaps as a consequence of the excitement and disturbance Walt suffered a setback in his convalescence. On October 3 he wrote Pete that the "blurs" and dizziness had returned and he promised to telegraph if his condition became really serious. Walt's independent nature made it difficult for George, too, and they probably had a quarrel: "My brother had a large room, very handsome, on second floor, with large bay window fronting west, built for me, but I moved up here [into a small room on the third floor] instead, it is much more retired, and has the sun—I am very comfortable here indeed, but my *heart* is blank and lonesome utterly." [25]

A few days later John Burroughs stopped for a day and night visit, and Walt also began to make the acquaintance of some of the neighbors, such as a thirteen-year-old boy, Rob Evans, who had lost an eye in an accident at play; and Tom Osler, a young railroad man, but he was killed very soon in a railroad disaster. Walt had become especially fond of him, partly because he reminded him of Pete. The newspapers were full of accounts of wrecks and accidents, and Walt worried a great deal about Pete's safety. In November he was able to hobble around a little more in good weather. He now frequently took tea with a Colonel Johnston and his family: "I get out every fair day—shall go out about 4 [November 9] to visit a family here, Col. Johnston, the jolliest man I ever met, an artist, a great talker, but real, natural first-rate off-hand cheerfulness and comical-sensible talk, a man of good information too, travelled in Europe—an hour or two does me real good—he has a wife, daughter, and son, all good —I go Sunday evenings to tea. . . ." [26]

Although Whitman's "bad spells" frequently returned, his condition in general improved during November and December. His locomotion continued to be quite difficult, but he had found it easy to make friends with the kind of men whom he had always liked most: "I have become sort of acquainted with most of the [letter] carriers, ferry men, car conductors and drivers, etc. etc., they are very good indeed—help me on and off the cars, here and in Philadelphia—they are nearly all young fellows—it all helps along. . . ." [27] Under these circumstances life was at least bearable.

II

By November Whitman had gained a little strength, and to relieve the tediousness of his many hours alone he began to write again. The editor of the New York *Daily Graphic*, who had printed five short poems of his during the previous March and April, was still friendly to him, and Whitman now sent him two fairly long articles on the capital. The first, printed November 24, 1873, was written as an eye-witness account of Washington on the eve of the impending opening of the Forty-third Congress.[28] It contained vivid descriptions of the House and Senate Chambers, the Rotunda, scenes on Capitol Hill, and reminiscences of some of the dramatic debates—especially in night sessions—that Whitman had heard. The second article, published November 29, concentrated on the Senate Chamber, the Supreme Court Room, and night scenes in the North Wing. This journalistic sight-seeing tour was a vicarious trip to the familiar haunts and sights which the crippled poet now looked back upon with almost unbearable nostalgia.

Whitman had sent Mrs. Gilchrist copies of the *Graphic* (as well as copies of the Philadelphia and New York newspapers), marking them according to a code she had suggested, and on December 18, she confided wistfully: "Perhaps if my hand were in yours, dear Walt, you would get along faster. Dearer and sweeter that lot than even to have been your bride in the full flush & strength and glory of your youth. I turn my face to the westward sky before I lie down to sleep, deep & steadfast within me the silent aspiration that every year, every month & week, may help something to prepare and make fitter me and mine to be your comfort and joy." [29]

At the beginning of 1874 loneliness continued to be Whitman's greatest burden. He had acquired a little dog that followed him around with great devotion, and he became quite fond of it, but it was no substitute for human companionship. On February 3, while writing Mrs. O'Connor about the death of a friend of theirs, he commented: "Poor, good Mr. Dille—Yet amid all its sombreness & terror how blessed to die 'by touch ethereal,' painless, instantaneous—Nelly Death has become to me a familiar thing—Yet, as I sit here writing, I do not feel a particle less of life in me, than ever." [30] And writing again on February 11, he confided: "I have twice hurriedly destroyed a large mass of letters & MSS.—to be ready for what might happen." [31]

Late in January Whitman began a series of articles in the *Weekly*

Graphic called " 'Tis But Ten Years Since," [32] based on—and in part copied verbatim from—the notes he had made in New York City early in the war, later in Virginia, in the Army hospitals of Washington, or written out from memory soon after the end of the war. This was to be the beginning of his first book of prose on the war years, to called *Memoranda During the War*. The first installment was published on January 24, and the last (the sixth) on March 7, 1874. On January 23 Walt remarked in a letter to Pete: "I keep myself some busy writing—have a piece in *Harper's Monthly* just out (February)—shall have another in the March number—Can't seem to do without occupying my mind through the day —nights are worst for me—I can't rest well—has been so now for a month. . . ." [33] The poem was "Song of the Redwood Tree," for which the editor of *Harper's* had paid $100 two months earlier and relinquished all future rights.

It is understandable that the necessity to keep his mind occupied should have led Whitman to the journalistic exploitation of his notebooks, but a close study of the two poems published in *Harper's* reveals that they served for more than means of combating boredom. Out of his fitful longings for the scenes and companions of Washington and his attempts to come somehow to terms with the life now forced upon him, Whitman found poems once more forming in his mind, as they had before under the pressure of great emotional stress. They were unlike the poems of former years and experiences, but they gave him some relief—if not the same exhilaration—that he had experienced in writing "Song of Myself" or some of the "Calamus" poems.

Perhaps in the Mercantile Library in Philadelphia, on one of those days when he was able to cross the river, Whitman read something about the Sequoias of California that led him to identify himself with one of those giants of the redwood forest being felled by an ax, and he tried to express its "death-chant." But these fancies did not shape into an elegy. Though Whitman felt a sympathetic identity with the dying tree, he was humbly, almost prayerfully, trying to reconcile himself not to death itself, but to waning life. What interested him in this symbol, therefore, was his old theme (as in "Pioneers! O Pioneers!") of the past preparing for the future:

Nor yield we mournfully, majestic brothers,
We who have grandly fill'd our time;
With Nature's calm content, with tacit, huge delight,

We welcome what we wrought for through the past,
And leave the field for them.

For them predicted long,
For a superber race—they too grandly fill their time,
For them we abdicate—in them ourselves, ye forest kings!
To them these skies and airs—these mountain peaks—Shasta—Nevadas,
These huge, precipitous cliffs—this amplitude, these valleys grand—far Yosemite,
To be in them absorb'd, assimilated.[34]

The real theme is the "superber race," the "loftier strain" running through all Whitman's poetic nationalism. In the "virgin lands" of the New World it was possible, as Whitman had said in the 1855 preface, for man to rival the amplitude of Nature:

Here may he hardy, sweet, gigantic grow—here tower proportionate to Nature,
Here climb the vast, pure spaces, unconfin'd, uncheck'd by wall or roof,
Here laugh with storm or sun—here joy—here patiently inure,
Here heed himself, unfold himself (not others' formulas heed,)—here fill his
    time, . . .

Thus the poet sees in the redwood tree "the promise of thousands of years, till now deferr'd."

Although the "Song of the Redwood Tree" grew out of Whitman's loneliness and near despair during the fall and winter of 1873–1874 and reflected his need for believing that what he had struggled in the past to accomplish would not be lost in the future, it was his second poem, "Prayer of Columbus," that was most colored, as he admitted to Peter Doyle,[35] with thoughts of himself; and to Ellen O'Connor he remarked, "I shouldn't wonder if I have unconsciously put a sort of autobiographical dash in it." [36] He prefaced the poem with this historical note:

It was near the close of his indomitable and pious life—on his last voyage, when nearly 70 years of age—that Columbus, to save his two remaining ships from foundering in the Carribean Sea in a terrible storm, had to run them ashore on the Island of Jamaica—where, laid up for a long and miserable year—1503—he was taken very sick, had several relapses, his men revolted, and death seemed daily imminent; though he was eventually rescued, and sent home to Spain to die, unrecognized, neglected and in want. . . .[37]

The most significant aspect of the poet's identification of himself with the "batter'd, wreck'd old man" was not his vicarious sympathy with Columbus in his illness, misfortune, and neglect, but the desire to communicate with God. Nearly every word of Columbus's prayer could have been Whitman's own prayer, part of which, however, sounded more like Job's assertion of his innocence than the prayer of a contrite heart:

> Thou knowest my years entire, my life,
> (My long and crowded life of active work—not adoration merely;)
> Thou knowest the prayers and vigils of my youth;
> Thou knowest my manhood's solemn and visionary meditations;
> Thou knowest how, before I commenced, I devoted all to come to Thee;
> Thou knowest I have in age ratified all those vows, and strictly kept them;
> Thou knowest I have not once lost nor faith nor ecstasy in Thee;
> (In shackles, prison'd, in disgrace, repining not,
> Accepting all from Thee—as duly come from Thee.) [38]

Like Job, the poet wondered what he had done to deserve such affliction, but he also wished to attain the faith of Columbus:

> My hands, my limbs grow nerveless;
> My brain feels rack'd, bewilder'd;
> Let the old timbers part—I will not part!
> I will cling fast to Thee, O God, though the waves buffet me;
> Thee, Thee, at least I know.

Like Columbus, Whitman also wondered what he knew or understood of his own life, and of his "work past or present"; he was sure only of the "dim-ever-shifting guesses" spread before him. But the more he suffered, the more he longed to believe that in future ages he would be saluted "in new tongues" as Columbus now was three centuries later:

> And these things I see suddenly—what mean they?
> As if some miracle, some hand divine unseal'd my eyes,
> Shadowy, vast shapes, smile through the air and sky,
> And on the distant waves sail countless ships,
> And anthems in new tongues I hear saluting me.

Mrs. Gilchrist knew instantly how much of the poet's own suffering had gone into this composition. As soon as she had read the "sacred Poem" she wrote: ". . . you too have sailed over stormy seas to your goal —surrounded with mocking disbelievers—you too have paid the great price of health—our Columbus." [39]

In the spring of 1874 Whitman received a "salute" in his own country from the literary society of Tufts College, at Medford, Massachusetts, which invited him to read a poem at the commencement in June. He accepted and wrote "Song of the Universal," but it had to be read by a proxy. The *Daily Graphic* printed it on June 17, and the *New Republic* in Camden reprinted it on June 20. This poem does not have much biographical significance, but it throws light on Whitman's intellectual history. He had been reading Hegel—or more accurately discussions of Hegel—for several years.[40] Traces of Hegelian influence may be seen in *Democratic Vistas*, in Whitman's belief that the "dialectic" of conflict and struggle will produce a more perfect society. Or as he re-expressed this idea more poetically in "Song of the Universal":

> In this broad earth of ours,
> Amid the measureless grossness and the slag,
> Enclosed and safe within its central heart,
> Nestles the seed perfection.
> .   .   .   .   .   .
> Out of the bulk, the morbid and the shallow,
> Out of the bad majority—the varied, countless frauds of men and States,
> Electric, antiseptic yet—cleaving, suffusing all,
> Only the Good is universal.[41]

This Whitman regarded as God's own plan for mankind, and he prayed for

> Belief in plan of Thee enclosed in Time and Space,
> Health, peace, salvation universal.
>
> Is it a dream?
> Nay, but the lack of it the dream,
> And, failing it, life's lore and wealth a dream,
> And all the world a dream.

Two days after his Tufts College poem had been reprinted in the *New Republic*, accompanied by an article on "Walt Whitman in Camden," Whitman wrote the President of the United States[42] asking to be retained in his clerkship in the office of the Solicitor of the Treasury, to which he had been transferred at his own request on March 10, 1873. (The newspapers had been printing accounts of impending reductions in Government personnel.) He still hoped to be able to return to work, and meanwhile the difference between his salary and his payments to his substitute was the only steady income he had. The President simply referred the letter to the Department of Justice, where it was passed on to the Solicitor of the Treasury, who recommended to the Attorney General on June 30 that Whitman be discharged for reasons of economy. On the same day Attorney General Williams wrote Whitman that his services would be terminated as of July 1, 1874, though in a few days the Attorney General granted two months' pay which was customary in such cases.[43] But even this left Whitman on September 1 without any dependable income. Although he had saved a few hundred dollars, this would not last long if he continued to pay board to his sister-in-law and helped to support Edward, who by this time had been sent to board with a family in the country. These new financial worries aggravated Walt's condition and he was able to do very little writing during the summer and early fall.

By mid-autumn Whitman had somewhat extended his acquaintances in Camden. One of his new friends was the principal of the Cooper School, who invited him to write a poem to be read at the dedication of a new public school building on Third and Linden streets.[44] The poet wrote "An Old Man's Thought of School," which the *Daily Graphic* published on November 3. It was a very ordinary occasional poem. Then on November 11 Whitman contributed "Death of a Fireman" to the *New Republic*. The editor of this paper, Mr. Harry Bonsall, had become another of Whitman's local friends, and during this and succeeding years he often helped the poet by printing little items about him or permitting him to use the *New Republic* printing office. There Whitman sometimes set up his own poems or supervised the printers in setting them up in order to provide copies in proof, as the Rome Brothers had done many years before in Brooklyn.

To a special Christmas number of the *Daily Graphic* Whitman contributed "A Christmas Garland," [45] composed of three new poems and a miscellany of prose on a variety of subjects. He began with some thoughts on the genius of Victor Hugo, George Sand, and Emerson. "I call it one of the chief acts of art," he declared, ". . . to hold the reins firmly and to preserve the mastery" in the wildest escapades of literary genius. But what he said of Hugo's literary excesses and "want of prudence" [46] in his novels might have been applied with equal pertinency to his own poems. Emerson, however, who had been kind to him many times during the past two decades, and whom he had once addressed as "master," Whitman accused of the opposite defect: ". . . is not his fault, finally, too great prudence, too rigid a caution?" During the past two or three years, stories of Emerson's disappointment with his Brooklyn poet—some of them almost certainly exaggerated—had reached Whitman's ears. But what really hurt most was that Emerson had failed to include in his 1872 anthology, *Parnassus*,[47] a single selection from *Leaves of Grass*, the book he had so warmly and impulsively praised in 1855. Perhaps unconsciously Whitman was trying to strike back, though the "rigid caution" that had excluded him from the charmed circle of Emerson's favorite poets could have caused Whitman to believe quite sincerely that there were blemishes in his idol's own "genius": ". . . I am disposed to think (picking out spots against the sun) that his constitutional distrust and doubt—almost finical in their nicety—have been too much for him—have not perhaps stopped him short of first-class genius, but have veiled it—have certainly clipped and pruned that free luxuriance of it which only satisfies the soul at last."[48] The tentative, uncertain wording of this reservation suggests the mixed emotions that caused the ailing poet in Camden to attempt to nick, ever so lightly, the armor of his hero.

Later in his manuscript Whitman formulated his theory of personality in literature (another, perhaps half-conscious, self-defense): ". . . poems of the first class (poems of the depth, as distinguished from those of the surface) are to be sternly tallied with the poets themselves, and tried by them and their lives." This theory he capped with some verses that he later adopted as an epigraph for *Leaves of Grass*:

> Go, said the Soul,
> Such verses for my Body write (for we are one),
> That, should I back again return unseen, or centuries hence,
> I shall with pleas'd smile resume all those verses,
> And fully confirm them.[49]

To make his own life a poem, and to communicate that life in compositions that would seem to the reader more real than art, had always been Whitman's ambition in *Leaves of Grass*, and now in his sickness and loneliness this theory was being tested as he had never dreamed it could be.

III

Early in 1875 Walt wrote to Pete: "I get desperate at staying in—not a human soul for cheer, or sociability or fun, and this continued week after week and month after month. . . ." On April 30 he wrote again:

Pete, the spring finds me pretty much in the same tedious and half way condition I have been lingering in now over two years—up and around every day, look not much different, and eat pretty well—but not a day passes without some bad spells, sometimes *very bad,* and never a real good night's sleep—yet still I have a sort of feeling not to give it up yet—keep real good spirits—don't get blue, even at my worst spells. . . . My sister is going away for some ten days tomorrow or next day, and I shall be quite alone in the house—wish you could come on and pay me a visit . . .[50]

During this dreary spring, however, Whitman began working on a new edition of his writings to be issued in 1876 with the opening of the Centennial Exposition at Philadelphia. For months the newspapers had been filled with plans for this great Exposition, and local residents watched with much interest the construction of the buildings and the laying out of the grounds in West Philadelphia. Fairs and exhibitions had always fascinated Whitman, and this one commemorating the first century of the American Republic was sure to excite him. Probably he hoped that the announcement of his Centennial Edition would influence the Philadelphia Exposition Committee to invite him to write the official poem for the opening, but the invitation went to Bayard Taylor. This was a double disappointment because ever since Taylor had satirized Walt's own performance at the New York Industrial Fair in 1871 Walt had detested his former friend. Nevertheless Whitman went stubbornly ahead with his plans for the new edition of his writings.

It was to be in two volumes, *Leaves of Grass* making the first, without the "Passage to India" annex, and the second to be composed of poetry and prose. The verse would include the poems recently published in *Harper's* and the *Graphic,* a few new short poems, and the New York Exhibition poem, "After All, Not to Create Only," retitled "Song of the Exposition"—with the muse now invited to migrate from Greece to Philadelphia. This second volume, to be called *Two Rivulets,* would be quite a hodgepodge, being filled with new material set up and printed at the New Republic Print Shop in Camden (notably "Memoranda During the War," which was also to be sold as a separate book), with several pamphlets printed from stereotype plates (*Democratic Vistas, Passage to India, After All, Not to Create Only,* and *As a Strong Bird on Pinions Free*) bound in. Thus the pagination would not be continuous and the table of contents confusing. But in his title Whitman found a motif that did symbolically fuse the miscellaneous contents.

The meaning of the title *Two Rivulets* Whitman explained in the Preface which he wrote (at least in part) on his fifty-sixth birthday, May 31, 1875:

For some reason—not explainable or definite to my own mind, yet secretly pleasing and satisfactory to it [an interesting revelation of Whitman's literary psychology]—I have not hesitated to embody in, and run through the Volume, two altogether distinct veins, or strata—Politics for one, and for the other, the pensive thought of Immortality. Thus, too, the prose and poetic, the dual forms of the present book. . . . [thus in original.] [51]

Even the form of the printed page in the "Two Rivulets" section, which introduced the *Two Rivulets* volume, emphasized this dual purpose. In his Preface Whitman stated his literary purposes and then in lengthy footnotes, sometimes taking up three-fourths of the page, he elaborated his intentions in *Leaves of Grass*. Below each poem he also gave prose comments on such topics as "Thoughts for the Centennial," "Democracy in the New World," "Nationality," "Darwinism," and other contemporary subjects and problems. He likewise played upon the poetic symbolism of the rivulets flowing across the broad land and eventually losing themselves in the ocean. The epigraph for the whole volume was:

> For the Eternal Ocean bound,
> These ripples, passing surges, streams of Death and Life.

And in the title poem these symbols acquired a multiple meaning, the "Two Rivulets" signifying "Companions, travelers, gossiping as they journey"; the "real and the Ideal"; the ebb and flow of time; night and day; and finally:

> In You whoe'er you are, my book perusing,
> In I myself—in all the World—these ripples flow,
> All, all, toward the mystic Ocean tending.
>
> (O yearnful waves! the kisses of your lips!
> Your breast so broad, with open arms, O firm, expanded shore!)

In a footnote Whitman returned to the same concern for history that he had shown in his first edition, the "precious legacies" that had come down to America "from all eras and all lands," Egypt, India, Greece and Rome, and Europe in later ages.[52] In his second poem, "Or from that Sea

of Time," he showed a still greater sense of the almost unimaginable contrast between finite experience and the infinity of Time and Eternity:

1

Or, from that Sea of Time,
Spray, blown by the wind—a double winrow-drift of weeds and shells;
.   .   .   .
Infinitessimals out of my life, and many a life,
(For not my life and years alone I give—all, all I give;)
These thoughts and Songs—waifs from the deep—here, cast high and dry,
Wash'd on America's shores.

2

Currents of starting a Continent new,
Overtures sent to the solid out of the liquid,
Fusion of ocean and land—tender and pensive waves,
(Not safe and peaceful only—waves rous'd and ominous too,
Out of the depths, the storm's abysms—Who knows whence? Death's waves,
Raging over the vast, with many a broken spar and tatter'd sail.)

Here the "two rivulets" of the book do merge and the poet's association of politics and death and immortality takes on biographical meaning. In the footnote he presents two thoughts, both reminiscent of *Democratic Vistas*: (1) Nearly every nation in history—and indeed almost
every age—has had its own characteristic masterpieces, such as Homeric
epics, the *Cid*, Dante's *Inferno*, or Shakespeare's dramas. But, "Where is
America's art-rendering . . .?" (2) Must not this "indispensable want
. . . be supplied?" [53] Thus the duality of Whitman's book becomes
clearer. As the poet took stock of his life on his fifty-sixth birthday, after
two years of sickness and impotence, he looked back upon his earlier
poems not only as poems of the body and healthy physiology but also as
promises of moral and spiritual development which he had not yet
achieved, any more than America had achieved the moral, esthetic, and
spiritual development which he had envisioned in his 1855 preface—and
been forced in *Democratic Vistas* to push still further into the future.
Whether Whitman fully perceived the parallel between his own duality
and that of the nation is not entirely clear, but his duality was one of the
ways in which he had come nearest achieving his intention of expressing the life of the nation through his own lyrics. The Civil War had
preserved the political Union, but a genuinely democratic union of the
citizens of the nation was as far from a reality as ever—perhaps farther
off. And for this as well as other reasons the would-be "poet of Democ-

racy" had gained no substantial acceptance in his own native land. Indeed, his most loyal following was in England, which he had always looked upon as feudal and aristocratic. Therefore, Whitman must look to the future for the fulfillment of both his personal ambitions and the creation of a true Democracy. These reflections brought his thoughts back to his earlier philosophy of *time*, and his poetic desire to bridge the past and future by his poetic intuitions in the present.

In his Preface to *Two Rivulets* Whitman had confessed still another duality. From the beginning he had had a double motive in writing his poems:

Something more may be added—for, while I am about it, I would make a full confession. I also sent out LEAVES OF GRASS to arouse and set flowing in men's and women's hearts, young and old, (my present and future readers,) endless streams of living, pulsating love and friendship, directly from them to myself, now and ever. To this terrible, irrepressible yearning, (surely more or less down underneath in most human souls,)—this never-satisfied appetite for sympathy, and this boundless offering of sympathy—this universal democratic comradeship—this old, eternal, yet ever-new interchange of adhesiveness, so fitly emblematic of America—I have given in that book, undisguisedly, declaredly, the openest expression. . . .[54]

But however private the emotional hungers which the poems were written to satisfy, Whitman thought that they had a larger social and political significance: "In my opinion it is by a fervent, accepted development of Comradeship, the beautiful and sane affection of man for man, latent in all the young fellows, North and South, East and West . . . that the United States of the future . . . are to be most effectually welded together, intercalated, anneal'd into a Living Union." [55]

IV

Only a few of Whitman's readers ever experienced the current of love that in writing his poems he had tried to set flowing between himself and them. Rossetti and Dowden, for example, admired his lyric power and accepted him as "the poet of democracy," but they never forgot that he was an author speaking through the medium of literary art. Those who read the poems (especially "Calamus") as love poems were mainly young university men, like John Addington Symonds, Edward Carpenter, Roden Noel, and Lionel Johnson. When Symonds first read *Leaves of Grass* at Trinity College, Cambridge, in 1865, he experienced "the naked, yet inebriating vision of a God-penetrated Universe." [56] But it was the "Calamus" poems that meant most to him. As Whitman himself summed it up after several years of correspondence with him: "What Mr. Symonds admires in my books is the comradeship; he says that he had often felt it, and wanted to express it, but dared not." [57]

With Carpenter, the experience was much the same. He read the Rossetti edition at Cambridge in 1868 or 1869, and "From that time forward a profound change" took place within him; he felt a "current of sympathy" flowing westward, across the ocean, to the poet in America. [58] He gave up his plans to take clerical orders and began doing social work in London. He felt himself, as he wrote Whitman at the beginning of 1876, dedicated "to carry on what you have begun." [59] He did not, like Charles Warren Stoddard in Hawaii, [60] or young Bram Stoker in Dublin, [61] write semi-love letters to the poet, but he made the doctrine of "manly love" his guiding inspiration in trying to bring about the "Living Union" of Whitman's dream. And the poet deeply appreciated this effect of his poems.

But when his poems set love flowing in the hearts of women readers, as they sometimes did, Whitman preferred that their responses remain impersonal and vicarious, as he had demonstrated in "Out of the Rolling Ocean the Crowd," [62] and was still in 1875 demonstrating in his infrequent letters to Mrs. Gilchrist. Since sending her the ring his letters had become a little more affectionate, but doubtless he felt safe in the distance that separated them—it would be different when she threatened to annihilate that distance. In July he wrote her a short, sympathetic letter, inquiring especially about her children. [63] As to his own condition, he had to report a return of the distressing sensations in his head—summers were usually worst for him. She replied on August 28, reporting the recent death of her mother. [64] Though she did not say so in this letter, now that she no longer had the responsibility of caring for her mother she began to plan on going to America. She hinted this plan in her letter of November 16, [65] but she did not definitely announce it, and Whitman did not immediately become alarmed.

Meanwhile Mrs. Gilchrist was corresponding with Whitman's friends and well-wishers in England about the best means of aiding him financially. [66] Rossetti had suggested buying up an edition of *Leaves of Grass* to give to public libraries, but realized that some libraries might refuse to accept copies and that this could damage Whitman's rising reputation in England. Mrs. Gilchrist thought the forthcoming book *Two Rivu-*

lets would be the safest for this plan. But the English group finally decided simply to subscribe individually to the two-volume set which Whitman was printing for 1876.

Whitman had some intimation that these plans were afoot, but he knew nothing about the details, and perhaps did not dare believe that he would receive any very substantial aid. As a matter of fact, during the fall of 1875 a number of things happened to hold his attention nearer home. On November 4 Lou's first child was born, and Walt felt highly pleased when she named her son for him, though the child was not strong and lived less than a year. While Lou was still in bed, Lord Houghton from England called at 431 Stevens Street to see the poet.[67] He had recently toured New England and met the Boston and Concord literary set. Longfellow, Lowell, and Holmes had tried to discourage him from calling on the awful Whitman, but Lord Houghton brought word that Emerson was still as loyal as ever, no matter what stories to the contrary had been circulated. This pleased Whitman almost more than the honor of having this distinguished Englishman hunt him up. The two men got along wonderfully well together. The only food in the house happened to be some baked apples, and when George arrived he found Walt and his guest calmly dining on them.[68] George was embarrassed but Walt was not.

About the middle of November Whitman went to Washington. He intended to stay only two days but he enjoyed the visit so much that he remained for over two weeks.[69] Soon after he arrived he went over to Baltimore to attend the public reburial of Poe's remains and the dedication of a monument to him. Whitman was invited to sit on the platform, and he accepted, though he refused to make a speech, according to the account printed in the Washington *Star* on November 16, probably written by Whitman himself. Here he was reported to have said in an informal interview that he had long had a distaste for Poe's writings, in which he missed the sunlight, fresh air, and health, but he had recently come to appreciate Poe's special place in literary history.[70]

Not long after his return from Washington, Whitman may have made his first trip to the Stafford farm, about twelve miles from Camden, which was soon to play a very important part in his life.[71] He had become acquainted with Harry Stafford, a boy who worked in the printing office where Walt was now having his new edition set up.[72] Some time in the late autumn of 1875 Harry took his new friend to visit his parents who lived about a mile and a half from the railroad station at Kirkwood.[73]

No details of this first visit to Mr. and Mrs. George Stafford have survived, and probably Whitman did little more than establish the basis for his later friendship with this plain, good-hearted farmer and his sympathetic wife.

Whitman also made a public appearance on the night of January 27, 1876, when he read popular poems (including, perhaps, a few of his own —not so popular) in Camden "in aid of the poor." [74] Considering his own circumstances, it was ironical that he should appear on the lecture platform in such a cause. And perhaps the irony of the situation caused him some bitter thought, too, for on the day preceding this performance the *West Jersey Press* of Camden printed a long article, "Walt Whitman's Actual American Position," that was almost unmistakably written by the poet himself.[75] The Springfield *Republican*, according to this article,[76] had recently published a long and friendly account of Whitman's reputation in England and America. One might suppose that he would have been pleased with this favorable publicity, but at the time he thought that the article had given an untrue impression of his American reception:

The real truth is that with the exception of a very few readers (women equally with men), Whitman's poems in their public reception have fallen stillborn in this country. They have been met, and are met today, with the determined denial, disgust and scorn of orthodox American authors, publishers and editors, and, in a pecuniary and worldly sense, have certainly wrecked the life of their author.[77]

This was followed by a circumstantial account of the history of *Leaves of Grass*, so filled with minute biographical details that no one except the author (or someone under his direction) could have written it. After telling of the poet's misfortunes in Washington (the Harlan affair and later paralysis), the article stated that he now lived "in a sort of half-sick, half-well condition, here in Camden—and that he remains singularly hearty in spirit and good natured, though, as he himself grimly expressed it lately, 'pretty well at the end of his rope. . . .'" But this heartiness of spirit was fictitious; the very act of his writing the article, as well as its whole tone, evidenced his bitterness and desperation. And, indeed, he had experienced much to embitter and discourage him. After twenty years, as stated in the article, his poems had made

Little or no impression, (at least ostensibly,) . . . Still he stands alone. No established publishing house will yet print his books. Most of the stores will not even sell them. In fact, his works have never been really published at all.

Worse still; for the past three years having left them in charge of book agents in New York City, who, taking advantage of the author's illness and helplessness, have, three of them, one after another, successively [and] thievishly embezzled every dollar of the proceeds!

The proof of this charge of embezzlement has not survived, and it is possible that the books had not been sold as Whitman thought they had. However, about this time or soon after a dishonest printer in New York named Worthington began printing pirated copies from the plates of the Thayer and Eldridge edition, Worthington having bought the plates after the bankruptcy of the Boston firm. In the winter of 1876 Whitman was also aggrieved because he had not sold any poems recently: the *Atlantic Monthly,* he said, "will not touch him"; *Scribner's* returned his "offerings . . . with insulting notes" and *"The Galaxy* the same." Even *Harper's* was now closed to him.[78]

Whitman's suffering and disappointment had probably led him to suspect a more rigid conspiracy against him than actually existed. One truth of the matter is that since the publication of "Song of the Redwood Tree" and "Prayer of Columbus" he had not been able to write any poems of comparable quality. His condition was truly pathetic, but editors are not noted for their charity. His complete *Leaves of Grass* was of course unacceptable both to British and to American publishers, and he would not permit the publication in America of such an expurgated volume as Rossetti had edited in England. His eccentricity of form and manners had also made him an easy target for newspaper satire, and contrary to his protested indifference, he was actually a very sensitive man. And now in sickness, loneliness, and poverty he was more sensitive than ever. This is the obvious explanation for the poet's next act in the *West Jersey Press* incident.

Whitman promptly clipped the article and sent it to William Rossetti, with the comment: "My theory is that the plain truth of the situation here is [that is, is here] best stated; it is even worse than described in the article." [79] Without delay Rossetti got the article printed in the London *Athenaeum* on March 11, 1876, and two days later Robert Buchanan followed it up in the London *Daily News* with a scathing and intemperate attack on the United States for neglecting her greatest man of letters.[80] He begged his countrymen to give the American poet "a substantial proof of the honour in which he is held here in the heart of England."

Buchanan's blast had several immediate effects. A few British magazines, notably the *Saturday Review,*[81] replied that so foul an author ought to be neglected, but with the British press in general the chance to show up American stupidity and cruelty was more appealing than the opportunity to censure the author of a questionable book. And naturally these attacks infuriated the American press. Bayard Taylor replied in the New York *Tribune,* quoting the *Saturday Press* and berating Buchanan.[82] The *Tribune* was the most persistent in the attacks on Whitman, though a great many other papers joined in the general hue and cry. In one of the *Tribune* attacks it was claimed that Washington authors had succeeded in having a father with four children ousted from his Government clerkship in order to make a place for Whitman,[83] an obvious fabrication because no "Washington authors" except O'Connor and Burroughs had ever supported Whitman in any of his job-seeking.

Although William O'Connor was still estranged from Walt, these falsehoods and misrepresentations in the *Tribune* were more than he could stand. He wrote another protest,[84] and John Burroughs also sent in a long and effective reply.[85] Both letters were printed, but these were almost the only defenses in America that Whitman received. However, even he himself now seemed to feel that his poverty and neglect had been overstated by himself and his friends. To Mrs. Gilchrist he protested that he was not in desperate need.[86] Frank Sanborn visited him early in April and sent a special dispatch from Philadelphia to the Springfield (Massachusetts) *Republican* in which he reported the poet

. . . though graver than formerly, is none the less cheerful, and has no complaints or reproaches against the Muse or against the power that rules the world. Certain statements made in his name about the neglect of critics and publishers, and the hardships of poverty, have come from him [note the giveaway] only as a mention of the simple fact, and not as reproaches or entreaties, and they ought not so to be interpreted.[87]

Later in the article Sanborn stated that, "Whitman lives comfortably and pleasantly, as an invalid can, with his brother, Col. George W. Whitman, who is inspector of gas-pipes in the city of Camden."

It is not easy to interpret Whitman's conduct in this whole episode. Had he simply in a period of emotional instability given way to his feelings, or had he deliberately planned the writing and use of the article to stir up sympathy for himself in Great Britain? Perhaps it is doubtful that he foresaw the repercussion in America. However we may judge his contradictory statements and conduct, we should remember that the poet was a very sick man, in mind as well as body. And although temporarily he received more unfavorable publicity in America than usual, in the long run he gained immense benefits from the international squabble over him. First of all, a long list of literary people in England subscribed for his Centennial Edition (on the title page called "Author's Edition"). Whitman set the price at ten dollars for the two volumes, but many of his British purchasers paid two or three times the price, and some bought several sets. The list included such names as Tennyson, the Rossetti brothers, Edmund Gosse, George Saintsbury, Lord Houghton, Justin McCarthy, Ford Madox Brown, and of course all those who had been corresponding with him—Mrs. Gilchrist, Robert Buchanan, Edward Carpenter, Moncure D. Conway, and many others.[88]

The money gave Whitman a temporary feeling of security, but best of all was the recognition. He called these good tidings "the blessed gales from the British Isles" and "deep medicines." [89] Publicity in the newspapers about this British support galled the Bayard Taylor clique in New York, but America could not help being impressed by such names as Tennyson and Dante Gabriel Rossetti. Although Whitman's reputation in America did not begin to climb immediately, there was an accumulative effect that became apparent a few years later. And the most important result of all was the boost to Whitman's morale. In the spring he returned to the Stafford farm for a prolonged stay, and his health began to improve almost immediately. It is difficult to say which helped more, the farm or the British subscribers, but certainly the "deep medicines" from across the Atlantic made it possible for nature to start the healing process.

Mrs. Gilchrist had meanwhile announced that she was coming to America, but this prospect hardly contributed to the invalid's recuperation. In her letter of January 18, 1876, she had told Whitman of her intention to sail on August 30 for Philadelphia, where she hoped to rent a house for herself and her three children, Beatrice, Herbert, and Grace.[90] Beatrice planned to study medicine at the University of Pennsylvania and Herbert would continue learning to paint. Mrs. Gilchrist asked if Walt could advise her about finding a boardinghouse where she could stay until she could rent a suitable house (she was bringing enough household goods to furnish it). He continued to mail newspapers and clippings but sent no advice, though she did not suspect the cause of his silence. On February 25 she wrote again, pointing out that "this is the last spring we shall be asunder," and imploring him: "Hold on but a little longer for me, my Walt—I am straining every nerve to hasten the day—I have enough for us all (with the simple, unpretentious ways we both love best)." [91] Then on March 11, she asked him: "Take from my picture a long, long look of tender love and joy and faith, deathless, ever young, ever growing, ever learning, aspiring love, tender, cherishing, domestic love." [92]

Before he had received this last message, Walt replied some time in March to the February 25 letter. After telling Mrs. Gilchrist that he had mailed her two volumes of his new edition and reporting that his health seemed "a shade better," he worked his way into the real purpose of his writing:

I even already vaguely contemplate plans (they may never be fulfilled, but yet again they may) of changes, journeys—even of coming to London & seeing you, visiting my friends, &c. [Notice his vagueness—and then his sudden clarity.] *My dearest friend, I do not approve your American trans-settlement. I see so many things here you have no idea of—the social, and almost every other kind of crudeness, meagerness, here (at least in appearance.)*

Don't do anything towards it nor resolve in it nor make any move at all in it without further advice from me. If I should get well enough to voyage, we will talk about it yet in London.[93]

Of course, this hint of his visiting London was merely an attempt to stall for time. However, she was not to be stopped so easily. On March 30 she retorted: "I will not act without 'further advice from you'; but as to not resolving on it, dear friend, I can't exactly obey that, for it has been my settled, steady purpose (resting on a deep, strong faith) ever since 1869." [94] And on April 21 she begged him: "Do not dissuade me from coming this autumn, my dearest Friend. I have waited patiently—7 years—patiently, yet often, especially since your illness, with such painful yearning your heart would yearn towards me if you realized it—I cannot wait any longer." [95] On May 18 she wrote that she planned to sail for Philadelphia around September 1. She did suggest that "if there be indeed an increasing hope of your coming here in the course of the summer" he should let her know immediately. Actually, Walt had no such hope, and he now knew how hopeless it was to stop this determined woman. But he had done everything he could to warn her; so with a clear conscience he went off to the Stafford farm and enjoyed the happiest summer he had known since his Long Island boyhood.

Whitman arrived at the Stafford farm for his first stay some time in late April or early May of 1876. George and Susan Stafford had five children, Edwin, Harry, Vandoran, and two small daughters. George Stafford was a quiet, serious, religious man, who occasionally preached in nearby Methodist churches. He and Whitman got along without friction but they never became intimate friends. However, Mrs. Stafford's maternal sympathies were immediately aroused by the semi-invalid who came to board with her and there quickly grew up between them a strong bond of understanding and affection. When she first saw the poet she thought he could not live more than a few months, but she wanted to do something to counteract his profound dejection; so she began to tell him about men she had known who had lived twenty years or more after a paralytic stroke.[96] This cheered him up more than anything the doctors had been able to say to him. When he came back in the spring of 1876, he began sitting out of doors. Soon one of the children started following him around with a light chair to sit in as soon as he was tired. At first he could go only a very short distance before having to rest, but gradually he increased the distance between the stops.

The Staffords lived in a pleasant house, part of it quite old, with maples and lilac bushes growing in the yard. The land sloped down to Timber Creek about 400 yards away, to which a rail-fenced lane led from a cow pasture near the house down to the water. Before long Whitman began advancing down the lane by easy stages, resting frequently in the chair and carefully estimating the strength needed for the return. It was several weeks before he finally reached the creek, but before the summer was over he could make the round trip unassisted. As he hobbled up and down the hill he became as minutely acquainted with its topography, scenery, plant, and animal life as Thoreau had been with Walden Pond. Like Thoreau, too, he kept notes, which he later used for some of the most charming prose in his *Specimen Days*.[97]

Near the foot of the hill a spring poured forth a stream of pure clear water as large as the poet's stout neck. Willows surrounded this refreshing spot, mint grew in profusion underfoot, and thickets of blackberries stood nearby. But the tree-lined creek interested Whitman most. There from June until September he bathed in the stream and took sunbaths on the grassy banks. At first one of the Stafford boys had to help him undress, but later he was able to be entirely independent and was left alone in this secluded spot. No houses were in sight and trespassers were rare, though apparently some of the neighbors did hear of this solitary nudity and were scandalized—perhaps thereby unintentionally giving him an even more exclusive possession of the creek. At this spot there was also an abandoned marl pit, and Whitman added mud baths to his routine, followed by vigorous scrubbing with a brush. For exercise he sang or declaimed at the top of his voice—popular songs, airs from the operas he had reveled in during his younger days in New York, and passages from Shakespeare or Homer or some other poet whom he had once recited to the waves on Long Island or shouted from the top of a Broadway stage in the midst of the traffic din. For hours at a time he simply sat or lay in the warm sunshine, but as soon as he had gained a little endurance he began wrestling with a limber sapling, and he believed that he could almost feel the strength of the young, healthy tree flowing into his half paralyzed limbs. To occupy his time and thoughts he also took notes. For years he had always carried little notebooks with him wherever he went, and scribbling down observations and impressions had become a fixed habit with him. Now he frequently made records of his rich sensory life at Timber Creek.

Although no object or creature was too small or insignificant to catch his attention, it was the trees that impressed him most during his first full summer at the creek. Perhaps having written a poem on the redwood tree (which he had never seen in reality) made him more observant of trees; but the sturdy oak he loved to sit under, or the tall poplar that he never tired of gazing at, had the qualities of strength, endurance, and passivity which he was doing his best to cultivate, and he thought of the trees quite literally as his companions.[98]

Occasionally Whitman returned to Camden for a few days. He probably called on Mrs. Gilchrist, or she on him, soon after her arrival in Philadelphia around the first of September. That first meeting was probably embarrassing for Walt and painful for Mrs. Gilchrist. To judge by her impassioned letters, her impulse to rush into his arms must have been almost overwhelming—and his reluctance to encourage her delusion was no doubt as strong as it had been throughout this strange one-sided courtship. But no one left any record whatever of that first meeting.

John Burroughs came down during the month to attend the Centennial and of course he visited Walt. Both men went over to see the Gilchrists in their Philadelphia hotel.[99] Burroughs wrote his wife that Whitman liked Mrs. Gilchrist and her family, and he himself helped her to find a house to rent, a new one at 1929 North 22nd Street. There a room was set aside for Walt any time he wished to use it, and during the next year and a half he did make use of it several times, occasionally staying a week or more. But more often, when the weather was good (and he was not at the Staffords'), he would catch the five o'clock ferry to Philadelphia, change to a streetcar, and arrive at the Gilchrists in time for "tea-supper." Mrs. Gilchrist's younger daughter, Grace, later described the after-supper scene:

After that was over, we would all take our chairs out, American fashion, beside the "stoop,"—that is, on to the pavement, below the front steps of the house. The poet sat in our midst, in a large bamboo rocking-chair, and we listened as he talked, on many subjects—human and literary. Walt Whitman was at this time fifty-eight, but he looked seventy. His beard and hair were snow-white, his complexion a fine colour, and unwrinkled. He had still, though stricken in 1873 by paralysis, a most majestic presence. He was over six feet, but he walked lame, dragging the left leg, and leaning heavily on a stick. He was dressed always in a complete suit of grey clothes with a large spotless white linen collar, his flowing white beard filling in the gap at his sunburnt throat. He possessed a full-toned, rather high, baritone voice, a little harsh and lacking in the finer modulations for sustained recitation; having an excellent memory, he declaimed many scenes from Shakespeare, poems by Tennyson, and occasionally his own. The "Mystic Trumpeter" was a favourite with him. . . .[100]

When he stayed overnight, the family observed that he sang while bathing and dressing—always fragments of songs, sometimes a bar from "The Star-Spangled Banner," or "snatches" from operas. He told the Gilchrists that he did not sing for pleasure in the music but for the exercise, though he often talked of the enjoyment he had experienced in the 1850's, in attending the opera. When the conversation turned to books he revealed the favorites and typical views which he had held for many years. George Sand remained his favorite author, and he thought Consuelo superior to any of Shakespeare's heroines. Actually, Shakespeare's heroines had never, he said, given him much satisfaction. He thought perhaps this was because boys had played the feminine roles in Shakespeare's day—though, in truth, he had never cared for Shakespeare's comedies, and preferred the more bombastic tragedies, such as Richard III, as we have seen before.[101] Most critics have found the heroines of Shakespeare's comedies to have far greater depth of character than the heroes, but Whitman seemed to have a congenital blindness to their subtle charms.

Our only clues to Mrs. Gilchrist's real feelings about Whitman while she was in Philadelphia and seeing him frequently are the comments she made in her letters to William Rossetti.[102] In these she insisted that she had not been disappointed in him, that he was all she expected him to be. But she must soon have realized that he simply could not return the affection for her that she felt for him. She was always to remain a loyal friend, but henceforth the friendship was to exist on the level that Whitman himself preferred—informal, companionable, but devoid of any sexual emotion whatever.

Even though he found that he liked Mrs. Gilchrist and her children, Whitman still derived most enjoyment during the fall of 1876 from the Stafford farm. The Centennial Exposition, which he had made the occasion of issuing a special edition of his works, seems to have meant very little to him after its opening. Perhaps the appointment of Bayard Taylor as the Centennial poet had spoiled it for him. Of course, it was also difficult for him to get around, and a large fair can be very exhausting. In his diaries preserved in *Specimen Days* he mentioned attending the Centennial only once and then he enjoyed his return on the ferry more than anything he had seen or heard at the Exposition.

Whitman seems to have gone back and forth between the farm and Camden a number of times during the autumn, but he was at Timber Creek during much of September, October, and November. He was in the country immediately following the equinoctial storm and was still there early in October. On the evening of October 20 he felt that he had never really seen the sky before, and from this time on for several years he seemed to derive his greatest pleasure from watching the clouds and the color of the sky during the day and the stars and constellations at night.[103]

Back in July Jeff and his two girls had arrived in Camden for a long visit; [104] and in December they took Walt down to the Jersey seashore. He was pleased by a five-mile drive in a carriage on the hard-packed sand, but his keenest delight came from a two-hour stroll all by himself on the deserted beach. This brought back to him many of his childhood and youthful memories on Long Island. For years at intervals, he had had a recurrent dream of "a stretch of interminable white-brown sand, hard and smooth and broad, with the ocean perpetually, grandly, rolling in upon it, with slow-measured sweep, with rustle and hiss and foam, and many a thump as of low bass drums. This scene, this picture, I say, has risen before me at times for years. Some times I wake at night and can hear and see it plainly." [105]

VI

January 28, 1877, was the one hundred and fortieth anniversary of the birth of Tom Paine, and Whitman felt sufficiently recovered to feel that he should commemorate it by a lecture. He preserved a résumé of the speech in Specimen Days,[106] and fortunately one of the few people who heard it has left a description of the occasion. This witness was Frank Harris, and the description is in My Life and Loves. Although this book does not enjoy a very good reputation for accuracy, the account of the lecture contains details that agree with the known facts of Whitman's life and opinions at this time and cannot be dismissed as fictitious. Harris did say that the lecture was given during late December, 1875, or January, 1876, whereas Whitman dated it 1877, given in Lincoln Hall, but this error would be an easy one to make some years after the event. Harris was attending for the purpose of taking notes for a friend of his on the editorial staff of the Philadelphia Press—though apparently the report was never printed.

According to this witness, on the evening of the lecture the weather was extremely disagreeable, with the thermometer near zero and a fierce wind driving the falling snow. Only about thirty people braved the storm to hear the lecture, and they sat huddled in an ill-lit, poorly heated hall large enough for a thousand. Whitman walked slowly and stiffly onto the stage, wearing a short jacket that cocked up behind like the tail of a Cochin China rooster which Harris remembered from his childhood. The poet spoke very slowly, but with honest conviction. He told his audience of having known a colonel in the Army (Colonel Fellows), who had been a friend of Paine, and he had assured Whitman that all the accusations against Paine's habits and character were false. "And the Colonel was an unimpeachable witness, . . . a man of the highest honor, and most scrupulous veracity." [107]

The cold weather continued into February. On the third Whitman spent two hours on a ferry trying unsuccessfully to make its way through the ice on the Delaware River to Philadelphia.[108] During the February thaw he went back to the Staffords', and on the eleventh he thought he "heard the first hum and preparation of awakening spring." But it was too cold to stay at Timber Creek and Walt returned to Camden. J. H. Johnston, the New York jeweler, had been urging him for several years to visit his family in New York, and in the last week of February Whitman accepted this standing invitation.[109] Johnston met him in Jersey City and took him over to 113 East 10th Street. There in the evening he met several people whom the Johnstons had invited to meet their guest. Whitman's host had also arranged with George W. Waters to paint his portrait, and the artist began the sittings the next morning. A day or so later Edmund Clarence Stedman called, and thereafter became an admirer and defender of the poet—though not always sufficiently ardent to satisfy him during his last years. On this first visit to the Johnstons Walt stayed a month, but it ended in sadness, for on the day he had planned to leave Mrs. Johnston became violently ill. He stayed over for one day, hoping to see a change in her condition, but he had to leave the family mourning her death.

For the next three months Walt went back and forth between Camden and the farm several times. On May 21 he was in Camden and spent a very delightful evening crossing and re-crossing the Delaware. An hour or two after sundown he observed "Venus like blazing silver well up in the west. The large pale thin crescent of the new moon, half an hour high, sinking languidly under a bar-sinister of cloud, and then emerging. Arcturus right overhead. A faint fragrant sea-odor wafted up from the south." As the evening advanced he became absorbed in watching the constellations, the Water-Serpent, the Swan, the northern Crown, the Eagle and Lyra. "All the usual sense of motion, all animal life, seem'd discarded, seem'd a fiction; a curious power, like the placid rest of Egyptian gods, took possession, none the less potent for being impalpable." [110] These moods, becoming more numerous as Whitman recovered his health, had the same mystical quality and emotional intensity that he had experienced in early manhood on Long Island and in Washington during the height of his poetic power.

Much of 1877 and the first half of 1878 Whitman spent at Timber Creek. During the summer of 1877 the sun bathing, mud baths, and outdoor exercises began to work a very perceptible improvement in his health. He still dragged his left foot in walking, but he felt better than he had at any time since his stroke. It was probably during this summer that Mrs. Gilchrist made a surprise visit to the Stafford farm and he became very angry, according to Mrs. Stafford.[111] In view of the pleasant disposition and even placidity of temperament that most of Whitman's biographers have depicted, Mrs. Stafford's testimony is especially interesting. Though she was devoted to him, she did not always find him genial or considerate. After he was able to walk with more ease he often stayed at the creek until midnight or after and sometimes he would awaken in the middle of the night and go out for an hour or two to watch the stars and the sky.[112] Mrs. Stafford greatly feared that he might have another stroke while wandering around at night alone and she always listened until he returned before she dared go back to sleep herself. In this way he caused her a great deal of worry and trouble of which he was unaware.

But Mrs. Stafford also reported that Whitman had the worst temper of anyone she had ever known. He would suddenly erupt like a volcano, after which he would be very quiet.[113] He always became angry when she straightened up his papers. About most things she humored him, but she insisted on cleaning his room and straightening his papers. She ignored his angry protests and in a few minutes he would burst into song. He also disliked being disturbed down at the creek, and she instructed the children never to go near him when he seemed to be enjoying a secluded spot.

Apparently Whitman's relations with young Harry Stafford were not always peaceful either, for in his diary notes for 1876–1877 Whitman refers to several "scenes" with "H.S." [114] The cause of these arguments is not clear, though Walt seems to have loaned Harry moderate sums of money at various times, and this could have caused friction. The only thing certain is that the friendship was almost shattered by emotional outbursts— probably on both sides.

VII

In all probability George and Lou often experienced Walt's sudden outbursts of anger, but few of his visitors suspected this side of his character and personality. On May 2, 1877, a young man from England who had corresponded with the poet for several years knocked at 431 Stevens Street.[115] He was Edward Carpenter, whose life had been changed by reading *Leaves of Grass* at Cambridge University. He was promptly admitted to a conventional middle-class American sitting room, with its ornamental tables, photograph albums, and "things under glass shades." Walt was called, probably by his sister-in-law, and he came hobbling down the stairs, leaning heavily on the banisters, ". . . at first sight quite an old man with long grey, almost white, beard, and shaggy head and neck, grey dress too; but tall, erect, and at closer sight not so old—a florid fresh complexion, pure grey-blue eye (no sign of age there) and full, strong, well-formed hands." [116]

As they talked Carpenter "was aware of a certain radiant power" in the man, "a large benign effluence and inclusiveness, as of the sun, which filled out the place where he was—yet with something of reserve and sadness in it too, and a sense of remoteness and inaccessibility." These impressions were deepened during the two or three weeks that Carpenter remained in the vicinity and visited Whitman for a part of nearly every day. On his first trip to Camden, Whitman suggested that they go over to Philadelphia and see the city, which they did mainly by streetcar. A day or so later he visited the poet at the Staffords', and shortly after both were house guests of Mrs. Gilchrist for a week. Then Carpenter accepted an invitation to visit John Burroughs on the Hudson, after which he toured New England and tried without success to defend Whitman before the Cambridge literati, Longfellow, Lowell, and Holmes.[117] He finally left America with the impression that "Whitman seemed to fill out 'Leaves of Grass,' and form an interpretation of it." Carpenter was convinced that the poems expressed only what the poet had experienced, and in both the man and his book "there were clearly enough visible the same strong and contrary moods, the same strange omnivorous egotism, controlled and restrained by that wonderful genius of his for human affection and love." [118]

During the summer of 1877 Whitman was visited in Camden by another man, this time a Canadian, who was to become an even more important friend of his than Edward Carpenter. This was Dr. Richard Maurice Bucke, superintendent of an insane asylum in London, Ontario, and a man with a truly remarkable background. He had grown up in the "bush" of western Canada, fought Indians in the United States, lost a foot from frostbite in an unsuccessful attempt to cross the Sierra Nevada Mountains in the winter of 1836, and yet despite this handicap had worked his way through medical school.[119] By the time he met Whitman he had earned a reputation as an alienist, and, as we shall see presently, he was also a pronounced mystic. Dr. Bucke had been reading *Leaves of Grass* for nearly ten years, and he decided to visit the poet on a trip to the Centennial Exposition, which was still in progress. His first sensation after knocking at 431 Stevens Street was much the same as Edward Carpenter's, but the poet made an even deeper impression on him than en the younger man, for in Whitman's presence Dr. Bucke experienced a "spiritual intoxication" that lasted for several weeks and was the "turning point" of his life: "It seemed to me at that time certain that he was either actually a god or in some sense clearly preterhuman." [120]

Joaquin Miller sometimes referred to Whitman in words almost as extravagant, though usually in a less serious mood than Dr. Bucke. In December, 1877, he came to Philadelphia to attend the opening of his play *The Danites*, and took tea with Mrs. Gilchrist and Walt. When his old friend entered the room, Miller exclaimed, "He looks like a god, tonight." Whitman took the Gilchrists to see Miller's play, and Mrs. Gilchrist described him "sitting in the recess of the box, and now and then nodding approval of the dialogue, but with the reserve of an old play-goer, who has seen the great artists." [121]

Mrs. Gilchrist thought Walt had made great progress in recovering his health, though his lameness did not abate, and she could not help noticing that he spoke sometimes of having " 'a wounded brain' and of being quite altered from his former self." Early in 1878 he suffered a minor and temporary setback—very likely from over-exposure to damp and cold.

One of the New York poets whom Whitman had met at the Johnstons', Richard Watson Gilder, suggested to Burroughs[122] as early as February 3, 1878, that Whitman's friends in New York (he mentioned especially John Swinton but he was also in touch with Johnston) arrange for him to give a lecture on Lincoln around April 14, or 15. Whitman was very receptive to the idea, but it finally had to be abandoned because of his weak physical condition.

Whitman's routine visits to Mrs. Gilchrist also ceased in the spring because she, by this time apparently cured of her romantic infatuation for him, decided to break up her household in Philadelphia, store her furniture, and leave for Massachusetts. Her daughter Beatrice was now an intern in a Boston hospital, and this may have influenced her to make this move. From Northfield, Massachusetts, Mrs. Gilchrist wrote Burroughs on May 1, 1878, about her plans and then reported on Walt's condition: "He is fairly well again—not so strong as before yet, but in a way to be so soon, now he can get out and be so constantly in the open air [at Timber Creek]. Dr. Weir Mitchell's opinion was encouraging . . . it was simply cold and rheumatism. Camden is a bad place for him; he wants mountain air, says the Dr., and I hope he will have some in the course of the summer." [123]

By June Whitman had recovered sufficiently to accept an invitation from J. H. Johnston and his second wife, Alma Calder, to be their house guest in their new home on upper Fifth Avenue.[124] Two hours before departure he saw a newspaper announcement of William Cullen Bryant's funeral next day and "Felt a strong desire to attend." At the Johnstons' he felt at home and at peace, "away up on Fifth Avenue, near Eighty-sixth Street, quiet, breezy, overlooking the dense woody fringe of the Park—plenty of space and sky, birds chirping, and air comparatively odorless." Next day John Burroughs came down from his home at Esopus and attended the funeral with Whitman, Swinton, Gilder, Stedman, and Dr. Bucke, who had also come from Canada for the occasion. A few days later Walt, accompanied by the Johnstons' young son, Albert, took a steamboat up the Hudson and spent a few days with Burroughs. There he picked currants and raspberries for his breakfasts, went driving with John and Albert, and immensely enjoyed the companionship, the scenery, and Mrs. Burroughs's good cooking. Before returning to Camden he spent a few more days in New York and found his greatest pleasure in a sailing trip out into the bay, southeast of Staten Island, past Sandy Hook and the highlands of Navesink.

The New York trip did Whitman much good, but he was glad to get back to Timber Creek, where he spent most of the summer. He now began to catalogue the flowers and birds of the vicinity, but as so many times in the past, his mystic rapport with nature came chiefly from watching the sky—"the full sky of the Bible, of Arabia, of the prophets, and of the oldest poems." [125] On the night of July 22, 1878, it seemed to him, "As if for the first time, indeed, creation noiselessly sank into and through me its placid and untellable lesson . . . the visible suggestion of God in space and time—now once definitely indicated if never again."

In October Mrs. Gilchrist wrote Walt of the pleasant time she was having in Concord, Massachusetts. She talked with all of Walt's Concord friends and visited Emerson. His memory had decayed so that he could not remember Thoreau's name, but "he looked very beautiful and talked in a friendly, pleasant manner." [126] During the fall Herbert Gilchrist was much with Whitman, painting his portrait, but in November he joined his mother in New York at 112 Madison Avenue, where she had decided to spend the winter. Both Herbert and his mother took great interest in the new plans of Whitman's friends to arrange for his Lincoln lecture in April. And this time it actually came off.

This first lecture on the death of Lincoln was given on April 14, 1879, in Steck Hall on Fourteenth Street.[127] How successful the performance was we have no proof. Whitman remained seated and read his manuscript. Next day the *Tribune* reported the lecture (perhaps under the influence of Mr. Johnston, who was a friend of Whitelaw Reid, the owner). Here it was stated that Whitman wished to have other lecture engagements. His old dream of a lecture tour had returned, but once again nothing came of it. All witnesses agree that he was not naturally a good public speaker. Mrs. O'Connor, who was certainly devoted to him, stated that when he began to read or speak in public he affected an artificial, theatrical delivery and the muscles of his throat seemed to become constricted, so that he lost the natural charm of his conversational voice.[128] In this lecture he sketched the various glimpses he had had of Lincoln, and then vividly described the theater and the living drama of the assassination—adopting the point of view of an eyewitness[129] though Whitman had been in Brooklyn at the time.

After the lecture Whitman stayed on at the Johnstons' until April 23, when he again went up the Hudson for a visit with John and Ursula Burroughs. This, his third and last visit to Riverby, the Burroughs home at Esopus, was his most leisurely and enjoyable one. On April 26 Burroughs wrote in his *Journal:*

These days I am happy. The days are perfection—sweet, bright, uncloying April days—and then Walt Whitman is here. He sits in the open bay window, reading, writing, musing, and looking down upon Smith and me grafting the trees or ploughing among the currants, or upon me alone wheeling baby Julian about the grounds. His white beard and ruddy face make a picture there I delight to see. Occasionally he comes out and strolls about, or sits on the wall on the brink of the hill, and looks out upon the scene. Presently I join him and we have much talk.[130]

Walt himself made extensive notes during this visit, some of which he later used in *Specimen Days*.[131] He was interested in everything he saw, heard, smelled, and tasted. Under the tutelage of his ornithologist friend he was especially observant of birds, though some of his notes show that he depended more on Burroughs's descriptions than on his own observations. The "grandest" sight he recorded was of a great eagle soaring over the Hudson, yet once again many of the details must have come from Burroughs, for he described its motions in storm and gale and different seasons of the year, not in the balmy spring weather of his visit.

But Whitman's enjoyment at Riverby was not confined to nature

study. Burroughs drove him over to Vassar College at Poughkeepsie, where he met Dr. Frederic L. Ritter, a composer and teacher
of music, and his wife, Mrs. Fannie Ritter.[132] Dr. Ritter had set some of
Whitman's poems to music, and he told the poet that he often read
Leaves of Grass to put him into "the free, exalted mood necessary to
compose music." He also said that Whitman's poems were easy to set to
music, because the music was already there and all the composer had
to do was to transcribe it.

On May 3 Burroughs wrote in his *Journal:* "Walt left today. The
weather has been nearly perfect, and his visit has been a great treat to
me—April days with Homer and Socrates for company." [133] Whitman returned to the Johnstons', where he remained until after Mrs. Gilchrist
sailed for England on June 7.[134] Curiously, though he devoted several
pages in *Specimen Days* to his experiences during these weeks in New
York, he did not once so much as allude to Mrs. Gilchrist. He wrote of
his walks in Central Park and his talks with policemen; his mingling with
the crowds downtown, which brought back to him the delightful sensations of his younger days; and an exhilarating experience on May 25: "A
three-hours' bay-trip from 12 to 3 this afternoon, accompanying the
City of Brussels down as far as the Narrows, in behoof of some Europe-
bound friends, to give them a good send off." [135] But these friends were
not the Gilchrists, who were not to sail for nearly two weeks, and they
did not go on the *City of Brussels.* However, Whitman enjoyed this experience so much that two days later he watched other famous ships start
for Europe. And apparently on the same day he took a three-hours' bay
trip and went aboard a United States warship, the *Minnesota,* where he
was particularly impressed by "the sight of the young fellows themselves,"
who gave a vocal concert while he was present. Next day one of the
lieutenants met Walt at the pier with a boat and rowed him out to the
warship, where he watched the boys drill, shared lunch with them, and
made new friends.[136]

Such experiences as these in a man's world meant more to Walt than
the drawing-room society of the Johnstons, the Gilders, or Mrs. Botta,
the wife of an Italian professor, where he met authors, artists, and mu-
sicians. Johnston himself made the observation that during Walt's previous visit "One day Whitelaw Reid called and staid two hours, and the
next day an old Broadway omnibus driver, with whom Walt had taken
many a ride called, and that night my wife remarked that she wondered
if Walt did not enjoy the Bus driver's call quite as much as he did

Whitelaw Reid's." [137] Walt appreciated the attention and kindness of all his friends, but there can be little doubt that Mrs. Johnston's surmise was correct as to his preference in companions.

During the Gilchrists' last weeks in America they were also house guests of the Johnstons, and on the day of their sailing, as Johnston later told Clara Barrus, Walt and Mrs. Gilchrist held a conference in the parlor and "both were deeply moved on rejoining the family. It was their real farewell. What passed between them was locked in their hearts. All their talks were ended." [138] Whether they sensed the fact or not, this was indeed their last talk, for Whitman would never be able to get to England, and Mrs. Gilchrist had only six more years to live. For some reason Whitman did not see the ship, the *Circassia*, depart, so that his last glimpse of Mrs. Gilchrist was at the Johnstons'.

The summer following Mrs. Gilchrist's departure Whitman spent at Timber Creek, with the same enjoyment and beneficial effects he had experienced for the past three summers. It was probably during the summer of 1879 that Longfellow crossed the Delaware to visit him,[139] but at the time this event did not especially impress Whitman. Longfellow came over with George W. Childs, a wealthy Philadelphian, but Walt was not at home. At the wharf one of the ferry men told them that Walt was on one of the boats (evidently riding back and forth, as he often did); so they waited for him. Because of the delay in finding Walt, the chat was brief and Longfellow did not say anything that was particularly interesting or memorable. A few years later, however, Walt looked back upon this meeting with a certain amount of pride.

In the following autumn Whitman finally got the opportunity to make a trip which he had dreamed of for many years—indeed, in his early poems had often made in his imagination. Colonel John W. Forney, publisher of the Philadelphia *Press*, and the Old Settlers of Kansas Committee invited him to be the guest of honor and visiting poet at the Kansas Quarter Centennial Celebration to be held in Lawrence, Kansas.[140] Perhaps this honor was not as flattering as a similar invitation to the Centennial Exposition would have been, but he had always wanted to see the West, and then also he would be able to visit Jeff and his nieces in St. Louis. The party, which included several others besides the poet and Colonel Forney, left West Philadelphia on the night of September 10. Sleeping cars were still a novelty and this was Whitman's first experience on one. Writing of it later he declared, half seriously: "They say the French Voltaire in his time designated the grand opera and a ship of war the most signal illustrations of the growth of humanity's and art's advance beyond primitive barbarism. Perhaps if the witty philosopher were here these days, and went in the same car with perfect bedding and feed from New York to San Francisco, he would shift his type and sample to one of our American sleepers." [141]

The train was supposed to reach St. Louis in thirty-six hours, but a "collision and bad locomotive smash" about two-thirds of the distance caused a delay, and Walt was able to spend only one night with his brother before continuing. He crossed Missouri in daylight and decided that this state stood "in the front rank of the Union. Of Missouri averaged politically and socially I have heard all sorts of talk, some pretty severe—but I should have no fear myself of getting along safely and comfortably anywhere among the Missourians."

The party changed trains at Kansas City and then sped on to Lawrence, Kansas, where Whitman and Colonel Forney were entertained in the home of Judge John P. Usher, who had been Secretary of the Interior under Lincoln and was now mayor of Lawrence. To Whitman's surprise he learned that he was expected to deliver a poem at a meeting in Topeka. Having no poem ready for the occasion, he wrote out a short speech to read, but he was so interested in talking to Judge Usher's sons, "true Westerners of the noblest type," that he forgot to go and deliver it.[142] The whole trip was sprinkled with such fiascoes, but the poet was not disturbed by them. He was interviewed for several newspapers, and he wrote out imaginary interviews for others. In all his public—or intended public—utterances he praised the Westerners for the heroic qualities which he had always imagined them to possess, some of which by this time had become the folklore of the nation. He continued to Denver, which completely captivated him. And after seeing Platte Canyon he declared, "I have found the law of my own poems."

Whitman left Denver by the Rio Grande and returned by the more southerly route. He saw Pike's Peak and was disappointed; he expected something more spectacular. At Pueblo he boarded the Atchison, Topeka and Santa Fe Railroad and headed east. As he traveled back across the prairies he mused on the country and the future:

Grand as is the thought that doubtless the child is already born who will see a hundred millions of people, the most prosperous and advanc'd of the world, inhabiting these Prairies, the great Plains, and the valley of the Mississippi, I could not help thinking it would be grander still to see all those inimitable American areas fused in the alembic of a perfect poem, or other esthetic work, entirely Western, fresh and limitless—altogether our own, without a trace or taste of Europe's soil, reminiscence, technical letter or spirit.[143]

Every "sight and feature" exhilarated him: the cactuses, buffalo grass, the "far circle-line of the horizon," the prairie dogs, and herds of antelope, the names of the towns (Eagle-Tail, Coyote, Cheyenne, Agate, Monotony, Kit Carson), the herds of cattle and ubiquitous cowboys—"to me a strangely interesting class, bright-eyed as hawks, with their swarthy complexions and their broad-brimm'd hats. . . ."[144]

Emotionally this trip was one of the most thrilling experiences of Whitman's life, and he had the illusion that it contributed to his intellectual development. But actually it only brought to the surface the accumulated beliefs and clichés of a lifetime. Everything he saw merely confirmed the ideas and theories which he had been expressing in his poems since 1855. But by the time he reached St. Louis he was physically exhausted and really ill. Partly because of the need for rest and partly for financial reasons—for Colonel Forney had gone on and left him entirely on his own resources—his visit to Jeff stretched into three months, and he became bored and restless. He tried to read in the Mercantile Library, but reached the typical conclusion that "all the prevalent book and library poets" were alien to America. To understand how shallow they were one must "dwell or travel awhile in Missouri, Kansas and Colorado, and get rapport with their people and country."[145]

On September 28 Whitman read that General Grant had arrived in San Francisco after a trip around the world, and this led him to declare, apparently completely oblivious of the corruption of Grant's administration:

What a man he is! what a history! what an illustration—his life—of the capacities of that American individuality common to us all! Cynical critics are wondering "what the people can see in Grant" to make such a hubbub about. They aver (and it is no doubt true) that he has hardly the average of our day's literary and scholastic culture, and absolutely no pronounc'd genius or conventional eminence of any sort. Correct: but he proves how an average Western farmer, mechanic, boatman, carried by tides of circumstances, perhaps caprices, into a position of incredible military or civic responsibilities (history has presented none more trying, no born monarch's, no mark more shining for attack or envy), may steer his way fitly and . . . with credit year after year. . . . Seems to me it transcends Plutarch. How those old Greeks, indeed, would have seized on him! A mere plain man—no art—no poetry—only practical sense, ability to do, or try his best to do, what devolv'd upon him. . . . The gods, the destinies, seem to have concentrated upon him.[146]

However, not everything in the West was perfect: he was disappointed in the women. Sitting in a store in Kansas City watching the crowds on the sidewalks flow by, he observed:

The ladies (and the same in Denver) are all fashionably drest, and have the look of "gentility" in face, manner and action, but they do *not* have, either in physique or the mentality appropriate to them, any high native originality of spirit or body (as the men certainly have, appropriate to them). They are "intellectual" and fashionable, but dyspeptic-looking and generally doll-like; their ambition evidently is to copy their Eastern sisters. Something far different and in advance must appear, to tally and complete the superb masculinity of the West, and maintain and continue it.[147]

It is difficult to understand why Jeff did not provide money for Walt's return, though maybe he thought Walt wished to pay him a prolonged visit—and Jeff had never been very perceptive of the needs of others. Also Walt was not entirely bored by his delayed return, for he did enjoy talking with his old friend W. T. Harris, editor of the Hegelian magazine *Speculative Philosophy*. In November he wrote John Burroughs that Alcott was expected to give a lecture in St. Louis and "I may see him." [148] (Apparently he did not.) But the enforced stay stretched through December. Finally James T. Fields sent Whitman a Christmas present of $100 through John Burroughs (Fields wanted the gift to remain anonymous) and as a consequence Walt was able to start back on January 4, 1880.

By the time Whitman reached George's he had covered over five thousand miles and seen what geographers have called the "heartland" of America. Before leaving St. Louis he had carefully traced the route of his travels on railroad maps which he sent to John Burroughs and Mrs. Gilchrist.[149] And for the remainder of his life he never tired of talking about his trip West. The poet who had begun his career by vicariously spanning the continent had now in reality traversed two-thirds of it.

After five months of rest in Camden, with frequent trips to Timber Creek, Whitman felt in the mood for more travel. Dr. Bucke had long been urging him to come to London, Ontario, for a long visit, and on the night of June 3, 1880, Walt took a sleeper in Philadelphia on the Lehigh Valley Railroad and started out on another thousand-mile trip. Next day he stopped at Niagara and saw the falls for the second time in his life. He was as deeply impressed by the view from the suspension bridge as any honeymooner or European tourist, and filed the picture away in his memory "with my life's rare and blessed bits of hours," such as a wild sea-storm he had once seen off Fire Island, the elder Booth playing Richard III, Alboni in the children's scene in *Norma,* or night scenes on the battlefields of Virginia.[150]

By six o'clock of that evening Whitman was in London, and Dr. Bucke took him to his home on the beautifully landscaped grounds of the asylum. On Sunday Whitman attended church services and watched the inmates of the institution instead of listening to the sermon: "I can only say that I took long and searching eye-sweeps as I sat there, and it . . . [aroused] unprecedented thoughts, problems unanswerable." [151] But despite such musings, he was not depressed by living so near these unfortunate people. He enjoyed strolling on the grounds, watching the haying operations on the institutional farm, and at night observing the stars much as he had in New Jersey. After short excursions on Lake St. Clair and Lake Huron, he and Dr. Bucke made a long, leisurely midsummer trip down the St. Lawrence, and up the Saguenay River, in the course of which they visited Montreal, Quebec, the Thousand Islands, Cape Eternity, Trinity Rock, and other historic points.[152] As usual Walt kept a diary, and his notes show that his interest in exact information was still as keen as ever. He continually asked questions and recorded geographical, economic, and historical details. While editing the *Eagle* some thirty-five years previously he had predicted the absorption of Canada into the United States,[153] and he came back from this trip still convinced that some day this British colony would add several stars to the American flag. So much for the benefits of travel! Whitman returned to Camden the first of September.

VIII

In the fall of 1880 several of Whitman's friends published articles about him and his poems. Perhaps the most important one was by Stedman in the November *Scribner's Magazine.*[154] Stedman tried to praise the poet judiciously, but he could not help condemning the use of sex in the poems. He compared the sexual passions and procreation to the mud and slime that Nature covers up. Burroughs thought that on the whole the article would do good, but he commented that "Nature covers up mud when she can, but she does not cover up procreation." [155] O'Connor never forgave Stedman for these reservations, and Whitman himself seemed to have a divided mind on the critic—and he never afterward entirely trusted him. However, a still newer friend, William Sloane Kennedy, who was on the editorial staff of the *Saturday Evening Post* in Philadelphia in 1880, was making similar reservations and protestations in an article which he was writing for the *Californian*—published the following February as "A Study of Whitman." [156] The truth of the matter was that the sex poems were no nearer being accepted in America in 1880 than they had been when Emerson had argued against them under the Boston elms twenty years before.

A matter that worried Whitman more at this time, however, was the surreptitious printing of copies of *Leaves of Grass* from the Thayer and Eldridge plates. While he was in St. Louis, Worthington had offered him $250 to authorize an edition from these plates.[157] Whitman had turned him down, even though at the time he needed the money for railroad fare back to Camden, and forbade the use of the plates, but in November he found a pirated copy in a Philadelphia bookstore and learned that the store had been ordering and selling copies for over a year.[158] What made this still more exasperating was that none of the Philadelphia stores would handle the authorized editions. Whitman wrote to Burroughs and R. W. Gilder, hoping that they could stop this pirating, and Dr. Bucke made investigations, but they could find no solution to the problem.

In January, 1881, Whitman got chilled one raw winter day and was sick for several weeks.[159] In February he felt too depressed to visit John Burroughs. But he was soon cheered up by an invitation to deliver his Lincoln lecture in Boston in the Hawthorne Room of the St. Botolph Club,[160] on or near the anniversary of the assassination. Hawthorne's son-in-law, G. P. Lathrop, had arranged for the lecture, John Boyle O'Reilly had engaged a hotel room at the Revere House, and Mrs. John T. Sargent had planned an informal reception.[161] Whitman went up on April 13 and gave his lecture on the 15th. Several newspapers printed favorable reports of it, and the *Herald* stated that, "Many of the leading literati were at his lecture, and among them Mr. [W. D.] Howells was most cordial in his greeting." During the week in Boston Whitman returned Longfellow's call. James T. Fields, the editor and publisher, also invited him to breakfast. But the most memorable experience he had in Boston during this trip was seeing a collection of J. F. Millet's paintings in the home of Quincy Shaw, who lived three or four miles from the city. After two rapt hours, Whitman decided that "Never before have I been so penetrated by this kind of expression," and he wondered, "Will America ever have such an artist out of her own gestation, body and soul?" [162]

In view of Whitman's disappointment with the women of Kansas City and Denver because of their delicate appearance and dressing like the women of the East, it is amusing to note his reaction to the women of Boston in the spring of 1881: "I never saw . . . so many *fine-looking gray-hair'd women*. At my lecture I caught myself pausing more than once to look at them, plentiful everywhere through the audience—healthy and wifely and motherly, and wonderfully charming and beautiful—I think such as no time or land but ours could show." [163]

Among the many callers who left (or sent in) visiting cards was James R. Newhall, now an attorney in Lynn, Massachusetts, who wrote on the back of his card: "Perhaps Mr. Whitman may remember the undersigned—New York, 1843, Aurora office. Came up from Lynn, this morning, on purpose to pay my respects." [164] On April 23 Whitman wrote in his diary: "It was well I got away in fair order, for if I had staid another week I should have been killed with kindness, and with eating and drinking." [165] The following week he wrote John Burroughs that his "Boston jaunt" had driven the last of his chill away.

Soon after Whitman left Boston his friend O'Reilly, editor of a Catholic paper called the *Pilot*, interested James R. Osgood, one of the leading American publishers, in publishing *Leaves of Grass*. At Osgood's own suggestion Whitman wrote him of his plans for a new edition, to be revised and expanded from the 1876 version, and stated emphatically (underscoring his words): *"Fair warning on one point, the sexuality odes about which the original row was started and kept up so long are all retained and must go in the same as ever."* [166] Osgood replied immediately, asking for the copy that Whitman said he was working on, inquiring about the existence of the Thayer and Eldridge plates, and adding: "I am sorry that I was absent from Boston during your visit: I should have been glad to renew the acquaintance I had with you in the old Pfaff days." [167]

Whitman explained fully about the plates in Worthington's hands, but insisted that he could and would stop him from using them—though he never did. After a considerable correspondence, during which Whitman repeatedly specified the kind of typography, paper, binding, and so on, which he wanted, a contract was agreed upon on terms dictated by the poet—he actually drove a shrewd bargain. The copyright was to remain in his name and the book was to sell for $2.00, for which the author was to receive twenty-five cents on each copy sold (10 per cent was the usual royalty). Typesetting was to begin in the fall.

Meanwhile the Staffords had moved to Glendale,[168] three or four miles from the farm at Timber Creek, Stafford having decided to give up farming in favor of storekeeping. Whitman spent several weeks with them in May and June, but of course he missed Timber Creek, though there were woods nearby, which he explored and used. However, more exciting experiences soon developed. In July Dr. Bucke met him in New York and together they took a number of trips by boat and carriage—to Far Rockaway on Long Island, to Long Branch, New Jersey, around Manhattan, and down toward the center of Long Island.[169]

Dr. Bucke had become interested in writing a biography of his friend and wanted to gather information about his early life and ancestral background. For this reason, as well as Walt's eagerness to see once more the scenes of his boyhood, the two men made a pilgrimage to the region of Huntington, which Walt had not seen for forty years. They rode around "the old familiar spots," stood on the hill at West Hills and surveyed the rolling acres once owned by Walt's grandfather and later by his father and Uncle Jesse. At West Hills they also visited the Whitman cemetery, and there, seated on an old grave, the silence broken only by the soughing wind, the poet wrote down his observations and impressions. He felt that three centuries of his family's history were concentrated "on this sterile acre." But, as might have been expected, he was even more deeply impressed by the Van Velsor cemetery, which he visited the next day, July 30.

From this atmospheric region of the Van Velsor cemetery, on top of a sterile hill overlooking Cold Spring, Whitman descended to the old homestead, and this brought back a flood of youthful memories, of sweet Grandmother Amy, jovial Grandfather Cornelius, and a delightful free and happy childhood among the fields and streams and bays of Long Island. Later Whitman continued these reminiscences through his boyhood in Brooklyn and New York City, and thus constructed the first chapters of his own biography,[170] which was to be published first by himself as an introduction to his *Specimen Days* and also utilized by Dr. Bucke in writing the first formal biography of Walt Whitman. Dr. Bucke had thus sought and participated in the creation of this record of the poet's background. But since Whitman had for many years, almost singlehandedly, fought his own battle for literary recognition, it is not surprising that he did not wish to leave the details of his origins and early years entirely to chance. He felt it his duty to provide what he regarded as the pertinent facts. And both he and Dr. Bucke hoped that the formal biography could be published as a fitting sequel to the Osgood edition of *Leaves of Grass*.

In August Whitman settled down with the Johnstons in their summer home at Mott Haven on the Harlem River, near 149th Street, to finish the editing of his new *Leaves of Grass*. After working on it two or three hours a day, he watched the boys swimming in the river, took leisurely walks in the region, or went into New York. One morning in August he went down to Twenty-fourth Street for breakfast at Pfaff's. Charlie of course was glad to see him, and after "first opening a big fat bottle of the best wine in the cellar," sat down to talk over old times of 1859 and 1860 and the jovial suppers at that other Pfaff's on Broadway near Bleecker Street:

Ah, the friends and names and frequenters, those times, that place! Most are dead—Ada Clare, Wilkins, Daisy Sheppard, O'Brien, Henry Clapp, Stanley, Mullin, Wood, Brougham, Arnold—all gone. And there Pfaff and I, sitting opposite each other at the little table, gave a remembrance to them in a style they would have themselves fully confirm'd, namely, big, brimming, fill'd-up champagne-glasses drain'd in abstracted silence, very leisurely, to the last drop.[171]

By the middle of August, 1881, Whitman's book was ready for the printers, and on the 19th he went up to Boston to see it through the press,[172] as he had done for his first Boston edition twenty-one years before. During the first couple of days he took a boyish delight in riding the horse cars out to Cambridge and back, sometimes going on to the barn, where he hobnobbed with the drivers. The printing was being done by Rand and Avery, at 117 Franklin Street, and there on August 23 he settled down, in a small office which he had almost entirely to himself, to read his first batch of proof. But this left him plenty of time for strolling on the Common, riding the streetcars, and meeting his friends. Judging by the number of calling cards which he took back to Camden with him—many with invitations on the backs and instructions as to how to reach the homes of the would-be hosts—he did not lack for entertainment. Cards were left by Sylvester Baxter, a journalist; T. H. Bartlett, well-known sculptor; Frank Hill Smith, editor of the Cambridge *Chronicle*; Linn B. Porter; John Boyle O'Reilly; Mrs. Ole Bull, American wife of the Norwegian violinist; C. H. Montague, reporter on the *Globe*; the Reverend Julius H. Ward, of Roxbury; Henry H. Clark, superintendent at Rand and Avery; and many others.[173]

Franklin Sanborn, the abolitionist whose trial Whitman had attended in 1860, came over on September 17 and took Whitman out to Concord for the week end. There he spent one "long and blessed evening with

Emerson." [174] It was now difficult for Emerson to carry on a conversation because of his failing memory; so he simply sat quietly and looked benign, but that was enough for the poet who had once addressed him as "Master." Whitman himself was content to sit in a corner, where he was not expected to say much, and look at the beloved sage. The Emersons also invited him for dinner the next day, and Horace Mann's daughter took him for a drive.[175]

Whitman saw the Old Manse, Concord battlefield, "Sleepy Hollow" Cemetery, where Hawthorne and Thoreau were buried, Walden Pond and the site of Thoreau's hut. He carried a stone and added it to the memorial cairn that other pilgrims to the spot had built up. Later at Emerson's he sat beside Mrs. Emerson, and she talked of Thoreau's personal life.

While Whitman was enjoying his weekend in Concord the condition of President Garfield, who had been shot by an assassin the previous July, became very grave, and he died near midnight after Walt's return to Boston. He had known General Garfield in Washington, while the young politician was an inexperienced Congressman from Ohio. After the poet's New York Exhibition performance, Garfield would always greet him by shouting, "After all not to create only," [176] and Walt was very fond of him. Therefore as the bells tolled on the night of September 19–20, the poet's thoughts naturally went back to those days in Washington when he had ridden on the streetcar and walked with Garfield on the streets of the capital.[177] Within the next day or two Whitman wrote a short poem, "The Sobbing of the Bells," which he inserted in "Songs of Parting," near the end of *Leaves of Grass*, just before the final pages were stereotyped.

Whitman remained in Boston for approximately three more weeks after his return from Concord. Every day from about eleven-thirty until one o'clock and again at sunset he sauntered under the elms on the Common, where he had listened twenty-one years ago to Emerson's eloquent arguments against the "Children of Adam" poems. In the crisp cool air the whole experience became more precious than gold to him, but he had no regrets over his stubborn resolve to ignore it. And so far as his reminiscences indicate, he had no premonition under those historic elms that the objections raised by Emerson might soon be revived by more formidable opponents in Boston. On the contrary, he apparently left about the middle of October for Camden with the feeling that *Leaves of Grass*, now properly published, would soon begin to win the respect at home that it had already received from many distinguished critics abroad.

IX

The Osgood edition of *Leaves of Grass*, copyrighted 1881 but dated 1881–82 on the title page, was a compact octavo book of 382 pages, bound in gold-colored cloth, with title and design on the backstrip, showing a butterfly resting on the forefinger of a hand,[178] stamped in gold. Whitman had always preferred books that he could carry in his pocket, and he requested that the margins be trimmed close to reduce the size of the book.[179] It was still rather large for most pockets, but it was a plain, neatly printed, serviceable, compact volume.

Although Whitman had added a few poems since 1876, this edition was notable more for the new arrangement of the poems than for any important change in the contents. For twenty years he had been trying to mould his collection of poems into an organic unity. Since one of his great ambitions in *Leaves of Grass* was to be the poetic voice of his country in the nineteenth century, and at the same time to put his own life on record (as he was to say later), the logical arrangement would have been a simple chronological one. But his constant revision of his poems, some of which had now several layers of revisions made in different periods, had already blurred chronology. And now in this final arrangement, to be kept in all future editions, with instructions to the executors to preserve it, the last semblance of chronology was demolished. Probably in 1881 Whitman did not foresee that he would live to write many more poems (though most of them short), which he would want to add to his book, but this problem could be solved by merely adding all future poems as annexes to the *Leaves*. Thus, perhaps inadvertently, the annexes came to be more logically arranged than the main body of the book.

In 1881 Whitman incorporated all annexes into *Leaves of Grass*, redistributing the individual poems according to his final plan—or so he thought. Actually his intentions had changed less since 1855 than he seemed to realize, for his major themes had always been *time, death,* and *resurrection*. What his final intention was in the arrangement of his poems we can only guess from his group titles, which began with "Inscriptions" and ended with "Whispers of Heavenly Death," "From Noon to Starry Night," and "Songs of Parting."

What Whitman was obviously trying to suggest was the journey through life from procreation through young manhood (for him the "Calamus" emotions dominant), to intellectual maturity (expressed in the sea-shore lyrics), and on past the war ("Drum-Taps," "Memories of President Lincoln"), to old age ("Autumn Rivulets") and intimations of death ("Whispers . . ."), ending with the final "So Long!" to the reader which he had used as an epilogue since 1860. In each of these groups the first poem fitted the group title, and sometimes the last poem. For example, the pioneers in "O Pioneers! O Pioneers!" might be regarded as "Birds of Passage," but only the abstract theme of "time," or identity in time and space, was present in all the poems of this group.

Some of Whitman's adaptations of poems to new groups, however, were clever. No longer having any use for "Two Rivulets" as an introduction to the book by the same title, he revised and combined these lines with the succeeding poem, "Or from that Sea of Time," to form "As Consequent, Etc.," with which he introduced "Autumn Rivulets":

> As consequent from store of summer rains,
> Or wayward rivulets in autumn flowing,
> Or many a herb-lined brook's reticulations,
> Or subterranean sea-rills making for the sea,
> Songs of continued years I sing.
>
> Life's ever-modern rapids first, (soon, soon to blend,
> With the old streams of death.)
> .   .   .   .
> In you, whoe'er you are my book perusing,
> In I myself, in all the world, these currents flowing,
> All, all toward the mystic ocean tending.
> .   .   .   .
> Or from the sea of Time . . .

From "Noon to Starry Night" was introduced by a new poem, "Thou Orb Aloft Full-Dazzling," a prayer-like ode to the sun. Although for many years Whitman had had to guard against sunstroke, he had really been a sun worshiper most of his adult life—perhaps influenced by his early study of Egyptian religion.[180] And recent sun bathing had greatly aided him in his recuperation. Now, when he was in the afternoon of his life and the "starry night" fast approaching, he appreciated more than ever the "fructifying heat and light."

Except for the revision of a word here and there, "So Long!" remained essentially as it was first printed in 1860, but perhaps the final lines had taken on deeper connotations during the past decade:

> Remember my words, I may again return,
> I love you, I depart from materials,
> I am as one disembodied, triumphant, dead.

The "sex odes," to use Whitman's term in his letter to Osgood, remained essentially as they had been for many years, except for shifting some poems both into and out of "Children of Adam" and "Calamus"—and for some strange reason "To a Common Prostitute" was now in "Autumn Rivulets." But the new edition did not in any way emphasize the sex poems. In fact, the new allegorical group titles tended to submerge them and to place more stress on the journey of the soul through life into eternity. However, it was these same poems which had offended so many people in the past that were to cause the poet the worst grief he had yet suffered for their sake.

The book was praised in most of the reviews. In December Whitman's good friend J. H. Johnston inquired of the publisher how it was selling and received the reply that it was having "a fair success . . . We have printed three editions, 2000 copies in all, and it is selling steadily."[181] But on March 1, 1882, the District Attorney of Boston notified Osgood and Co. that he had officially classified *Leaves of Grass* as obscene literature, and on March 4 the firm wrote Whitman:

We enclose a letter from the District Attorney, dated March 1st, and received by us yesterday, March 3d. Please read and return it, keeping copy of it if you so desire. We are not at present informed what portions of the book are objected to. We are, however, naturally reluctant to be identified with any legal proceedings in a matter of this nature. We are given to understand that if certain parts of the book should be withdrawn its further circulation would not be objected to. Will you advise us whether you would consent to the withdrawal of the present edition and the substitution of an edition lacking the obnoxious features?

Whitman replied that he was "not afraid of the District Attorney's threat," but that he wanted the publisher to be satisfied, and that he would be willing to revise or cancel the offensive passages, adding that they "wouldn't be . . . more than half a dozen . . . words or phrases." He felt so confident that this did "not amount to anything" that he urged the publication of Dr. Bucke's biography of him, which was now finished. But when he received the list of the changes demanded by the District Attorney he replied: "The list whole and several is rejected by me, and will not be thought of under any circumstances."[182] He then submitted his own list of suggested changes, which in turn failed to satisfy the District Attorney, and Osgood replied: "We do not think the official mind will be satisfied with the changes you propose. They seem to think it necessary that the two poems, *A Woman Waits for Me* and *Ode to a Common Prostitute*, should be omitted altogether. If you consent to this we think the matter can be arranged without any other serious changes." [183]

Whitman took his time in replying; he did not make a hasty decision. But he refused to give in, finally suggesting that Osgood cease to be his publisher, and asked what terms they could propose for a settlement. Osgood replied that Whitman had $405.50 royalties to his credit. The plates had cost the company $475, and 225 copies of the book in unbound sheets were on hand. Osgood offered the plates (including the steel engraving from the 1855 edition which Whitman had sold them for $74) and the unbound sheets in exchange for his royalties. Actually, the company did better than that, for on May 1, Mr. Osgood called on Whitman in person at Camden with this agreement:

Memorandum of Agreement between James R. Osgood and Co., of Boston, Mass., & Walt Whitman of Camden, N.J. J.R.O. & Co. agree to surrender to W. W. the plates, dies, steel portrait, and 225 copies (more or less), in sheets of *Leaves of Grass,* and pay W. W. the sum of $100 in cash.

W. W. agrees to accept the same in lieu of all claims for copyright, &c., in full.

The publication of said work to be discontinued by J.R.O. & Co., the contract for the same to be cancelled, & no copies issued hereafter with their imprint.[184]

Whitman signed the agreement.

As soon as O'Connor heard the news he began to erupt as he had when Secretary Harlan had discharged the "good gray poet." Entirely forgotten now was his quarrel with Walt. And as before, he saw a larger issue at stake than an injustice to the poet; the freedom of the press was at stake—as indeed it was. He thought Osgood cowardly not to fight the District Attorney's charges in court. O'Connor wrote more letters to the newspapers, and perhaps did some good, for the press as a whole condemned the Boston District Attorney. But whether or not O'Connor deserved the credit for this editorial support of Whitman (one of the few times in his life when he received such support), he may have performed one other valuable service. The District Attorney had succeeded in getting the Boston postmaster to ban *Leaves of Grass* from the mails, but this order was soon lifted, possibly as a result of protests by O'Connor to the Attorney General.[185]

In defense of the publisher, it should be said that the firm looked at the whole matter from a business point of view. They thought it would be unprofitable to take this controversy into court—and quite possibly they did not believe that they could win before a Boston jury. On the other hand, they tried to get Whitman to take out the two short poems in order to forestall prosecution. Actually these were not very good poems anyway and their deletion would not have injured *Leaves of Grass*. But to Whitman any yielding to censorship was a compromise of his principles, and it was not his nature to compromise, as we have seen many times in the past.

Perhaps Whitman's reputation in America might have grown more rapidly and steadily if Osgood had continued to publish his poems. But, after having little success in selling his books himself, the following autumn he found a publisher nearby. This was Rees Welsh & Co., in Philadelphia. Actually David McKay, who worked for Rees Welsh & Co., mainly a publisher of lawbooks, was responsible for the new arrangement, and before the year was out he took over *Leaves of Grass* and agreed to publish a volume of prose under his own imprint. The publicity of the Boston suppression had called attention to *Leaves of Grass*, and for a year or more it sold better than it ever had before. For a while it even looked as though Whitman had at least gained financially from being "banned in Boston" —as many an author since has. But unfortunately American literary taste had not really changed, and the artificial stimulation of sales gradually subsided.[186]

⋘ XI ⋙

CLEAR MIDNIGHT

This is thy hour O Soul, thy free flight into the wordless,
Away from books, away from art, the day erased, the lesson done,
Thee fully forth emerging, silent, gazing, pondering the themes thou lovest
    best,
Night, sleep, death and the stars.[1]

I

BEFORE he had any intimation of trouble in Boston with the District Attorney over the Osgood edition, Whitman had already begun preparation
of what was later in the year (1882) to become *Specimen Days*. He had
hoped to have it published by Osgood, but after the suppression of the
1881 *Leaves of Grass* it was first brought out by Rees Welsh & Co., and
then taken over by David McKay. In a footnote to *Specimen Days* Whitman said that "pages from 1 to 28 are nearly verbatim [from] an offhand
letter of mine in January, 1882, to an insisting friend." [2] The friend was,
of course, Dr. R. M. Bucke, who had been working for several years on a
biography of Whitman.

In writing to Osgood about his plans for the 1881 edition of *Leaves of
Grass*, Whitman had insisted that "The book has not hitherto been really
published at all." [3] And now that it had been he felt the time had come
for a general summing up of his career and a consolidation of his literary
position. Then, too, he had reached the time of life when reminiscences
came naturally to his mind and pen; hence the delight he had taken the
previous summer in that trip with Dr. Bucke to West Hills,[4] and the readiness with which he now recorded his knowledge of his childhood and early
manhood. The events of 1882 also encouraged him to feel that he had
reached the end of an epoch and that it was time for him to put his literary
house in order.

The first of these events was the visit of Oscar Wilde on the afternoon of January 18.[5] The famous British esthete was on a sensational lecture tour of America, and he had just the day before lectured in Philadelphia, where he had been so coldly received that he had considered saying to his audience, "You don't like this, and there is no use my going on." After the lecture George W. Childs, owner of the Philadelphia *Public Ledger*, had given a dinner in his honor. Childs was a friend of Whitman, and he may have encouraged his guest to call on the poet, but such encouragement was really unnecessary, for Wilde had admired Whitman since his early youth, his mother, Lady Wilde, having had an early edition of *Leaves of Grass*.

Oscar Wilde, wearing his brown velvet suit, crossed over to Camden with J. M. Stoddart, the publisher. They were admitted to the Whitman home on Stevens Street by Walt's sister-in-law, who offered them elderberry wine. Wilde drank it off as if it "were the nectar of the gods," and confided to Stoddard later that, "If it had been vinegar, I would have drunk it all the same, for I have an admiration for that man which I can hardly express." The two poets got along splendidly together. Walt called him "Oscar," and the younger man sat at his feet on a low stool, with his hand on the poet's knee. Next day to a Philadelphia *Press* reporter Whitman stated for publication that he thought Wilde "was glad to get away from lecturing, and fashionable society, and spend a time with an 'old rough.' We had a very happy time together. I think him genuine, honest, and manly." [6]

Walt did not agree with some of his guest's esthetic theories, but he was captivated by the man: "He seemed to me like a great big, splendid boy . . . He is so frank, and outspoken, and manly. I don't see why such mocking things are written of him." The old poet was delighted to hear Wilde say that, "We in England think there are only two [American poets]—Walt Whitman and Emerson." Wilde acknowledged Longfellow to be a poet, but he had "contributed little to literature that might not have come just as well from European sources." After drinking a milk punch made by Walt himself, Oscar departed, feeling properly awed by the "grand old man," while Walt felt pleasantly exhilarated by the charming flattery of the "splendid boy."

About a week after Oscar Wilde's visit Walt wrote a letter[7] to his young friend Harry Stafford that throws a good deal of light on the poet's life at the time and his vicarious paternalism for Harry:

DEAR HARRY

Yours rec'd—I am just starting off a few miles out from Phila—probably a day or two only—will look up the book you require (if I can find one) soon as I come back—& send you—I am ab't as usual—nothing very new—Hank if I'd known you was coming home last Sunday would have come down Saturday & staid till Monday any way—You say you wrote a *blue letter* but didn't send it to me—dear boy the only way is to dash ahead and "whistle dull care away"— after all its mostly in one's self one gets blue & not from outside—life is like the weather—you've got to take what comes, & you can make it all go pretty well if only [you] think so (& provide in reason for rain & snow)—I wish it was so you could all your life come in & see me often for an hour or two—You see I think I understand you better than any one—(& like you more too)— (You may not fancy so, but it is so)—& I believe Hank there are many things, confidences, questions, candid *says* you would like to have with me, you have never yet broached—me the same—

—Have you read about Oscar Wilde? He has been to see me & spent an afternoon—He is a fine large handsome youngster—had the *good sense* to take a great fancy to *me!*—I was invited to reception in Phila. am'g the big bugs & a grand dinner to him by Mr & Mrs Childs—but did not go to any—Awful cold here, this is now the third day—but you know all about *that*—

—(You say you know you are *a great fool*—dont you know every cute fellow secretly knows that about himself—I do)—God bless you my darling boy— Keep a brave heart—

WW

Two months later the news of Longfellow's death reached Whitman while he was at Glendale with the Staffords. In spite of the fact that he enjoyed being told that he was more important than Longfellow, Whitman did not really harbor a grudge against him, as he did against Lowell and Holmes, whose adverse comments had been quoted to him by several English visitors.[8] Besides, Longfellow had taken the trouble to come over to Camden to see him while the Centennial Exposition was in progress.[9] The report of Longfellow's death reached Whitman (probably through newspapers) on a "clear forenoon, deep in the shade of pines and cedars, and a tangle of old laurel-trees and vines." [10] After he had returned to Camden, on April 3 he wrote a memorial tribute which was printed five days later in the New York *Critic*. Here he praised the gentle poet as the "counteractant most needed for our materialistic, self-assertive, money-worshipping, Anglo-Saxon races, and especially for the present age in America. . . ." He now even defended Longfellow from the charge of lacking "racy nativity," and repeated with approval "what I have heard

Longfellow himself say [perhaps in Cambridge the previous spring],[11] that ere the New World can be worthily original, and announce herself and her own heroes, she must be well saturated with the originality of others. . . ." Whitman himself had obviously mellowed as a result of his two talks with Longfellow.

Scarcely more than a month later (April 27) Emerson died, and on May 6 Whitman also paid his respects to him in the *Critic*. He praised him not for any of his literary accomplishments but as a symbol of "conscience, simplicity, culture, humanity's attributes at their best," a life which formed "in its entirety one of the few (alas! how few!) perfect and flawless excuses for being. . . ." Thus it was finally Emerson the man, the personality, not the poet or philosopher, whose memory Whitman cherished. This was not a new idea with him; yet as his own life drew nearer to a close, he seemed to hold on more tenaciously than ever to his belief in the supremacy of personality.

Perhaps this judging of all lives in terms of personality was what the psychologists call "compensating." Whatever the cause, Whitman had certainly spent a lifetime trying to embody his literary ideals and ambitions in a personality of his own creation—or at least cultivation. And perhaps this was but another aspect of his life-long loneliness. He had had many friends, and seldom if ever more than now. Aside from his literary admirers in England, and a sprinkling in France, Denmark, and Germany, he had many personal friends in Washington, New York, Brooklyn, Boston, and recently in Camden and Philadelphia. He was not unaware of this. On May 31, his sixty-third birthday, he wrote to "a German Friend": ". . . the principal object of my life seems to have been accomplish'd—I have the most devoted and ardent of friends, and affectionate relatives—and of enemies I really make no account." [12] Yet recently he had jotted down in a little notebook the plan to write a "Poemet embodying the idea [:] I wander along my life hardly ever meeting comrades. . . . For I have not met them[.] Therefore I have put my passionate love of comrades in my poems[.]" [13]

No decisive rupture had occurred in Whitman's friendship with his closest comrade, Peter Doyle, but correspondence between the two men had dwindled and finally stopped. Perhaps Harry Stafford came nearest to filling Peter's place, but he seems to have lacked Peter's stability, and it is doubtful that Whitman himself was still capable of the same intense personal interest in anyone that he had taken in the young Washington streetcar conductor. Dr. Bucke thought the poet almost superhuman in his poise and self-control, but he either did not know or overlooked his friend's impatience, his gnawing dissatisfaction, and his increasing hypochondria. Whitman would indeed have been superhuman if his failures and loneliness had left him unscathed, and that he was unscathed is pure myth.

Although Camden was a grimy suburb of Philadelphia, inhabited mainly by day laborers, it did have a number of professional men who were interested in literature, and for several years they were friendly with Whitman. One was Geoffrey Buckwalter, teacher and author of spelling books.[14] Another was James M. Scovel, a lawyer who became famous for his success in homicide cases. When Whitman first knew him he was co-publisher (with Harry Bonsall) of the Camden *New Republic*. He once went to New York and frightened Worthington into paying Whitman $50 for the use he had made of the Thayer and Eldridge plates.[15] Dr. J. M. Ridge, a physician and surgeon and owner of a drugstore on Third and Mickle streets, liked to talk about literature. But the most colorful figure of this group was Dr. Reynell Coates, the holder of an M.D. degree but experienced in several other professions.[16] He was about eighty when Whitman first met him, and he had spent an active life in literature (or journalism), law, and politics as well as science—he was organizing an expedition to the South Pole when the Civil War broke out. In 1852 he had been nominated by the Native American party for the Vice Presidency but had refused to speak on the same rostrum with Daniel Webster, the Natives' candidate for the Presidency. Colonel Johnston, the artist, in whose home Whitman often had tea during his first years in Camden,[17] was also an amateur critic of art and literature. None of these men except Buckwalter cared for Whitman's poetry, but they enjoyed arguing with him and often met for spirited discussions until *Leaves of Grass* was banned in Boston, after which Johnston and Coates became less friendly if not outright hostile.

However, several other professional men in Camden, mainly lawyers, remained loyal to the poet until the end of his life. The oldest of this group was Samuel H. Grey, in whose office Charles G. Garrison and John W. Westcott studied, both of whom later became prominent lawyers and finally district judges. All three greatly admired Whitman both as a poet and man. Westcott, a native of Camden County, had returned in 1878 after twelve years of school and college in New England. He met

Whitman the following year, and frequently called on him thereafter. His son, Ralph W. Westcott, recalls that his father "was fond of declaiming *Leaves of Grass* at home and regarded Whitman almost as a saint." [18]

Whitman was not without friends across the river, either. Philadelphia was characteristically respectable, conventional, and intolerant, and most Philadelphians were either indifferent to *Leaves of Grass* or abominated the book as unpoetic and indecent. Yet some distinguished residents of the Quaker City became warmly attached to the notorious poet in Camden. Several were newspaper men. Colonel J. W. Forney, owner of the Philadelphia *Press*, has already been mentioned as one of the sponsors of Whitman's trip to the West. [19] The editor of the Philadelphia *Ledger*, William V. McKean, did not like Whitman, but the owner, George W. Childs, had invited him to his home and in future years generously helped him financially. [20] In 1881 a man with a very unusual background joined the staff of the *Press*. He was Talcott Williams, who had spent his youth in Turkey and had learned most of the languages of the Near East. [21] After graduating from Amherst in 1873 he had worked on the New York *Sun* and *World*, the San Francisco *Chronicle*, and the Springfield *Republican* before coming to Philadelphia. He was always to have reservations about *Leaves of Grass*, but he was a collector of celebrities, and he tried to collect Walt Whitman. When Walt felt like it he took dinner with Williams but never entirely trusted him.

Professor Horace Howard Furness, the great Shakespeare scholar at the University of Pennsylvania, also became fond of Whitman personally without entirely approving of *Leaves of Grass*. [22] Another member of the University of Pennsylvania faculty, Professor Daniel Garrison Brinton, who taught American linguistics (that is, Indian languages) and archaeology, became so devoted to Walt that he often went over to Camden alone to talk with him. [23] Some years later Walt called him "a master-man—stern, resolute, loyal—yes, what I like (in the best sense) to call adhesive: a good comrade, a ripe intellect." [24]

Conservative Philadelphia had a number of writers and artists who were little appreciated at home, and several of them befriended the neglected Camden poet. Four especially deserve mention: George Henry Boker, the dramatist and poet; Charles Godfrey Leland, translator of Heine and author of a book on gypsies, who helped to start an Industrial Art School in Philadelphia in 1881; [25] Elizabeth Robins, niece of Leland, magazine writer; and Joseph Pennell, later one of the country's most distinguished etchers, who in 1881 had suddenly become famous as a magazine illustrator and in 1882 married Miss Robins.[26]

Miss Robins and her uncle first met Whitman in Philadelphia on a streetcar in the spring of 1881. "He was quite charming," Leland wrote in his diary, "and asked us to come and see him when in Camden." [27] Since gypsies were in the habit of camping in or near Camden, Leland and his niece often went over, and they usually saw the poet at some time during the trip. As Miss Robins remembered, they sometimes "found him sitting in a big chair by the fruit stall at the foot of Market Street [Philadelphia] gossiping with the Italian who kept it, eating peanuts, shaking hands with the horse-car drivers, whose stopping-place was just in front." [28] At other times they saw him getting on or off the ferry, or on the streetcar in Philadelphia. He almost always wanted to hear about the gypsies, but Miss Robins thought he himself would rather "come across them by chance. not by design."

Leland recalled this incident:

Once, when I had first made his acquaintance, we met at the corner of Sansom and Seventh Streets. He took me into a very common little bar-room where there was a table, and introduced me to several rather shabby common-looking men,—not workmen, but looking like Bohemians and bummers. I drank ale and talked, and all easily and naturally enough—I had in my time been *bon compagnon* with Gypsies, tinkers, and all kinds of loose fish, and thought nothing of it all. But when we came forth Whitman complimented me very earnestly on having been so companionable and said he had formed a very different idea of me, in short he did not know the breadth of my capacity. I had evidently risen greatly in his opinion.[29]

When his book on gypsies was published, Leland presented Whitman with a copy, in which he had written a short complimentary poem, and in return he asked Whitman if he would not write a few original verses in the copy of *Leaves of Grass* which he had given Leland's brother, Henry, who had praised Whitman's poems in 1860, to the poet's everlasting gratitude, and who had died during the Civil War. Whitman bluntly replied that he wrote only for money. His exact words were: "Sometimes when a fellow says to me, 'Walt, here's ten or five dollars—write me a poem for it,' I do so. And then seeing a look of disappointment or astonishment in my face, he added: 'But I will give you my photograph and autograph,' which he did."

In 1856 Whitman himself had read Leland's translation of Heine's *Pic-*

tures of Travel, from which he may have received a hint or two for one of his great poems, "Out of the Cradle Endlessly Rocking," [30] but if he ever mentioned this book to the translator, neither Miss Robins nor her uncle took note of it in their reminiscences. However, at this period Whitman evidently admired Leland most for his easy association with "Bohemians and bummers." And this fact throws a great deal of light on his increasing unpopularity with the average citizen of Camden and Philadelphia. Whitman, of course, had always enjoyed mixing with all sorts of "loose fish," to use Leland's term, and by the early 1880's his little excursions to the waterfront bars of Market Street provided one of his few means of escape from the boredom of George's dull home. To conventionally-minded people this conduct appeared to be not only loafing but deliberate association with disreputable characters. It was bad enough for Charles Leland to write a book about gypsies, but for a man to enjoy the society of "bummers" was looked upon as nothing less than disgraceful. And naturally the newspaper publicity about the banning of *Leaves of Grass* in Boston only confirmed the popular suspicions. As a result gossip about Whitman's indecency, and some even said immorality, circulated freely in Camden and men like Coates stopped associating with him. His literary, artist, and professional friends in Philadelphia were more sophisticated, and most of them remained loyal (though Professor Furness and several others thought the poet was foolish to sacrifice a good publisher for a few silly poems on sex). Most Philadelphians, however, were simply indifferent to the man and his book.

II

There was a little flurry of interest in *Leaves of Grass* in Philadelphia when Rees Welsh brought out a reprint of the Boston edition in July, 1882. The first printing of one thousand copies is said to have been sold out in one day (not all in local sales, of course) and a second printing in five days.[31] In the fall Rees Welsh & Co. published *Specimen Days and Collect* (dated 1882–83), and later in the year both books, uniform in format, were issued under the imprint of David McKay (probably from sheets printed by Rees Welsh, with only the title page changed). Both books sold for $2.00 and Whitman received thirty-five cents a copy on *Leaves of Grass* (for which he now owned the plates) and twenty-two cents on *Specimen Days.* Before the end of the year David McKay took over Rees Welsh's contract for these books, and in McKay's royalty statements of December 1, 1882, Whitman was credited with $1,091.30 on *Leaves of Grass* and $203.50 on *Specimen Days*, for a total of $1294.80.[32] This was much better than the Osgood edition had done, and so far as known was the most that Whitman ever earned in half a year on *Leaves of Grass*.

Whitman was naturally greatly encouraged by the sale of *Leaves of Grass* during the summer and autumn of 1882. The sale of *Specimen Days* was disappointing, but of course Whitman hoped it would eventually win acceptance. By mid-December he could feel that at last he was beginning to win his battle for literary success. And during the last week in December he had some visitors who gave him further assurance of his widening influence. Mary Whitall Smith, daughter of the wealthy glass manufacturer in Philadelphia and former Quaker evangelist, Robert Pearsall Smith, arrived home from Smith College for the Christmas vacation with a strong determination to visit an old, neglected poet in Camden about whose life and writing she had recently heard.[33] A Boston woman (name not given) had lectured on Whitman at Smith College, and Miss Smith had been surprised to learn that he lived so near her own home. When she told her parents of her intentions, they strongly opposed her visit. They had never read *Leaves of Grass*, but they had heard that its author was disreputable. However, Mary insisted on going to Camden, and her father decided that he would drive her over himself to protect her from any harm.

They located George Whitman's house without difficulty and Walt was at home. To his surprise, Smith found the old poet charming, and acting on a sudden impulse invited him to ride back to Germantown with them and spend the night. With scarcely a moment's hesitation Walt accepted. His sister-in-law packed a few necessities for him and he set off with his new friends. Moreover, he enjoyed the visit so much that he spent two nights, and was given a standing invitation to return at any time he wished.

Many years later Smith's son, Logan Pearsall, wrote a rather fanciful account of this first visit, placing it during the Easter vacation, but there is no doubt that the Smiths did become Whitman's warm friends and that he visited them several times before their departure for Europe in 1886. The account of his conduct as a house guest also parallels Grace Gilchrist's. He sang while taking his morning bath, was otherwise quiet and courteous in his manners, and especially enjoyed driving in the park with his host.

The following year was less eventful than 1881–1882, but during the summer Dr. Bucke's *Walt Whitman* was published by McKay. As with Burroughs's *Notes*, Whitman aided his friend in writing this book, but it was not, as some critics have asserted, a self-written biography—except for the sketch of his ancestry and early life, which the following year he admitted writing.[34] The most surprising thing about this admission is that the biographical account contains several glaring inaccuracies. For example, Whitman was said to have spent a whole year in New Orleans (actually only two months), and in an introductory chronological table (which may or may not have been written by Whitman) this was given as having taken place in 1848–1849. In general the poet's travels and his knowledge of American life were exaggerated, and much of his journalistic experiences passed over in silence. His editorship of the Brooklyn *Times* was not mentioned at all, or his earlier editing of New York papers. It is difficult to understand how Whitman's memory could have tricked him so egregiously about the New Orleans sojourn, but the omissions could easily have been accidental. Probably Whitman wrote this sketch in haste, without attempting to verify the facts; yet it is difficult not to suspect that he deliberately stretched the period of his stay in the deep South. This may be a minor detail, but it shows that the poet was willing to make some adjustments in the facts in order to present his biography as he wished it to be.

In an Appendix to Part I Dr. Bucke reprinted O'Connor's *The Good Gray Poet* and a long pyrotechnical letter from O'Connor regarding the Harlan affair.[35] Dr. Bucke also consulted and interviewed several of Whitman's Brooklyn and New York friends, whose reminiscences he quoted at length. Some of these, and especially Miss Helen Price's letter, preserved valuable information for any study of the poet's life and early background —perhaps the most valuable part, in fact, of the whole book.

Dr. Bucke's own impressions of Whitman's personality and character (which he frankly presented as only his own) also showed a limited, and sometimes fanciful, understanding of his subject. To Dr. Bucke, as we have already noticed,[36] Whitman had the character of a saint: always perfectly self-controlled, never petulant or even impatient, and indifferent to praise or abuse. Dr. Bucke never heard the poet swear or utter a single word in anger.[37] However, he talked with a friend of Whitman who thought he had a "double nature," and this opinion Dr. Bucke gave in summary. The name of this witness was not given, but he was said to be an elderly gentleman, a portrait painter, and "a distant relative of the poet."

. . . [He] tells me that Walt Whitman, in the elements of his character, had deepest sternness and hauteur, not easily aroused, but coming forth at times, and then well understood by those who know him best as something not to be trifled with. . . . His theory is, in almost his own words, that there are two natures in Walt Whitman. The one is of immense suavity, self-control, a mysticism like the occasional fits of Socrates, and a pervading Christ-like benevolence, tenderness, and sympathy. . . . But these qualities, though he has enthroned them, and for many years governed his life by them, are duplicated by far sterner ones. No doubt he has mastered the latter, but he has them.[38]

In the inclusion of such opinions as this and in the reprinting of reviews of *Leaves of Grass*, both favorable and unfavorable, Dr. Bucke attempted to counterbalance what he knew to be his own idealistic interpretation. There seems to be no reason for assuming that the doctor did not write as honest and accurate a book as he was capable of writing.

The portion of this book of least permanent value was Part II, in which Dr. Bucke tried to analyze the poems—for form, content, and esthetic qualities. Although he had read fairly widely, he was not a competent judge of poetry, and Whitman's own comments had been of little help to him. Of course, Dr. Bucke defended the sex themes as wholesome and insisted on the deep spiritual purpose underlying all the poems in *Leaves of Grass*. He thought the poet a forerunner of a new type of spiritual mentality—"cosmic consciousness" he was to call it in a future book.[39] He accepted without question Whitman's conviction that above all else he had put a real person into his poems for the first time in the history of literature. He also accepted quite literally Whitman's contention that he had no literary sources whatever and that books and libraries had had little influence on the creation of his poems, although Dr. Bucke himself observed that the poet usually read at least two hours a day, even on vacations.[40]

Although Whitman was only partly responsible for the limitations of this biography and critical study, it conformed so well with his views of himself and his poems that he was thoroughly satisfied with it. For the remainder of his life he repeatedly praised it, and he several times expressed the hope that no other biography of him would ever be written.[41] He knew that it was superficial, and he admitted that it lacked objectivity. Perhaps he feared that more penetrating biographers and critics would demolish his cherished conception of himself—the self that he had striven so long to become, and that Dr. Bucke thought he had truly become. In 1883 this book made Whitman feel that he was now properly installed in the Pantheon of great poets. His poetry and prose were collected in two volumes and his official biography had already been published. Few poets live to see their works and lives so completely prepared for future generations.

III

Whitman had not seen John Burroughs since John's return to America from England, where he had spent the summer of 1882, during which time he had visited Mrs. Gilchrist and most of the prominent writers and journalists who had befriended Whitman.[42] On August 17, 1883, Burroughs acknowledged receiving a copy of Dr. Bucke's book on Whitman, but he had to admit: "I cannot say that I care much for what Dr. Bucke has to say; he gives me no new hint or idea." [43] Probably it was difficult for Whitman to understand this sour comment, but in truth Dr. Bucke had added very little either in biographical information or in literary criticism to Burroughs's own book on the poet. Of all Whitman's personal friends (at least those in America), Burroughs was the only one who grew in literary judgment throughout the years—which was to be one of the causes of Whitman's doubting his loyalty. In the same August 17 letter Burroughs also showed his impatience with O'Connor's uncontrolled exuberance: "Wm. O'Connor's letter [printed by Dr. Bucke as a preface to *The Good Gray Poet*] is a treat, with a little too much seasoning. If Wm. would only practice a little more self-denial, he would be much more effective. He *could* write so that his critics could not laugh at him. . . ."

These frank comments of Burroughs did not immediately affect his friendship with Whitman. On September 26 Walt met him at Ocean Grove, New Jersey, at a hotel called the Sheldon House. The resort season was over, and the two men had the beach to themselves. On September 29 Burroughs wrote in his diary:

Long autumn days by the sea with Whitman. Much and copious talk. His presence loosens my tongue, that has been so tied since I came here. I feel as if under the effects of some rare tonic or cordial all the time. There is something grainy and saline in him, as in the voice of the sea. Sometimes his talk is choppy and confused, or elliptical and unfinished; again there comes a long splendid roll of thought that bathes one from head to foot, or swings you quite free from your moorings. I leave him and make long loops off down the coast, or back inland, while he moves slowly along the beach, or sits, often with bare head, in some nook sheltered from the wind and sun. . . .[44]

Whitman kept a diary too, and the difference between his and Burroughs's is very striking. Burroughs, the naturalist, enjoyed the scenery and the ocean air, but his chief delight was the companionship of his old friend. Walt, however, was interested in every physical detail of the trip, the time of leaving Camden, the distance covered (about sixty miles), the stations passed by the train, and his sense impressions of the beach, the ocean, the sun, and the sky at night. On September 30 Whitman wrote in his diary:

Still here. J B has just left for New York. I walk along the beach. A partial tempest of wind from north, following a heavy rain storm last night. The waves rolling and dashing and combing. An unusual show of foam and white froth, not only on shore but out everywhere as far as you can see. Not a sail in sight. I am having a capital week—eat well and sleep well.

.   .   .   .

Sometimes if the temperature allows, go down and walk or sit till quite late— have the whole performance to myself—beyond all operas or finest vocalism or band. Ever that ceaseless, sulking, guttural of the sea as if to me its wrongs and toils in confidence—ever those muffled distant lion roars—. . . Some vast soul like a planet stopt, arrested, tied—some mighty freedom pent denied —some cosmic right withheld.[45]

Whether the poet began recording these impressions with the intention of making a poem of them is not obvious, but by this time the thought had occurred to him and he began making a list of "Adverbs, adjectives &c suggested by the sea surf," and jotting down the key images for the poem forming in his mind—and notebook. He liked so much having "the whole performance" to himself that one wonders if he really missed "JB." But perhaps his pleasure was merely that of a practiced poet absorbed in the act of composing. At any rate, the old-time joy of finding soul-satisfying words came back to him, and from his notes grew the poem "With Husky-Haughty Lips, O Sea!"

With husky-haughty lips, O sea!
Where day and night I wend thy surf-beat shore,
Imaging to my sense thy varied strange suggestions,
(I see and plainly list thy talk and conference here,)
Thy troops of white-maned racers racing to the goal,
Thy ample, smiling face, dash'd with the sparkling dimples of the sun,
Thy brooding scowl and murk—thy unloos'd hurricanes,
Thy unsubduedness, caprices, wilfulness;
Great as thou art above the rest, thy many tears—a lack from all eternity in thy
    content,

(Naught but the greatest struggles, wrongs, defeats, could make thee greatest—
    no less could make thee,)
Thy lonely state—something thou ever seek'st and seek'st, yet never gain'st,
Surely some right withheld—some voice, in huge monotonous rage, of freedom-
    lover pent,
Some vast heart, like a planet's, chain'd and chafing in those breakers,
By lengthen'd swell, and spasm, and panting breath,
And rhythmic rasping of thy sands and waves,
And serpent hiss, and savage peals of laughter,
And undertones of distant lion roar,
(Sounding, appealing to the sky's deaf ear—but now, rapport for once,
A phantom in the night thy confidant for once,)
The first and last confession of the globe,
Outsurging, muttering from thy soul's abysms,
The tale of cosmic elemental passion,
Thou tellest to a kindred soul.

Many of these images and conceits are obviously subjective. The poet calls himself "a kindred soul," and doubtless he also felt unsubdued, capricious, willful, in his own "lonely state." But he liked to think that he shared something more important with the "vast heart . . . chain'd and chafing in those breakers": "Naught but the greatest struggles, wrongs, defeats, could make thee greatest—no less could make thee . . ." His most fervent wish and prayer was that out of the struggles and defeats of his own life a great, elemental poet had been, or could yet be made.

Whitman completed the poem after he returned to Camden, and during the remainder of the autumn he worked leisurely on his manuscripts, revising and planning for new editions. He spent the Christmas holidays in Philadelphia as a guest of Francis H. Williams, a minor poet and dramatist who supported his family by clerking in a bank. Whitman especially enjoyed playing with the Williams' small son, "Churchy," and going sleigh riding, which he mentioned in a letter to Harry Stafford.[46]

IV

For several years George Whitman had cherished the plan of building a house on a small farm he had bought near Burlington, about twelve miles from Camden.[47] His wife did not encourage the idea, and as for Walt, he said nothing but had no intention of living where he would not have ready access to the ferries to Philadelphia. Nevertheless, George completed his house in the country, this time providing a room on the third floor for Walt, since that seemed to be his favorite location, and arranged to move early in 1884. He could hardly believe his ears when Walt announced he would not go, and no amount of persuasion had any effect on him. Evidently angry words passed between the two brothers, and after he moved George refused to see Walt for several years.

Actually Walt had never become reconciled to living permanently with George. Soon after he lost his position in Washington he had bought a small lot, twenty by one hundred feet, on Roydon Street, in Camden, intending to build a small house for himself as soon as he could spare the money, though he was never to find such a time. Probably for a few weeks after George and Lou left Camden, Walt boarded, but in March he purchased a house at 328 Mickle Street (later changed to 330). The owners had been asking $1800, but offered it to him for $1750 cash.[48] Walt still had $1250 from the royalties he had received from McKay (mostly for 1882), and he borrowed $500 from George W. Childs—which he later repaid, according to his own statement.[49]

This house was a mediocre frame structure, two stories high, with six cramped rooms. It was badly in need of repairs, had no furnace, and was in a poor location.[50] It was only a block from the railroad tracks, on which there was almost constant traffic day and night. When excursion trains to the sea-shore resorts were not dashing through, long freight trains were rumbling past, or switch engines huffed and banged empty cars around, meanwhile blanketing the neighborhood with coal smoke and soot. The inhabitants of the street were a nondescript lot, some respectable and some not. A run-down church across the street had a bell with a harsh tone, and every Sunday morning its choir made more noise than music. Still worse, when the wind blew from the southwest it brought an extremely pungent odor from a fertilizer factory on the Philadelphia side of the Delaware River. But a tree grew in front of the house and a lilac bush in the back yard, and the streetcars to the ferries stopped only a block away.

Those ferries were almost a life-necessity to the crippled poet. They were owned by the Pennsylvania Railroad, from which Thomas Donaldson, a lawyer friend of Whitman, secured annual passes for him.[51] Donaldson also offered Whitman a comfortable house in Philadelphia rent free, but he chose to provide his own house. However, he accepted Donaldson's hospitality when he felt like it, and it was at his home that Whitman met the great English actor Henry Irving, and his young manager Bram Stoker, in April, 1884.[52] Whitman was pleased to be told by these British visitors that he looked like Tennyson. But best of all was meeting Bram Stoker, the Irish boy who had written so uninhibitedly nearly a decade ago. Both Stoker and Irving were to remain ardent friends for the remainder of the poet's life.

Edward Carpenter also returned to America in June and on the 17th called at 328 Mickle Street,[53] one of the first pilgrims to stop at the sorry little house that within a few years was to be visited by dozens of distinguished men and women from foreign countries. This was one justification for Whitman's refusal to live with George and Louisa in that house in the country. Probably many of these pilgrims would have found their way to Burlington, but Mickle Street was easy to reach from Philadelphia, and here Walt could receive them at any time and entertain them in his own way.

When Whitman bought the Mickle Street house a Mr. and Mrs. Lay were renting it, and he agreed to their staying on provided they would board him. Carpenter observed that he "was on easy terms" with them, and so far as he could see it was a satisfactory arrangement. On his second visit Carpenter took supper in the kitchen with Walt and Mr. and Mrs. Lay. "They seemed homely decent people, rather dull and quiet. Whitman, who was dressed just in shirt and trousers—for the weather was hot —kept things going." [54] After supper they sat in the front room, where they were joined by Folger McKinsey, "a young Philadelphian of literary leanings."

On this second trip to America Carpenter saw Whitman a number of times, both in Camden and Philadelphia, and he took notes on his impressions of the poet. On the day of his first call, Walt talked of Dr. Bucke's book: "not much cared for by my friends—but I like it." [55] On this occasion he said that he himself had written the account of his "birthplace and antecedents which occupies the first twenty-four pages of the book." Nor did he agree with Burroughs about O'Connor's letter to the newspapers: ". . . I must say I like them. They are comforting. Just as any woman likes a man to fall in love with her—whether she returns it or not—so to have once aroused so eloquent and passionate a declaration is reassuring and a help to me."

Although Carpenter liked Whitman personally as much as he had on his first visit in 1877, he was more convinced than ever that the mind and character of the man were paradoxical:

I am impressed more than ever with W.'s contradictory, self-willed, tenacious, obstinate character, strong and even extreme moods, united with infinite tenderness, wistful love, and studied tolerance; also great caution (he says: the "phrenologists always say that caution is my chief characteristic—did you know that?") and a certain artfulness, combined with keen, penetrating and determined candour; the wild-hawk look still there, "untamable, untranslatable," yet with that wonderful tenderness at bottom.[56]

On his last visit to Camden, the morning of June 30, Carpenter found Whitman in an intimate, affectionate mood, inclined to make confessions about *Leaves of Grass:*

"What lies behind 'Leaves of Grass' is something that few, very few, only one here and there, perhaps oftenest women, are at all in a position to seize. It lies behind almost every line; but concealed, studiedly concealed; some passages left purposely obscure. There is something in my nature *furtive* like an old hen! You see a hen wandering up and down a hedgerow, looking apparently quite unconcerned, but presently she finds a concealed spot, and furtively lays an egg, and comes away as though nothing had happened! That is how I felt in writing 'Leaves of Grass.' Sloan Kennedy calls me 'artful'—which about hits the mark. I think there are truths which it is necessary to envelop or wrap up." [57]

These are extremely revealing confessions, especially for the poet who made an issue of telling all, concealing nothing, and had resisted all attempts to get him to use a few fig leaves on his "Children of Adam." He gave Carpenter no hints as to the truths he had felt it necessary to envelop, but the young man had a suspicion. Afterward, looking back upon all his impressions of Whitman, he decided that there was "a great tragic element in his nature—and [one which] possibly prevented him ever being quite what is called 'happy in love affairs.' " [58] To this Carpenter added: "He celebrates in his poems the fluid, all-solvent disposition, but often was himself less the river than the rock." Dr. Bucke was not capable of making such an acute observation. But Robert Pearsall Smith told Carpenter that what impressed him most about Walt was his "magnificent No!" when invited out, or asked to do something he did not wish to do, "and yet, as a rule with a large sunny amiability which made offense impossible." [59]

Probably the Lays did not find living with this strong-willed man easy or agreeable. They may have resented the way he monopolized the front room, or more likely Mrs. Lay became impatient with the irregular hours of his meals, which appear to have been the cause of much friction at

George and Lou's. Whatever the cause, the arrangement proved unsatisfactory and the Lays moved out, leaving Walt alone in an empty house,
for he had no furniture or household equipment. Somewhere he picked
up a cheap oil stove, a pan or two, a few dishes and some wooden boxes for
chairs and tables. Probably at this time Lou turned over his mother's bed
to him, but his housekeeping was as primitive as it had been in his fourth-
floor Washington bedroom. No doubt many of his friends would have
donated furniture and kitchen utensils, but he carried himself with such
an independent air that they hesitated to try. Actually he usually accepted
all gifts graciously, but he certainly did not solicit them, though he did
not mind borrowing from a friend willing and able to lend. In July he
borrowed $200 from Dr. Bucke, and the doctor was glad to help.[60] Dur-
ing this year Whitman also became acquainted with Thomas B. Harned,
a lawyer in Camden, who invited him to have dinner every Sunday at his
home on Federal Street.[61] Whitman spent some of his happiest hours with
these kind and congenial people. There he also became better acquainted
with a young bank clerk, Horace Traubel, a brother-in-law of Harned,
who was soon to play a very important role in his life. When Whitman
first came to live in Camden he had often met Traubel, then a boy of fifteen, on Stevens Street and sometimes chatted with him, and Traubel's
interest in the poet had steadily grown during the intervening years.[62]

In spite of the kindness of his many friends, the winter of 1884–1885
was a hard one for Whitman. His royalties continued to dwindle. They
dropped from over $300 in 1883 to exactly $42.77 in 1885.[63] A will that
Whitman drew up in 1882, before McKay had paid him his December
royalties, indicated that he had a total of about $3,000 in two savings
banks,[64] one in Brooklyn and one in Camden, and it is likely that he still
had this secret "nest-egg" two years later, but was probably trying to keep
it intact. It was not his habit to draw on his savings, and besides he was always conscious of Edward's dependency on him. Even during his most
trying years he paid Edward's board every other week. Walt's sister-in-law
came to see him as often as she could, and brought him little gifts of food
from the farm.[65] Walt appreciated her kindness, but it was not enough to
give him much relief from his poverty and discouragement. And he was
almost as discouraged as he had been ten years earlier, except that now he
could hobble around. But living alone in an unfurnished, unheated house
in midwinter was a miserable existence for an elderly cripple.

Sometime during 1884 Whitman became acquainted with a widow,
Mrs. Mary Oakes Davis, who mended his clothes and on January 25,

1885 began preparing one meal a day for him.[66] She had had a very hard life and since her childhood had tended and nursed older people in their final years. The first was a blind aunt, and recently she had taken care of an aged seaman, Captain Fritzinger, whose wife had died leaving two boys. While tending Captain Fritzinger, Mary Oakes had secretly married a Captain Davis, but shortly afterward he was drowned when his ship went down in a storm. Meanwhile the two Fritzinger boys, Harry and Warren, ran away to sea at the ages of fourteen and seventeen respectively, and they were away when their father died leaving his property and savings to be divided equally between Mrs. Davis and them. She was living near Stevens Street when Whitman got acquainted with her. While she was alone she had taken in an orphan girl, but waiting on elderly people had become a fixed habit with her; so her sympathy went out to the crippled poet hobbling around in the snow and ice late in 1884. He was said to be so poor at this time that he was trying to peddle his own books in Philadelphia, but since McKay was still his publisher, in whom he never lost confidence, this story seems doubtful—although he may have occasionally delivered copies of the 1876 edition which he still had on hand.

But of Whitman's personal distress and need for a housekeeper there can be no doubt. Consequently, he suggested that if Mrs. Davis would move her furniture into his house and act as his housekeeper he would provide her with a house. No formal agreement was signed and it is impossible now to know the exact details of the arrangement, but Mrs. Davis moved to 328 Mickle Street. After Whitman's death she claimed that she paid most of the grocery bills and her biographer has represented the poet as unreasonable, demanding, parsimonious, and tyrannical.[67] He had always been irregular in his habits and he probably did take Mrs. Davis's attentions and sacrifices too much for granted. Naturally, too, in his old age and sickness he may have become childish and petulant. But Mrs. Davis had always allowed herself to be imposed on by somebody, and continued to do so after Whitman's death. Thus it is difficult to know how far his impositions were intentional; the whole truth cannot now be extracted from the conflicting testimony of the partisan witnesses. It is sufficient to say that Mrs. Davis devoted her whole energy to taking care of Walt Whitman, and it is difficult to imagine how he could have managed during the last years of his life without her devoted care and assistance. Mrs. Davis also sacrificed her reputation by keeping house for the author of the notorious *Leaves of Grass*. Many conventionally-minded

people in Camden regarded this menage as highly improper, and slander-
ous gossip was circulated in the town. Whitman had never cared what his
neighbors thought, but the woman was more sensitive.

When Mrs. Davis moved in she brought all her possessions, including a
dog, a cat, four birds (a canary, a pair of turtle doves, and a robin she had
rescued from a cat), and some hens, as well as the curios of the late Captain Fritzinger, which included a ship model and souvenirs from many
parts of the world.[68] The little house was filled to overflowing. Mrs. Davis
had planned to assign the small back bedroom upstairs to the orphan girl,
but Whitman insisted on keeping both it and the large bedroom for
himself, so that the two women had to sleep in the little room downstairs
adjoining the kitchen. In the shed attached to the kitchen she made a bed
for the cat, let the dog sleep on the lounge, and placed her hens in an out-
house. On a shelf in the dining room she placed her clock, some china
vases, and a stuffed parakeet. The only spot she could find for the flour
barrel was the back hallway, which was always dark, and strangers usually
collided with it in going to the kitchen. But Whitman's little house was
now furnished—doubtless even more than he wished.

Not long after this heterogeneous family of people and animals was settled, Edmund Gosse called.[69] He was touring the United States and had
come to Philadelphia especially to visit the poet, whom he had supposed
from reports in Boston to be bedridden, but the hotel porter in Philadelphia said he could often be seen strolling on Chestnut Street. On the
morning of January 3, 1885, Gosse crossed over to Camden, which
seemed to him one of the most grimy, deserted towns he had ever seen.
After wandering around for some time he happened on 328 Mickle
Street and knocked, and a "melancholy woman opened the door." Then
a "very old gentleman" greeted him from the stairs.

There was a good deal of greeting on the stairs, and then the host, moving
actively, though clumsily, and with a stick, advanced to his own dwelling-room
on the first storey. [Second floor in American usage]. The opening impression
was, as the closing one would be, of extreme simplicity. A large room, without
carpet on the scrubbed planks, a small bedstead, a little round stove with a
stack-pipe in the middle of the room, one chair—that was all the furniture.
On the walls and in the fireplace such a miserable wall-paper—tinted, with a
spot—as one sees in the bedrooms of labourers' cottages; no pictures hung in
the room, but pegs and shelves loaded with objects. Various boxes lay about,
and one huge clamped trunk, and heaps, mountains of papers in a wild confusion, swept up here and there into stacks and peaks; but all the room, and

the old man himself, clean in the highest degree, raised to the nth power of stainlessness, scoured and scrubbed to such a pitch that dirt seemed defied for all remaining time. Whitman, in particular, in his suit of hodden grey and shirt thrown wide open at the throat, his grey hair and whiter beard voluminously flowing, seemed positively blanched with cleanliness; the whole man sand-white with spotlessness, like a deal table that has grown old under the scrubbing-brush.[70]

Whitman sat in the only chair, leaving an upright box for his guest. As they talked the poet kept feeding and "irritating" the stove, and at times the conversation subsided entirely. In his passive dignity he reminded Gosse of "a great old grey Angora Tom," or an Oriental sage. The only pictures Gosse observed were in the back room, "a print of a Red Indian," which Whitman said had been given him by the artist Catlin, and a photograph of "a very handsome young man in a boat, sculling," whom Whitman identified as a special friend of his in Canada, a professional oarsman. As time passed Gosse felt himself more and more captivated by his unusual host. To his surprise he discovered that the old man had a sly sense of humor. But mostly "he seemed dwelling in a vague pastoral life, the lovely days when he was young, and went about with 'the boys' in the sun."

When Gosse left the house his "heart was full of affection for this beautiful old man" who had just said "Good-bye, my friend!"

I felt that the experience of the day was embalmed by something that a great poet had written long ago, but I could not find what it was till we started once more to cross the frosty Delaware; then it came to me, and I knew that when Shelley spoke of

> Peace within and calm around,
> And that content, surpassing wealth,
> The sage in meditation found,
> And walk'd with inward glory crown'd,

he had been prophesying of Walt Whitman, nor shall I ever read those lines again without thinking of the old rhapsodist in his empty room, glorified by patience and philosophy.[71]

In an article which Whitman published in February, 1885, under a pseudonym, he gave his own description of the room in which Gosse had spent several hours with him.[72] Like Gosse he mentioned the simple furnishings and clutter of books and manuscripts, but he enumerated more pictures on the walls, including photographs of his father, mother, and sisters, "a portrait of a sweetheart of long ago, a large print of Osceola the Seminole chief (given to Whitman many years ago by Catlin the artist), [and] some rare old engravings by Strange, and 'Banditti Regaling' by Mortimer." He liked to think of this room as the cabin of a ship, and in his descriptions various objects and pieces of furniture took on symbolical massiveness and strength, such as "a mighty trunk" with double locks and bands of iron, and "a great cane-seat chair, with posts and rungs like ship's spars; altogether the most imposing, heavy-timbered, broad-armed and broad-bottomed edifice of the kind possible. It was the Christmas gift of the young son and daughter of Thomas Donaldson, of Philadelphia, and was specially made for the poet." [73]

Whitman's feline or Oriental passivity and poise, of which Gosse had been acutely aware, was not altogether unconscious, either. "I never knew a man," Whitman declared in his pseudonymous article, "who—for all he takes an absorbing interest in politics, literature, and what is called 'the world'—seems to be so poised on himself alone." Strangers, like Edmund Gosse, were impressed by this outward equanimity, and thought it natural. It was not altogether ungenuine, and Whitman had cultivated it so assiduously that he could now control his impatience and console himself by a kind of auto-suggestion. But this state of mind had had to be deliberately cultivated; it was never unconscious.

V

During the winter of 1884–1885 Whitman's lameness grew worse, and when spring finally came he was greatly disappointed not to be able to get out as much as he had for the past several years. In August the thought occurred to Donaldson[74] (or possibly Mrs. Davis suggested it to him)[75] that a horse and buggy would bring the poet much pleasure. Donaldson wrote to thirty-five prominent men, most but not all personal friends of Whitman, asking if they would contribute ten dollars apiece for this purpose, and thirty-two promptly made the contribution. The contributors included R. W. Gilder, Charles Dudley Warner, Mark Twain, Whittier, Holmes, Edwin Booth, Talcott Williams, George H. Boker, and other friends of Whitman in Philadelphia, Boston, New York, and Washington. Whittier replied:

DEAR FRIEND: I am sorry to hear of the physical disabilities of the man who tenderly nursed the wounded Union soldiers and as tenderly sung the dirge of their great captain. I have no doubt, in his lameness, that a kind, sober-paced roadster would be more serviceable to him than the untamed, rough-jolting Pegasus he has been accustomed to ride—without check or snaffle. I inclose my mite, for the object named in thy note, with all good wishes.

I need not say perhaps that I have been pained by some portions of W. W.'s writings, which for his own sake, and that of his readers, I wish could be omitted.[76]

A phaeton was especially built for the poet in Columbus, Ohio, at cost —everything was bought for far below the usual price. A horse was found that was deemed safe, an attractive sorrel pony named Frank, that had been driven at the seashore during the summer by women and children. About four o'clock on September 15 Donaldson dropped in at 328 Mickle Street and presently called attention to a horse and buggy stopping in front of the house. A strange man was driving and Donaldson's young son was riding with him. After Whitman had admired the turnout, he was told that it was his, and Donaldson handed him an envelope containing $135.40, the unexpended balance of the contributions. With tears in his eyes Walt was assisted into the new phaeton and he drove until dark.[77]

About a week later someone at the stable where the horse and buggy were being kept took the harness by mistake and for several days Whitman's friends had great fun with poetic protests in the Philadelphia *News* and *Press*,[78] but the harness was returned and the poet resumed his driving. In fact, he drove Frank so furiously that the horse's knees began to tremble. One day Donaldson saw Walt driving a new horse and asked what had happened to Frank. "Sold," Walt replied. "I sold him. He was groggy in the knees and too slow. Did you want a pair of cripples to drive out—Frank and myself? This horse is a goer and delights me with his motion. . . ." At this time a teen-age boy named Bill Duckett, whose mother had recently died, was boarding with Mrs. Davis, and he usually accompanied Whitman on his drives, assisting with the lines when necessary. Walt enjoyed this recreation until 1888, when he became too weak to continue it. But for three years the horse and phaeton afforded him much pleasure.

Meanwhile Whitman had lost his most loyal friend in England. On December 15, 1885, he received a letter from Herbert Gilchrist which told of the death of his mother on November 29. Whitman replied immediately.

DEAR HERBERT,

I have received your letter.

Nothing now remains but a sweet and rich memory—none more beautiful all time, all life all the earth—

I cannot write anything of a letter to-day, I must sit alone and think.

WALT WHITMAN.[79]

Although no one else could be quite as devoted to him as Mrs. Gilchrist had been, Whitman's remaining friends tactfully and generously provided financial assistance during the last years of his life. Each April for several years they gave him a planked shad and champagne dinner at Billy Thompson's popular resort on the Delaware River about two miles below Camden. And in 1886 they arranged for a resumption of his Lincoln lectures. On April 15, 1886, he read his lecture at the Chestnut Street Opera House in Philadelphia and received $692 for his performance.[80] The house was well filled and George W. Childs and Dr. S. Weir Mitchell each paid $100 for their tickets, while the manager of the Opera House donated the use of the hall.

In May Whitman also received from William Rossetti the fifth installment of funds that Rossetti had been collecting in England since the previous fall, which now totaled approximately £156, or around $850. The list of contributors included Oliver Elton, Henry James, Robert Louis Stevenson, Havelock Ellis, George Saintsbury, and about eighty others.[81] It is interesting that these funds were raised as a result of a letter that Charles Aldrich, a librarian in Iowa, who strongly disapproved of Whitman's poems, had written to Rossetti in June, 1885. Aldrich wrote of visiting the poet in his home and finding him alone and in great want. This report had greatly distressed Rossetti and Mrs. Gilchrist (only a few months before her death) and they immediately began making plans for his relief. The first step that Rossetti took was the futile one of writing to President Cleveland,[82] calling his attention to Whitman's services to the Union during the war and suggesting that he ought to be placed on a pension.

Several months later the idea of a pension also occurred to Sylvester Baxter in Boston and he took more practical measures to obtain it.[83] He got Congressman Henry B. Lovering of Lynn, Massachusetts, to introduce a bill in the House of Representatives to provide Whitman a pension of $25.00 a month. This bill was reported favorably to the House and would probably have passed if Whitman, when he heard of it, had not replied that he was not a dependent and did not wish to receive a pension, whereupon the bill was quietly dropped. Actually the contributions from England had relieved his acute need.

In Boston Sylvester Baxter and W. S. Kennedy (now living in Boston) also began raising a fund to build a cottage for Whitman on Timber Creek, and this netted $800, which was turned over to the poet without any restrictions.[84] He did not build the cottage immediately, and later, with the permission of the donors, the money was used for more pressing needs. But he had received unmistakable evidence of the loyalty and generosity of his friends in America as well as in England.

In the latter part of 1886 some of Whitman's friends in England promoted a fund for him through the *Pall Mall Gazette,* which amounted to £80 when it was sent to him as a New Year's gift (1887).[85] The following spring his New York friends arranged for him to give his Lincoln lecture in Madison Square Theater.[86] This raised another $600, thanks to a check from Andrew Carnegie for $350. Carnegie, the millionaire author of *Triumphant Democracy* (1886), wrote to J. H. Johnston, the chief organizer of this benefit performance: "When the *Pall Mall Gazette* raised a subscription for Mr. Whitman, I felt triumphant democracy disgraced. Whitman is the great poet of America so far." [87] Other notables, such as Mark Twain, James Russell Lowell, and Augustus Saint-Gaudens attended the lecture, and a reception was given afterward at the Westminster Hotel, with an attendance of two hundred people. Apparently Whitman did not know that José Martí, a Cuban journalist then in exile because of his liberal political views, also heard the lecture and wrote a highly eulogistic account which spread Whitman's fame throughout Latin America as the semi-divine author of *Leaves of Grass.*

A few weeks after Whitman's return from New York, Sidney Morse arrived to make a clay model of a bust for future casting.[88] Mrs. Davis managed to clear enough space in the crowded parlor for the sitter, the sculptor, and his pile of clay, though she was disturbed by the messiness of the clay. But before the bust was well begun Herbert Gilchrist arrived from England to paint a portrait of Whitman and to bring him personal news of the death of Mrs. Gilchrist, whom Whitman now referred to as his "noblest woman friend." Walt had given written consent for Herbert's portrait but had forgotten to tell Mrs. Davis of the artist's expected arrival.[89] Herbert was now a painter of some renown, having been recently admitted to the Royal Academy. Morse, seeing that there was no room for Herbert to set up his easel, moved his clay to the back yard and worked there with frequent trips back and forth through the house to look at his subject posing in the parlor for Gilchrist.

This year marked a climax in Whitman's popularity as an artist's model. In the fall J. W. Alexander painted his portrait, in an uncharacteristic, saintly pose,[90] but Alexander was a famous artist and sold his portrait to the Metropolitan Museum in New York, where it still hangs. And Thomas Eakins of Philadelphia also started a portrait—eventually to become the most famous of all—which he finished the following spring.[91] Saint-Gaudens planned to sculpture the poet too,[92] after he had finished a commission on which he was working, but Whitman's illness prevented his carrying out this plan. Nevertheless, no other American poet had been painted, sculptured, and photographed so often and so competently for posterity.

On the whole 1887 was perhaps the most satisfying year that Whitman had had since coming to Camden. But many of his friends were disturbed (he himself said little) by an article that Swinburne published in the August number of the *Fortnightly Review*. After referring to his earlier praise, Swinburne specifically asserted that he had "no recantation to intone," and he summarized some of the American poet's "laudable and valuable qualities," but then he went on to point out his deficiencies as a thinker, his lack of prosodic form, and to compare his Eve to "a drunken apple woman, indecently sprawling in the slush and garbage of the gutter amid the rotten refuse of her overturned fruit-stall," and to liken his Venus to "a Hottentot wench under the influence of cantharides and adulterated rum." Sir Edmund Gosse labeled this a "recantation,"[93] and Whitman's closest friends felt outraged.[94]

A great deal has been written about this change in Swinburne's attitude toward the poet to whom he had addressed an ode in 1871.[95] Watts-Dunton has been blamed for turning him against Whitman,[96] and of course it is impossible not to suspect that the American poet's intemperate British champion Robert Buchanan, Swinburne's bitter enemy, helped to provoke the writing of the "drunken apple-woman" piece.[97] But as suggested in an earlier chapter, Swinburne had at first taken a position from which he would almost inevitably have to retreat.[98] Furthermore, it was Whitman the American democrat rather than Whitman the lyric poet whom he had endorsed, and he may have been annoyed by the propaganda use that some of Whitman's partisans had made of his endorsement and his name.

The importance of this episode in Whitman's life has been exaggerated, anyway. He was amazed by Swinburne's apparent change of mind—to a friend he exclaimed, "Aint he the damnedest simalcrum!" [99]—but on the whole Walt himself was less disturbed than he would have been a few years earlier. The many manifestations of affection for himself and tributes to his poetry which he had received during the past year had given him the real confidence and genuine poise for which he had sought so long.

VI

The New Year (1888) began without any portents of change in Whitman's life. During 1887 he had done more writing than in any recent year, especially articles for magazines, and at the end of the year Julius Chambers, the new managing editor of the New York *Herald*, had put him on the pay roll as the "poet laureate" of the paper, of course with the consent of the owner of the paper, James Gordon Bennett (the younger). Throughout the first half of 1888 Whitman contributed short poems at about the rate of two a week. One of these poems Chambers never forgot. On March 11, the day before the famous "blizzard of '88," he received from Walt a charming little poem entitled "The First Violet of Spring."

I marked it for the editorial page and went home earlier than usual. It was a beautiful, clear, frosty night. When the paper was on the streets next morning, the joke was on me. . . . Naturally I did not hear the last of *The First Violet* for many a day. Poor Walt felt badly about the incident, and when I last saw him, shortly before his death, he recurred to the upset of the Weather Bureau.[100]

The Harneds gave a birthday party for Whitman at their home, and he enjoyed it immensely.[101] Two or three days later he was still feeling exhilarated and drove his horse later than usual. Before returning home he rode down to the river and sat for some time at the edge of the water, enjoying the sunset and late spring air. But the weather was cooler than he realized and that night he suffered another stroke.[102] Someone—perhaps Dr. S. Weir Mitchell—sent for Dr. William Osler to examine him, and on June 8 Dr. Bucke unexpectedly arrived from Canada. After spending the night at Walt's bedside, Dr. Bucke was convinced that he could not live more than a few hours, or at most a few days, and Dr. Osler also thought he was on "tenter-hooks." [103]

Dr. Bucke and Thomas Harned were especially concerned for fear the poet had not made a will—they were particularly anxious about his literary estate—and on June 9, accompanied by Donaldson, they called on him to persuade him to attend to this matter. But Walt was in no hurry, and they mercifully desisted. However, Dr. Bucke telegraphed J. H. Johnston, on vacation at Saratoga Springs, that Walt was dying and asked him to see if Robert G. Ingersoll, the great freethinking orator, would speak at the funeral. Ingersoll happened to be at Saratoga Springs also, but he refused Dr. Bucke's request because at the time he had a low opinion of *Leaves of Grass,* though he admitted to Johnston that he had never carefully read the book. Johnston made him promise to do so, and the result was that Whitman soon afterward gained another enthusiastic friend.[104]

On June 10 Walt's condition became still more alarming, and Dr. Bucke obtained a male nurse for him, Dr. Nathan D. Baker,[105] probably a young physician from Philadelphia. Walt did not want anyone, but Mrs. Davis was already exhausted from nursing him and he obviously had to have constant and skilled attention. His condition improved by July, though he was no longer capable of doing any sustained writing and on July 3 he wrote the New York *Herald:* "Thanks best thanks dear Mr. Bennett & dear Mr. Chambers & all you dear *Herald* boys—but have not sent you a line for a month & probably will not any more—as I am ill from breaking out of old war-paralysis—I return the check & take my name from the roll." [106]

For some months Horace Traubel had been visiting Whitman almost daily—sometimes two or three times a day—and since the previous March he had been inconspicuously taking notes on his conversations with the old poet. Walt knew that Horace was planning to write some sort of book about him, and as he rummaged around in the piles of letters and manuscripts in his room he selected items to turn over to his young friend. When he was feeling well enough he usually asked Traubel to read the letters aloud before taking them away, and this often brought out reminiscences or stimulated the expression of opinions that this would-be Boswell devotedly recorded. Traubel also ran many errands for the invalid, and during the summer and fall of 1888 he was almost as indispensable to Whitman as his nurse or doctors.

As a matter of fact, Traubel soon became acting treasurer for the group which had assumed the responsibility of supplying Whitman with a nurse. Dr. Bucke took the initiative in engaging a nurse, though several friends in Camden and Philadelphia agreed to provide the funds for this expense. At first Harned acted as treasurer, but he soon relinquished this task to Traubel. When Dr. Baker left on July 14, Dr. Bucke secured a man named Musgrove to take his place, but Whitman did not like him and in November Dr. Bucke sent down Edward Wilkins to replace him.[107] Probably by this time Traubel was collecting money for payment of the nurse, though the names of the contributors were never made public. Once when Whitman inquired about how the nurse was being paid Traubel assured him that it was being taken care of and that he was not to worry.[108] This satisfied him and he never mentioned the subject again. But providing a nurse proved to be a considerable strain, for the patient lived on in this semi-invalid condition for four years, not always bedridden but constantly in need of physical assistance.

At the time of Whitman's collapse he had been working on a new collection of prose and poetry, to be called *November Boughs*. With Horace Traubel's assistance, he resumed the printing of this book, in midsummer. Horace carried "copy" to the printer, brought back the proofs to the author, and acted as business manager. McKay published the book in November and an English edition was issued in 1889 under the imprint of Alexander Gardner.

November Boughs, a slender book of 140 pages, contained a very important long preface called "A Backward Glance O'er Travel'd Roads," which combined two articles that Whitman had published in 1884 and 1887.[109] He had thus spent several years in a thoughtful summing up of his literary theories and practices, and here he gave the frankest and most judicial discussion of them he had ever achieved. He now admitted: ". . . I have not gain'd the acceptance of my own time, but have fallen back on fond dreams of the future. . . ." [110] Without bitterness he also admitted that *Leaves of Grass* had always been a financial failure, yet he was satisfied: ". . . I have had my say entirely my own way, and put it unerringly on record—the value thereof to be decided by time." From first to last, the work was an experiment anyway, "as, in the deepest sense, I consider our American Republic itself to be. . . ." At least he could feel sure that he had "positively gain'd a hearing," [111] as indeed he had.

Here Whitman also reiterated his primary purpose in his poems, which was "to exploit that Personality [his own], identified with place and date, in a far more candid and comprehensive sense than any hitherto poem or book." [112] With this purpose Whitman was still completely satisfied, but he was not so sure of his secondary intention to give expression to modern "science and democracy" [113] in his poems. The basis of this doubt he did not make clear. Perhaps he was beginning to fear the outcome of his country's material progress during the nineteenth century, but he had certainly arrived at no definite conclusion on this subject.

Regarding his poetic form he was now overly modest, perhaps having been affected finally by the reservations of such learned friends as Professor Furness: "in verbal melody and all the conventional technique of poetry, not only the divine works that to-day stand ahead in the world's reading, but dozens more, transcend (some of them immeasurably transcend) all I have done, or could do." [114] He still believed, however, that "there must imperatively come a readjustment of the whole theory and nature of Poetry," but he had been shaken in his earlier belief that his own poems had their own superb music and rhythm.

The poems in *November Boughs* Whitman grouped under the section title "Sands at Seventy," which four years later he annexed to *Leaves of Grass*. In the clarity of his newly gained self-knowledge he realized that these poems lacked his old-time lyric power, but he was thankful that he could at least continue to write them "in joy and hope." In "A Carol Closing Sixty-Nine" he summed up his situation:

The body wreck'd, old, poor and paralyzed—the strange inertia falling pall-
    like round me,
The burning fires down in my sluggish blood not yet extinct,
The undiminish'd faith—the groups of loving friends.

But he feared that 1888 might see the end of his long poetic career, as he admitted in "Queries to My Seventieth Year":

    Approaching, nearing, curious,
    Thou dim, uncertain spectre—bringest thou life or death?
    Strength, weakness, blindness, more paralysis and heavier?
    Or placid skies and sun? Wilt stir the waters yet?
    Or haply cut me short for good? Or leave me here as now,
    Dull, parrot-like and old, with crack'd voice harping, screeching?

Whitman appropriately closed "Sands at Seventy" with a poem, "After the Supper and Talk," that accurately described his mood at the time the book was published:

After the supper and talk—after the day is done,
As a friend from friends his final withdrawal prolonging,

Good-bye and Good-bye with emotional lips repeating,
(So hard for his hand to release those hands—no more will they meet,
No more for communion of sorrow and joy, of old and young,
A far-stretching journey awaits him, to return no more,)
Shunning, postponing severance—seeking to ward off the last word ever so
    little,
E'en at the exit-door turning—charges superfluous calling back—e'en as he
    descends the steps,
Something to eke out a minute additional—shadows of nightfall deepening,
Farewells, messages lessening—dimmer the forthgoer's visage and form,
Soon to be lost for aye in the darkness—loth, O so loth to depart!
Garrulous to the very last.

This was the real Walt Whitman, "loth to depart," and "Garrulous to the very last." So garrulous that Horace Traubel would be able to record six or more thick volumes of his talk.

With Traubel's help Whitman was also able to publish late in 1888 a large one-volume collected edition of his poetry and prose. Of course, he used the 1881 plates of *Leaves of Grass* and the plates of the McKay editions of *Specimen Days* and *November Boughs*, but there was still page proof to examine and plans for the binding to be settled. These problems provided numerous errands for Traubel and hours of conversation for the two men. The title of this edition was *Walt Whitman: Complete Poems and Prose, 1855–1888*. Only six hundred numbered copies were printed and today it is a much-valued collector's item.[115]

<h2 style="text-align:center">VII</h2>

The remaining tedious, pain-wracked three years and three months of Whitman's life have been so minutely recorded by Horace Traubel that it would be almost impossible to find anything new for a biographer to tell. Although everyone who is interested in Whitman's life must be grateful to Traubel for his industry and zeal, this voluminous record actually —and unintentionally—is one of the cruelest in literary history. Day after day, sometimes even in semi-delirium, the poet's thoughts, opinions, moods, appearance, and gestures were preserved by the relentless reporter's pencil. Sometimes Whitman's talk sparkled and he made statements that illuminated his past life and literary productions. But more often he was banal, or repetitious, or merely agreed with a suggestion thrown out by his questioner.

Some friends of the poet, notably John Burroughs, have questioned the accuracy of Traubel's recordings.[116] For example, these printed conversations frequently contained "hell" and "damn," and Burroughs, Bucke, and several others have stated that they never heard Whitman swear. However, as we have noticed many times, he was always capable of meeting different friends on their own footing. It was not that his own personality was chameleon-like, but that he had many facets to his personality, and he could exhibit different ones to different people. Thus the contradictions between the Whitman described by Burroughs, Bucke, Mrs. O'Connor, Eldridge, and Traubel need not be attributed to anyone's inaccuracy or falsification; each knew only so much of this remarkable man as he was capable of knowing, and not one of them understood the whole man—nor did Whitman himself. Perhaps least of all Whitman himself, for he was an intellectual who distrusted intellectuals. He wanted to write for the common man, and preferred the simple uneducated men for his daily companions, though they were incapable of understanding his poetry.

Traubel, of course, was not so simple as Peter Doyle or Harry Stafford. His father, Maurice Traubel, who had emigrated in his young manhood from Germany, was an excellent lithographer and a fair artist (he made a very good crayon sketch of Whitman), and Horace grew up in a home in which Goethe, Heine, Schiller, and the great German authors were known and respected. He also possessed native intellectual independence, and by the time he knew Whitman he was a socialist and an agnostic. Although Whitman believed in no one creed or church, he was at heart deeply religious. Traubel often said this about him, though his leading questions usually brought out the "freethinker" in the poet. Sometimes he deliberately tried to convert Whitman to socialism (actually a rather mild and vague socialism), and Walt would agree that maybe after all he was more of a socialist than he had realized, but he always retained too much of his old-fashioned Jeffersonianism to be much of a socialist. At times this persistent questioner was a vexation to the sick old man and he would make an angry retort, only to make amends in a moment by agreeing with some opinion or observation of Traubel's. Therefore, even though the volumes of *With Walt Whitman in Camden* may contain an accurate record of Whitman's conversations with Traubel, and they probably do, there were depths of Whitman's mind, character, and life scarcely even hinted in them. In the first place, Traubel never knew Whitman in his prime—and he would not have understood him, the poet of the great sea-shore lyrics, the poet of the 1850's and 1860's, even if he had known him. But to say this is not to detract from Traubel's very great service to Whitman. Without his assistance American literature might have been deprived of *November Boughs, Good-Bye My Fancy*, and the final edition of *Leaves of Grass*.

VIII

The pattern of Whitman's life established in 1888 held for the remainder of his life. Mrs. Davis ran the house in the same way, Traubel continued to run errands and to copy conversations, a male nurse was on duty nearly all the time, a physician called almost daily, and visitors from both America and Europe frequently dropped in.

In February, 1889, Mrs. Davis went to court to collect a large board bill from Bill Duckett,[117] the orphan boy she had taken in four years ago. On the witness stand Bill swore that Walt Whitman had invited him to stay at the house. Walt, of course, could not go to court to contradict this testimony and he was greatly upset over it, especially since he had trusted and liked the boy. Yet his sympathy was also with Mrs. Davis, who had been tricked by her charitable impulses. In spite of Duckett's false testimony Mrs. Davis secured a judgment against him, but whether she ever collected any money is not known.

There is no evidence of any friction between Mrs. Davis and Whitman. A year or so later Dr. Bucke distrusted her for a time, but he finally came to realize the sacrifices she was making, although there is no evidence that he arranged for Mrs. Davis's financial relief.[118] The orphan girl probably left before Bill Duckett began staying at the house, but meanwhile Mrs. Davis had exhausted the few hundred dollars she had inherited from Captain Fritzinger, and the entertainment of Whitman's frequent guests was a burden.

With Traubel's assistance, Whitman realized a long-cherished ambition on his seventieth birthday by publishing a handy pocket-size edition of his *Leaves* bound in leather, compactly printed on thin paper, with photograph tipped in, and autographed with a prefatory note on the title page. Whitman's friends in Camden decided to give him a mammoth birthday party on May 31, 1889. A local committee, including H. L. Bonsall, Thomas Harned, Geoffrey Buckwalter, and several other business and professional men, hired Morgan Hall, employed caterers to prepare a banquet, and sent notices all over the world to Whitman's correspondents and favorable critics, and to leading authors. Whitman himself was not strong enough to attend the dinner, but he was carried in afterward and listened to some of the speeches and the reading of the eulogistic letters and telegrams, which were later printed and presented to him as *Camden's Compliment*.[119] The program was that of a typical "testimonial dinner," and the eulogies were no more exaggerated than they usually are on such occasions. But this was not an ordinary testimonial dinner. The whole atmosphere was that of a religious cult, and that was what these birthday celebrations for the poet were coming to be. The celebrants were disciples of a new Messiah. They praised his poetry, but as Scripture, not as literature. Whitman complained afterward that they "laid it on too thick," but he encouraged the cult by thinking and speaking of his critical reception as a cultural movement which "we" were spreading to all parts of the world. That "we" removed (or disguised) much of the egotism, but it perhaps gave his "disciples" the delusion that they had more of a "movement" than was actually the case. What precisely did this cult stand for, besides the doctrine that Walt Whitman was a great poet? The speakers—and Whitman himself—could mention only the standard ideals of nineteenth century romanticism and democratic liberalism: the sacredness of the individual and the Godhead in every man, the rights of the "common man," more humanitarian laws and government, the beauty of the human body, the need for a democratic esthetics. Whitman in his life and writings embraced and exemplified all of these, but this did not make him unique, or the leader of a new movement. As a *poet* he was indeed unique, and the greatest American poet of his generation, but it would only be possible for future generations to discern and begin to understand his real uniqueness. However, this dinner had a greater practical purpose, too, and that was fully achieved. The celebrants bought a stout and useful wheelchair for the invalid. It was now possible on fine days for his nurse to wheel him down to the docks, where he could at least see the river and watch the ferries coming and departing.

Nothing else in 1889 equaled the excitement and pleasure of the birthday dinner, although a visit by Sir Edwin Arnold in September greatly pleased both the poet and his friends.[120] Sir Edwin, author of a widely read book called *The Light of Asia*, was returning to England from Japan by way of America in order to talk with Whitman. And at the end of the year came an even more welcome recognition of Whitman's importance: E. C. Stedman gave him thirteen pages in his anthology, *Library of American Literature*, in which no other poet received more than three pages.

In October Edward Wilkins, the Canadian nurse, left and Warren Fritzinger, who had recently retired from the sea, took his place.[121] He was greatly devoted to his patient and remained with Whitman until his death, though shortly before the end a professional nurse, Mrs. Elizabeth Leavitt Keller, was employed. Of all the nurses Whitman had, "Warry" was his favorite.

In 1890 the poet was a little stronger, and he managed with much assistance in going and coming, to read his Lincoln lecture at the Contemporary Club in Philadelphia,[122] of which Horace Traubel was an active member. The birthday dinner this year was held in Philadelphia, and this time Whitman was well enough to attend.[123] The main speaker was Robert Ingersoll, who spoke for forty-five minutes. Whitman always felt buoyed up by Colonel Ingersoll's enthusiasm and eloquence, and of course he was grateful for any praise of *Leaves of Grass*, but he could never agree with the agnostic's doubts about immortality. On this occasion he turned to Ingersoll after his speech and asked, "Unless there is a definite object for it all, what in God's name, is it all for?" [124]

About this time a question of a very different sort was also bothering Whitman. For years John Addington Symonds had been persistently asking him the meaning of the "Calamus" poems.[125] Most readers were content merely to take them, as Mrs. Gilchrist had done, as a general plea for love and understanding, or as symbolizing brotherhood and friendship. But to Symonds a more poignant confession seemed to be concealed in them. Finally, on August 19, 1890, Whitman wrote him:

About the questions on Calamus, etc; they quite daze me. Love is only to be rightly construed by and within its own atmosphere and essential character— all of its pages and pieces so coming strictly under—: that the Calamus part has even allowed the possibility of such construction as mentioned is terrible— I am fain to hope the pp themselves are not to be even mentioned for such gratuitory and quite at the time undreamed and unv[ou]ched possibility of morbid inferences which are disavowed by me and seem damnable.

.　.　.　.　.　.　.　.　.　.　.

My life, young manhood, mid-age, times South, etc., have been jolly bodily, and doubtless open to criticism. Though unmarried, I have had six children— two are dead—one living Southern grandchild—fine boy writes to me occasionally—circumstances (connected with their benefit and fortune) have separated me from intimate relations.[126]

For two or three years before his death Walt frequently hinted to Traubel that he had a great secret to confide to him, but he was never in the right mood to make the confession. Once he told Traubel that a few hours earlier in the day his grandson had visited him, and when Traubel expressed regret that he had not met him, Whitman exclaimed, "God forbid!" [127] On another occasion Traubel and Harned went to him with the announcement that they had come for the confession, but Whitman suddenly became desperately ill before their eyes, according to Traubel, and could not talk.[128]

Were there any children? Traubel never knew, though he took Whitman's word that there were some. Harned wrote in his "Reminiscences" (still unpublished):

Whitman more than a year before his death, told me that he was the father of some children. He expressed an intention to give me the details. I frequently urged him, but he always put me off. He said there would be no legal trouble. As I knew nothing definite, I did not deem it necessary to write about it after his death. I was greatly surprised when Edward Carpenter published Whitman's letter to Symonds. Burroughs said that he did not believe in the "children" story. I can't see why Whitman should say what he did to me, or write to Symonds, if it were not true, *but* he speaks of "Times South." He only went south once, so far as we know, and then he was twenty-eight years old, and he stayed away only three months. He speaks of a *grand*-child, fine boy who writes him. Some claim that this *could not* be. Where [are] these letters? And none of these children have been heard from. Are they only children of psychology? [129]

To the present day no trace whatever has been found of any of these children, and it is extremely doubtful that any evidence ever will be found. They were, in all probability, "the children of psychology."

Whitman doubtless believed that the fiction of his illegitimate children would allay any suspicions that Symonds might have concerning the normal heterosexuality of the poet of *Calamus*. But this was a misunderstanding, for Symonds himself was married and had children, though he was by nature homosexual.[130] Psychologists today know that the distinction between the two sexual types is often not as definite and categorical as popularly believed. Whitman, as we have already noticed many times in this biography, was strongly homoerotic, but this does not mean that he could not have begotten a child or two—though *six* is highly improbable, and this large number increases the suspicion that the children were entirely imaginary.

In the following October (1890) Ingersoll gave a benefit lecture for Whitman in the Horticultural Hall in Philadelphia, on the subject of

"Liberty in Literature." J. H. Johnston had arranged this lecture, which realized $870. Some orthodox Philadelphians objected to letting the notorious agnostic have the hall, but the lecture took place without incident. Whitman sat on the stage, and at the end Colonel Ingersoll handed him the lecture neatly printed and bound.[131]

The last birthday celebration was held at 328 Mickle Street to make it easier for Whitman to attend. The program was less formal than in 1889, and Whitman himself participated more freely in it, while a stenographer took down everything that was said.[132] Tennyson sent his greetings, and Eakins made a short speech in which he said that in painting Whitman he had found "that the ordinary methods wouldn't do—that technique, rules and traditions would have to be thrown aside; that, before all else, he was to be treated as a *man*, whatever became of what are commonly called the principles of art." [133] This was a tribute of the poet's own caliber, and the sincerest flattery for being (perhaps) unconsciously a paraphrase of his own literary theory. But William O'Connor had died several months before, and Whitman was saddened to think he could not be present. John Burroughs was absent also, and that rankled. Walt several times referred to his not being there, and perhaps suspected that these orgies of flattering the old poet sickened his more reserved friend.

As the midnight of the poet's life drew nearer, the pilgrims continued to come. For some years a group of men in Bolton, England, had been meeting to read and discuss *Leaves of Grass*. It included a physician and several ordinary men without much education, and they had humorously named themselves "Bolton College." In 1890 they had decided to send one of their group to see the great poet and bring back a report. Accordingly on July 15 Dr. John Johnston arrived in Camden, and then he made a visit to Brooklyn, where he talked with a ferry pilot who had known Whitman. Afterward he visited the poet's birthplace and talked with some of the older residents of West Hills and Huntington. He completed his tour with a visit to John Burroughs. The following year another member of "Bolton College," J. W. Wallace, came over, had a talk with the poet (which he duly wrote down), collected more information about the great man's life, and returned to make his report to the group. Later the two reports were published in one of the most interesting of the early books on Whitman's life.[134]

The saddest event in Walt's life during 1890 was the death of Jeff in St. Louis on November 25. In the obituary that Walt himself wrote for the *Engineering Record* he said that his brother "had been troubled of late years from a bad throat and from gastric affection, tending on typhoid." [135] Probably the ambiguous disease was tuberculosis, to which the Whitman family seemed especially susceptible.[136] Jeff had always been Walt's favorite brother, and his death was a very severe shock to the aged poet.

Nothing particularly significant happened during the winter of 1891, but one event of the spring which deserves mention in Whitman's biography was the marriage of Horace Traubel to Anne Montgomerie in the poet's bedroom.[137] She had taken a great interest in Whitman for several years, and had suggested to Horace that he keep records of the conversations. Whitman himself devised a special wedding ceremony for the couple, and their mutual friend, J. H. Clifford, pastor of a Unitarian Church in Germantown, officiated. Reverend Clifford had attended many of the Sunday dinners at the Harneds when Walt was present, had participated in all the birthday celebrations, and had often quoted *Leaves of Grass* in his sermons.[138] The ceremony over, Walt kissed the bride (or she him) and gave the young husband and wife his blessing—a simple and unpremeditated gesture, but, like so many of his final acts, proper conduct for a venerable "prophet."

With Traubel's continued help, Whitman published still one more book of poetry and prose in 1891, which he called *Good-Bye My Fancy*. The prose was a miscellany of literary essays, reminiscences of his life in Brooklyn and Long Island, and thoughts on death. It included the obituary of his brother Jeff, and an essay on death called "A Death Bouquet." Whitman was well aware that his end was near, and his poems revealed this awareness. But he was not morbidly brooding on death, nor was he anxious to embrace it. Rather he was nostalgically looking back upon a life for which, with all its disappointments, he had no regrets; and now, meditatively, he liked to play with the imagery of departing ships, sunsets and twilights, and to muse on the prospects of *Leaves of Grass* in future ages. This thin book of poems ended with a "Good-bye and hail!" to the faculty which for at least thirty-five years Whitman had regarded as his other self ("I always think of myself as two").[139]

GOOD-BYE MY FANCY!

GOOD-BYE my Fancy!
Farewell dear mate, dear love!
I'm going away, I know not where,
Or to what fortune, or whether I may ever see you again,
So Good-bye my Fancy.

Now for my last—let me look back a moment;
The slower fainter ticking of the clock is in me,
Exit, nightfall, and soon the heart-thud stopping.

Long have we lived, joy'd, caress'd together;
Delightful!—now separation—Good-bye my Fancy.

Yet let me not be too hasty,
Long indeed have we lived, slept, filter'd, become really blended into one;
Then if we die we die together, (yes, we'll remain one,)
If we go anywhere we'll go together to meet what happens,
May-be we'll be better off and blither, and learn something,
May-be it is yourself now really ushering me to the true songs, (who knows?)
May-be it is you the mortal knob really undoing, turning—so now finally,
Good-bye—and hail! my Fancy.

IX

Wallace left Camden on November 3, 1891, and soon after he reached home he and Dr. Johnston each received a copy of the final edition of *Leaves of Grass*.[140] It was dated 1892, but Walt had had a few advance copies bound up to use as Christmas presents. This was a two-volume edition, *Leaves of Grass* with the various annexes ("Good-Bye My Fancy" being last) and all the collected prose, including that of *November Boughs* and *Good-Bye My Fancy*. For many years Whitman had prepared each edition as if it were the last, but this time he knew that it was the last, and he inserted "An Executor's Diary Note, 1891," in which he placed upon the executor "the injunction that whatever may be added to the *Leaves* shall be supplementary, avowed as such, leaving the book complete as I left it, consecutive to the point I left off, marking always an unmistakable, deep down, unobliteratable division line. In the long run the world will do as it pleases with the book. I am determined to have the world know what I was pleased to do."

Meanwhile Whitman had made his last will and testament, appointing Dr. Bucke, Thomas B. Harned, and Horace Traubel as his literary executors and leaving the bulk of his savings and property for the use of Edward, still boarding in the country near Camden. He made one will in 1888,[141] but a final one on December 24, 1891, in which he left $1,000 each to his sisters Mary and Hannah, and a like amount to Mrs. Davis. His sister-in-law, Mrs. George Whitman, was designated executrix and was requested to use the Mickle Street property for the support of Edward. In this will Whitman left his gold watch to Harry Stafford and a silver one to Peter Doyle, but in a codicil dated January 1, 1892, he gave the gold watch to Horace Traubel and the silver one to Harry Stafford instead of Peter Doyle, from whom Whitman had apparently not heard for several years. In this codicil he also reduced the bequest to his sister Mary to $200, and designated $250 for his name-sake Walt Whitman Fritzinger (the new-born son of Harry Fritzinger).[142]

The poet who never forgot that the phrenologists had found him well-endowed with "caution" had even prepared his tomb. The previous Christmas he had ridden out to Harleigh Cemetery to select a lot, and then signed a contract for building a small mausoleum, borrowing a design from William Blake. In these negotiations he had shown a complete lack of business sense, for he had apparently commissioned the construction of the tomb without any agreement as to the cost. Harned learned that he was greatly worried over the matter, and on inquiry discovered that the contractor intended to charge him several thousand dollars.[143] Harned settled for $1500—which he probably paid himself.

Why did Whitman want a mausoleum? It was not entirely for himself. He wanted his family united in death—as it had never really been in life. Accordingly, he requested that the remains of his father and mother be removed to places provided for them, and also his nephew Walter. (Of Mrs. George Whitman's stillborn child, which she had requested to have buried with her, nothing remained to move.)[144] For the removal of the brothers Andrew, Jesse, and Jeff he made no plans—doubtless in the case of Jeff because he had been buried with his wife in St. Louis. But he left instructions that Hannah, George, and Louisa, and Edward were to be buried beside him—and they were.

In the last years of his life Whitman had welcomed scores of visitors to his Mickle Street home, and some had even made pilgrimages to his birthplace. He knew that if *Leaves of Grass* lived—and he thought it might—his tomb would become a shrine, as it has. He showed good judgment in choosing the simple design from Blake, with a triangular capstone, and the location at the base of a small hill covered with laurel and oak trees.

Dr. John Johnston and J. W. Wallace had scarcely received their copies of *Leaves of Grass* (later called the "Deathbed" edition) before Whitman was seized by a chill on December 17 and helped to bed.[145] Next day Dr. Longaker found him suffering from congestion in the right lung, and on the 21st the physicians decided that his case was hopeless. Dr. Bucke came next day from Canada, and at once re-planned the funeral, this time engaging Ingersoll to speak. But Walt did not die immediately. John Burroughs arrived on December 26, and found that "though he had been very near death for many days, I am sure I had never seen his face so beautiful. There was no breaking-down of the features, or the least sign of decrepitude, such as we usually note in old men. The expression was full of pathos, but it was as grand as that of a god. I could not think of him as near death, he looked so unconquered." [146]

In January Whitman rallied, and he lingered until March 26. Most of this time he suffered excruciating pain, but the doctors, his nurse, and his few visitors marveled that he did not complain, though toward the last he expressed the wish that death would soon relieve him. Throughout these weeks of pain and waiting, letters and cables arrived almost every day from Europe and various parts of the United States. These were read to Whitman, and sometimes he dictated messages in reply. Traubel kept Dr. Johnston and J. W. Wallace informed. Wallace closed his record of these communications with this summary: "on the evening of Saturday, March 26th—the daylight fading and a gentle rain falling outside—the end came, simply and peacefully—Whitman conscious to the last, calm and undisturbed, his right hand resting in that of Horace Traubel." [147]

X

Walt Whitman died at approximately six-forty on Saturday evening, in time for the reporters to prepare long accounts for the Sunday papers, March 27, 1892. Although Emerson had perhaps been more famous, and Longfellow certainly more universally loved, no other American author had aroused so much controversy or possessed so colorful a personality. For these reasons his death was sure to be widely and lengthily reported. Naturally the Philadelphia papers gave liberal space to his passing, but so did the papers in all the large cities, and especially New York. Athough the poet's friend Julius Chambers had left the New York *Herald* for the *World*, the *Herald* gave three columns, or half a page, to his death. The *Times* gave over two columns, and the *Tribune* nearly two. A Reuter's reporter cabled two columns and a quarter to the London *Chronicle*, which were printed on Monday. It is safe to say that in his death Whitman received more newspaper space than he had during his whole lifetime.

Certainly newspaper space is a crude measurement of literary fame, but the longer articles summarized Whitman's biography (drawing details mainly from Dr. Bucke's *Walt Whitman* and the autobiography in *Specimen Days*) and listed his books, sometimes with critical interpretations. Thus at his death Whitman's life and works became more widely known and appreciated. Of the three New York newspapers mentioned above, the *Tribune* gave the most factual, impartial account, neither condemning nor approving the poetry, nor attempting to guess the poet's place in literary history. The *Herald* stated that, "To the mass of people Whitman's poetry will always remain as a sealed book, but there are few who are not able to appreciate the beauty of . . . 'O Captain! My Captain!'" The account ended by prophesying that "Whitman's death will excite a new interest in his poetry, and may lead to a better understanding of his genius."

The *Times* gave the frankest summary and appraisal, which began: "The old poet who for so many years has made the public his confidant during the slow stages of his departure from the world is now at rest." The journalist thought that in his death "the City of New-York has lost the most remarkable literary character since Washington Irving." Though "his merits are not conceded so generally as those of Irving," he was said to have only one rival in originality, Poe, and "Whitman had the honor of causing Alfred Lord Tennyson to change his style late in life, as appears from the Jubilee Ode published in honor of Queen Victoria in 1887." But New Yorkers "never cared for Walt Whitman or bought his books or read them." This was attributed largely to Whitman's discarding rhyme and meter, for most readers still thought these essential to poetry. Here the author of the obituary suggested a parallel with Rembrandt, who also displeased the citizens of his native city, Amsterdam, by artistic innovations which posterity was to cherish. The *Times* account ended by saying that, "It is impossible to forecast what Whitman's place in American literature is going to be." But "posterity is not going to judge him as harshly as some of the virtuous of to-day have done, for how can the men of the future fail to be won over by a man who believes so rapturously in the essential goodness of all created things—even of that pit, the soul of man!"

XI

Mrs. Davis objected to an autopsy, but Mrs. George Whitman gave her consent and a post-mortem was performed by Professor Henry W. Cattell, demonstrator of Gross Morbid Anatomy at the University of Pennsylvania, in the presence of Dr. Daniel Longaker, Professor F. X. Dercum,

Dr. Alexander McAlister, Whitman's Camden physician, and Horace L. Traubel.[148] The physicians decided that "The cause of death was pleurisy of the left side, consumption of the right lung, general miliary tuberculosis and parenchymatous nephritis. There was also found a fatty liver, gallstone, a cyst in the adrenal, tubercular abscesses, involving the bones, and pachymeningitis." [149]

The left lung was collapsed, so that no air could enter, and "only about one-eighth of the right lung was suitable for breathing purposes." Tubercles were found also in the stomach, intestines, kidney, and liver. The abscess on the left side had completely eroded through the fifth rib so that the ends grated when moved. A huge stone almost filled the gall bladder. Dr. Longaker declared in his report: "It is, indeed, marvelous that respiration could have been carried on for so long a time with the limited amount of useful lung tissue found at the autopsy. It was no doubt due largely to that indomitable will pertaining to Walt Whitman. Another would have died much earlier with one half of the pathological changes which existed in his body." [150] This was an ironical end for the poet who had set out to chant the songs of health and sound physiology. But the diagnosis of the causes of his death confirms the reality of his fancied vitality and physical endurance. He must have inherited a remarkably strong body to have survived these multiple diseases as long as he did.

The funeral was held on March 30. From 11.00 A.M. until 2:00 P.M. the body was on view at 328 Mickle Street. Several thousand people passed through the house to view the coffin, and the street was still thronged when it was closed.[151] One of the thousands who came was Peter Doyle. At first he was not recognized, and a policeman was turning him away from the door when fortunately someone who knew him caught sight of him just in time and he was admitted for one last look at the mortal remains of his old "comrade." [152] Probably many had come out of morbid curiosity, in response to the newspaper publicity, but literally thousands followed the funeral procession the two miles to Harleigh Cemetery, where a large tent had been erected for the services.[153] No minister officiated, but the following speakers took their places on the slightly elevated platform: Thomas B. Harned, Robert G. Ingersoll, Richard Maurice Bucke, Francis Howard Williams, and Daniel G. Brinton.[154]

Williams read passages from "Out of the Cradle Endlessly Rocking." Harned spoke briefly on Whitman's life in Camden and his belief in immortality. Williams read selections from the writings of Confucius, Gautama, and the words of Jesus. Professor Brinton spoke briefly on

Whitman's "teaching." Williams read from the Koran, Isaiah, and St. John. Dr. Bucke spoke on immortality. Williams read from the Zend-Avesta and Plato. And Ingersoll closed the service with a brief oration. He could not very well speak on immortality, but he chose the next best theme: "Again we, in the mystery of Life, are brought face to face with the mystery of Death." His final words were:

He has lived, he has died, and death is less terrible than it was before. Thousands and millions will walk down into the "dark valley of the shadow" holding Walt Whitman by the hand. Long after we are dead the brave words he has spoken will sound like trumpets to the dying.

And so I lay this little wreath upon this great man's tomb. I loved him living, and I love him still.

NOTES

ABBREVIATIONS

Barrus, *Comrades* Clara Barrus, *Whitman and Burroughs: Comrades*, Boston, 1931.

CW *The Complete Writings of Walt Whitman*, ed. Richard Maurice Bucke, Thomas B. Harned, and Horace L. Traubel, New York and London, 1902. 10 vols.

Civil War *Walt Whitman and the Civil War: A Collection of Original Articles and Manuscripts*, cd. Charles I. Glicksberg, Philadelphia, 1933.

DAB *Dictionary of American Biography*, ed. Allen Johnson and Dumas Malone, New York, 1928–1936. 20 vols.

FC *Faint Clews & Indirections: Manuscripts of Walt Whitman and His Family*, ed. Clarence Gohdes and Rollo G. Silver, Durham, N.C., 1949.

GF *The Gathering of the Forces: Editorials, Essays, Literary and Dramatic Reviews and Other Material Written by Walt Whitman as Editor of the Brooklyn Daily Eagle in 1846 and 1847*, ed. Cleveland Rodgers and John Black, New York and London, 1920. 2 vols.

ISL *I Sit and Look Out: Editorials from the Brooklyn Daily Times*, ed. Emory Holloway and Vernolian Schwarz, New York, 1932.

In Re *In Re Walt Whitman*, ed. by his literary executors, Philadelphia, 1893.

NYD *New York Dissected: A Sheaf of Recently Discovered Newspaper Articles by the Author of Leaves of Grass*, ed. Emory Holloway and Ralph Adimari, New York, 1936.

Nonesuch *Walt Whitman, Complete Poetry & Selected Prose and Letters*, ed. Emory Holloway, London, the Nonesuch Press, 1938.

UPP *Uncollected Poetry and Prose of Walt Whitman: Much of Which Has Been But Recently Discovered with Various Early Manuscripts Now First Published*, ed. Emory Holloway, New York, 1932. 2 vols.

W–G Wells, Carolyn, and Goldsmith, Alfred F., *A Concise Bibliography of the Works of Walt Whitman*, Boston, 1922.

WWC Horace L. Traubel, *With Walt Whitman in Camden*. Vol. I: *March 28–July 14, 1888*, Boston, 1906. Vol. II: *July 16–October 31, 1888*, New York, 1908. Vol. III: *November 1, 1888–January 20, 1889*, New York, 1914. Vol. IV: *January 21–April 7, 1889*, Philadelphia, 1953.

Workshop *Walt Whitman's Workshop*, ed. Clifton Joseph Furness, Cambridge, Mass., 1928.

COLLECTIONS

Bayley	W. D. Bayley Collection, Ohio Wesleyan University.
Berg	Berg Collection, New York Public Library.
Einstein	Private Collection of Milton I. D. Einstein, New York City.
Feinberg	Private Collection of Charles E. Feinberg, Detroit, Michigan.
Hanley	Private Collection of T. E. Hanley, Bradford, Pennsylvania.
Trent	Josiah Trent Collection, Duke University Library.
Lion	Formerly Private Collection of Oscar Lion, New York City, now in Rare Book Room of New York Public Library.
Van Sinderen	Van Sinderen Collection, Yale University Library.

CHAPTER I

[1] "Starting from Paumanok," Sec. 2.

[2] Brown leather notebook in Library of Congress.

[3] "Van" was probably part of the surname, but the newspapers gave neither initials nor first name.

[4] New York *Evening Post* and New York *Daily Advertiser*, May 28, 1823.

[5] See *The Diary of Philip Hone, 1828–1851*, ed. by Bayard Tuckerman (New York, 1889), I, 75. On May 27, 1833, Hone had a similar experience in trying to get to Brooklyn from eastern Long Island.

[6] See CW, I, xvi.

[7] See p. 362.

[8] R. M. Bucke, *Walt Whitman* (Philadelphia, 1883), 13. See also FC, 48.

[9] Daniel G. Brinton and Horace L. Traubel, "A Visit to West Hills," *Walt Whitman Fellowship Papers*, No. 10, Dec., 1894, 62.

[10] FC, 47.

[11] *Ibid.*, 45.

[12] CW, IV, 17; VII, 41.

[13] See Ralph Foster Weld, *Brooklyn Village, 1816–1834* (New York, 1938), 279.

[14] Cf. Weld, *op. cit.*, 22.

[15] See *ibid.*, Chapter I, and Francis Guy's painting reproduced opposite p. 180.

[16] *Ibid.*, 41.

[17] *Ibid.*, 28.

[18] UPP, II, 86.

[19] CW, IV, 17; see Appendix B, pp. 596–600.

[20] UPP, II, 86.

[21] CW, IV, 17.

[22] Barrus, *Comrades*, 254. Walt also thought his father's drinking might have been responsible for the feeble-mindedness of Edward (born 1833).

[23] WWC, I, 256.

[24] See Appendix B.

[25] WWC, I, 79.

[26] Moncure D. Conway, *The Life of Thomas Paine* (New York, 1892), II, 422.

[27] CW, VI, 241.

[28] See David Goodale, "Some of Walt Whitman's Borrowings," *American Literature*, X, 202–213 (May, 1938).

[29] WWC, II, 205.

[30] CW, I, xvi.

[31] See p. 308.

[32] CW, VII, 41.

[33] UPP, II, 256–257.

[34] UPP, II, 256; CW, VII, 42; *Lafayette in Brooklyn* (New York, George D. Smith, 1905).

[35] *Walt Whitman's Diary in Canada*, ed. by W. S. Kennedy (Boston, 1904), 5.

[36] UPP, II, 265; but the daughter of Whitman's teacher said the school was on Sands Street—*ibid.*, I, xxvi, note 9. Probably this was a later location; the poet's memory was usually accurate on the details of his early youth.

[37] Weld, *op. cit.*, 183 ff.

[38] UPP, I, xxvi, note 9.

[39] Grace Gilchrist, "Chats with Walt Whitman," *Temple Bar Magazine*, CXIII, 200–212 (Feb., 1898).

[40] UPP, II, 265–266.

[41] *Ibid.*

[42] CW, VI, 256.

[43] *Journal of the Life and Religious Labors of Elias Hicks* (New York, 1832), 438.

[44] FC, 48.

[45] *Ibid.*, 45.

[46] "Old Salt Kossabone."

[47] FC, 45.

[48] *Ibid.*, 46.

[49] *Ibid.*, 43.

[50] CW, IV, 12.

[51] *Ibid.*

[52] *Ibid.*, 14.

[53] *Ibid.*, 16.

[54] *Ibid.*, 17–18.

[55] WWC, II, 98.

[56] UPP, II, 248.

[57] A political faction organized in 1815 to oppose the administration of Governor De Witt Clinton; some members of the group wore a tail of a buck in their hats.

[58] UPP, II, 3.

[59] Weld, *op. cit.*, 169.

[60] CW, V, 33.

[61] UPP, II, 246–248.

[62] CW, IV, 18.

[63] Henry R. Stiles, A *History of the City of Brooklyn* (Brooklyn, 1870), 635.

[64] Weld, *op. cit.*, 61–62.

[65] *Ibid.*, 78.

[66] UPP, II, 293.

[67] *In Re*, 38.

[68] Weld, *op. cit.*, 81.

[69] CW, IV, 22.

[70] Weld, *op. cit.*, 45.

[71] *Ibid.*, 159.

[72] UPP, II, 86.

[73] CW, IV, 19.

[74] See pp. 138–139.

[75] See Katharine Molinoff, *Some Notes on Whitman's Family* (Brooklyn, 1941), 20–21.

[76] UPP, I, 118.

[77] "The shower of meteors—this occurred in the night of 12th and 13th Nov. 1833—toward morning—myriads in all directions, some with long shining white trains, some falling over each other like falling water—leaping silent, white apparitions around up there in the sky over my head [.]" Holograph in Berg Collection.

[78] CW, V, 33–34.

[79] *Civil War*, 54.

[80] CW, IV, 19.

[81] *Civil War*, 54.

[82] Of course, he could have lived in Brooklyn and commuted. But later, when he worked in New York as printer and editor, he boarded near his office. See p. 61.

[83] Hone, *op. cit.*, I, 153.

[84] *Ibid.*, 204.

[85] UPP, II, 86.

[86] Published in *Union Magazine of Literature and Art*, II, 280–281 (June, 1848); reprinted in UPP, I, 229–234.

[87] CW, IV, 20.

[88] UPP, II, 13.

[89] *Ibid.*

[90] See Katharine Molinoff, *Whitman's Teaching at Smithtown, 1837–38* (Brooklyn, 1942).

[91] *Ibid.*, 21–22.

[92] UPP, II, 86–87.

[93] *In Re*, 39.

[94] A. J. G. Perkins and Theresa Wolfson, *Frances Wright: Free Enquirer: The Study of a Temperament* (New York, 1939), 331.

[95] WWC, II, 204.

[96] *Ibid.*, 205.

[97] *Ibid.*, 500.

[98] CW, I, xvi.

[99] Published in the *Rover*, III, No. 5 (April, 1844); reprinted in *Short Stories of Walt Whitman*, ed. by T. O. Mabbott (New York, 1927), 109–113.

[100] Molinoff, *Some Notes on Whitman's Family*, 3.

[101] UPP, II, 87.

[102] CW, I, xvi.

[103] Katharine Molinoff, *An Unpublished Whitman Manuscript: The Record of the Smithtown Debating Society, 1837–38* (Brooklyn, 1941).

[104] CW, V, 34.

[105] *In Re*, 34.

[106] Brinton and Traubel, *op. cit.*, 62.

[107] Willis Steell, "Walt Whitman's Early Life on Long Island," *Munsey's Magazine*, XL, 497–502 (Jan., 1909). This story sounds aprocryphal, and one wonders why the defendant was tried before a jury instead of a justice of the peace, but George insisted that the arrest and trial actually took place.—*In Re*, 35.

[108] The earliest was "Effects of Lightning," reprinted in *Long Island Democrat*, Aug. 8, 1838. Installments of the "Sun-Down Papers" were printed in April 28, Aug. 11, Sept. 29, Oct. 20, and Nov. 28, 1840; July 6, 1841. One was printed in the *Long Island*

Farmer (Jamaica), July 20, 1841. Poems printed in the *Long Island Democrat*: "Our Future Lot," Oct. 31, 1838; "Young Grimes," Jan. 1, 1839; "Fame's Vanity," Oct. 23, 1839; "My Departure," Nov. 27, 1839; "The Inca's Daughter," May 5, 1840; "The Love that is Hereafter," May 19, 1840; "We All Shall Rest at Last," July 14, 1840; "The Spanish Lady," Aug. 4, 1840; "The End of All," Sept. 22, 1840; "The Columbian's Song," Oct. 27, 1840; "The Winding Up," June 22, 1841. All reprinted UPP.

[109] UPP, I, xxxiii n.

[110] Horace L. Traubel, "Walt Whitman, Schoolmaster: Notes of a Conversation with Charles A. Roe, 1894," *Walt Whitman Fellowship Papers*, No. 14, April, 1895, 81–87.

[111] Perkins and Wolfson, *op. cit.*, 337.

[112] "The Punishment of Pride," *New World*, Dec. 18, 1841; reprinted UPP.

[112a] J. Johnston, M.D. and J. W. Wallace, *Visits to Walt Whitman in 1890–1891* (London, 1917), 70.

[113] Ellen M. Calder in manuscript version of "Personal Recollections of Walt Whitman" from copy made by C. J. Furness. This passage was omitted in publication of the article in the *Atlantic Monthly*, June, 1907.

[114] UPP, I, 32 ff.

[115] *Ibid.*, 37.

[116] *Ibid.*, 10.

[117] Joseph Jay Rubin, "Whitman in 1840: A Discovery," *American Literature*, IX, 239–242 (May, 1937).

[118] *Ibid.*, 239.

[119] *Ibid.*, 240.

[120] UPP, II, 86.

CHAPTER II

[1] "Roots and Leaves. . . ," a "Calamus" poem.

[2] UPP, II, 87.

[3] Frederic Hudson, *Journalism in the United States from 1690–1872* (New York, 1873), 456.

[4] See Merle M. Hoover, *Park Benjamin, Poet and Editor* (New York, 1948), 95 ff.

[5] UPP, I, 51.

[6] See Lawrence Sargent Hall, "Young America," in *Hawthorne: Critic of Society* (New Haven, 1944), 104.

[7] Long after he had become fully aware of the faults of these early stories, Whitman liked to recall his connection with the *Democratic Review*, and he reprinted several of these stories as "Pieces in Early Youth" in an appendix to *Specimen Days and Collect*.

[8] *Democratic Review*, IX, 177–181 (Aug., 1841); reprinted in CW, VI, 5–15.

[9] *Democratic Review*, IX, 476–482 (Nov., 1841); reprinted in CW, VI, 39–49.

[10] *Democratic Review*, IX, 560–568 (Dec., 1841); reprinted in UPP, I, 52–60.

[11] UPP, I, 10–11, note 1.

[12] *Ibid.*, I, 17–19.

[13] See Chapter I, note 108.

[14] UPP, I, 19–20.

[15] See *Walt Whitman of the New York Aurora: Editor at Twenty-two*, ed. by Joseph Jay Rubin and Charles H. Brown (State College, Pa., 1950), 2.

[16] *Ibid.*, 1.

[17] CW, V, 35.

[18] *Walt Whitman . . . Aurora*, 135.

[19] Hoover, *op. cit.*, 103.

[20] UPP, II, 103.

[21] *Walt Whitman . . . Aurora*, 110.

[22] Hoover, *op. cit.*, 130.

[23] *Walt Whitman . . . Aurora*, 2.

[24] *Ibid.*, 4.

[25] *Ibid.*, 35.

[26] William Cauldwell, "Walt Whitman as a Young Man," New York *Times*, Jan. 26, 1901; reprinted in the *Conservator*, XX, 76 (July, 1901); quoted in *Walt Whitman . . . Aurora*, 140, note 28.

[27] *Walt Whitman . . . Aurora*, 44.

[28] *Ibid.*, 120.

[29] *Ibid.*, 140, note 28.

[30] *Ibid.*, 116.

[31] *Ibid.*, 117.

[32] *Ibid.*

[33] *Ibid.*, 24.

[34] *Ibid.*, 9.

[35] *Ibid.*, 10; CW, VI, 292.

[36] *Walt Whitman . . . Aurora*, 58.

[37] *Ibid.*, 82–83.

[38] *Ibid.*, 140, note 26.

[39] *Ibid.*, 99–100.

[40] *Ibid.*, 99.

[41] *Ibid.*, 105.

[42] CW, VII, 55.

[43] *Walt Whitman . . . Aurora*, 115; UPP, I, 67–72.

[44] *Ibid.*, 12.

[45] *Ibid.*

[46] James Robinson Newhall, *The Legacy of an Octogenarian* (Lynn, Mass., 1897), 130 ff.

[47] *Walt Whitman . . . Aurora*, 2.

[48] Hoover, *op. cit.*, 101 ff. Benjamin never publicly admitted being joint editor.

[49] *Walt Whitman . . . Aurora*, 13.

[50] Issue of Thursday, Aug. 11, 1842; a copy of this issue is in the Union College Library.

[51] "The Tomb-Blossoms," *Democratic Review*, X, 62–68 (Jan., 1842); reprinted in *Voices from the Press* (James J. Brenton, editor), 1850, and UPP, I, 60–67. "The Last of the Sacred Army," *Democratic Review*, X, 259–264 (March, 1842); reprinted, *Democratic Review*, XXIX, 463–466 (Nov., 1851), and UPP, I, 72–78. "The Child Ghost; a Story of the Last Loyalist," *Democratic Review*, X, 451–459 (May, 1842); reprinted, revised, retitled, "The Last Loyalist," CW, VI, 28–38. "A Legend of Life and Love," *Democratic Review*, XI, 83–86 (July, 1842); reprinted in New York *Tribune*, July 6, 1842, *Brother Jonathan*, July 9, 1842, Brooklyn *Eagle*, June 11, 1846, and UPP, I, 78–83 and GF, II, 377–386. "The Angel of Tears," *Democratic Review*, XI, 282–284 (Sept., 1842); reprinted Brooklyn *Evening Star*, Feb. 28, 1846, and UPP, I, 83–86.

[52] Emory Holloway, UPP, I, 83, note 1; and Bliss Perry, *Walt Whitman, His Life and Work* (Boston, 1906), 24.

[53] UPP, I, 84.

[54] UPP, II, 103–104.

[55] Walt Whitman, *Franklin Evans; or The Inebriate: A Tale of the Times*, ed. by Emory Holloway (New York, 1929), xviii.

[56] WWC, I, 93.

[57] J. G. Schumaker, New York *Tribune*, April 4, 1892, quoted by Perry, *op. cit.*, 28.

[58] *Franklin Evans*, ed. Holloway, vii.

[59] *Ibid.*, 4.

[60] FC, 45.

[61] *Franklin Evans*, xv.

[62] UPP, II, 87.

[63] *Ibid.*

[64] CW, IV, 168.

[65] UPP, I, 7.

[66] *Ibid.*, II, 88.

[67] *Ibid.*, I, 86–89.

[68] CW, VI, 85–88.

[69] UPP, I, 90–92.

[70] CW, VII, 55.

[71] See Herbert Asbury, *The Gangs of New York* (New York, 1927), 21 ff.

[72] *Walt Whitman . . . Aurora*, 57.

[73] Asbury, *op. cit.*, 34–37.

[74] *Walt Whitman . . . Aurora*, 21.

[75] George C. D. Odell, *Annals of the New York Stage* (New York, 1931), V, 373.

[76] UPP, II, 88.

[77] GF, II, 6.

[78] UPP, I, 161, note.

[79] John Arthur Garraty, *Silas Wright* (New York, 1949).

[80] UPP, II, 86.

[81] Reprinted in *Short Stories by Walt Whitman*, ed. by T. O. Mabbott (New York, 1927), 87–97.

[82] CW, VI, 15–28. Whitman revised the ending, shortening it and making it less sentimental.

CHAPTER III

[1] "Song of the Broad-Axe," Secs. 10–12.

[2] UPP, I, 33, note.

[3] See p. 101.

[4] UPP, II, 87.

[5] Hearn's Directory for 1845–1846 listed Walter Whitman, carpenter, at Prince and Willoughby, but this seems to have been the same house later listed as 71 Prince Street.

[6] Emory Holloway, "More Light on Whitman," *American Mercury*, I, 183–189 (Feb., 1924), 184.

[7] CW, VII, 48–49.

[8] *Ibid.*, 48.

[9] UPP, II, 87.

[10] Unpublished MS in Whitman's handwriting, dated Nov. 23rd. "62 Portland Ave." Transcribed by C. J. Furness.

[11] Holloway, "More Light . . ." *op. cit.*

[12] Florence Bernstein Freedman, *Walt Whitman Looks at the Schools* (New York, 1950), 65–67.

[13] *Ibid.*, 66.

[14] *Ibid.*, 46.

[15] *Ibid.*, 71.

[16] Some of the articles were signed with Whitman's initials, and Emory Holloway has identified as Whitman's a series of "Postscript Letters," supposedly sent to the *Star* over the signature "O.P.Q." See "More Light . . ." *op. cit.*, 184.

[17] *Star*, Oct. 27, 1845.

[18] Holloway, "More Light . . ." *op. cit.*, 185.

[19] *Ibid.*, signed "O.P.Q."

[20] "The author desires us to say, for him, that he pretends to no scientific knowledge of music. He merely claims to appreciate so much of it (a sadly disdained department, just now) as affects, in the language of the deacons, 'the natural heart of man.' It is scarcely necessary to add that we agree with our correspondent throughout. Ed. B.J." [Edgar Allan Poe]. UPP, I, 104 n.

[21] CW, IV, 22.

[22] *Ibid.*, VII, 49 ff.

[23] UPP, I, 105–106.

[24] *Star*, Nov. 28, 1845.

[25] Freedman, *op. cit.*, 89.

[26] *Ibid.*, 214–215 (Oct. 22, 24; Nov. 28, 1845).

[27] *Ibid.*, 88 ff.

[28] *Star*, Nov. 18, 1845.

[29] Freedman, *op. cit.*, 72; *Star*, Dec. 29, 1845.

[30] Freedman, *op. cit.*, 69.

[31] *Ibid.*

[32] *Star*, Dec. 4, 1845; Freedman, *op. cit.*, 81.

[33] *Star*, Jan. 8, 1846; Freedman, *op. cit.*, 85; see also note 317, p. 250.

[34] Holloway, "More Light . . ." *op. cit.*

[35] Freedman, *op. cit.*, 150, 155–157, 158–159.

[36] Theodore A. Zunder, "William B. Marsh—The First Editor of the Brooklyn Daily Eagle," *American Book Collector*, IV, 93–95 (Aug., 1933).

[37] Cf. p. 19.

[38] GF, I, xix.

[39] Holloway, "More Light . . ." *op. cit.*, 183.

[40] GF, II, 7–8.

[41] *Ibid.*, II, 11.

[42] *Ibid.*, I, xxi. Cleveland Rodgers, editor of the Brooklyn *Eagle* in the 1920's, discovered and interviewed Henry Sutton.

[43] "The Play Ground," June 1, 1846 (UPP, I, 21); "Ode to be Sung at Fort Greene: 4th of July, 1846," July 2, 1846 (UPP, I, 22–23); "The Child and the Profligate," Jan. 27, 28, 29, 1847 (CW, VI, 60–73); "A Legend of Life and Love," June 11, 1846 (UPP, I, 78–83); *Franklin Evans*, Nov. 16–30, 1846 (UPP, II, 103–221); "The Love of Eris, a Spirit Record," Aug. 18, 1846 (UPP, I, 86–89); "Dumb Kate; Story of an Early Death," July 13, 1846 (CW, VI, 85–88); "The Half-Breed" ("Arrow-Tip"), June 1–6, 8, 9, 1846; "The Boy Lover," Jan. 4–5, 1848 (CW, VI, 49–60); "One Wicked Im-

pulse," Sept. 7–8, 1846 (CW, VI, 15–28); "A Fact Romance of Long Island," Dec. 16, 1846; "The Old Black Widow," Nov. 12, 1846 (UPP, I, 138–139); "An Incident on Long Island Forty Years Ago," Dec. 24, 1846 (UPP, I, 149–151).

[44] UPP, II, 103, note.

[45] GF, I, xxxviii–ix.

[46] Brooklyn *Eagle*, May 23, 1846. See Theodore A. Zunder, "Whitman Interviews Barnum," *Modern Language Notes*, XLVIII, 40 (Jan., 1933).

[47] UPP, I, 115.

[48] *Ibid.*, 118–121.

[49] *Ibid.*, 22–23.

[50] *Ibid.*, 141–144.

[51] See p. 18.

[52] George C. D. Odell, *Annals of the New York Stage* (New York, 1931), V, 252.

[53] *Ibid.*, 256.

[54] GF, II, 140–144.

[55] UPP, I, 112–113.

[56] *Ibid.*, 117.

[57] GF, I, 148–151.

[58] UPP, I, 137.

[59] *Ibid.*, 128.

[60] *Ibid.*, 131; GF, II, 305–306.

[61] UPP, I, 126–137.

[62] *Ibid.*, 127–130.

[63] GF, II, 212–213.

[64] Bernard DeVoto, *The Year of Decision* (Boston, 1943).

[65] See e.g., Robert Selph Henry, *The Story of the Mexican War* (Indianapolis, 1950), 49–50.

[66] GF, I, 187.

[67] *Ibid.*, I, 80–83.

[68] DeVoto, *op. cit.*, 128 *et passim*.

[69] GF, I, 85–86.

[70] *Ibid.*, 240–242.

[71] DeVoto, *op. cit.*, 205.

[72] GF, I, 242–243.

[73] *Ibid.*, 23.

[74] *Ibid.*

[75] *Ibid.*, 247.

[76] *Ibid.*, 10–11.

[77] *Ibid.*, 13.

[78] CW, IV, 202–203. Cf. Charles I. Glicksberg, "Whitman and Bryant," *Fantasy*, V, 31–36 (No. 2, 1935).

[79] GF, II, 188.

[80] *Ibid.*, I, 249.

[81] *Ibid.*, 250.

[82] *Ibid.*, 16–17.

[83] See John Arthur Garraty, *Silas Wright* (New York, 1949), especially Chapter XVI.

[84] GF, II, 6.

[85] *Ibid.*, 30.

[86] *Ibid.*, 37.

[87] *Ibid.*, I, 4, 5, 6.

[88] *Ibid.*, 194.

[89] *Ibid.*, 197.

[90] *Ibid.*, 203.

[91] *Ibid.*, 25–26.

[92] *Ibid.*, 221–222.

[93] *Ibid.*, 227–228.

[94] See note 43, above.

[95] UPP, II, 88. Cf. GF, I, xxxii.

[96] GF, I, xxxiv–xxxv.

[97] A workingmen's party which once held a meeting in New York City by the light of friction matches called "locofocos." See Arthur M. Schlesinger, Jr., *The Age of Jackson* (Boston, 1945), 190 ff.

[98] GF, I, xxxiii.

[99] CW, V, 35.

[100] *Ibid.*, IV, 27.

[101] UPP, I, 181 ff.

[102] *Ibid.*, 181–190.

[103] *Ibid.*, II, 77–78.

[104] *Ibid.*, 77.

[105] *Ibid.*, I, 187.

[106] *Ibid.*, 188.

[107] Letter from Jefferson Whitman to his mother [Feb. 27, 1848], sent from New Orleans. Quoted from transcription made by Clifton J. Furness from the Bucke Collection—original not seen.

[108] New Orleans letter from Jefferson Whitman to his mother, March 14, 1848 (see note 107, above).

[109] *Ibid.*

[110] *Ibid.*

[111] UPP, II, 77.

[112] *Ibid.*

[113] Letter from Jefferson Whitman to his mother, March 14, 1848 (see note 107, above).

[114] *Ibid.*, March 27, 1848.

[115] *Ibid.*

[116] *Ibid.*, April 23, 1848.

[117] UPP, I, 191.

[118] *Ibid.*, 191–192.

[119] *Ibid.*, 193–195.

[120] *Ibid.*, 199–218.

[121] See p. 48.

[122] UPP, I, 225–228.

[123] Henry Bryan Binns, *A Life of Walt Whitman* (London, 1905), Chapter IV.

[124] Typescript of an article by J. William Lloyd enclosed in a letter addressed to Clifton J. Furness dated June 20, 1936 (now in present author's possession).

[125] UPP, I, 204.

[126] Letter from Jefferson Whitman to his mother, March 27, 1848 (see note 107, above).

[127] *Ibid.*, March 28, 1848.

[128] *Ibid.*, April 23, 1848.

[129] *Ibid.*, March 27, 1848.

[130] CW, VI, 208–216.

[131] *Ibid.*, 210.

[132] *Ibid.*, 211.

[133] *Ibid.*, 212; UPP, II, 78.

[134] UPP, II, 78.

[135] *Ibid.*, 77–79.

[136] Holloway, "More Light . . ." *op. cit.*

[137] *Ibid.*

[138] CW, IV, 16.

[139] Not previously quoted.

[140] UPP, I, lii, note 8. Only one copy of the *Freeman* has survived, that of Saturday, Sept. 9, 1848, now in the Trent Collection.

[141] That the father's health was failing this early is only a deduction. Dr. R. M. Bucke said (in an unpublished MS transcribed by Clifton J. Furness) that he died after an exhausting illness, from paralysis, and Binns, *op. cit.*, 86, reports Walter Whitman's health as failing in 1853. The fact that the family moved in with Walt in the spring of 1848 is an indication that the father was not able to take care of them.

[142] See Appendix B, p. 599.

[143] See p. 98.

[144] UPP, II, 88, note 8. For picture see GF, II, 242.

[145] Holloway in UPP, I, lii, note 8, gives the third place where the *Freeman* was printed as 96 Myrtle Avenue, and the Brooklyn *Directory* for 1849–50 listed Walter Whitman, Jr., as editor of the Brooklyn *Freeman*, "Fulton at Middagh, h. 106 Myrtle Avenue." Probably he did not move his printing office to 106 Myrtle until after he gave up editing the *Freeman*.

[146] Edward Hungerford, "Walt Whitman and His Chart of Bumps," *American Literature*, II, 357–358 (Jan., 1931).

[147] *Ibid.*, 363.

[148] UPP, I, 25–27.

[149] *Ibid.*, 26, note.

[150] No title in 1855; in 1860 given title "Europe, the 72d and 73d Years of These States." UPP, I, 27–30.

[151] The allusion is general rather than specific. The language is Biblical and perhaps alludes to the second coming of Christ.

[152] Cf. Gay W. Allen, "Biblical Echoes in Whitman's Works," *American Literature*, VI, 302–315 (Nov., 1934).

CHAPTER IV

[1] "A Word Out of the Sea" (1860 version of "Out of the Cradle Endlessly Rocking").

[2] Cf. "Notes from Conversations with George W. Whitman, 1893; mostly in his own words," by Horace L. Traubel, in *In Re*, 33–34; "There was a great boom in Brooklyn in the early fifties, and he had his chance then, but you know he made nothing of that chance. Some of us reckoned that he had by this neglect wasted his best opportunity. . . ."

³ Reprinted in UPP, I, 239.

⁴ Brooklyn *Evening Star*, May 12, 1851, quoted by Henry R. Stiles, A *History of the City of Brooklyn* (Brooklyn, 1870), II, 291.

⁵ UPP, II, 88, note 8; for a picture of the house see GF, II, 242. There has been speculation that Whitman made a second trip to the South in the fall of 1849 (see UPP, I, liii, note 4, and 24, note 1), but no actual evidence has been cited. Since Whitman kept detailed notes of his trip to New Orleans, it would seem likely that he would have kept some written record (diary, letters, etc.) of a second trip. No member of his family, so far as known, ever referred to such a trip or his absence from Brooklyn at this time. Moreover, the fact that Walt had recently built a house and was running a printing shop and bookstore on the first floor makes it seem unlikely that he would wander off for six months, leaving his business unattended. Actually, the hypothesis of this second trip has frequently been used to bolster the other hypothesis of a love affair and illegitimate children in the South.

⁶ See UPP, I, 234–235, 241–247.

⁷ *Ibid.*, 236–241, 247–259.

⁸ UPP, II, 88, note 8.

⁹ See Edward Hungerford, "Walt Whitman and His Chart of Bumps," *American Literature*, II, 350–384 (Jan., 1931).

¹⁰ UPP, I, 236–238.

¹¹ WWC, II, 506.

¹² *Ibid.*, 502.

¹³ See DAB.

¹⁴ Four were reproduced in UPP, I, facing p. 194.

¹⁵ Horatio Greenough, *Aesthetics in Washington* (1851) and *The Travels, Observations and Experiences of a Yankee Stonecutter* (1852). The best of Greenough's essays have been collected and edited by Harold A. Small, *Form and Function, Remarks on Art by Horatio Greenough* (Berkeley, Calif., 1947). F. O. Matthiessen has discussed Greenough's "functional" theories of art in relation to Whitman's poetic theory in *American Renaissance* (New York, 1941), 141–152.

¹⁶ Small, *op. cit.*, 111.

¹⁷ *Ibid.*, 50.

¹⁸ *Ibid.*, 120.

¹⁹ *Ibid.*, 53.

²⁰ Especially in *Aesthetics in Washington*, but mentioned, *passim*, in Small, *op. cit.*

²¹ "Art and Artists [:] Remarks of Walt Whitman before the Brooklyn Art Union, on the Evening of March 31, 1851," Brooklyn *Daily Advertiser*, April 3, 1851; reprinted UPP, I, 241–247.

²² "In the temple of Juno at Elis, Sleep and his twin-brother, Death, were represented as children reposing in the arms of Night. On various funeral monuments of the ancients, the Genius of Death is sculptured as a beautiful youth, leaning on an inverted torch, in the attitude of repose, his wings folded, and his feet crossed. In such peaceful and attractive forms did the imagination of the ancient poets and sculptors represent death. And these were men in whose souls the religion of Nature was like the light of stars, beautiful, but faint and cold! Strange, that, in later days, this angel of God, which leads us with a gentle hand into the 'land of the great departed, into the silent land,' should have been transformed into a monstrous and terrific thing! such is the spectral rider on the white horse;—such is the ghastly skeleton with scythe and hour-glass;—the Reaper whose name is Death!" *Hyperion*, Book IV, Chapter VIII.

[23] Michael Angelo's definition in Longfellow's poem "Michael Angelo," *Complete Works* (Boston, 1886–1904), VI, 144.

[24] See UPP, I, 244, note 1. On March 10 Parke Godwin gave an address on "The Philosophy of Art" at the Academy of Design. The following evening Daniel Huntington gave an address before the American Artists' Association in New York on "Christian Art." This last was repeated on March 25 for the benefit of the public. Holloway thinks the latter may have been the lecture to which Whitman alluded.

[25] Similar attitudes toward Greek art and life may be found in "Pictures." See note 170, below.

[26] *In Re*, 35.

[27] "Letters from Paumanok," [No. 1] Greenport, L.I., June 25; [No. 2] June 28; reprinted in UPP, I, 247–254.

[28] "A Plea for Water," signed by Whitman; reprinted in UPP, I, 254–255.

[29] See Grace Adams and Edward Hutter, *The Mad Forties* (New York, 1942), 34–57.

[30] Stiles, *op. cit.*, II, 292.

[31] Published Aug. 14, 1851; reprinted in UPP, I, 255–259.

[32] This was a reminiscence of an earlier performance; *Don Pasquale* was given on Aug. 11, 1851. See George C. D. Odell, *Annals of The New York Stage* (New York, 1927–38), VI, 98.

[33] UPP, I, 257. For a later opinion see CW, IV, 27; VII, 53, 56.

[34] This subject has been studied and ably presented by Robert D. Faner, *Walt Whitman & Opera* (Philadelphia, 1951).

[35] *Ibid.*, Chapter II.

[36] CW, IV, 26.

[37] *Ibid.*, VII, 50.

[38] J. Johnston and J. W. Wallace, *Visits to Walt Whitman in 1890–1891* (London, 1918), 162.

[39] Faner, *op. cit.*, 26 ff.

[40] FC, 19.

[41] CW, IV, 292.

[42] WWC, II, 174.

[43] Quoted by Faner, *op. cit.*, 30.

[44] See CW, IV, 26; V, 217; VII, 50.

[45] Quoted by Faner, *op. cit.*, 30.

[46] *Ibid.*, 31.

[47] *Ibid.*, 66. See also CW, VIII, 252–254, and the poem "Vocalism."

[48] CW, VII, 21–22.

[49] "Proud Music of the Storm."

[50] "Shut Not Your Doors, Proud Libraries."

[51] A letter from Sarah H. Wicks to Hannah Whitman, Oct. 8, 1848 (now in Library of Congress), refers to Jeff's study of music.

[52] *In Re*, 38.

[53] See Katherine Molinoff, *Some Notes on Whitman's Family* (Brooklyn, 1941), 24–43.

[54] The letters of Hannah have never been collected, but a few have been published. See FC, 209–212. A very revealing letter from Mrs. Heyde to her mother written July 19, 1855 (soon after the death of Walter Whitman, Sr.), was published in *Life in Letters: American Autograph Journal*, II, 99–103.

[55] FC, 49.

[56] CW, IV, 27. Later he changed the years to "1852–54," CW, VII, 64.

[57] *In Re*, 33.
[58] See Esther Shephard, *Walt Whitman's Pose* (New York, 1938).
[59] See Johnston and Wallace, *op. cit.*, 64–66.
[60] Cf. *The Diary of Philip Hone*, ed. by Bayard Tuckerman (New York, 1889), I, 203.
[61] See Lloyd Morris, *Incredible New York, 1850–1950* (New York, 1951), 4.
[62] CW, IV, 23–24.
[63] John Burroughs, *Whitman: A Study* (Boston, 1896), 24.
[64] UPP, II, 6.
[65] NYD, 140.
[66] CW, VII, 57.
[67] Fred Lewis Pattee, *The Feminine Fifties* (New York, 1940), 164–166.
[68] See picture in Morris, *op. cit.*, 10.
[69] Cf. Pattee, *op. cit.*, 165. In 1858 the building burned to the ground.
[70] CW, VII, 32.
[71] Quoted by Pattee, *op. cit.*, 166.
[72] CW, IX, 133–134.
[73] See J. T. Trowbridge, *My Own Story* (Boston, 1903), 366.
[74] See NYD, 27–30.
[75] Published Dec. 8, 1851; reprinted NYD, 30–40.
[76] Clipped from the *North British Review*, American edition, XI, 283–306 (Aug., 1849). Now in the Trent Collection. See *Catalogue of the Whitman Collection . . . Being a Part of the Trent Collection . . .*, compiled by Ellen Frances Frey (Durham, N.C., 1945), 73.
[77] NYD, 38.
[78] CW, IX, 104–105.
[79] Part of the imagery in a strange poem, "Scented Herbage of My Breast," came from a picture of the burial of Osiris. See Esther Shephard, "Possible Sources of Some of Whitman's Ideas and Symbols . . .", *Modern Language Quarterly*, XIV, 74, note 37 (March, 1953).
[80] Joseph Beaver, *Walt Whitman—Poet of Science* (New York, 1951).
[81] The Brooklyn *Daily Eagle*, March 20, 1847; reprinted in GF, II, 146–149.
[82] UPP, I, 128, note.
[83] Quoted by Beaver, *op. cit.*, 157, note 24.
[84] "Song of Myself," Sec. 33.
[85] Beaver, *op. cit.*, 66.
[86] "Poets to Come" (in "Inscriptions," *Leaves of Grass*).
[87] "Song of Myself," Sec. 33.
[88] Beaver, *op. cit.*, 58.
[89] *Ibid.*, especially Chapter II.
[90] *Ibid.*, 11.
[91] E.g., in his notebook dated 1847 (UPP, II, 64) Whitman reminded himself to ask Mr. ——— Dwight about the highest numeral term known. CW, IX, 129–130 (talk with a Mrs. Rose about the life of Frances Wright); *ibid.*, X, 25, "Get from Mr. ——— Arkhurst the names of all insects." See also *ibid.*, IX, 135 ("Iron Works"); *ibid.*, 136 ("The Whale"); many other examples in Whitman's notes.
[92] *In Re*, 39. Frederic Saunders, *New York in a Nutshell, or Visitor's Handbook to the City of New York*, 1853, says that the New York Society Library was said to have 50,000 volumes, and the Mercantile Library Association probably had as many. The Astor Library was incorporated in 1849. A librarian was employed and sent to Europe

to buy books, and by Jan., 1851, 30,000 volumes had been accumulated, according to the *Index of Books in Astor Library*, published by the trustees, in 1851. These were housed temporarily at 32 Bond Street, and the books were available for limited use. In Jan., 1851, this library contained around 150 volumes on Egypt and Egyptology. In American literature, nothing by Emerson, Hawthorne, Poe. Shakespeare was well represented. The Astor Library was opened to the public on May 1, 1853, in a new building on the east side of Lafayette Place, with over 60,000 volumes.

[93] See CW, X, 63–97. Many of these are now in the Trent Collection; see Frey, *op. cit.*

[94] Some of these have been printed in CW, IX, 45–230; the original MSS are in the Library of Congress and the private library of Mr. Charles E. Feinberg in Detroit.

[95] Trent Collection.

[96] *Ibid.*

[97] See "The Organic Principle" in G. W. Allen, *Walt Whitman Handbook* (Chicago, 1946), 292 ff.

[98] Cf. W. S. Kennedy, *Reminiscences of Walt Whitman* (London, 1896), 150 ff.

[99] See Maurice O. Johnson, "Walt Whitman as a Critic of Literature," *University of Nebraska Studies in Language, Literature and Criticism* (Lincoln, Neb., 1938), No. 16, especially 12.

[100] See note 97 above. The two last studies: Gregory Paine, "The Literary Relations of Whitman and Carlyle . . ." *Studies in Philology*, XXXVI, 550–563 (July, 1939), and Fred N. Smith, "Whitman's Debt to Sartor Resartus," *Modern Language Quarterly*, III, 51–65 (March, 1942).

[101] Several annotated extracts from this work are in the Trent Collection.

[102] All three are in the Trent Collection.

[103] *Ibid.*

[104] In Library of Congress.

[105] John Stafford, *The Literary Criticism of "Young America," A Study in the Relationship of Politics and Literature, 1837–1850* (Berkeley, Calif., 1952).

[106] See p. 44.

[107] Stafford, *op. cit.*, 11.

[108] See L. S. Hall, *Hawthorne as Critic of Society* (New Haven, 1944), 104 ff.

[109] Reprinted in Willard Thorp (ed.), *Herman Melville: Representative Selections* (New York, 1938), 327–345.

[110] Stafford, *op. cit.*, 67.

[111] *Ibid.*, 69.

[112] *Ibid.*, 55.

[113] Quoted by Adams and Hutter, *op. cit.*, 170.

[114] Stafford, *op. cit.*, 57–58.

[115] See Frey, *op. cit.*, 77.

[116] *Ibid.*

[117] *Ibid.*, 78.

[118] *Edinburgh Review*, April, 1849, 187.

[119] Frey, *op. cit.*

[120] *Ibid.*, 78.

[121] *Ibid.*

[122] *Ibid.*, 72–73.

[123] *Ibid.*, 72.

[124] *Ibid.*, 80.

[125] Now in the Harned Collection of Library of Congress.

¹²⁶ UPP, II, 63 ff.

¹²⁷ See p. 116.

¹²⁸ Whitman's personal copy in Bayley Collection.

¹²⁹ UPP, II, 63.

¹³⁰ *Ibid.*

¹³¹ See p. 19.

¹³² UPP, II, 64.

¹³³ From Heine's *Germany* as quoted by John Firman Coar, *Studies in German Literature in the Nineteenth Century* (New York, 1903), 181–182. A French version of "On the History of German Religion and Philosophy" was published in *Revue des Deux Mondes* in 1834. Possibly no English version was available to Whitman in the 1850's. However, similar ideas might have been found in Herder's *Outlines of a Philosophy of the History of Man* (London, 1803), or *The Autobiography of Goethe,* translated by Parke Godwin, which Whitman reviewed in the Brooklyn *Daily Eagle,* Nov. 19, 1846. See UPP, I, 139.

¹³⁴ UPP, II, 64–65.

¹³⁵ *Ibid.,* 65.

¹³⁶ Quoted by Kuno Francke, *A History of German Literature as Determined by Social Forces,* 4th ed. (New York, 1901), 521.

¹³⁷ Recorded for July 16, 1851.

¹³⁸ CW, VII, 27.

¹³⁹ UPP, II, 65.

¹⁴⁰ *Ibid.,* 66. Heine's *Pictures of Travel,* which Whitman read in Charles Godfrey Leland's translation (1855), contains striking parallels to Whitman's description of the effect of the seashore at night on his soul, though this notebook was perhaps written before 1855. See Esther Shephard, "An Inquiry into Whitman's Method of Turning Prose into Poetry," *Modern Language Quarterly,* XIV, 54 (March, 1953).

¹⁴¹ UPP, II, 66.

¹⁴² See Gustav Bychowski, "Walt Whitman: A Study in Sublimation," *Psychoanalysis and the Social Sciences,* II, 223–261 (1950).

¹⁴³ Cf. Allen, *op. cit.,* 248.

¹⁴⁴ Frances Wright, *A Few Days in Athens: Being the Translation of A Greek Manuscript Discovered in Herculaneum* (London, 1822; New York, 1831).

¹⁴⁵ David Goodale, "Some of Walt Whitman's Borrowings," *American Literature,* X, 202–213 (May, 1938).

¹⁴⁶ *A Few Days in Athens,* 147.

¹⁴⁷ Holograph in Library of Congress.

¹⁴⁸ See p. 110.

¹⁴⁹ Whitman's reference to *A Few Days in Athens* indicates that he read it in his youth, along with Volney's *Ruins;* see WWC, II, 445.

¹⁵⁰ WWC, II, 71–72.

¹⁵¹ *Ibid.,* II, 229, 264, 332; III, 186.

¹⁵² UPP, II, 67.

¹⁵³ *Walt Whitman of the New York Aurora: Editor at Twenty-two,* ed. by Joseph J. Rubin and Charles H. Brown (State College, Pa., 1950), pp. 39, 41.

¹⁵⁴ Henry D. Thoreau, *Letters to Various Persons* (Boston, 1865), 148.

¹⁵⁵ CW, III, 55.

¹⁵⁶ See Allen, *op. cit.,* 457 ff.

¹⁵⁷ Dorothy Frederica Mercer, in an unpublished thesis, "Leaves of Grass and the Bhagavad Gita: A Comparative Study" (1933), quoted by Allen, *op. cit.,* 460.

[158] The main source of time concepts in twentieth century literature has been Vico, and after him Bergson, who has taught that *time* and not space is the true measure of existence. What he has called *durée*, time ever growing and accumulating (not objective time), is "the continuous progress of the past which gnaws into the future and which swells as it advances" (*Creative Evolution*, p. 7). Proust tried to recapture and relive imaginatively—immerse himself in—"suspended time." Eliot, a real scholar of comparative literature from Sanskrit to the French Symbolists and widely read in philosophy, has so absorbed the great literature of the past that it has become a part of his own mind and memory, and we are told that in *The Waste Land* the images of the past (both remote past, *i.e.*, preserved in mythology, and the historical past) join the images of the sordid present on one level of time, so that in the poem there is only an endless present.

[159] UPP, II, 76.

[160] *Ibid.*, 79–80.

[161] *Ibid.*, 70.

[162] *Ibid.*

[163] *Ibid.*, 85.

[164] *Ibid.*, 72; cf. "Song of Myself," Secs. 28–29.

[165] UPP, II, 73.

[166] *Ibid.*, 88.

[167] *Ibid.*, 89.

[168] *Ibid.*, 81. One idea Whitman jotted down but never used was "Poem incarnating the mind of an old man . . ." If he had used it, the poem would hardly have resembled Eliot's "Gerontion."

[169] Cf. p. 38.

[170] The manuscript is now in the Van Sinderen Collection of Yale University Library. Edited and published by Emory Holloway, *Pictures: An Unpublished Poem of Walt Whitman* (New York, 1927).

[171] *Ibid.*, 13.

[172] On July 29, 1881, Whitman wrote: "After more than forty years' absence, (except a brief visit, to take my father there once more, two years before he died,) went down Long Island on a week's jaunt to the place where I was born. . . ." CW, IV, 7. In "A Week at West Hills," published in the New York *Tribune*, Aug. 4, 1881, Whitman reported that he had not "been in Huntington village for over 40 years, and only once briefly at the Hills during that time."

[173] Cf. Binns, *A Life of Walt Whitman*, 65; *Walt Whitman's Diary in Canada*, 66.

[174] Perhaps the best contemporary description of the Anthony Burns episode is Theodore Parker's *Life and Correspondence*, ed. by John Weiss (New York, 1864), II, 125 ff.

[175] UPP, I, 259–264.

[176] MS of Mrs. W. D. O'Connor, formerly in Bucke Collection.

[177] *The Free Press* (London, Ont.), June 5, 1880.

[178] *In Re*, 35.

[179] WWC, II, 471.

[180] Johnston and Wallace, *op. cit.*, 116–117.

[181] See p. 149.

[1182] See Appendix B, p. 600.

[183] UPP, II, 88, note 8.

[184] *In Re*, 35.

CHAPTER V

[1] "In Paths Untrodden," the first poem in the "Calamus" section.

[2] Ralph Adimari has done the most research on this problem. See his "Leaves of Grass—First Edition," *American Book Collector*, V, 150–152 (May–June, 1934). Also discussed by Clifton J. Furness in his Introduction to *Leaves of Grass by Walt Whitman: Reproduced from the First Edition* (1855) (New York, 1939). The New York *Tribune* was not published on July 5 because the *Tribune* was a morning paper and was written and printed the night before, which would have been the national holiday. However, if it was the intention of Whitman and the Fowlers to "publish" *Leaves of Grass* on July 4, it should have been announced on July 3.

[3] Letter from Whitman to a Mr. Ford, Aug. 23, 1867; original in the J. Pierpont Morgan Library.

[4] Cf. Furness, *op. cit.*, vi–vii.

[5] *Ibid.*, viii, details given by Hollyer in letters now in the J. Pierpont Morgan Library.

[6] Whitman several times gave the figure of a thousand copies. See Furness *op. cit.*, xv.

[7] Adimari, *op. cit.*, 152.

[8] See p. 179, *post*.

[9] WWC, III, 115–116.

[10] See Harold Blodgett, *Walt Whitman in England* (Ithaca, N.Y., 1934), 14 ff.

[11] Taken from transcription made by Clifton J. Furness. Original letter not located. "Laura" has not been identified.

[12] Henry R. Stiles, A *History of the City of Brooklyn* (Brooklyn, 1869), III, 504.

[13] Published in *Life in Letters: American Autograph Journal*, II, 102–103 (June, 1939).

[14] Facsimile of original in WWC, IV, between pp. 152–153.

[15] See Henry Seidel Canby, *Walt Whitman: An American* (Boston, 1943), 121.

[16] *Leaves of Grass* (Brooklyn, 1855), iv.

[17] *Ibid.*, v.

[18] *Ibid.*, vi.

[19] *Ibid.*

[20] See Willie T. Weathers, "Whitman's Poetic Translations of His 1855 Preface," *American Literature*, XIX, 21–40 (March, 1947).

[21] *Leaves of Grass, op. cit.*, vi.

[22] William James, A *Pluralistic Universe* (New York, 1909).

[23] *Leaves of Grass, op. cit.*, ix–x.

[24] All quotations in this paragraph are from Emerson's essay on "The Poet."

[25] Cf. "Nature," an uncompleted essay.

[26] In essay "Inspiration," quoted by Sherman Paul, *Emerson's Angle of Vision* (Cambridge, Mass., 1952), 170.

[27] In this discussion of the 1855 edition all quotations are from the original version, many of which were revised in subsequent editions. E.g., "I celebrate myself, and sing myself."

[28] Section 46 (1881 version), p. 46 in the 1855 edition.

[29] Section 24 (1881 version), p. 29 in the 1855 edition.

[30] See p. 461, *post*.

[31] Section 24; p. 29 and p. 30 in 1855 edition.

[32] Section 5, p. 15 in 1855 edition.

[33] Cf. Henry Seidel Canby, *op. cit.*, 113; and Frederick Schyberg, *Walt Whitman* (New York, 1951), 113–114.

[34] Section 6, p. 16 in 1855 edition. Many critics have speculated, often unprofitably, on Whitman's title. The poet probably thought "leaves" more connotative and musical than the more idiomatic "blades." "Grass" was a slang term meaning either a casual worker in the printing office or "copy" of little value that he set up. Clifton J. Furness in his Introduction for the Facsimile Edition of the 1855 *Leaves of Grass, op. cit.*, p. x, thinks that Whitman ironically applied this slang term to his book, which the printers at Rome Brothers probably thought of little value. To the author of this biography such reasoning seems unconvincing.

[35] See p. 139.

[36] Section 19, p. 25 in 1855 edition.

[37] *Ibid.*, 21; p. 27.

[38] *Ibid.*, 24; p. 29.

[39] *Ibid.*, 28; p. 32.

[40] *Ibid.*, 3; p. 14.

[41] *Ibid.*, 28; p. 33.

[42] UPP, II, 64 ff.

[43] Section 44, p. 50 in 1855 edition.

[44] *Ibid.*, 49; p. 54.

[45] *Ibid.*, 51; p. 55.

[46] *Ibid.*, 52; p. 56.

[47] Cf. Henri Frankford and others, *Before Philosophy: A Study of Egypt and Mesopotamia* . . . (Penguin Books, 1951).

[48] Cf. Herbert Asbury, *Gangs of New York* (New York, 1928), 201–202.

[49] Although corn is sometimes red, edible corn is usually white or yellow; "rose" probably has a phallic symbolism.

[50] See *Poets of the English Language*, ed. by W. H. Auden and N. H. Pearson (New York, 1950), V, xxiv.

[51] See Matthew 25:13.

[52] Adimari, *op. cit.*

[53] Moncure Daniel Conway, *Autobiography: Memories and Experiences* (Boston, 1905), I, 215–216.

[54] Reprinted in second issue of first edition. These two books were also jointly reviewed in the *Crayon*, III, 30–32 (Jan., 1856).

[54a] *In Re*, 13, 27.

[55] Reprinted in second issue of first edition.

[56] *Ibid.* The reviewer was actually Charles Eliot Norton. See note 63, below.

[57] WWC, III, 125.

[58] The copy Whitman sent to Longfellow, with the clipping still in it, is in the Craigie House at Cambridge, Mass.

[59] Ralph Rusk, *The Life of Ralph Waldo Emerson* (New York, 1949), 373.

[60] Bliss Perry, *Walt Whitman* (Boston, 1906), 100, note 2.

[61] *Ibid.*, 101.

[62] *Ibid.*

[63] *A Leaf of Grass from Shady Hill, With a Review of Walt Whitman's Leaves of Grass*, written by Charles Eliot Norton in 1855 (Cambridge, Mass., 1928).

[64] *Ibid.*, 11–12.

[65] Henry B. Rankin, *Personal Recollections of Abraham Lincoln* (New York, 1916), 125–126.

⁶⁶ See p. 382.

⁶⁷ Reprinted in NYD, 18 ff.

⁶⁸ *Ibid.*, 52.

⁶⁹ *Ibid.*, 166.

⁷⁰ Blodgett, *op. cit.*, 13.

⁷¹ See Milton E. Flower, *James Parton, The Father of Modern Biography* (Durham, N.C., 1951), 25 ff.

⁷² NYD, 162–163.

⁷³ *Ibid.*, 171.

⁷⁴ Cf. *The Animal Magnetism; or History, Phenomena and Curative Effects of Animal Magnetism* . . . By a Physician (Philadelphia, 1841).

⁷⁵ See p. 139.

CHAPTER VI

¹ "Scented Herbage of My Breast" (1860 reading).

² Reprinted NYD, 80–84.

³ See *ibid.*, 105.

⁴ *Ibid.*, 108–114.

⁵ It is not known in what printing office (Rome Brothers, Brooklyn *Times*, *Life Illustrated*, or other) the proofs were made. The tract was not published until 1928, when it was brought out in France and the United States: *The Eighteenth Presidency!* . . . with notes by Jean Catel (Montpelier, France, 1928), 31 pp.; Clifton J. Furness, *Walt Whitman's Workshop* (Cambridge, 1928), 85–113.

⁶ The name of Mrs. Price's husband is given in "Letters of Walt Whitman," *Putnam's Monthly*, V, 163–169 (Nov., 1908). (This article was published anonymously, but must have been written either by Mrs. Price or with her collaboration.) Smith's *Brooklyn City Directory* for 1856–57 lists Edward Price at 31 Hicks St., but Lain's (Consolidated Directory for 1857–58) gives Edmund Price at this address— evidently correct. A James Price, cabinetmaker, lived at 22 Classon Avenue in 1856–57, and at 84 Classon in 1857–58. The Whitmans were living at 91½ Classon, just across the street from 84. Possibly James was a relative of Edmund Price, and Mrs. Abby Price could have met Mrs. Whitman while visiting the James Prices.

⁷ R. M. Bucke, *Walt Whitman* (Philadelphia, 1883), 27.

⁸ Cf. Moncure D. Conway, "Walt Whitman," *Fortnightly Review*, VI, 538 ff. (Oct. 15, 1866).

⁹ Bucke, *op. cit.*, 32–33.

¹⁰ *The Journals of Bronson Alcott*, selected and edited by Odell Shepard (Boston, 1938), 286–287.

¹¹ *Ibid.*, 289.

¹² *In Re*, 36.

¹³ Alcott's *Journals*, *op. cit.*, 290.

¹⁴ *Ibid.*, 291.

¹⁵ See DAB.

¹⁶ Alcott's *Journals*, *op. cit.*, 293–294.

¹⁷ *Letters to Various Persons*, by Henry David Thoreau (Boston, 1865), 142.

¹⁸ *Ibid.*, 146–148

[19] WWC, I, 212.

[20] *Ibid.*, III, 318.

[21] *Anne Gilchrist: Her Life and Writings*, ed. by Herbert Harlakenden Gilchrist (London, 1887), 237.

[22] Alcott's *Journals*, 294.

[23] WWC, II, 130.

[24] Ralph Rusk, *The Life of Ralph Waldo Emerson* (New York, 1949), 374.

[25] *In Re*, 35.

[26] See NYD, 151–153, 232; WWC, III, 235–239; Barrus, *Comrades*, 177–178.

[27] ISL, 8–20.

[28] *Ibid.*, 10.

[29] *Ibid.*, 12–20.

[30] Letter to Charles Skinner, quoted by Skinner in "Whitman as Editor," *Atlantic Monthly*, XCII, 679–686 (Nov., 1903).

[31] Cf. ISL, 17.

[32] See p. 130.

[33] WWC, III, 238.

[34] ISL, 53–54.

[35] WWC, III, 235–236. After his death one of Whitman's friends remarked that Fanny Fern was once "sweet" on him (NYD, 153), but this could have been an allusion to her praise of *Leaves of Grass*, if based on anything tangible.

[36] July 20, 1857, reprinted in ISL, 103–104.

[37] See p. 72.

[38] Oct. 22, 1858.

[39] Skinner, *op. cit.*, 679. A young German printer and poet, Frederick Huene, who worked in the composing room of the *Times* while Whitman was editor, gave a similar description. Whitman hoped that Huene would translate *Leaves of Grass* into German, but Huene decided that he was unequal to the task. See ISL, 12–13.

[40] ISL, 13–15.

[41] July 16, 1858.

[42] See p. 99.

[43] Henry Bryan Binns, *A Life of Walt Whitman* (London, 1905), 112.

[44] ISL, 13.

[45] Skinner, *op. cit.*, 679.

[46] E.g., "A Bad Subject for a Newspaper Article" (prostitution), July 20, 1857; and the review of Sanger's *History of Prostitution*, Dec. 9, 1858, reprinted in ISL, 118–119.

[47] Cf. Index of WWC; and CW, IV, 168–171.

[48] Notebook in Library of Congress, quoted UPP, II, 91, note I; and ISL, 15.

[49] Katharine Molinoff, *Some Notes on Whitman's Family* (Brooklyn, 1941), 7.

[50] The notebook also contained a photograph of a young woman (UPP, II, 70) who has never been identified, and romantic biographers (e.g., Frances Winwar) have speculated that this was a picture of Whitman's mistress or sweetheart. It could have been Mrs. Beach's photograph (see p. 262).

[51] UPP, II, 88, note 8.

[52] CW, IX, 154–155.

[53] Whitman's literary executors, obviously following his own attitudes, made such a claim. For summary see G. W. Allen, *Walt Whitman Handbook* (Chicago, 1946), 107–108.

[54] Original in the Huntington Library, ed. by Rollo G. Silver, "Seven Letters of Walt Whitman," *American Literature*, VII, 78 (March, 1935).

[55] Quoted in ISL, 20. (When Holloway examined this letter it was in the Valentine Manuscripts—see note 56, below—it is not there now and its whereabouts is unknown to the present biographer.)

[56] From the Rome Brothers these manuscripts passed to a family named Valentine, and they are frequently called the "Valentine MSS." The present owner is Mr. Clifton Waller Barrett, of Long Island, a graduate of the University of Virginia. Professor Fredson Bowers, University of Virginia, is editing the manuscripts for publication by the University of Chicago Press.

[57] Quoted by permission of Mr. Clifton Waller Barrett and Professor Fredson Bowers (see note 56).

[58] *Ibid.*

[59] Trent Collection.

[60] Trent Collection. Clifton J. Furness transcribed the MS while it was in Dr. R. M. Bucke's collection and published it, without attempting to date it, in "Walt Whitman's Politics," *American Mercury*, XVI, 459–466 (April, 1929).

[61] See note 56, above.

[62] See p. 525.

[63] Bowers (see note 56) has worked out the chronology. There were two kinds of white paper, Williamsburg tax blanks (probably an unused supply that Whitman found in the *Times* printing office) and white stationery that Whitman used last of all; but the transcriptions on the back of the tax forms and on the white stationery seem to have been made about the same time. Details to be given in Bowers's forthcoming edition, scheduled for publication in 1955 by the University of Chicago Press.

[64] A phrenological term, see p. 103.

[65] See note 56.

[66] See note 56. The twelve "Calamus-Leaves" poems correspond to the poems in the "Calamus" group as follows: I, No. 14; II, No. 20; III, No. 11; IV, No. 23; V, No. 8; VI, No. 32; VII, No. 10; VIII, No. 9; IX, No. 34; X, No. 40; XI, No. 36; XII, No. 42. The praise in the Capitol alluded to in III might have been a review of *Leaves of Grass* in the *National Intelligencer*, Washington, D.C., Feb. 18, 1856 (see p. 174).

[67] See p. 218.

[68] In 1881 and later editions of *Leaves of Grass* the "Calamus" group has still another arrangement.

[69] "Calamus" No. 20 in 1860 edition (see note 56, above). This and the other eleven "Calamus" poems numbered with Roman numerals in the Valentine-Barrett MSS. have been published by Fredson Bowers, "Whitman's Manuscripts for the Original 'Calamus' Poems," *Studies in Bibliography: Papers of the Bibliographical Society of the University of Virginia*, VI, 257–265 (1953–1954).

[70] No. 8 in 1860 edition (see note 56, above).

[71] No. 10 in 1860 edition (see note 56, above).

[72] No. 9 in 1860 edition (see note 56, above).

[73] Sections 35–36 (see note 56, above).

[74] Leaf No. 15 in MS (see note 56 above): "States!/You do not need maternity only . . ." Verso: "Calamus-Leaves IV—later in MS repeated as No. III, corresponding to 1860 "Calamus" No. 11.

[75] Section 38; cf. "Out of the Cradle Endlessly Rocking," p. 234.

[76] Section 42, end of white paper insertions (see note 56).

[77] Section 61 (see note 56)—these lines on blue paper, immediately following pink paper insertions.

[78] Section 62 (see note 56).

[79] Albert Parry, *Garrets and Pretenders: A History of Bohemianism in America* (New York, 1933), 14–48.

[80] *Ibid.*, 19.

[81] *Ibid.*, 35–37.

[82] Skinner, *op. cit.*, 680; cf. WWC, I, 417.

[83] W. D. Howells, *Literary Friends and Acquaintances* (New York, 1900), 68–76.

[84] *Ibid.*, 69.

[85] *Ibid.*, 74.

[86] WWC, II, 375.

[87] In *November Boughs* (CW, VI, 111) Whitman said he had been in Boston in 1859, but his letters written in the spring of 1860 imply that he had never been in Boston before. Cf. note 111, below.

[88] Reprinted in *A Child's Reminiscence* by Walt Whitman, collected [and edited] by Thomas Ollive Mabbott and Rollo G. Silver (Seattle, Wash., 1930), 10.

[89] *Ibid.*, 19–20.

[90] See p. 217.

[91] Cf. p. 114.

[92] Quoted by R. M. Bucke, *op. cit.*, 29.

[93] Emory Holloway, *Whitman: An Interpretation in Narrative* (New York, 1926), 162, says: "Surely some lover had died, and he could find solace only in song."

[94] So arranged in later editions: (1) an introduction or prelude, (2) the song of the bird (in italics), and (3) the poet's interpretation of the bird's song.

[95] Only in the *Saturday Press* version.

[96] This version reprinted in *A Child's Reminiscence* (see note 88 above). Revised for the 1867 and 1871 editions. For example, the staccato first line became in 1871 the rhythmical "Out of the cradle endlessly rocking."

[97] For an excellent critical analysis of thought and style of this poem, see Leo Spitzer "'Explication de Texte' Applied to Walt Whitman's 'Out of the Cradle Endlessly Rocking'" ELH: *A Journal of English Literary History*, XVI, 229–249 (Sept., 1949).

[98] See Joseph Beaver, *Walt Whitman—Poet of Science* (New York, 1951), 3–4.

[99] In the etymological sense: from L. *dæmon*, spirit.

[100] Thayer and Eldridge letter in Feinberg Collection; contract not located. Richard J. Hinton claimed to have called the attention of Thayer and Eldridge to *Leaves of Grass*. See W. S. Kennedy, *The Fight of a Book for the World* (West Yarmouth, Mass., 1926), 242.

[101] CW, V, 26–27.

[102] Nonesuch, 886–887.

[103] Cf. Emerson's essays on "Love" and "Friendship."

[104] Discovered by Kenneth Walter Cameron; see Cameron's *Ralph Waldo Emerson's Reading* (Raleigh, N.C., 1941), 141, under section "Names of Strangers Introduced" [1849–1865], [notebook] III, 215.

[105] Franklin B. Sanborn gave this information in an address on Whitman (manuscript in the John Pierpont Morgan Library); see also "Emerson in His Home," the *Arena*, XV, 16–21 (Dec., 1895), 20.

[106] Original in the John Pierpont Morgan Library.

[107] Rochester, N.Y., *Express*, March 7, 1868.

[108] WWC, IV, 437.

[109] Redpath remained Whitman's friend and helper; frequently mentioned in WWC, especially in Vol. II.

[110] Sanborn, *op. cit.*

[111] CW, VI, 111. Whitman also "remembered" in old age (WWC, II, 99) that he alternated between the meetings of Theodore Parker and Father Taylor, but here his memory failed him, for Theodore Parker was then mortally ill with tuberculosis and had departed for Europe on Feb. 8. Perhaps Whitman heard Parker in New York.

[112] Original in the Walt Whitman House in Camden, N.J. Quoted by permission of the Walt Whitman Foundation.

[113] Trent Collection.

[114] From transcription made by Clifton J. Furness while the letter was still in the Bucke collection.

[115] Trent Collection.

[116] See note 114 above.

[117] Trent Collection.

[118] Manuscript reminiscence of Mrs. Ellen Calder (Mrs. W. D. O'Connor); published in part in "Personal Recollections of Walt Whitman," *Atlantic Monthly*, XCIX, 825–839 (June, 1907).

[119] J. T. Trowbridge, *My Own Story* (Boston, 1903), 360.

[120] *Ibid.*, 367.

[121] A copy of the *Saturday Press* issue of April 28, 1860, is in the New-York Historical Society Library.

[122] NYD, 181–182.

[123] Original in the Walt Whitman House, Camden, N.J. Quoted by permission of the Walt Whitman Foundation.

[124] WWC, IV, 195.

[125] See note 123, above.

[126] WWC, IV, 195.

[127] *Ibid.*

[128] W–G., 8.

[129] See p. 221.

[130] Among the old poems (from the 1855 edition) were: "Great Are the Myths," "Song of the Answerer," "This Compost," and "Song of Prudence."

[131] Title used in *Atlantic Monthly*, April, 1860.

[132] Cf. similar theme in "Out of the Cradle," p. 235.

[133] See note 131, above.

[134] CW, X, 18.

[135] Edward Hungerford, "Walt Whitman and His Chart of Bumps," *American Literature*, II, 350–384 (Jan., 1931).

[136] CW, IX, 150.

[137] See note 56, above.

[138] *Ibid.*

[139] See p. 200.

[140] See p. 186.

[141] See note 56, above.

[142] See p. 228.

CHAPTER VII

[1] "As Toilsome I Wander'd Virginia's Woods," in *Drum-Taps*.

[2] In addition to advertisements in newspapers, Thayer and Eldridge printed and distributed gratis a little booklet called *Leaves of Grass Imprints*, composed of reviews and critical comments on the first two editions.

[3] T. O. Mabbott and R. G. Silver, editors of A *Child's Reminiscence* [a critical edition of the first version of "Out of the Cradle Endlessly Rocking"] (Seattle, 1930), suggest that this review may have been written by Whitman, or that at least he assisted the writer. However, in the reviews that Whitman had written of the earlier editions, he stressed personality instead of "the philosophic mind," and he would almost certainly have defended the sex poems instead of saying that they "should never have been published at all." Moreover, the style does not sound like Whitman, for the most part.

[4] Quoted from photostat of the May 19, 1860, New York *Saturday Press* supplied by the Pennsylvania Historical Society. Also reprinted in A *Child's Reminiscence*, 22–28.

[5] See p. 243.

[6] Quoted from photostat of *Saturday Press*. See note 4.

[7] UPP, I, lviii, note 15.

[8] Clara Barrus, *The Life and Letters of John Burroughs* (Boston, 1925), I, 120 n.

[9] Allen Lesser, *Enchanting Rebel: The Secret of Adah Isaacs Menken* (New York, 1947), 61 ff.

[10] *Ibid.*, 64.

[11] WWC, III, 117.

[12] See p. 420.

[13] See p. 199, *passim*.

[14] Letter to John Burroughs, dated May 10, 1892, quoted by Barrus, *Comrades*, 304.

[15] A copy of the London *Spectator* review in Whitman's hand is now in the Lion Collection.

[16] Listed in A *Child's Reminiscence*, 44.

[17] See p. 130.

[18] See p. 195.

[19] See p. 193.

[20] Admiral Matthew Calbraith Perry sailed in 1853 with the intention of negotiating a treaty with Japan, then closed to all intercourse with the Occident, and in 1854 succeeded in making a trade treaty with Japan.

[21] CW, IV, 21. The New York *Times* for June 16, 1860, reported the expected arrival of the Japanese aboard the *Alida* at the Battery about two o'clock. Over 5,000 troops were to parade. Special rooms had been prepared for the ambassadors at the Metropolitan Hotel, frescoed with Japanese scenes.

[22] Quoted from the New York *Times*, June 27, 1860. The punctuation of this version differs considerably from the *Drum-Taps* and *Leaves of Grass* versions.

[23] The R. M. Bucke collection of Whitman manuscripts once contained Whitman's notes on his contract with Thayer and Eldridge, but it now seems impossible to locate them.

[24] John Burroughs, *Notes on Walt Whitman as Poet and Person* (New York, 1871), 21.

[25] "Banner at Day-Break," retitled "Song of the Banner at Day-Break"; "Washington's First Battle" became "The Centenarian's Story, Volunteer of 1861 (At Washington Park, Brooklyn, assisting the Centenarian)"; "Pictures," not published by Whitman but

edited by Emory Holloway (New York, 1927); "Quadrel," probably "Chanting the Square Deific"; "Sonnets," probably some of the "Calamus" poems—see note, *ante*, p. 566, n. 66.

[26] In an article (without title) published by Henry Stoddard in "World of Letters," *The Mail and Express* (New York), June 20, 1898, p. 30.

[27] See p. 197.

[28] WWC, I, 417.

[29] In an 1862 notebook in Library of Congress; quoted in UPP, II, 92.

[30] Henry Bryan Binns, *A Life of Walt Whitman* (London, 1905), 178.

[31] CW, V, 241–244. Apparently Whitman did not hear Lincoln give his Cooper Institute address in New York.

[32] The "unknown-looking persons" were the Western bodyguards who accompanied Lincoln. CW, V, 243–244.

[33] *Ibid.*, IV, 28–29.

[34] Binns, *op. cit.*, 181.

[35] The main source for this story is W. S. Kennedy, *Reminiscences of Walt Whitman* (Philadelphia, 1896), 69. Kennedy claims to have heard Whitman himself tell the story, but he also cites a denial by a member of the Pfaff group.

[36] Nonesuch, 1909. Full name: John Frederick Schiller Gray.

[37] Letter to Myron Benton, Barrus, *Comrades*, 2.

[38] CW, IV, 31.

[39] *Civil War*, 86.

[40] FC, 69.

[41] CW, IV, 31.

[42] *Ibid.*, 35.

[43] *Ibid.*, 37.

[44] This *Drum-Taps* version varies in punctuation from the *Leaves of Grasss* version.

[45] *Civil War*, 86.

[46] In a letter printed in Nonesuch, 934, Whitman says that Andrew had been a soldier. His military record can be found at Albany, N.Y. Cf. Molinoff, *Some Notes on Whitman's Family* (Brooklyn, 1941), 18–19.

[47] The most vehement was T. W. Higginson. See W. S. Kennedy, *The Fight of a Book for the World* (West Yarmouth, Mass., 1926), 70 ff.

[48] See p. 293.

[49] FC, 69.

[50] Quoted from the *Leader*.

[51] UPP, II, 222–321.

[52] *Ibid.*, 312.

[53] *Ibid.*, 223.

[54] *Civil War*, 42.

[55] *Ibid.*

[56] The first article, mainly devoted to history and general description of how the hospital functioned, was printed on March 15, and the series ran until May 17. These articles were signed "Velsor Brush," but there is no doubt that Walt Whitman wrote them, for aside from the fact that his maternal grandmother was a Brush and his mother a Van Velsor, his notebooks and manuscripts show conclusively that he was the author. *Civil War*, 17 ff.

[57] *Ibid.*, 35.

[58] *Ibid.*, 42–43.

[59] *Ibid.*, 62.

[60] The copy used, now in the Lion Collection, New York Public Library, has a notation that it was given to "J. C. F." by Dr. G. P. Wiksell: "He knew nothing of the writer, and did not know who had the original." On Sept. 28, 1904, Henry Bryan Binns wrote to Edward Carpenter (letter now in Bayley Collection, Ohio Wesleyan University), "Traubel showed me a love letter from Ellen Eyre (? of New York) in 1862—and J. H. Johnston a photo of a young N.Y. actress who had been 'one of Walt's sweethearts.'" The letter was likely the original of the copy in the Lion Collection, but there is no evidence whatever that "Ellen Eyre" was a New York actress—nor any evidence that she was not.

[61] Notebook in Library of Congress. Quoted by Louis Untermeyer in *The Poetry and Prose of Walt Whitman* (New York, 1949), 53.

[62] Barrus, *Comrades*, 3.

[63] *Ibid.* Burroughs said that only one contributor to the *Leader*, a woman who lived in Albany, received payments, but this may have been an exaggeration.

[64] The imagery and emotions of "Give Me the Splendid Silent Sun" also indicate that it was written before Whitman left Brooklyn.

[65] *Civil War*, 126.

[66] *Ibid.*, 86.

[67] FC, 153–154.

[68] R. M. Bucke, *Walt Whitman* (Philadelphia, 1883), 34, stated that the Whitman family saw George's name in the New York *Herald* and subsequent biographers accepted the statement. The present biographer examined the New York dailies for Dec. 16, 1862.

[69] There was no official list; each paper printed the names compiled by its correspondents.

[70] CW, VII, 131–132.

[71] Cf. Bucke, *op. cit.*, 34.

[72] *Ibid.*; also diary in 1862 notebook, now in Library of Congress.

[73] CW, VII, 128.

[74] *Ibid.*, 129.

[75] *Ibid.*, 91, 135.

[76] *Ibid.*, 163.

[77] *Ibid.*, 129; also diary in 1862 notebook, now in Library of Congress. See map on p. 282.

[78] CW, VII, 129.

[79] Unpublished letter from George to Jeff Whitman, Jan. 8, 1863, in Hanley Collection.

[80] *Civil War*, 71; CW, VII, 130.

[81] CW, VII, 130–131.

[82] Letter to Nat and Fred Gray, March 19, 1863, printed by Holloway, Nonesuch edition, 895.

[83] *Civil War*, 71, note 24.

[84] *Ibid.*, 79 (germ of poem); the *Drum-Taps* poem quoted.

[85] *Civil War*, 81.

[86] CW, IV, 39–40.

[87] *Ibid.*, 40.

[88] Ellen [O'Connor] Calder, "Personal Recollections of Walt Whitman," *Atlantic Monthly*, XCIX, 825–826 (June, 1907).

[89] CW, VII, 133.

[90] *Ibid.*

[91] *Ibid.*, 134–135.

[92] Sec. 33, line 123.

[93] Sec. 40, lines 22–27.

[94] CW, VII, 125–126.

[95] *Ibid.*, IV, 62.

[96] Margaret Leech, *Reveille in Washington: 1860–1865* (New York, 1941), 207–208.

[97] Whitman's letters to his mother frequently mention the number of sick in the hospitals. Cf. CW, VII, 231.

[98] Discussed in *Civil War*, 3–6.

[99] CW, VII, 168.

[100] WWC, I, 371.

[101] Cf. *Civil War*, 93.

[102] Armory Square most often mentioned in *Specimen Days* and *Wound Dresser*. See CW, VII, 171, 208. On Jan. 29, 1865, he called this a "model hospital" (CW, IV, 101).

[103] Barrus, *Comrades*, xxix.

[104] Binns, *op. cit.*, 198.

[105] *Civil War*, 4.

[106] Brooklyn *Eagle*, March 19, 1863.

[107] DAB.

[108] CW, VII, 152 and 178.

[109] See J. T. Trowbridge, *My Own Story* (Boston, 1903), 385.

[110] CW, VII, 140.

[111] *Ibid.*, 163–164.

[112] Leech, *op. cit.*, 5 ff.

[113] "Conflict of Conviction."

[114] CW, VII, 140.

[115] Letter from Jeff Whitman to Walt, Jan. 13, 1863, formerly in Bucke Collection (transcription made by Clifton J. Furness—original not available).

[116] FC, 155.

[117] CW, VII, 137.

[118] Letter from Jeff Whitman to Walt, Feb. 18, 1863 (see note 115).

[119] CW, VII, 180.

[120] Letters from Mrs. Whitman to Walt, March, 1863, and March 19, 1863. Trent Collection.

[121] Letter from Mrs. Whitman to Walt [late April, 1863], now in Hanley Collection.

[122] Letter of March, 1863. Trent Collection.

[123] CW, VII, 147.

[124] See *ibid.*, 151; cf. *ibid.*, 146.

[125] Molinoff, *op. cit.*. 18.

[126] CW, VII, 146.

[127] *Ibid.*, 147.

[128] *Ibid.*, 158.

[129] Cf. *ibid.*, IV, 130.

[130] CW, VII, 158 *passim*.

[131] *Ibid.*, 167.

[132] *Ibid.*, 169.

[133] *Ibid.*, 179.

[134] *Ibid.*, 166.

[135] *Ibid.*, 167.

[136] *Ibid.*, 172.

[137] Typewritten biographical sketch of Lewis Kirke Brown in Manuscript Division of Library of Congress.

[138] Drafts of five letters have survived, written between April and November, 1863—see note 139, below.

[139] Holograph in the Berg Collection, New York Public Library. All of these holographs seem to be rough drafts.

[140] *Ibid.* Many phrases were deleted—not indicated in these quotations. For example, after "dear Comrade" Whitman first wrote and then crossed out, "What I am writing is pretty strong talk, but it is exactly what I say."

[141] See p. 273.

[142] Barrus, *Comrades*, 4.

[143] *Ibid.*, 5–6.

[144] *Ibid.*

[145] *Ibid.*, 6.

[146] *Ibid.*, 7.

[147] Calder, *op. cit.*, 830.

[148] See note 115, above.

[149] Herbert Asbury, *Gangs of New York* (New York, 1928), 118 ff.

[150] *Ibid.*

[151] CW, VII, 175.

[152] *Ibid.*, 183.

[153] In May, 1864, Jeff's name had still not been drawn (*ibid.*, 269). But a letter from George to his mother dated Sept. 30, 1864, implies that Jeff has had to pay a substitute (FC, 178).

[154] See note 115, above.

[155] CW, VII, 179, 183–184, 191.

[156] Trent Collection.

[157] In a letter to Lewis Brown, written Nov. 8, 1863, Whitman said he arrived in Brooklyn between eight and nine o'clock, Nov. 2 (WWC, III, 101).

[158] FC, 185.

[159] *Civil War*, 138.

[160] *Ibid.*, 138–139.

[161] WWC, III, 101; Nonesuch, 931.

[162] *Civil War*, 139.

[163] Lion Collection. Bliss Perry, *Walt Whitman* (Boston, 1906), 142–143, printed this letter, but he did not accurately follow Whitman's punctuation and misread "my" for "many" in the phrase "amid many troubles."

[164] *Civil War*, 139.

[165] Einstein Collection.

[166] FC, 187–190.

[167] *Ibid.*, 188.

[168] See note 115, above.

[169] Letter dated "December, 1863," in Trent Collection.

[170] *Ibid.*

[171] Trent Collection.

[172] In 1868 Nancy gave birth to illegitimate twins, and sent her other children to beg in the streets. See p. 395.

[173] Christmas, 1863, letter—Trent Collection.

[174] Letter from Redpath, Oct. 28, 1863, in WWC, IV, 418. A manuscript prospectus for the book is in the Van Sinderen Collection, Yale University.

[175] WWC, IV, 416.
[176] Partly influence of Taylor-Scott rivalry—see p. 86.
[177] Barrus, *Comrades*, 16.
[178] *Ibid.*, 17.
[179] *Ibid.*, 18.
[180] Trowbridge, *op. cit.*, 370.
[181] *Ibid.*, 377.
[182] *Ibid.*, 378.
[183] *Ibid.*, 381.
[184] *Ibid.*, 388.
[185] *Ibid.*, 390.
[186] CW, VII, 224.
[187] *Ibid.*, 226.
[188] *Ibid.*, 229.
[189] *Ibid.*, 232.
[190] Perry, *op. cit.*, 145.
[191] CW, IV, 85.
[192] *Ibid.*, VII, 236.
[193] *Ibid.*, 237.
[194] *Ibid.*, 242.
[195] *Ibid.*, 244.
[196] *Ibid.*, 247.
[197] *Ibid.*, 249.
[198] *Ibid.*, 265.
[199] See p. 140.
[200] CW, VII, 268.
[201] *Ibid.*, 271.
[202] *Ibid.*, 275.
[203] *Ibid.*, 279.
[204] Trent Collection.
[205] Van Sinderen Collection.
[206] See note 137, above.
[207] Barrus, *Comrades*, 19.
[208] WWC, III, 338.
[209] Berg Collection.
[210] Barrus, *Comrades*, 19–20.
[211] Manuscript version in *Civil War*, 63–83.
[212] Reprinted in "Hospital Visits," CW, VII, 101–127.
[213] *Ibid.*, 118–119.
[214] *Ibid.*, 122.
[215] Molinoff, *op. cit.*, 20.
[216] This transcription is from the photostat which Mrs. Molinoff reproduces on p. 21. Her own transcription is slightly inaccurate.
[217] The catalogue of the sale of Dr. Bucke's Collection of *Manuscripts, Autograph Letters, First Editions and Portraits of Walt Whitman*, Anderson Galleries, Inc., 1936, p. 64, listed letters by Mattie Whitman to Walt which told of the violent outbreaks of Jesse Whitman which finally led to his being placed in an asylum, but the present owner of these letters has not been located.
[218] Holograph in American Literature Collection, Yale University Library.
[219] *Civil War*, 178.

[220] WWC, II, 401.

[221] Perry, *op. cit.*, 150.

[222] Cf. Joseph Beaver, *Walt Whitman, Poet of Science* (New York, 1951), 55–56.

[223] Perry, *op. cit.*, 152.

[224] WWC, III, 470–471.

[225] See note 115, above.

[226] Molinoff, *op. cit.*, 21. On Jesse's record someone wrote at the bottom of the page after Walt's name: "Washington, D.C., Jan. 22, 1865."

[227] Berg Collection.

[228] See Dixon Wecter, "Walt Whitman as Civil Servant," *PMLA*, LVIII, 1094–1109 (Dec., 1943). Wecter examined the Government files on Whitman's employment and thought this letter was sent to Brooklyn, but other facts cited here contradict that assumption. Moreover, the letter was addressed to "Walt Whitman, Esq. of New York," not to Brooklyn, as in Mr. Otto's previous letter.

CHAPTER VIII

[1] "Over the Carnage Rose Prophetic a Voice," published in *Drum-Taps*, a revision of the 1860 "Calamus" poem No. 5.

[2] CW, VI, 158.

[3] Many years later Whitman was strangely confused about the name of the Secretary of the Interior at this time; he gave it as Caleb Smith (CW, VI, 219), though Smith had been forced to resign late in 1862.

[4] Einstein Collection.

[5] Letter to Jefferson Whitman, Jan. 30, 1865, WWC, III, 539–540.

[6] Einstein Collection.

[7] Knowing that the great need of the Confederacy was for man power, Grant had stopped all exchanges of prisoners in the spring of 1864. See Margaret Leech, *Reveille in Washington* (New York, 1941), 359.

[8] See p. 380.

[9] WWC, III, 292.

[10] Einstein Collection.

[11] See p. 113.

[12] Einstein Collection.

[13] WWC, II, 426.

[14] *Civil War*, 100.

[15] See letter to Trowbridge, *ibid.*

[16] Formerly in the Bucke Collection: from transcription made by Clifton J. Furness; original not available.

[17] CW, IV, 105–106.

[18] *Ibid.*, 106.

[19] *Ibid.*, 107.

[20] See note 16, above.

[21] Hanley Collection (unpublished). Undated except for "Sunday afternoon," which would have had to be February 26 because events alluded to do not fit the preceding or following Sunday.

[22] See note 16, above. The letter read:

ANNAPOLIS Feb 19th, 1865

MRS. LOUISA WHITMAN:
 MADAM,
   I enclose the memorandum your son gave me Feb. 14th. If I can tell you anything further, myself, about him I shall be happy to do so.

I am very respectfully,
WILLIAM COOK
Capt, 9th U.S.C.S.

94 W. 10 Str.
New York

[23] See note 16, above. The enclosed slip read:
George W. Whitman
Capt. 51st Regt. N. Y. Vols.
Prisoner of war at Danville Va. in tip top health and spirits.
 Mother's address Mrs. Louisa Whitman
Portland ave near Myrtle ave.
Brooklyn, N.Y.

[24] WWC, III, 202–203.

[25] Trent Collection; FC, 179–180.

[26] CW, IV, 115.

[27] *Ibid.*, 109.

[28] *Ibid.*

[29] *Ibid.*, 110.

[30] Leech, *op. cit.*, 370.

[31] CW, IV, 72.

[32] *Ibid.*, 112.

[33] *Ibid.*, 113.

[34] FC, 190–191.

[35] See letter written to O'Connor March 26, 1865, quoted in Section II below. On April 7, 1865, Whitman again wrote that his leave had been extended two weeks and that he planned to arrive back in Washington April 16 or 17 (doubtless Sunday evening or early Monday morning, after a night trip).

[36] See note 16, above.

[37] Whitman in his April 7 letter to O'Connor said he planned to return the 16th or 17th; since the latter was Monday his leave was no doubt up that day. See note 16, above.

[38] *Ibid.*

[39] *Ibid.*

[40] CW, IV, 37.

[41] Notebook formerly in the Bucke Collection, quoted *Civil War*, 174.

[42] See Leech, *op. cit.*, 401.

[43] See p. 11.

[44] Leech, *op. cit.*, 403.

[45] Barrus, *Comrades*, 20.

[46] *Ibid.*, 20–21.

[47] See p. 233.

[48] Burroughs wrote a friend in mid-September, 1865, that Whitman was "deeply interested in what I tell him of the Hermit Thrush, and says he has used largely the information I have given him in one of his principal poems." Barrus, *Comrades*, 24.

[49] Hospital Notebook No. 3 in Library of Congress, quoted, *Civil War*, 128.

[50] WWC, III, 471.

[51] Jeff's letter of May 14, 1865, Einstein Collection (unpublished).

[52] Leech, *op. cit.*, 415 ff.

[53] Nonesuch edition, 958–960.

[54] June 3, 1865; Trent Collection.

[55] The first issue of *Drum-Taps*, printed in New York by Peter Eckler and bound by Abraham Simpson, was a thin, 12mo., book of 72 pages, printed on poor-quality paper and bound in unattractive brown, pebble-grain cloth. The typography was neat and clear, but the whole book showed the economy which the times and Whitman's limited income forced upon him. Biographers have long said that after a few copies were distributed Whitman called in the issue and stopped the sale in order that he might add his elegy on Lincoln to the collection. (So stated by H. B. Binns, *A Life of Walt Whitman* [London, 1905, 212], and nearly all biographers since.) But of actual bibliographical facts we have very few; however, by taking all known details into consideration, these deductions can be made: Some of the poems were already in type when Whitman returned to Washington before the Lincoln funeral was held. But the book was probably not printed before early or mid-May because Whitman was still able to insert his short poem on the burial, April 19, which he had to mail to New York, wait for proof, and then wait for page proof—and Whitman was much too careful about the typography of his books to rush or omit any of these routine stages. When the book finally went to press, he probably had five hundred or more sets of the sheets run off, but did not have many bound at that time—today copies of the first issue are extremely rare. The unused sheets Whitman held to be bound in with the supplement he was already planning—though since he had the plates stereotyped, additional copies could readily be printed. However, if Whitman "called in" any copies, he probably did so because they were not selling rather than for some other reason. See "A Walt Whitman Manuscript," by Oral Sumner Coad, *The Journal of Rutgers University Library*, II, 6–10 (Dec., 1938).

[56] See p. 267.

[57] Cf. CW, IV, 94–96.

[58] *Ibid.*, 100.

[59] See p. 320.

[60] Added in 1881 edition of *Leaves of Grass*.

[61] The thought of this passage first appeared in the 1860 "Calamus" group, poem No. 5, which was adapted in "Over the Carnage Rose Prophetic a Voice."

[62] See p. 262.

[63] See p. 436 ff.

[64] Notebook in Library of Congress; quoted UPP, II, 93.

[65] *Ibid.*; Civil War, 79.

[66] See p. 61.

[67] See p. 298.

[68] CW, IV, 286–287.

[69] A group title first used in 1871 in *Passage to India* annex.

[70] Transferred in 1871.

[71] Einstein Collection (unpublished).

[72] FC, 204.

[73] WWC, III, 471.

[74] CW, VI, 219–221.

[75] See p. 311.

[76] WWC, III, 472.

[77] *Ibid.*, 471.

[78] Barrus, *Comrades*, 28–29.

[79] Whitman's summary of the interview as told to him by Ashton in July, 1865, WWC, III, 472.

[80] Barrus, *Comrades*, 29.

[81] Einstein Collection (unpublished).

[82] Lion Collection.

[83] "Song of Myself," Sec. 42.

[84] "By Blue Ontario's Shore," Sec. 7.

[85] Final title, "City of Orgies."

[86] FC, 182.

[87] See note 16, above.

[88] WWC, III, 178–179. See William E. Barton, *Abraham Lincoln and Walt Whitman* (Indianapolis, 1928), 95–105. He has questioned the authenticity of this letter, but his book is exceedingly biased and this specific argument not convincing.

[89] Trent Collection.

[90] Trent Collection; letter dated Aug. 29, 1865.

[91] *Ibid.*

[92] Trent Collection.

[93] *Ibid.*

[94] FC, 192.

[95] The title page read: "SEQUEL TO DRUM-TAPS./ (SINCE THE PRECEDING CAME FROM THE PRESS.)/ WHEN LILACS LAST IN THE DOOR-YARD BLOOM'D./ AND OTHER PIECES./ WASHINGTON./ 1865–6". This pamphlet contained no copyright notice, and was probably not copyrighted. Some of the reviewers of *Drum-Taps* listed it separately, a fact which suggests that Whitman used the pamphlet for review copies rather than the second edition of *Drum-Taps* with the *Sequel* bound in as an annex.

[96] Gibson Brothers was one of the printing houses most prominently advertised in the Washington, D.C., *Directory* for this year.

[97] CW, V, 246.

[98] See p. 122.

[99] H. Pongs, "Walt Whitman und Stefan George," *Comparative Literature*, IV, 289–322 (Fall, 1952), says this passage has the simplicity of medieval allegory: "Es ist Allegorik mittelalterlicher Einfalt, aufschliessende Tiefe des Symbols zu gewinnen, durch Spaltung in das 'Wissen um den Tod' und den 'Gedanken an den Tod.' . . . 315.

[100] By Gustav Holst, Normand Lockwood, F. L. Ritter, Charles Wood, and others.

[101] See G. L. Sixbey, "Chanting the Square Deific: A Study in Whitman's Religion," *American Literature*, IX, 171–195 (May, 1937).

[102] See p. 276.

[103] See pp. 260–264.

[104] Barrus, *Comrades*, 10–11.

[105] See p. 230.

[106] Reprinted by Louis Untermeyer in *The Poetry and Prose of Walt Whitman* (New York, 1949), 1033–1338. James later was ashamed of this youthful review and confessed to a friend (in an unpublished letter, dated 10 Oct. 1903—quoted here by courtesy of Leon Edel and the Henry James Estate): ". . . I can, however, bring out a thank you for your intimation in respect to the little atrocity I mentioned remembering to have perpetrated (on W[alt] W[hitman]) in the gross impudence of youth—yea, even a thank-you-very-much-indeed. But nothing would induce me to reveal the where-

abouts of my disgrace, which I only recollect as deep and damning. The place I dimly remember, but the year is utterly vague to me—I only know that I haven't seen the accursed thing for more than thirty years, and that if it were to cross my path nothing would induce me to look at it. I am so far from 'keeping' the abominations of my early innocence that I destroy them wherever I spy them—which, thank goodness, occurs rarely."

[107] Trent Collection.

[108] Nathan Resnick, *Walt Whitman and the Authorship of the Good Gray Poet* (Brooklyn, 1948).

[109] ". . . O'Connor has the sole honor of inventing it [the title]. It was suggested to him, he told me, by a line in Tennyson's ode on the Death of the Duke of Wellington—'The good grey head which all men knew.' "—C. W. Eldridge to Dewitt C. Lockwood (1893). Quoted in Barrus, *Comrades*, 312.

[110] WWC, I, 83.

[111] The quotation in O'Connor's monograph shows this to have been the review published in the London *Leader*, June 30, 1860.

[112] WWC, I, 86.

[113] Trent Collection.

[114] *Ibid.*

[115] Doyle remembered the time as the winter of 1866 (see CW, VIII, 5). But Whitman first mentioned him in his Diary in Dec., 1865, CW, IV, 133.

[116] CW, VIII, 5.

[117] See p. 269.

[118] Barrus, *Comrades*, 35. *The Good Gray Poet* was reprinted by Bucke, with some emendations, in his *Walt Whitman* (Philadelphia, 1883), 99–130.

[119] Published in *Putnam's Magazine*, Jan., 1868; reprinted in *Three Tales* (Boston, 1892), 211–326.

[120] Bucke, *op. cit.*, 102.

[121] See p. 361.

[122] Bucke, *op. cit.*, 115.

[123] *Ibid.*, 122.

[124] *Ibid.*, 124–125.

[125] *Ibid.*, 130.

[126] *Ibid.*, 131.

[127] Jan. 27, 1866, pp. 51–52, signed "F."

[128] Unsigned but attributed to Sanborn in the Saunders-Furness Bibliography (unpublished), and internal evidence indicates his authorship.

[129] *In Re*, 149–157.

[130] CW, VIII, 173 ff.

[131] Trent Collection.

[132] CW, VIII, 175–176.

[133] Typewritten letter Eldridge to J. H. Johnston, Washington, D.C., May 29, 1902. Original (signed) in Berg Collection, New York Public Library. Quoted in part in Barrus, *Comrades*, 334–335.

[134] Letter of March 31, 1866, Trent Collection.

[135] *Ibid.*, June 7, 1866.

[136] CW, VIII, 180–181.

[137] Letters of July 30 and Aug. 1, 1866, now in Morgan Library, New York City; several times published.

[138] *Ibid.*

[139] Van Sinderen Collection.

[140] Lion Collection.

[141] See note 16, above.

[142] "Walt Whitman," by Moncure D. Conway, *Fortnightly Review*, VI, 538–548 (Oct. 15, 1866).

[143] CW, VIII, 183.

[144] Barrus, *Comrades*, 40.

[145] See p. 203.

[146] See p. 384.

[147] CW, VIII, 184–185.

[148] *Ibid.*, 186.

[149] See note 55, above.

[150] The title page read: LEAVES/ OF/ GRASS./ New-York./ 1867. Like the first edition, the author's name did not appear, except in the copyright notice on verso. Though printed and copyrighted in 1866, this is known as the 1867 edition (from the date on the title page). And the edition is bibliographically confusing in other ways, because small batches were bound up at different times, often with varying contents and occasionally with slightly different arrangements. Four main issues are distinguished by bibliographers, but more could be counted. See W–G, 12–14.

[151] See p. 226 for 1860 version.

[152] "As I Sat Alone by Blue Ontario's Shore," Sec. 4.

[153] Cf. opening lines of "So Long!", 1860 version.

[154] "Walt Whitman and his 'Drum-Taps'," by John Burroughs, *Galaxy*, II, 606–615 (Dec. 1, 1866).

[155] CW, VIII, 186–187.

[156] Burroughs, *op. cit.*, 613.

[157] WWC, III, 521.

[158] CW, VIII, 190.

[159] *Ibid.*, 192–193.

[160] Feinberg Collection.

CHAPTER IX

[1] "In Cabin'd Ships at Sea," in "Inscriptions."

[2] CW, VIII, 198.

[3] *Ibid.*, 193.

[4] Letter of March 21, 1867, Trent Collection.

[5] *Ibid.*, Feb. 27, 1867.

[6] CW, VIII, 200.

[7] *Ibid.*, 207.

[8] *Ibid.*, 210.

[9] *Ibid.*, 195.

[10] Letter of March 28, 1867, Trent Collection.

[11] Trent Collection.

[12] CW, VIII, 212.

[13] Correspondence with Mrs. Abby Price, John Pierpont Morgan Library.

[14] Trent Collection.

[15] CW, VIII, 216.

[16] Letter of May 3, 1867, Trent Collection.

[17] On July 1, 1868, Mrs. Whitman wrote Walt: "one year ago this fourth i was here with the boxes and barrels all piled up around me it dont seem like a year since we moved here . . ." Trent Collection.

[18] Letter of Nov. 19, 1867, Trent Collection.

[19] See letter of Feb. 12, 1868, Trent Collection.

[20] Harold Blodgett, *Walt Whitman in England* (Ithaca, N.Y., 1934), 16.

[21] *Ibid.*, 18.

[22] *Rossetti Papers, 1862–1870*, a compilation by William Michael Rossetti (New York, 1903), 181.

[23] *Ibid.*, 230.

[24] Barrus, *Comrades*, 47.

[25] *Ibid.*, 48.

[26] WWC, III, 506.

[27] *Ibid.*, II, 419.

[28] Bliss Perry, *Walt Whitman* (Boston, 1906), 185.

[29] Barrus, *Comrades*, 47.

[30] WWC, III, 296.

[31] *Workshop*, 151.

[32] "So Long!", 1860.

[33] *Workshop*, 153.

[34] WWC, III, 298.

[35] *Ibid.*, 299.

[36] *Ibid.*, 300.

[37] *Rossetti Papers*, 244.

[38] WWC, III, 301 ff.

[39] *Ibid.*, 306 ff.

[40] *Rossetti Papers*, 297.

[41] Blodgett, *op. cit.*, 32.

[42] See Edward F. Grier, "Walt Whitman, the Galaxy, and Democratic Vistas," *American Literature*, XXIII, 333 (Nov., 1951).

[43] *Ibid.*, 336.

[44] *Ibid.*

[45] *Ibid.*

[46] See p. 346.

[47] Grier, *op. cit.*, 337.

[48] *Ibid.*, 337–338.

[49] *Ibid.*, 338.

[50] See p. 196.

[51] Speech delivered in New York City on June 2, 1948, published as "Of American Democracy," *Twice A Year*, 10th Anniversary Issue, 1948, p. 568.

[52] Grier, *op. cit.*, 341.

[53] Barrus, *Comrades*, 49.

[54] CW, VIII, 219–220.

[55] Barrus, *Comrades*, 50.

[56] John Morley, *Recollections* (New York, 1917), II, 105.

[57] A. C. Swinburne, *William Blake* (London, 1868), 337.

[58] Odell Shepard, *Pedlar's Progress: The Life of Bronson Alcott* (Boston, 1937), 494.

[59] *Ibid.*

[60] Albert C. Knudson, *The Philosophy of Personalism* (New York, 1927), 17–18.

[61] *The Journals of Bronson Alcott*, ed. by Odell Shepard (Boston, 1938), 306, note.

[62] *Ibid.*, 391.

[63] WWC, III, 245.

[64] CW, V, 69.

[65] Trent Collection.

[66] *Ibid.*

[67] *Ibid.*

[68] CW, VIII, 227.

[69] *Ibid.*, 227–228.

[70] Mentioned in letter of July 15, Trent Collection.

[71] Trent Collection.

[72] DAB.

[73] CW, VIII, 229–230.

[74] *Ibid.*, 233 ff.

[75] *Ibid.*, 230.

[76] *Ibid.*, 231.

[77] *Ibid.*, 234–235.

[78] Letter to William O'Connor, Sept. 27, 1868, Berg Collection.

[79] CW, VIII, 21–23.

[80] Barrus, *Comrades*, 50–51.

[81] Original in Morgan Library.

[82] Harry Law-Robertson, *Walt Whitman in Deutschland* (Giessen, Germany, 1935), 8.

[83] Original in Berg Collection. O'Connor's letter in WWC, II, 431.

[84] *Ibid.*, 326.

[85] Berg Collection.

[86] CW, VIII, 25–26.

[87] *Ibid.*, 30–31.

[88] *North American Review*, CIII, 611 (Oct., 1868).

[89] E.g., A *Fable for Critics*.

[90] Berg Collection.

[91] CW, VIII, 34.

[92] See p. 206.

[93] CW, VIII, 35.

[94] *Ibid.*, 38.

[95] Trent Collection.

[96] Letter of Nov. 18, 1868, Trent Collection.

[97] WWC, IV, 269–270.

[98] CW, VIII, 237.

[99] WWC, II, 22.

[100] *Ibid.*

[101] *Ibid.*, I, 216.

[102] Mrs. Whitman to Walt, Dec. 5, 1868, Trent Collection.

[103] Exact date not given, Trent Collection. An illegible squiggle follows "100," possibly intended for "Drs."

[104] See Emory Holloway, "Whitman as His Own Press Agent," *American Mercury*, XVIII, 482–488 (Dec., 1929), 484–485.

[105] CW, VIII, 238.

[106] Letter [Feb. or March], 1869, Trent Collection.

[107] Trent Collection.

[108] *Ibid.*, exact date not given.

[109] Trent Collection.

[110] *Ibid.*

[111] Holloway, ". . . Press Agent," *op. cit.*, 482.

[112] *Ibid.*, 483.

[113] Letter of acceptance, WWC, I, 216. Why the poem was not printed is not known.

[114] Trent Collection.

[115] Letter of Aug. 23, 1869.

[116] CW, VIII, 40–41, note.

[117] *Ibid.*, 40–41.

[118] Berg Collection, Aug. 23, 1869.

[119] CW, VIII, 43.

[120] *Ibid.*, 45.

[121] See Whitman's letter to Rossetti, Dec. 9, 1869, quoted below.

[122] *Rossetti Papers*, 418.

[123] Thomas B. Harned (ed.), *The Letters of Anne Gilchrist and Walt Whitman* (New York, 1918), 56–57.

[124] H. H. Gilchrist, *Anne Gilchrist: Her Life and Writings* (London, 1887), 177.

[125] *Ibid.*, 177–179. Also in Clarence H. Gohdes and P. F. Baum, *Letters of William Rossetti* (Durham, N.C., 1934), 23.

[126] Harned, *op. cit.*, 3–4.

[127] *Rossetti Papers*, 403.

[128] *Ibid.*, 418.

[129] *Ibid.*, 492.

[130] Justin McCarthy, *Reminiscences* (New York, 1899), I, 225–228.

[131] Katherine Molinoff, *Some Notes on Whitman's Family* (Brooklyn, 1941), 22. Whitman evidently received the report promptly because on March 24, 1870 (letter in Trent Collection), Mrs. Whitman commented on the news in Walt's letter to her.

[132] Trent Collection.

[133] Reprinted in Harned, *op. cit.*, 3–22.

[134] See pp. 261–263.

[135] Berg Collection.

[136] Trent Collection.

[137] Notebook in Library of Congress; quoted in UPP, II, 95.

[138] *Ibid.*, 96.

[139] CW, VIII, 7.

[140] Letter to Burroughs from Eldridge, March 7, 1896, in Berg Collection. Quoted in Barrus, *Comrades*, 322.

[141] Edward Hungerford, "Walt Whitman and His Chart of Bumps," *American Literature*, II, 350–384 (Jan., 1931).

[142] Oscar Cargill, unpublished.

[143] CW, VIII, 48.

[144] UPP, II, 96.

[145] MS in Van Sinderen Collection, Yale.

[146] CW, VIII, 58.

[147] The exact terms of Whitman's contract with Redfield are not known, for the new *Leaves of Grass* did not carry the Redfield imprint, though all three books were printed uniformly and Whitman had exclusive possession of the plates, made by Smith & McDougal of 82 Beekman Street, from which he later printed several issues and edi-

tions without the imprint of any publisher. But J. S. Redfield also issued a second edition of John Burroughs's *Notes on Walt Whitman as Poet and Person* in 1871. Probably Redfield was unwilling to bear the much larger cost of setting up and printing *Leaves of Grass*, which, after all, was only a revision of a book for which there had been no great demand in four previous editions.

[148] CW, VIII, 51.

[149] *Ibid.*

[150] *Ibid.*, 60.

[151] *Ibid.*, 63.

[152] *Ibid.*, 65.

[153] WWC, II, 487.

[154] Cf. "Out of the Cradle Endlessly Rocking" or "On the Beach At Night Alone"— placed in the 1871–72 edition in a group appropriately called "Sea-Shore Memories."

[155] An advertisement on the back cover of *Passage to India* listed bookstores where Whitman's recent publications were for sale. They included three book dealers in New York, three in Washington, one in Boston, one in Brooklyn, and Trubner in London.

[156] See pp. 128–129.

[157] See p. 262.

[158] CW, VIII, 69–75.

[159] Gohdes and Baum, *op. cit.*, 78.

[160] *Rossetti Papers*, 517.

[161] CW, VIII, 72.

[162] WWC, I, 326.

[163] *Ibid.*, 328–329.

[164] The plans were in the report reprinted by Whitman in *After All, Not to Create Only*.

[165] See Holloway, ". . . Press Agent," *op. cit.*, 486.

[166] *Ibid.*

[167] *Ibid.*

[168] *Ibid.*, 487.

[169] *Ibid.*, 486.

[170] *Ibid.*, Roden Noel, "A Study of Walt Whitman," *Dark Blue*, Oct.–Nov., 1871; reprinted in *Essays on Poetry and Poets* (London, 1886), 304–341.

[171] Holloway, ". . . Press Agent," *op. cit.*, 484.

[172] WWC, I, 328–329.

[173] Gohdes and Baum, *op. cit.*, 78.

[174] *Ibid.*, 80.

[175] Harned, *op. cit.*, 59 (originals in Library of Congress).

[176] *Ibid.*, 60–61.

[177] *Ibid.*, 63.

[178] *Ibid.*, 64.

[179] *Ibid.*, 66.

[180] *Ibid.*, 67.

[181] *Ibid.*, 68–69.

[182] *Ibid.*, 70.

[183] From original in University of Pennsylvania Library; hitherto unpublished.

[184] See p. 341.

[185] Harned, *op. cit.*, 77.

[186] Barrus, *Comrades*, 158.

[187] Harned, *op. cit.*, 78.

[188] CW, VIII, 78.

[189] *Ibid.*, 81.

[190] Carl Roos (ed.), "Walt Whitman's Letters to a Danish Friend," *Orbis Litterarum*, Tome VII, Fasc. 1–2, pp. 31–60 (1949).

[191] Barrus, *Comrades*, 72.

[192] Perry, *op. cit.*, 203 ff.

[193] Holloway, ". . . Press Agent," *op. cit.*, found no items in print.

[194] Perry, *op. cit.*, 204.

[195] CW, VIII, 85.

[196] *Ibid.*, 87.

[197] *Ibid.*, 240.

[198] *Ibid.*, 242.

[199] In Trent Collection, unpublished.

[200] CW, VIII, 243.

[201] Barrus, *Comrades*, 96.

[202] Blodgett, *op. cit.*, 76.

[203] Quoted, *ibid.*, 79–80.

[204] Algernon Charles Swinburne, *Under the Microscope* (London, 1872), 45.

[205] *Ibid.*, 47.

[206] Once, by a slip of the pen, Whitman gave the date as Jan. 3, 1873 (Harned, *op. cit.*, 94).

[207] R. M. Bucke, *Walt Whitman* (Philadelphia, 1883), 45–46.

[208] *In Re*, 74.

[209] Holograph in Yale Library.

[210] *In Re*, 73.

CHAPTER X

[1] "Last of Ebb, and Daylight Waning," in "Fancies at Navesink."

[2] WWC, IV, 472.

[3] See pp. 421–422.

[4] *In Re*, 74.

[5] *Ibid.*, 77.

[6] *Ibid.*, 78.

[7] *Ibid.*, 79.

[8] *Ibid.*, 80.

[9] Barrus, *Comrades*, 81.

[10] *In Re*, 88 ff.

[11] Trent Collection.

[12] Quoted by Jacob Schwartz, *Manuscripts, Autograph Letters, First Editions and Portraits of Walt Whitman* [sale of Dr. R. M. Bucke property] (Anderson Galleries, New York, 1936), 85.

[13] Trent Collection.

[14] Unpublished letter in Hanley Collection.

[15] WWC, IV, 514.

[16] CW, VIII, 99; Barrus, *Comrades*, 83.

[17] Barrus, *Comrades*, 83.

[18] CW, VIII, 94; Barrus, *Comrades*, 84.

[19] CW, VIII, 96.

[20] Thomas B. Harned (ed.), *The Letters of Anne Gilchrist and Walt Whitman* (New York, 1918), 95.

[21] *Ibid.*, 97.

[22] Berg Collection.

[23] WWC, I, 227.

[24] CW, VIII, 107.

[25] *Ibid.*, 108–109.

[26] *Ibid.*, 117.

[27] *Ibid.*, 125.

[28] Reprinted UPP, II, 42–49.

[29] Harned, *op. cit.*, 103. A dash under "London," in the address meant Whitman was better.

[30] Berg Collection.

[31] *Ibid.*

[32] Reprinted by T. O. Mabbott and R. G. Silver, " 'Tis But Ten Years Since," *American Literature*, XV, 51–62 (March, 1943).

[33] CW, VIII, 133.

[34] Quoted from *Harper's Monthly*, XLVIII, 366–367 (Feb., 1874). There are many differences in punctuation between this and later versions.

[35] CW, VIII, 137.

[36] Berg Collection.

[37] *Harper's Monthly* (see note 34, above).

[38] *Harper's Monthly*, XLVIII, 524–525 (March, 1874).

[39] Harned, *op. cit.*, 108.

[40] For summary of studies of Hegel's influence see G. W. Allen, *Walt Whitman Handbook* (Chicago, 1946), index (many references).

[41] Text of *Daily Graphic* quoted.

[42] Dixon Wecter, "Walt Whitman as Civil Servant," PMLA, LVIII, 1106–1107 (Dec., 1943). Letter dated June 22, 1874.

[43] *Ibid.* Notification of dismissal printed in WWC, III, 476, but not agreement on severance pay.

[44] See poem "An Old Man's Thought of School."

[45] Reprinted in UPP, II, 53–58.

[46] *Ibid.*, 53.

[47] Emerson's memory was failing by this time and he was only able to edit the anthology with the assistance of his daughter, Edith, whose literary taste was conventional. See R. W. Rusk, *The Life of Ralph Waldo Emerson* (New York, 1949), 451 *passim*.

[48] UPP, II, 54.

[49] *Ibid.*, 56.

[50] CW, VIII, 153.

[51] *Two Rivulets*, Author's Edition (Camden, N.J., 1876), 6.

[52] *Ibid.*, 15.

[53] *Ibid.*, 16–17.

[54] *Ibid.*, 11, note.

[55] *Ibid.*

[56] Harold Blodgett, *Walt Whitman in England* (Ithaca, N.Y., 1934), 59.

[57] *Ibid.*, 58.

[58] *Ibid.*, 203.

[59] *Ibid.*, 202.

[60] WWC, IV, 267–268.

[61] *Ibid.*, 181–185.

[62] See p. 341.

[63] Holograph in University of Pennsylvania Library.

[64] Harned, *op. cit.*, 129–130.

[65] *Ibid.*, 136.

[66] *Workshop*, 244.

[67] Blodgett, *op. cit.*, 141–143.

[68] *In Re*, 36.

[69] Barrus, *Comrades*, 94.

[70] CW, IV, 286.

[71] Cf. *ibid.*, 181.

[72] Edward Carpenter, *Days with Walt Whitman* (London, 1906), 11.

[73] The post office was Kirkwood, and Whitman sometimes referred to the place as Whitehorse, though today there is no such town in the vicinity; however, there is a nearby Whitehorse Highway.

[74] *Workshop*, 246.

[75] *Ibid.*, 245.

[76] Whitman's reference seems to imply a recent article in the Springfield *Republican*, but it has not been located. On Dec. 8, 1872, this paper reprinted "Walt Whitman in Europe" from the Dec., 1872, *Kansas Magazine*.

[77] *Workshop*, 245.

[78] *Ibid.*, 246.

[79] Quoted by Blodgett, *op. cit.*, 36.

[80] *Ibid.*, 81.

[81] *Ibid.*

[82] *Ibid.*, 81–82.

[83] R. M. Bucke, *Walt Whitman* (Philadelphia, 1883), 215.

[84] Barrus, *Comrades*, 128.

[85] *Ibid.*, 125–128.

[86] Harned, *op. cit.*, 146.

[87] The Springfield (Mass.) *Daily Republican*, April 19, 1876. The article was unsigned but the allusions to Sanborn's trial in Boston in 1860 establish the authorship. Cf. p. 242.

[88] Thomas Donaldson, *Walt Whitman the Man* (New York, 1896), 28–29.

[89] Barrus, *Comrades*, 122.

[90] Harned, *op. cit.*, 139–140.

[91] *Ibid.*, 141.

[92] *Ibid.*, 143–144.

[93] *Ibid.*, 145.

[94] *Ibid.*, 147.

[95] *Ibid.*, 149.

[96] J. Johnston and J. W. Wallace, *Visits to Walt Whitman in 1890–1891* (London, 1917), 186.

[97] CW, IV, 144 ff.

[98] *Ibid.*, 157.

[99] Barrus, *Comrades*, 138.

[100] Grace Gilchrist, "Chats with Walt Whitman," *Temple Bar Magazine*, CXIII, 200–212 (Feb., 1898).

[101] See pp. 24, 79.

[102] Quoted by Herbert H. Gilchrist, *Anne Gilchrist: Her Life and Writings* (London, 1887), 229 *passim*.

[103] CW, IV, 163–164.

[104] Henry Bryan Binns, *A Life of Walt Whitman* (London, 1905), 265.

[105] CW, IV, 168.

[106] *Ibid.*, 168–171.

[107] Frank Harris, *My Life and Loves* (Paris, n.d.), Book I, Chapter XIII.

[108] CW, IV, 172.

[109] J. H. Johnston in Charles N. Elliot (ed.), *Walt Whitman As Man, Poet, and Friend* (Boston, 1915), 150.

[110] CW, IV, 178–179.

[111] Johnston and Wallace, *op. cit.*, 186.

[112] *Ibid.*, 186. Cf. CW, IV, 215.

[113] Johnston and Wallace, *op. cit.*, 186.

[114] Notebook in Library of Congress. Quoted by Edward L. Naumburg, Jr., "A Collector Looks at Walt Whitman," *Princeton University Library Chronicle*, III, 12 (Nov., 1941).

[115] Carpenter, *op. cit.*, 3.

[116] *Ibid.*, 4.

[117] *Ibid.*, 28–31.

[118] *Ibid.*, 31–32.

[119] Binns, *op. cit.*, 269.

[120] *Fellowship Papers*, No. 6 (Nov., 1894), p. 38.

[121] H. Gilchrist, *op. cit.*, 231.

[122] Barrus, *Comrades*, 171–173.

[123] *Ibid.*, 146.

[124] Elliot, *op. cit.*, 152; CW, IV, 202.

[125] CW, IV, 212.

[126] Harned, *op. cit.*, 162.

[127] Barrus, *Comrades*, 182.

[128] Ellen Calder, "Personal Recollections of Walt Whitman," *Atlantic Monthly*, XCIX, 825–834 (June, 1907), 828.

[129] CW, V, 239–256.

[130] Barrus, *Comrades*, 184.

[131] CW, IV, 234–240.

[132] Barrus, *Comrades*, 186.

[133] *Ibid.*, 184.

[134] H. Gilchrist, *op. cit.*, 249; Barrus, *Comrades*, 146.

[135] CW, IV, 245.

[136] *Ibid.*, 248.

[137] Elliot, *op. cit.*, 152.

[138] Barrus, *Comrades*, 146–47.

[139] WWC, I, 129.

[140] Robert R. Hubach, *Walt Whitman and the West* (abstract of Ph.D. thesis) (Indiana University, 1943), 10.

[141] CW, IV, 253.

[142] *Ibid.*, 255.

[143] *Ibid.*, 270.

[144] *Ibid.*, 271.

[145] *Ibid.*, 276.

[146] *Ibid.*, 279–280.

[147] *Ibid.*, 278–279.

[148] Barrus, *Comrades*, 188.

[149] *Ibid.*, between 188–189; H. Gilchrist, *op. cit.*, facing 253.

[150] CW, IV, 292.

[151] *Ibid.*, 294.

[152] *Diary in Canada*, 16.

[153] See p. 84.

[154] Title: "Walt Whitman," reprinted in *Poets of America* (Boston, 1885), 349–395.

[155] Barrus, *Comrades*, 194.

[156] Vol. III, 149–158.

[157] Barrus, *Comrades*, 196.

[158] *Ibid.*, 197.

[159] *Ibid.*, 205.

[160] W. S. Kennedy, *Reminiscences of Walt Whitman* (London, 1896), 3.

[161] Barrus, *Comrades*, 205.

[162] CW, V, 11.

[163] *Ibid.*, 7.

[164] Card now in Library of Congress, Harned Collection.

[165] CW, V, 11.

[166] CW, VIII, 276.

[167] *Ibid.*, 277.

[168] Binns, *op. cit.*, 280.

[169] CW, IV, 7 ff.

[170] *Ibid.*, 9.

[171] *Ibid.*, V, 21.

[172] Diary notes (unpublished) in Library of Congress.

[173] See note 164, above.

[174] CW, V, 23.

[175] Described in letter to Mrs. George Whitman, Sept. 18, 1881; in Feinberg Collection.

[176] WWC, I, 324–325; on another occasion Whitman spoke very disparagingly of Garfield (WWC, III, 129).

[177] New York *Daily Tribune*, April 4, 1892, p. 8. J. G. Schumaker recalled having introduced Whitman to Garfield on a Washington streetcar.

[178] For speculation on the symbolism see Esther Shephard, *Walt Whitman's Pose* (New York, 1938), 250 ff.

[179] CW, VIII, 281.

[180] See pp. 122–123.

[181] CW, VIII, 288.

[182] For a complete list of omissions demanded see Bucke, *op. cit.*, 149.

[183] CW, VIII, 295.

[184] *Ibid.*, 298.

[185] The person who reported *Leaves of Grass* to the Boston District Attorney was never definitely identified. O'Connor believed at first it was Anthony Comstock, but some of Whitman's friends in Boston thought that it was a narrow-minded preacher.

Some years later Mr. Stevens admitted that he had not carefully read the book before he threatened Osgood & Co. with prosecution and he had decided in the intervening years that he had made a mistake. Obviously he was pushed by someone. Cf. W. S. Kennedy, *The Fight of a Book for the World* (West Yarmouth, Mass., 1926), 248.

[186] McKay's royalty statements for Dec. 14, 1882, are in the University of Pennsylvania Library.

CHAPTER XI

[1] "A Clear Midnight," in "From Noon to Starry Night."

[2] CW, IV, 3, note.

[3] *Ibid.*, VIII, 278.

[4] See p. 493.

[5] Lloyd Morris and Henry Justin Smith, *Oscar Wilde Discovers America* (New York, 1936), 63–77.

[6] Quoted, *ibid.*, 75.

[7] Unpublished letter in Feinberg Collection.

[8] Cf. Edward Carpenter, *Days with Walt Whitman* (London, 1906), 30; WWC, I, 101.

[9] CW, V, 8.

[10] *Ibid.*, 30.

[11] *Ibid.*, 32–33.

[12] *Ibid.*, 39.

[13] Inaccurately quoted by Thomas Donaldson, *Walt Whitman the Man* (New York, 1896), 7–8. Original owned by Donaldson's granddaughter, Mrs. Benedict of Philadelphia.

[14] Henry Chupak, *Walt Whitman in Camden* (New York University Ph.D. thesis, 1952), 122–126.

[15] WWC, I, 250.

[16] Chupak, *op. cit.*

[17] CW, VIII, 117.

[18] Letter to Henry Chupak, *op. cit.*, 133–134.

[19] See p. 486.

[20] See p. 502. Letter from Whitman to Childs, accepting a dinner invitation (Pennsylvania Historical Society Library).

[21] Elizabeth Dunbar, *Talcott Williams* (Brooklyn, 1936).

[22] H. B. F. Jayne (ed.), *The Letters of Horace Howard Furness* (New York, 1922), I, 345–346.

[23] Charles N. Elliot (ed.), *Walt Whitman As Man, Poet and Friend* (Boston, 1915), 39–40.

[24] WWC, I, 128.

[25] Elizabeth Robbins Pennell, *Charles Godfrey Leland* (Boston, 1906), II, 98 ff.

[26] Elizabeh Robbins Pennell, *The Life and Letters of Joseph Pennell* (Boston, 1929), I, 99 ff.

[27] Pennell, *Leland, op. cit.*, II, 110.

[28] *Ibid.*, 192.

[29] *Ibid.*, 193–194.

[30] Cf. Chapter IV, note 140.

[31] Joseph Jackson, *Printing in Philadelphia* (Philadelphia, n.d.).

[32] MSS in University of Pennsylvania Library.

[33] Logan Pearsall Smith, *Unforgotten Years* (Boston, 1939), 92 ff.

[34] Carpenter, *op. cit.*, 37.

[35] R. M. Bucke, *Walt Whitman* (Philadelphia, 1883), 73–98.

[36] See p. 510.

[37] Bucke, *op. cit.*, 51, 69.

[38] *Ibid.*, 56.

[39] R. M. Bucke, *Cosmic Consciousness* (New York, 1923).

[40] Bucke, *Whitman, op. cit.*, 52.

[41] *In Re*, 311. Many references in WWC.

[42] Barrus, *Comrades*, 149.

[43] *Ibid.*, 244.

[44] *Ibid.*, 245.

[45] Quoted from holographs in Lion Collection. Published in part in Barrus, *Comrades*, 246, note.

[46] Berg Collection.

[47] Details in the paragraph drawn from an unpublished account, "A Child's Memories of the Whitmans," by Amy Haslam Dowe, niece of Mrs. George Whitman.

[48] Signed agreement now in Walt Whitman House, Camden, N.J.

[49] WWC, I, 291.

[50] Cf. Donaldson, *op. cit.*, 66–69.

[51] *Ibid.*, 190.

[52] *Ibid.*, 53 ff. See also Bram Stoker, *Reminiscences of Henry Irving* (New York, 1906), II, 92 ff.

[53] Carpenter, *op. cit.*, 35.

[54] *Ibid.*, 41.

[55] *Ibid.*, 36.

[56] *Ibid.*, 38.

[57] *Ibid.*, 43.

[58] *Ibid.*, 47.

[59] *Ibid.*, 49.

[60] From correspondence in the Bucke Collection transcribed by Clifton J. Furness.

[61] Harned's unpublished reminiscences.

[62] David Karsner, *Horace Traubel: His Life and Work* (New York, 1919), 59 ff. Cf. WWC, III, 407.

[63] See note 32, above.

[64] Original now in Walt Whitman House, Camden, N.J.

[65] Dowe, *op. cit.*

[66] Elizabeth Leavitt Keller, *Walt Whitman in Mickle Street* (New York, 1921), 12 ff. Mrs. Keller represents Whitman as taking his meals at Mrs. Davis's. But more likely she was the woman who went daily to his house "to look after him" before Mrs. Davis moved to 328 Mickle Street. See Clarence Gohdes and P. F. Baum (eds.), *Letters of William Michael Rossetti* (Durham, N.C., 1934), 189.

[67] *Ibid.*, 55 ff.

[68] *Ibid.*, 24–25.

[69] Edmund Gosse, *Critical Kit-Kats* (New York, 1896), 100 ff.

[70] *Ibid.*, 102.

[71] *Ibid.*, 106. The Shelley quotation is from "Stanzas Written in Dejection, Near Naples," somewhat adapted by Gosse to fit occasion.

[72] "Walt Whitman in Camden," the *Critic*, III, 97–98 (Feb. 28, 1885); reprinted in UPP, II, 58–62.

[73] *Ibid.*, 60–61.

[74] Donaldson, *op. cit.*, 172.

[75] Keller, *op. cit.*, 48.

[76] Donaldson, *op. cit.*, 175.

[77] *Ibid.*, 183.

[78] *Ibid.*, 188–189.

[79] Herbert H. Gilchrist, *Anne Gilchrist* (London, 1887), 284.

[80] Donaldson, *op. cit.*, 107.

[81] Gohdes and Baum, *op. cit.*, 185.

[82] *Ibid.*, 181–183.

[83] Donaldson, *op. cit.*, 162 ff; William Sloane Kennedy, *Reminiscences of Walt Whitman* (London), 23.

[84] Manuscript records of Walt Whitman Cottage Fund in Boston Public Library. Barrus, *Comrades*, *op. cit.*, 268; Kennedy, *op. cit.*, 54.

[85] Kennedy, *op. cit.*, 24; Barrus, *Comrades*, *op. cit.*, 269–270.

[86] Barrus, *Comrades*, *op. cit.*, 264.

[87] Kennedy, *op. cit.*, 29.

[88] *In Re*, 367 ff; Keller, *op. cit.*, 73–86.

[89] Keller, *op. cit.*, 77.

[90] For Whitman's opinions see WWC, I, 132.

[91] *Ibid.*, 131.

[92] Kennedy, *op. cit.*, 28.

[93] *The Life of Algernon Charles Swinburne* (New York, 1917), 376.

[94] Barrus, *Comrades*, *op. cit.*, 265–266.

[95] See especially W. B. Cairns, "Swinburne's Opinion of Whitman," *American Literature*, III, 125–135 (May, 1931); W. S. Munroe, "Swinburne's Recantation of Walt Whitman," *Revue-Anglo-Américaine*, VII, 138–141 (Aug., 1941).

[96] Harold Blodgett, *Walt Whitman in England* (Ithaca, N.Y., 1934), 115–116.

[97] Reprinted in *Studies in Prose and Poetry* (London, 1894).

[98] See p. 431.

[99] Barrus, *Comrades*, *op. cit.*, 266.

[100] Julius Chambers, *News Hunting on Three Continents* (New York, 1921), 303.

[101] WWC, I, 238–239; *In Re*, 119.

[102] WWC, I, 259–260.

[103] *Ibid.*, 305.

[104] Elliot, *op. cit.*, 158.

[105] WWC, I, 298.

[106] Chambers, *op. cit.*, 305 (facsimile).

[107] WWC, III, 29.

[108] Keller, *op. cit.*, 107.

[109] See Sculley Bradley and John R. Stevenson, *Walt Whitman's Backward Glances* (Philadelphia, 1947), 1–13.

[110] CW, III, 42.

[111] *Ibid.*, 43.

[112] *Ibid.*, 44.

[113] *Ibid.*, 45.

[114] *Ibid.*, 50.

[115] W–G, 31–32.

[116] Barrus, *Comrades, op. cit.,* 287.

[117] WWC, IV, 64–66.

[118] Keller, *op. cit.,* 158 *passim.*

[119] Horace L. Traubel (ed.), *Camden's Compliment to Walt Whitman May 31, 1889 . . .* (Philadelphia, 1889).

[120] Barrus, *Comrades,* 262; Elliot, *op. cit.,* 168 ff.

[121] Keller, *op. cit.,* 119 ff.

[122] *In Re,* 131.

[123] *Ibid.,* 349–351.

[124] Henry Bryan Binns, *Walt Whitman* (London, 1905), 332.

[125] WWC, I, 202–203; Barrus, *Comrades,* 336–338; Carpenter, *op. cit.,* 142 ff.

[126] Carpenter, *op. cit.,* 142–145, quotes part of the letter (second paragraph quoted here); the other paragraph Symonds quoted in an unpublished letter (now in Bayley Collection, Ohio Wesleyan University) to Edward Carpenter (dated Feb. 13, 1893).

[127] Binns, *op. cit.,* 349. Told in an unpublished letter from Traubel to Edward Carpenter, dated Feb. 28, 1902. Bayley Collection.

[128] Letter from Traubel to Edward Carpenter, dated Dec. 27, 1901. Bayley Collection. See also Binns, *op. cit.,* 349.

[129] From transcription made by Clifton J. Furness from Harned manuscript.

[130] Obvious in correspondence between Symonds and Edward Carpenter. Bayley Collection.

[131] *Liberty in Literature: Testimonial to Walt Whitman,* by Robert G. Ingersoll (New York, 1890); reprinted in *In Re,* 253–283. Cf. Donaldson, *op. cit.,* 109.

[132] *In Re,* 297–327.

[133] *Ibid.,* 322.

[134] J. Johnston and J. W. Wallace, *Visits to Walt Whitman in 1890–1891* (London, 1917).

[135] Reprinted CW, VII, 47–49.

[136] Cf. Josiah Trent, "Walt Whitman—A Case History," *Surgery, Gynecology and Obstetrics,* Vol. 87, p. 114 (July, 1948).

[137] From Clifton J. Furness's Notes (unpublished) of Conservations with Mrs. Traubel.

[138] Harned's reminiscences (unpublished); Clifford mentioned frequently in WWC.

[139] See p. 138.

[140] Johnston and Wallace, *op. cit.,* 231.

[141] Printed by William Sloane Kennedy, *The Fight of a Book for the World,* 289–291.

[142] Some details of this carefully planned will were upset by events of the year following Whitman's death. His sister-in-law, the executrix, died the following August and Edward in November. Mrs. Whitman had promised to re-imburse Mrs. Davis for expenditures she had made during Walt's last years, but George thought the housekeeper had been sufficiently provided for in the will. As a result Mrs. Davis sued the estate in 1894 and was awarded compensation for her time and expenses. Keller, *op. cit.,* 182–186.

[143] Barrus, *Comrades,* 340–341.

[144] Dowe, *op. cit.*

[145] Johnston and Wallace, *op. cit.,* 231.

[146] John Burroughs, *Whitman: A Study* (Boston, 1896), 53.

[147] Johnston and Wallace, *op. cit.,* 240.

[148] Donaldson, *op. cit.,* 269; Trent, *op. cit.,* 118.

[149] *In Re*, 409.

[150] *Ibid.* Dr. Trent, *op. cit.*, decided after examining Whitman's medical record that he had probably suffered from hypertension since the 1860's.

[151] *In Re*, 437.

[152] Binns, *op. cit.*, 344.

[153] The pallbearers (active and honorary) were: George W. Childs, Julian Hawthorne, Robert G. Ingersoll, Horace Howard Furness, Daniel G. Brinton, John Burroughs, Lincoln L. Eyre, J. H. Johnston, J. H. Stoddart, Francis Howard Williams, R. M. Bucke, Talcott Williams, Thomas B. Harned, Horace L. Traubel, Judge Charles G. Garrison, H. L. Bonsall, Reverend J. H. Clifford, Harrison S. Morris, Richard Watson Gilder, H. D. Bush, Julius Chambers, Thomas Eakins, A. G. Cattell, Edmund Clarence Stedman, David McKay, and Thomas Donaldson (Donaldson, *op. cit.*, 272).

[154] *In Re*, 438 (whole funeral program printed here 437–452).

APPENDIX A

GENEALOGY OF WHITMAN FAMILY

[Holograph of R. M. Bucke, doubtless prepared from data supplied by Walt Whitman, now in Trent Collection, Duke University Library.]

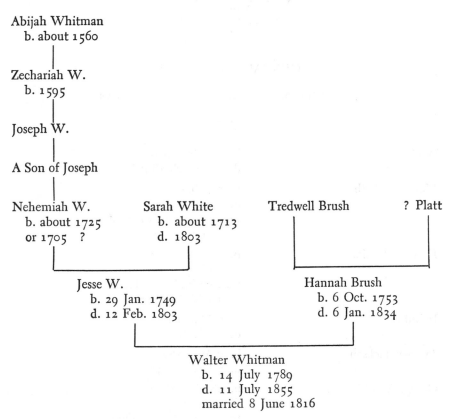

ANCESTORS OF WALTER WHITMAN

Abijah Whitman
   b. about 1560

Zechariah W.
   b. 1595

Joseph W.

A Son of Joseph

Nehemiah W.   Sarah White   Tredwell Brush   ? Platt
   b. about 1725   b. about 1713
   or 1705 ?   d. 1803

          Jesse W.   Hannah Brush
             b. 29 Jan. 1749   b. 6 Oct. 1753
             d. 12 Feb. 1803   d. 6 Jan. 1834

                    Walter Whitman
                       b. 14 July 1789
                       d. 11 July 1855
                       married 8 June 1816

ANCESTORS OF LOUISA VAN VELSOR

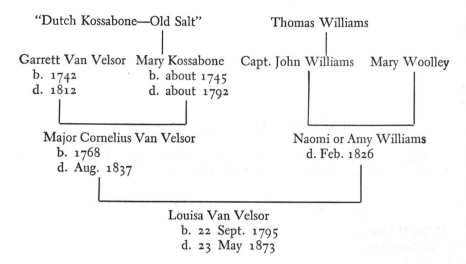

"Dutch Kossabone—Old Salt"　　　　Thomas Williams

Garrett Van Velsor　Mary Kossabone　　Capt. John Williams　Mary Woolley
　b. 1742　　　　　b. about 1745
　d. 1812　　　　　d. about 1792

　　Major Cornelius Van Velsor　　　　　　Naomi or Amy Williams
　　　b. 1768　　　　　　　　　　　　　　d. Feb. 1826
　　　d. Aug. 1837

Louisa Van Velsor
b. 22 Sept. 1795
d. 23 May 1873

GENEALOGICAL DATA

CHILDREN OF WALTER AND LOUISA WHITMAN

Jesse
　　　　　　　　　　　　　　b. 2 March 1818
　　　　　　　　　　　　　　d. 21 March 1870 [1]

Walt
　　　　　　　　　　　　　　b. 31 May 1819
　　　　　　　　　　　　　　d. 26 March 1892 [2]

Mary Elizabeth
　　　　　　　　　　　　　　b. 3 Feb. 1821
　　　　　　　　　　　　　　d. 6 Aug. 1899 [5]
　　　　　　　　　　　　　　m. Ansel Van Nostrand
　　　　　　　　　　　　　　　2 Jan. 1840

Hannah Louisa
　　　　　　　　　　　　　　b. 28 Nov. 1823
　　　　　　　　　　　　　　d. 18 July 1908 [2]
　　　　　　　　　　　　　　m. Charles Louis Heyde
　　　　　　　　　　　　　　　16 March 1852

Infant
　　　　　　　　　　　　　　b. 2 March 1825 [6]
　　　　　　　　　　　　　　d. 14 Sept. 1825 [5]

Andrew Jackson
　　　　　　　　　　　　　　b. 7 April 1827
　　　　　　　　　　　　　　d. 3 Dec. 1863 [3]

George Washington
　　　　　　　　　　　　　　b. 28 Nov. 1829
　　　　　　　　　　　　　　d. 20 Dec. 1901 [2]
　　　　　　　　　　　　　　m. Louisa Orr Haslam
　　　　　　　　　　　　　　　14 April 1871

Thomas Jefferson   b. 18 July 1833
d. 25 Nov. 1890 [4]
m. Martha E. Mitchell
     23 Feb. 1859

Edward   b. 9 Aug. 1835
d. 30 Nov. 1892 [2]

Mannahatta (Daughter of Thomas Jefferson)   b. 9 June 1860
     d. 3 Sept. 1886

Jessie Louisa (Daughter of Thomas Jefferson)   b. 17 June 1863[1]

Martha E. Whitman (Wife of Thomas Jefferson)   d. 19 Feb. 1873

Walter Orr (Son of George Washington)   b. 4 Nov. 1875
  (Interred in vault with his mother)   d. 12 July 1876

Louisa Orr (Wife of George Washington)   b. 2 March 1842
     d. 9 Aug. 1892[2]

---

[1] Family record written by Whitman in a Bible presented to his sister, Mrs. Mary Elizabeth Van Nostrand, Christmas, 1878–1879. See Katharine Molinoff, *Some Notes on Whitman's Family* (Brooklyn, 1941), pp. 7–8.
[2] Official Records of Harleigh Cemetery, Camden, N.J.
[3] Letter written by Mrs. Louisa Whitman to Walt, dated Dec. 5, 1863, in Trent Collection, Duke University Library.
[4] Obituary of Thomas Jefferson Whitman, *Complete Writings of Walt Whitman*, VII, 48.
[5] Molinoff, *op. cit.*, p. 9.
[6] There is a discrepancy in the date given here (in Dr. Bucke's holograph, Trent Collection) and that in the Family Record as reported by Molinoff, where the date of birth is given as April 12, 1825.

APPENDIX B

PROPERTY TRANSFERS OF THE WHITMAN FAMILY
HALL OF RECORDS, BROOKLYN, N. Y.

[Note: Mrs. Katharine Molinoff several years ago had the legal records in Brooklyn searched for real-estate transfers of Louisa and Walter Whitman and Walter Whitman, Jr. The transactions listed in Appendix B are condensed from the transcriptions made for Mrs. Molinoff, who generously permitted their use. Evidently, however, a few of the records have either been lost or were not found by the searchers, because in his notebook Walt Whitman indicated some transactions not included here.—See *Uncollected Poetry and Prose*, edited by Emory Holloway (New York, 1921), II, 88, note 8.]

Liber 15, p. 467:   Property bought September 1, 1824, from Evan M. Johnson of Newtown, minister, and wife, Maria, by Walter Whitman, carpenter, for $250. Property begins 75 feet East from S. E. Corner of Washington and Johnson streets on south side of Johnson Street. [Lot 25 by 100 feet.]

Liber 17, p. 425:   Property bought March 1, 1825, from William Lupton Johnson of Trenton, Hunterdon County, N.J., minister, and wife, Mary Elizabeth, for $250, by Walter Whitman, carpenter. Property begins northwest corner of Tillary and Adams Street. [Lot 25 by 100 feet.]

Liber 19, p. 106ff.:   Recorded February 13, 1826. William Beers, shoemaker in Brooklyn, leased or bought from Evan M. Johnson of Newtown, Queens County, the property beginning 175 feet south from the southwest corner of Johnson and Adams Street on the west side of Adams Street.
Beers assigned this indenture over to Walter Whitman for $25.
Whitman for $40 turned indenture over to Nathaniel W. Brown. Effingham Brown appeared for Walter Whitman to record the transaction.

Liber 30, p. 142: Leased from William Lupton Johnson of Trenton, Hunterdon County, N.J., minister by Walter Whitman, carpenter, property beginning 25 feet from N.W. corner of Tillary and Adams St. [Lot 25 by 100 feet.]; 21-year lease; $15 yearly rental in quarterly payments; Whitman to pay all taxes.
Recorded March 3, 1831. Edwd. M. M. Clarke commissioner for Kings County.

Liber 30, p. 146: Indenture made on 2nd March 1831.
Walter Whitman, housecarpenter and Ann [sic] Louisa, his wife, for $1,250. Beginning N. E. corner of Adams and Tillary St. north along west side of Adams St. 100 ft. . . . Contains 2500 sq. ft. Conveyed to said Walter Whitman by William Lupton Johnson and Mary Elizabeth, his wife, by Indenture bearing date of 1st day of March in 1825 as recorded in Liber 17. [Liber 17 says N. W. corner. Liber 30 says N. E. corner.]

Liber 55, p. 499: Indenture made 2nd day of Nov. 1835 between John F. Garrison and wife Sarah and Walter Whitman for the sum of $1023 sold forever. Property in 7th Ward of Brooklyn and is: Bounded southeasterly by Clason Ave. . . . and southerly by Myrtle St. 215 ft. Together with the privileges (if any exist) of a landing at the Dock or landing place purchased by Silas Butler for the United States according to the reservations in the deed. . .
Recorded on 24th Nov. 1845 at 4 P.M. by Sam'l Garrison comr. deeds in and for city of Brooklyn.

Liber 164, p. 319: Indenture made October 25, 1844 between Austin Reeves and Mary Ann, his wife, and Walter Whitman for $1200. Property in 7th Ward of Brooklyn. N.E. corner of Willoughby and Prince St. beginning 200 ft. north of corner on east side of Prince St. running 25 ft. north along east side of Prince St. [Lot 25 by 85 ft.] Subject to mortgage given by Reeves to Long Island Insurance Co. for $900 (recorded in Liber 82 p. 411) and assumed by Whitman.
Recorded May 29, 1847 at 9 A.M. before James H. Cornwell, comr. deeds.

Liber 164, p. 321: May 25, 1847 between Walter Whitman and wife Louisa and Walter Whitman Jr. for $1360 property described in Liber 164 p. 319.
Recorded May 29, 1847.

Liber 189, p. 16:   Indenture made on October 30, 1848, between Joseph F. Bridges and wife Sarah and Walter Whitman Jr. for $1000 forever. Property in 7th Ward of Brooklyn beginning southside of Myrtle Ave. 40 ft. 3 inches east of S. E. corner of Myrtle Avenue and Duffield St. running South with Duffield St. 75 ft. [Lot 75 by 20 feet.]

Liber 283, p. 202: Indenture on May 15, 1852 between William B. Nichols and Walter Whitman Jr. for $800. Property in 11th late 7th Ward of city of Brooklyn, beginning at point on west side of Cumberland St. 303 ft 10 in. north from N. W. corner of Cumberland St. and Atlantic Ave., running thence north along W. line of Cumberland St. 28 ft. [Lot 100 by 28 ft.]

Jefferson Whitman was witness to signing of deed and appeared before comr. of deeds, C. H. Thomas to swear to it June 2d., 1852 at 9 A.M.

[J. W.'s signature appeared as "J. Whitman."]

Liber 397, p. 320: May 24, 1855 between Edward Macomber and Louisa Whitman wife of Walter Whitman for $1840 forever, land and dwelling house in 7th ward—beginning point on east side of Ryerson St. 380 ft. from N. E. corner of Ryerson and Myrtle. [Lot 100 by 20 ft.] Louisa to have full power over property "without concurrence of her husband at any time during the present or any future coverture by deeds or any instrument in writing to grant mortgages or devise said premises." Sealed and delivered in the presence of * E. A. Strausbury, N. Y. County, certified by Richard J. Connelly, clerk N. Y. County, June 9, 1855.

Liber 421, p. 273: April 10, 1856 John H. and George Wheeler, New York City and Louisa Whitman, Brooklyn for $375 in the 7th Ward of Brooklyn, N. W. corner Graham St. and Willoughby Ave., 141 ft. and ½ in. running west with Willoughby 100 ft. and 7½ in., thence north parallel with Graham St. 25 ft. 2 and 1 in. [Lot irregular in shape.]

Sealed and delivered on 11th April 1856—Recorded 24th April 1856 at 3:45 P.M.

* The words Louisa Whitman on the first page written on erasure before execution.

INDEX